THE CRB ENCYCLOPEDIA OF COMMODITY AND FINANCIAL PRICES
2006

 Commodity Research Bureau

WILEY

John Wiley & Sons, Inc.

Copyright © 2006 by Commodity Research Bureau, a Barchart company. All rights reserved.

Published by John Wiley & Sons, Inc., Hoboken, New Jersey
Published simultaneously in Canada.

No part of this publication may be reproduced, stored in a retrieval system, or transmitted in any form or by any means, electronic, mechanical, photocopying, recording, scanning, or otherwise, except as permitted under Section 107 or 108 of the 1976 United States Copyright Act, without either the prior written permission of the Publisher, or authorization through payment of the appropriate per-copy fee to the Copyright Clearance Center, Inc., 222 Rosewood Drive, Danvers, MA 01923, (978) 750-8400, fax (978) 750-4470, or on the web at www.copyright.com. Requests to the Publisher for permission should be addressed to the Permissions Department, John Wiley & Sons, Inc., 111 River Street, Hoboken, NJ 07030, (201) 748-6011, fax (201) 748-6008, or online at http://www.wiley.com/go/permissions.

Limit of Liability/Disclaimer of Warranty: While the publisher and author have used their best efforts in preparing this book, they make no representations or warranties with respect to the accuracy or completeness of the contents of this book and specifically disclaim any implied warranties of merchantability or fitness for a particular purpose. No warranty may be created or extended by sales representatives or written sales materials. The advice and strategies contained herein may not be suitable for your situation. You should consult with a professional where appropriate. Neither the publisher nor author shall be liable for any loss of profit or any other commercial damages, including but not limited to special, incidental, consequential, or other damages.

For general information on our other products and services or for technical support, please contact our Customer Care Department within the United States at (800) 762-2974, outside the United States at (317) 572-3993 or fax (317) 572-4002.

Wiley also publishes its books in a variety of electronic formats. Some content that appears in print may not be available in electronic books. For more information about Wiley products, visit our web site at www.wiley.com.

ISBN 13 978-0-471-78443-2
ISBN 10 0-471-78443-5

Printed in the United States of America

10 9 8 7 6 5 4 3 2 1

CRB believes that the information and opinions contained herein are reliable, but CRB does not make any warranties whatsoever, expressed or implied, and CRB assumes no liability for reliance on or use of information and opinion contained herein.

Commodity Research Bureau Editorial Board

Editor in Chief	**Associate Editor**	**Contributing Author**
Christopher J. Lown	Amy L. Kelley	Richard W. Asplund

Commodity Research Bureau
330 South Wells Street, Suite 612
Chicago, Illinois 60606-7110 USA

Phone: +1.312.554.8456 or 800.621.5271
Fax: +1.312.939.4135
Web: www.crbtrader.com
Email: info@crbtrader.com

TABLE OF CONTENTS

PAGE 5 Introduction
6 Key World and Market Events

10 Currencies

12 U.S. Dollar Index
16 Australian Dollar
21 British Pound
26 Canadian Dollar
32 Euro FX
36 Japanese Yen
42 Mexican Peso
46 Swiss Franc
52 Cross-Rates

60 Energy

62 Crude Oil, WTI
68 Gasoline, Unleaded
73 Heating Oil
78 Natural Gas
84 Propane

88 Financial Instruments

90 EuroDollars, 3-Month
92 Federal Funds, 30-Day
94 Libor, 1-Month
96 Treasury Note, 2-Year
100 Treasury Note, 5-Year
104 Treasury Note, 10-Year
108 Treasury Note, 30-Year
112 International Interest Rates
120 Economic Indicators

138 Foods & Fibers

140 Cocoa
146 Coffee
152 Orange Juice
154 Sugar
160 Cotton
166 Lumber

172 Grains & Oilseeds

176 Corn
182 Oats
188 Rice
194 Wheat, Chicago
200 Wheat, Kansas City
204 Wheat, Minneapolis
208 Canola
210 Soybeans
216 Soybean Meal
222 Soybean Oil

228 Indexes - Commodities

230 Reuters-CRB Index (CCI)
232 Reuters/Jefferies-CRB Index
234 CRB Industrials Sub-Index
236 CRB Grains & Oilseeds Sub-Index
238 CRB Livestock & Meats Sub-Index
240 CRB Energy Sub-Index
242 CRB Precious Metals Sub-Index
244 CRB Softs Sub-Index
246 CRB Spot Index
248 CRB Metals Sub-Index
250 CRB Textiles Sub-Index
252 CRB Raw Industrials Sub-Index
254 CRB Foodstuffs Sub-Index
256 CRB Fats & Oils Sub-Index
258 CRB Livestock Sub-Index
260 Goldman Sachs Commodity Index

262 Indexes - Stocks

266 Dow Jones Industrials Index
270 Dow Jones Transports Index
272 Dow Jones Utilities Index
274 CBOE Volatility Index
276 NASDAQ 100 Index
278 NASDAQ Composite Index
280 S&P 500 Index
284 S&P MidCap 400 Index
286 S&P 100 Index
288 Russell 2000 Index
290 Value Line Index
292 International Stock Indexes

304 Livestock & Meats

306 Cattle, Feeder
312 Cattle, Live
318 Hogs, Lean
324 Pork Bellies
330 Hides
332 Tallow

334 Metals

336 Aluminum
342 Copper
350 Gold
356 Lead
358 Nickel
360 Palladium
364 Platinum
368 Silver
374 Tin
376 Zinc

378 CD Instructions

NOTE: 2006 data through March 31

Commodity Research Bureau Product Overview

Commodity Research Bureau is the oldest and most respected information provider in the industry. CRB was founded in 1934 and is widely recognized in the industry for its accurate and professional products.

CRB's products are tailored for individual traders and brokerage firms. All of our products are available to brokerage firms on a bulk and private-label basis.

Product samples and pricing are located on our web site at www.crbtrader.com.

Please contact us for a free consultation about how our products can help your trading or your business.

Call +1.312.554.8456, or e-mail us at info@crbtrader.com

Commodity Research Bureau

330 South Wells Street, Suite 612
Chicago, Illinois 60606-7110

Phone: +1.312.554.8456
or 800.621.5271
Fax: +1.312.939.4135
Email: info@crbtrader.com
Website: www.crbtrader.com

Price Data	
CRB DataCenter	End-of-day daily price files on futures, Commitments of Traders, options on futures, options volatility (implied/historic), equities and mutual funds. Available in various formats for direct upload to your chart/analysis software.
CRB InfoTech CD	The most comprehensive collection of commodity market information available anywhere, with decades of prices on over 600 cash, futures, foreign exchange, index markets, and option volatilities (implied/historic).
Custom Historical Data	Order a one-time package of price information according to your needs.

Charts	
CRB PriceCharts	Weekly 104-page magazine of charts on over 70 futures markets. Available in print and PDF formats.
PriceCharts.com	Over 400 pages of charts and technical studies covering the 77 major US, Europe, and Asia futures markets. Available in PDF format.
Wall Charts	Large poster-size charts on 35 futures markets with volume/open interest and Commitment of Traders data. Published annually each fall or on demand with your company logo.
Historical Desk Sets	Spiral-bound set of 86 charts on 48 markets with volume/open interest and Commitment of Traders data. Published each spring and fall.

Fundamental and Technical Research and Trading Systems	
Futures Market Service	Weekly 8-page newsletter on futures market fundamentals available in print or PDF formats.
Trends In Futures	Bi-weekly 4-page newsletter on futures market technicals. Available in print and PDF format.
Electronic Futures Trend Analyzer	Computerized daily trading system started in 1963 with specific entry and exit points for over 60 Futures Markets.

Books	
CRB Commodity Yearbook	Annual publication of fundamental data, including supply/demand and production/consumption and price data, on over 100 commodity markets. Concise introductory articles that describe the salient features of each commodity. Available as a hardcover book with CD.
CRB Encyclopedia of Commodity and Financial Prices	Concise introductory articles on the fundamental market factors moving commodity and financial prices, providing a valuable complement to understanding price behavior on the long-term historical price charts. Available as a hardcover book with CD.

For more information and current specials, visit www.crbtrader.com or call +1.312.554.8456 or 800.621.5271

INTRODUCTION

The purpose of this book is to present the "big picture" for the commodity and financial markets by providing a (1) a complete array of long-term price charts, (2) a brief written history and outlook for each commodity and financial sector, and (3) a CD-ROM with comprehensive supporting data.

The long-term charts in this book are difficult to find anywhere else. Commodity Research Bureau (CRB) has been in business since 1934 and CRB has developed the most complete database of commodity and financial price history available in the industry. Many of the chart services that are available on the web, and even the more expensive terminal-based chart services, have limited price histories and a limited graphical ability to display long-term charts. This book fills that gap by providing a handy reference guide with easy-to-access long-term price charts. This book also includes inflation-adjusted charts for a variety of commodity markets, which provide an interesting perspective on long-term prices.

The brief written histories of the key commodity and financial sectors give market participants an easy way to get up to speed on the main events that have moved the markets in the post-war period. Understanding what has happened in the past is critical for forecasting the markets looking ahead. In just a few pages, readers can quickly gain an overview of what has been happening in each major commodity and financial sector and also gain an important understanding of the key factors that are likely to drive each market in the future.

In the historical commentary, we often use data from the *CRB Commodity Yearbook 2006* to explain the supply/demand factors that have moved the markets. The *CRB Commodity Yearbook 2006* is the companion book for this publication since it contains a host of fundamental data on the commodity and financial markets. This data provides an important means to gain a deeper understanding of the fundamental supply/demand factors that move the markets.

There are a number of charts that stand out in the publication in hand. For example, commodity prices are currently in the second largest bull market in post-war history. The Reuters/Jefferies CRB index recently rallied to a new record high, taking out the previous high seen in 1980. It is interesting to note, however, that the RJ/CRB index is only trading at about one-half the level seen in the 1960s when viewed on an inflation-adjusted basis, suggesting the current commodity rally still has plenty of room on the upside.

The charts in this book also show why there has been wrenching change in the US farm industry over the last 30 years. Grain and soybean prices are currently trading far below the levels seen in the 1960s on an inflation-adjusted basis, explaining why many small family farms have been forced out of business. Cattle and hog prices are also trading far below the levels seen in the 1960s on an inflation-adjusted basis.

Gold and silver prices, by contrast, have rallied to the highest levels in more than two decades. Yet, gold and silver prices are still well below the record highs seen in 1980s and are even farther below those record highs when viewed on an inflation-adjusted basis.

The long-term charts on the US stock market make it clear that the natural direction for stock prices is upward, even on an inflation-adjusted basis. US stocks have rallied sharply since 1900, with only a few extended periods of very poor returns (e.g., the Great Depression and the 1970s).

The long-term charts of US interest rates show how volatile US interest rates were during the 1970s and 1980s when inflation reached runaway levels and the Federal Reserve finally had to crack down with higher short-term rates. In recent years, it is striking to note how low US interest rates have fallen, and how the volatility of interest rates has fallen sharply as well.

The dollar, on the other hand, continues to be volatile due to shifting monetary policies and major global trade imbalances. The dollar plunged in 2002-04 on the Fed's accommodative monetary policy and the rising US current account deficit. The dollar in 2005 showed a modest recovery rally, but remains on thin ice due to the massive US current account deficit.

Oil prices have rallied sharply to record highs over the last several years because of new demand from China and limited investment by oil producers in new production capacity. Oil prices will continue to be a key factor for the world economic outlook in coming years.

The charts and commentary in this book illustrate the general prosperity that the world has enjoyed in the post-war period. The US Federal Reserve, after a difficult period in the 1970s, has since become very successful in containing inflation. That has been the single greatest contribution to promoting low interest rates, a strong stock market, and favorable economic conditions for businesses and consumers. China has also become an important positive element for world prosperity in the past decade with its rapid development and huge demand for products and services.

The last several decades have provided exciting times for those involved in the commodity and financial markets. These exciting times will continue as new and unforeseen events buffet the markets. Our goal is to provide the reader with the tools and the knowledge to understand and forecast these markets.

Richard Asplund, CRB Chief Economist

KEY WORLD AND MARKET EVENTS

Federal Reserve Established—1913—Congress creates the modern Federal Reserve after a series of runs on national banks makes clear the need for a centralized monetary authority to manage the money supply and act as the lender of last resort to commercial banks.

World War I begins—1914-1918—First World War lasts from August 1914 to November 1918.

1929 Stock Market Crash—October 28-29, 1929—Dow Jones Industrial Average plunges 23.6% in just two days and then plunges by an overall 90% to the low in 1932.

Smoot-Hawley Act—1930—Congress passes the protectionist Smoot-Hawley Act which helps cause the 1929 Stock Market Crash and deepens the Great Depression by causing a sharp drop in US trade.

Great Depression—1929-33—The Great Depression lasts nearly 4 years (Aug 1929 to March 1933) and devastates the US economy and social structure. The Great Depression is later shown to result in part from an inadvertent deflationary monetary policy by the Federal Reserve.

Bretton Woods Conference—July 22, 1944—US and UK, looking ahead to the end of World War II, meet in Bretton Woods, New Hampshire and create a post-war monetary system based on fixed exchange rates and the fixed convertibility of the dollar into gold. The Bretton Woods conference also sets the stage for the creation of the World Bank, the International Monetary Fund (IMF), and the General Agreement on Tariffs and Trade (GATT). The Bretton Woods currency system is highly successful for over two decades but finally breaks down in 1971 under stress from US inflation and trade deficit and the need for more global flexibility.

World War II ends—1945—World War II ends in Europe on May 8, 1945, with the surrender of Germany and Italy. World War II ends in the Pacific with Japan's surrender on August 15, 1945.

Korean War—1950-53—Korean War lasts from 1950-1953 as US fights communism.

William McChesney Martin becomes Fed Chairman—April 2, 1951—William McChesney Martin Jr. begins his long 19-year term as Fed Chairman (through Jan 31, 1970).

OPEC is formed—September 1960—OPEC is formed among several Middle East Arab countries to gain negotiating leverage with the major oil companies.

Berlin Wall is built—1961—Soviet Union builds Berlin Wall as Cold War emerges between the Soviet Union and the US and its allies.

Cuban Missile Crisis—October 16, 1962—Cold War reaches its peak with the Cuban Missile Crisis which ends with the Soviet Union removing its missiles from Cuba.

Kennedy assassination—November 22, 1963—President Kennedy is assassinated in Dallas by Lee Harvey Oswald. Vice President Lyndon Johnson becomes President.

Gulf of Tonkin incident—August 1964—US military involvement in Vietnam starts to escalate into an all-out war after a North Vietnamese gunboat fires on an American destroyer. Major US involvement in the Vietnam War finally ends 9 years later in 1973 with the Paris Peace Accords.

1967 Arab-Israeli War—June 5-10, 1967—Israel launches a pre-emptive attack in a war with Egypt, Syria and Jordan, and takes control of Sinai Peninsula, the West Bank, and about half of the Golan Heights. Sinai is returned to Egypt when Israel and Egypt declare peace in the Camp David Accords, signed on September 17, 1978.

Arthur Burns becomes Fed Chairman—February 1, 1970—Arthur Burns begins his 8-year term as Fed Chairman (through Jan 31, 1978).

Nixon closes the gold window, ending Bretton Woods—August 15, 1971—President Nixon announces that the US government will no longer exchange gold for dollars. That effectively ends the Bretton Woods monetary system that had been in place since 1945. Major currencies are freely floating by 1973. Along with the gold announcement, Nixon also announces 90-day wage and price controls and a 10% import surcharge in an attempt to curb inflation and the US trade deficit.

Nixon travels to China—February 21-28, 1972—Nixon travels to China to seek rapprochement with the Communist nation. US and China announce they will work toward full diplomatic relations. China's long isolation starts to thaw.

Soviet Grain Purchases—Summer 1972—The Soviet Union during the summer of 1972 purchases a huge amount of corn, wheat, soybeans and soybean meal from the US in response to poor domestic crops, thus causing grain and soybean prices to soar in late 1972 and early 1973.

Yom Kippur War—October 6, 1973—Israel barely wins the war that started with a surprise attack on Yom Kippur by Egypt and Syria in an attempt to win back Sinai and Golan Heights, respectively.

Arab Oil Embargo—October 17, 1973—Arab members of OPEC halt exports of oil to the US in retaliation for supporting Israel during the Yom Kippur War. Oil prices triple from $3.50 to the $10-11 per barrel range by 1974-75. The embargo lasts only 5 months (until March 1974) but the long-term impact is severe.

KEY WORLD AND MARKET EVENTS

1973-75 US recession and stock bear market—Serious US stock bear market emerges in response to the Arab Oil Embargo and the major US economic recession from Nov-1973 to March-1975.

President Nixon resigns—August 4, 1974—President Nixon resigns due to the Watergate scandal. Vice President Gerald Ford becomes President.

Whip Inflation Now—October 8, 1974—President Ford's "Whip Inflation Now" campaign illustrates US government's poor understanding of the monetarist causes of inflation. It would be 5 more years before inflation is attacked with a tight monetary policy.

US citizens can legally own gold—1975—US allows its citizens to own gold bullion. Owning gold was illegal from 1933-1974 except for jewelry and coin collecting.

China begins economic liberalization—1978—The People's Republic of China starts reforming its economy from a centrally-planned economy to a market-oriented economy, but retains communist political structure. Rapid Chinese economic growth begins (average annual Chinese GDP growth is +9.7% from 1978-2005).

C. William Miller becomes Fed Chairman—March 8, 1978—C. William Miller is appointed Fed Chairman by President Jimmy Carter and begins his short 1-year term.

Paul Volcker becomes Fed Chairman—August 6, 1979—Paul Volcker is appointed Federal Reserve Chairman by President Jimmy Carter and begins his 8-year term. Volcker cracks down on money supply to force inflation lower, causing double dip recessions in 1980 and 1981-82. The federal funds rate target peaks at 20% in March 1980 and again in May 1981.

Shah is deposed by Iranian Revolution—January 16, 1979—Shah of Iran is deposed by popular protest and is replaced by an Islamic theocracy headed by Ayatollah Khomeini, who arrives in Iran on February 1, 1979, two weeks after the Shah fled on January 16, 1979. Oil prices surge as Iran's oil production is devastated by the revolution.

1979 Oil Crisis—Crude oil prices more than double from about $15 to $40 per barrel on oil supply disruptions caused initially by the Iranian revolution, which severely cut Iranian oil production. Americans experience long lines at the gas pumps as shortages are worsened by President Carter's gasoline price controls.

Soviet Grain Embargo—January 4, 1980—President Carter announces an embargo on grain exports to the Soviet Union in retaliation for the Soviet Union's invasion of Afghanistan.

Gold and silver hit record highs—January 1980—Gold reaches a record high of $850.00 (London PM gold fix on Jan 21, 1980) and silver in New York reaches a record high of $48.00 (NY daily close) due to inflationary 1970s, but precious metals prices then plunge as Volcker cracks down on inflation.

1980 US Recession—US recession (January 1980 to July 1980) is caused by Fed's crack-down on money supply and inflation and the surge in oil prices tied to the Iranian revolution. First dip of the "double-dip" recession.

Iran-Iraq War begins—September 22, 1980—The Iran-Iraq War lasts from 1980-1988 and causes sharp cutbacks in Iranian and Iraqi oil production and puts new upward pressure on oil prices. A ceasefire is finally declared on August 20, 1988.

1981-82 US Recession—US economy enters another recession (the second dip of the "double-dip recession") from July 1981 to November 1982 as the US economy continues to suffer from high oil prices and the Fed's crack-down on inflation.

Latin American Debt Crisis—Early-1980s—Latin America countries (Brazil, Argentina and Mexico in particular) are unable to pay large debts owed to global banks due to world recession and oil price spike.

President Reagan's first term begins—January 20, 1981—Ronald Reagan's 8-year term as President begins with his mission of "supply side economics." Reagan terminates oil price controls and forces a 25% tax cut through Congress, which eventually produces a huge federal budget deficit but also stimulates the economy.

US stocks begin bull market—1982—After plunging on an inflation-adjusted basis from 1973-1982, the US stock market finally enters a long-term bull market that lasts until 2000, with corrections in 1987 and 1990.

Plaza Accord—September 1985—G5 nations agree on plan to drive the dollar lower via currency market intervention.

Louvre Accord—February 21-22, 1987—G5 nations agreed to stabilize currencies and halt the dollar's decline

Greenspan becomes Fed Chairman—August 11, 1987—Alan Greenspan is appointed as Federal Reserve Chairman by President Reagan and begins his long 18-1/2 year term (through January 31, 2006).

1987 "Black Monday" Stock Market Crash—October 19, 1987—US stock market crashes -20.5% but recovers its losses within just 9 months as Fed successfully manages the crisis by flooding the banking system with liquidity.

KEY WORLD AND MARKET EVENTS

Berlin Wall Falls—November 9, 1989—Berlin Wall, which was originally built in 1961 by the Soviets to separate East and West Germany, falls. Unification of East and West Germany follows in 1990, creating economic dislocations for Germany.

Nikkei index peaks and Japan's bubble later bursts—December 1989—Japan's stock market peaks and the stock and property bubble starts to burst. Japan suffers more than a decade of deflation and sub-par economic growth. The Nikkei index plunges by three-quarters and Tokyo land prices fall by one-half.

Iraq invades Kuwait—August 2, 1990—Iraqi dictator Saddam Hussein invades Kuwait to take control of oil fields, with likely intention to move on to Saudi Arabia.

"Desert Storm" Gulf War—January 17, 1991—US and coalition forces go to war against Iraq to force Iraq out of Kuwait. US stops short of Baghdad and leaves Saddam Hussein in power.

1990-91 US Recession—US economy is in recession from July 1990 to March 1991 due mainly to the oil price spike caused by Iraq's invasion of Kuwait and the subsequent US-Coalition war against Iraq.

Soviet Union dissolves—December 26, 1991—The Supreme Soviet, the highest governmental body of the Soviet Union, dissolves itself and Russia and other republics later become independent nations.

S&L Bailout—1991—Congress bails out the US savings and loan banking sector which is insolvent due to high short-term rates and rampant speculation. Bailout costs some $350 billion but is disposed of fairly quickly by the Resolution Trust Corporation.

NAFTA—1993—US Congress approves North American Free Trade Zone among the US, Mexico and Canada.

Mexican Peso Crisis—1994—Mexican peso collapses by 40% in two weeks. President Clinton bails out Mexico with a $50 billion loan and the fall-out is contained.

Uruguay Round is completed—April 1994—After 7-1/2 years, the Uruguay Round of world trade talks finally concludes successfully with agreement among 125 countries, creating the World Trade Organization (replacing the General Agreement on Tariffs and Trade, or GATT) and promoting a major expansion in world trade. Previous world trade agreements include the Tokyo Round (1979), the Kennedy Round (1967), and five others.

Fed Chairman Greenspan's "Irrational Exuberance" speech—December 5, 1996—Fed Chairman Greenspan in a now-famous speech refers to "irrational exuberance" in the US stock market but the Fed allows equity bubble to proceed before it finally bursts on its own accord in 2000.

China takes over Hong Kong sovereignty—July 1, 1997—UK hands over sovereignty of Hong Kong to China.

Asian financial crisis—July 1997—Run starts on East Asian Tiger currencies causing a collapse in the East Asian stock markets and an economic recession. Countries most affected were Thailand, South Korea and the Philippines. The crisis convinces Asian foreign central banks of the need to acquire large foreign currency reserves, which they continue to do today. In response to the rolling crisis, Dow Jones plunges 7.2% (554 points) on October 27, 1997. Asian economic shock undercuts oil prices and other commodity prices.

Russian debt default—August 17, 1998—Russia defaults on its foreign sovereign debt and devalues the ruble due to high debt from Soviet era, limited success with market reforms, high inflation, and low currency reserves due in part to spending $6 billion to defend the ruble during the Asian currency crisis in 1997. The ruble is floated in the wake of the crisis.

LTCM hedge fund bailout—September 1998—Federal Reserve orchestrates bailout of Long-Term Capital Management hedge fund in order to prevent systemic financial system crisis.

European Monetary Union—January 1, 1999—European Monetary Union is completed and the Euro comes into existence to replace individual currencies such as the mark, franc and lira. The European Central Bank takes over responsibility for Euro-Zone monetary policy.

US stock market hits record high but bubble subsequently bursts—March 2000—The S&P 500, the Nasdaq Composite and other key stock market indices hit record highs in March 2000 but subsequently enter a bear market through 2002 after the equity bubble bursts.

Fed slashes interest rates—January 2001—The Fed slashes its federal funds rate target from 6.50% in late 2000 to 1.75% by the end of 2001, and further to 1.00% by mid-2003 in order to prevent deflation.

2001 US Recession—US economy enters recession from March 2001 to November 2001 due to bursting of equity bubble and post-Y2K technology spending bust.

9/11 terrorist attacks on US—September 11, 2001—Al-Qaeda attacks US with airplanes crashing into World Trade Center and the Pentagon. As a result, US enters two wars (Afghanistan and Iraq) and military spending, along with the US budget deficit, soar.

US invades Afghanistan—October 7, 2001—US invades Afghanistan to oust Taliban government and deny safe haven to al-Qaeda.

KEY WORLD AND MARKET EVENTS

Doha Round begins—November 2001—In an attempt to extend Uruguay Round success, the Doha Round of world trade talks begins but little progress is made through early 2006 due to objections by Brazil and others about G7 government agricultural subsidies to local farmers.

Congress passes Sarbanes-Oxley—July 30, 2002—Congress passes Sarbanes-Oxley Act which creates corporate governance reforms and enhanced financial disclosure in response to the string of corporate frauds that developed during the stock bubble, including Enron (bankruptcy Dec 2001), Worldcom (bankruptcy July 2002), Tyco, and others.

SARS outbreak begins—February 2003—SARS, a new and particularly deadly type of pneumonia, is first reported in Asia in February 2003 and quickly spreads to various locations around the world, hurting economic growth in Asia, Canada and elsewhere. The disease is contained, however, and no cases are reported after late- 2004.

US launches war against Iraq's Saddam Hussein—March 20, 2003—US and UK begin "Operation Iraqi Freedom" against Iraq and topple Saddam Hussein. President Bush on May 1, 2003 declares that major combat operations are complete but serious insurgency continues 3 years later. Saddam Hussein is captured by US forces on December 13, 2003, and is put on trial in Iraq.

First case of Mad Cow is found in Canada—May 20, 2003—The first case of Mad Cow disease (BSE) is found in Canada. US and other countries suspend the import of live cattle from Canada.

First case of Mad Cow is found in US—December 2003—The US first case of Mad Cow disease (BSE) is found in a Canadian-born dairy cow in Washington state. More than 50 countries suspend imports of US cattle and beef products.

Fed begins 2-year rate hike regime—June 2004—Fed on June 2004 starts raising its funds rate target from the 1% level that prevailed during 2003-04. Federal funds rate target rises to 4.75% by March 2006, and further rate hikes are expected later in 2006.

Avian flu starts to emerge—August 2004—Sporadic outbreaks of avian flu are seen in August-October 2004 in Vietnam and Thailand. Avian flu progressively spreads into other parts of Asia and then to Africa and Europe by early 2006. Aside from killing people, avian flu causes a sharp drop in poultry consumption by consumers in affected countries. Concern emerges about possible global pandemic if virus mutates to become easily transmissible by human-to-human contact.

Hurricane Ivan hits Gulf coast— September 16, 2004—Hurricane Ivan, the strongest hurricane of the 2004 season, hits landfall in the Gulf of Mexico near Gulf Shores, Alabama. Ivan causes widespread damage to oil rigs and ocean-floor pipelines in Gulf of Mexico and drives oil prices sharply higher in Q4-2004.

China revalues Yuan and moves to crawling peg—July 21, 2005—China announces a one-time revaluation in the yuan by 2.1%, and then allows the yuan to crawl higher by 1% in the subsequent 6 months in a nod to international demands that China allow its currency to rise to help curb its soaring trade surplus.

CAFTA is signed into law—August 2, 2005—President Bush signs into law the Central American Free Trade Agreement, which reduces trade barriers among the participants (US, Costa Rica, Dominican Republic, El Salvador, Guatemala, Honduras, and Nicaragua). Sugar is a particularly contentious issue in CAFTA debate due to US protectionism.

Hurricane Katrina causes widespread devastation—August 29, 2005—Hurricane Katrina makes landfall near New Orleans and causes widespread devastation including the flooding and shut-down of New Orleans. Katrina is followed by Hurricane Rita on September 24, which hits near Houston and causes further damage to oil rig production in the Gulf of Mexico. Gulf oil production is still 25% below normal 6 months later.

China becomes world's 4th-largest economy—December 2005—China announces one-time hike in the size of its GDP by $282 billion (+17%) after a census finds numerous uncounted small businesses, thus vaulting China to the 4th largest world economy (behind only the US, Japan, and Germany). In purchasing power parity terms, China was already the second largest in the world behind only the US (after taking account of the severely undervalued Chinese currency), according to the CIA Fact Book.

Bernanke becomes Fed Chairman—February 1, 2006—Economist, former Fed Governor and Bush-advisor, Ben Bernanke, is appointed Fed Chairman by President George W. Bush, taking over from Alan Greenspan, who retired after an extremely successful 18-1/2 year term.

CURRENCIES

Current Dollar Outlook

The dollar rallied sharply during 2005, surprising many market participants who expected further weakness in the dollar based on the huge US current account deficit. The dollar index in 2005 rallied by +12.8% and retraced 30% of the plunge seen in 2002-04. The dollar in Q1-2006 consolidated mildly below the 2005 highs.

The main factor driving the dollar higher in 2005 was the sharp rise in US interest rate differentials, as seen in the nearby interest rate spread chart (i.e., the 3-month US Eurodollar Libor rate minus the European Libor rate). Higher US short-term interest rates encouraged foreign investors to put their cash into the US money markets to earn a higher yield than they could earn in Europe or Japan. The Fed's tighter monetary policy also meant that the Fed was pumping fewer dollar reserves into the nation's banking system, making dollars a bit less plentiful.

The US Federal Reserve started raising its federal funds rate target in June 2004 from the 1.00% level that prevailed during the previous 12 months. The Fed from June 2004 through March 2006 raised its funds rate target by a total of 375 basis points, from 1.00% to 4.75%. As of March 2006, the market consensus was that the Fed would likely raise its funds rate target by another 25-50 basis points by autumn 2006.

Over the course of the Fed's 375 basis point tightening, the European Central bank implemented only two small 25 basis point rate hikes to 2.50% (in Dec 2005 and March 2006). The Bank of Japan reduced its excess reserve target in March 2006 but left in place its extraordinarily accommodative zero-interest-rate monetary policy. Thus, US interest rate differentials rose by roughly 325-375 basis points against European and Japanese short-term rates from mid-2004 through Q1-2006.

Despite the rally in the dollar in 2005, the US trade deficit continues to be a major bearish factor for the dollar. The US trade deficit in 2005 widened to $726 billion, posting a new record for the fourth straight year. Meanwhile, the US current account balance (which is the broadest measure of US trade with the rest of the world and includes goods, services, and transfer payments) reached a record high of 7.0% of GDP by Q4-2005.

There are many reasons for the massive US current account deficit. Short-term factors include (1) the surge in oil prices seen in 2002-06, which sharply boosted the dollar value of imported oil, (2) the fact that the US business cycle remained ahead of its key trading partners which meant that US demand for imports was relatively strong and foreign demand for US exports was relatively weak, and (3) importers into the US did not raise prices substantially in response to the weak dollar but instead accepted lower profit margins to preserve their market shares, meaning there was no significant drop-off in US import demand.

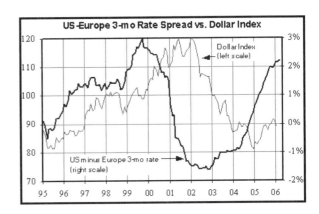

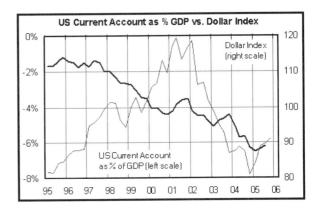

Long-term structural factors behind the US current account deficit include (1) the huge US appetite for foreign imported oil, (2) the improved comparative advantage of nations such as China and India which have cheap labor and the resources to employ that labor into export powerhouses, and (3) the poor US household savings rate and the massive US federal budget deficit, which means the US must import a huge amount of capital to cover its capital needs (boosting the capital account surplus and the US current account deficit as well).

The US trade deficit with China also continues to be a key factor behind the rising US trade deficit. The US trade deficit with China reached a new record high of $202 billion in 2005, up 25% from the $162 billion deficit in 2004. The US trade deficit with China by itself comprised 28% of the overall US trade deficit in 2005. The US trade deficit with China is a source of major discontent in the US because China is fixing its currency at an undervalued level, giving China a greater competitive advantage than it deserves. China revalued the yuan by a slight 2.1% in July 2005, but that was a drop in the bucket compared to estimates that the Chinese yuan is undervalued by as much as 30-50%. China appears to be intent on keeping the yuan fixed at undervalued levels for at least the next several years.

CURRENCIES

Dollar History

Modern floating rate currency era begins in 1973

Exchange rates from 1945 to 1971 were fixed by the Bretton Woods agreement. Major world currencies were fixed in terms of the dollar, which was the system's "reserve currency," and the dollar in turn was fixed and convertible into gold by the US government at $35 per ounce. The Bretton Woods era of fixed exchange rates effectively ended on August 15, 1971 when President Nixon announced that the US government would close the gold window and no longer exchange gold for dollars. With the gold convertibility of the system removed, the system of fixed exchange rates slowly broke down and by 1973 the major world currencies were trading in a floating-rate currency system where the market determines the value of a currency rather than government fiat.

The Bretton Woods system broke down mainly because the US by the early 1970s was seeing increased inflation and a balance of payments deficit. When currencies started floating freely in 1973, the US dollar depreciated through most of the rest of the 1970s due to the relatively high US inflation rate seen during the 1970s, which averaged +7.1% annually, up sharply from +2.3% in the 1960s and +2.1% in the 1950s.

Dollar strength during the Volcker Era

Paul Volcker was appointed Federal Reserve Chairman in August 1979 and he raised interest rates sharply to crack down on money supply growth and to halt run-away inflation. Sharply higher US interest rates quickly allowed the dollar to stabilize in the 1979-1980 period. The dollar then rallied sharply starting in mid-1980 as US inflation started to fall and as investors bought dollars to take advantage of high US yields.

Plaza Accord of 1985

The dollar index nearly doubled in value from mid-1981 to the record high in 1985, driven higher by (1) declining US inflation, (2) a stimulative fiscal policy caused by the Reagan tax cuts and budget deficits, and (2) the sharp rally in the US stock market which attracted foreign capital into the US. The Reagan administration took a lassie-faire attitude to the surge in the dollar and made little effort to curb the dollar's gains.

By 1985, however, US manufacturers and the US auto industry in particular were screaming because their export goods were no longer competitive in the world market. US exports plunged and imports rose, thus causing the US current account deficit to soar to a then-record of 3.2% of GDP by the end of 1985. The Reagan administration finally arranged the Plaza Accord in September 1985 where the

G5 countries (US, UK, West Germany, France and Canada) agreed to force a depreciation in the dollar, mainly through currency market intervention. The central banks spent $10 billion intervening in the currency markets. The outcome was very successful and the dollar fell sharply, giving back all of its 1981-85 rally. The sharp decline became alarming, however, as the market commentators started spinning doomsday dollar melt-down scenarios. In order to halt the plunge in the dollar seen in 1985-87, the G5 nations signed the Louvre Accord in February 1987, in which they agreed to halt the decline in the dollar.

The Louvre Accord was successful in halting the plunge in the dollar. However, the dollar from 1987 through 1995 continued to trade on a weak note, undercut by the declining trend in US interest rates during that timeframe and the generally high US current account deficit.

The dollar then rallied sharply during the 1995-2002 period after the Fed raised its funds rate target to the 6% area in 1994 and as the US technology boom and stock market bubble drew huge amounts of foreign capital into the US. The dollar then plunged during the 2002-04 time frame due to (1) the bursting of the US equity bubble, (2) the Fed's sharp cut in the funds rate to an extraordinary low 1.00%, and (3) the sharp increase in the US current account deficit from about 4% of GDP in 2002 to 6.3% by the end 2004. The dollar's plunge in 2002-04 sparked a huge rally in the US commodity markets.

Introduction of Euro in January 1999

The euro was introduced January 1, 1999 as part of the European Economic and Monetary Union (EMU). Eleven European countries initially participated in the common currency, which replaced each nation's individual currencies (Deutschemark, franc, lira, etc). The idea was to create a common economic area with free flow of trade and eliminate the inefficiencies caused by having individual currencies. The European Central Bank took over the duties of setting monetary policy for the Euro-Zone countries. The euro has been a success and has become a critical component of the global financial system.

U.S. DOLLAR INDEX

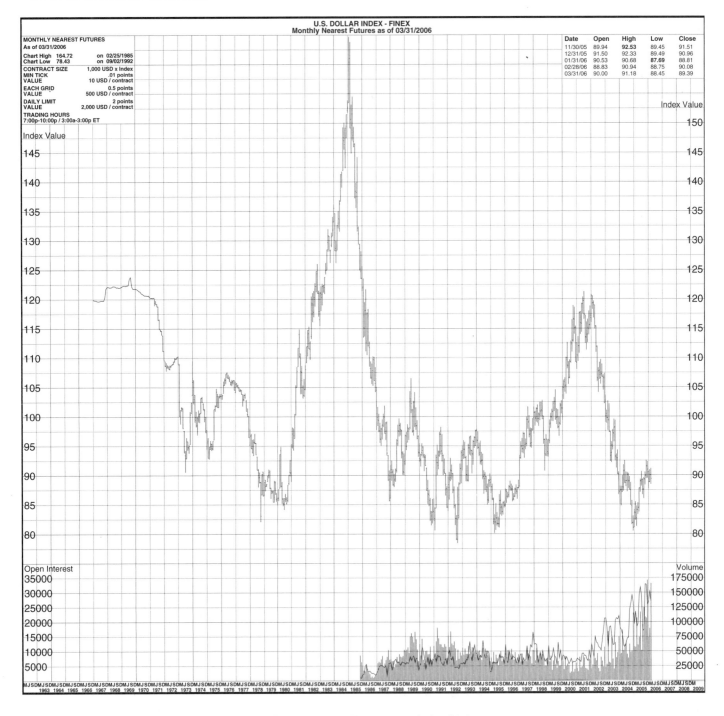

Annual High, Low and Close of U.S. Dollar Index Futures   Index Value

Year	High	Low	Close	Year	High	Low	Close	Year	High	Low	Close
1968	122.22	121.95	121.96	1981	114.88	88.95	104.69	1994	97.85	84.95	88.69
1969	123.82	121.74	121.74	1982	126.02	104.62	117.91	1995	89.79	80.14	84.83
1970	121.75	120.55	120.64	1983	134.05	115.43	131.79	1996	89.20	84.51	87.86
1971	120.55	111.16	111.21	1984	151.47	126.18	151.47	1997	101.68	88.01	99.57
1972	111.27	107.76	110.14	1985	164.72	123.24	123.55	1998	102.82	90.74	93.96
1973	110.31	90.54	102.39	1986	125.62	104.20	104.24	1999	104.60	93.12	101.42
1974	109.50	96.86	97.29	1987	105.02	85.55	85.66	2000	118.90	99.40	109.28
1975	104.81	92.82	103.51	1988	99.70	86.07	92.29	2001	121.29	108.04	117.21
1976	107.60	102.91	104.56	1989	106.52	91.75	93.93	2002	120.80	102.26	102.26
1977	106.01	96.44	96.44	1990	95.44	81.46	83.89	2003	103.67	86.70	87.26
1978	97.87	82.07	86.50	1991	98.23	80.60	84.69	2004	92.50	80.48	81.00
1979	91.02	85.43	85.82	1992	94.20	78.43	93.87	2005	92.53	81.11	90.96
1980	94.88	84.12	90.39	1993	97.69	88.92	97.63	2006	91.18	87.69	89.39

Source: New York Board of Trade

U.S. DOLLAR INDEX

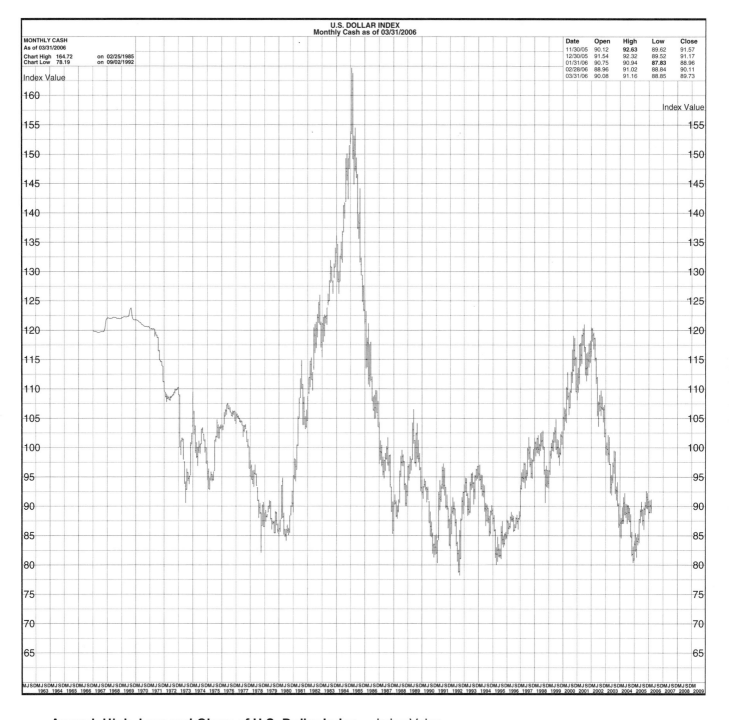

Annual High, Low and Close of U.S. Dollar Index   Index Value

Year	High	Low	Close	Year	High	Low	Close	Year	High	Low	Close
1968	122.22	121.95	121.96	1981	114.88	88.95	104.69	1994	97.10	84.91	88.73
1969	123.82	121.74	121.74	1982	126.02	104.62	117.91	1995	89.63	80.05	84.76
1970	121.75	120.55	120.64	1983	134.05	115.43	131.79	1996	89.14	84.48	88.18
1971	120.55	111.16	111.21	1984	151.47	126.18	151.47	1997	101.79	88.15	99.65
1972	111.27	107.76	110.14	1985	164.72	123.24	123.46	1998	102.88	90.57	94.17
1973	110.31	90.54	102.39	1986	125.21	103.55	103.58	1999	104.88	93.05	101.87
1974	109.50	96.86	97.29	1987	104.35	85.33	85.42	2000	119.07	99.71	109.56
1975	104.81	92.82	103.51	1988	99.61	85.87	92.50	2001	121.02	108.09	116.82
1976	107.60	102.91	104.56	1989	106.56	91.77	93.21	2002	120.51	101.80	101.85
1977	106.01	96.44	96.44	1990	94.72	81.27	83.07	2003	103.20	86.36	86.92
1978	97.87	82.07	86.50	1991	97.32	80.34	83.52	2004	92.29	80.39	80.85
1979	91.02	85.43	85.82	1992	92.52	78.19	92.36	2005	92.63	80.77	91.17
1980	94.88	84.12	90.39	1993	96.85	88.37	96.84	2006	91.16	87.83	89.73

Source: New York Board of Trade

U.S. DOLLAR INDEX

Quarterly High, Low and Close of U.S. Dollar Index Futures — Index Value

Quarter	High	Low	Close	Quarter	High	Low	Close	Quarter	High	Low	Close
09/1996	88.20	85.50	87.72	12/1999	102.73	96.65	101.42	03/2003	103.67	97.62	99.49
12/1996	89.20	85.95	87.86	03/2000	106.63	99.40	105.16	06/2003	102.19	92.16	95.11
03/1997	96.30	88.01	94.47	06/2000	112.66	103.85	106.58	09/2003	99.57	92.43	93.23
06/1997	97.36	92.93	95.40	09/2000	116.52	106.44	113.00	12/2003	94.32	86.70	87.26
09/1997	101.68	94.88	96.92	12/2000	118.90	109.27	109.28	03/2004	89.95	84.77	87.95
12/1997	99.68	94.65	99.57	03/2001	117.78	108.04	117.63	06/2004	92.50	87.30	89.00
03/1998	101.65	97.05	101.37	06/2001	120.37	114.01	119.75	09/2004	90.49	87.20	87.51
06/1998	102.47	98.40	100.98	09/2001	121.29	111.35	113.96	12/2004	88.79	80.48	81.00
09/1998	102.82	95.31	96.02	12/2001	118.85	112.62	117.21	03/2005	85.46	81.11	84.05
12/1998	96.95	90.74	93.96	03/2002	120.80	116.00	119.06	06/2005	89.35	83.31	88.98
03/1999	100.58	93.12	99.92	06/2002	118.95	105.97	106.55	09/2005	90.66	86.02	89.35
06/1999	103.28	99.18	102.53	09/2002	109.75	104.12	107.26	12/2005	92.53	88.35	90.96
09/1999	104.60	97.92	98.20	12/2002	108.95	102.26	102.26	03/2006	91.18	87.69	89.39

Source: New York Board of Trade

U.S. DOLLAR INDEX

Quarterly High, Low and Close of U.S. Dollar Index   Index Value

Quarter	High	Low	Close	Quarter	High	Low	Close	Quarter	High	Low	Close
09/1996	88.32	85.63	87.94	12/1999	102.76	96.94	101.87	03/2003	103.20	97.57	99.06
12/1996	89.14	86.04	88.18	03/2000	106.86	99.71	105.44	06/2003	101.81	91.88	94.73
03/1997	96.32	88.15	94.72	06/2000	112.86	104.23	106.84	09/2003	99.49	92.10	92.85
06/1997	97.47	93.07	95.67	09/2000	116.75	106.70	113.25	12/2003	94.13	86.36	86.92
09/1997	101.79	95.14	97.11	12/2000	119.07	109.46	109.56	03/2004	89.84	84.56	87.61
12/1997	99.73	94.73	99.65	03/2001	117.63	108.09	117.37	06/2004	92.29	87.02	88.80
03/1998	101.69	97.67	101.50	06/2001	120.33	113.86	119.43	09/2004	90.29	87.00	87.36
06/1998	102.45	98.57	101.17	09/2001	121.02	111.31	113.48	12/2004	88.64	80.39	80.85
09/1998	102.88	95.41	96.17	12/2001	118.26	112.27	116.82	03/2005	85.44	80.77	84.06
12/1998	96.94	90.57	94.17	03/2002	120.51	115.54	118.62	06/2005	89.48	83.36	89.11
03/1999	100.79	93.05	100.10	06/2002	118.75	105.37	106.11	09/2005	90.77	85.99	89.52
06/1999	103.48	99.35	102.85	09/2002	109.77	103.54	106.87	12/2005	92.63	88.53	91.17
09/1999	104.88	98.26	98.54	12/2002	108.74	101.80	101.85	03/2006	91.16	87.83	89.73

Source: New York Board of Trade

AUSTRALIAN DOLLAR

Annual High, Low and Close of Australian Dollar Futures In USD per AUD

Year	High	Low	Close	Year	High	Low	Close	Year	High	Low	Close
1968	1.1198	1.1084	1.1089	1981	1.1890	1.1225	1.1280	1994	.7795	.6762	.7730
1969	1.1143	1.1081	1.1143	1982	1.1308	.9339	.9801	1995	.7725	.7055	.7401
1970	1.1184	1.1087	1.1112	1983	.9910	.8542	.8985	1996	.8210	.7276	.7936
1971	1.1888	1.1124	1.1887	1984	.9668	.8187	.8258	1997	.8005	.6475	.6518
1972	1.2732	1.1880	1.2732	1985	.8230	.6350	.6822	1998	.7005	.5465	.6085
1973	1.4885	1.2710	1.4825	1986	.7490	.5715	.6650	1999	.6743	.6123	.6583
1974	1.4875	1.3025	1.3245	1987	.7395	6288	.7170	2000	.6693	.5075	.5590
1975	1.3655	1.2518	1.2545	1988	.8810	.6940	.8450	2001	.5725	.4774	.5074
1976	1.2610	1.0054	1.0890	1989	.8880	.7315	.7760	2002	.5773	.5033	.5548
1977	1.1410	1.0822	1.1380	1990	.8335	.7330	.7656	2003	.7475	.5578	.7455
1978	1.1860	1.1230	1.1500	1991	.7985	.7493	.7565	2004	.7980	.6730	.7790
1979	1.1518	1.0902	1.1057	1992	.7670	.6775	.6869	2005	.7992	.7214	.7325
1980	1.1814	1.0670	1.1814	1993	.7242	.6392	.6770	2006	.7579	.7006	.7157

Source: Chicago Mercantile Exchange

AUSTRALIAN DOLLAR

Annual High, Low and Close of Australian Dollar   In USD per AUD

Year	High	Low	Close	Year	High	Low	Close	Year	High	Low	Close
1968	1.1198	1.1084	1.1089	1981	1.1890	1.1225	1.1280	1994	.7789	.6773	.7764
1969	1.1143	1.1081	1.1143	1982	1.1308	.9339	.9801	1995	.7764	.7077	.7437
1970	1.1184	1.1087	1.1112	1983	.9910	.8542	.8985	1996	.8211	.7313	.7943
1971	1.1888	1.1124	1.1887	1984	.9668	.8187	.8258	1997	.8012	.6463	.6515
1972	1.2732	1.1880	1.2732	1985	.8230	.6350	.6822	1998	.6880	.5503	.6101
1973	1.4885	1.2710	1.4825	1986	.7490	.5715	.6650	1999	.6745	.6106	.6568
1974	1.4875	1.3025	1.3245	1987	.7395	.6380	.7215	2000	.6685	.5075	.5585
1975	1.3655	1.2518	1.2545	1988	.8833	.6955	.8540	2001	.5725	.4778	.5106
1976	1.2610	1.0054	1.0890	1989	.8967	.7270	.7880	2002	.5796	.5052	.5615
1977	1.1410	1.0822	1.1380	1990	.8480	.7392	.7718	2003	.7537	.5614	.7521
1978	1.1860	1.1230	1.1500	1991	.8038	.7500	.7595	2004	.8003	.6777	.7825
1979	1.1518	1.0902	1.1057	1992	.7705	.6783	.6885	2005	.7990	.7234	.7335
1980	1.1814	1.0670	1.1814	1993	.7253	.6413	.6793	2006	.7586	.7016	.7157

Source: Forex

AUSTRALIAN DOLLAR

Quarterly High, Low and Close of Australian Dollar Futures   In USD per AUD

Quarter	High	Low	Close	Quarter	High	Low	Close	Quarter	High	Low	Close
09/1996	.8020	.7670	.7889	12/1999	.6665	.6300	.6583	03/2003	.6178	.5578	.5987
12/1996	.8210	.7810	.7936	03/2000	.6693	.5962	.6082	06/2003	.6703	.5887	.6674
03/1997	.8005	.7554	.7856	06/2000	.6107	.5651	.5980	09/2003	.6817	.6335	.6746
06/1997	.7888	.7442	.7542	09/2000	.6025	.5360	.5431	12/2003	.7475	.6700	.7455
09/1997	.7558	.7170	.7270	12/2000	.5598	.5075	.5590	03/2004	.7980	.7255	.7589
12/1997	.7425	.6475	.6518	03/2001	.5725	.4848	.4852	06/2004	.7649	.6730	.6910
03/1998	.7005	.6328	.6633	06/2001	.5329	.4774	.5084	09/2004	.7304	.6850	.7233
06/1998	.6638	.5804	.6188	09/2001	.5389	.4802	.4895	12/2004	.7938	.7140	.7790
09/1998	.6344	.5465	.5955	12/2001	.5237	.4888	.5074	03/2005	.7992	.7475	.7685
12/1998	.6487	.5811	.6085	03/2002	.5320	.5033	.5309	06/2005	.7819	.7469	.7564
03/1999	.6545	.6123	.6354	06/2002	.5773	.5231	.5600	09/2005	.7761	.7336	.7601
06/1999	.6743	.6230	.6662	09/2002	.5680	.5214	.5392	12/2005	.7622	.7214	.7325
09/1999	.6722	.6287	.6536	12/2002	.5682	.5369	.5548	03/2006	.7579	.7006	.7157

Source: Chicago Mercantile Exchange

AUSTRALIAN DOLLAR

Quarterly High, Low and Close of Australian Dollar   In USD per AUD

Quarter	High	Low	Close	Quarter	High	Low	Close	Quarter	High	Low	Close
09/1996	.8023	.7685	.7913	12/1999	.6660	.6302	.6568	03/2003	.6179	.5614	.6041
12/1996	.8211	.7821	.7943	03/2000	.6685	.6010	.6075	06/2003	.6738	.5924	.6726
03/1997	.8012	.7555	.7856	06/2000	.6103	.5650	.5964	09/2003	.6871	.6343	.6808
06/1997	.7894	.7439	.7536	09/2000	.6018	.5367	.5425	12/2003	.7537	.6760	.7521
09/1997	.7556	.7148	.7251	12/2000	.5594	.5075	.5585	03/2004	.8003	.7258	.7655
12/1997	.7414	.6463	.6515	03/2001	.5725	.4853	.4854	06/2004	.7692	.6777	.6972
03/1998	.6880	.6320	.6619	06/2001	.5316	.4778	.5111	09/2004	.7348	.6857	.7278
06/1998	.6629	.5802	.6184	09/2001	.5390	.4823	.4912	12/2004	.7947	.7187	.7825
09/1998	.6333	.5503	.5940	12/2001	.5251	.4900	.5106	03/2005	.7990	.7507	.7731
12/1998	.6478	.5818	.6101	03/2002	.5357	.5052	.5334	06/2005	.7841	.7477	.7605
03/1999	.6548	.6106	.6342	06/2002	.5796	.5258	.5635	09/2005	.7765	.7370	.7629
06/1999	.6745	.6228	.6668	09/2002	.5713	.5230	.5434	12/2005	.7646	.7234	.7335
09/1999	.6718	.6290	.6525	12/2002	.5692	.5402	.5615	03/2006	.7586	.7016	.7157

Source: Forex

AUSTRALIAN DOLLAR

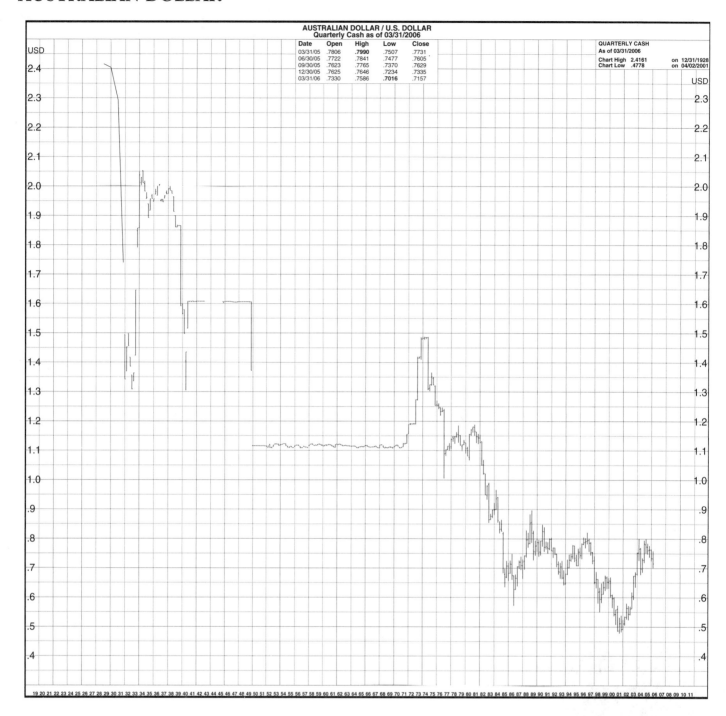

Annual High, Low and Close of Australian Dollar — In USD per AUD

Year	High	Low	Close	Year	High	Low	Close	Year	High	Low	Close
1929	2.4042	2.4042	2.4042	1942	1.6075	1.6075	1.6075	1955	1.1166	1.1090	1.1166
1930	2.2930	2.2930	2.2930	1943	1.6075	1.6075	1.6075	1956	1.1186	1.1086	1.1096
1931	1.8648	1.3425	1.3425	1944	na	na	na	1957	1.1179	1.1087	1.1179
1932	1.4970	1.3075	1.3089	1945	1.6071	1.6035	1.6071	1958	1.1224	1.1169	1.1171
1933	2.0488	1.3360	2.0375	1946	1.6071	1.6054	1.6054	1959	1.1221	1.1149	1.1149
1934	2.0527	1.9576	1.9614	1947	1.6061	1.6045	1.6061	1960	1.1209	1.1155	1.1185
1935	1.9726	1.8928	1.9564	1948	1.6062	1.6058	1.6062	1961	1.1217	1.1105	1.1194
1936	2.0053	1.9477	1.9550	1949	1.6062	1.1158	1.1158	1962	1.1216	1.1159	1.1169
1937	1.9908	1.9463	1.9905	1950	1.1158	1.1155	1.1155	1963	1.1175	1.1142	1.1142
1938	1.9991	1.8603	1.8603	1951	1.1158	1.1131	1.1131	1964	1.1153	1.1090	1.1118
1939	1.8667	1.5633	1.5657	1952	1.1205	1.1087	1.1179	1965	1.1170	1.1119	1.1164
1940	1.6079	1.3040	1.6075	1953	1.1231	1.1167	1.1197	1966	1.1171	1.1111	1.1116
1941	1.6085	1.6056	1.6075	1954	1.1229	1.1105	1.1105	1967	1.1185	1.1088	1.1185

Source: Forex

BRITISH POUND

Annual High, Low and Close of British Pound   In USD per GBP

Year	High	Low	Close	Year	High	Low	Close	Year	High	Low	Close
1929	4.8816	4.8482	4.8816	1942	4.0350	4.0348	4.0350	1955	2.8026	2.7836	2.8026
1930	4.8707	4.8564	4.8566	1943	4.0350	4.0350	4.0350	1956	2.8077	2.7825	2.7850
1931	4.8649	3.3737	3.3737	1944	4.0350	4.0350	4.0350	1957	2.8058	2.7827	2.8058
1932	3.7500	3.2753	3.2787	1945	4.0350	4.0249	4.0337	1958	2.8171	2.8033	2.8034
1933	5.1497	3.3614	5.1159	1946	4.0338	4.0294	4.0294	1959	2.8165	2.7984	2.7984
1934	5.1534	4.9408	4.9458	1947	4.0313	4.0271	4.0313	1960	2.8135	2.7997	2.8073
1935	4.9699	4.7762	4.9288	1948	4.0315	4.0307	4.0315	1961	2.8154	2.7874	2.8096
1936	5.0363	4.8880	4.9078	1949	4.0314	2.8007	2.8007	1962	2.8153	2.8009	2.8033
1937	4.9964	4.8851	4.9964	1950	2.8007	2.8000	2.8000	1963	2.8048	2.7965	2.7965
1938	5.0180	4.6703	4.6703	1951	2.8007	2.7949	2.7949	1964	2.7994	2.7834	2.7906
1939	4.6857	3.9247	3.9301	1952	2.8079	2.7812	2.8059	1965	2.8037	2.7908	2.8021
1940	4.0356	3.2736	4.0350	1953	2.8190	2.8028	2.8103	1966	2.8039	2.7888	2.7901
1941	4.0350	4.0248	4.0350	1954	2.8281	2.7874	2.7874	1967	2.7992	2.4063	2.4063

Source: Forex

BRITISH POUND

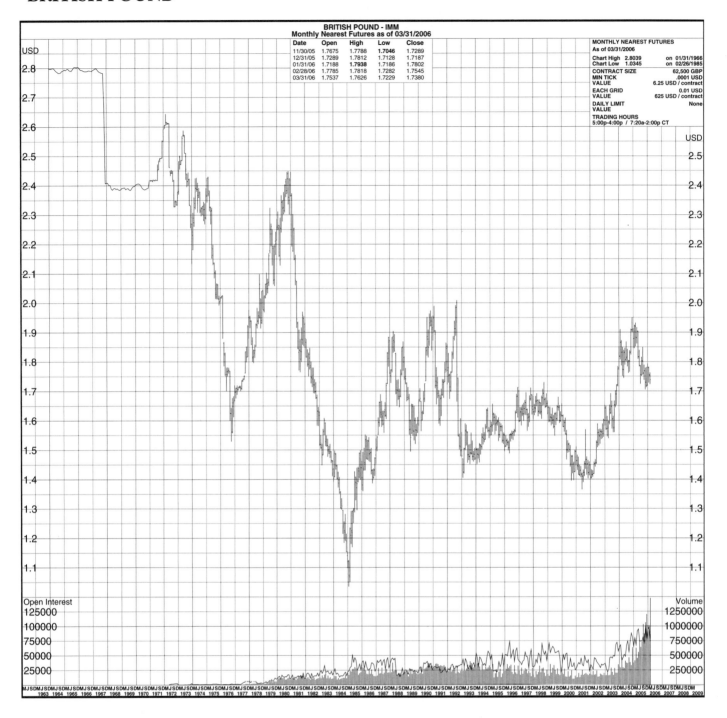

Annual High, Low and Close of British Pound Futures   In USD per GBP

Year	High	Low	Close	Year	High	Low	Close	Year	High	Low	Close
1968	2.4092	2.3842	2.3842	1981	2.4475	1.7645	1.9040	1994	1.6436	1.4522	1.5670
1969	2.3973	2.3840	2.3973	1982	1.9340	1.5820	1.6295	1995	1.6570	1.5200	1.5514
1970	2.4061	2.3853	2.3906	1983	1.6310	1.4105	1.4625	1996	1.7128	1.4880	1.7124
1971	2.5538	2.3938	2.5520	1984	1.4975	1.1525	1.1540	1997	1.7114	1.5650	1.6466
1972	2.6440	2.3270	2.3342	1985	1.4975	1.0345	1.4390	1998	1.7300	1.6042	1.6568
1973	2.5880	2.2550	2.2940	1986	1.5525	1.3600	1.4720	1999	1.6798	1.5476	1.6190
1974	2.4270	2.1340	2.2910	1987	1.8845	1.4530	1.8825	2000	1.6578	1.3952	1.4948
1975	2.4300	1.9920	2.0040	1988	1.9045	1.6456	1.7992	2001	1.5700	1.3652	1.4486
1976	2.0255	1.5290	1.6640	1989	1.8180	1.4940	1.5888	2002	1.6052	1.4004	1.6022
1977	1.9250	1.6670	1.9195	1990	1.9740	1.5640	1.9094	2003	1.7843	1.5390	1.7739
1978	2.0985	1.7960	2.0410	1991	1.9898	1.5824	1.8448	2004	1.9500	1.7436	1.9071
1979	2.3245	1.9685	2.2015	1992	2.0088	1.4780	1.4986	2005	1.9318	1.7046	1.7187
1980	2.4485	2.1280	2.4185	1993	1.5904	1.4050	1.4684	2006	1.7938	1.7186	1.7380

Source: Chicago Mercantile Exchange

BRITISH POUND

Annual High, Low and Close of British Pound   In USD per GBP

Year	High	Low	Close	Year	High	Low	Close	Year	High	Low	Close
1968	2.4092	2.3842	2.3842	1981	2.4320	1.7610	1.9100	1994	1.6440	1.4545	1.5660
1969	2.3973	2.3840	2.3973	1982	1.9390	1.5840	1.6180	1995	1.6570	1.5213	1.5507
1970	2.4061	2.3853	2.3906	1983	1.6310	1.4105	1.4500	1996	1.7163	1.4898	1.7140
1971	2.5538	2.3938	2.5520	1984	1.4950	1.1560	1.1575	1997	1.7145	1.5678	1.6480
1972	2.6440	2.3312	2.3478	1985	1.5015	1.0345	1.4475	1998	1.7365	1.6085	1.6628
1973	2.5843	2.3055	2.3222	1986	1.5590	1.3660	1.4865	1999	1.6791	1.5475	1.6150
1974	2.4370	2.1780	2.3460	1987	1.8875	1.4640	1.8870	2000	1.6581	1.3955	1.4926
1975	2.4343	2.0173	2.0237	1988	1.9055	1.6565	1.8115	2001	1.5100	1.3688	1.4555
1976	2.0358	1.5745	1.7006	1989	1.8305	1.4935	1.6110	2002	1.6133	1.4044	1.6100
1977	1.9195	1.6950	1.9170	1990	1.9875	1.5885	1.9320	2003	1.7944	1.5463	1.7860
1978	2.1050	1.8040	2.0420	1991	2.0040	1.5995	1.8655	2004	1.9553	1.7482	1.9188
1979	2.3325	1.9780	2.2130	1992	2.0100	1.4965	1.5095	2005	1.9326	1.7047	1.7208
1980	2.4555	2.1255	2.3875	1993	1.5971	1.4082	1.4760	2006	1.7935	1.7191	1.7365

Source: Forex

BRITISH POUND

Quarterly High, Low and Close of British Pound Futures In USD per GBP

Quarter	High	Low	Close	Quarter	High	Low	Close	Quarter	High	Low	Close
09/1996	1.5716	1.5334	1.5646	12/1999	1.6798	1.5914	1.6190	03/2003	1.6524	1.5448	1.5724
12/1996	1.7128	1.5600	1.7124	03/2000	1.6578	1.5620	1.5940	06/2003	1.6920	1.5390	1.6468
03/1997	1.7028	1.5830	1.6386	06/2000	1.6090	1.4670	1.5186	09/2003	1.6672	1.5596	1.6536
06/1997	1.6692	1.5986	1.6606	09/2000	1.5236	1.3952	1.4770	12/2003	1.7843	1.6444	1.7739
09/1997	1.6960	1.5650	1.6114	12/2000	1.5000	1.3966	1.4948	03/2004	1.9102	1.7720	1.8316
12/1997	1.7114	1.5940	1.6466	03/2001	1.5110	1.4150	1.4158	06/2004	1.8490	1.7436	1.8057
03/1998	1.6834	1.6042	1.6656	06/2001	1.4486	1.3652	1.4094	09/2004	1.8683	1.7612	1.8023
06/1998	1.6922	1.6142	1.6608	09/2001	1.5700	1.3900	1.4668	12/2004	1.9500	1.7650	1.9071
09/1998	1.7076	1.6052	1.6924	12/2001	1.4772	1.4028	1.4486	03/2005	1.9318	1.8456	1.8826
12/1998	1.7300	1.6424	1.6568	03/2002	1.4486	1.4004	1.4190	06/2005	1.9168	1.7829	1.7863
03/1999	1.6680	1.5940	1.6108	06/2002	1.5308	1.4184	1.5244	09/2005	1.8492	1.7242	1.7603
06/1999	1.6430	1.5732	1.5792	09/2002	1.5900	1.5086	1.5626	12/2005	1.7894	1.7046	1.7187
09/1999	1.6520	1.5476	1.6464	12/2002	1.6052	1.5362	1.6022	03/2006	1.7938	1.7186	1.7380

Source: Chicago Mercantile Exchange

BRITISH POUND

Quarterly High, Low and Close of British Pound   In USD per GBP

Quarter	High	Low	Close	Quarter	High	Low	Close	Quarter	High	Low	Close
09/1996	1.5724	1.5350	1.5645	12/1999	1.6791	1.5913	1.6150	03/2003	1.6570	1.5539	1.5838
12/1996	1.7163	1.5608	1.7140	03/2000	1.6581	1.5620	1.5919	06/2003	1.6904	1.5463	1.6555
03/1997	1.7115	1.5858	1.6389	06/2000	1.6070	1.4655	1.5163	09/2003	1.6760	1.5610	1.6631
06/1997	1.6725	1.6010	1.6637	09/2000	1.5216	1.3955	1.4749	12/2003	1.7944	1.6534	1.7860
09/1997	1.6982	1.5678	1.6189	12/2000	1.4979	1.3966	1.4926	03/2004	1.9142	1.7788	1.8443
12/1997	1.7145	1.5994	1.6480	03/2001	1.5100	1.4158	1.4161	06/2004	1.8605	1.7482	1.8192
03/1998	1.6890	1.6096	1.6721	06/2001	1.4498	1.3688	1.4155	09/2004	1.8772	1.7709	1.8124
06/1998	1.6969	1.6162	1.6672	09/2001	1.4785	1.3936	1.4740	12/2004	1.9553	1.7747	1.9188
09/1998	1.7130	1.6085	1.6998	12/2001	1.4844	1.4044	1.4555	03/2005	1.9326	1.8509	1.8901
12/1998	1.7365	1.6453	1.6628	03/2002	1.4559	1.4044	1.4259	06/2005	1.9218	1.7872	1.7914
03/1999	1.6653	1.5955	1.6113	06/2002	1.5380	1.4248	1.5304	09/2005	1.8500	1.7272	1.7639
06/1999	1.6430	1.5720	1.5768	09/2002	1.5847	1.5153	1.5688	12/2005	1.7903	1.7047	1.7208
09/1999	1.6513	1.5475	1.6458	12/2002	1.6133	1.5415	1.6100	03/2006	1.7935	1.7191	1.7365

Source: Forex

CANADIAN DOLLAR

Annual High, Low and Close of Canadian Dollar   In USD per CAD

Year	High	Low	Close	Year	High	Low	Close	Year	High	Low	Close
1929	.9975	.9834	.9907	1942	.8996	.8717	.8788	1955	1.0350	1.0005	1.0005
1930	1.0012	.9889	.9990	1943	.9064	.8940	.8940	1956	1.0409	1.0008	1.0409
1931	.9998	.8271	.8271	1944	.9051	.8933	.8975	1957	1.0547	1.0230	1.0230
1932	.9123	.8513	.8660	1945	.9083	.8991	.9073	1958	1.0416	1.0154	1.0366
1933	1.0118	.8351	1.0055	1946	.9678	.9060	.9544	1959	1.0551	1.0258	1.0512
1934	1.0294	.9917	1.0131	1947	.9569	.8836	.8836	1960	1.0515	1.0178	1.0178
1935	1.0018	.9858	.9905	1948	.9323	.8906	.9225	1961	1.0127	.9589	.9589
1936	1.0012	.9950	1.0006	1949	.9552	.8841	.8841	1962	.9568	.9191	.9292
1937	1.0015	.9986	.9995	1950	.9604	.8921	.9491	1963	.9285	.9233	.9262
1938	1.0002	.9906	.9906	1951	.9741	.9348	.9741	1964	.9310	.9247	.9304
1939	.9977	.8762	.8762	1952	1.0417	.9949	1.0300	1965	.9311	.9228	.9294
1940	.8802	.8007	.8656	1953	1.0301	1.0055	1.0275	1966	.9304	.9232	.9232
1941	.8913	.8369	.8739	1954	1.0344	1.0157	1.0329	1967	.9315	.9238	.9256

Source: Forex

CANADIAN DOLLAR

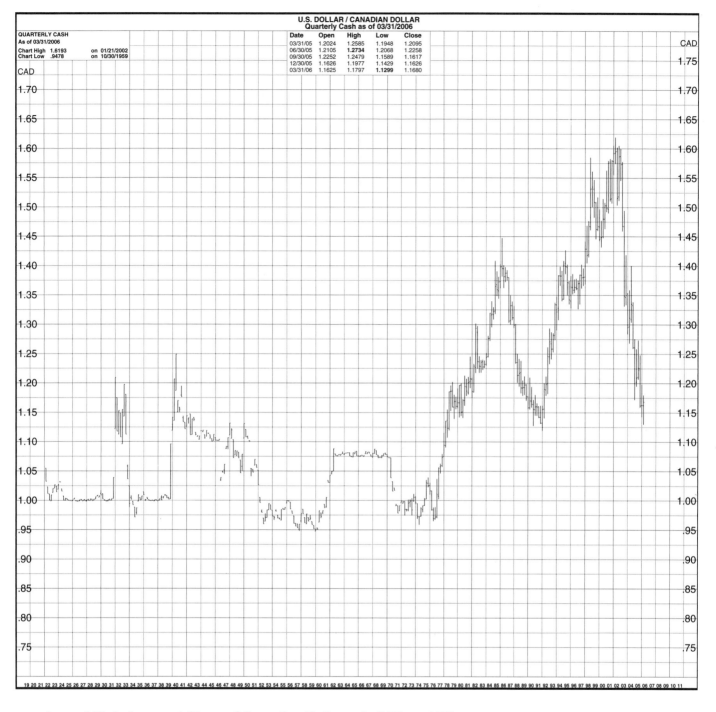

Annual High, Low and Close of Canadian Dollar   In CAD per USD

Year	High	Low	Close	Year	High	Low	Close	Year	High	Low	Close
1929	1.0169	1.0025	1.0094	1942	1.1472	1.1116	1.1379	1955	.9995	.9662	.9995
1930	1.0112	.9988	1.0010	1943	1.1186	1.1033	1.1186	1956	.9992	.9607	.9607
1931	1.2090	1.0002	1.2090	1944	1.1194	1.1049	1.1142	1957	.9775	.9481	.9775
1932	1.1747	1.0961	1.1547	1945	1.1122	1.1010	1.1022	1958	.9848	.9601	.9647
1933	1.1975	.9883	.9945	1946	1.1038	1.0333	1.0478	1959	.9748	.9478	.9513
1934	1.0084	.9714	.9871	1947	1.1317	1.0450	1.1317	1960	.9825	.9510	.9825
1935	1.0144	.9982	1.0096	1948	1.1228	1.0726	1.0840	1961	1.0429	.9875	1.0429
1936	1.0050	.9988	.9994	1949	1.1311	1.0469	1.1311	1962	1.0880	1.0452	1.0762
1937	1.0014	.9985	1.0005	1950	1.1210	1.0412	1.0536	1963	1.0831	1.0770	1.0797
1938	1.0095	.9998	1.0095	1951	1.0697	1.0266	1.0266	1964	1.0814	1.0741	1.0748
1939	1.1413	1.0023	1.1413	1952	1.0051	.9600	.9709	1965	1.0837	1.0740	1.0760
1940	1.2489	1.1361	1.1553	1953	.9945	.9708	.9732	1966	1.0832	1.0748	1.0832
1941	1.1949	1.1220	1.1443	1954	.9845	.9667	.9681	1967	1.0825	1.0735	1.0804

Source: Forex

CANADIAN DOLLAR

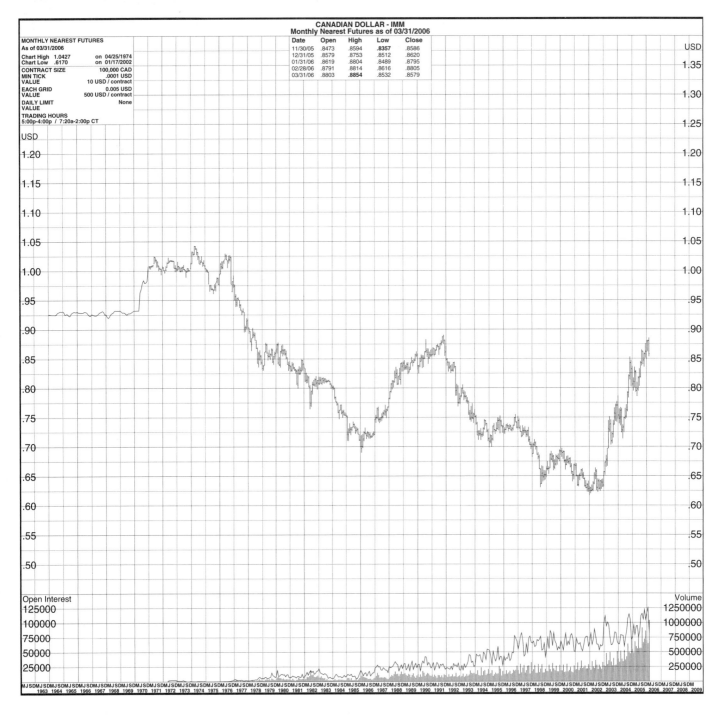

Annual High, Low and Close of Canadian Dollar Futures   In USD per CAD

Year	High	Low	Close	Year	High	Low	Close	Year	High	Low	Close
1968	.9321	.9196	.9318	1981	.8490	.7992	.8406	1994	.7638	.7088	.7128
1969	.9321	.9253	.9308	1982	.8420	.7641	.8128	1995	.7530	.6983	.7331
1970	.9842	.9318	.9828	1983	.8196	.7990	.8043	1996	.7551	.7216	.7332
1971	1.0248	.9933	1.0024	1984	.8042	.7469	.7538	1997	.7524	.6954	.7007
1972	1.0260	.9961	1.0051	1985	.7569	.7097	.7114	1998	.7120	.6305	.6520
1973	1.0160	.9892	1.0001	1986	.7328	.6898	.7210	1999	.6947	.6473	.6922
1974	1.0427	1.0040	1.0090	1987	.7715	.7213	.7679	2000	.6992	.6403	.6679
1975	1.0100	.9610	.9775	1988	.8440	.7667	.8362	2001	.6719	.6225	.6276
1976	1.0296	.9640	.9822	1989	.8625	.8233	.8561	2002	.6640	.6170	.6322
1977	.9924	.8951	.9141	1990	.8828	.8246	.8555	2003	.7772	.6318	.7694
1978	.9181	.8355	.8437	1991	.8906	.8520	.8602	2004	.8530	.7135	.8322
1979	.8777	.8305	.8597	1992	.8718	.7685	.7815	2005	.8753	.7855	.8620
1980	.8780	.8294	.8385	1993	.8060	.7401	.7557	2006	.8854	.8489	.8579

Source: Chicago Mercantile Exchange

CANADIAN DOLLAR

Annual High, Low and Close of Canadian Dollar   In CAD per USD

Year	High	Low	Close	Year	High	Low	Close	Year	High	Low	Close
1968	1.0874	1.0728	1.0732	1981	1.2453	1.1753	1.1860	1994	1.4088	1.3078	1.4017
1969	1.0807	1.0728	1.0743	1982	1.3017	1.1844	1.2291	1995	1.4268	1.3276	1.3641
1970	1.0732	1.0161	1.0175	1983	1.2517	1.2180	1.2444	1996	1.3865	1.3265	1.3703
1971	.9990	.9785	.9990	1984	1.3397	1.2442	1.3218	1997	1.4415	1.3346	1.4289
1972	1.0014	.9747	.9953	1985	1.4086	1.3180	1.3986	1998	1.5848	1.4048	1.5349
1973	1.0112	.9747	.9963	1986	1.4475	1.3625	1.3808	1999	1.5468	1.4428	1.4458
1974	.9947	.9587	.9911	1987	1.3805	1.2945	1.2990	2000	1.5627	1.4318	1.4987
1975	1.0393	.9910	1.0167	1988	1.3010	1.1830	1.1922	2001	1.6052	1.4901	1.5918
1976	1.0368	.9648	1.0101	1989	1.2118	1.1560	1.1585	2002	1.6193	1.5035	1.5730
1977	1.1151	1.0022	1.0942	1990	1.2097	1.1273	1.1600	2003	1.5776	1.2840	1.2956
1978	1.1959	1.0905	1.1862	1991	1.1661	1.1195	1.1556	2004	1.4002	1.1719	1.1997
1979	1.2021	1.1392	1.1667	1992	1.2936	1.1405	1.2708	2005	1.2734	1.1429	1.1626
1980	1.2127	1.1409	1.1946	1993	1.3481	1.2408	1.3218	2006	1.1797	1.1299	1.1680

Source: Forex

CANADIAN DOLLAR

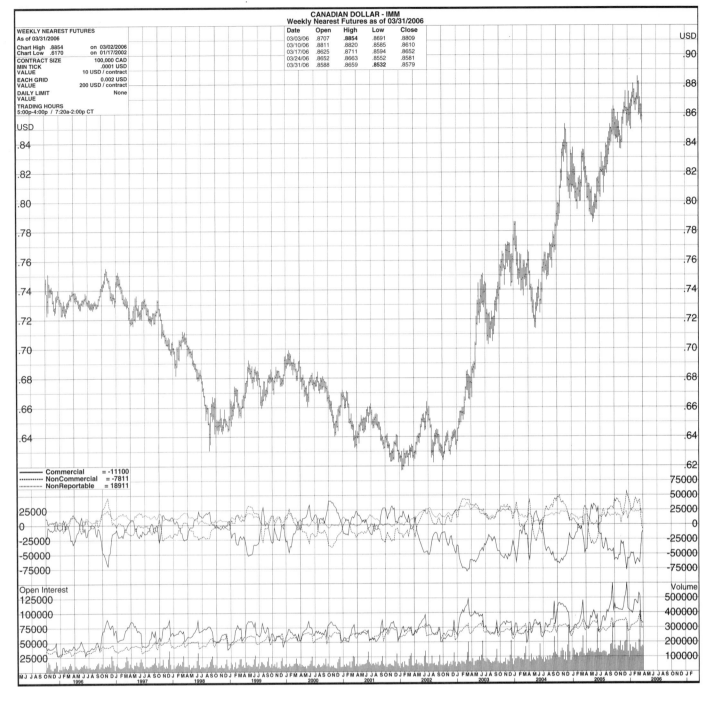

Quarterly High, Low and Close of Canadian Dollar Futures   In USD per CAD

Quarter	High	Low	Close	Quarter	High	Low	Close	Quarter	High	Low	Close
09/1996	.7371	.7261	.7366	12/1999	.6947	.6687	.6922	03/2003	.6853	.6318	.6774
12/1996	.7551	.7310	.7332	03/2000	.6992	.6782	.6911	06/2003	.7513	.6666	.7374
03/1997	.7524	.7257	.7259	06/2000	.6922	.6604	.6767	09/2003	.7458	.7027	.7377
06/1997	.7362	.7155	.7276	09/2000	.6844	.6641	.6660	12/2003	.7772	.7372	.7694
09/1997	.7346	.7160	.7270	12/2000	.6712	.6403	.6679	03/2004	.7863	.7356	.7611
12/1997	.7335	.6954	.7007	03/2001	.6719	.6325	.6346	06/2004	.7656	.7135	.7494
03/1998	.7120	.6815	.7061	06/2001	.6610	.6320	.6600	09/2004	.7935	.7465	.7920
06/1998	.7083	.6780	.6822	09/2001	.6627	.6315	.6328	12/2004	.8530	.7830	.8322
09/1998	.6859	.6305	.6538	12/2001	.6422	.6225	.6276	03/2005	.8370	.7945	.8269
12/1998	.6667	.6401	.6520	03/2002	.6349	.6170	.6269	06/2005	.8295	.7855	.8163
03/1999	.6745	.6473	.6629	06/2002	.6640	.6235	.6586	09/2005	.8650	.8027	.8624
06/1999	.6922	.6629	.6831	09/2002	.6608	.6223	.6287	12/2005	.8753	.8357	.8620
09/1999	.6861	.6593	.6825	12/2002	.6450	.6240	.6322	03/2006	.8854	.8489	.8579

Source: Chicago Mercantile Exchange

CANADIAN DOLLAR

Quarterly High, Low and Close of Canadian Dollar   In CAD per USD

Quarter	High	Low	Close	Quarter	High	Low	Close	Quarter	High	Low	Close
09/1996	1.3784	1.3589	1.3617	12/1999	1.4967	1.4428	1.4458	03/2003	1.5776	1.4590	1.4678
12/1996	1.3756	1.3265	1.3703	03/2000	1.4771	1.4318	1.4490	06/2003	1.4943	1.3310	1.3481
03/1997	1.3855	1.3346	1.3849	06/2000	1.5143	1.4477	1.4798	09/2003	1.4188	1.3335	1.3501
06/1997	1.4023	1.3617	1.3802	09/2000	1.5079	1.4630	1.5030	12/2003	1.3541	1.2840	1.2956
09/1997	1.3960	1.3665	1.3808	12/2000	1.5627	1.4923	1.4987	03/2004	1.3588	1.2683	1.3114
12/1997	1.4415	1.3692	1.4289	03/2001	1.5793	1.4901	1.5751	06/2004	1.4002	1.3038	1.3351
03/1998	1.4686	1.4048	1.4182	06/2001	1.5824	1.5104	1.5141	09/2004	1.3384	1.2593	1.2611
06/1998	1.4763	1.4149	1.4673	09/2001	1.5810	1.5070	1.5791	12/2004	1.2755	1.1719	1.1997
09/1998	1.5848	1.4610	1.5312	12/2001	1.6052	1.5552	1.5918	03/2005	1.2585	1.1948	1.2095
12/1998	1.5610	1.5007	1.5349	03/2002	1.6193	1.5741	1.5949	06/2005	1.2734	1.2068	1.2258
03/1999	1.5468	1.4828	1.5090	06/2002	1.6023	1.5035	1.5157	09/2005	1.2479	1.1589	1.1617
06/1999	1.5093	1.4458	1.4623	09/2002	1.6051	1.5111	1.5863	12/2005	1.1977	1.1429	1.1626
09/1999	1.5173	1.4598	1.4673	12/2002	1.5994	1.5454	1.5730	03/2006	1.1797	1.1299	1.1680

Source: Forex

EURO FX

Annual High, Low and Close of Euro FX Futures   In USD per EUR

Year	High	Low	Close	Year	High	Low	Close	Year	High	Low	Close
1968	.4923	.4874	.4895	1981	1.0149	.7583	.8735	1994	1.3160	1.1067	1.2624
1969	.5306	.4866	.5306	1982	.8770	.7528	.8221	1995	1.4549	1.2496	1.3620
1970	.5386	.5302	.5367	1983	.8397	.7037	.7170	1996	1.3670	1.2431	1.2690
1971	.5998	.5343	.5998	1984	.7712	.6171	.6196	1997	1.2712	1.0345	1.0874
1972	.6219	.6085	.6110	1985	.8031	.5621	.8015	1998	1.2320	1.0537	1.1768
1973	.8606	.6087	.7233	1986	1.0195	.7863	1.0187	1999	1.1925	1.0000	1.0160
1974	.8166	.6773	.8107	1987	1.2469	1.0084	1.2454	2000	1.0464	.8245	.9428
1975	.8592	.7329	.7467	1988	1.2521	1.0160	1.1044	2001	.9615	.8342	.8878
1976	.8304	.7467	.8297	1989	1.1677	.9550	1.1566	2002	1.0473	.8549	1.0471
1977	.9330	.8050	.9320	1990	1.3369	1.1270	1.3109	2003	1.2623	1.0302	1.2534
1978	1.1395	.9062	1.0749	1991	1.3559	1.0617	1.2885	2004	1.3687	1.1745	1.3558
1979	1.1448	1.0167	1.1328	1992	1.4101	1.1614	1.2073	2005	1.3593	1.1661	1.1880
1980	1.1495	.9625	.9965	1993	1.2493	1.1189	1.1245	2006	1.2359	1.1835	1.2179

Source: Chicago Mercantile Exchange

EURO FX

Annual High, Low and Close of Euro FX   In USD per EUR

Year	High	Low	Close	Year	High	Low	Close	Year	High	Low	Close
1968	.4923	.4874	.4895	1981	1.0149	.7583	.8735	1994	1.3160	1.1067	1.2624
1969	.5306	.4866	.5306	1982	.8770	.7528	.8221	1995	1.4549	1.2496	1.3620
1970	.5386	.5302	.5367	1983	.8397	.7037	.7170	1996	1.3670	1.2431	1.2690
1971	.5998	.5343	.5998	1984	.7712	.6171	.6196	1997	1.2712	1.0345	1.0874
1972	.6219	.6085	.6110	1985	.8031	.5621	.8015	1998	1.2320	1.0537	1.1717
1973	.8606	.6087	.7233	1986	1.0195	.7863	1.0187	1999	1.1890	.9992	1.0088
1974	.8166	.6773	.8107	1987	1.2469	1.0084	1.2454	2000	1.0413	.8230	.9422
1975	.8592	.7329	.7467	1988	1.2521	1.0160	1.1044	2001	.9592	.8352	.8912
1976	.8304	.7467	.8297	1989	1.1677	.9550	1.1566	2002	1.0505	.8565	1.0493
1977	.9330	.8050	.9320	1990	1.3369	1.1270	1.3109	2003	1.2649	1.0336	1.2588
1978	1.1395	.9062	1.0749	1991	1.3559	1.0617	1.2885	2004	1.3666	1.1760	1.3567
1979	1.1448	1.0167	1.1328	1992	1.4101	1.1614	1.2073	2005	1.3581	1.1641	1.1837
1980	1.1495	.9625	.9965	1993	1.2493	1.1189	1.1245	2006	1.2324	1.1802	1.2116

Source: Forex

EURO FX

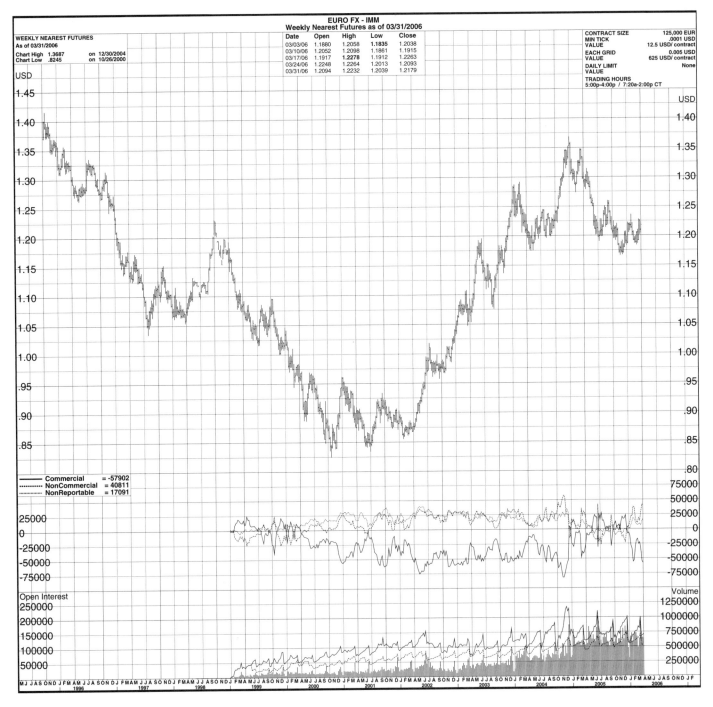

Quarterly High, Low and Close of Euro FX Futures   In USD per EUR

Quarter	High	Low	Close	Quarter	High	Low	Close	Quarter	High	Low	Close
09/1996	1.3352	1.2768	1.2827	12/1999	1.0958	1.0000	1.0160	03/2003	1.1082	1.0302	1.0868
12/1996	1.3135	1.2431	1.2690	03/2000	1.0464	.9440	.9607	06/2003	1.1960	1.0534	1.1469
03/1997	1.2712	1.1366	1.1677	06/2000	.9805	.8861	.9581	09/2003	1.1715	1.0759	1.1620
06/1997	1.1759	1.1200	1.1207	09/2000	.9639	.8478	.8854	12/2003	1.2623	1.1365	1.2534
09/1997	1.1244	1.0345	1.1118	12/2000	.9430	.8245	.9428	03/2004	1.2919	1.2025	1.2280
12/1997	1.1532	1.0871	1.0874	03/2001	.9615	.8761	.8796	06/2004	1.2366	1.1745	1.2178
03/1998	1.1162	1.0550	1.0586	06/2001	.9094	.8411	.8482	09/2004	1.2449	1.1959	1.2432
06/1998	1.1320	1.0537	1.1085	09/2001	.9339	.8342	.9084	12/2004	1.3687	1.2219	1.3558
09/1998	1.1865	1.0955	1.1865	12/2001	.9221	.8712	.8878	03/2005	1.3593	1.2735	1.2982
12/1998	1.2304	1.1545	1.1768	03/2002	.9040	.8549	.8682	06/2005	1.3143	1.2012	1.2137
03/1999	1.1925	1.0730	1.0802	06/2002	.9956	.8686	.9885	09/2005	1.2598	1.1900	1.2059
06/1999	1.0921	1.0255	1.0399	09/2002	1.0185	.9571	.9834	12/2005	1.2249	1.1661	1.1880
09/1999	1.0855	1.0156	1.0729	12/2002	1.0473	.9666	1.0471	03/2006	1.2359	1.1835	1.2179

Source: Chicago Mercantile Exchange

EURO FX

Quarterly High, Low and Close of Euro FX   In USD per EUR

Quarter	High	Low	Close	Quarter	High	Low	Close	Quarter	High	Low	Close
09/1996	1.3352	1.2768	1.2827	12/1999	1.0909	.9992	1.0088	03/2003	1.1083	1.0336	1.0931
12/1996	1.3135	1.2431	1.2690	03/2000	1.0413	.9406	.9554	06/2003	1.1933	1.0562	1.1514
03/1997	1.2712	1.1366	1.1677	06/2000	.9751	.8847	.9525	09/2003	1.1739	1.0764	1.1661
06/1997	1.1759	1.1200	1.1207	09/2000	.9595	.8443	.8831	12/2003	1.2649	1.1377	1.2588
09/1997	1.1244	1.0345	1.1118	12/2000	.9425	.8230	.9422	03/2004	1.2929	1.2046	1.2307
12/1997	1.1532	1.0871	1.0874	03/2001	.9592	.8759	.8759	06/2004	1.2389	1.1760	1.2196
03/1998	1.1162	1.0550	1.0586	06/2001	.9087	.8414	.8493	09/2004	1.2462	1.1970	1.2439
06/1998	1.1151	1.0537	1.0818	09/2001	.9330	.8352	.9112	12/2004	1.3666	1.2225	1.3567
09/1998	1.1773	1.0673	1.1724	12/2001	.9244	.8737	.8912	03/2005	1.3581	1.2732	1.2958
12/1998	1.2320	1.1409	1.1717	03/2002	.9063	.8565	.8718	06/2005	1.3125	1.1981	1.2102
03/1999	1.1890	1.0685	1.0766	06/2002	.9988	.8713	.9913	09/2005	1.2589	1.1868	1.2029
06/1999	1.0881	1.0266	1.0338	09/2002	1.0212	.9610	.9875	12/2005	1.2205	1.1641	1.1837
09/1999	1.0825	1.0112	1.0695	12/2002	1.0505	.9688	1.0493	03/2006	1.2324	1.1802	1.2116

Source: Forex

JAPANESE YEN

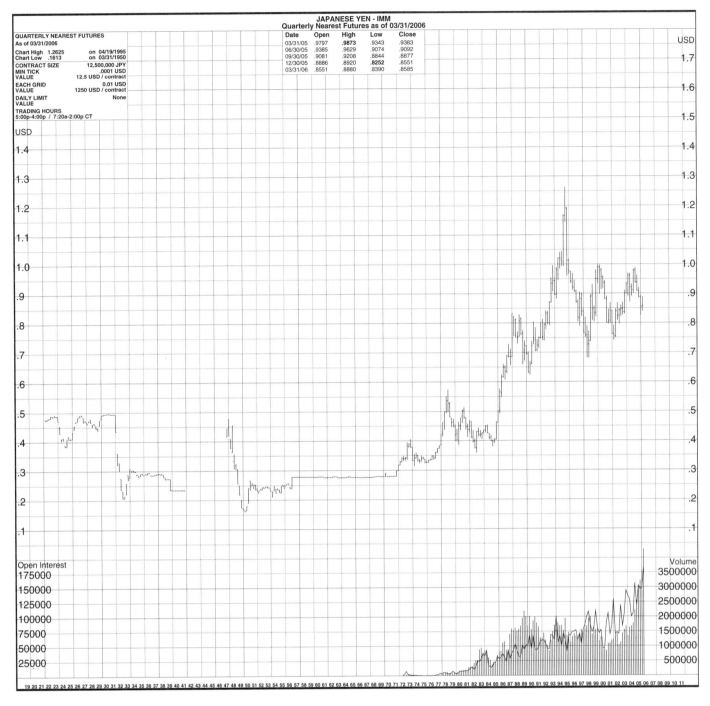

Annual High, Low and Close of Japanese Yen   In USD per JPY

Year	High	Low	Close	Year	High	Low	Close	Year	High	Low	Close
1929	.4896	.4388	.4896	1942	na	na	na	1955	.2513	.2247	.2494
1930	.4962	.4909	.4962	1943	na	na	na	1956	.2779	.2392	.2779
1931	.4944	.4346	.4346	1944	na	na	na	1957	.2779	.2779	.2779
1932	.3599	.2062	.2073	1945	na	na	na	1958	.2779	.2779	.2779
1933	.3074	.2074	.3074	1946	na	na	na	1959	.2779	.2776	.2776
1934	.3031	.2868	.2882	1947	.4762	.4167	.4202	1960	.2787	.2768	.2781
1935	.2932	.2798	.2874	1948	.4545	.3030	.3226	1961	.2786	.2762	.2762
1936	.2941	.2851	.2851	1949	.3058	.1681	.1681	1962	.2790	.2762	.2790
1937	.2909	.2849	.2908	1950	.2667	.1613	.2353	1963	.2789	.2755	.2756
1938	.2905	.2721	.2721	1951	.2597	.2312	.2312	1964	.2784	.2757	.2784
1939	.2730	.2344	.2344	1952	.2439	.2247	.2410	1965	.2786	.2759	.2769
1940	.2344	.2343	.2344	1953	.2469	.2299	.2299	1966	.2770	.2757	.2758
1941	.2344	.2344	.2344	1954	.2469	.2105	.2358	1967	.2763	.2758	.2763

Source: Forex

JAPANESE YEN

Annual High, Low and Close of Japanese Yen — In JPY per USD

Year	High	Low	Close	Year	High	Low	Close	Year	High	Low	Close
1929	227.89	204.25	204.25	1942	na	na	na	1955	445.00	398.00	401.00
1930	203.71	201.53	201.53	1943	na	na	na	1956	418.00	359.84	359.84
1931	230.10	202.27	230.10	1944	na	na	na	1957	359.84	359.84	359.84
1932	484.97	277.85	482.39	1945	na	na	na	1958	359.84	359.84	359.84
1933	482.16	325.31	325.31	1946	na	na	na	1959	360.23	359.84	360.23
1934	348.68	329.92	346.98	1947	240.00	210.00	238.00	1960	361.27	358.81	359.58
1935	357.40	341.06	347.95	1948	330.00	220.00	310.00	1961	362.06	358.94	362.06
1936	350.75	340.02	350.75	1949	595.00	327.00	595.00	1962	362.06	358.42	358.42
1937	351.00	343.76	343.88	1950	620.00	375.00	425.00	1963	362.98	358.55	362.84
1938	367.51	344.23	367.51	1951	432.50	385.00	432.50	1964	362.71	359.20	359.20
1939	426.62	366.30	426.62	1952	445.00	410.00	415.00	1965	362.45	358.94	361.14
1940	426.80	426.62	426.62	1953	435.00	405.00	435.00	1966	362.71	361.01	362.58
1941	426.62	426.62	426.62	1954	475.00	405.00	424.00	1967	362.58	361.93	361.93

Source: Forex

JAPANESE YEN

Annual High, Low and Close of Japanese Yen Futures   In USD per JPY

Year	High	Low	Close	Year	High	Low	Close	Year	High	Low	Close
1968	.2794	.2760	.2794	1981	.5128	.4115	.4624	1994	1.0442	.8818	1.0108
1969	.2795	.2781	.2795	1982	.4669	.3596	.4315	1995	1.2625	.9601	.9773
1970	.2896	.2783	.2796	1983	.4438	.4048	.4371	1996	.9755	.8676	.8713
1971	.3175	.2790	.3175	1984	.4543	.3984	.3987	1997	.9050	.7623	.7736
1972	.3480	.3175	.3410	1985	.5018	.3794	.5004	1998	.8974	.6807	.8884
1973	.4055	.3320	.3329	1986	.6608	.4922	.6354	1999	.9990	.8040	.9892
1974	.3600	.3130	.3310	1987	.8320	.6283	.8316	2000	.9974	.8794	.8827
1975	.3503	.3240	.3260	1988	.8288	.7296	.8069	2001	.8907	.7600	.7629
1976	.3500	.3260	.3407	1989	.8187	.6588	.6968	2002	.8685	.7415	.8447
1977	.4228	.3406	.4216	1990	.8046	.6254	.7384	2003	.9384	.8220	.9318
1978	.5735	.4140	.5270	1991	.7993	.7031	.7991	2004	.9825	.8710	.9797
1979	.5306	.3995	.4197	1992	.8419	.7402	.8004	2005	.9873	.8252	.8551
1980	.5056	.3847	.5025	1993	.9959	.7915	.8959	2006	.8880	.8390	.8585

Source: Chicago Mercantile Exchange

JAPANESE YEN

Annual High, Low and Close of Japanese Yen   In JPY per USD

Year	High	Low	Close	Year	High	Low	Close	Year	High	Low	Close
1968	362.32	357.91	357.91	1981	246.36	198.60	219.92	1994	113.58	96.15	99.71
1969	359.58	357.78	357.78	1982	278.70	217.20	234.85	1995	104.65	79.78	103.46
1970	359.32	345.30	357.65	1983	247.64	226.50	231.74	1996	116.43	103.18	115.93
1971	379.00	313.00	313.00	1984	251.95	221.04	251.95	1997	131.58	110.63	130.20
1972	321.00	294.12	301.75	1985	263.85	199.92	200.08	1998	147.62	111.73	113.88
1973	302.39	254.45	280.27	1986	203.58	151.85	158.10	1999	124.78	101.30	102.18
1974	304.88	273.97	301.11	1987	159.75	120.90	121.10	2000	115.05	101.36	114.34
1975	306.84	284.58	305.16	1988	137.30	120.30	125.00	2001	132.08	113.57	131.56
1976	306.00	285.96	292.83	1989	151.90	123.20	143.95	2002	135.14	115.54	118.79
1977	292.83	237.47	240.10	1990	160.40	123.75	135.45	2003	121.88	106.74	107.38
1978	243.90	176.30	194.14	1991	142.10	124.79	124.84	2004	114.89	101.83	102.43
1979	251.19	193.12	240.73	1992	134.95	118.65	124.80	2005	121.40	101.69	117.96
1980	261.85	201.98	203.00	1993	126.21	100.40	111.83	2006	119.40	113.44	117.69

Source: Forex

JAPANESE YEN

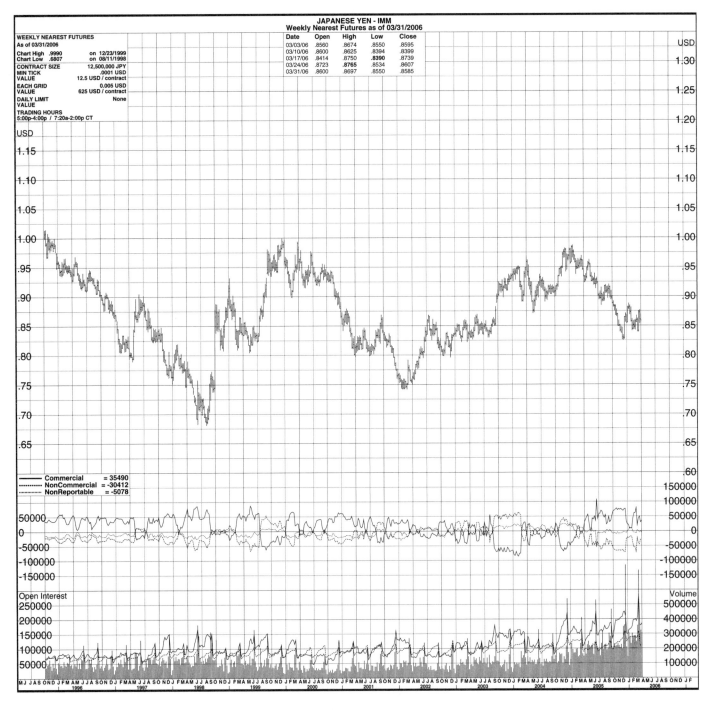

Quarterly High, Low and Close of Japanese Yen Futures — In USD per JPY

Quarter	High	Low	Close	Quarter	High	Low	Close	Quarter	High	Low	Close
09/1996	.9465	.9046	.9076	12/1999	.9990	.9345	.9892	03/2003	.8607	.8220	.8482
12/1996	.9120	.8676	.8713	03/2000	.9974	.8978	.9908	06/2003	.8698	.8265	.8369
03/1997	.8786	.8044	.8178	06/2000	.9855	.9142	.9577	09/2003	.9111	.8296	.8996
06/1997	.9050	.7894	.8826	09/2000	.9600	.9175	.9373	12/2003	.9384	.8979	.9318
09/1997	.9014	.8220	.8392	12/2000	.9445	.8794	.8827	03/2004	.9695	.8904	.9604
12/1997	.8480	.7623	.7736	03/2001	.8907	.8005	.8008	06/2004	.9688	.8710	.9220
03/1998	.8197	.7512	.7587	06/2001	.8470	.7962	.8079	09/2004	.9322	.8905	.9127
06/1998	.7903	.6820	.7266	09/2001	.8688	.7983	.8415	12/2004	.9825	.9002	.9797
09/1998	.7725	.6807	.7390	12/2001	.8416	.7600	.7629	03/2005	.9873	.9343	.9383
12/1998	.8974	.7378	.8884	03/2002	.7920	.7415	.7567	06/2005	.9629	.9074	.9092
03/1999	.9319	.8089	.8486	06/2002	.8481	.7501	.8403	09/2005	.9208	.8844	.8877
06/1999	.8574	.8040	.8348	09/2002	.8685	.8082	.8243	12/2005	.8920	.8252	.8551
09/1999	.9810	.8217	.9500	12/2002	.8478	.7956	.8447	03/2006	.8880	.8390	.8585

Source: Chicago Mercantile Exchange

JAPANESE YEN

Quarterly High, Low and Close of Japanese Yen   In JPY per USD

Quarter	High	Low	Close	Quarter	High	Low	Close	Quarter	High	Low	Close
09/1996	111.70	106.40	111.40	12/1999	107.98	101.30	102.18	03/2003	121.88	116.35	117.91
12/1996	116.43	110.65	115.93	03/2000	111.73	101.36	102.75	06/2003	121.12	115.07	119.75
03/1997	124.83	114.93	123.80	06/2000	110.03	102.85	106.05	09/2003	120.69	110.12	111.49
06/1997	127.47	110.63	114.63	09/2000	109.80	104.83	108.09	12/2003	111.60	106.74	107.38
09/1997	123.06	111.99	120.30	12/2000	115.05	106.84	114.34	03/2004	112.33	103.41	104.39
12/1997	131.58	118.75	130.20	03/2001	126.34	113.57	126.25	06/2004	114.89	103.49	108.80
03/1998	134.40	122.43	133.20	06/2001	126.81	118.37	124.72	09/2004	112.50	107.59	110.07
06/1998	146.73	127.40	138.86	09/2001	126.12	115.84	119.41	12/2004	111.47	101.83	102.43
09/1998	147.62	129.08	136.47	12/2001	132.08	119.30	131.56	03/2005	107.70	101.69	107.22
12/1998	136.85	111.73	113.88	03/2002	135.14	126.40	132.73	06/2005	110.99	104.20	110.90
03/1999	123.73	108.25	118.78	06/2002	133.84	118.40	119.54	09/2005	113.72	108.78	113.47
06/1999	124.78	117.50	121.18	09/2002	124.21	115.54	121.79	12/2005	121.40	113.02	117.96
09/1999	122.87	103.25	106.29	12/2002	125.69	118.31	118.79	03/2006	119.40	113.44	117.69

Source: Forex

MEXICAN PESO

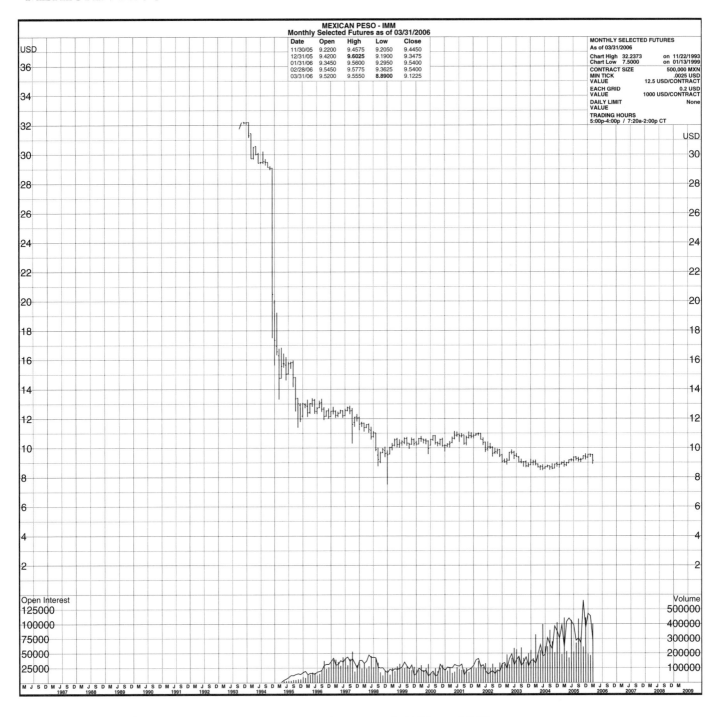

Annual High, Low and Close of Mexican Peso Futures   In USD per MXN

Year	High	Low	Close	Year	High	Low	Close	Year	High	Low	Close
				1997	12.8800	10.3000	12.0600	2002	11.0300	9.3600	9.4925
1993	32.2373	30.8642	32.1750	1998	12.1400	8.7500	9.6100	2003	9.8800	8.6650	8.8300
1994	32.2061	17.4978	20.4708	1999	10.7400	7.5000	10.2900	2004	9.2350	8.4600	8.8575
1995	20.0803	11.4000	11.9800	2000	10.8600	9.5700	10.1275	2005	9.6025	8.6425	9.3475
1996	13.4000	11.9100	12.1350	2001	11.1400	9.7400	10.7825	2006	9.5775	8.8900	9.1225

Source: Chicago Mercantile Exchange

MEXICAN PESO

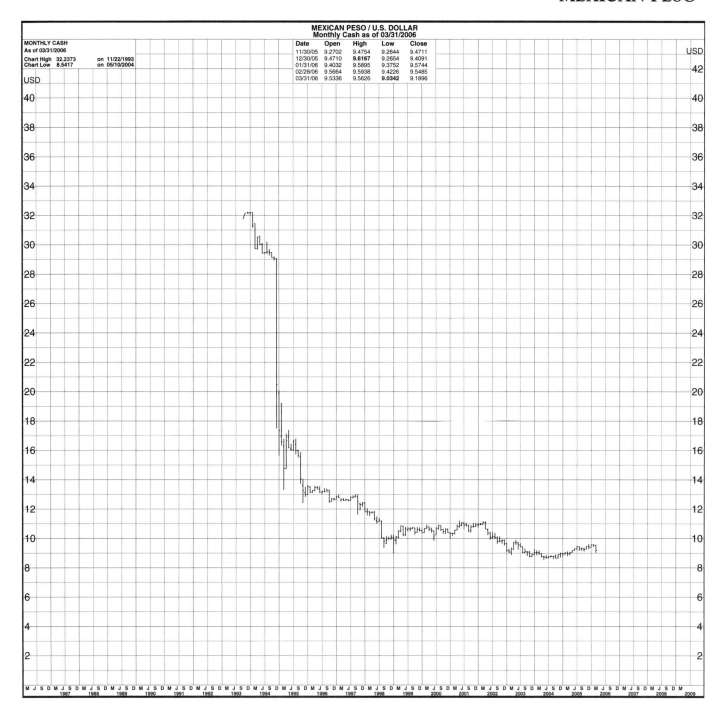

Annual High, Low and Close of Mexican Peso In USD per MXN

Year	High	Low	Close	Year	High	Low	Close	Year	High	Low	Close
				1997	12.9870	11.6279	12.4069	2002	11.1669	9.5279	9.6339
1993	32.2373	30.8642	32.1750	1998	12.4688	9.3589	10.0650	2003	9.9162	8.7276	8.9049
1994	32.2061	17.4978	20.4708	1999	10.8640	8.9710	10.5290	2004	9.2878	8.5417	8.9804
1995	20.0803	12.4069	13.0039	2000	10.9390	9.8570	10.3950	2005	9.6167	8.7443	9.4091
1996	13.6426	12.4224	12.6968	2001	11.2110	10.0050	10.9200	2006	9.5938	9.0342	9.1896

Source: Forex

MEXICAN PESO

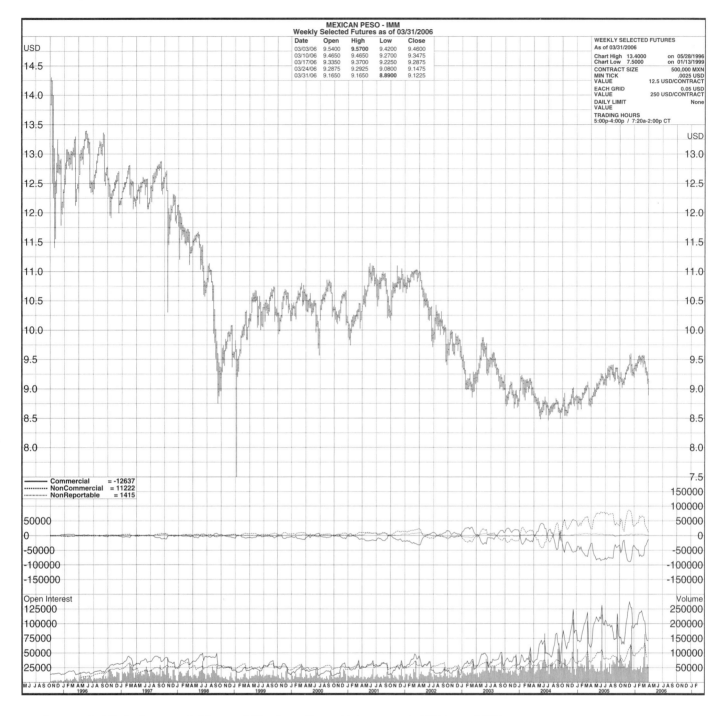

Quarterly High, Low and Close of Mexican Peso Futures   In USD per MXN

Quarter	High	Low	Close	Quarter	High	Low	Close	Quarter	High	Low	Close
09/1996	13.3600	12.3200	12.6500	12/1999	10.7000	9.9300	10.2900	03/2003	9.5800	8.8500	9.1500
12/1996	12.7900	11.9100	12.1350	03/2000	10.8050	10.1500	10.6125	06/2003	9.8800	9.1100	9.4775
03/1997	12.8100	12.0600	12.2325	06/2000	10.6300	9.5700	9.9625	09/2003	9.6300	8.9350	9.0250
06/1997	12.6100	12.0600	12.2000	09/2000	10.8600	10.1700	10.3450	12/2003	9.1250	8.6650	8.8300
09/1997	12.8800	12.1700	12.5275	12/2000	10.6800	10.0800	10.1275	03/2004	9.2350	8.7900	8.8950
12/1997	12.7200	10.3000	12.0600	03/2001	10.4600	9.7400	10.3175	06/2004	8.9225	8.4600	8.5975
03/1998	12.1400	11.1100	11.3950	06/2001	11.1400	10.3150	10.8850	09/2004	8.8375	8.4900	8.6825
06/1998	11.6700	10.5700	10.7475	09/2001	10.9900	10.2000	10.3050	12/2004	9.0250	8.5300	8.8575
09/1998	11.1400	8.7500	9.2175	12/2001	11.1000	10.1600	10.7825	03/2005	9.1200	8.6425	8.8300
12/1998	10.0825	8.9600	9.6100	03/2002	11.0300	10.6250	10.9675	06/2005	9.2650	8.7400	9.1700
03/1999	10.3350	7.5000	10.1675	06/2002	11.0100	9.7100	9.8650	09/2005	9.4125	9.0450	9.1850
06/1999	10.6800	10.0000	10.3250	09/2002	10.4275	9.4000	9.6250	12/2005	9.6025	9.0150	9.3475
09/1999	10.7400	10.1400	10.3200	12/2002	10.0000	9.3600	9.4925	03/2006	9.5775	8.8900	9.1225

Source: Chicago Mercantile Exchange

MEXICAN PESO

Quarterly High, Low and Close of Mexican Peso   In USD per MXN

Quarter	High	Low	Close	Quarter	High	Low	Close	Quarter	High	Low	Close
09/1996	13.4228	13.0293	13.2538	12/1999	10.7790	10.2620	10.5290	03/2003	9.7087	8.8775	9.2687
12/1996	13.3333	12.4224	12.6968	03/2000	10.9390	10.3690	10.7810	06/2003	9.9162	9.2366	9.5630
03/1997	12.9870	12.5125	12.6904	06/2000	10.7980	9.8570	10.1620	09/2003	9.6840	9.0119	9.0988
06/1997	12.7551	12.5313	12.6103	09/2000	10.9220	10.2410	10.5910	12/2003	9.1501	8.7276	8.9049
09/1997	12.9870	12.5747	12.9870	12/2000	10.7010	10.3020	10.3950	03/2004	9.2878	8.8498	8.9807
12/1997	12.9870	11.6279	12.4069	03/2001	10.5880	10.0050	10.5690	06/2004	8.9914	8.5417	8.7048
03/1998	12.4688	11.5327	11.7371	06/2001	11.2110	10.5600	11.0610	09/2004	8.8460	8.5953	8.7866
06/1998	11.8624	11.0193	11.1297	09/2001	11.1360	10.4220	10.5110	12/2004	9.0319	8.6357	8.9804
09/1998	11.4025	9.3589	9.8184	12/2001	11.0619	10.4004	10.9200	03/2005	9.1226	8.7443	8.9526
12/1998	10.2500	9.6154	10.0650	03/2002	11.1669	10.7486	11.0681	06/2005	9.3190	8.8684	9.3046
03/1999	10.5400	8.9710	10.5010	06/2002	11.1632	9.9182	10.0492	09/2005	9.4882	9.1611	9.2920
06/1999	10.8640	10.1580	10.6560	09/2002	10.4306	9.6316	9.7953	12/2005	9.6167	9.1124	9.4091
09/1999	10.7910	10.4640	10.7470	12/2002	10.1317	9.5279	9.6339	03/2006	9.5938	9.0342	9.1896

Source: Forex

SWISS FRANC

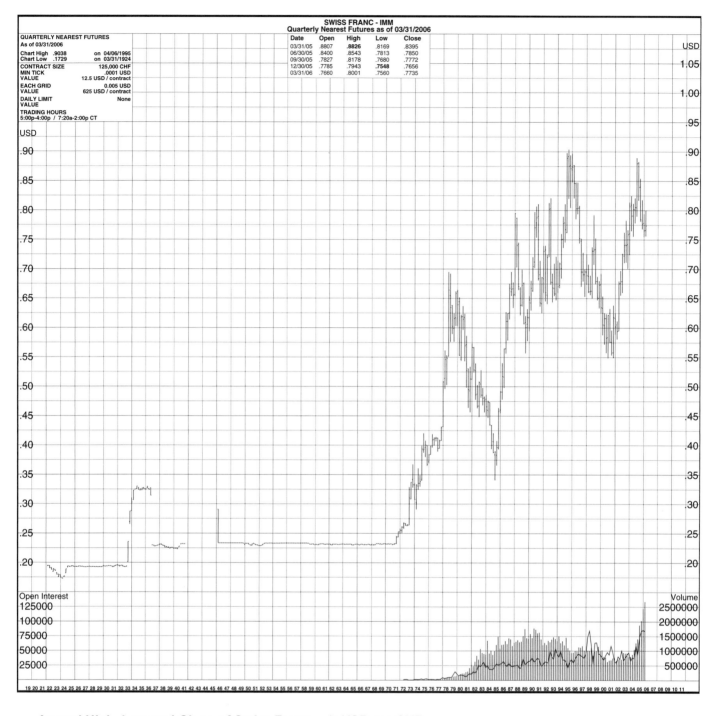

Annual High, Low and Close of Swiss Franc   In USD per CHF

Year	High	Low	Close	Year	High	Low	Close	Year	High	Low	Close
1929	.1944	.1923	.1944	1942	na	na	na	1955	.2334	.2332	.2334
1930	.1944	.1929	.1940	1943	na	na	na	1956	.2334	.2333	.2334
1931	.1960	.1924	.1948	1944	na	na	na	1957	.2334	.2331	.2334
1932	.1951	.1924	.1924	1945	na	na	na	1958	.2334	.2330	.2332
1933	.3102	.1928	.3025	1946	.2907	.2336	.2336	1959	.2320	.2304	.2313
1934	.3302	.3064	.3241	1947	.2336	.2336	.2336	1960	.2323	.2305	.2323
1935	.3275	.3231	.3243	1948	.2336	.2336	.2336	1961	.2322	.2310	.2317
1936	.3303	.2298	.2298	1949	.2336	.2308	.2329	1962	.2317	.2301	.2317
1937	.2315	.2279	.2312	1950	.2329	.2294	.2320	1963	.2317	.2310	.2317
1938	.2323	.2260	.2261	1951	.2330	.2288	.2290	1964	.2317	.2311	.2317
1939	.2267	.2242	.2242	1952	.2333	.2288	.2333	1965	.2316	.2300	.2316
1940	.2320	.2225	.2320	1953	.2333	.2325	.2329	1966	.2317	.2304	.2313
1941	.2322	.2320	.2321	1954	.2333	.2331	.2333	1967	.2317	.2303	.2316

Source: Forex

SWISS FRANC

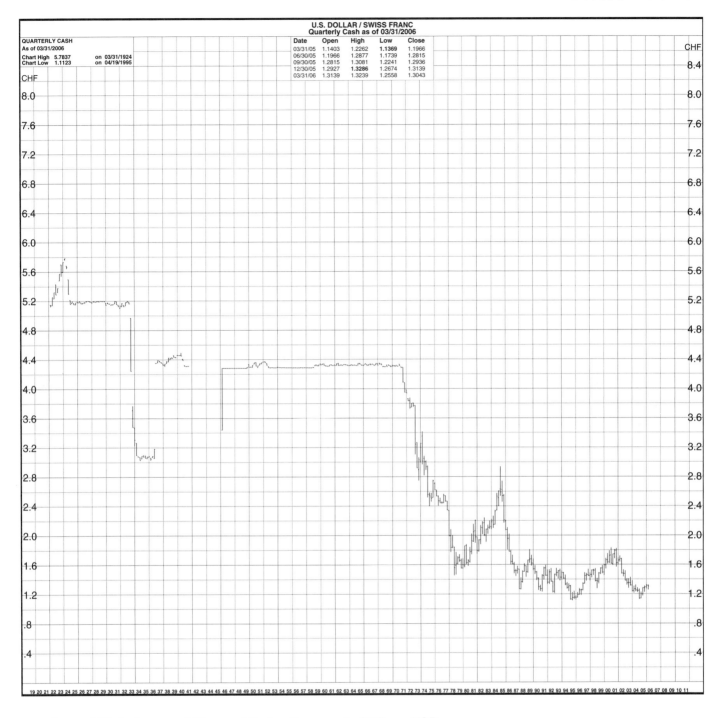

Annual High, Low and Close of Swiss Franc In CHF per USD

Year	High	Low	Close	Year	High	Low	Close	Year	High	Low	Close
1929	5.2002	5.1440	5.1440	1942	na	na	na	1955	4.2882	4.2845	4.2845
1930	5.1840	5.1440	5.1546	1943	na	na	na	1956	4.2863	4.2845	4.2845
1931	5.1975	5.1020	5.1335	1944	na	na	na	1957	4.2900	4.2845	4.2845
1932	5.1975	5.1256	5.1975	1945	na	na	na	1958	4.2918	4.2845	4.2882
1933	5.1867	3.2237	3.3058	1946	4.2808	3.4400	4.2808	1959	4.3403	4.3103	4.3234
1934	3.2637	3.0285	3.0855	1947	4.2808	4.2808	4.2808	1960	4.3384	4.3048	4.3048
1935	3.0950	3.0534	3.0836	1948	4.2808	4.2808	4.2808	1961	4.3290	4.3066	4.3159
1936	4.3516	3.0276	4.3516	1949	4.3328	4.2808	4.2937	1962	4.3459	4.3159	4.3159
1937	4.3879	4.3197	4.3253	1950	4.3592	4.2937	4.3103	1963	4.3290	4.3159	4.3159
1938	4.4248	4.3048	4.4228	1951	4.3706	4.2918	4.3668	1964	4.3271	4.3159	4.3159
1939	4.4603	4.4111	4.4603	1952	4.3706	4.2863	4.2863	1965	4.3478	4.3178	4.3178
1940	4.4944	4.3103	4.3103	1953	4.3011	4.2863	4.2937	1966	4.3403	4.3159	4.3234
1941	4.3103	4.3066	4.3085	1954	4.2900	4.2863	4.2863	1967	4.3422	4.3159	4.3178

Source: Forex

SWISS FRANC

Annual High, Low and Close of Swiss Franc Futures   In USD per CHF

Year	High	Low	Close	Year	High	Low	Close	Year	High	Low	Close
1968	.2327	.2299	.2326	1981	.5865	.4566	.5668	1994	.8108	.6680	.7673
1969	.2327	.2312	.2320	1982	.5675	.4486	.5070	1995	.9038	.7616	.8731
1970	.2326	.2309	.2319	1983	.5280	.4507	.4658	1996	.8772	.7439	.7520
1971	.2580	.2316	.2554	1984	.4763	.3870	.3879	1997	.7520	.6529	.6897
1972	.2685	.2511	.2644	1985	.4928	.3408	.4908	1998	.7920	.6503	.7331
1973	.3676	.2642	.3078	1986	.6268	.4779	.6247	1999	.7525	.6258	.6347
1974	.3993	.2908	.3935	1987	.7955	.6144	.7950	2000	.6536	.5488	.6217
1975	.4202	.3652	.3838	1988	.7877	.6215	.6728	2001	.6382	.5492	.6020
1976	.4189	.3843	.4122	1989	.6773	.5569	.6474	2002	.7265	.5808	.7249
1977	.5094	.3895	.5079	1990	.8068	.6296	.7875	2003	.8138	.7010	.8066
1978	.6951	.4961	.6347	1991	.8108	.6254	.7300	2004	.8892	.7554	.8796
1979	.6648	.5764	.6394	1992	.8209	.6405	.6781	2005	.8826	.7548	.7656
1980	.6516	.5430	.5697	1993	.7212	.6436	.6702	2006	.8001	.7560	.7735

Source: Chicago Mercantile Exchange

SWISS FRANC

Annual High, Low and Close of Swiss Franc   In CHF per USD

Year	High	Low	Close	Year	High	Low	Close	Year	High	Low	Close
1968	4.3497	4.2974	4.2992	1981	2.2123	1.7421	1.7901	1994	1.4950	1.2363	1.3088
1969	4.3253	4.2974	4.3103	1982	2.2416	1.7790	2.0092	1995	1.3188	1.1123	1.1534
1970	4.3309	4.2992	4.3122	1983	2.2212	1.9113	2.1815	1996	1.3538	1.1490	1.3413
1971	4.2950	3.9400	3.9400	1984	2.6102	2.1003	2.6068	1997	1.5387	1.3398	1.4616
1972	3.8775	3.7286	3.7693	1985	2.9385	2.0712	2.0777	1998	1.5470	1.2747	1.3751
1973	3.7707	2.7473	3.2531	1986	2.1097	1.6025	1.6090	1999	1.6021	1.3404	1.5913
1974	3.4153	2.5157	2.5523	1987	1.6360	1.2695	1.2700	2000	1.8300	1.5427	1.6140
1975	2.7563	2.3981	2.6212	1988	1.6155	1.2630	1.5010	2001	1.8219	1.5680	1.6585
1976	2.6192	2.4050	2.4456	1989	1.8090	1.4870	1.5410	2002	1.7225	1.3810	1.3835
1977	2.5654	1.9861	1.9940	1990	1.5895	1.2395	1.2720	2003	1.4274	1.2310	1.2398
1978	2.0833	1.4550	1.6200	1991	1.5936	1.2319	1.3585	2004	1.3227	1.1285	1.1398
1979	1.7437	1.5451	1.5987	1992	1.5496	1.2105	1.4665	2005	1.3286	1.1369	1.3139
1980	1.8801	1.5637	1.7771	1993	1.5520	1.3823	1.4883	2006	1.3239	1.2558	1.3043

Source: Forex

SWISS FRANC

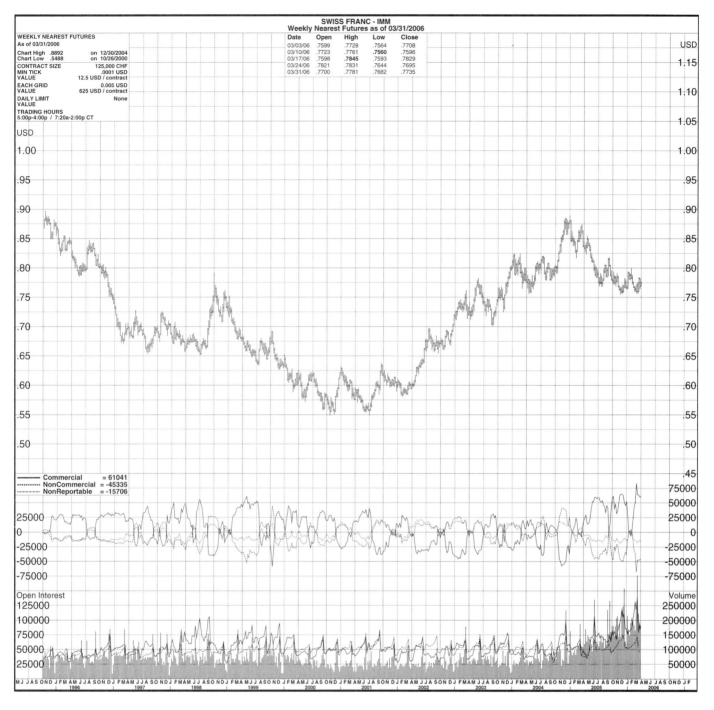

Quarterly High, Low and Close of Swiss Franc Futures   In USD per CHF

Quarter	High	Low	Close	Quarter	High	Low	Close	Quarter	High	Low	Close
09/1996	.8475	.7938	.8039	12/1999	.6924	.6258	.6347	03/2003	.7621	.7107	.7404
12/1996	.8081	.7439	.7520	03/2000	.6536	.5880	.6055	06/2003	.7829	.7115	.7406
03/1997	.7520	.6705	.6956	06/2000	.6255	.5721	.6162	09/2003	.7664	.7010	.7589
06/1997	.7281	.6792	.6908	09/2000	.6235	.5576	.5828	12/2003	.8138	.7247	.8066
09/1997	.6998	.6529	.6956	12/2000	.6225	.5488	.6217	03/2004	.8249	.7648	.7908
12/1997	.7258	.6744	.6897	03/2001	.6326	.5750	.5762	06/2004	.8116	.7554	.8017
03/1998	.7080	.6601	.6618	06/2001	.5959	.5535	.5580	09/2004	.8209	.7785	.8054
06/1998	.6892	.6560	.6628	09/2001	.6382	.5492	.6178	12/2004	.8892	.7900	.8796
09/1998	.7375	.6503	.7308	12/2001	.6255	.5890	.6020	03/2005	.8826	.8169	.8395
12/1998	.7920	.7077	.7331	03/2002	.6115	.5808	.5943	06/2005	.8543	.7813	.7850
03/1999	.7525	.6747	.6792	06/2002	.6795	.5951	.6756	09/2005	.8178	.7680	.7772
06/1999	.6873	.6472	.6510	09/2002	.6975	.6552	.6791	12/2005	.7943	.7548	.7656
09/1999	.6803	.6336	.6733	12/2002	.7265	.6601	.7249	03/2006	.8001	.7560	.7735

Source: Chicago Mercantile Exchange

SWISS FRANC

Quarterly High, Low and Close of Swiss Franc   In CHF per USD

Quarter	High	Low	Close	Quarter	High	Low	Close	Quarter	High	Low	Close
09/1996	1.2661	1.1850	1.2548	12/1999	1.6021	1.4540	1.5913	03/2003	1.4083	1.3231	1.3496
12/1996	1.3538	1.2466	1.3413	03/2000	1.6888	1.5427	1.6633	06/2003	1.4079	1.2785	1.3511
03/1997	1.4923	1.3398	1.4473	06/2000	1.7529	1.6109	1.6340	09/2003	1.4274	1.3096	1.3184
06/1997	1.4823	1.3783	1.4616	09/2000	1.7925	1.6151	1.7242	12/2003	1.3805	1.2310	1.2398
09/1997	1.5387	1.4413	1.4484	12/2000	1.8300	1.6110	1.6140	03/2004	1.3078	1.2140	1.2664
12/1997	1.4902	1.3831	1.4616	03/2001	1.7435	1.5904	1.7428	06/2004	1.3227	1.2323	1.2503
03/1998	1.5280	1.4220	1.5235	06/2001	1.8079	1.6846	1.7938	09/2004	1.2859	1.2207	1.2450
06/1998	1.5367	1.4543	1.5203	09/2001	1.8219	1.5680	1.6207	12/2004	1.2685	1.1285	1.1398
09/1998	1.5470	1.3686	1.3778	12/2001	1.6959	1.5986	1.6585	03/2005	1.2262	1.1369	1.1966
12/1998	1.4149	1.2747	1.3751	03/2002	1.7225	1.6357	1.6813	06/2005	1.2877	1.1739	1.2815
03/1999	1.4925	1.3404	1.4824	06/2002	1.6822	1.4738	1.4809	09/2005	1.3081	1.2241	1.2936
06/1999	1.5569	1.4680	1.5500	09/2002	1.5304	1.4360	1.4750	12/2005	1.3286	1.2674	1.3139
09/1999	1.5892	1.4773	1.4959	12/2002	1.5170	1.3810	1.3835	03/2006	1.3239	1.2558	1.3043

Source: Forex

EURO / SWISS FRANC

Annual High, Low and Close of Euro / Swiss Franc   In CHF per EUR

Year	High	Low	Close	Year	High	Low	Close	Year	High	Low	Close
1968	2.1247	2.0939	2.1012	1981	1.8404	1.5261	1.5636	1994	1.6997	1.5963	1.6522
1969	2.2903	2.0951	2.2877	1982	1.7023	1.5244	1.6517	1995	1.7085	1.5086	1.5709
1970	2.3276	2.2798	2.3131	1983	1.7130	1.5440	1.5642	1996	1.7098	1.5518	1.7080
1971	2.3632	2.2495	2.3632	1984	1.6891	1.5323	1.6152	1997	1.7258	1.5795	1.5966
1972	2.3775	2.2919	2.3030	1985	1.7072	1.5590	1.6425	1998	1.6675	1.5489	1.6218
1973	2.4801	2.1494	2.3530	1986	1.7041	1.5353	1.6390	1999	1.6302	1.5783	1.5998
1974	2.3744	2.0359	2.0691	1987	1.7174	1.5582	1.5816	2000	1.6174	1.4942	1.5210
1975	2.1221	1.9545	1.9573	1988	1.6870	1.5381	1.6576	2001	1.5480	1.4399	1.4780
1976	2.0326	1.8155	2.0291	1989	1.8126	1.6274	1.7823	2002	1.4882	1.4442	1.4503
1977	2.0994	1.8386	1.8584	1990	1.8535	1.5685	1.6674	2003	1.5748	1.4484	1.5605
1978	1.9746	1.4547	1.7413	1991	1.7820	1.5959	1.7504	2004	1.5867	1.5037	1.5463
1979	1.8566	1.7212	1.8110	1992	1.8398	1.6420	1.7705	2005	1.5661	1.5295	1.5555
1980	1.8928	1.6928	1.7709	1993	1.8547	1.6264	1.6736	2006	1.5821	1.5407	1.5803

Source: Forex

EURO / SWISS FRANC

Quarterly High, Low and Close of Euro / Swiss Franc   In CHF per EUR

Quarter	High	Low	Close	Quarter	High	Low	Close	Quarter	High	Low	Close
09/1996	1.6658	1.5540	1.6095	12/1999	1.6170	1.5850	1.5998	03/2003	1.4811	1.4484	1.4751
12/1996	1.7098	1.5890	1.7080	03/2000	1.6174	1.5843	1.5894	06/2003	1.5563	1.4744	1.5558
03/1997	1.7258	1.6697	1.6930	06/2000	1.5932	1.5393	1.5567	09/2003	1.5624	1.5280	1.5372
06/1997	1.6963	1.6091	1.6457	09/2000	1.5667	1.5056	1.5229	12/2003	1.5748	1.5368	1.5605
09/1997	1.6510	1.5900	1.6136	12/2000	1.5364	1.4942	1.5210	03/2004	1.5867	1.5466	1.5587
12/1997	1.6429	1.5795	1.5966	03/2001	1.5471	1.5058	1.5269	06/2004	1.5693	1.5037	1.5243
03/1998	1.6179	1.5696	1.6142	06/2001	1.5480	1.5126	1.5238	09/2004	1.5544	1.5132	1.5487
06/1998	1.6675	1.5995	1.6492	09/2001	1.5284	1.4399	1.4770	12/2004	1.5557	1.5078	1.5463
09/1998	1.6656	1.5716	1.6119	12/2001	1.4915	1.4514	1.4780	03/2005	1.5634	1.5344	1.5504
12/1998	1.6334	1.5489	1.6218	03/2002	1.4882	1.4571	1.4661	06/2005	1.5574	1.5295	1.5509
03/1999	1.6302	1.5783	1.5974	06/2002	1.4785	1.4490	1.4686	09/2005	1.5661	1.5400	1.5559
06/1999	1.6158	1.5830	1.6027	09/2002	1.4747	1.4442	1.4565	12/2005	1.5653	1.5354	1.5555
09/1999	1.6121	1.5909	1.6002	12/2002	1.4789	1.4497	1.4503	03/2006	1.5821	1.5407	1.5803

Source: Forex

EURO / BRITISH POUND

Annual High, Low and Close of Euro / British Pound   In GBP per EUR

Year	High	Low	Close	Year	High	Low	Close	Year	High	Low	Close
1968	.2073	.2044	.2065	1981	.4794	.3856	.4573	1994	.8230	.7463	.8061
1969	.2223	.2040	.2219	1982	.5127	.4447	.5081	1995	.9012	.8034	.8783
1970	.2273	.2212	.2258	1983	.5546	.4804	.4945	1996	.8820	.7420	.7420
1971	.2378	.2231	.2348	1984	.5399	.4916	.5353	1997	.7557	.6371	.6630
1972	.2619	.2347	.2602	1985	.5576	.4801	.5537	1998	.7164	.6303	.7104
1973	.3446	.2587	.3115	1986	.6934	.5478	.6853	1999	.7183	.6199	.6253
1974	.3462	.3041	.3456	1987	.7130	.6487	.6600	2000	.6415	.5685	.6309
1975	.3797	.3448	.3690	1988	.6602	.6034	.6097	2001	.6444	.5953	.6123
1976	.5180	.3690	.4879	1989	.7233	.5946	.7179	2002	.6543	.6072	.6517
1977	.5062	.4683	.4862	1990	.7193	.6426	.6785	2003	.7254	.6470	.7049
1978	.5418	.4742	.5264	1991	.6907	.6526	.6907	2004	.7108	.6545	.7071
1979	.5309	.4609	.5119	1992	.8163	.6645	.7998	2005	.7095	.6611	.6879
1980	.5114	.4117	.4174	1993	.8416	.7552	.7619	2006	.6985	.6784	.6978

Source: Forex

EURO / BRITISH POUND

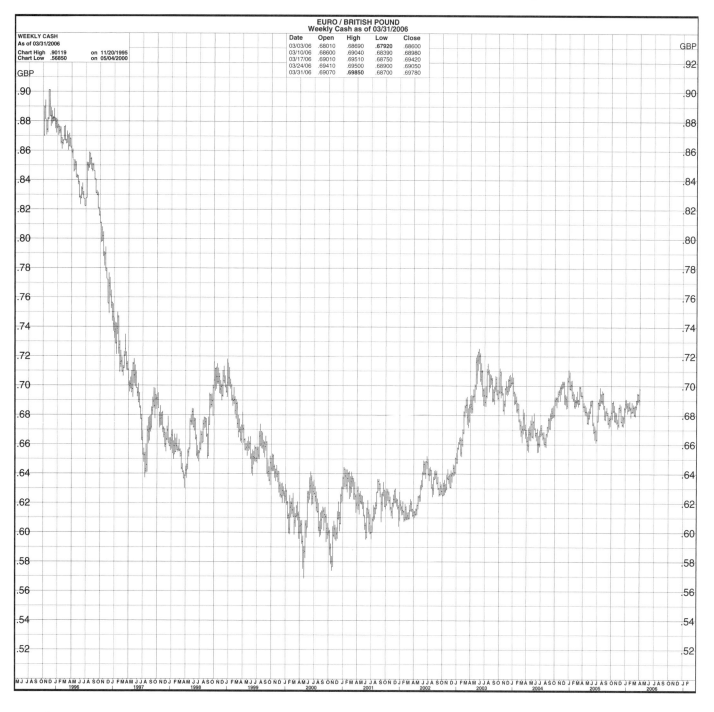

Quarterly High, Low and Close of Euro / British Pound   In GBP per EUR

Quarter	High	Low	Close	Quarter	High	Low	Close	Quarter	High	Low	Close
09/1996	.8589	.8198	.8199	12/1999	.6535	.6199	.6253	03/2003	.6927	.6470	.6900
12/1996	.8198	.7420	.7420	03/2000	.6329	.5956	.5999	06/2003	.7254	.6813	.6957
03/1997	.7557	.7064	.7128	06/2000	.6415	.5685	.6279	09/2003	.7153	.6859	.7012
06/1997	.7184	.6753	.6753	09/2000	.6359	.5934	.5985	12/2003	.7120	.6806	.7049
09/1997	.6986	.6371	.6884	12/2000	.6312	.5738	.6309	03/2004	.7059	.6612	.6673
12/1997	.6951	.6548	.6630	03/2001	.6444	.6133	.6183	06/2004	.6816	.6545	.6704
03/1998	.6702	.6303	.6333	06/2001	.6315	.5953	.5997	09/2004	.6879	.6580	.6864
06/1998	.6845	.6318	.6493	09/2001	.6365	.5955	.6179	12/2004	.7108	.6843	.7071
09/1998	.6949	.6483	.6873	12/2001	.6300	.6040	.6123	03/2005	.7095	.6849	.6856
12/1998	.7164	.6872	.7104	03/2002	.6279	.6072	.6114	06/2005	.6904	.6611	.6756
03/1999	.7183	.6607	.6688	06/2002	.6521	.6090	.6479	09/2005	.6989	.6713	.6819
06/1999	.6820	.6385	.6553	09/2002	.6502	.6241	.6294	12/2005	.6908	.6707	.6879
09/1999	.6739	.6321	.6495	12/2002	.6543	.6249	.6517	03/2006	.6985	.6784	.6978

Source: Forex

BRITISH POUND / JAPANESE YEN

Annual High, Low and Close of British Pound / Japanese Yen   In JPY per GBP

Year	High	Low	Close	Year	High	Low	Close	Year	High	Low	Close
1968	926.28	879.65	884.00	1981	494.40	401.18	420.05	1994	169.63	149.13	156.18
1969	900.38	884.20	900.38	1982	468.62	375.34	379.99	1995	164.52	128.33	160.48
1970	904.26	869.33	904.26	1983	387.18	331.17	336.02	1996	198.89	156.47	198.75
1971	909.44	799.69	799.69	1984	354.56	288.01	291.63	1997	218.95	181.36	215.20
1972	832.26	701.75	708.45	1985	341.77	268.91	289.62	1998	240.91	186.54	189.40
1973	717.92	627.23	650.84	1986	298.53	218.36	235.02	1999	201.89	161.05	165.05
1974	718.14	641.89	706.41	1987	249.24	225.18	228.52	2000	179.76	148.28	170.71
1975	713.43	612.80	617.55	1988	241.90	220.83	226.56	2001	191.61	165.45	191.43
1976	621.45	462.27	497.98	1989	233.14	216.37	231.82	2002	197.23	179.23	191.35
1977	500.67	435.58	460.26	1990	286.94	232.81	262.16	2003	199.50	179.48	191.77
1978	472.50	358.29	396.43	1991	264.46	220.62	232.66	2004	208.05	190.15	196.51
1979	550.35	393.06	532.74	1992	249.19	186.70	188.46	2005	213.02	189.60	202.95
1980	573.72	481.32	484.66	1993	195.37	147.29	165.10	2006	211.16	200.59	204.34

Source: Forex

BRITISH POUND / JAPANESE YEN

Quarterly High, Low and Close of British Pound / Japanese Yen   In JPY per GBP

Quarter	High	Low	Close	Quarter	High	Low	Close	Quarter	High	Low	Close
09/1996	174.90	164.10	174.32	12/1999	178.87	161.05	165.05	03/2003	198.01	184.29	186.75
12/1996	198.89	173.37	198.75	03/2000	179.76	162.78	163.88	06/2003	199.50	185.16	198.23
03/1997	203.69	192.97	202.95	06/2000	170.88	156.33	160.83	09/2003	199.16	181.37	185.40
06/1997	207.33	181.49	190.74	09/2000	166.40	148.28	159.46	12/2003	191.93	179.48	191.77
09/1997	197.73	181.36	194.80	12/2000	171.83	151.56	170.71	03/2004	208.05	190.25	192.47
12/1997	218.95	193.06	215.20	03/2001	179.07	165.50	178.82	06/2004	205.08	190.15	197.90
03/1998	224.25	199.85	222.78	06/2001	181.41	165.45	176.58	09/2004	204.75	193.70	199.47
06/1998	239.98	213.24	231.55	09/2001	178.91	169.21	176.05	12/2004	203.68	191.05	196.51
09/1998	240.91	216.19	232.03	12/2001	191.61	173.47	191.43	03/2005	202.72	189.60	202.61
12/1998	232.55	186.54	189.40	03/2002	192.43	180.25	189.25	06/2005	205.35	194.20	198.68
03/1999	198.96	176.87	191.43	06/2002	192.58	180.07	182.98	09/2005	203.47	192.80	200.12
06/1999	201.89	188.63	191.12	09/2002	193.25	179.23	191.05	12/2005	213.02	199.21	202.95
09/1999	193.63	166.05	174.98	12/2002	197.23	187.72	191.35	03/2006	211.16	200.59	204.34

Source: Forex

EURO / JAPANESE YEN

Annual High, Low and Close of Euro FX / Japanese Yen   In JPY per EUR

Year	High	Low	Close	Year	High	Low	Close	Year	High	Low	Close
1968	190.13	181.17	182.58	1981	205.21	175.92	192.10	1994	128.94	112.99	125.87
1969	199.81	182.64	199.81	1982	213.63	188.51	193.06	1995	144.37	110.60	140.91
1970	204.74	193.74	204.17	1983	197.66	164.93	166.16	1996	149.11	132.46	147.63
1971	205.73	187.74	187.74	1984	181.35	149.67	156.11	1997	148.01	121.75	142.62
1972	195.55	182.91	184.37	1985	169.36	146.12	160.36	1998	162.57	132.36	135.10
1973	228.58	174.63	202.72	1986	163.59	140.66	161.05	1999	135.16	102.10	103.25
1974	244.11	198.71	244.11	1987	169.45	148.39	150.81	2000	111.96	88.97	107.75
1975	251.20	221.37	227.86	1988	158.75	134.13	138.05	2001	117.30	99.98	117.23
1976	242.96	221.89	242.96	1989	168.32	132.30	166.49	2002	125.60	111.30	124.64
1977	243.99	209.72	223.77	1990	188.93	159.76	177.56	2003	140.96	124.13	135.17
1978	233.94	177.43	208.68	1991	179.11	144.59	160.86	2004	141.63	125.83	138.98
1979	285.34	205.94	272.70	1992	175.41	148.60	150.67	2005	143.61	130.61	139.62
1980	278.06	201.11	202.29	1993	155.73	115.15	125.75	2006	143.42	137.11	142.59

Source: Forex

EURO / JAPANESE YEN

Quarterly High, Low and Close of Euro FX / Japanese Yen   In JPY per EUR

Quarter	High	Low	Close	Quarter	High	Low	Close	Quarter	High	Low	Close
09/1996	146.75	139.69	142.89	12/1999	116.49	102.10	103.25	03/2003	130.78	124.13	128.88
12/1996	149.11	140.32	147.63	03/2000	111.96	97.56	98.19	06/2003	140.96	127.50	137.88
03/1997	148.01	138.20	144.62	06/2000	103.15	94.93	101.03	09/2003	138.59	125.07	129.99
06/1997	145.39	126.70	128.99	09/2000	103.28	90.09	95.47	12/2003	135.24	124.19	135.17
09/1997	135.83	121.75	134.18	12/2000	107.86	88.97	107.75	03/2004	139.04	126.58	128.46
12/1997	145.51	132.43	142.62	03/2001	113.20	104.18	110.61	06/2004	137.88	125.83	132.71
03/1998	144.56	132.36	140.98	06/2001	113.72	99.98	105.95	09/2004	137.56	131.25	136.89
06/1998	159.03	137.19	150.37	09/2001	110.75	104.71	108.82	12/2004	141.63	134.06	138.98
09/1998	162.57	148.00	159.58	12/2001	117.30	106.72	117.23	03/2005	140.72	133.00	138.91
12/1998	162.37	133.95	135.10	03/2002	119.68	111.30	115.67	06/2005	140.49	130.61	134.23
03/1999	135.16	124.59	127.87	06/2002	119.50	113.46	118.53	09/2005	138.85	132.54	136.48
06/1999	133.08	122.67	125.30	09/2002	121.96	114.25	120.24	12/2005	143.61	135.86	139.62
09/1999	125.69	106.98	113.71	12/2002	125.60	120.01	124.64	03/2006	143.42	137.11	142.59

Source: Forex

ENERGY

Crude Oil Market Outlook

Crude oil and petroleum products represent the single most important commodity group for the world economy. There is no other commodity that has periodically spiked higher in price and single-handedly caused three US economic recessions (1973-74, 1980, 1990-91). Moreover, oil price movement will remain critical going forward given that crude oil has tripled in price in the past several years and the possibility for a super-spike above $100 per barrel exists if there are any major supply disruptions.

Oil prices have rallied sharply in the past 3 years mainly because of strong world demand, and particularly strong demand from China. At the same time, world production is straining to meet demand and there is very little excess supply capacity. Recent supply disruptions included a 20% cut in Nigerian production due to rebel attacks in February 2006 and a continuing 25% cut in oil production from the Gulf of Mexico due to Hurricane Katrina in August 2005. In addition, the market remains very nervous that Iran may eventually decide to cut-off oil exports to retaliate for pressure from the US and Europe to halt its nuclear research program.

Production capacity is the key issue facing the oil industry and oil consuming nations. The oil industry needs to invest some $2.2 trillion over the next 30 years in exploration and production in order to meet oil demand in the future, according to a study released by the International Energy Agency (IEA) in 2003. Moreover, the alarming fact is that 75% of that investment is needed to simply replace the reserves that are currently being depleted. Only 25% of that investment is needed to meet new demand. The US passed its prime in oil production in the early 1970s, and there is now a debate about whether world oil production is in the process of peaking due to the lack of investment in exploration and new production facilities.

Crude Oil Price History

1973 oil crisis

The world oil market from the 1930s through the early 1970s was tightly controlled by the major oil companies, which were referred to as the "Seven Sisters." However, in the early 1970s, Middle East countries started to nationalize their oil facilities and take control of their own oil production destiny. This gave the Arab countries the leverage to announce an oil embargo on the US in 1973 in retaliation for US support for Israel during the Yom Kippur War, when Israel suffered a surprise attack by Egypt and Syria.

In the space of a few months, oil prices (for West Texas Intermediate oil) spiked higher and roughly tripled from $3.56 per barrel in mid-1973 to $10.11 in early 1974. The shock to US consumers came not only from the hike in prices but also shortages and long lines at the gas pumps. Shortages quickly arose because of ill-conceived US oil price

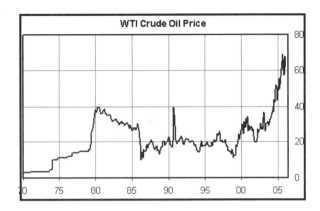

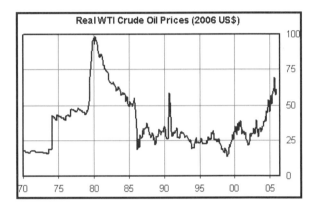

controls and rationing that were imposed by President Nixon and Congress in the early 1970s. Those price controls discouraged exploration and production and reduced the supply of gasoline available to US consumers at the gas pump (President Reagan finally dismantled oil price controls and regulation in 1981). The Arab Oil Embargo on US oil exports did not work particularly well from a technical standpoint since the US could simply buy oil from other sellers from the pool of oil that sloshes around world. However, the embargo did succeed in raising prices sharply and alerting the world to OPEC's impressive pricing power.

OPEC was initially formed in 1960 in order to present a united front in negotiations with the major oil companies. OPEC currently has 11 members (Saudi Arabia, Iran, Venezuela, Iraq, UAE, Kuwait, Nigeria, Libya, Indonesia, Algeria, Qatar). OPEC members together account for some two-thirds of world oil reserves. OPEC is not a true cartel since it does not account for 100% of oil production. However, OPEC does seek to stabilize world oil prices by acting as the "swing producer," increasing or decreasing production in order to keep the market relatively stable. OPEC wants to maximize its long-term oil revenues, but OPEC does not want to push oil prices too high because a price spike would (1) cause oil demand to plunge from a world recession, (2) cause non-OPEC oil production to become economical in higher-expense areas, and (3) encourage the development of alternative sources of energy.

1979 oil crisis

After the 1973 Arab Oil Embargo was over, oil prices did not fall back but instead rose steadily through the latter half of the 1970s as OPEC enforced its newly-found pricing power and as oil demand grew. Oil prices then spiked higher in 1979 on the Iranian revolution against the Shah of Iran in January 1979, which devastated Iranian oil production. The Iran-Iraq war, which began in September 1980, then caused a sharp reduction in both Iranian and Iraqi oil output. OPEC production plunged by half, from 30 million barrels per day (bpd) in 1978 to only 15 million bpd by 1984. In response to those events, oil prices spiked higher in 1979 from about $15 per barrel in late-1978 to $38 per barrel at the end of 1979 and to a then-record of $39.50 in June 1980 (which is equivalent to $94 per barrel in current 2006 dollars). After peaking in 1980, oil prices then moved steadily lower through 1985 as the world adjusted to the Iranian-Iraqi oil production disruptions and as other sources of supply came online. In addition, oil prices were undercut by the double-dip US recessions seen in 1980 and 1981-82.

1986 oil price collapse

Oil prices then plunged in 1986 to $10 per barrel as Iranian and Iraqi oil production started to come back on-line, even though the Iraq-Iraq war did not officially end until 1988. Iranian oil production started rising sharply in 1986 from about 2.0 mln bpd in 1985 to 3.2 mln bpd by early 1989. Iraqi production roughly doubled from 1.5 mln bpd in 1984 to 2.7 mln bpd by early 1987. Other OPEC members failed to cut production fast enough to accommodate rising Iran-Iraq production, thus causing a collapse in oil prices. Oil prices finally recovered in 1987 back to the $20 area after OPEC reinstalled some production discipline.

1990 spike on first Gulf war

Oil prices were relatively steady and averaged $19 per barrel from the late-1980s through 1996. There was, however, a brief upward spike to nearly $40 per barrel seen in 1990 when the US and coalition forces went to war against Iraq to push Saddam Hussein out of Kuwait and to protect Saudi Arabia and its oil fields.

1998 oil price collapse and 1999-2000 recovery

After moving sideways near $20 per barrel during much of the 1990s, oil prices in 1997-99 plunged due to (1) reduced Asian oil demand tied to the 1997 Asian currency crisis, (2) a four-fold increase in Iraqi production (from 500,000 bpd at the end of 1996 to 2 million bpd in mid-1998) as the UN oil-for-food program allowed for a restoration of Iraq's oil production, and (3) the failure of OPEC to cut production fast enough to accommodate increased Iraqi production. Saudi Arabia in particular was reluctant to allow its production to fall below 8.0 mln bpd. However, after oil prices plunged to $10 per barrel and some OPEC nations were forced to borrow heavily to meet their financial

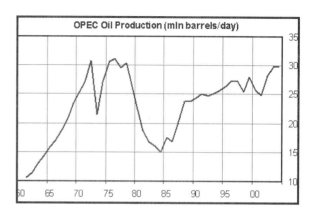

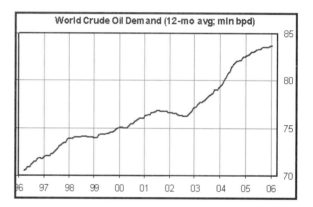

obligations, OPEC finally agreed to new production discipline and oil prices then more than tripled from $10 to over $30 by 2000. However, oil prices then fell sharply in 2000-02 from the $30 area to a low of $20 in 2002 due to reduced oil demand caused by the US recession in 2001 and soft global economy that followed the bursting of the equity bubble.

2002-06 supply/demand squeeze

After hitting a low of $20 per barrel in 2002, oil prices more than tripled to a record high of $70 per barrel in August 2005. That rally was driven by (1) stronger worldwide demand with the global economic recovery, and particularly stronger oil import demand from China (China's oil imports doubled from 60 million tons in mid-2002 to over 120 million tons in early 2005), (2) various temporary supply disruptions, and (3) the lack of any significant world excess capacity that could be quickly ramped up to meet new demand.

In addition, US oil production in the Gulf of Mexico was severely disrupted by Hurricane Ivan in September 2004, which caused long-term and severe damage to oil rigs and undersea oil pipelines. Hurricanes Katrina and Rita, a year later in August and September 2005, then caused even more damage to oil rigs and undersea pipelines. US production in the Gulf of Mexico was completely shut-down right after Katrina and 25% of production remained offline even 6 months after Katrina.

CRUDE OIL

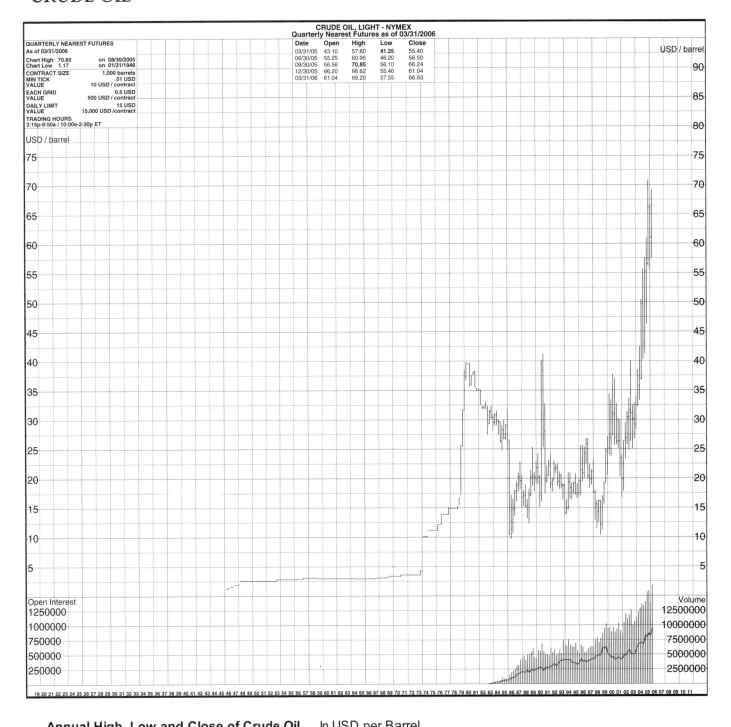

Annual High, Low and Close of Crude Oil   In USD per Barrel

Year	High	Low	Close	Year	High	Low	Close	Year	High	Low	Close
				1952	2.57	2.57	2.57	1960	2.97	2.97	2.97
				1953	2.82	2.57	2.82	1961	2.97	2.97	2.97
1946	1.62	1.17	1.62	1954	2.82	2.82	2.82	1962	2.97	2.97	2.97
1947	2.07	1.62	2.07	1955	2.82	2.82	2.82	1963	2.97	2.97	2.97
1948	2.57	2.57	2.57	1956	2.82	2.82	2.82	1964	2.97	2.92	2.92
1949	2.57	2.57	2.57	1957	3.07	2.82	3.00	1965	2.92	2.92	2.92
1950	2.57	2.57	2.57	1958	3.07	3.00	3.00	1966	2.97	2.92	2.97
1951	2.57	2.57	2.57	1959	3.00	2.97	2.97	1967	3.07	2.97	3.07

Source: New York Mercantile Exchange

CRUDE OIL

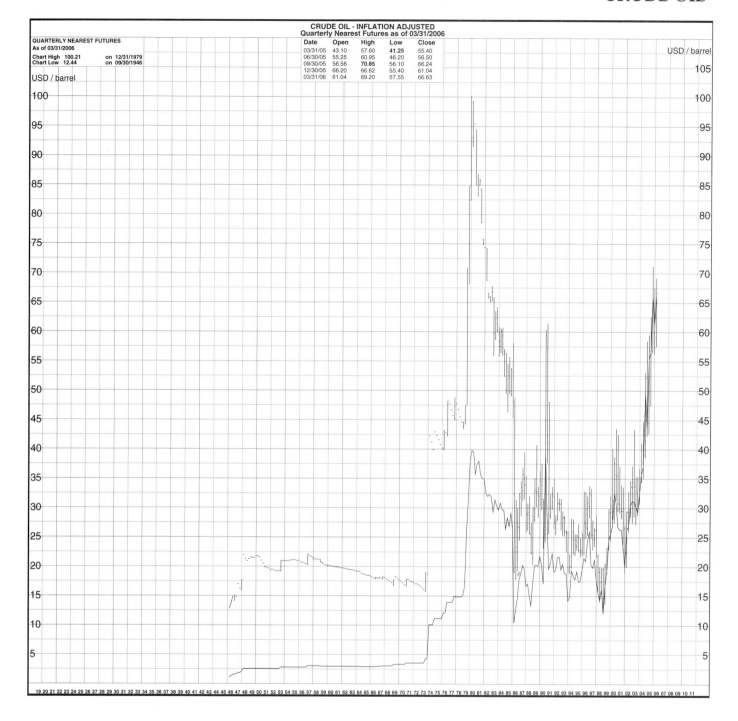

CRUDE OIL

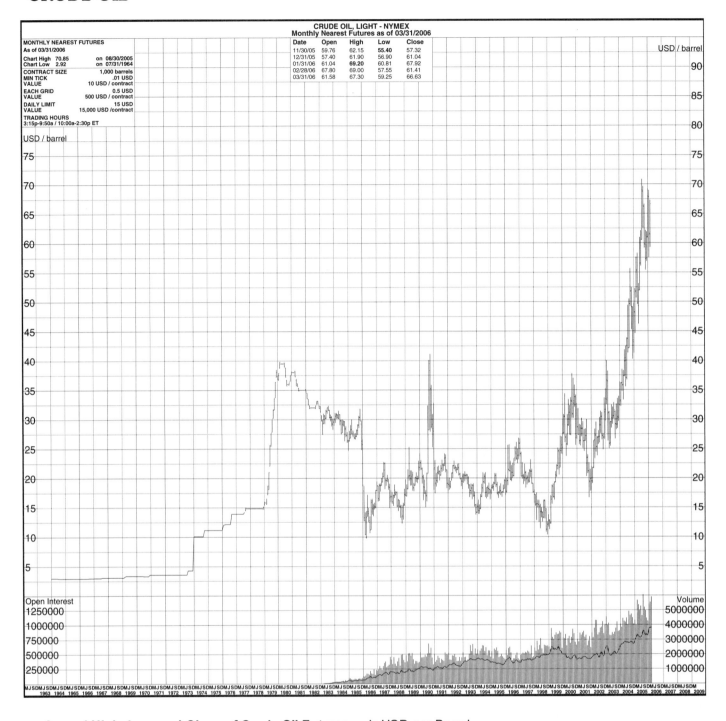

Annual High, Low and Close of Crude Oil Futures   In USD per Barrel

Year	High	Low	Close	Year	High	Low	Close	Year	High	Low	Close
1968	3.07	3.07	3.07	1981	38.25	34.87	35.00	1994	20.98	13.88	17.76
1969	3.35	3.07	3.35	1982	35.12	31.87	31.87	1995	20.82	16.60	19.55
1970	3.56	3.31	3.56	1983	32.35	27.40	29.60	1996	26.80	17.08	25.92
1971	3.56	3.56	3.56	1984	31.50	26.04	26.41	1997	26.74	17.50	17.64
1972	3.56	3.56	3.56	1985	31.82	24.66	26.30	1998	18.06	10.35	12.05
1973	4.31	3.56	4.31	1986	26.60	9.75	17.94	1999	27.15	11.26	25.60
1974	11.16	10.11	11.16	1987	22.76	14.90	16.70	2000	37.80	23.70	26.80
1975	11.16	11.16	11.16	1988	18.92	12.28	17.24	2001	32.70	16.70	19.84
1976	13.90	11.16	13.90	1989	25.30	16.91	21.82	2002	33.65	17.85	31.20
1977	14.97	13.78	14.85	1990	41.15	15.06	28.44	2003	39.99	25.04	32.52
1978	15.14	14.72	15.14	1991	32.75	17.45	19.12	2004	55.67	32.20	43.45
1979	38.47	15.48	38.01	1992	22.95	17.72	19.50	2005	70.85	41.25	61.04
1980	39.81	35.75	37.48	1993	21.14	13.75	14.17	2006	69.20	57.55	66.63

Source: New York Mercantile Exchange

CRUDE OIL

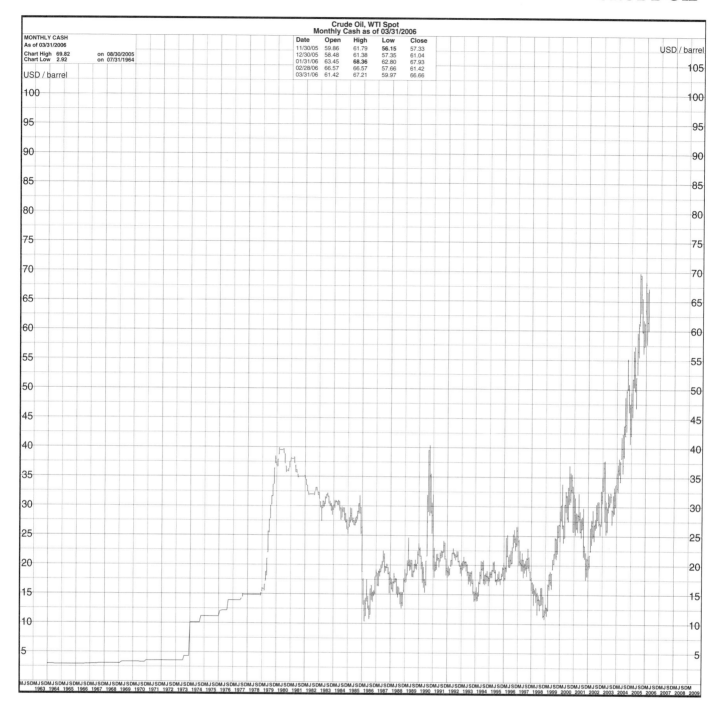

Annual High, Low and Close of Crude Oil   In USD per Barrel

Year	High	Low	Close	Year	High	Low	Close	Year	High	Low	Close
1968	3.07	3.07	3.07	1981	38.25	34.87	35.00	1994	20.87	13.86	17.78
1969	3.35	3.07	3.35	1982	35.12	31.87	31.87	1995	20.71	16.67	19.47
1970	3.56	3.31	3.56	1983	32.25	27.40	29.60	1996	26.56	17.26	25.91
1971	3.56	3.56	3.56	1984	31.00	26.05	26.40	1997	26.61	17.53	17.63
1972	3.56	3.56	3.56	1985	31.80	25.20	26.30	1998	17.81	10.80	11.66
1973	4.31	3.56	4.31	1986	26.55	10.40	17.95	1999	26.94	11.36	26.92
1974	11.16	10.11	11.16	1987	22.40	15.15	16.70	2000	37.00	23.84	25.76
1975	11.16	11.16	11.16	1988	18.60	12.60	17.25	2001	32.30	17.48	19.78
1976	13.90	11.16	13.90	1989	24.65	17.05	21.80	2002	32.73	17.98	31.23
1977	14.97	13.78	14.85	1990	40.40	15.30	28.45	2003	37.83	25.23	32.55
1978	15.14	14.72	15.14	1991	32.00	17.85	19.10	2004	55.23	32.48	43.46
1979	38.47	15.48	38.01	1992	22.89	17.85	19.48	2005	69.82	42.13	61.04
1980	39.81	35.75	37.48	1993	21.43	13.79	14.13	2006	68.36	57.66	66.66

Source: New York Mercantile Exchange

CRUDE OIL

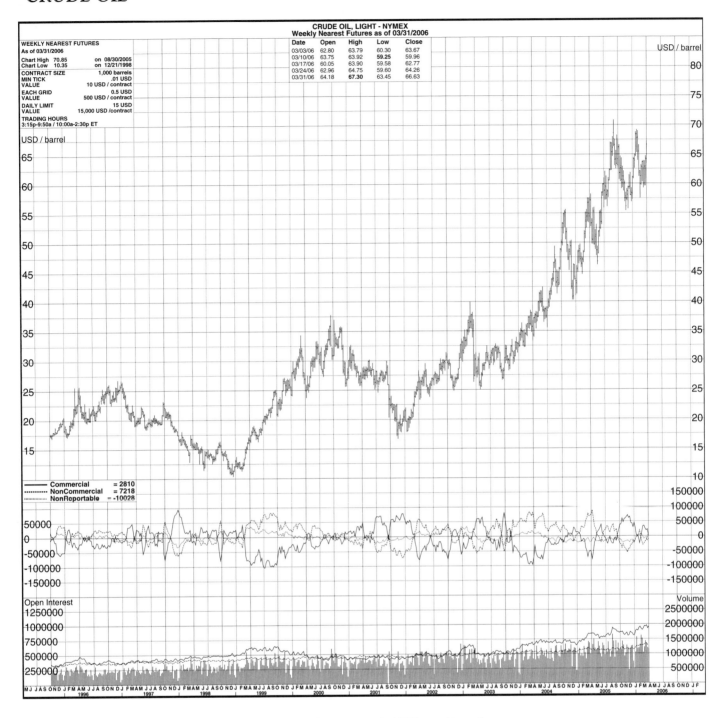

Quarterly High, Low and Close of Crude Oil Futures   In USD per Barrel

Quarter	High	Low	Close	Quarter	High	Low	Close	Quarter	High	Low	Close
09/1996	25.35	19.98	24.38	12/1999	27.15	20.55	25.60	03/2003	39.99	26.30	31.04
12/1996	26.80	22.47	25.92	03/2000	34.37	24.02	26.90	06/2003	32.50	25.04	30.19
03/1997	26.74	19.86	20.41	06/2000	33.40	23.70	32.50	09/2003	32.85	26.65	29.20
06/1997	22.40	18.35	19.80	09/2000	37.80	27.26	30.84	12/2003	33.93	28.26	32.52
09/1997	21.48	18.88	21.18	12/2000	37.00	25.58	26.80	03/2004	38.50	32.20	35.76
12/1997	23.15	17.50	17.64	03/2001	32.70	25.70	26.29	06/2004	42.45	33.30	37.05
03/1998	18.06	12.80	15.61	06/2001	30.20	25.10	26.25	09/2004	50.47	36.69	49.64
06/1998	16.30	11.40	14.18	09/2001	29.98	20.30	23.43	12/2004	55.67	40.25	43.45
09/1998	16.20	12.56	16.14	12/2001	23.98	16.70	19.84	03/2005	57.60	41.25	55.40
12/1998	16.36	10.35	12.05	03/2002	26.38	17.85	26.31	06/2005	60.95	46.20	56.50
03/1999	17.05	11.26	16.76	06/2002	29.54	23.31	26.86	09/2005	70.85	56.10	66.24
06/1999	19.37	15.61	19.29	09/2002	31.39	25.73	30.45	12/2005	66.62	55.40	61.04
09/1999	25.12	19.22	24.51	12/2002	33.65	24.82	31.20	03/2006	69.20	57.55	66.63

Source: New York Mercantile Exchange

CRUDE OIL

Quarterly High, Low and Close of Crude Oil In USD per Barrel

Quarter	High	Low	Close	Quarter	High	Low	Close	Quarter	High	Low	Close
09/1996	25.31	20.11	24.37	12/1999	26.94	21.04	26.92	03/2003	37.83	27.50	31.03
12/1996	26.56	22.53	25.91	03/2000	33.85	24.04	26.80	06/2003	32.38	25.23	30.18
03/1997	26.61	20.01	20.41	06/2000	32.60	23.84	31.80	09/2003	32.38	26.93	29.23
06/1997	22.11	17.87	19.76	09/2000	37.00	27.48	30.45	12/2003	33.73	28.48	32.55
09/1997	21.25	18.10	21.17	12/2000	35.76	25.76	25.76	03/2004	38.18	32.48	35.78
12/1997	22.89	17.53	17.63	03/2001	32.15	25.17	26.46	06/2004	42.35	34.28	37.05
03/1998	17.81	13.20	15.96	06/2001	32.30	25.62	25.74	09/2004	49.91	38.38	49.65
06/1998	16.14	11.55	14.15	09/2001	29.78	21.45	23.43	12/2004	55.23	40.72	43.46
09/1998	16.14	12.30	16.13	12/2001	23.33	17.48	19.78	03/2005	56.62	42.13	55.41
12/1998	16.14	10.80	11.66	03/2002	26.33	17.98	26.33	06/2005	59.65	46.81	56.50
03/1999	16.79	11.36	16.75	06/2002	29.38	23.48	26.88	09/2005	69.82	55.49	66.25
06/1999	18.92	15.82	18.57	09/2002	30.83	26.08	30.45	12/2005	65.48	56.15	61.04
09/1999	24.77	19.34	24.47	12/2002	32.73	25.15	31.23	03/2006	68.36	57.66	66.66

Source: New York Mercantile Exchange

GASOLINE, UNLEADED

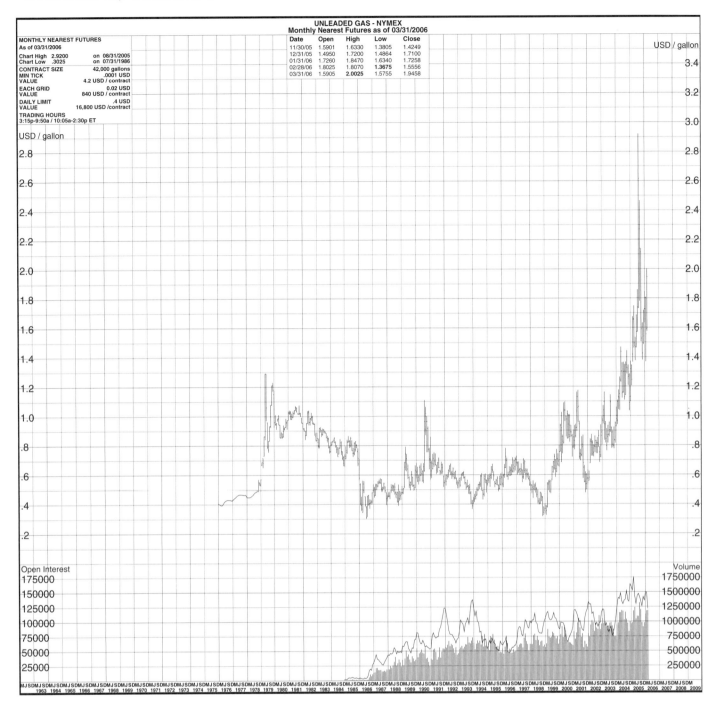

Annual High, Low and Close of Unleaded Gasoline Futures   In USD per Gallon

Year	High	Low	Close	Year	High	Low	Close	Year	High	Low	Close
				1985	.9000	.6575	.7125	1996	.7810	.5150	.7067
				1986	.7260	.3025	.4790	1997	.7290	.5250	.5281
1976	.4300	.3920	.4260	1987	.5785	.3950	.4367	1998	.5600	.3160	.3570
1977	.4670	.4270	.4650	1988	.5450	.3895	.4788	1999	.7720	.3240	.6910
1978	.5700	.4470	.5375	1989	.7920	.4660	.6322	2000	1.0960	.6540	.7858
1979	1.2900	.5250	1.1800	1990	1.1100	.5350	.7092	2001	1.1750	.4780	.5725
1980	1.1750	.8500	.9725	1991	.8600	.5175	.5487	2002	.9400	.5310	.8648
1981	1.0750	.9550	.9550	1992	.6775	.5025	.5404	2003	1.1630	.7630	.9492
1982	1.0400	.8325	.8325	1993	.6250	.3670	.3877	2004	1.4700	.9290	1.0887
1983	.9275	.7475	.7600	1994	.6105	.4010	.5590	2005	2.9200	1.0980	1.7100
1984	.8575	.6525	.6575	1995	.6740	.4870	.5886	2006	2.0025	1.3675	1.9458

Source: New York Mercantile Exchange

GASOLINE, UNLEADED

Annual High, Low and Close of Unleaded Gasoline In USD per Gallon

Year	High	Low	Close	Year	High	Low	Close	Year	High	Low	Close
				1985	.9000	.6575	.7125	1996	.7464	.4755	.6915
				1986	.7260	.3050	.4625	1997	.7639	.4924	.4924
1976	.4300	.3920	.4260	1987	.5800	.4130	.4360	1998	.5167	.2907	.3408
1977	.4670	.4270	.4650	1988	.5900	.4270	.4850	1999	.7788	.2930	.6755
1978	.5700	.4470	.5375	1989	.7575	.4675	.6350	2000	1.1093	.6380	.7553
1979	1.2900	.5250	1.1800	1990	1.1075	.5225	.7035	2001	1.0120	.4622	.5478
1980	1.1750	.8500	.9725	1991	.8420	.5300	.5525	2002	.9328	.5010	.8468
1981	1.0750	.9550	.9550	1992	.6655	.4950	.5400	2003	1.1231	.6831	.9580
1982	1.0400	.8325	.8325	1993	.6160	.3499	.3855	2004	1.4240	.9297	1.0885
1983	.9275	.7475	.7600	1994	.6155	.3970	.5115	2005	3.1340	1.0965	1.7700
1984	.8575	.6525	.6575	1995	.6663	.4605	.5251	2006	1.9807	1.3812	1.8718

Source: New York Mercantile Exchange

GASOLINE, UNLEADED

Quarterly High, Low and Close of Unleaded Gasoline Futures   In USD per Gallon

Quarter	High	Low	Close	Quarter	High	Low	Close	Quarter	High	Low	Close
09/1996	.6700	.5925	.6271	12/1999	.7720	.5830	.6910	03/2003	1.1630	.8050	.9444
12/1996	.7190	.6130	.7067	03/2000	1.0250	.6540	.9169	06/2003	.9600	.7630	.8699
03/1997	.7290	.6000	.6368	06/2000	1.0960	.7430	1.0378	09/2003	1.1436	.7790	.8865
06/1997	.6760	.5485	.5830	09/2000	1.0350	.8415	.8694	12/2003	.9590	.7760	.9492
09/1997	.7100	.5650	.6263	12/2000	1.0100	.7200	.7858	03/2004	1.1775	.9290	1.1244
12/1997	.6400	.5250	.5281	03/2001	.9450	.7700	.9190	06/2004	1.4700	1.0380	1.1562
03/1998	.5600	.4410	.5031	06/2001	1.1750	.7050	.7211	09/2004	1.3660	1.1075	1.3444
06/1998	.5450	.4460	.4642	09/2001	.8700	.5750	.6799	12/2004	1.4450	1.0350	1.0887
09/1998	.4970	.3950	.4774	12/2001	.6630	.4780	.5725	03/2005	1.6750	1.0980	1.6549
12/1998	.4780	.3160	.3570	03/2002	.8450	.5310	.8249	06/2005	1.7491	1.3770	1.5721
03/1999	.5470	.3240	.5414	06/2002	.8740	.7220	.7938	09/2005	2.9200	1.5700	2.1381
06/1999	.5650	.4700	.5562	09/2002	.8640	.7440	.8135	12/2005	2.1390	1.3805	1.7100
09/1999	.7400	.5610	.7236	12/2002	.9400	.6840	.8648	03/2006	2.0025	1.3675	1.9458

Source: New York Mercantile Exchange

GASOLINE, UNLEADED

Quarterly High, Low and Close of Unleaded Gasoline   In USD per Gallon

Quarter	High	Low	Close	Quarter	High	Low	Close	Quarter	High	Low	Close
09/1996	.6544	.5846	.6248	12/1999	.7624	.5828	.6755	03/2003	1.0880	.7717	.9169
12/1996	.7330	.6175	.6915	03/2000	.9843	.6380	.8294	06/2003	.8829	.6831	.8277
03/1997	.7090	.5902	.6083	06/2000	1.1093	.6591	.9441	09/2003	1.1231	.7896	.8678
06/1997	.6466	.5251	.5500	09/2000	1.0493	.7658	.8682	12/2003	.9595	.8128	.9580
09/1997	.7639	.5532	.6276	12/2000	1.0274	.6939	.7553	03/2004	1.1283	.9297	1.1017
12/1997	.6387	.4924	.4924	03/2001	.8897	.7514	.7992	06/2004	1.4240	1.0030	1.1234
03/1998	.5019	.3903	.4694	06/2001	1.0120	.6144	.6581	09/2004	1.3529	1.1176	1.3407
06/1998	.5167	.4184	.4367	09/2001	.8555	.6142	.6762	12/2004	1.4204	1.0010	1.0885
09/1998	.4680	.3799	.4636	12/2001	.6789	.4622	.5478	03/2005	1.5313	1.0965	1.5313
12/1998	.4765	.2907	.3408	03/2002	.7534	.5010	.7474	06/2005	1.6048	1.3223	1.4731
03/1999	.5339	.2930	.5339	06/2002	.7961	.6702	.7364	09/2005	3.1340	1.5001	2.1231
06/1999	.5384	.4450	.5300	09/2002	.8340	.6952	.7973	12/2005	2.1047	1.4119	1.7700
09/1999	.7788	.5416	.7224	12/2002	.9328	.7079	.8468	03/2006	1.9807	1.3812	1.8718

Source: New York Mercantile Exchange

GASOLINE, UNLEADED

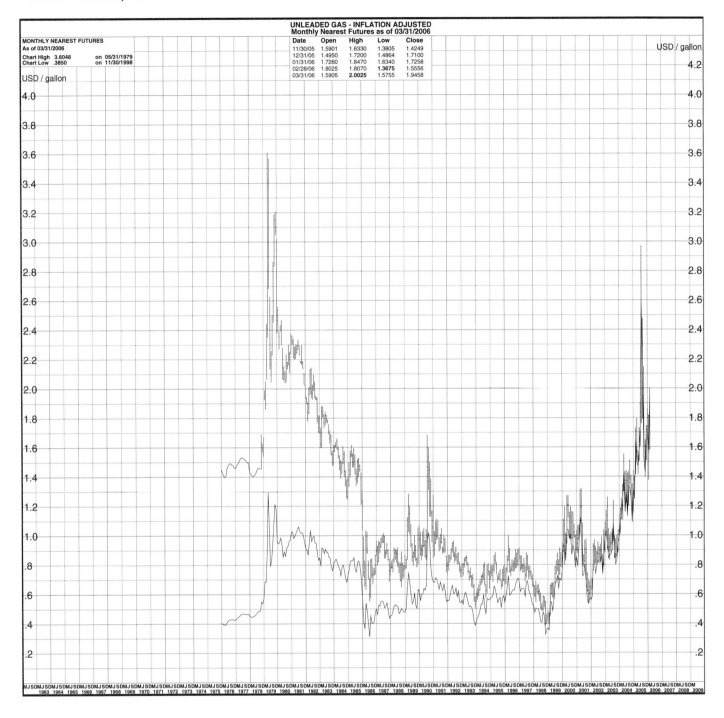

HEATING OIL

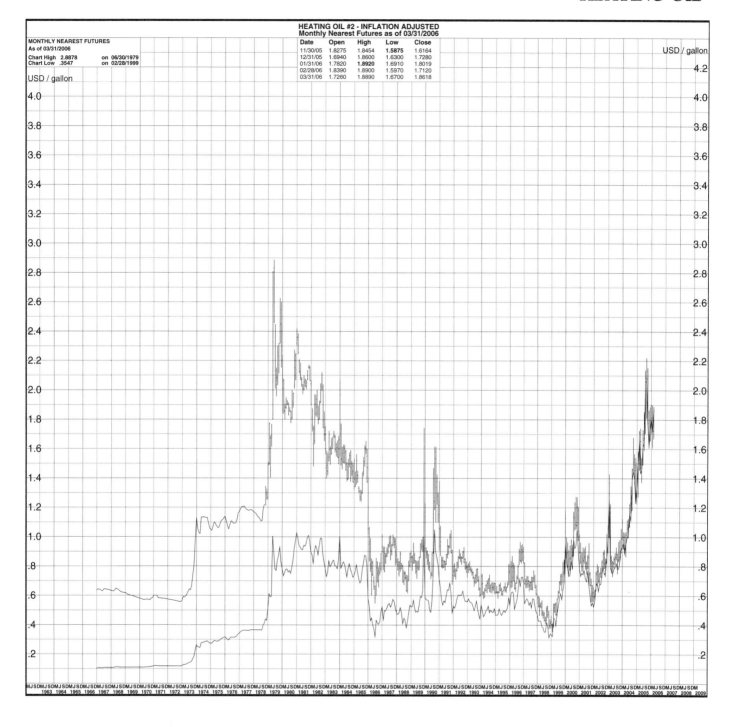

HEATING OIL

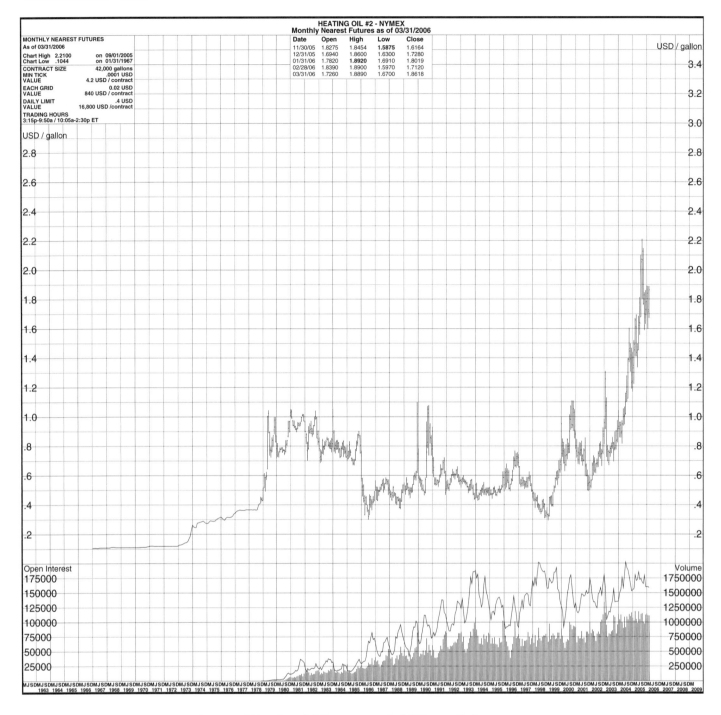

Quarterly High, Low and Close of Heating Oil Futures   In USD per Gallon

Quarter	High	Low	Close	Quarter	High	Low	Close	Quarter	High	Low	Close
09/1996	.7280	.5375	.7151	12/1999	.7150	.5340	.6903	03/2003	1.3100	.7250	.7924
12/1996	.7675	.6515	.7284	03/2000	.9975	.6355	.7833	06/2003	.8070	.6690	.7808
03/1997	.7450	.5215	.5672	06/2000	.8500	.6275	.8414	09/2003	.8605	.6938	.7778
06/1997	.5910	.5070	.5355	09/2000	1.0760	.7490	.9240	12/2003	.9760	.7690	.9127
09/1997	.5885	.5140	.5793	12/2000	1.1100	.8500	.9066	03/2004	1.0430	.8560	.8864
12/1997	.6260	.4890	.4908	03/2001	.8979	.6770	.7550	06/2004	1.0674	.8150	1.0055
03/1998	.4985	.3770	.4302	06/2001	.8350	.6735	.7125	09/2004	1.3960	1.0120	1.3917
06/1998	.4645	.3640	.3815	09/2001	.8575	.5950	.6635	12/2004	1.6030	1.1900	1.2297
09/1998	.4320	.3350	.4211	12/2001	.6793	.4930	.5507	03/2005	1.6700	1.1680	1.6576
12/1998	.4375	.3080	.3400	03/2002	.6865	.4990	.6689	06/2005	1.6950	1.3340	1.6191
03/1999	.4525	.2920	.4468	06/2002	.7350	.5995	.6796	09/2005	2.2100	1.5560	2.0673
06/1999	.4860	.3850	.4785	09/2002	.8183	.6540	.8018	12/2005	2.1470	1.5875	1.7280
09/1999	.6280	.4835	.6154	12/2002	.9255	.6630	.8655	03/2006	1.8920	1.5970	1.8618

Source: New York Mercantile Exchange

HEATING OIL

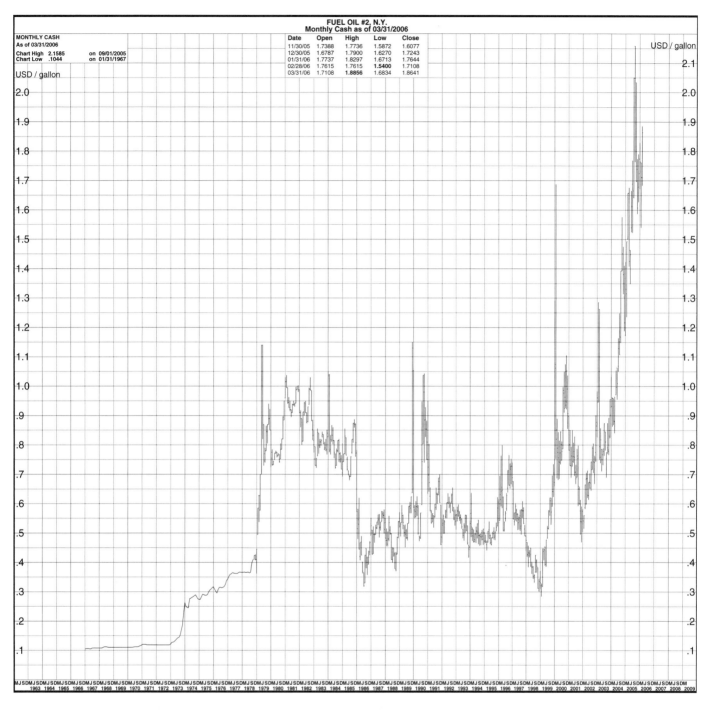

Quarterly High, Low and Close of Heating Oil In USD per Gallon

Quarter	High	Low	Close	Quarter	High	Low	Close	Quarter	High	Low	Close
09/1996	.7149	.5401	.7083	12/1999	.7350	.5285	.7055	03/2003	1.2847	.7512	.7952
12/1996	.7659	.6525	.7282	03/2000	1.6878	.6595	.7896	06/2003	.8571	.7110	.7791
03/1997	.7409	.5266	.5687	06/2000	.8465	.6816	.8447	09/2003	.8732	.6898	.7748
06/1997	.6019	.5108	.5353	09/2000	1.0498	.7468	.9253	12/2003	.9562	.7666	.9027
09/1997	.5817	.4955	.5788	12/2000	1.1052	.8551	.9074	03/2004	1.0330	.8628	.8822
12/1997	.6089	.4906	.4906	03/2001	.8983	.6895	.7630	06/2004	1.0629	.8405	1.0096
03/1998	.4921	.3841	.4335	06/2001	.8512	.6952	.7068	09/2004	1.3930	1.0506	1.3930
06/1998	.4501	.3610	.3828	09/2001	.7983	.5926	.6605	12/2004	1.5758	1.1882	1.2165
09/1998	.4253	.3315	.4253	12/2001	.6591	.4691	.5495	03/2005	1.6579	1.1740	1.6579
12/1998	.4111	.3008	.3355	03/2002	.6652	.5049	.6652	06/2005	1.6760	1.3491	1.6124
03/1999	.4473	.2842	.4473	06/2002	.7133	.5975	.6733	09/2005	2.1585	1.5227	2.0486
06/1999	.4773	.3866	.4773	09/2002	.7960	.6450	.7893	12/2005	2.0334	1.5872	1.7243
09/1999	.6207	.4827	.6102	12/2002	.9017	.6680	.8648	03/2006	1.8856	1.5400	1.8641

Source: New York Mercantile Exchange

HEATING OIL

Quarterly High, Low and Close of Heating Oil Futures   In USD per Gallon

Quarter	High	Low	Close	Quarter	High	Low	Close	Quarter	High	Low	Close
09/1996	.7280	.5375	.7151	12/1999	.7150	.5340	.6903	03/2003	1.3100	.7250	.7924
12/1996	.7675	.6515	.7284	03/2000	.9975	.6355	.7833	06/2003	.8070	.6690	.7808
03/1997	.7450	.5215	.5672	06/2000	.8500	.6275	.8414	09/2003	.8605	.6938	.7778
06/1997	.5910	.5070	.5355	09/2000	1.0760	.7490	.9240	12/2003	.9760	.7690	.9127
09/1997	.5885	.5140	.5793	12/2000	1.1100	.8500	.9066	03/2004	1.0430	.8560	.8864
12/1997	.6260	.4890	.4908	03/2001	.8979	.6770	.7550	06/2004	1.0674	.8150	1.0055
03/1998	.4985	.3770	.4302	06/2001	.8350	.6735	.7125	09/2004	1.3960	1.0120	1.3917
06/1998	.4645	.3640	.3815	09/2001	.8575	.5950	.6635	12/2004	1.6030	1.1900	1.2297
09/1998	.4320	.3350	.4211	12/2001	.6793	.4930	.5507	03/2005	1.6700	1.1680	1.6576
12/1998	.4375	.3080	.3400	03/2002	.6865	.4990	.6689	06/2005	1.6950	1.3340	1.6191
03/1999	.4525	.2920	.4468	06/2002	.7350	.5995	.6796	09/2005	2.2100	1.5560	2.0673
06/1999	.4860	.3850	.4785	09/2002	.8183	.6540	.8018	12/2005	2.1470	1.5875	1.7280
09/1999	.6280	.4835	.6154	12/2002	.9255	.6630	.8655	03/2006	1.8920	1.5970	1.8618

Source: New York Mercantile Exchange

HEATING OIL

Quarterly High, Low and Close of Heating Oil In USD per Gallon

Quarter	High	Low	Close	Quarter	High	Low	Close	Quarter	High	Low	Close
09/1996	.7149	.5401	.7083	12/1999	.7350	.5285	.7055	03/2003	1.2847	.7512	.7952
12/1996	.7659	.6525	.7282	03/2000	1.6878	.6595	.7896	06/2003	.8571	.7110	.7791
03/1997	.7409	.5266	.5687	06/2000	.8465	.6816	.8447	09/2003	.8732	.6898	.7748
06/1997	.6019	.5108	.5353	09/2000	1.0498	.7468	.9253	12/2003	.9562	.7666	.9027
09/1997	.5817	.4955	.5788	12/2000	1.1052	.8551	.9074	03/2004	1.0330	.8628	.8822
12/1997	.6089	.4906	.4906	03/2001	.8983	.6895	.7630	06/2004	1.0629	.8405	1.0096
03/1998	.4921	.3841	.4335	06/2001	.8512	.6952	.7068	09/2004	1.3930	1.0506	1.3930
06/1998	.4501	.3610	.3828	09/2001	.7983	.5926	.6605	12/2004	1.5758	1.1882	1.2165
09/1998	.4253	.3315	.4253	12/2001	.6591	.4691	.5495	03/2005	1.6579	1.1740	1.6579
12/1998	.4111	.3008	.3355	03/2002	.6652	.5049	.6652	06/2005	1.6760	1.3491	1.6124
03/1999	.4473	.2842	.4473	06/2002	.7133	.5975	.6733	09/2005	2.1585	1.5227	2.0486
06/1999	.4773	.3866	.4773	09/2002	.7960	.6450	.7893	12/2005	2.0334	1.5872	1.7243
09/1999	.6207	.4827	.6102	12/2002	.9017	.6680	.8648	03/2006	1.8856	1.5400	1.8641

Source: New York Mercantile Exchange

NATURAL GAS

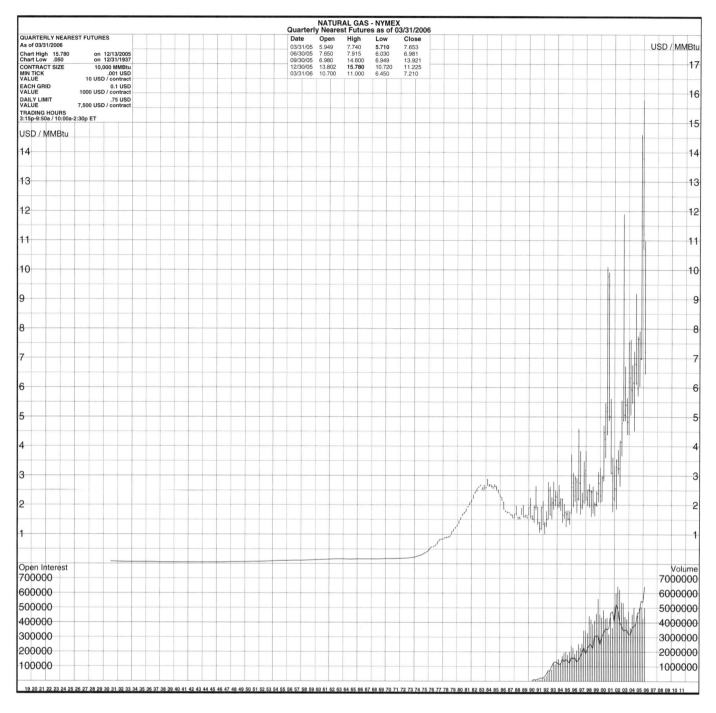

Annual High, Low and Close of Natural Gas   In USD per MMBtu

Year	High	Low	Close	Year	High	Low	Close	Year	High	Low	Close
				1942	.050	.050	.050	1955	.100	.100	.100
1930	.080	.080	.080	1943	.050	.050	.050	1956	.110	.110	.110
1931	.070	.070	.070	1944	.050	.050	.050	1957	.110	.110	.110
1932	.060	.060	.060	1945	.050	.050	.050	1958	.120	.120	.120
1933	.060	.060	.060	1946	.050	.050	.050	1959	.130	.130	.130
1934	.060	.060	.060	1947	.060	.060	.060	1960	.140	.140	.140
1935	.060	.060	.060	1948	.060	.060	.060	1961	.150	.150	.150
1936	.060	.060	.060	1949	.060	.060	.060	1962	.160	.160	.160
1937	.050	.050	.050	1950	.070	.070	.070	1963	.160	.160	.160
1938	.050	.050	.050	1951	.070	.070	.070	1964	.150	.150	.150
1939	.050	.050	.050	1952	.080	.080	.080	1965	.160	.160	.160
1940	.050	.050	.050	1953	.090	.090	.090	1966	.160	.160	.160
1941	.050	.050	.050	1954	.100	.100	.100	1967	.160	.160	.160

Source: New York Mercantile Exchange

NATURAL GAS

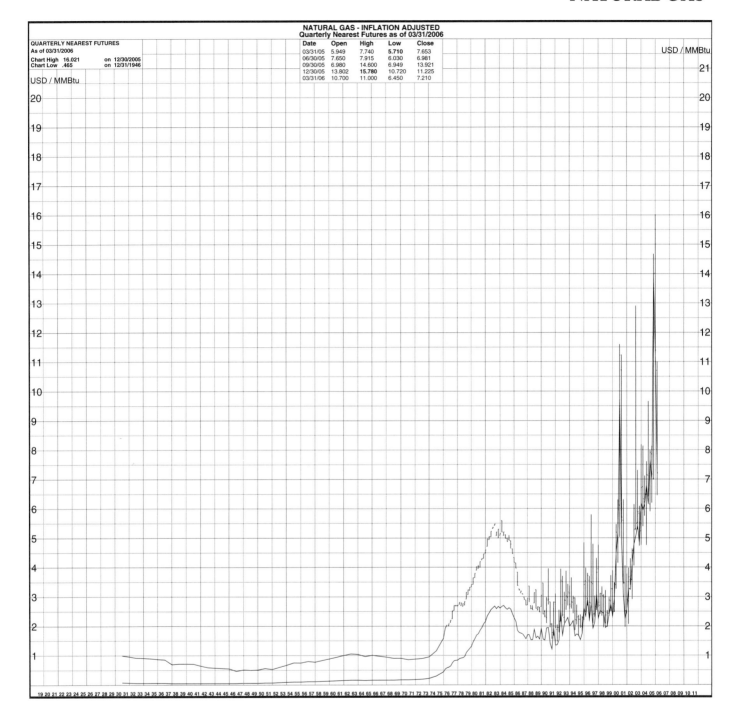

NATURAL GAS

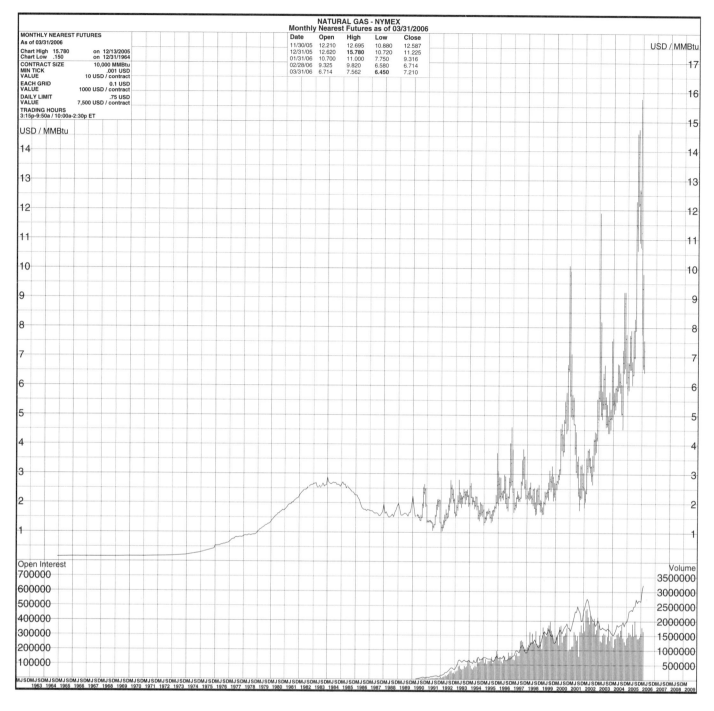

Annual High, Low and Close of Natural Gas Futures   In USD per MMBtu

Year	High	Low	Close	Year	High	Low	Close	Year	High	Low	Close
1968	.160	.160	.160	1981	2.160	1.770	2.160	1994	2.690	1.395	1.725
1969	.170	.170	.170	1982	2.620	2.230	2.620	1995	3.720	1.250	2.619
1970	.170	.170	.170	1983	2.680	2.520	2.610	1996	4.600	1.735	2.757
1971	.180	.180	.180	1984	2.870	2.570	2.570	1997	3.850	1.680	2.264
1972	.190	.190	.190	1985	2.710	2.280	2.280	1998	2.725	1.600	1.945
1973	.220	.220	.220	1986	2.260	1.730	1.760	1999	3.275	1.625	2.329
1974	.300	.300	.300	1987	1.740	1.560	1.700	2000	10.100	2.125	9.775
1975	.440	.440	.440	1988	1.960	1.520	1.890	2001	9.916	1.760	2.570
1976	.640	.540	.640	1989	1.980	1.550	1.920	2002	5.560	1.850	4.789
1977	.840	.670	.840	1990	2.650	1.396	1.950	2003	11.899	4.390	6.189
1978	.960	.870	.960	1991	2.140	1.060	1.343	2004	9.200	4.520	6.149
1979	1.310	1.020	1.310	1992	2.790	1.020	1.687	2005	15.780	5.710	11.225
1980	1.760	1.370	1.740	1993	2.800	1.521	1.997	2006	11.000	6.450	7.210

Source: New York Mercantile Exchange

NATURAL GAS

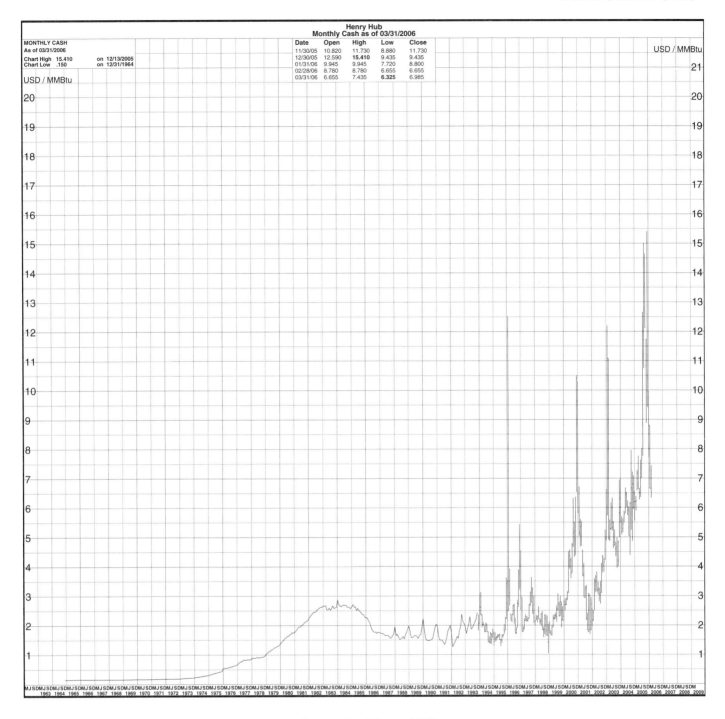

Annual High, Low and Close of Natural Gas   In USD per MMBtu

Year	High	Low	Close	Year	High	Low	Close	Year	High	Low	Close
1968	.160	.160	.160	1981	2.160	1.770	2.160	1994	3.130	1.345	1.705
1969	.170	.170	.170	1982	2.620	2.230	2.620	1995	3.625	1.280	2.750
1970	.170	.170	.170	1983	2.680	2.520	2.610	1996	12.500	1.695	4.050
1971	.180	.180	.180	1984	2.870	2.570	2.570	1997	4.550	1.785	2.265
1972	.190	.190	.190	1985	2.710	2.280	2.280	1998	2.635	1.035	1.935
1973	.220	.220	.220	1986	2.260	1.730	1.760	1999	3.075	1.645	2.305
1974	.300	.300	.300	1987	1.740	1.560	1.700	2000	10.500	2.140	10.415
1975	.440	.440	.440	1988	1.960	1.520	1.890	2001	10.295	1.695	2.720
1976	.640	.540	.640	1989	1.980	1.550	1.920	2002	5.250	1.980	4.585
1977	.840	.670	.840	1990	2.230	1.470	2.040	2003	12.200	3.965	5.825
1978	.960	.870	.960	1991	2.000	1.340	2.000	2004	7.960	4.385	6.185
1979	1.310	1.020	1.310	1992	2.380	1.260	2.070	2005	15.410	5.560	9.435
1980	1.760	1.370	1.740	1993	2.430	1.720	2.080	2006	9.945	6.325	6.985

Source: New York Mercantile Exchange

NATURAL GAS

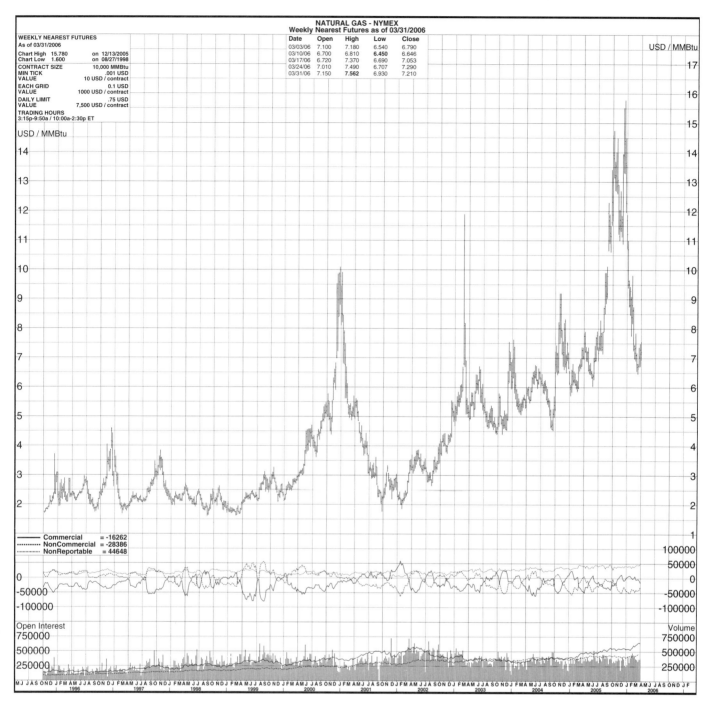

Quarterly High, Low and Close of Natural Gas Futures In USD per MMBtu

Quarter	High	Low	Close	Quarter	High	Low	Close	Quarter	High	Low	Close
09/1996	2.920	1.735	2.214	12/1999	3.275	2.080	2.329	03/2003	11.899	4.850	5.060
12/1996	4.600	2.165	2.757	03/2000	2.980	2.125	2.945	06/2003	6.719	4.865	5.411
03/1997	3.840	1.680	1.926	06/2000	4.715	2.815	4.476	09/2003	5.640	4.390	4.830
06/1997	2.430	1.850	2.139	09/2000	5.479	3.610	5.186	12/2003	7.550	4.390	6.189
09/1997	3.480	2.051	3.082	12/2000	10.100	4.380	9.775	03/2004	7.630	5.060	5.933
12/1997	3.850	2.140	2.264	03/2001	9.916	4.870	5.025	06/2004	6.760	5.460	6.155
03/1998	2.530	1.960	2.522	06/2001	5.620	3.055	3.096	09/2004	7.230	4.520	6.795
06/1998	2.725	1.915	2.469	09/2001	3.620	1.760	2.244	12/2004	9.200	6.100	6.149
09/1998	2.520	1.600	2.433	12/2001	3.340	2.140	2.570	03/2005	7.740	5.710	7.653
12/1998	2.640	1.710	1.945	03/2002	3.560	1.850	3.283	06/2005	7.915	6.030	6.981
03/1999	2.095	1.625	2.013	06/2002	3.875	3.050	3.245	09/2005	14.600	6.949	13.921
06/1999	2.480	1.950	2.394	09/2002	4.200	2.640	4.138	12/2005	15.780	10.720	11.225
09/1999	3.130	2.100	2.744	12/2002	5.560	3.670	4.789	03/2006	11.000	6.450	7.210

Source: New York Mercantile Exchange

NATURAL GAS

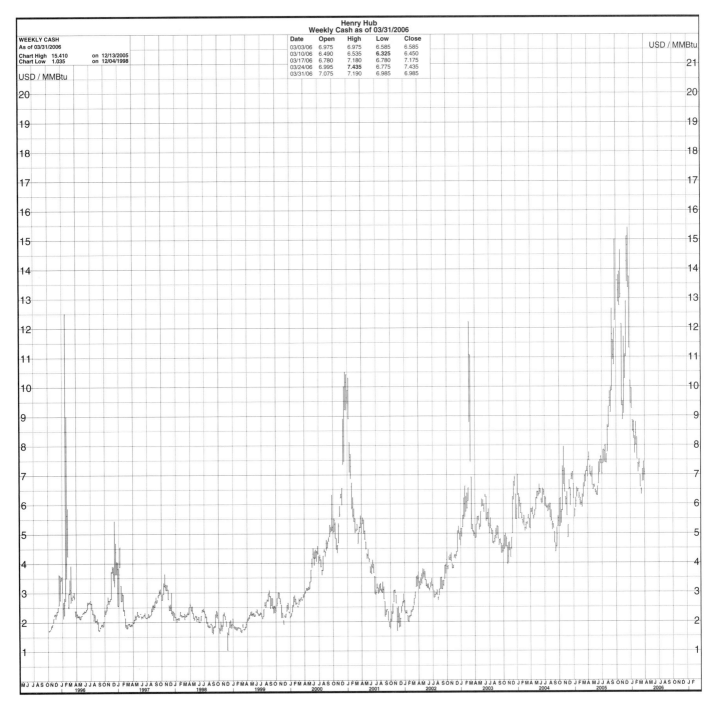

Henry Hub Weekly Cash as of 03/31/2006

Date	Open	High	Low	Close
03/03/06	6.975	6.975	6.585	6.585
03/10/06	6.490	6.535	6.325	6.450
03/17/06	6.780	7.180	6.780	7.175
03/24/06	6.995	7.435	6.775	7.435
03/31/06	7.075	7.190	6.985	6.985

WEEKLY CASH As of 03/31/2006
Chart High 15.410 on 12/13/2005
Chart Low 1.035 on 12/04/1998
USD / MMBtu

Quarterly High, Low and Close of Unleaded Gasoline — In USD per Gallon

Quarter	High	Low	Close	Quarter	High	Low	Close	Quarter	High	Low	Close
09/1996	2.725	1.695	1.865	12/1999	3.005	1.920	2.305	03/2003	12.200	4.880	4.985
12/1996	5.445	1.930	4.050	03/2000	2.935	2.140	2.870	06/2003	6.335	4.860	5.330
03/1997	4.550	1.785	1.900	06/2000	4.585	2.845	4.330	09/2003	5.530	4.345	4.580
06/1997	2.365	1.850	2.155	09/2000	6.325	3.585	5.130	12/2003	6.950	3.965	5.825
09/1997	3.125	2.130	3.125	12/2000	10.500	4.340	10.415	03/2004	7.015	5.080	5.445
12/1997	3.635	2.065	2.265	03/2001	10.295	4.670	5.355	06/2004	6.680	5.485	6.030
03/1998	2.345	2.000	2.320	06/2001	5.545	2.955	2.955	09/2004	6.235	4.385	6.165
06/1998	2.635	1.985	2.375	09/2001	3.355	1.820	1.820	12/2004	7.960	4.865	6.185
09/1998	2.465	1.600	2.210	12/2001	3.085	1.695	2.720	03/2005	7.275	5.560	7.170
12/1998	2.340	1.035	1.935	03/2002	3.585	1.980	3.205	06/2005	7.760	6.290	7.025
03/1999	2.105	1.645	1.995	06/2002	3.805	3.050	3.215	09/2005	15.000	7.035	15.000
06/1999	2.420	1.930	2.325	09/2002	4.100	2.730	4.100	12/2005	15.410	8.880	9.435
09/1999	3.075	2.110	2.310	12/2002	5.250	3.780	4.585	03/2006	9.945	6.325	6.985

Source: New York Mercantile Exchange

PROPANE

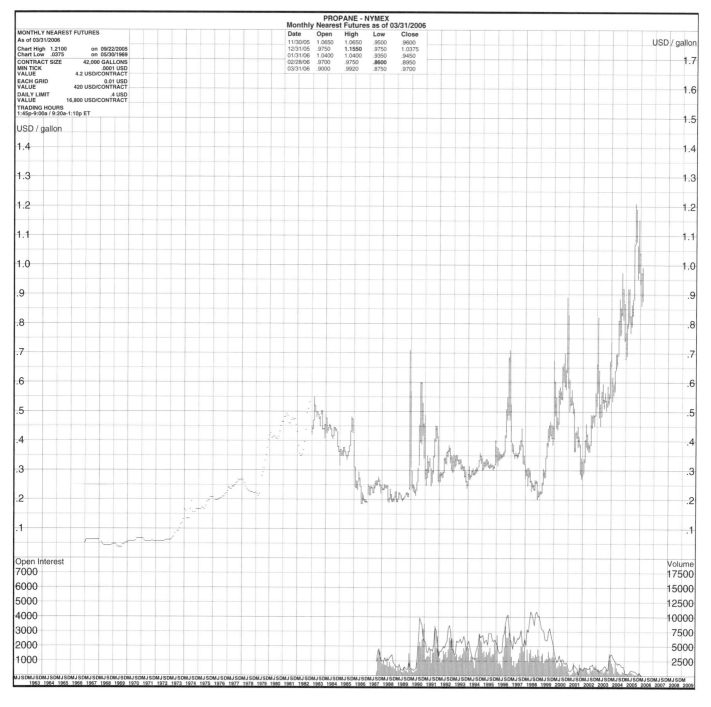

Annual High, Low and Close of Propane Futures   In USD per Gallon

Year	High	Low	Close	Year	High	Low	Close	Year	High	Low	Close
1968	.0625	.0425	.0455	1981	.4930	.4550	.4550	1994	.3600	.2485	.3329
1969	.0525	.0375	.0525	1982	.5320	.3490	.5320	1995	.4025	.3000	.3935
1970	.0673	.0545	.0673	1983	.5500	.4075	.4550	1996	.7100	.3150	.4900
1971	.0673	.0573	.0573	1984	.4925	.3625	.3625	1997	.5260	.3200	.3292
1972	.0621	.0573	.0621	1985	.4825	.3150	.4275	1998	.3200	.2000	.2125
1973	.1328	.0621	.1328	1986	.4000	.1850	.1900	1999	.4675	.2125	.4450
1974	.1928	.1348	.1664	1987	.2775	.2150	.2375	2000	.8900	.4050	.8650
1975	.2075	.1662	.2075	1988	.2525	.1890	.2235	2001	.8300	.2700	.3260
1976	.2213	.1975	.2213	1989	.7085	.1900	.7080	2002	.5650	.2750	.5400
1977	.2680	.2290	.2670	1990	.6000	.2125	.4478	2003	.8200	.4510	.6600
1978	.2700	.2210	.2210	1991	.4900	.2450	.2750	2004	.9740	.5350	.7450
1979	.4040	.2120	.4040	1992	.3850	.2560	.3300	2005	1.2100	.6800	1.0375
1980	.4650	.4060	.4650	1993	.3535	.2385	.2495	2006	1.0400	.8600	.9700

Source: New York Mercantile Exchange

PROPANE

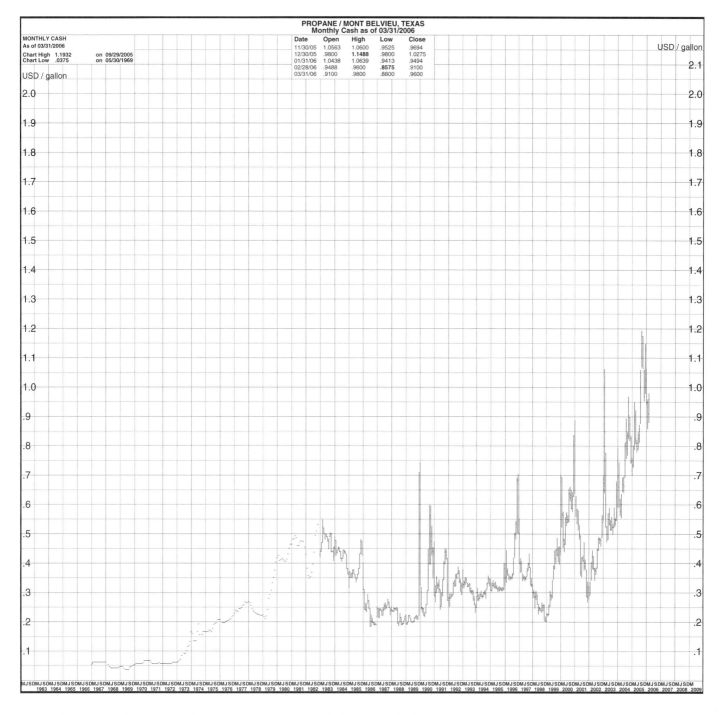

Annual High, Low and Close of Propane   In USD per Gallon

Year	High	Low	Close	Year	High	Low	Close	Year	High	Low	Close
1968	.0625	.0425	.0455	1981	.4930	.4550	.4550	1994	.3585	.2500	.3325
1969	.0525	.0375	.0525	1982	.5320	.3490	.5320	1995	.4013	.3025	.3825
1970	.0673	.0545	.0673	1983	.5500	.4075	.4550	1996	.7050	.3225	.5025
1971	.0673	.0573	.0573	1984	.4925	.3625	.3625	1997	.5525	.3188	.3263
1972	.0621	.0573	.0621	1985	.4825	.3150	.4275	1998	.3298	.2025	.2025
1973	.1328	.0621	.1328	1986	.4000	.1850	.1900	1999	.4869	.2025	.4575
1974	.1928	.1348	.1664	1987	.2775	.2150	.2375	2000	.8375	.4288	.8338
1975	.2075	.1662	.2075	1988	.2525	.1875	.2200	2001	.8875	.2675	.3200
1976	.2213	.1975	.2213	1989	.7100	.1900	.7100	2002	.5650	.2775	.5400
1977	.2680	.2290	.2670	1990	.7400	.2163	.4425	2003	1.0625	.4725	.6675
1978	.2700	.2210	.2210	1991	.4750	.2410	.2735	2004	.9688	.5550	.7463
1979	.4040	.2120	.4040	1992	.3890	.2510	.3250	2005	1.1932	.7000	1.0275
1980	.4650	.4060	.4650	1993	.3790	.2312	.2535	2006	1.0639	.8575	.9600

Source: New York Mercantile Exchange

PROPANE

Quarterly High, Low and Close of Propane Futures   In USD per Gallon

Quarter	High	Low	Close	Quarter	High	Low	Close	Quarter	High	Low	Close
09/1996	.5075	.3475	.5075	12/1999	.4675	.3875	.4450	03/2003	.8200	.4800	.5125
12/1996	.7100	.4700	.4900	03/2000	.6725	.4050	.4800	06/2003	.5950	.4510	.5400
03/1997	.5260	.3575	.3575	06/2000	.5850	.4375	.5775	09/2003	.5650	.5025	.5250
06/1997	.3625	.3400	.3475	09/2000	.6650	.5405	.6250	12/2003	.6725	.5180	.6600
09/1997	.4030	.3450	.3993	12/2000	.8900	.5750	.8650	03/2004	.7400	.5350	.5800
12/1997	.4440	.3200	.3292	03/2001	.8300	.5000	.5280	06/2004	.7000	.5675	.6675
03/1998	.3200	.2470	.2800	06/2001	.5750	.3625	.3750	09/2004	.8850	.6925	.8335
06/1998	.3090	.2275	.2470	09/2001	.4500	.3640	.4025	12/2004	.9740	.7400	.7450
09/1998	.2675	.2325	.2560	12/2001	.4150	.2700	.3260	03/2005	.9200	.6800	.8750
12/1998	.2665	.2000	.2125	03/2002	.4050	.2750	.4000	06/2005	.9200	.7675	.8300
03/1999	.2600	.2125	.2575	06/2002	.4600	.3625	.3775	09/2005	1.2100	.8250	1.1800
06/1999	.3450	.2525	.3425	09/2002	.4900	.3625	.4810	12/2005	1.1900	.9500	1.0375
09/1999	.4550	.3425	.4460	12/2002	.5650	.4500	.5400	03/2006	1.0400	.8600	.9700

Source: New York Mercantile Exchange

PROPANE

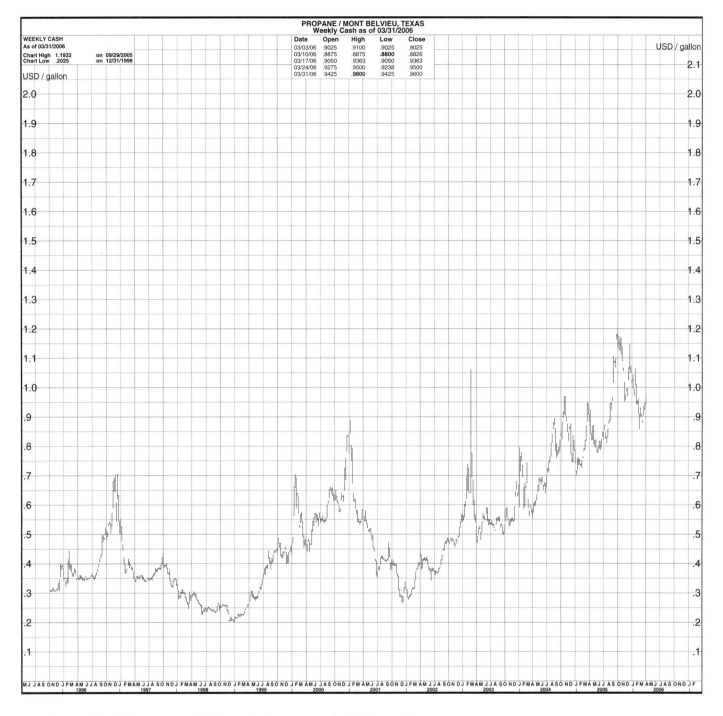

Quarterly High, Low and Close of Propane   In USD per Gallon

Quarter	High	Low	Close	Quarter	High	Low	Close	Quarter	High	Low	Close
09/1996	.5025	.3463	.5025	12/1999	.4869	.3975	.4575	03/2003	1.0625	.5238	.5238
12/1996	.7050	.4813	.5025	03/2000	.7025	.4288	.4813	06/2003	.5894	.4725	.5375
03/1997	.5525	.3675	.3708	06/2000	.5725	.4388	.5725	09/2003	.5582	.4981	.5225
06/1997	.3645	.3383	.3475	09/2000	.6625	.5375	.6250	12/2003	.6800	.5232	.6675
09/1997	.4025	.3425	.3988	12/2000	.8375	.5750	.8338	03/2004	.7957	.5619	.5763
12/1997	.4338	.3188	.3263	03/2001	.8875	.5325	.5838	06/2004	.6950	.5550	.6625
03/1998	.3298	.2460	.2860	06/2001	.5800	.3588	.3669	09/2004	.8950	.6938	.8363
06/1998	.3060	.2260	.2398	09/2001	.4725	.3525	.4025	12/2004	.9688	.7400	.7463
09/1998	.2663	.2325	.2550	12/2001	.4138	.2675	.3200	03/2005	.9500	.7000	.8907
12/1998	.2600	.2025	.2025	03/2002	.4038	.2775	.4038	06/2005	.9225	.7788	.8257
03/1999	.2600	.2025	.2563	06/2002	.4450	.3413	.3763	09/2005	1.1932	.8113	1.1750
06/1999	.3413	.2538	.3413	09/2002	.4882	.3613	.4813	12/2005	1.1738	.9525	1.0275
09/1999	.4475	.3460	.4438	12/2002	.5650	.4575	.5400	03/2006	1.0639	.8575	.9600

Source: New York Mercantile Exchange

FINANCIAL INSTRUMENTS

US interest rates started rising in mid-2004, but are currently still very low from an historical perspective. This is primarily the result of the Federal Reserve's success in fighting inflation. The Fed is now focused almost exclusively on maintaining price stability, knowing that a stable inflation situation will keep (1) US interest rates low, (2) the US economy operating at its highest non-inflationary potential, and (3) employment at its maximum level. The long-term outlook for US interest rates is generally favorable because the Federal Reserve now has the knowledge, will, and political independence to do what it takes to keep inflation at relatively low levels, thus keeping US interest rates at relatively low levels going forward.

The most striking aspect of the nearby long-term chart of the 10-year T-note yield is that current US interest rates are not only low, but that volatility has dropped sharply. This is part of a trend dubbed "The Great Moderation," where the variability of GDP and inflation has dropped sharply since the 1980s. There are three reasons behind the Great Moderation: (1) improved performance of monetary policy and government macroeconomic policies in general, (2) the improved ability of the US economy to absorb shocks due to structural improvements (e.g., inventory management) and globalization (global trade, cross-border investment flows, flexible exchange rates), and (3) "luck" with a reduced number of external shocks. But getting to the Great Moderation required some severe pain as the Federal Reserve and the US government learned the lessons from the 1970s and 1980s.

Current US Interest Rate Outlook

The 10-year Treasury note yield has been moving sideways for the past several years, but has recently moved higher and as of March 2006 is challenging the upper boundary of its 3-year trading range of 3.07% to 4.90%.

The 10-year T-note yield moved higher in early 2006 because of three main factors: (1) the cumulative effect of the Fed's long tightening regime which started in June 2004, (2) inflation concerns tied to steep energy price increases, and (3) the recent increase in global as well as US short-term interest rates which is ending the cheap financing that investors used to finance purchases of T-notes (i.e., the "carry trade" where investors borrowed in the money markets at cheap rates and invested in the long-end at higher yields to take advantage of the steep yield curve spread seen over that period).

As of the end of March 2006, the markets were expecting the Fed to boost the federal funds rate target by another 25 basis points to 5.00% by spring 2006 and were discounting a strong chance of a further 25 basis point rate hike to 5.25% by autumn 2006.

However, the rise in T-note yields is likely to be limited

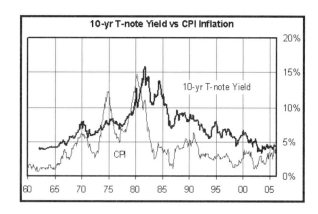

because the Fed's tightening before long will curb the economy and will keep a damper on inflation. By the time the Fed is done tightening, the Fed will have steadily raised interest rates for two straight years. That tighter monetary policy will eventually catch up with the US economy and allow interest rates to fall back again. It is unlikely that the Fed will allow inflation to enter into a runaway mode, which would cause long-term interest rates to soar. Rather, the Fed is likely to fulfill its mission of keeping inflation under control, thus keeping long-term interest rates under control as well.

US Interest Rate History

The 1970s to 1990s

US interest rates rose sharply in the period of 1965 to the early 1980s mainly because the Fed let inflation get out of control. The CPI rose sharply in 1973-75 to +11.8%, fell back in 1976-77, but then soared to a peak of +13.6% in 1980. Upward pressure on inflation in the 1970s stemmed from (1) deficit spending for the Vietnam War and President Johnson's Great Society, (2) the end of the Bretton Woods fixed-currency system in 1971 which resulted in the dollar's depreciation, and (3) the Arab oil embargo in 1973.

The Fed should have tightened monetary policy during that time, but instead kept interest rates targeted too low and allowed inflation to reach runaway levels. Finally, President Jimmy Carter appointed Paul Volcker as Fed Chairman in 1979. Mr. Volcker used strict monetarist policies to clamp down on reserve and money supply growth, which is the root cause of inflation. The Fed raised its federal funds rate target as high as 20% in 1980 and again in 1981. The Fed's tight monetary policy caused US interest rates to spike higher and caused a double-dip recession in 1980 (Jan-July) and again in 1981-82 (July 1981 to Nov 1982).

Throughout the remainder of the 1980s, the 10-year T-note yield moved steadily lower as inflation stabilized in the 4-6% range and as the US economy experience a long period of expansion. That expansion was interrupted by a recession in 1990-91, which was caused by the first Iraq war and its related oil spike. Yet over the 1982-2003 time frame, the 10-year T-note yield moved steadily lower on the Fed's impressive inflation-fighting regime. US interest rates were able to fall even further in the 1990s as the CPI was able to stabilize at the low average of 2.5-3.0%. The 10-year T-note yield in the 1990s eased from 8% at the end of 1989 to as low as 4.16% by the end of 1998.

Interest Rates During the 2000 Equity Bubble

The latter half of the 1990s was the time of the extraordinary Internet and technology boom. US GDP in the latter half of the 1990s averaged +4.0%, which was significantly stronger than the long-run average of +3.4%. The Fed allowed GDP to run at the high level of +4.0% in the late 1990s because Fed Chairman Greenspan recognized that productivity showed a permanent upward shift in the late-1990s due to technology improvements.

However, the technology boom, along with modest interest rates and speculative Internet fever, produced a massive bubble in the stock market. The Fed by mid-1999 realized that it needed to start taking away the punch bowl and raised the funds rate target from 4.75% in mid-1999 to a 10-year high of 6.5% by mid-2000. The Fed's tighter monetary policy finally popped the stock market bubble in early 2000. The plunge in the stock market that started in 2000, along with the post Y2K technology spending bust, led to a US recession in 2001 (March-November).

In response, the Fed in 2001 slashed its funds rate target from 6.5% to 1.75%, and then cut the funds rate further to 1.00% in 2002 and early-2003 due to the additional shock to the economy from the al-Qaeda terrorist attack on September 11, 2001. The war between the US and Iraq in 2003 provided another negative factor for the US economy during that period. The Fed eased monetary policy sharply in order to prevent the possibility of deflation, which the Fed knew had devastated the Japanese economy in the 1990s. The Fed's easy monetary policy, combined with a benign inflation environment, allowed the 10-year T-note yield to fall to a low of 3.07% in June 2003, a level in long-term yields not seen since the 1960s.

By mid-2004, the Fed recognized that the US economy had finally entered a sustained expansion and the Fed started to raise the federal funds rate target in 25 basis point rate increments at each consecutive Federal Open Market Committee meeting. The US economy continued to perform well in the 2004-05 period despite the Fed's tighter monetary policy and the sharp rise in oil prices that occurred over that time-frame. As of early 2006, the Fed's tightening process was still in progress and the Fed was expected to continue tightening to 5.00%-5.25%.

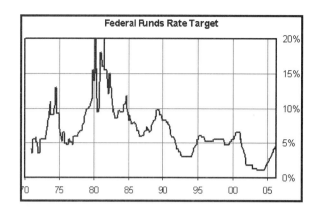

The 2004-05 Long-Term Rate "Conundrum"

During the course of the Fed's tightening regime that started in June 2004, the 10-year T-note yield was able to trade sideways until late-2005 and did not see upward pressure from the ongoing rise in short-term rates. The Fed raised its federal funds rate target by a total of 3.25 percentage points to 4.25% through the end of 2005 from the 1.00% level that prevailed in late 2003 and early 2004. Yet, during 2004 and 2005, the 10-year T-note yield traded in the narrow range of 3.65%-4.90% and did not show any significant upward movement in response to the Fed's tightening process for short-term rates.

Fed Chairman Alan Greenspan, in testimony to Congress delivered on February 16, 2005, used the term "conundrum" to refer to the observation that long-term interest rates were remaining remarkably low despite the Fed's action to raise short-term rates. The Fed had expected to see long-term rates show some upward movement in response to higher short-term rates.

The general consensus is that long-term rates were held down from late-2004 through 2005 by several main factors: (1) market confidence in the Fed's inflation-fighting intentions and the benign core inflation outlook during that period, (2) the "carry trade" where global investors used cheap financing from Japan and Europe to fund the purchase of higher-yielding US Treasury securities, and (3) heavy purchases of Treasury securities by foreign central banks (mainly Japan, China and South Korea) who needed to invest the dollars they acquired through their large trade surpluses with the US. Foreign central banks in 2005 purchased an average of about 40% of all Treasury coupon auctions, a huge percentage that helped keep yields low.

Mr. Greenspan's "conundrum" was largely eliminated in late-2005 and early-2006, however, when US T-note yields started to move higher as global interest rates started to increase and as the Fed's tighter monetary policy started to bite harder into the long-end of the yield curve. By March 2006, the 10-year T-note yield was near the top of the 2004-05 range of 4.90%.

EURODOLLARS, 3-MONTH

Annual High, Low and Close of Eurodollar, 3-Month Futures   In Points of 100%

Year	High	Low	Close	Year	High	Low	Close	Year	High	Low	Close
				1989	92.2200	88.7600	91.9800	1998	95.3050	94.2000	95.0450
1981	86.7600	84.6900	85.5800	1990	92.8800	91.0800	92.8000	1999	95.1500	93.8000	93.8350
1982	90.7000	82.8400	90.7000	1991	96.0100	92.5200	95.9600	2000	94.1550	93.0100	94.1100
1983	91.2700	89.0200	89.6500	1992	97.0100	95.0900	96.3600	2001	98.1600	94.1350	98.0250
1984	91.0800	86.6300	90.4800	1993	96.8600	96.3400	96.4900	2002	98.7000	97.3700	98.6800
1985	92.5900	89.2500	92.2500	1994	96.6900	92.7500	92.7700	2003	99.1000	98.6150	98.7750
1986	94.3600	91.7400	93.8900	1995	94.6900	92.7300	94.6800	2004	98.8950	97.0650	97.0950
1987	94.1200	90.1500	92.4400	1996	94.8600	94.0200	94.4400	2005	97.1300	95.1900	95.2250
1988	93.2700	90.4200	90.6200	1997	94.5300	93.9550	94.2250	2006	95.3200	94.7800	94.7950

Source: Chicago Mercantile Exchange

EURODOLLARS, 3-MONTH

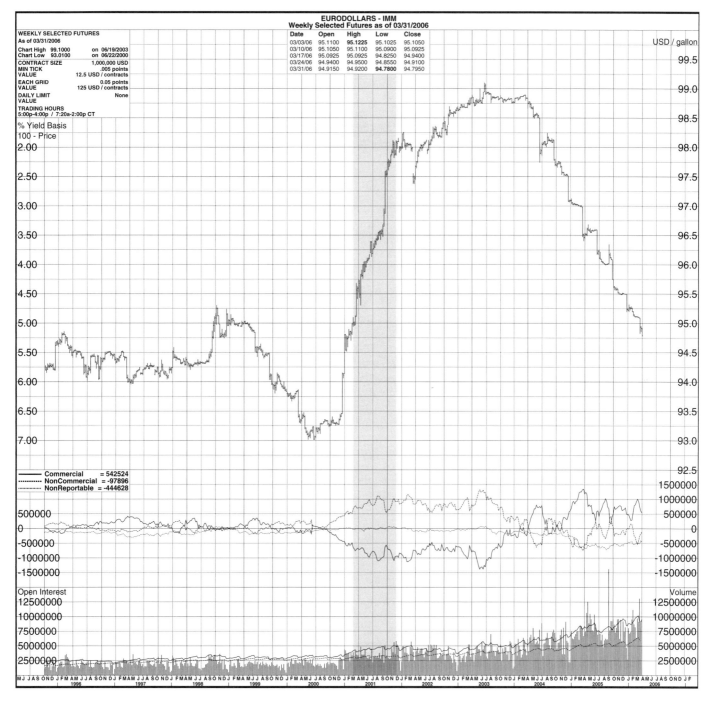

Quarterly High, Low and Close of Eurodollar, 3-Month Futures   In Points of 100%

Quarter	High	Low	Close	Quarter	High	Low	Close	Quarter	High	Low	Close
09/1996	94.4800	94.0200	94.2400	12/1999	94.1550	93.8000	93.8350	03/2003	98.8850	98.6150	98.8500
12/1996	94.5200	94.2000	94.4400	03/2000	93.8700	93.2900	93.3450	06/2003	99.1000	98.6950	98.9250
03/1997	94.5300	93.9850	94.0050	06/2000	93.5000	93.0100	93.0650	09/2003	98.9500	98.7550	98.8650
06/1997	94.2450	93.9550	94.1200	09/2000	93.3600	93.0450	93.2600	12/2003	98.8850	98.7450	98.7750
09/1997	94.3200	94.1100	94.1700	12/2000	94.1550	93.2350	94.1100	03/2004	98.8950	98.7500	98.8300
12/1997	94.3750	94.0400	94.2250	03/2001	95.6850	94.1350	95.5900	06/2004	98.8350	97.7400	97.9800
03/1998	94.5900	94.2100	94.2950	06/2001	96.3950	95.3000	96.1850	09/2004	98.2450	97.6700	97.6950
06/1998	94.4200	94.2000	94.3050	09/2001	97.6150	96.1750	97.5400	12/2004	97.7650	97.0650	97.0950
09/1998	95.0350	94.2950	94.9500	12/2001	98.1600	97.5200	98.0250	03/2005	97.1300	96.4000	96.4850
12/1998	95.3050	94.7425	95.0450	03/2002	98.2600	97.3700	97.4700	06/2005	96.6850	96.1400	96.1500
03/1999	95.1500	94.9350	94.9900	06/2002	98.1275	97.4450	98.0450	09/2005	96.3450	95.6100	95.6150
06/1999	95.0400	94.4200	94.5950	09/2002	98.5250	98.0350	98.5100	12/2005	95.6350	95.1900	95.2250
09/1999	94.6500	94.0100	94.0350	12/2002	98.7000	98.2050	98.6800	03/2006	95.3200	94.7800	94.7950

Source: Chicago Mercantile Exchange

FEDERAL FUNDS, 30-DAY

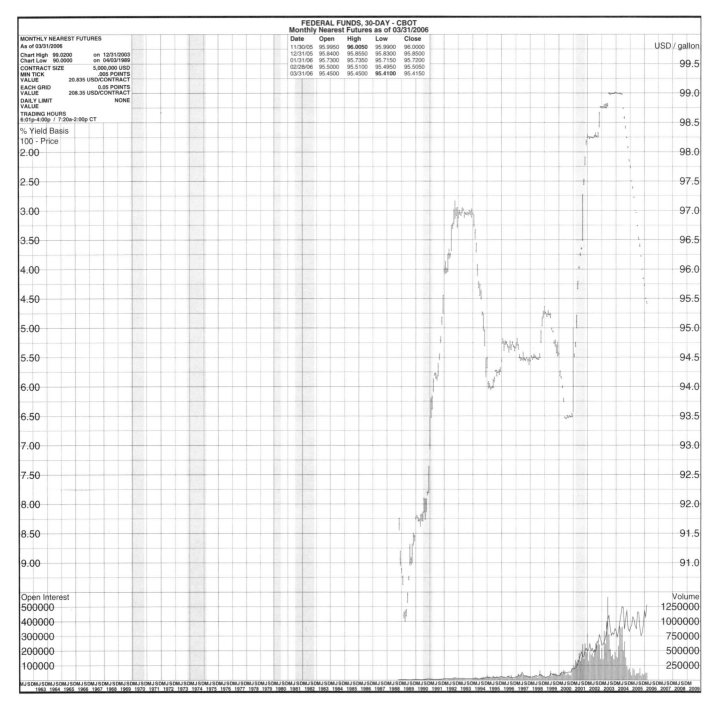

Annual High, Low and Close of Federal Funds, 30-Day Futures   In Points of 100%

Year	High	Low	Close	Year	High	Low	Close	Year	High	Low	Close
				1993	97.0500	96.8700	97.0300	2000	94.5950	93.4450	93.4900
				1994	96.9800	94.1600	94.4800	2001	98.2100	93.5750	98.1800
1988	91.7900	90.9500	91.2000	1995	94.5100	93.9500	94.3200	2002	98.7750	98.2150	98.7600
1989	91.5100	90.0000	91.4500	1996	94.8250	94.4150	94.6600	2003	99.0200	98.7350	99.0150
1990	92.6400	91.6100	92.6400	1997	94.8200	94.3650	94.4900	2004	99.0100	97.8350	97.8400
1991	95.5600	92.9300	95.5500	1998	95.2850	94.4300	95.2850	2005	97.7600	95.8300	95.8500
1992	97.1700	95.9100	97.0500	1999	95.3700	94.5100	94.6900	2006	95.7350	95.4100	95.4150

Source: Chicago Board of Trade

FEDERAL FUNDS, 30-DAY

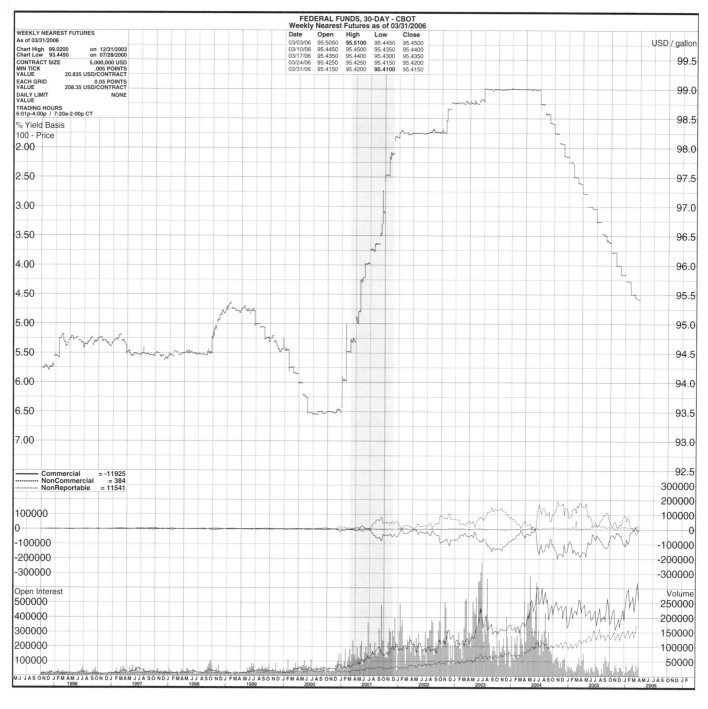

Quarterly High, Low and Close of Federal Funds, 30-Day Futures   In Points of 100%

Quarter	High	Low	Close	Quarter	High	Low	Close	Quarter	High	Low	Close
09/1996	94.7800	94.5750	94.7050	12/1999	94.7950	94.5100	94.6900	03/2003	98.8050	98.7350	98.7500
12/1996	94.7750	94.6000	94.6600	03/2000	94.5950	94.1350	94.1400	06/2003	98.8300	98.7400	98.7850
03/1997	94.8200	94.6300	94.6350	06/2000	94.0200	93.4650	93.4700	09/2003	99.0100	98.9650	98.9900
06/1997	94.5550	94.4400	94.4650	09/2000	93.5150	93.4450	93.4800	12/2003	99.0200	98.9800	99.0150
09/1997	94.5950	94.4350	94.4500	12/2000	93.5500	93.4700	93.4900	03/2004	99.0100	98.9900	98.9950
12/1997	94.5100	94.3650	94.4900	03/2001	95.0000	93.5750	94.6850	06/2004	99.0000	98.9700	98.9750
03/1998	94.5350	94.4300	94.5050	06/2001	96.0500	94.9900	96.0200	09/2004	98.7450	98.3950	98.4000
06/1998	94.5550	94.4650	94.4800	09/2001	97.2800	96.2300	96.8950	12/2004	98.2550	97.8350	97.8400
09/1998	94.5700	94.4550	94.4950	12/2001	98.2100	97.4350	98.1800	03/2005	97.7600	97.3700	97.3750
12/1998	95.2850	94.7450	95.2850	03/2002	98.3050	98.2150	98.2550	06/2005	97.2300	96.9600	96.9650
03/1999	95.3700	95.1800	95.1900	06/2002	98.2600	98.2350	98.2400	09/2005	96.7450	96.3750	96.3800
06/1999	95.3050	95.1600	95.2300	09/2002	98.3300	98.2450	98.2500	12/2005	96.2300	95.8300	95.8500
09/1999	95.0050	94.7250	94.7800	12/2002	98.7750	98.2450	98.7600	03/2006	95.7350	95.4100	95.4150

Source: Chicago Board of Trade

LIBOR, 1-MONTH

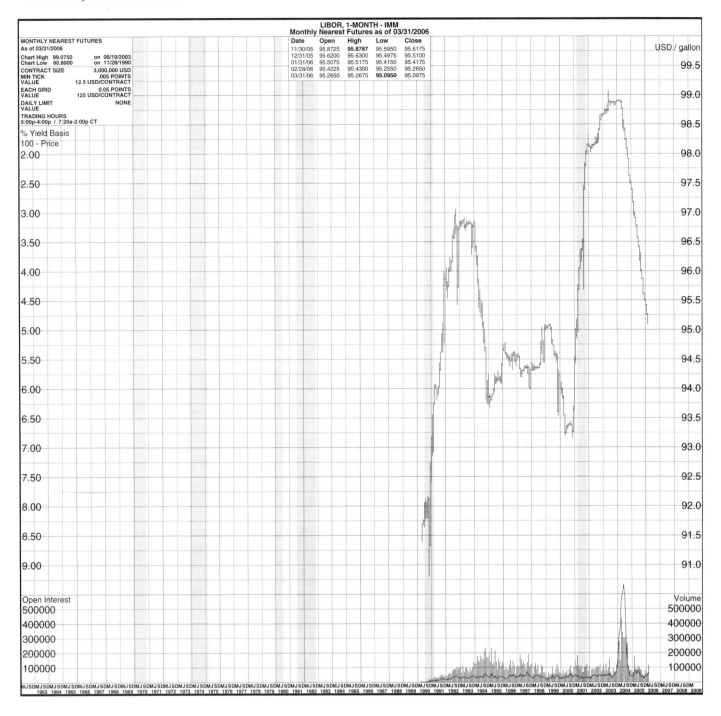

Annual High, Low and Close of Libor, 1-Month Futures   In Points of 100%

Year	High	Low	Close	Year	High	Low	Close	Year	High	Low	Close
				1995	94.4300	93.6600	94.4100	2001	98.1700	93.6300	98.1650
1990	92.7400	90.8000	92.6400	1996	94.7900	94.3100	94.5700	2002	98.6800	98.0150	98.6575
1991	96.0000	92.4000	95.8700	1997	94.6100	93.9800	94.3200	2003	99.0750	98.6125	98.8850
1992	97.0600	95.4200	96.7000	1998	95.0850	94.2900	95.0200	2004	98.9150	97.4850	97.5275
1993	96.9100	96.2800	96.7600	1999	95.0975	93.5375	94.2300	2005	97.5325	95.4975	95.5100
1994	96.8800	93.7300	93.8600	2000	94.2300	93.1600	93.6225	2006	95.5175	95.0950	95.0975

Source: Chicago Mercantile Exchange

LIBOR, 1-MONTH

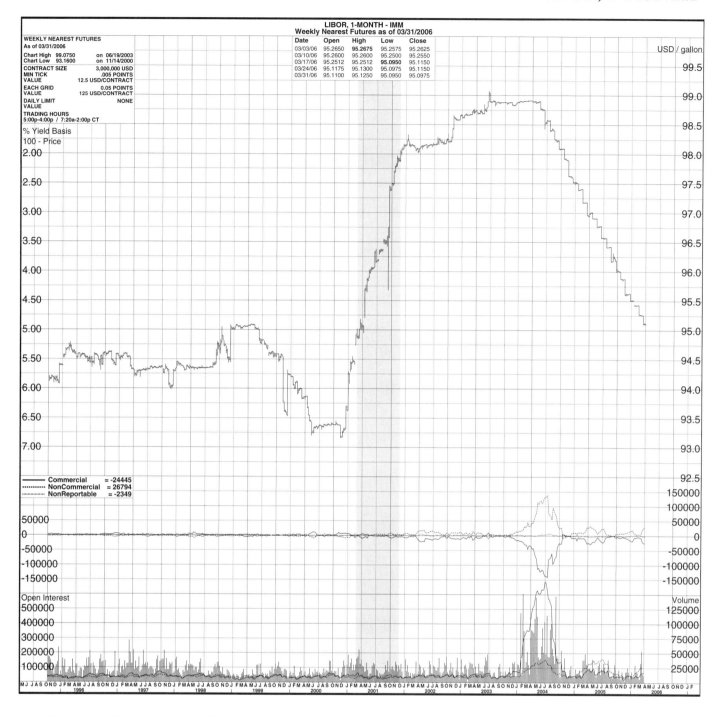

Quarterly High, Low and Close of Libor, 1-Month Futures   In Points of 100%

Quarter	High	Low	Close	Quarter	High	Low	Close	Quarter	High	Low	Close
09/1996	94.6000	94.3100	94.5700	12/1999	94.6100	93.5375	94.2300	03/2003	98.7725	98.6125	98.7350
12/1996	94.6400	94.3800	94.5700	03/2000	94.2300	93.8200	93.8575	06/2003	99.0750	98.6750	98.8875
03/1997	94.6100	94.3250	94.3350	06/2000	93.8800	93.2000	93.3625	09/2003	98.9150	98.8150	98.8800
06/1997	94.3500	94.1850	94.3100	09/2000	93.4250	93.3000	93.3950	12/2003	98.8900	98.8250	98.8850
09/1997	94.3900	94.2950	94.3550	12/2000	93.7050	93.1600	93.6225	03/2004	98.9150	98.8750	98.9100
12/1997	94.4100	93.9800	94.3200	03/2001	95.1850	93.6300	95.0525	06/2004	98.9100	98.4250	98.5500
03/1998	94.4600	94.2900	94.3450	06/2001	96.3750	94.9500	96.1650	09/2004	98.5850	98.0750	98.0950
06/1998	94.4000	94.3050	94.3450	09/2001	97.4600	95.6800	97.3850	12/2004	98.0950	97.4850	97.5275
09/1998	94.8000	94.3400	94.6900	12/2001	98.1700	97.3800	98.1650	03/2005	97.5325	96.9350	96.9775
12/1998	95.0850	94.4350	95.0200	03/2002	98.3300	98.0150	98.0875	06/2005	97.0150	96.5675	96.5700
03/1999	95.0900	94.9900	95.0575	06/2002	98.1900	98.0800	98.1550	09/2005	96.5850	95.9900	96.0125
06/1999	95.0975	94.7500	94.8175	09/2002	98.3400	98.1500	98.3275	12/2005	96.0200	95.4975	95.5100
09/1999	94.8375	94.5200	94.5775	12/2002	98.6800	98.1900	98.6575	03/2006	95.5175	95.0950	95.0975

Source: Chicago Mercantile Exchange

TREASURY NOTE, 2-YEAR

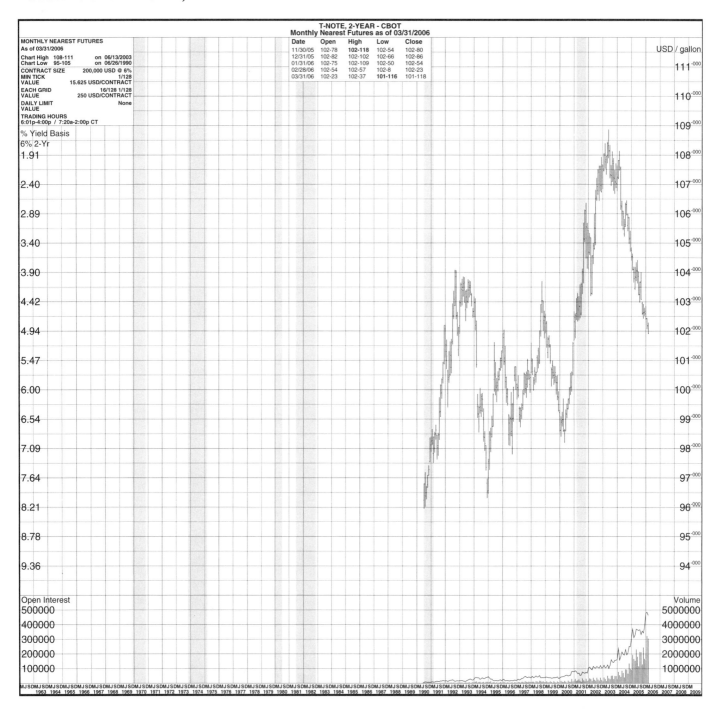

Annual High, Low and Close of Treasury Note, 2-Year Futures   Nominal Value

Year	High	Low	Close	Year	High	Low	Close	Year	High	Low	Close
				1995	101 160	96 118	101 084	2001	106 094	101 176	104 126
1990	98 096	95 210	98 000	1996	102 012	97 204	100 084	2002	107 240	103 050	107 152
1991	102 050	97 130	102 050	1997	101 014	98 186	100 106	2003	108 222	106 172	107 006
1992	104 022	99 102	102 028	1998	103 180	99 248	102 124	2004	108 036	104 180	104 204
1993	103 220	101 232	102 168	1999	102 150	99 066	99 078	2005	104 216	102 108	102 172
1994	103 048	96 080	96 140	2000	101 162	98 048	101 148	2006	102 218	101 232	101 236

Source: Chicago Board of Trade

TREASURY NOTE, 2-YEAR

Annual High, Low and Close of Treasury Note, 2-Year Yield   In Percent

Year	High	Low	Close	Year	High	Low	Close	Year	High	Low	Close
1976	7.260	5.310	5.340	1985	10.890	7.940	7.980	1996	6.517	4.771	5.859
1977	7.260	5.420	7.220	1986	8.380	5.880	6.310	1997	6.536	5.427	5.617
1978	9.980	7.240	9.980	1987	9.430	6.110	7.760	1998	5.726	3.566	4.511
1979	12.630	8.920	11.230	1988	9.229	6.984	9.133	1999	6.386	4.379	6.218
1980	15.360	8.360	13.060	1989	9.929	7.373	7.840	2000	6.947	5.056	5.108
1981	16.950	12.110	13.630	1990	9.075	7.075	7.130	2001	5.108	2.287	3.047
1982	15.180	9.480	9.480	1991	7.231	4.661	4.751	2002	3.753	1.558	1.598
1983	11.410	9.090	10.850	1992	5.915	3.572	4.542	2003	2.140	1.056	1.819
1984	13.170	9.830	10.020	1993	4.658	3.644	4.225	2004	3.138	1.446	3.065
1979	38.47	15.48	38.01	1994	7.768	3.999	7.680	2005	4.502	3.049	4.400
1980	39.81	35.75	37.48	1995	7.732	5.141	5.150	2006	4.841	4.292	4.816

Source: Federal Reserve Board

TREASURY NOTE, 2-YEAR

Quarterly High, Low and Close of Treasury Note, 2-Year Futures   Nominal Value

Quarter	High	Low	Close	Quarter	High	Low	Close	Quarter	High	Low	Close
09/1996	99 236	97 204	99 008	12/1999	100 126	99 066	99 078	03/2003	108 104	106 214	107 196
12/1996	100 204	98 234	100 084	03/2000	99 076	98 104	98 252	06/2003	108 222	107 084	108 038
03/1997	100 124	98 232	99 040	06/2000	99 180	98 048	99 048	09/2003	108 088	106 242	107 204
06/1997	99 252	98 186	99 222	09/2000	100 020	99 008	100 016	12/2003	107 230	106 172	107 006
09/1997	100 160	99 186	100 144	12/2000	101 162	99 210	101 148	03/2004	108 036	106 194	107 150
12/1997	101 014	99 230	100 106	03/2001	103 032	101 176	102 254	06/2004	107 154	105 112	105 228
03/1998	101 154	99 248	100 084	06/2001	103 152	102 084	102 146	09/2004	106 116	105 056	105 250
06/1998	101 046	100 044	101 000	09/2001	105 176	102 136	105 034	12/2004	106 002	104 180	104 204
09/1998	102 234	100 188	102 230	12/2001	106 094	104 032	104 126	03/2005	104 216	103 168	103 204
12/1998	103 180	101 192	102 124	03/2002	105 110	103 050	103 076	06/2005	104 108	103 104	104 008
03/1999	102 150	101 020	101 184	06/2002	106 000	103 062	105 132	09/2005	104 008	102 250	103 020
06/1999	101 218	100 028	100 176	09/2002	107 132	104 236	107 116	12/2005	103 000	102 108	102 172
09/1999	100 254	100 042	100 150	12/2002	107 240	106 112	107 152	03/2006	102 218	101 232	101 236

Source: Chicago Board of Trade

TREASURY NOTE, 2-YEAR

Quarterly High, Low and Close of Treasury Note, 2-Year Yield   In Percent

Quarter	High	Low	Close	Quarter	High	Low	Close	Quarter	High	Low	Close
09/1996	6.517	5.860	6.093	12/1999	6.386	5.608	6.218	03/2003	1.872	1.314	1.490
12/1996	6.109	5.557	5.859	03/2000	6.734	6.252	6.474	06/2003	1.732	1.056	1.300
03/1997	6.444	5.718	6.411	06/2000	6.947	6.093	6.349	09/2003	2.072	1.221	1.466
06/1997	6.536	5.912	6.050	09/2000	6.476	5.932	5.983	12/2003	2.140	1.426	1.819
09/1997	6.093	5.698	5.758	12/2000	6.067	5.056	5.108	03/2004	1.972	1.446	1.572
12/1997	5.903	5.427	5.617	03/2001	5.108	4.086	4.159	06/2004	2.938	1.564	2.677
03/1998	5.668	4.982	5.533	06/2001	4.554	3.862	4.213	09/2004	2.815	2.323	2.605
06/1998	5.726	5.289	5.450	09/2001	4.240	2.713	2.815	12/2004	3.138	2.450	3.065
09/1998	5.509	4.261	4.261	12/2001	3.356	2.287	3.047	03/2005	3.899	3.049	3.783
12/1998	4.804	3.566	4.511	03/2002	3.753	2.689	3.715	06/2005	3.816	3.418	3.633
03/1999	5.225	4.379	4.966	06/2002	3.740	2.572	2.827	09/2005	4.181	3.567	4.165
06/1999	5.775	4.784	5.507	09/2002	2.932	1.675	1.691	12/2005	4.502	4.149	4.400
09/1999	5.797	5.387	5.583	12/2002	2.214	1.558	1.598	03/2006	4.841	4.292	4.816

Source: Federal Reserve Board

TREASURY NOTE, 5-YEAR

Annual High, Low and Close of Treasury Note, 5-Year Futures — Nominal Value

Year	High	Low	Close	Year	High	Low	Close	Year	High	Low	Close
				1993	106 014	99 006	103 002	2000	103 112	96 064	103 072
				1994	104 078	92 004	92 076	2001	110 058	102 112	105 106
1988	91 024	87 124	88 052	1995	102 058	92 016	102 056	2002	114 074	103 046	113 032
1989	94 098	86 044	93 008	1996	103 076	95 120	99 040	2003	117 102	110 060	111 080
1990	93 098	88 022	93 026	1997	101 046	96 048	100 110	2004	115 036	107 108	109 068
1991	100 032	91 076	100 018	1998	107 052	100 076	105 044	2005	110 000	105 046	106 044
1992	102 090	94 078	99 040	1999	105 052	98 002	98 002	2006	106 116	104 038	104 056

Source: Chicago Board of Trade

TREASURY NOTE, 5-YEAR

Annual High, Low and Close of Treasury Note, 5-Year Yield — In Percent

Year	High	Low	Close	Year	High	Low	Close	Year	High	Low	Close
1968	6.360	5.420	6.330	1981	16.270	12.210	13.970	1994	7.904	4.927	7.823
1969	8.330	6.110	8.220	1982	15.020	10.090	10.090	1995	7.935	5.374	5.388
1970	8.300	5.850	5.980	1983	11.950	9.720	11.570	1996	6.917	5.120	6.199
1971	7.030	4.740	5.500	1984	13.840	10.830	11.080	1997	6.899	5.602	5.701
1972	6.320	5.470	6.260	1985	11.700	8.480	8.490	1998	5.807	3.889	4.542
1973	8.130	6.230	6.830	1986	9.000	6.390	6.820	1999	6.353	4.387	6.346
1974	8.790	6.720	7.360	1987	10.110	6.540	8.414	2000	6.834	4.880	4.967
1975	8.560	6.930	7.500	1988	9.244	7.542	9.146	2001	5.108	3.246	4.334
1976	7.820	5.990	6.130	1989	9.761	7.394	7.856	2002	4.877	2.533	2.730
1977	7.580	6.160	7.540	1990	9.137	7.526	7.636	2003	3.617	1.997	3.218
1978	9.350	7.580	9.320	1991	8.082	5.895	5.924	2004	4.101	2.608	3.607
1979	11.500	8.700	10.380	1992	7.186	5.087	6.029	2005	4.578	3.551	4.355
1980	14.120	8.860	12.590	1993	6.073	4.536	5.193	2006	4.846	4.229	4.814

Source: Federal Reserve Board

TREASURY NOTE, 5-YEAR

Quarterly High, Low and Close of Treasury Note, 5-Year Futures Nominal Value

Quarter	High	Low	Close	Quarter	High	Low	Close	Quarter	High	Low	Close
09/1996	99 010	95 120	98 016	12/1999	100 050	98 002	98 002	03/2003	115 028	111 044	113 064
12/1996	100 110	98 002	99 040	03/2000	98 080	96 064	98 064	06/2003	117 102	112 046	115 016
03/1997	99 124	96 110	97 000	06/2000	100 002	96 064	99 002	09/2003	115 062	110 072	113 060
06/1997	98 124	96 048	98 054	09/2000	100 090	98 054	100 070	12/2003	113 076	110 060	111 080
09/1997	100 064	98 048	100 020	12/2000	103 112	100 020	103 072	03/2004	115 036	110 106	113 072
12/1997	101 046	99 034	100 110	03/2001	106 038	102 112	105 066	06/2004	113 084	107 108	108 088
03/1998	102 112	100 088	101 056	06/2001	106 008	103 022	103 044	09/2004	111 118	108 070	110 096
06/1998	102 054	100 076	101 124	09/2001	108 096	103 032	108 024	12/2004	111 100	109 014	109 068
09/1998	106 102	101 066	106 098	12/2001	110 058	104 088	105 106	03/2005	110 000	106 016	107 012
12/1998	107 052	104 006	105 044	03/2002	107 074	103 046	103 094	06/2005	109 122	106 106	108 114
03/1999	105 052	101 110	103 006	06/2002	108 096	103 064	107 054	09/2005	109 064	106 076	106 110
06/1999	103 118	99 074	100 118	09/2002	114 056	107 024	114 036	12/2005	106 124	105 046	106 044
09/1999	101 060	99 056	100 060	12/2002	114 074	111 016	113 032	03/2006	106 116	104 038	104 056

Source: Chicago Board of Trade

TREASURY NOTE, 5-YEAR

T-Note Yield, 5-Year
Weekly Cash as of 03/31/2006

Date	Open	High	Low	Close
03/03/06	4.629	4.720	4.578	4.710
03/10/06	4.731	4.802	4.719	4.766
03/17/06	4.793	4.795	4.580	4.621
03/24/06	4.633	4.736	4.592	4.662
03/31/06	4.670	4.846	4.666	4.814

WEEKLY CASH As of 03/31/2006
Chart High 6.930 on 05/01/1995
Chart Low 1.997 on 06/13/2003

Quarterly High, Low and Close of Treasury Note, 5-Year Yield   In Percent

Quarter	High	Low	Close	Quarter	High	Low	Close	Quarter	High	Low	Close
09/1996	6.917	6.198	6.453	12/1999	6.353	5.756	6.346	03/2003	3.204	2.474	2.738
12/1996	6.471	5.791	6.199	03/2000	6.807	6.278	6.320	06/2003	3.010	1.997	2.423
03/1997	6.899	6.016	6.748	06/2000	6.834	5.936	6.171	09/2003	3.617	2.346	2.823
06/1997	6.865	6.253	6.379	09/2000	6.316	5.803	5.833	12/2003	3.519	2.792	3.218
09/1997	6.413	5.875	5.981	12/2000	5.938	4.880	4.967	03/2004	3.401	2.608	2.781
12/1997	6.129	5.602	5.701	03/2001	5.092	4.351	4.557	06/2004	4.101	2.776	3.808
03/1998	5.807	5.074	5.602	06/2001	5.108	4.411	4.934	09/2004	3.875	3.212	3.370
06/1998	5.797	5.340	5.454	09/2001	4.962	3.246	3.780	12/2004	3.774	3.205	3.607
09/1998	5.539	4.200	4.221	12/2001	4.696	3.448	4.334	03/2005	4.385	3.559	4.174
12/1998	4.745	3.889	4.542	03/2002	4.877	4.038	4.824	06/2005	4.224	3.551	3.725
03/1999	5.349	4.387	5.093	06/2002	4.875	3.789	4.062	09/2005	4.288	3.735	4.195
06/1999	5.949	4.891	5.634	09/2002	4.104	2.548	2.578	12/2005	4.578	4.182	4.355
09/1999	6.043	5.487	5.749	12/2002	3.404	2.533	2.730	03/2006	4.846	4.229	4.814

Source: Federal Reserve Board

TREASURY NOTE, 10-YEAR

Annual High, Low and Close of Treasury Note, 10-Year Futures   Nominal Value

Year	High	Low	Close	Year	High	Low	Close	Year	High	Low	Close
				1989	90 36	79 28	88 32	1998	112 40	100 10	106 18
				1990	88 40	80 50	87 00	1999	108 14	95 46	95 55
1982	77 56	60 30	76 10	1991	94 44	84 16	94 30	2000	105 36	93 43	104 55
1983	77 44	67 60	70 30	1992	98 60	87 62	94 38	2001	112 26	102 44	105 09
1984	72 56	61 62	71 26	1993	106 28	93 50	102 14	2002	116 28	101 58	115 03
1985	82 54	68 34	82 12	1994	104 02	85 56	88 22	2003	121 06	109 39	112 17
1986	95 34	79 28	91 50	1995	103 18	87 04	102 24	2004	117 62	107 51	111 60
1987	93 44	74 32	82 62	1996	104 28	91 50	97 32	2005	114 32	107 31	109 26
1988	87 36	79 28	81 28	1997	101 56	92 36	101 32	2006	110 13	106 08	106 25

Source: Chicago Board of Trade

TREASURY NOTE, 10-YEAR

Annual High, Low and Close of Treasury Note, 10-Year Yield   In Percent

Year	High	Low	Close	Year	High	Low	Close	Year	High	Low	Close
1968	6.270	5.340	6.160	1981	15.840	12.110	13.980	1994	8.062	5.548	7.820
1969	8.050	5.950	7.880	1982	14.950	10.360	10.360	1995	7.928	5.574	5.581
1970	8.220	6.210	6.500	1983	12.200	10.120	11.820	1996	7.123	5.501	6.418
1971	6.950	5.380	5.890	1984	13.990	11.240	11.550	1997	7.016	5.659	5.725
1972	6.620	5.850	6.410	1985	12.020	8.990	9.000	1998	5.849	4.084	4.654
1973	7.580	6.400	6.900	1986	9.490	6.950	7.230	1999	6.453	4.558	6.440
1974	8.160	6.930	7.400	1987	10.230	7.010	8.830	2000	6.834	4.998	5.102
1975	8.590	7.220	7.760	1988	9.410	8.110	9.133	2001	5.563	4.101	5.033
1976	8.000	6.800	6.810	1989	9.550	7.634	7.917	2002	5.475	3.559	3.818
1977	7.820	6.840	7.780	1990	9.113	7.880	8.063	2003	4.668	3.074	4.257
1978	9.160	7.820	9.150	1991	8.434	6.659	6.701	2004	4.904	3.650	4.216
1979	11.020	8.760	10.330	1992	7.723	6.164	6.701	2005	4.693	3.803	4.395
1980	13.650	9.470	12.430	1993	6.789	5.143	5.790	2006	4.884	4.289	4.853

Source: Federal Reserve Board

TREASURY NOTE, 10-YEAR

Quarterly High, Low and Close of Treasury Note, 10-Year Futures   Nominal Value

Quarter	High	Low	Close	Quarter	High	Low	Close	Quarter	High	Low	Close
09/1996	97 28	91 50	95 02	12/1999	99 33	95 46	95 55	03/2003	117 58	112 11	114 56
12/1996	100 18	94 52	97 32	03/2000	98 14	93 43	98 05	06/2003	121 06	113 08	117 28
03/1997	98 44	94 18	94 42	06/2000	99 60	94 52	98 31	09/2003	117 61	109 39	114 40
06/1997	97 38	92 36	96 46	09/2000	100 46	97 40	100 14	12/2003	114 48	110 31	112 17
09/1997	100 30	95 56	99 10	12/2000	105 36	99 43	104 55	03/2004	117 62	111 02	115 26
12/1997	101 56	98 20	101 32	03/2001	107 33	103 38	106 13	06/2004	115 32	107 51	109 21
03/1998	104 16	100 34	101 42	06/2001	106 55	102 44	103 01	09/2004	114 24	109 11	112 40
06/1998	103 42	100 10	102 40	09/2001	109 59	102 44	108 50	12/2004	114 10	110 63	111 60
09/1998	108 28	102 08	108 26	12/2001	112 26	103 46	105 09	03/2005	113 25	107 53	109 17
12/1998	112 40	105 32	106 18	03/2002	107 43	101 58	102 29	06/2005	114 32	108 54	113 30
03/1999	108 14	102 10	103 18	06/2002	108 61	102 12	107 15	09/2005	113 43	109 50	109 59
06/1999	104 48	97 56	99 57	09/2002	116 13	106 56	115 58	12/2005	110 05	107 31	109 26
09/1999	100 56	97 01	98 52	12/2002	116 28	111 32	115 03	03/2006	110 13	106 08	106 25

Source: Chicago Board of Trade

TREASURY NOTE, 10-YEAR

Quarterly High, Low and Close of Treasury Note, 10-Year Yield   In Percent

Quarter	High	Low	Close	Quarter	High	Low	Close	Quarter	High	Low	Close
09/1996	7.123	6.460	6.701	12/1999	6.453	5.871	6.440	03/2003	4.203	3.549	3.823
12/1996	6.718	6.006	6.418	03/2000	6.834	5.994	6.000	06/2003	4.080	3.074	3.528
03/1997	6.920	6.229	6.905	06/2000	6.593	5.700	6.018	09/2003	4.668	3.459	3.937
06/1997	7.016	6.353	6.496	09/2000	6.184	5.656	5.799	12/2003	4.491	3.912	4.257
09/1997	6.522	5.994	6.107	12/2000	5.897	4.998	5.102	03/2004	4.418	3.650	3.837
12/1997	6.209	5.659	5.725	03/2001	5.365	4.687	4.923	06/2004	4.904	3.831	4.617
03/1998	5.849	5.283	5.647	06/2001	5.563	4.846	5.392	09/2004	4.641	3.963	4.119
06/1998	5.827	5.347	5.438	09/2001	5.438	4.501	4.572	12/2004	4.420	3.943	4.216
09/1998	5.555	4.389	4.406	12/2001	5.395	4.101	5.033	03/2005	4.693	3.977	4.496
12/1998	4.991	4.084	4.654	03/2002	5.473	4.791	5.415	06/2005	4.541	3.803	3.945
03/1999	5.455	4.558	5.238	06/2002	5.475	4.600	4.822	09/2005	4.435	3.942	4.328
06/1999	6.075	4.996	5.780	09/2002	4.867	3.567	3.607	12/2005	4.682	4.317	4.395
09/1999	6.169	5.620	5.870	12/2002	4.351	3.559	3.818	03/2006	4.884	4.289	4.853

Source: Federal Reserve Board

TREASURY NOTE, 30-YEAR

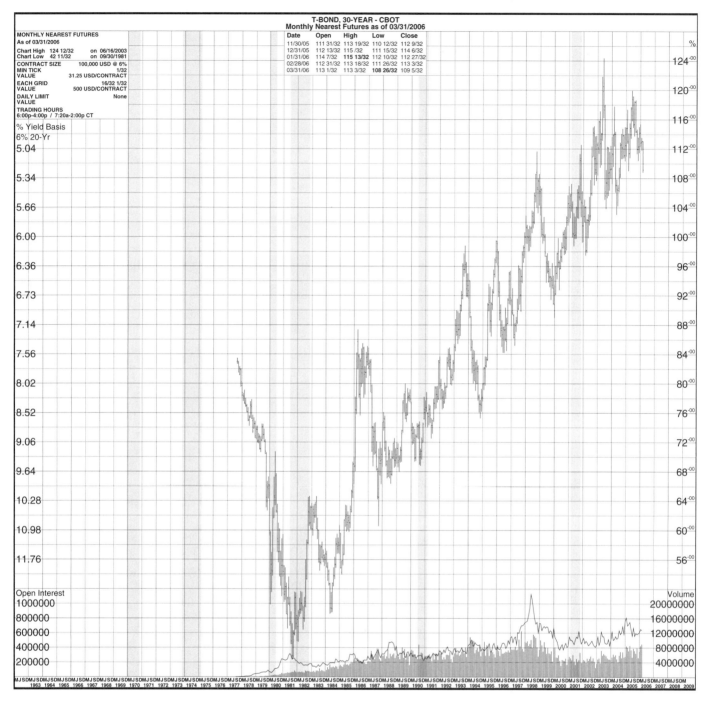

Annual High, Low and Close of Treasury Note, 30-Year Futures   Nominal Value

Year	High	Low	Close	Year	High	Low	Close	Year	High	Low	Close
1977	83 19	79 17	80 07	1987	84 29	60 18	70 11	1997	100 21	85 06	100 01
1978	80 02	72 17	72 26	1988	76 04	66 11	70 09	1998	111 21	98 02	106 09
1979	74 16	62 21	66 08	1989	80 01	67 31	77 28	1999	106 31	90 25	90 30
1980	70 23	49 28	55 25	1990	78 06	68 26	76 03	2000	105 23	89 00	104 20
1981	59 15	42 11	47 09	1991	83 06	72 16	83 04	2001	112 19	98 24	101 17
1982	64 20	44 25	63 03	1992	84 30	76 16	82 24	2002	115 04	97 16	112 22
1983	64 20	54 15	56 08	1993	98 26	81 19	93 12	2003	124 12	103 27	109 10
1984	59 17	48 19	58 09	1994	95 02	75 09	78 02	2004	117 26	103 02	112 16
1985	69 11	53 30	69 00	1995	99 17	77 19	99 13	2005	119 30	109 00	114 06
1986	87 12	66 11	82 17	1996	99 15	84 07	91 22	2006	115 13	108 26	109 05

Source: Chicago Board of Trade

TREASURY NOTE, 30-YEAR

Annual High, Low and Close of Treasury Note, 30-Year Yield   In Percent

Year	High	Low	Close	Year	High	Low	Close	Year	High	Low	Close
1968	5.650	5.040	5.650	1981	15.210	11.670	13.650	1994	8.187	6.154	7.883
1969	6.810	5.740	6.810	1982	14.800	10.330	10.430	1995	7.962	5.938	5.956
1970	6.990	5.970	5.970	1983	12.150	10.270	11.870	1996	7.250	5.922	6.639
1971	5.960	5.440	5.620	1984	13.940	11.320	11.540	1997	7.189	5.850	5.915
1972	6.560	5.570	6.340	1985	11.970	9.270	9.270	1998	6.092	4.685	5.092
1973	7.450	6.530	7.010	1986	9.650	7.120	7.490	1999	6.491	5.030	6.479
1974	8.290	7.180	7.620	1987	10.250	7.290	8.950	2000	6.762	5.380	5.457
1975	8.330	7.520	8.050	1988	9.542	8.320	8.995	2001	5.919	4.661	5.472
1976	7.910	7.200	7.200	1989	9.337	7.753	7.973	2002	5.872	4.606	4.783
1977	8.060	7.350	8.030	1990	9.203	7.962	8.240	2003	5.495	4.135	5.068
1978	8.990	8.070	8.960	1991	8.622	7.394	7.396	2004	5.597	4.620	4.822
1979	10.530	8.800	10.110	1992	8.146	7.201	7.403	2005	4.931	4.151	4.547
1980	13.170	9.490	11.980	1993	7.493	5.771	6.341	2006	4.921	4.460	4.893

Source: Federal Reserve Board

TREASURY NOTE, 30-YEAR

Quarterly High, Low and Close of Treasury Note, 30-Year Futures — Nominal Value

Quarter	High	Low	Close	Quarter	High	Low	Close	Quarter	High	Low	Close
09/1996	90 12	84 07	88 05	12/1999	96 15	90 25	90 30	03/2003	117 05	108 13	112 24
12/1996	95 13	88 05	91 22	03/2000	97 28	89 00	97 22	06/2003	124 12	109 26	117 11
03/1997	93 01	86 06	86 10	06/2000	99 28	92 24	97 11	09/2003	118 01	103 27	112 05
06/1997	91 19	85 06	89 27	09/2000	101 00	96 19	98 21	12/2003	112 15	105 20	109 10
09/1997	96 05	89 26	94 20	12/2000	105 23	97 23	104 20	03/2004	117 26	107 08	114 02
12/1997	100 21	93 23	100 01	03/2001	107 08	101 31	104 06	06/2004	114 12	103 02	106 12
03/1998	102 30	98 02	99 29	06/2001	104 28	98 24	100 10	09/2004	114 03	106 04	112 07
06/1998	103 20	98 03	102 27	09/2001	107 02	99 25	105 16	12/2004	115 00	110 11	112 16
09/1998	108 19	101 06	108 18	12/2001	112 19	99 08	101 17	03/2005	117 12	109 00	111 12
12/1998	111 21	103 08	106 09	03/2002	105 04	97 16	98 05	06/2005	119 30	110 25	118 24
03/1999	106 31	99 03	100 11	06/2002	105 16	97 27	102 25	09/2005	119 04	113 24	114 13
06/1999	102 24	93 25	96 19	09/2002	114 31	102 08	114 08	12/2005	115 00	110 12	114 06
09/1999	97 26	93 05	94 20	12/2002	115 04	107 02	112 22	03/2006	115 13	108 26	109 05

Source: Chicago Board of Trade

TREASURY NOTE, 30-YEAR

Quarterly High, Low and Close of Treasury Note, 30-Year Yield   In Percent

Quarter	High	Low	Close	Quarter	High	Low	Close	Quarter	High	Low	Close
09/1996	7.250	6.672	6.921	12/1999	6.491	5.997	6.479	03/2003	5.094	4.603	4.837
12/1996	6.942	6.310	6.639	03/2000	6.762	5.826	5.831	06/2003	5.056	4.135	4.566
03/1997	7.102	6.499	7.097	06/2000	6.252	5.623	5.894	09/2003	5.495	4.526	4.884
06/1997	7.189	6.637	6.782	09/2000	5.976	5.628	5.884	12/2003	5.331	4.873	5.068
09/1997	6.800	6.283	6.399	12/2000	5.950	5.380	5.457	03/2004	5.219	4.620	4.777
12/1997	6.472	5.850	5.915	03/2001	5.691	5.217	5.458	06/2004	5.597	4.777	5.313
03/1998	6.092	5.666	5.930	06/2001	5.919	5.429	5.736	09/2004	5.352	4.757	4.891
06/1998	6.091	5.573	5.621	09/2001	5.776	5.297	5.411	12/2004	5.066	4.703	4.822
09/1998	5.792	4.954	4.973	12/2001	5.721	4.661	5.472	03/2005	4.931	4.351	4.766
12/1998	5.421	4.685	5.092	03/2002	5.872	5.311	5.815	06/2005	4.825	4.151	4.219
03/1999	5.709	5.030	5.624	06/2002	5.863	5.321	5.519	09/2005	4.618	4.205	4.568
06/1999	6.202	5.401	5.961	09/2002	5.559	4.606	4.662	12/2005	4.879	4.479	4.547
09/1999	6.274	5.842	6.047	12/2002	5.214	4.631	4.783	03/2006	4.921	4.460	4.893

Source: Federal Reserve Board

STERLING, 3-MONTH

Quarterly High, Low and Close of Sterling, 3-Month Futures   In Points of 100%

Quarter	High	Low	Close	Quarter	High	Low	Close	Quarter	High	Low	Close
09/1996	94.320	93.980	94.020	12/1999	94.310	93.550	93.620	03/2003	96.560	96.050	96.550
12/1996	94.070	93.250	93.290	03/2000	93.800	93.370	93.460	06/2003	96.610	96.330	96.570
03/1997	93.760	93.260	93.330	06/2000	93.810	93.410	93.680	09/2003	96.690	96.070	96.210
06/1997	93.510	92.880	92.880	09/2000	93.820	93.640	93.780	12/2003	96.220	95.760	95.800
09/1997	92.990	92.540	92.580	12/2000	94.400	93.720	94.240	03/2004	95.880	95.420	95.460
12/1997	92.720	92.250	92.420	03/2001	94.980	94.250	94.870	06/2004	95.530	94.760	94.950
03/1998	92.720	92.350	92.510	06/2001	94.950	94.510	94.540	09/2004	95.070	94.840	95.030
06/1998	92.610	92.030	92.100	09/2001	95.800	94.540	95.670	12/2004	95.170	94.980	95.140
09/1998	93.140	92.080	93.030	12/2001	96.220	95.590	95.880	03/2005	95.230	94.910	94.990
12/1998	94.510	93.020	94.480	03/2002	96.070	95.410	95.520	06/2005	95.510	94.980	95.500
03/1999	95.040	94.360	95.030	06/2002	95.820	95.480	95.630	09/2005	95.770	95.390	95.500
06/1999	95.040	94.690	94.920	09/2002	96.280	95.600	96.230	12/2005	95.600	95.340	95.500
09/1999	94.990	93.840	93.910	12/2002	96.270	95.950	96.160	03/2006	95.540	95.330	95.370

Source: Euronext LIFFE

CANADIAN BANKERS' ACCEPTANCE, 3-MONTH

Quarterly High, Low and Close of Canadian Bankers' Acceptance, 3-Month Futures   In Points of 100%

Quarter	High	Low	Close	Quarter	High	Low	Close	Quarter	High	Low	Close
09/1996	96.100	94.730	95.770	12/1999	95.000	94.360	94.610	03/2003	97.180	96.450	96.560
12/1996	97.070	95.750	96.460	03/2000	94.700	94.140	94.190	06/2003	97.150	96.430	97.005
03/1997	96.930	96.000	96.010	06/2000	94.380	93.840	94.020	09/2003	97.460	96.820	97.435
06/1997	96.840	95.760	96.020	09/2000	94.270	94.040	94.200	12/2003	97.495	97.150	97.475
09/1997	96.410	95.810	95.830	12/2000	94.590	94.020	94.560	03/2004	98.075	97.470	98.060
12/1997	96.100	94.540	94.930	03/2001	95.810	94.590	95.470	06/2004	98.080	97.420	97.670
03/1998	95.410	94.780	95.030	06/2001	95.950	95.290	95.520	09/2004	97.900	97.175	97.215
06/1998	95.190	94.630	94.780	09/2001	97.230	95.510	97.080	12/2004	97.430	97.100	97.370
09/1998	94.970	93.590	94.850	12/2001	98.130	97.090	98.110	03/2005	97.470	97.025	97.160
12/1998	95.420	94.830	95.170	03/2002	98.270	96.800	97.040	06/2005	97.430	97.155	97.320
03/1999	95.250	94.880	95.230	06/2002	97.400	96.750	96.860	09/2005	97.310	96.675	96.695
06/1999	95.610	94.770	95.050	09/2002	97.310	96.790	97.070	12/2005	96.740	96.015	96.015
09/1999	95.180	94.700	94.880	12/2002	97.300	96.930	97.200	03/2006	96.240	95.805	95.840

Source: Montreal Exchange

EURIBOR, 3-MONTH

Quarterly High, Low and Close of Euribor, 3-Month Futures — In Points of 100%

Quarter	High	Low	Close	Quarter	High	Low	Close	Quarter	High	Low	Close
12/1998	96.920	96.835	96.850	06/2001	95.890	95.260	95.755	12/2003	97.990	97.780	97.890
03/1999	97.190	96.875	97.180	09/2001	96.650	95.660	96.585	03/2004	98.190	97.820	98.125
06/1999	97.450	97.180	97.255	12/2001	96.910	96.525	96.855	06/2004	98.145	97.715	97.820
09/1999	97.310	96.720	96.780	03/2002	96.905	96.310	96.360	09/2004	97.925	97.725	97.775
12/1999	96.765	96.340	96.390	06/2002	96.615	96.310	96.485	12/2004	97.850	97.725	97.795
03/2000	96.445	95.795	95.920	09/2002	97.050	96.450	97.000	03/2005	97.875	97.720	97.790
06/2000	96.010	95.160	95.210	12/2002	97.440	96.810	97.350	06/2005	97.995	97.790	97.945
09/2000	95.250	94.805	94.845	03/2003	97.700	97.275	97.690	09/2005	97.995	97.680	97.785
12/2000	95.270	94.745	95.270	06/2003	98.125	97.510	98.030	12/2005	97.795	97.270	97.295
03/2001	95.805	95.230	95.735	09/2003	98.065	97.820	97.975	03/2006	97.390	96.910	96.925

Source: Euronext LIFFE

EURO-BUND (FGBL)

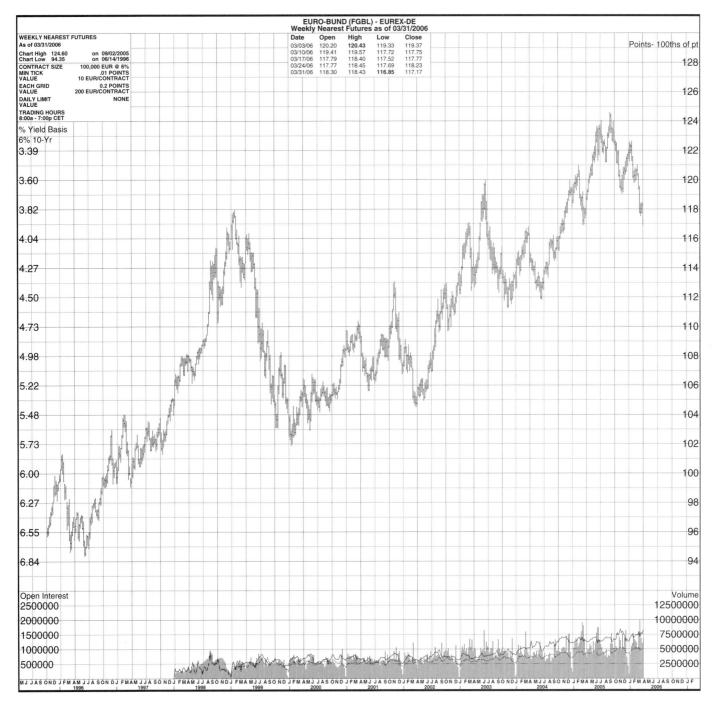

Quarterly High, Low and Close of Euro-Bund Futures Nominal Value

Quarter	High	Low	Close	Quarter	High	Low	Close	Quarter	High	Low	Close
09/1996	99.02	94.85	98.62	12/1999	108.28	103.05	104.14	03/2003	117.10	112.18	114.72
12/1996	102.99	98.58	100.84	03/2000	105.70	101.85	105.41	06/2003	120.00	112.65	116.83
03/1997	104.04	99.30	99.98	06/2000	106.78	102.90	105.07	09/2003	117.14	112.29	115.16
06/1997	102.65	99.06	101.52	09/2000	106.26	104.15	105.30	12/2003	115.45	111.24	113.12
09/1997	103.58	101.41	102.96	12/2000	108.74	104.91	108.45	03/2004	116.81	112.53	116.07
12/1997	105.17	101.28	104.33	03/2001	110.39	108.00	109.56	06/2004	116.21	111.81	113.15
03/1998	108.17	103.96	107.37	06/2001	109.63	105.61	106.51	09/2004	116.23	112.93	115.65
06/1998	108.62	106.12	108.36	09/2001	109.51	106.12	108.65	12/2004	119.97	115.12	118.59
09/1998	114.90	108.18	114.60	12/2001	113.11	106.75	106.79	03/2005	120.98	116.89	118.61
12/1998	116.74	110.15	115.78	03/2002	109.16	104.50	104.78	06/2005	123.78	118.51	123.50
03/1999	117.94	112.67	114.00	06/2002	108.23	104.63	107.42	09/2005	124.60	121.16	122.53
06/1999	116.36	108.84	110.41	09/2002	112.94	106.89	112.75	12/2005	122.71	119.03	121.84
09/1999	111.27	104.71	105.83	12/2002	113.70	109.67	113.54	03/2006	122.65	116.85	117.17

Source: Eurex

JAPANESE GOVERNMENT BOND, 10-YEAR

Quarterly High, Low and Close of Japanese Government Bond, 10-Year Futures — Nominal Value

Quarter	High	Low	Close	Quarter	High	Low	Close	Quarter	High	Low	Close
09/1996	122.60	117.77	122.13	12/1999	133.10	129.10	132.83	03/2003	143.45	141.70	143.06
12/1996	127.00	122.04	124.11	03/2000	134.40	130.17	131.54	06/2003	145.04	141.20	141.74
03/1997	127.02	123.52	125.90	06/2000	133.95	130.62	132.75	09/2003	142.50	134.24	137.14
06/1997	127.33	119.75	124.12	09/2000	134.21	130.80	132.38	12/2003	138.96	135.77	137.84
09/1997	129.18	123.50	128.64	12/2000	136.08	132.48	134.90	03/2004	140.45	136.89	137.36
12/1997	131.10	128.20	129.81	03/2001	140.88	134.65	139.31	06/2004	139.03	133.16	135.01
03/1998	131.15	127.95	130.18	06/2001	141.30	137.10	140.46	09/2004	138.49	134.09	138.04
06/1998	134.44	128.50	132.68	09/2001	141.50	138.50	139.47	12/2004	139.50	136.77	138.38
09/1998	139.21	131.50	138.93	12/2001	140.94	137.85	138.20	03/2005	139.96	137.22	139.40
12/1998	139.60	127.10	128.05	03/2002	138.16	135.72	137.96	06/2005	141.35	138.95	141.27
03/1999	134.10	125.70	132.50	06/2002	139.45	137.48	139.15	09/2005	141.35	137.36	137.67
06/1999	137.24	128.00	129.18	09/2002	141.69	138.44	140.38	12/2005	138.49	135.90	137.35
09/1999	132.95	128.35	131.47	12/2002	142.39	140.26	142.09	03/2006	138.56	132.81	133.26

Source: Singapore Exchange

EURO-SWISS, 3-MONTH

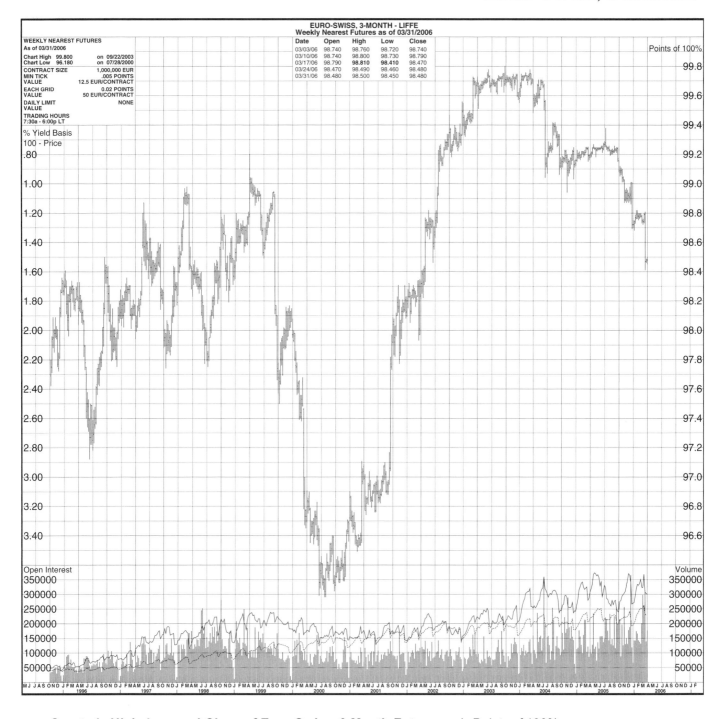

Quarterly High, Low and Close of Euro-Swiss, 3-Month Futures In Points of 100%

Quarter	High	Low	Close	Quarter	High	Low	Close	Quarter	High	Low	Close
09/1996	98.500	97.180	98.370	12/1999	98.170	97.500	98.100	03/2003	99.730	99.320	99.690
12/1996	98.450	97.750	98.250	03/2000	98.080	96.650	96.730	06/2003	99.780	99.510	99.680
03/1997	98.360	98.010	98.160	06/2000	96.910	96.190	96.360	09/2003	99.800	99.610	99.720
06/1997	98.870	97.940	98.470	09/2000	96.600	96.180	96.280	12/2003	99.750	99.570	99.620
09/1997	98.630	98.140	98.240	12/2000	96.710	96.260	96.680	03/2004	99.780	99.550	99.690
12/1997	98.440	97.740	98.280	03/2001	97.110	96.490	97.040	06/2004	99.710	99.040	99.100
03/1998	98.980	98.170	98.400	06/2001	97.090	96.740	96.890	09/2004	99.420	99.060	99.160
06/1998	98.480	97.770	97.940	09/2001	97.970	96.820	97.900	12/2004	99.250	98.940	99.160
09/1998	98.500	97.750	98.440	12/2001	98.310	97.770	98.120	03/2005	99.253	99.150	99.210
12/1998	98.820	98.190	98.430	03/2002	98.350	97.930	98.230	06/2005	99.290	99.180	99.270
03/1999	98.800	98.350	98.770	06/2002	98.820	98.210	98.650	09/2005	99.380	99.080	99.090
06/1999	99.200	98.550	98.580	09/2002	99.470	98.630	99.390	12/2005	99.120	98.690	98.720
09/1999	98.950	97.890	97.990	12/2002	99.560	99.180	99.510	03/2006	98.820	98.410	98.480

Source: Euronext LIFFE

PRIME RATE AND DISCOUNT RATE

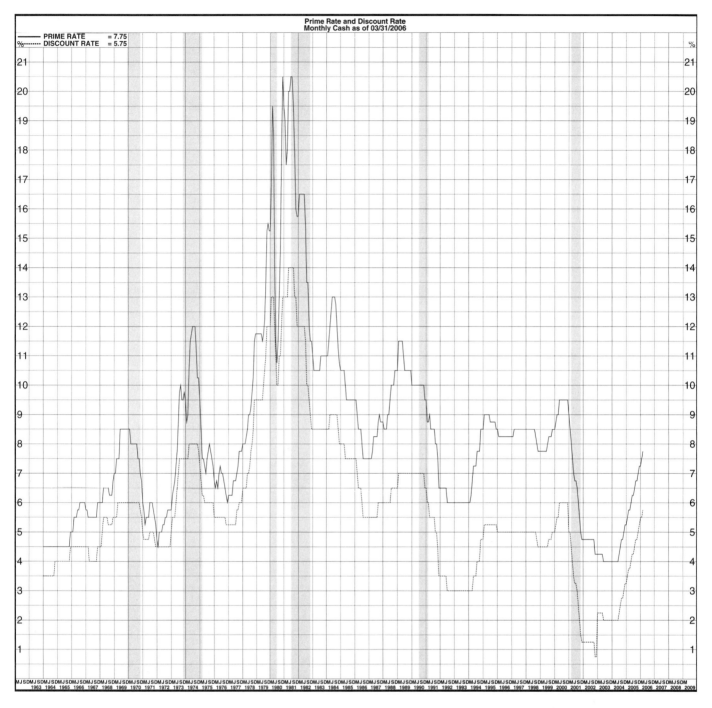

Annual High, Low and Close of Prime Rate   In Percent

Year	High	Low	Close	Year	High	Low	Close	Year	High	Low	Close
1968	6.75	6.00	6.75	1981	20.50	15.75	15.75	1994	8.50	6.00	8.50
1969	8.50	7.00	8.50	1982	17.00	11.50	11.50	1995	9.00	8.50	8.50
1970	8.50	6.75	6.75	1983	11.50	10.50	11.00	1996	8.50	8.25	8.25
1971	6.50	5.25	5.25	1984	13.00	10.75	10.75	1997	8.50	8.25	8.50
1972	5.75	4.50	5.75	1985	10.75	9.50	9.50	1998	8.50	7.75	7.75
1973	10.00	5.75	9.75	1986	9.50	7.50	7.50	1999	8.50	7.75	8.50
1974	12.00	8.75	10.25	1987	9.25	7.50	8.75	2000	9.50	8.50	9.50
1975	10.00	7.00	7.25	1988	10.50	8.50	10.50	2001	9.50	4.75	4.75
1976	7.25	6.00	6.00	1989	11.50	10.50	10.50	2002	4.75	4.25	4.25
1977	7.75	6.00	7.75	1990	10.50	9.50	9.50	2003	4.25	4.00	4.00
1978	11.75	7.75	11.75	1991	9.50	6.50	6.50	2004	5.25	4.00	5.25
1979	15.75	11.50	15.25	1992	6.50	6.00	6.00	2005	7.25	5.25	7.25
1980	21.50	10.75	20.50	1993	6.00	6.00	6.00	2006	7.75	7.25	7.75

Source: Federal Reserve Board

PRIME RATE AND DISCOUNT RATE

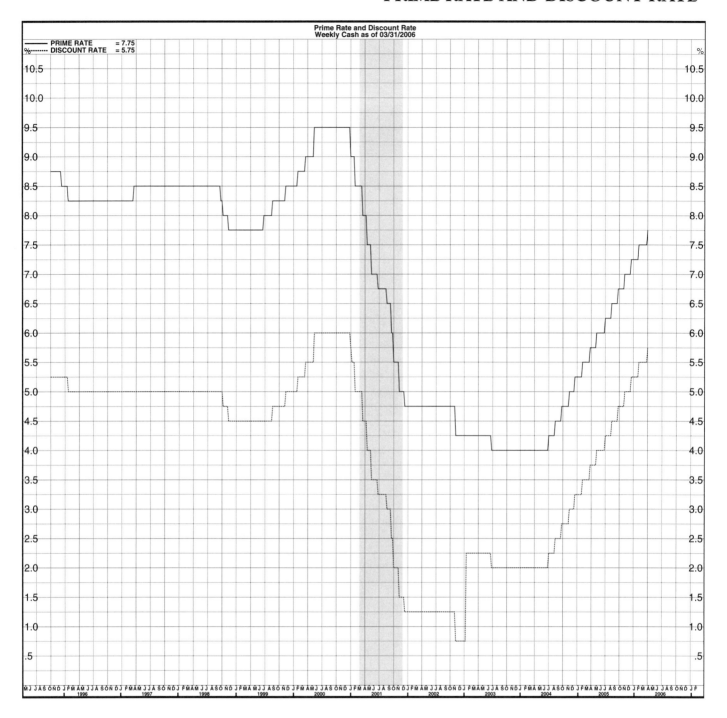

Annual High, Low and Close of Discount Rate   In Percent

Year	High	Low	Close	Year	High	Low	Close	Year	High	Low	Close
1968	5.50	5.00	5.50	1981	14.00	12.00	12.00	1994	4.75	3.00	4.75
1969	6.00	6.00	6.00	1982	12.00	8.50	8.50	1995	5.25	4.75	5.25
1970	5.75	5.50	5.50	1983	8.50	8.50	8.50	1996	5.25	5.00	5.00
1971	5.25	4.50	4.50	1984	9.00	8.00	8.00	1997	5.00	5.00	5.00
1972	4.50	4.50	4.50	1985	8.00	7.50	7.50	1998	5.00	4.50	4.50
1973	7.50	5.00	7.50	1986	7.50	5.50	5.50	1999	5.00	4.50	5.00
1974	8.00	7.75	7.75	1987	6.00	5.50	6.00	2000	6.00	5.00	6.00
1975	7.25	6.00	6.00	1988	6.50	6.00	6.50	2001	6.00	1.25	1.25
1976	6.00	5.25	5.25	1989	7.00	6.50	7.00	2002	1.25	0.75	0.75
1977	6.00	5.25	6.00	1990	7.00	6.50	6.50	2003	2.25	0.75	2.00
1978	9.50	6.00	9.50	1991	6.50	3.50	3.50	2004	3.25	2.00	3.25
1979	12.00	9.50	12.00	1992	3.50	3.00	3.00	2005	5.25	3.25	5.25
1980	13.00	10.00	13.00	1993	3.00	3.00	3.00	2006	5.75	5.25	5.75

Source: Federal Reserve Board

CONSUMER PRICE INDEX

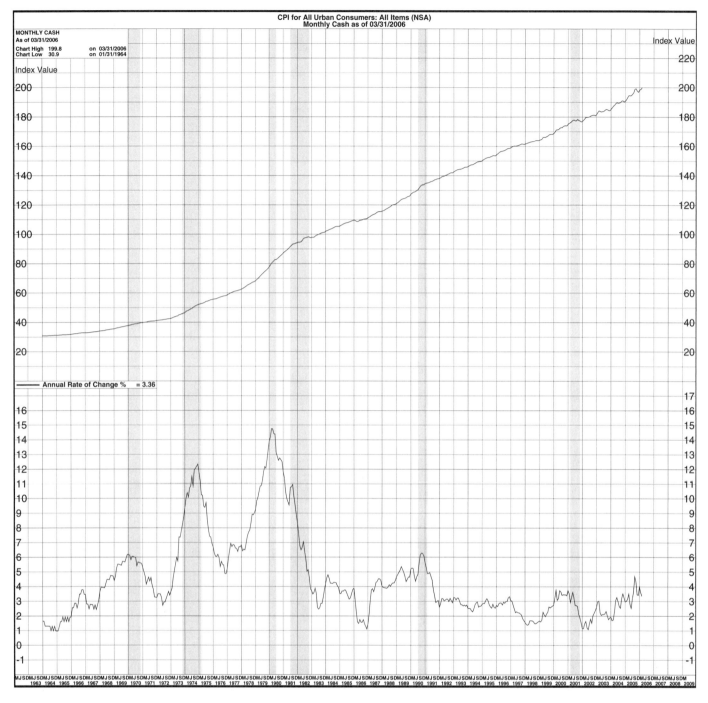

Annual High, Low and Close of CPI: All Items   Index Value

Year	High	Low	Close	Year	High	Low	Close	Year	High	Low	Close
1968	35.5	34.1	35.5	1981	94.0	87.0	94.0	1994	149.7	146.2	149.7
1969	37.7	35.6	37.7	1982	98.2	94.3	97.6	1995	153.7	150.3	153.5
1970	39.8	37.8	39.8	1983	101.3	97.8	101.3	1996	158.6	154.4	158.6
1971	41.1	39.8	41.1	1984	105.3	101.9	105.3	1997	161.6	159.1	161.3
1972	42.5	41.1	42.5	1985	109.3	105.5	109.3	1998	164.0	161.6	163.9
1973	46.2	42.6	46.2	1986	110.5	108.6	110.5	1999	168.3	164.3	168.3
1974	51.9	46.6	51.9	1987	115.4	111.2	115.4	2000	174.1	168.8	174.0
1975	55.5	52.1	55.5	1988	120.5	115.7	120.5	2001	178.3	175.1	176.7
1976	58.2	55.6	58.2	1989	126.1	121.1	126.1	2002	181.3	177.1	180.9
1977	62.1	58.5	62.1	1990	133.8	127.4	133.8	2003	185.2	181.7	184.3
1978	67.7	62.5	67.7	1991	137.9	134.6	137.9	2004	191.0	185.2	190.3
1979	76.7	68.3	76.7	1992	142.0	138.1	141.9	2005	199.2	190.7	196.8
1980	86.3	77.8	86.3	1993	145.8	142.6	145.8	2006	199.8	198.3	199.8

Not seasonally adjusted.   Source: U.S. Department of Labor: Bureau of Labor Statistics

CONSUMER PRICE INDEX

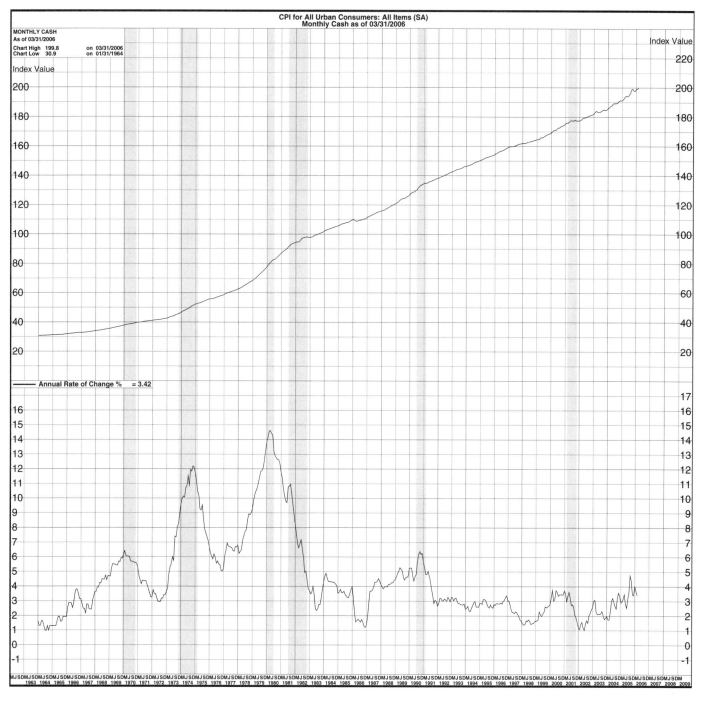

Annual High, Low and Close of CPI: All Items Index Value

Year	High	Low	Close	Year	High	Low	Close	Year	High	Low	Close
1968	35.6	34.1	35.6	1981	94.1	87.2	94.1	1994	150.1	146.3	150.1
1969	37.7	35.7	37.7	1982	98.1	94.4	97.7	1995	153.9	150.5	153.9
1970	39.8	37.9	39.8	1983	101.4	97.9	101.4	1996	159.1	154.7	159.1
1971	41.1	39.9	41.1	1984	105.5	102.1	105.5	1997	161.8	159.4	161.8
1972	42.5	41.2	42.5	1985	109.5	105.7	109.5	1998	164.4	162.0	164.4
1973	46.3	42.7	46.3	1986	110.8	108.7	110.8	1999	168.8	164.7	168.8
1974	51.9	46.8	51.9	1987	115.6	111.4	115.6	2000	174.6	169.3	174.6
1975	55.6	52.3	55.6	1988	120.7	116.0	120.7	2001	178.1	175.6	177.3
1976	58.4	55.8	58.4	1989	126.3	121.2	126.3	2002	181.6	177.7	181.6
1977	62.3	58.7	62.3	1990	134.2	127.5	134.2	2003	185.0	182.3	185.0
1978	67.9	62.7	67.9	1991	138.2	134.7	138.2	2004	191.2	185.9	191.2
1979	76.9	68.5	76.9	1992	142.3	138.3	142.3	2005	199.1	191.3	197.7
1980	86.4	78.0	86.4	1993	146.3	142.8	146.3	2006	199.8	199.0	199.8

Seasonally adjusted. Source: U.S. Department of Labor: Bureau of Labor Statistics

PRODUCER PRICE INDEX

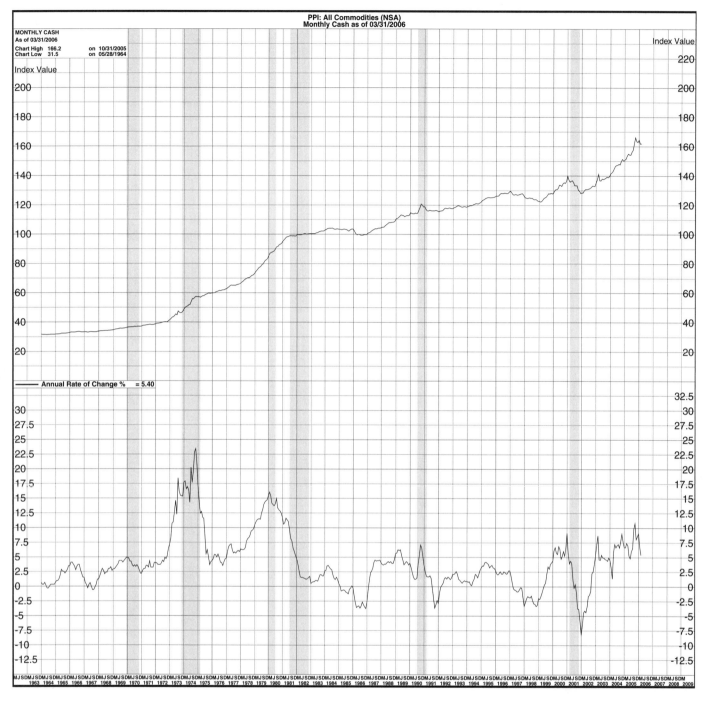

Annual High, Low and Close of PPI: All Commodities   Index Value

Year	High	Low	Close	Year	High	Low	Close	Year	High	Low	Close
1968	34.6	33.8	34.6	1981	99.0	95.2	98.8	1994	121.9	119.1	121.9
1969	36.3	34.8	36.3	1982	100.5	99.6	100.5	1995	125.7	122.9	125.7
1970	37.1	36.5	37.1	1983	102.3	100.2	102.3	1996	129.1	126.2	129.1
1971	38.6	37.3	38.6	1984	104.2	102.9	103.5	1997	129.7	126.8	126.8
1972	41.1	38.8	41.1	1985	103.6	102.1	103.6	1998	125.4	122.8	122.8
1973	47.5	41.6	47.4	1986	103.2	99.3	99.7	1999	128.3	122.3	127.8
1974	57.4	49.0	57.3	1987	104.2	100.5	104.2	2000	136.2	128.3	136.2
1975	59.8	56.9	59.7	1988	109.0	104.6	109.0	2001	140.0	128.1	128.1
1976	62.5	59.9	62.5	1989	113.2	110.5	113.0	2002	133.2	128.4	132.9
1977	66.2	62.8	66.2	1990	120.8	114.1	118.7	2003	141.2	135.3	139.5
1978	72.7	66.8	72.7	1991	119.0	115.9	115.9	2004	151.4	141.4	150.2
1979	83.4	73.8	83.4	1992	118.1	115.6	117.6	2005	166.2	150.9	163.0
1980	93.8	85.2	93.8	1993	119.7	118.0	118.6	2006	164.6	161.9	162.0

Not seasonally adjusted.   *Source: U.S. Department of Labor: Bureau of Labor Statistics*

PRODUCER PRICE INDEX

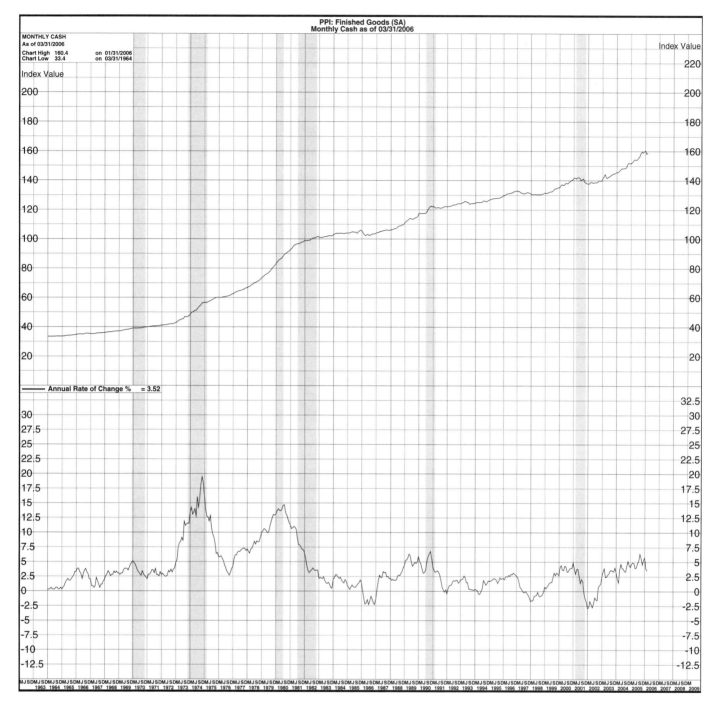

Annual High, Low and Close of PPI: Finished Goods   Index Value

Year	High	Low	Close	Year	High	Low	Close	Year	High	Low	Close
1968	37.1	36.1	37.1	1981	98.3	92.8	98.3	1994	126.6	124.8	126.6
1969	38.9	37.2	38.9	1982	101.8	98.8	101.8	1995	129.3	126.9	129.3
1970	39.8	39.0	39.8	1983	102.3	101.0	102.3	1996	132.9	129.7	132.9
1971	41.1	39.9	41.1	1984	104.0	103.0	104.0	1997	133.0	130.9	131.4
1972	42.7	41.0	42.7	1985	106.0	103.8	106.0	1998	131.3	130.4	131.3
1973	47.6	43.0	47.6	1986	105.5	102.3	103.6	1999	135.2	131.2	135.2
1974	56.4	48.8	56.4	1987	106.2	104.1	105.8	2000	140.5	135.2	140.5
1975	60.1	56.6	60.1	1988	110.0	106.3	110.0	2001	142.2	138.0	138.0
1976	62.4	59.9	62.4	1989	115.5	111.1	115.5	2002	140.0	137.7	139.7
1977	66.7	62.5	66.7	1990	122.6	117.4	122.0	2003	145.3	141.2	145.3
1978	72.8	67.0	72.8	1991	122.6	121.1	122.3	2004	152.1	145.6	151.7
1979	82.2	73.7	82.2	1992	124.2	122.0	124.2	2005	159.9	151.7	159.9
1980	91.8	83.4	91.8	1993	125.7	123.9	124.4	2006	160.4	158.2	159.0

Seasonally adjusted.   *Source: U.S. Department of Labor: Bureau of Labor Statistics*

U.S. UNEMPLOYMENT RATE

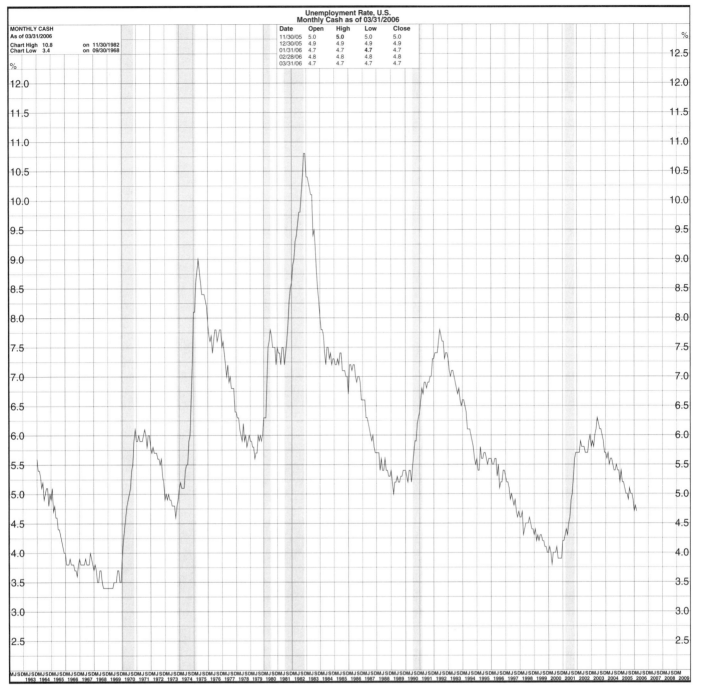

Annual High, Low and Close of U.S. Unemployment Rate   In Percent

Year	High	Low	Close	Year	High	Low	Close	Year	High	Low	Close
1968	3.8	3.4	3.4	1981	8.5	7.2	8.5	1994	6.6	5.5	5.5
1969	3.7	3.4	3.5	1982	10.8	8.6	10.8	1995	5.8	5.4	5.6
1970	6.1	3.9	6.1	1983	10.4	8.3	8.3	1996	5.6	5.1	5.4
1971	6.1	5.8	6.0	1984	8.0	7.2	7.3	1997	5.3	4.6	4.7
1972	5.8	5.2	5.2	1985	7.4	7.0	7.0	1998	4.7	4.3	4.4
1973	5.0	4.6	4.9	1986	7.2	6.6	6.6	1999	4.4	4.0	4.0
1974	7.2	5.1	7.2	1987	6.6	5.7	5.7	2000	4.1	3.8	3.9
1975	9.0	8.1	8.2	1988	5.7	5.3	5.3	2001	5.7	4.2	5.7
1976	7.9	7.4	7.8	1989	5.4	5.0	5.4	2002	6.0	5.7	6.0
1977	7.6	6.4	6.4	1990	6.3	5.2	6.3	2003	6.3	5.7	5.7
1978	6.4	5.8	6.0	1991	7.3	6.4	7.3	2004	5.7	5.4	5.4
1979	6.0	5.6	6.0	1992	7.8	7.3	7.4	2005	5.4	4.9	4.9
1980	7.8	6.3	7.2	1993	7.3	6.5	6.5	2006	4.8	4.7	4.7

Source: U.S. Department of Labor: Bureau of Labor Statistics

U.S. UNEMPLOYED

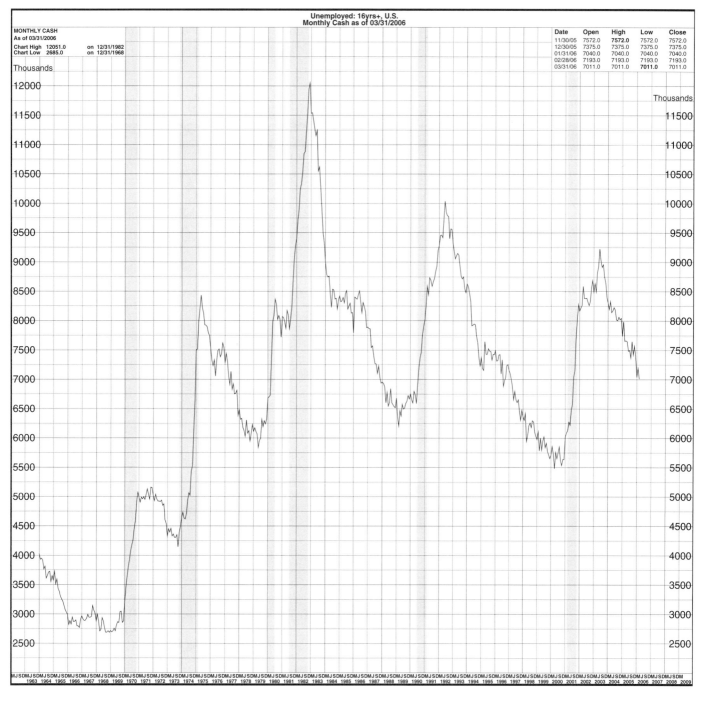

Annual High, Low and Close of U.S. Unemployed, 16yrs+   In Thousands

Year	High	Low	Close	Year	High	Low	Close	Year	High	Low	Close
1968	3,001	2,685	2,685	1981	9,267	7,863	9,267	1994	8,630	7,230	7,230
1969	3,049	2,692	2,884	1982	12,051	9,397	12,051	1995	7,645	7,153	7,423
1970	5,076	3,201	5,076	1983	11,545	9,331	9,331	1996	7,491	6,882	7,253
1971	5,161	4,903	5,154	1984	9,008	8,198	8,358	1997	7,158	6,308	6,476
1972	5,038	4,543	4,543	1985	8,513	8,128	8,138	1998	6,422	5,941	6,032
1973	4,489	4,144	4,489	1986	8,508	7,795	7,883	1999	6,111	5,653	5,653
1974	6,636	4,618	6,636	1987	7,892	6,936	6,936	2000	5,858	5,481	5,634
1975	8,433	7,501	7,744	1988	6,953	6,518	6,518	2001	8,281	6,017	8,281
1976	7,620	7,053	7,545	1989	6,725	6,205	6,667	2002	8,691	8,165	8,691
1977	7,443	6,386	6,386	1990	7,901	6,590	7,901	2003	9,228	8,399	8,399
1978	6,489	5,947	6,228	1991	9,198	8,015	9,198	2004	8,330	8,005	8,047
1979	6,325	5,840	6,325	1992	10,040	9,283	9,557	2005	7,988	7,367	7,375
1980	8,363	6,683	7,718	1993	9,325	8,477	8,477	2006	7,193	7,011	7,011

Source: U.S. Department of Labor: Bureau of Labor Statistics

U.S. CIVILIAN LABOR FORCE

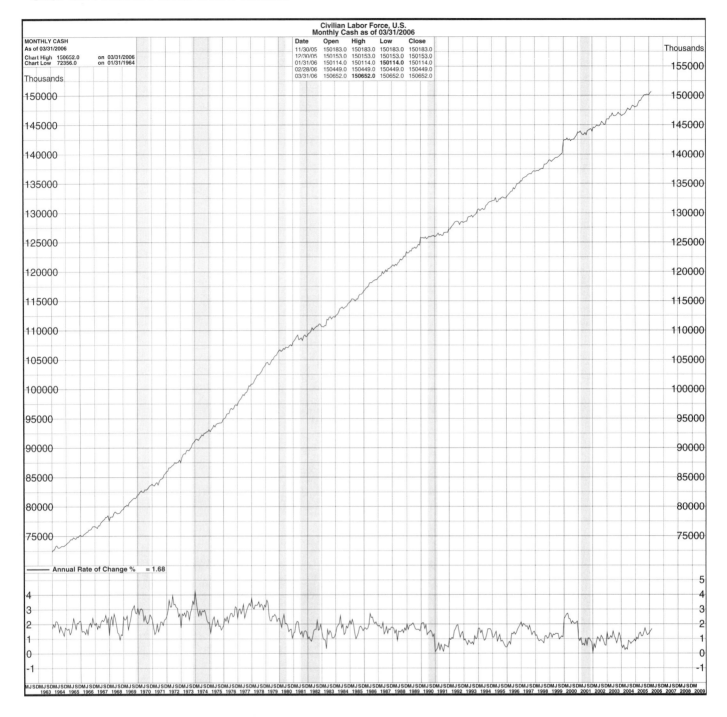

Annual High, Low and Close of U.S. Civilian Labor Force   In Thousands

Year	High	Low	Close	Year	High	Low	Close	Year	High	Low	Close
1968	79,463	77,578	79,463	1981	109,236	108,026	108,912	1994	131,951	130,400	131,951
1969	81,624	79,523	81,624	1982	111,083	109,089	111,083	1995	132,716	131,851	132,511
1970	83,670	81,981	83,670	1983	112,327	110,587	112,327	1996	135,113	132,616	135,113
1971	85,625	83,575	85,625	1984	114,581	112,209	114,581	1997	137,155	135,400	137,155
1972	87,943	85,978	87,943	1985	116,354	114,725	116,354	1998	138,634	137,095	138,634
1973	90,890	87,487	90,890	1986	118,634	116,682	118,611	1999	140,177	138,730	140,177
1974	92,780	91,199	92,780	1987	120,729	118,845	120,729	2000	143,248	142,267	143,248
1975	94,409	92,776	94,409	1988	122,637	120,913	122,622	2001	144,324	143,301	144,324
1976	97,348	94,934	97,348	1989	124,637	123,135	124,497	2002	145,573	143,858	145,091
1977	100,576	97,208	100,491	1990	126,142	125,573	126,142	2003	147,109	145,914	146,808
1978	103,809	100,837	103,809	1991	126,701	125,955	126,664	2004	148,313	146,529	148,203
1979	106,258	104,057	106,258	1992	128,613	127,207	128,554	2005	150,183	147,979	150,153
1980	107,568	106,442	107,352	1993	129,941	128,400	129,941	2006	150,652	150,114	150,652

Source: U.S. Department of Labor: Bureau of Labor Statistics

U.S. NON-FARM PAYROLLS

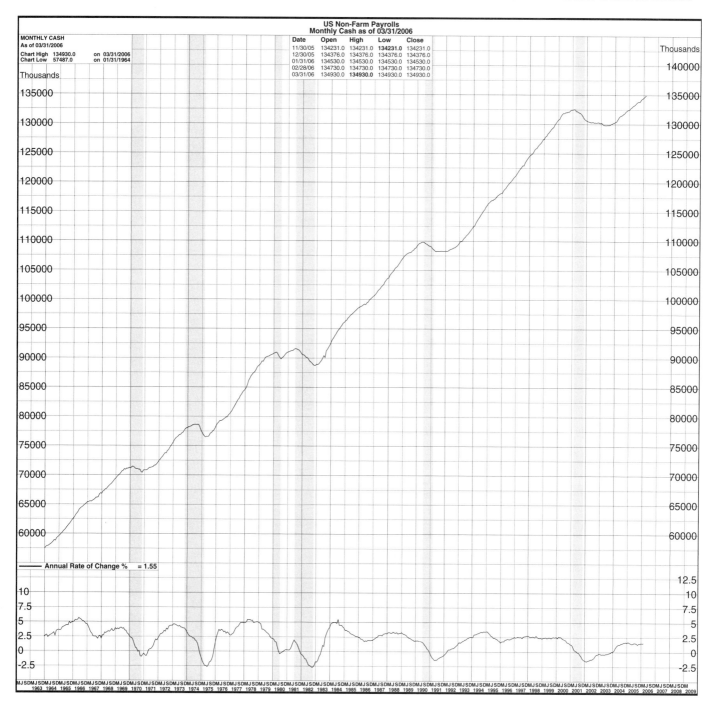

Annual High, Low and Close of U.S. Non-Farm Payrolls   In Thousands

Year	High	Low	Close	Year	High	Low	Close	Year	High	Low	Close
1968	69,245	66,805	69,245	1981	91,594	90,884	90,884	1994	116,056	112,473	116,056
1969	71,240	69,438	71,240	1982	90,557	88,756	88,756	1995	118,210	116,377	118,210
1970	71,453	70,409	70,790	1983	92,210	88,903	92,210	1996	121,003	118,192	121,003
1971	72,108	70,805	72,108	1984	96,087	92,657	96,087	1997	124,361	121,232	124,361
1972	75,270	72,445	75,270	1985	98,587	96,353	98,587	1998	127,364	124,629	127,364
1973	78,035	75,620	78,035	1986	100,484	98,710	100,484	1999	130,536	127,477	130,536
1974	78,634	77,657	77,657	1987	103,634	100,655	103,634	2000	132,484	130,781	132,484
1975	78,017	76,463	78,017	1988	106,871	103,728	106,871	2001	132,546	130,705	130,705
1976	80,448	78,506	80,448	1989	108,809	107,133	108,809	2002	130,581	130,161	130,161
1977	84,408	80,692	84,408	1990	109,820	109,118	109,118	2003	130,255	129,827	130,255
1978	88,674	84,595	88,674	1991	108,998	108,203	108,261	2004	132,449	130,372	132,449
1979	90,669	88,811	90,669	1992	109,418	108,242	109,418	2005	134,376	132,471	134,376
1980	90,991	89,832	90,936	1993	112,203	109,725	112,203	2006	134,930	134,530	134,930

Source: U.S. Department of Labor: Bureau of Labor Statistics

U.S. INITIAL JOBLESS CLAIMS

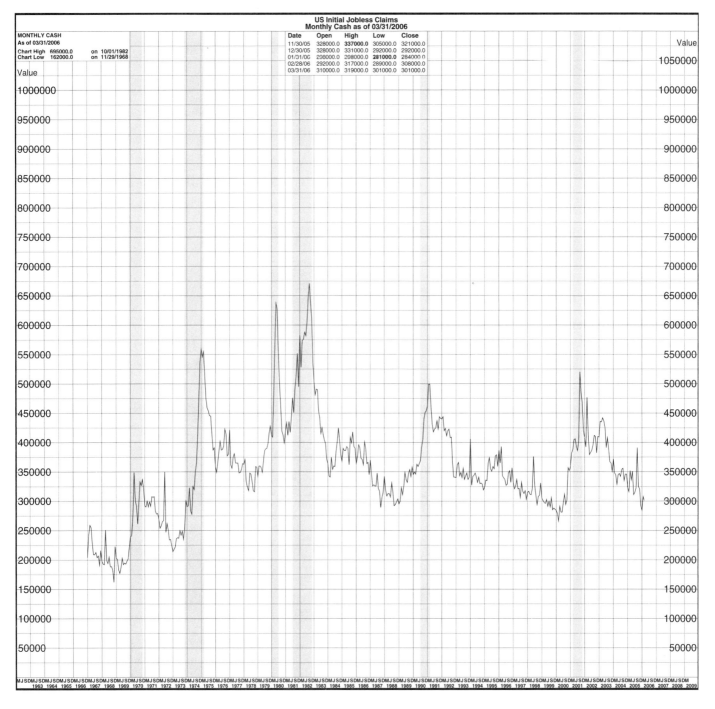

Annual High, Low and Close of U.S. Initial Jobless Claims   In Number

Year	High	Low	Close	Year	High	Low	Close	Year	High	Low	Close
1968	251,000	162,000	223,000	1981	558,000	392,000	495,000	1994	406,000	314,000	319,000
1969	232,000	177,000	223,000	1982	695,000	489,000	534,000	1995	390,000	324,000	359,000
1970	374,000	230,000	321,000	1983	515,000	362,000	372,000	1996	426,000	326,000	357,000
1971	359,000	244,000	279,000	1984	439,000	333,000	379,000	1997	347,000	301,000	303,000
1972	350,000	225,000	225,000	1985	426,000	359,000	390,000	1998	376,000	294,000	331,000
1973	326,000	214,000	300,000	1986	416,000	344,000	345,000	1999	345,000	268,000	286,000
1974	537,000	269,000	537,000	1987	370,000	289,000	315,000	2000	365,000	257,000	352,000
1975	575,000	365,000	391,000	1988	361,000	284,000	304,000	2001	520,000	317,000	421,000
1976	423,000	333,000	380,000	1989	407,000	282,000	358,000	2002	477,000	377,000	410,000
1977	565,000	334,000	364,000	1990	474,000	331,000	454,000	2003	447,000	351,000	351,000
1978	429,000	304,000	358,000	1991	509,000	408,000	441,000	2004	372,000	321,000	346,000
1979	471,000	336,000	428,000	1992	564,000	313,000	341,000	2005	435,000	292,000	292,000
1980	642,000	394,000	399,000	1993	415,000	290,000	341,000	2006	319,000	281,000	301,000

Source: U.S. Department of Labor: Bureau of Labor Statistics

U.S. INITIAL JOBLESS CLAIMS

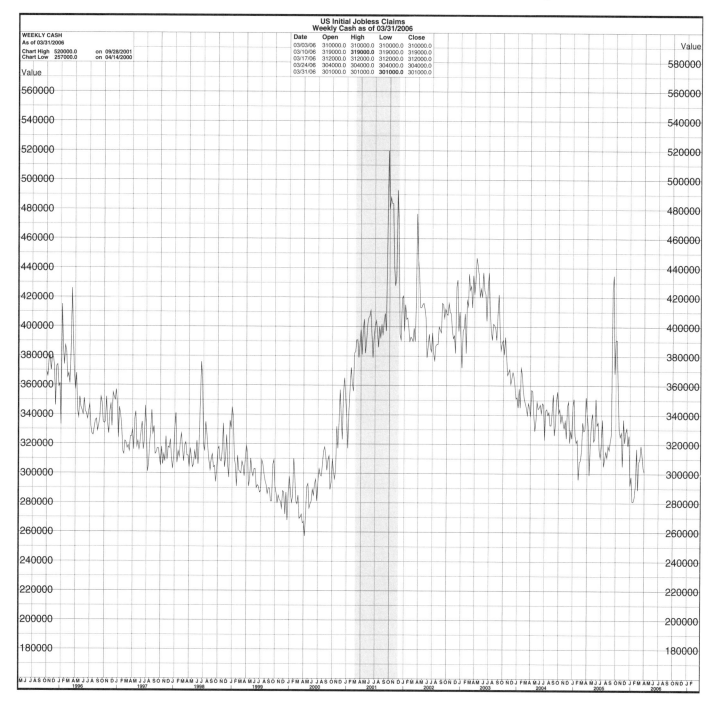

Quarterly High, Low and Close of U.S. Initial Jobless Claims   In Number

Quarter	High	Low	Close	Quarter	High	Low	Close	Quarter	High	Low	Close
09/1996	352,000	326,000	348,000	12/1999	309,000	268,000	286,000	03/2003	436,000	372,000	435,000
12/1996	357,000	327,000	357,000	03/2000	310,000	266,000	266,000	06/2003	447,000	404,000	426,000
03/1997	347,000	313,000	325,000	06/2000	296,000	257,000	281,000	09/2003	437,000	384,000	389,000
06/1997	342,000	316,000	322,000	09/2000	318,000	289,000	294,000	12/2003	393,000	351,000	351,000
09/1997	346,000	301,000	317,000	12/2000	365,000	296,000	352,000	03/2004	372,000	340,000	345,000
12/1997	325,000	303,000	303,000	03/2001	391,000	317,000	388,000	06/2004	357,000	329,000	347,000
03/1998	341,000	307,000	312,000	06/2001	411,000	379,000	393,000	09/2004	356,000	323,000	356,000
06/1998	376,000	304,000	376,000	09/2001	520,000	386,000	520,000	12/2004	349,000	321,000	346,000
09/1998	362,000	294,000	294,000	12/2001	493,000	391,000	421,000	03/2005	352,000	296,000	352,000
12/1998	336,000	297,000	331,000	03/2002	477,000	390,000	477,000	06/2005	351,000	299,000	311,000
03/1999	345,000	291,000	298,000	06/2002	446,000	379,000	383,000	09/2005	435,000	305,000	391,000
06/1999	319,000	290,000	291,000	09/2002	416,000	377,000	412,000	12/2005	391,000	292,000	292,000
09/1999	309,000	281,000	306,000	12/2002	432,000	382,000	410,000	03/2006	319,000	281,000	301,000

Source: U.S. Department of Labor: Bureau of Labor Statistics

U.S. AVERAGE HOURLY EARNINGS

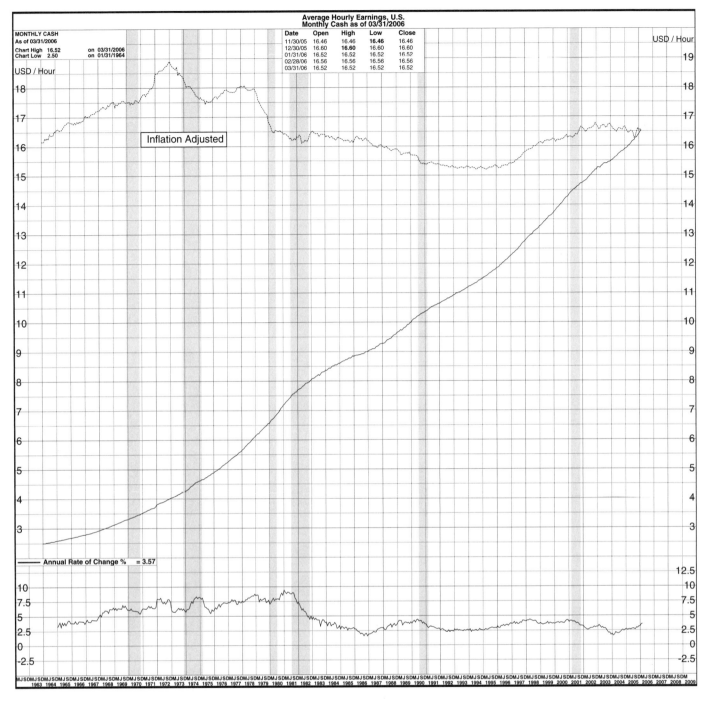

Annual High, Low and Close of U.S. Average Hourly Earnings   In Dollars per Hour

Year	High	Low	Close	Year	High	Low	Close	Year	High	Low	Close
1968	3.11	2.94	3.11	1981	7.63	7.18	7.63	1994	11.46	11.19	11.46
1969	3.30	3.12	3.30	1982	8.01	7.71	8.01	1995	11.79	11.47	11.79
1970	3.50	3.31	3.50	1983	8.32	8.05	8.32	1996	12.23	11.84	12.23
1971	3.73	3.52	3.73	1984	8.60	8.36	8.60	1997	12.73	12.27	12.73
1972	4.01	3.80	4.01	1985	8.86	8.60	8.86	1998	13.19	12.77	13.19
1973	4.25	4.03	4.25	1986	9.00	8.84	9.00	1999	13.68	13.25	13.68
1974	4.60	4.26	4.60	1987	9.27	9.01	9.27	2000	14.26	13.73	14.26
1975	4.87	4.61	4.87	1988	9.59	9.28	9.59	2001	14.73	14.27	14.73
1976	5.22	4.89	5.22	1989	9.97	9.64	9.97	2002	15.19	14.73	15.19
1977	5.60	5.25	5.60	1990	10.33	10.00	10.33	2003	15.45	15.19	15.45
1978	6.09	5.65	6.09	1991	10.63	10.36	10.63	2004	15.85	15.48	15.85
1979	6.56	6.13	6.56	1992	10.88	10.63	10.88	2005	16.35	15.90	16.35
1980	7.12	6.56	7.12	1993	11.17	10.92	11.17	2006	16.52	16.40	16.52

Source: U.S. Department of Labor: Bureau of Labor Statistics

ISM MANUFACTURING: PMI COMPOSITE INDEX

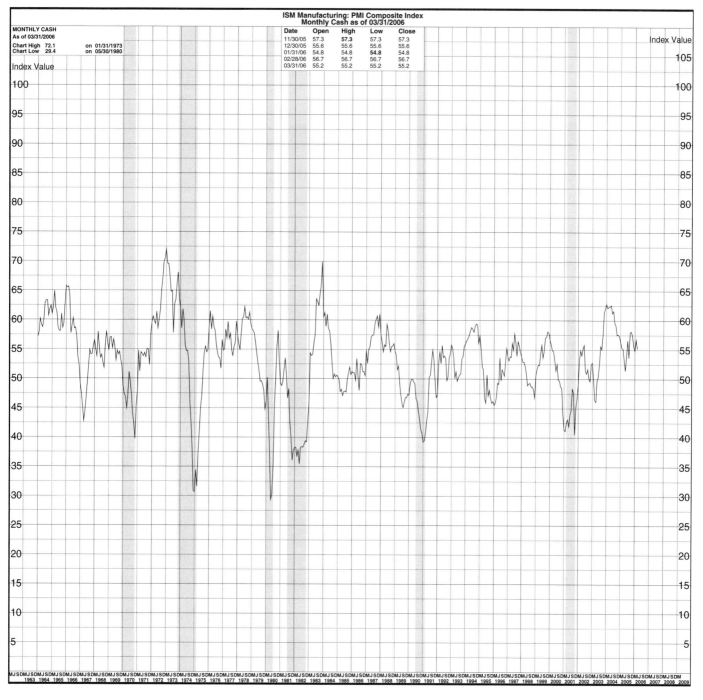

Annual High, Low and Close of ISM Manufacturing: PMI Index   Index Value

Year	High	Low	Close	Year	High	Low	Close	Year	High	Low	Close
1968	58.1	51.8	56.1	1981	53.5	36.1	37.8	1994	59.4	56.0	56.1
1969	57.1	52.0	52.0	1982	42.8	35.5	42.8	1995	57.4	45.9	46.2
1970	51.1	39.7	45.4	1983	69.9	46.0	69.9	1996	55.2	45.5	55.2
1971	57.6	47.9	57.6	1984	61.3	50.0	50.6	1997	57.7	53.1	54.5
1972	70.5	58.6	70.5	1985	52.0	47.1	50.7	1998	53.8	46.8	46.8
1973	72.1	57.8	63.6	1986	53.4	48.0	50.5	1999	58.1	50.6	57.8
1974	62.1	30.9	30.9	1987	61.0	52.6	61.0	2000	56.7	43.9	43.9
1975	55.5	30.7	54.9	1988	59.3	54.6	56.0	2001	48.3	40.5	46.7
1976	61.5	51.7	56.6	1989	54.7	45.1	47.4	2002	55.8	49.1	52.5
1977	59.8	53.9	59.8	1990	50.0	40.8	40.8	2003	62.1	46.1	62.1
1978	62.2	55.0	59.4	1991	54.9	39.2	46.8	2004	62.8	57.3	57.3
1979	58.5	44.8	44.8	1992	55.7	47.3	54.2	2005	58.1	51.4	55.6
1980	58.2	29.4	53.0	1993	55.8	49.6	55.6	2006	56.7	54.8	55.2

Source: Institute for Supply Management

U.S. GROSS DOMESTIC PRODUCT

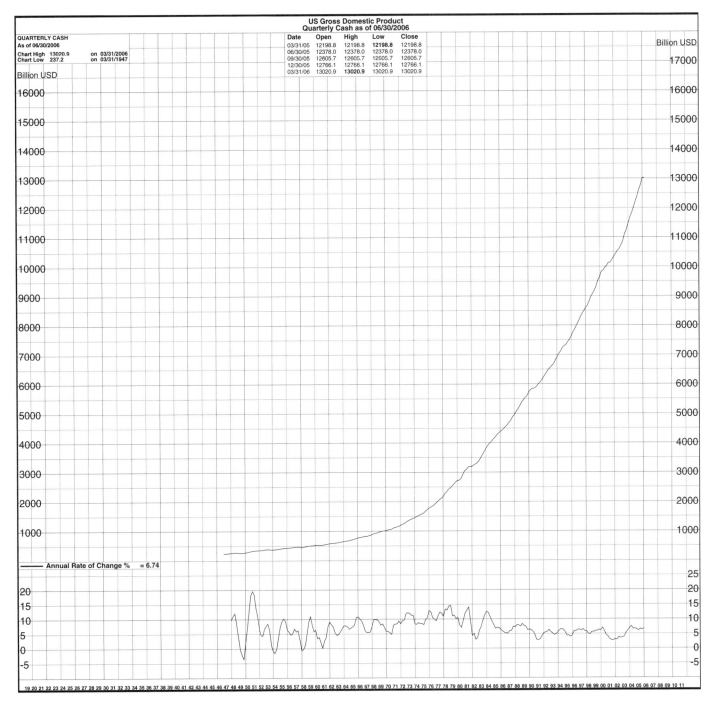

Annual High, Low and Close of U.S. Gross Domestic Product   In Billions of Dollars

Year	High	Low	Close	Year	High	Low	Close	Year	High	Low	Close
1968	936.3	879.9	936.3	1981	3,196.4	3,052.7	3,196.4	1994	7,232.2	6,911.0	7,232.2
1969	1,004.6	961.0	1,004.6	1982	3,314.4	3,186.8	3,314.4	1995	7,522.5	7,298.3	7,522.5
1970	1,052.9	1,017.3	1,052.9	1983	3,690.4	3,382.9	3,690.4	1996	8,000.4	7,624.1	8,000.4
1971	1,151.7	1,098.3	1,151.7	1984	4,036.3	3,809.6	4,036.3	1997	8,471.2	8,113.8	8,471.2
1972	1,287.0	1,190.6	1,287.0	1985	4,321.8	4,119.5	4,321.8	1998	8,953.8	8,586.7	8,953.8
1973	1,432.3	1,335.5	1,432.3	1986	4,546.1	4,385.6	4,546.1	1999	9,519.5	9,066.6	9,519.5
1974	1,553.4	1,447.0	1,553.4	1987	4,886.3	4,613.8	4,886.3	2000	9,953.6	9,629.4	9,953.6
1975	1,714.6	1,570.0	1,714.6	1988	5,253.7	4,951.9	5,253.7	2001	10,226.3	10,021.5	10,226.3
1976	1,885.3	1,772.6	1,885.3	1989	5,584.3	5,367.1	5,584.3	2002	10,591.1	10,333.3	10,591.1
1977	2,111.6	1,939.3	2,111.6	1990	5,849.4	5,716.4	5,848.8	2003	11,236.0	10,717.0	11,236.0
1978	2,417.0	2,150.0	2,417.0	1991	6,095.8	5,888.0	6,095.8	2004	11,995.2	11,457.1	11,995.2
1979	2,660.5	2,464.4	2,660.5	1992	6,484.3	6,196.1	6,484.3	2005	12,766.1	12,198.8	12,766.1
1980	2,916.9	2,725.3	2,916.9	1993	6,800.2	6,542.7	6,800.2	2006	13,020.9	13,020.9	13,020.9

Source: U.S. Department of Commerce: Bureau of Economic Analysis

U.S. GROSS FEDERAL DEBT

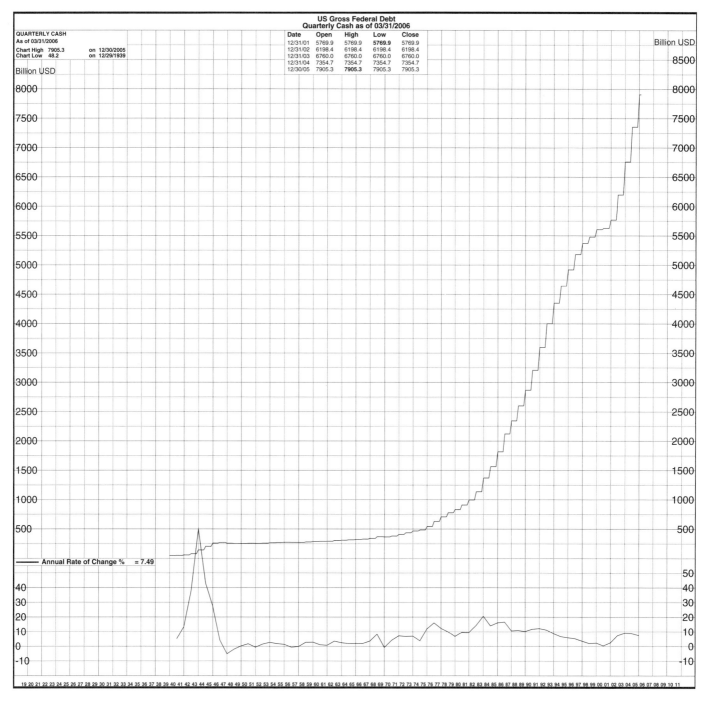

Annual High, Low and Close of U.S. Gross Federal Debt — In Billions of Dollars

Year	High	Low	Close	Year	High	Low	Close	Year	High	Low	Close
1967	340.4	340.4	340.4	1980	909.0	909.0	909.0	1993	4,351.0	4,351.0	4,351.0
1968	368.7	368.7	368.7	1981	994.8	994.8	994.8	1994	4,643.3	4,643.3	4,643.3
1969	365.8	365.8	365.8	1982	1,137.3	1,137.3	1,137.3	1995	4,920.6	4,920.6	4,920.6
1970	380.9	380.9	380.9	1983	1,371.7	1,371.7	1,371.7	1996	5,181.5	5,181.5	5,181.5
1971	408.2	408.2	408.2	1984	1,564.6	1,564.6	1,564.6	1997	5,369.2	5,369.2	5,369.2
1972	435.9	435.9	435.9	1985	1,817.4	1,817.4	1,817.4	1998	5,478.2	5,478.2	5,478.2
1973	466.3	466.3	466.3	1986	2,120.5	2,120.5	2,120.5	1999	5,605.5	5,605.5	5,605.5
1974	483.9	483.9	483.9	1987	2,346.0	2,346.0	2,346.0	2000	5,628.7	5,628.7	5,628.7
1975	541.9	541.9	541.9	1988	2,601.1	2,601.1	2,601.1	2001	5,769.9	5,769.9	5,769.9
1976	629.0	629.0	629.0	1989	2,867.8	2,867.8	2,867.8	2002	6,198.4	6,198.4	6,198.4
1977	706.4	706.4	706.4	1990	3,206.3	3,206.3	3,206.3	2003	6,760.0	6,760.0	6,760.0
1978	776.6	776.6	776.6	1991	3,598.2	3,598.2	3,598.2	2004	7,354.7	7,354.7	7,354.7
1979	829.5	829.5	829.5	1992	4,001.8	4,001.8	4,001.8	2005	7,905.3	7,905.3	7,905.3

Source: The White House: Council of Economic Advisors

U.S. FEDERAL SURPLUS OR DEFICIT

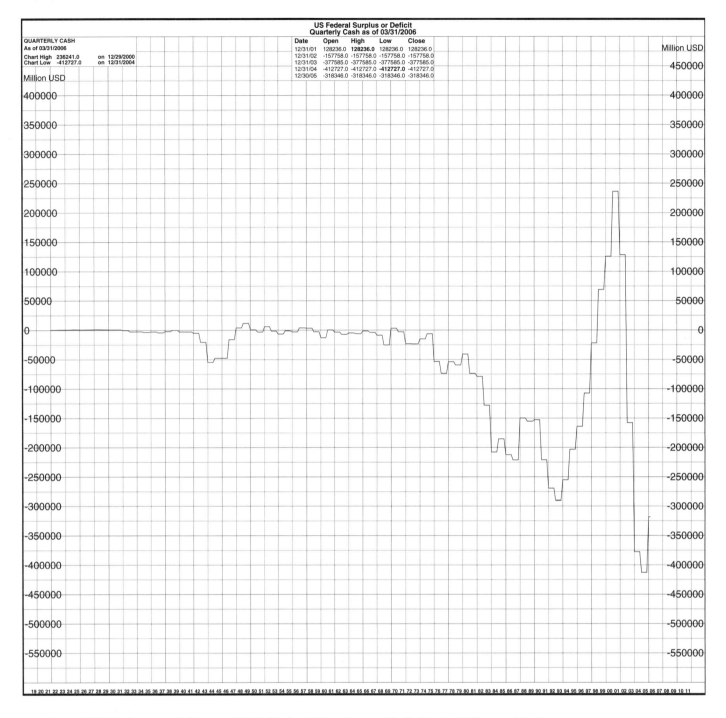

Annual High, Low and Close of U.S. Federal Surplus or Deficit   In Millions of Dollars

Year	High	Low	Close	Year	High	Low	Close	Year	High	Low	Close
1967	-8,643	-8,643	-8,643	1980	-73,830	-73,830	-73,830	1993	-255,051	-255,051	-255,051
1968	-25,161	-25,161	-25,161	1981	-78,968	-78,968	-78,968	1994	-203,186	-203,186	-203,186
1969	3,242	3,242	3,242	1982	-127,977	-127,977	-127,977	1995	-163,952	-163,952	-163,952
1970	-2,842	-2,842	-2,842	1983	-207,802	-207,802	-207,802	1996	-107,431	-107,431	-107,431
1971	-23,033	-23,033	-23,033	1984	-185,367	-185,367	-185,367	1997	-21,884	-21,884	-21,884
1972	-23,373	-23,373	-23,373	1985	-212,308	-212,308	-212,308	1998	69,270	69,270	69,270
1973	-14,908	-14,908	-14,908	1986	-221,227	-221,227	-221,227	1999	125,610	125,610	125,610
1974	-6,135	-6,135	-6,135	1987	-149,730	-149,730	-149,730	2000	236,241	236,241	236,241
1975	-53,242	-53,242	-53,242	1988	-155,178	-155,178	-155,178	2001	128,236	128,236	128,236
1976	-73,732	-73,732	-73,732	1989	-152,639	-152,639	-152,639	2002	-157,758	-157,758	-157,758
1977	-53,659	-53,659	-53,659	1990	-221,036	-221,036	-221,036	2003	-377,585	-377,585	-377,585
1978	-59,185	-59,185	-59,185	1991	-269,238	-269,238	-269,238	2004	-412,727	-412,727	-412,727
1979	-40,726	-40,726	-40,726	1992	-290,321	-290,321	-290,321	2005	-318,346	-318,346	-318,346

Source: The White House: Office of Management and Budget

U.S. RETAIL SALES (EXCEPT AUTOS)

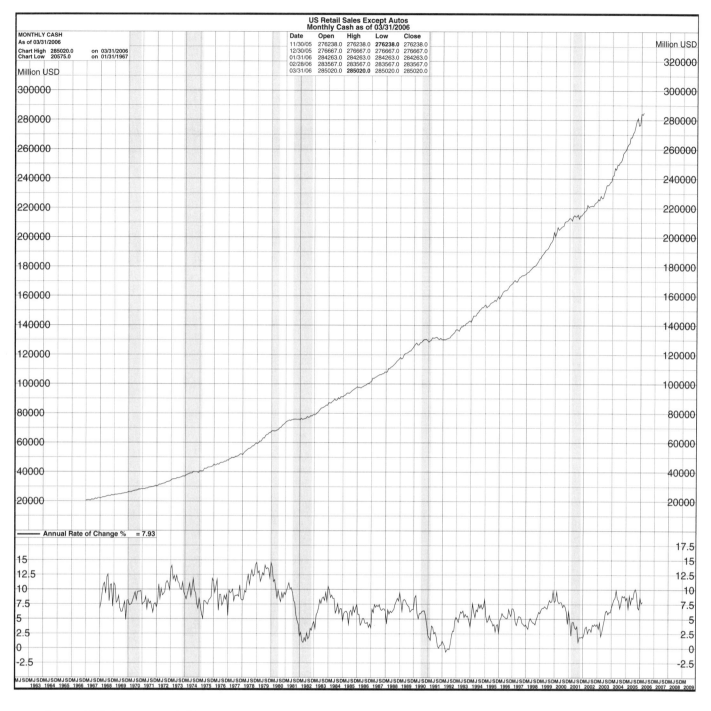

Annual High, Low and Close of U.S. Retail Sales, Except Autos   In Millions of Dollars

Year	High	Low	Close	Year	High	Low	Close	Year	High	Low	Close
1968	24,415	21,961	24,014	1981	76,020	73,970	76,020	1994	153,249	142,199	153,249
1969	25,960	24,394	25,960	1982	79,095	75,481	79,095	1995	159,533	152,039	159,533
1970	28,494	26,325	28,494	1983	85,534	78,920	85,408	1996	168,243	157,931	168,243
1971	30,678	28,330	30,678	1984	91,288	87,027	91,146	1997	174,675	168,637	174,675
1972	33,717	30,298	33,717	1985	97,340	91,352	97,340	1998	185,466	175,486	185,466
1973	37,211	34,384	36,928	1986	101,366	97,248	101,366	1999	203,493	185,933	203,493
1974	40,224	37,455	39,428	1987	108,160	101,539	108,160	2000	211,968	200,548	211,968
1975	44,107	40,601	44,107	1988	116,869	107,927	116,869	2001	216,123	211,323	216,123
1976	48,143	44,502	48,143	1989	124,644	117,030	124,644	2002	224,381	217,134	224,381
1977	52,170	47,752	52,170	1990	130,530	125,981	129,765	2003	238,132	225,259	238,132
1978	59,577	51,638	59,577	1991	131,920	128,683	130,476	2004	259,384	241,876	259,384
1979	66,693	59,189	66,693	1992	136,677	130,261	136,677	2005	281,332	261,623	276,667
1980	73,021	67,810	73,021	1993	143,105	136,063	143,105	2006	285,020	283,567	285,020

Source: U.S. Department of Commerce: Census Bureau

U.S. INTERNATIONAL TRADE BALANCE

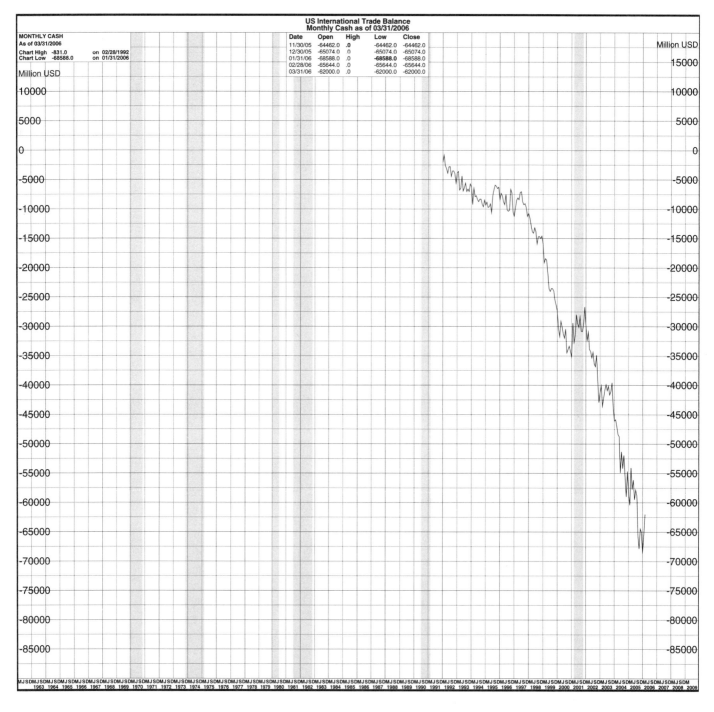

Quarterly High, Low and Close of U.S. Trade Balance, Goods and Services   In Millions of Dollars

Quarter	High	Low	Close	Quarter	High	Low	Close	Quarter	High	Low	Close
09/1996	-10,195	-10,195	-10,195	12/1999	-26,367	-26,367	-26,367	03/2003	-43,543	-43,543	-43,543
12/1996	-10,475	-10,475	-10,475	03/2000	-31,732	-31,732	-31,732	06/2003	-39,882	-39,882	-39,882
03/1997	-8,477	-8,477	-8,477	06/2000	-31,279	-31,279	-31,279	09/2003	-41,645	-41,645	-41,645
06/1997	-7,174	-7,174	-7,174	09/2000	-34,474	-34,474	-34,474	12/2003	-43,742	-43,742	-43,742
09/1997	-9,254	-9,254	-9,254	12/2000	-34,154	-34,154	-34,154	03/2004	-46,966	-46,966	-46,966
12/1997	-11,250	-11,250	-11,250	03/2001	-32,700	-32,700	-32,700	06/2004	-54,894	-54,894	-54,894
03/1998	-12,796	-12,796	-12,796	06/2001	-29,498	-29,498	-29,498	09/2004	-51,939	-51,939	-51,939
06/1998	-13,189	-13,189	-13,189	09/2001	-30,782	-30,782	-30,782	12/2004	-54,672	-54,672	-54,672
09/1998	-14,714	-14,714	-14,714	12/2001	-26,679	-26,679	-26,679	03/2005	-54,055	-54,055	-54,055
12/1998	-14,608	-14,608	-14,608	03/2002	-30,920	-30,920	-30,920	06/2005	-59,493	-59,493	-59,493
03/1999	-18,424	-18,424	-18,424	06/2002	-35,329	-35,329	-35,329	09/2005	-65,585	-65,585	-65,585
06/1999	-23,502	-23,502	-23,502	09/2002	-36,842	-36,842	-36,842	12/2005	-65,074	-65,074	-65,074
09/1999	-23,527	-23,527	-23,527	12/2002	-42,917	-42,917	-42,917	03/2006	-62,000	-62,000	-62,000

Source: U.S. Department of Commerce: Bureau of Economic Analysis

U.S. HOUSING STARTS

Annual High, Low and Close of U.S. Housing Starts   In Thousands of Units

Year	High	Low	Close	Year	High	Low	Close	Year	High	Low	Close
1968	1,630	1,380	1,548	1981	1,547	837	910	1994	1,564	1,272	1,455
1969	1,769	1,229	1,327	1982	1,372	843	1,303	1995	1,461	1,249	1,431
1970	1,893	1,085	1,893	1983	1,910	1,472	1,688	1996	1,557	1,370	1,370
1971	2,295	1,741	2,295	1984	2,260	1,586	1,612	1997	1,566	1,355	1,566
1972	2,494	2,221	2,366	1985	1,942	1,632	1,942	1998	1,792	1,525	1,792
1973	2,481	1,526	1,526	1986	1,972	1,623	1,833	1999	1,748	1,553	1,708
1974	1,752	975	975	1987	1,784	1,400	1,400	2000	1,737	1,463	1,532
1975	1,360	904	1,321	1988	1,573	1,271	1,563	2001	1,670	1,540	1,568
1976	1,804	1,367	1,804	1989	1,621	1,251	1,251	2002	1,829	1,592	1,788
1977	2,142	1,527	2,142	1990	1,551	969	969	2003	2,083	1,629	2,057
1978	2,197	1,718	2,044	1991	1,103	798	1,079	2004	2,062	1,807	2,050
1979	1,913	1,498	1,498	1992	1,297	1,099	1,227	2005	2,228	1,833	2,002
1980	1,523	927	1,482	1993	1,533	1,083	1,533	2006	2,265	1,996	1,996

Seasonally adjusted.   *Source: U.S. Department of Commerce: Census Bureau*

FOODS & FIBERS

Sugar

Sugar prices are currently in a major bull market that started in 2004. Sugar prices during this 2004-06 bull market have quadrupled in price from 5 cents per pound in 2004 to the current level near 20 cents per pound. Sugar prices are currently at 24-year highs, levels not seen since 1981.

Bullish factors driving the current rally include (1) strong worldwide demand for sugar for human consumption and also for ethanol production in Brazil, (2) the forecast by the International Sugar Organization for a production deficit of 1.5-2.0 million metric tons in the 2005-06 marketing year and three straight years of inventory draw-downs, (3) a smaller-than-expected crop for Brazil, (4) tight US sugar supplies after Hurricane Wilma damaged cane crops in Florida in autumn 2005, and (5) active buying by speculative and commodity index funds. Demand for sugar to produce ethanol is likely to grow sharply in coming years as gasoline prices remain high and make ethanol even more price-competitive. Historically, key sugar market events include:

1974 rally—Sugar rallies to a record 66 cents per pound on strong demand, extremely low inventories in 1974, and general commodity market strength tied to inflation and speculation.

1980 rally—Sugar rallies to 45 cents per pound on a drop in sugar production in 1980 and general commodity strength tied to speculation and the spike in US inflation to a record high of 14% in 1980.

1988-90 rally—Sugar rallies to 16 cents per pound as strong demand outpaces production for five consecutive years and as production deficits cause inventories to fall to the lowest levels since 1980-81.

1994 rally—Sugar rallies to the 15 cent per pound area as sugar production dips in 1993-94, causing inventories to drop to low levels in 1994.

1997-99 bear market—Sugar prices fall to 10-year lows after Asian currency crisis causes a sharp drop in demand and sugar inventories reach near-record highs.

2004-06 bull market—Sugar prices soar on strong demand, tight supplies, and the commodity bull market.

Coffee

Coffee prices rallied to a new 6-year high in March 2005 but then consolidated below that high in the following year through March 2006. The coffee market is in balance at the moment with the International Coffee Organization forecasting a small production surplus of 5 million bags (i.e., demand of 116 million bags against production of 121 million bags, where 1 bag = 60 kg or 132.3 lbs). However, world inventories are currently low and that could lead to a rally on any supply disruptions. Historically, key coffee market events include:

1976-1977 rally—Coffee prices rally to record high of 337.5 cents per pound on a devastating frost in Brazil in 1975 and general commodity market strength.

1979 rally—Coffee prices rally to 230 cents per pound on light frost in Brazil and general commodity price strength.

1981-1985 trading range—Coffee prices trade in a narrow range due to International Coffee Agreement (ICA) quotas.

1985-1986 rally—Coffee prices spike higher to 275 cents per pound on extreme drought in Brazil and a sharp draw-down in inventories.

1989-1993 bear market—Coffee prices fall as ICA quotas end and as ending stocks are near record highs.

1994 rally—Coffee prices spike higher on a severe frost in Brazil.

1997 rally—Coffee prices spike higher on strong demand and steady inventory draw-downs in 1995-97.

1998-2001 bear market—Coffee prices fall on growing world supply.

2002-2006 bull market—Coffee prices more than triple due to strong demand, lagging production due to poor tree tending during bear market, inventory draw-downs, and general commodity strength.

Cocoa

Cocoa prices rallied sharply in 2000-02 on strong demand and a sharp drop in ending stocks in the 2000-01 and 2001-02 marketing years. However, cocoa prices then fell back and traded in a relatively narrow range of $1300-1800 per metric ton from 2003 through early-2006. Cocoa prices settled back in 2003-06 after three big crops in the 20002-03, 2003-04 and 2004-05 marketing years. That allowed inventories to rebound upward, although they remained at relatively tight levels. The cocoa market has seen volatility based on the ongoing conflict between the Ivory Coast government and rebels in the north, which periodically causes disruptions of cocoa exports from the world's largest cocoa producer (the Ivory Coast accounts for 40% of the world's cocoa production). Historically, key cocoa market events include:

1976-78 rally—Cocoa prices rally sharply on a series of poor crops in the early 1970s which caused the stocks-to-grindings ratio to drop from 35% at the beginning of the 1970s to a record low of 18% in the 1976-77 marketing year. The cocoa market came into the 1970s with poor production capacity because low cocoa prices seen in the 1950s and 1960s caused poor investment in and maintenance of cocoa farms.

1984-92 bear market—Starting in the 1984-85 marketing year, cocoa production grows sharply, causing a big increase in inventories. The stocks-to-grindings ratio reaches a record high of 66% in 1991-92.

1993-98 Brazil production plunges—Brazilian cocoa production is devastated by the fungus "witch's broom," causing production to drop by half from 305,000 metric tons in 1992-93 to 124,000 MT in 1999-2000. Production has so far only recovered to 160,000 MT.

2001-02 rally—Cocoa prices rally on strong demand and a sharp drop in the ending stocks in the 2000-01 and 2001-02 marketing years.

2004 Ivory Coast ceasefire violation—Cocoa prices rally sharply in November 2004 when Ivory Coast government troops bomb a French peacekeeping force and the French military responds by destroying all the Ivory Coast's military aircraft. The incident causes a temporary disruption of cocoa shipments from the Ivory Coast.

Orange Juice

Orange juice futures prices have nearly tripled from 55 cents per pound in mid-2004 to a 14-year high of 150 cents per pound in early 2006. The rally has been driven by the 33% drop in Florida orange production seen in the 2004-05 and 2005-06 marketing years due to hurricane damage. Four hurricanes devastated the Florida orange groves in fall 2004 and slashed Florida production to 150 million 90-lb boxes. Hurricane Wilma then hit Florida on October 24, 2005, causing the second year of severe damage to the Florida orange crop and allowing an increase of only 5% in the crop size to 154 million boxes. Historically, key orange market events include:

1980s Florida freezes—Major freezes in Florida in the 1980s (particularly in December 1983 and 1985) destroy one-third of Florida's orange trees and lead to a sharp reduction in Florida and US orange production in 1981 through 1992. Orange juice futures prices spiked higher numerous times during the 1980s.

1988 Brazilian production record—Brazilian orange production surges to a then-record high in 1998-90 and grows further in the 1990s, adding to world supply and curbing orange juice price spikes in 1990s. Brazil's share of world orange production grows to 37% in 2004 from 10% in 1970, while the US share falls to 18% in 2004 from 45% in 1970.

1990s California freezes—Freezes in 1991 and 1998 cause California orange production to plunge by 60% in 1990-91 and 40% in 1998-99 from the 5-year trend.

1992 Florida production surge—Starting in 1992, Florida orange production surges and remains high through most of the rest of the 1990s, leading to generally weak prices.

2003-04 bear market—Orange juice futures prices plunge to a 29-year low on a near-record crop in 2003-04 and the Atkins diet fad which reduced demand for high-carb orange juice.

2004-05 hurricanes—Four hurricanes in 2004 and Hurricane Wilma in 2005 devastate Florida orange groves and result in production dropping by one-third in 2004-05 and 2005-06.

Cotton

Cotton prices generally strengthened in 2005 and early 2006 on strong demand from China. Cotton was able to rally despite a record US cotton crop in 2005-06 of 23.7 million bales and a sharp 25% increase in the US carry-over to 6.9 million bales. However, the global carry-over in 2005-06 fell slightly by -2% yr/yr to 50.77 million bales, showing that supply on a global scale was roughly in balance with demand in 2005-06. Demand for cotton has risen sharply from 2001 through 2005, mainly because of increased clothing demand in China and India where wealth is growing. Strong demand has absorbed supply and prevented cotton stocks from getting out of hand. Going into 2006, the size of the US cotton crop may hit a new record high due to increased acreage and a continuation of the very high yields seen in the past 2 years. This is likely to cap cotton prices in 2006, barring any weather disasters. Historically, key cotton market events include:

1970s price spikes—Cotton prices spike higher along with other US field crops in the 1970s due to inflation and general strength in commodity prices.

1983 and 1988 droughts—Cotton prices in 1983 and again in 1988 spike higher in response to US droughts.

1994-95 rally—Cotton prices rally to their modern day record of $1.172 per pound in April 1996 as a result of strong demand and sharply reduced crops in various Asian producing countries (China, Pakistan, India, Uzbekistan and Turkmenistan) due to dry weather, insect infestation and disease. The rally came despite a record US cotton crop in the 1994-95 marketing year.

2001 bear market—Cotton prices fall sharply in 2001 to 30 cents per pound as the US produces a then-record crop of 20.3 million bales. World ending stocks rise to a near-record high in the 2001-02 marketing year.

COCOA

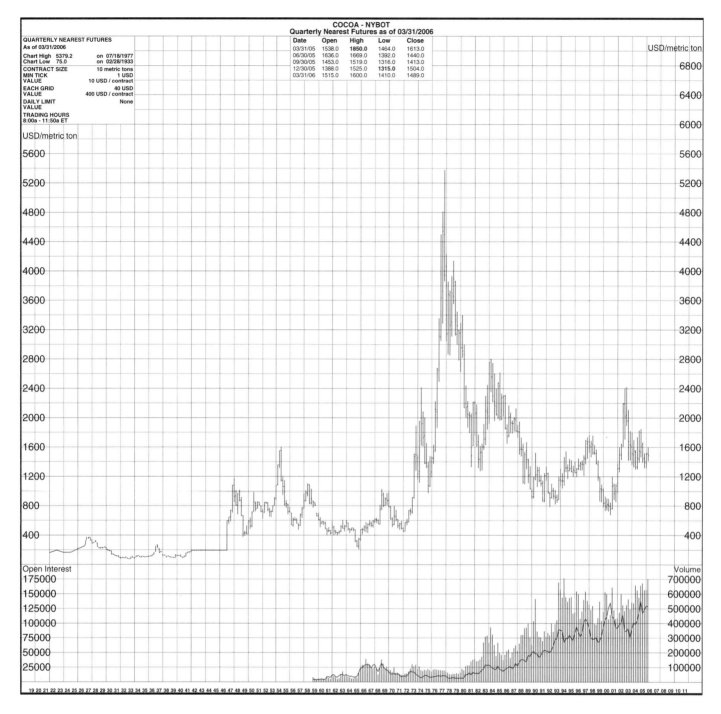

Annual High, Low and Close of Cocoa   In Dollars per Metric Ton

Year	High	Low	Close	Year	High	Low	Close	Year	High	Low	Close
1929	238	201	201	1942	192	187	192	1955	1,149	683	711
1930	205	134	134	1943	192	192	192	1956	703	513	560
1931	131	88	88	1944	192	192	192	1957	970	472	871
1932	102	82	82	1945	192	192	192	1958	1,105	816	891
1933	107	75	91	1946	595	192	595	1959	865	648	648
1934	122	99	108	1947	1,179	551	926	1960	672	518	521
1935	113	101	109	1948	1,020	661	667	1961	623	430	538
1936	246	113	246	1949	667	375	592	1962	554	430	477
1937	268	119	119	1950	979	485	755	1963	639	466	598
1938	129	98	100	1951	857	626	716	1964	592	472	516
1939	133	92	128	1952	847	650	714	1965	529	251	513
1940	130	93	116	1953	1,075	645	1,075	1966	623	463	601
1941	188	112	188	1954	1,601	948	1,061	1967	711	573	692

Source: New York Board of Trade

COCOA

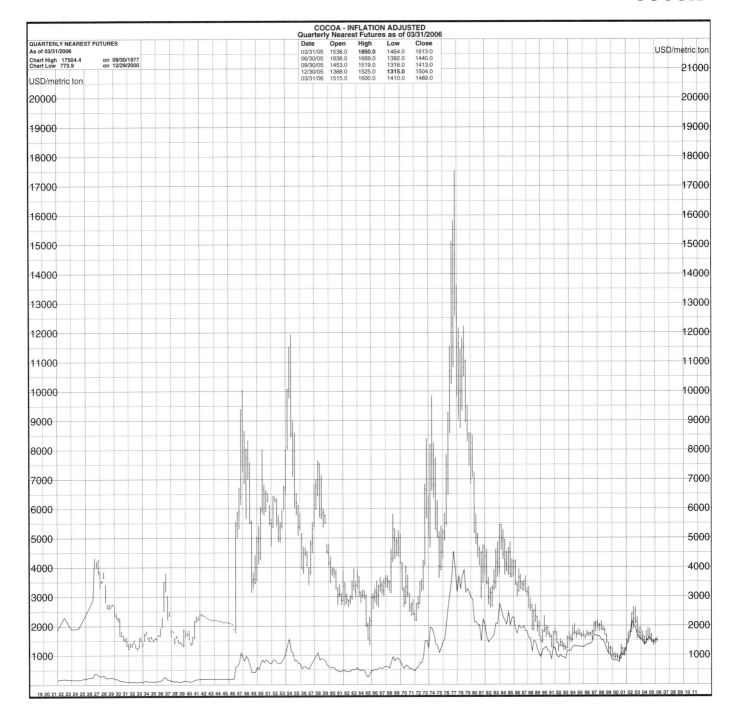

COCOA

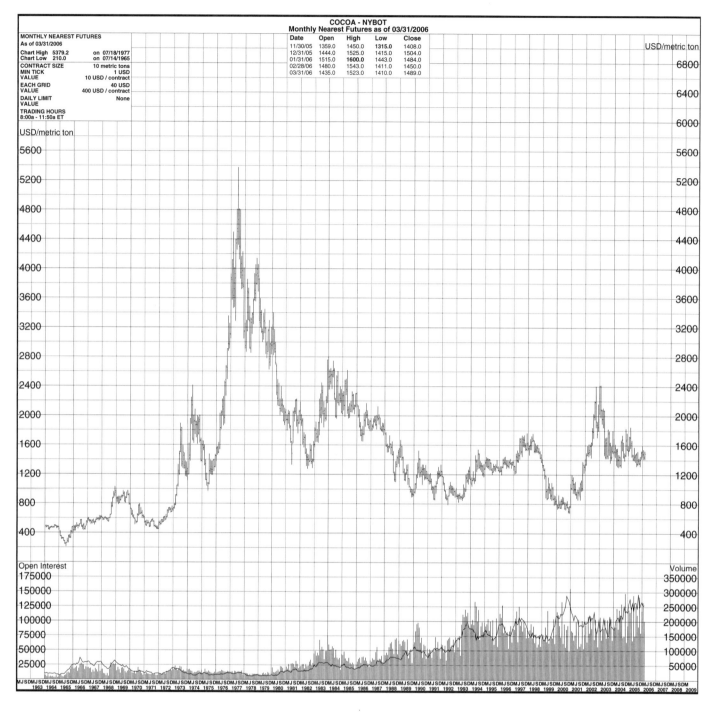

Annual High, Low and Close of Cocoa Futures   In Dollars per Metric Ton

Year	High	Low	Close	Year	High	Low	Close	Year	High	Low	Close
1968	1,032	549	944	1981	2,230	1,330	2,054	1994	1,543	1,041	1,280
1969	974	777	786	1982	2,184	1,275	1,603	1995	1,442	1,200	1,258
1970	795	511	620	1983	2,759	1,565	2,755	1996	1,447	1,196	1,374
1971	619	446	455	1984	2,805	1,960	2,052	1997	1,766	1,210	1,630
1972	765	453	720	1985	2,620	1,963	2,298	1998	1,758	1,368	1,379
1973	1,896	694	1,237	1986	2,315	1,648	1,935	1999	1,422	782	837
1974	2,414	1,116	1,381	1987	2,128	1,732	1,814	2000	929	674	758
1975	1,657	972	1,450	1988	1,950	1,103	1,500	2001	1,380	752	1,310
1976	3,357	1,371	3,114	1989	1,670	890	925	2002	2,405	1,260	2,021
1977	5,379	3,047	3,138	1990	1,525	905	1,150	2003	2,420	1,360	1,515
1978	4,142	2,852	3,897	1991	1,337	850	1,245	2004	1,830	1,299	1,547
1979	3,869	2,623	2,954	1992	1,254	785	936	2005	1,850	1,315	1,504
1980	3,401	1,870	2,050	1993	1,310	820	1,144	2006	1,600	1,410	1,489

Source: New York Board of Trade

COCOA

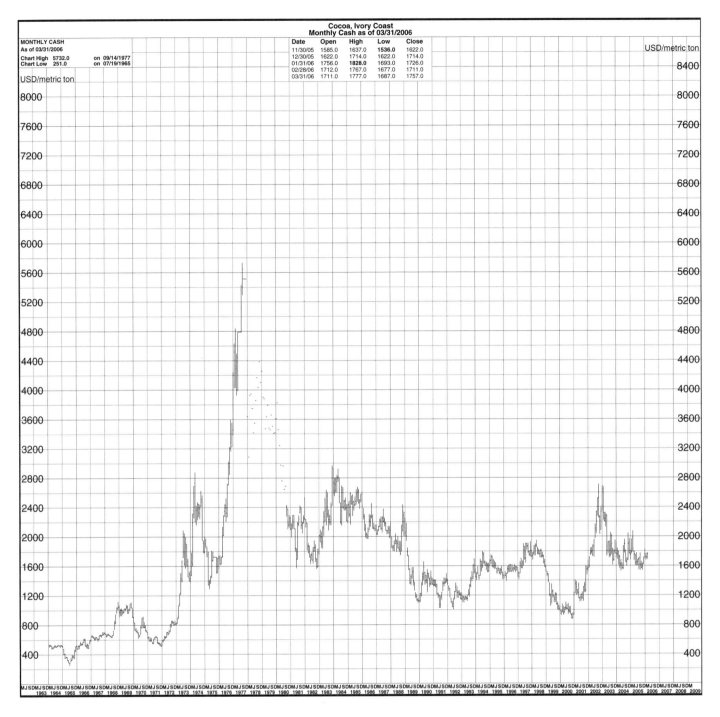

Annual High, Low and Close of Cocoa   In Dollars per Metric Ton

Year	High	Low	Close	Year	High	Low	Close	Year	High	Low	Close
1968	1,121	634	1,047	1981	2,425	1,571	2,246	1994	1,795	1,403	1,582
1969	1,105	904	909	1982	2,542	1,562	1,832	1995	1,751	1,419	1,419
1970	918	617	708	1983	2,962	1,755	2,962	1996	1,623	1,393	1,534
1971	700	510	510	1984	2,926	2,156	2,215	1997	1,930	1,412	1,802
1972	862	518	821	1985	2,680	2,163	2,580	1998	1,949	1,583	1,583
1973	2,089	796	1,488	1986	2,597	1,967	2,155	1999	1,616	988	1,017
1974	2,877	1,378	1,786	1987	2,377	1,975	2,052	2000	1,106	876	930
1975	2,006	1,290	1,709	1988	2,435	1,744	2,317	2001	1,596	925	1,565
1976	3,594	1,565	3,456	1989	2,247	1,097	1,128	2002	2,711	1,524	2,336
1977	5,732	3,390	5,512	1990	1,661	1,099	1,348	2003	2,686	1,614	1,763
1978	4,387	3,086	4,101	1991	1,496	1,027	1,413	2004	2,044	1,526	1,770
1979	4,255	3,406	3,417	1992	1,415	1,007	1,154	2005	2,074	1,535	1,714
1980	3,825	2,100	2,285	1993	1,695	1,098	1,499	2006	1,828	1,677	1,757

Source: New York Board of Trade

COCOA

Quarterly High, Low and Close of Cocoa Futures   In Dollars per Metric Ton

Quarter	High	Low	Close	Quarter	High	Low	Close	Quarter	High	Low	Close
09/1996	1,404	1,284	1,377	12/1999	1,040	782	837	03/2003	2,420	1,892	1,960
12/1996	1,418	1,286	1,374	03/2000	929	730	800	06/2003	2,110	1,420	1,681
03/1997	1,490	1,210	1,453	06/2000	905	740	820	09/2003	1,820	1,420	1,626
06/1997	1,700	1,368	1,684	09/2000	898	725	797	12/2003	1,800	1,360	1,515
09/1997	1,735	1,445	1,679	12/2000	846	674	758	03/2004	1,698	1,328	1,549
12/1997	1,766	1,529	1,630	03/2001	1,202	752	1,073	06/2004	1,562	1,299	1,336
03/1998	1,689	1,465	1,652	06/2001	1,109	880	974	09/2004	1,738	1,300	1,453
06/1998	1,758	1,500	1,523	09/2001	1,100	854	1,077	12/2004	1,830	1,390	1,547
09/1998	1,629	1,500	1,512	12/2001	1,380	977	1,310	03/2005	1,850	1,464	1,613
12/1998	1,570	1,368	1,379	03/2002	1,598	1,260	1,494	06/2005	1,669	1,392	1,440
03/1999	1,422	1,145	1,192	06/2002	1,648	1,428	1,630	09/2005	1,519	1,316	1,413
06/1999	1,189	860	1,038	09/2002	2,206	1,610	2,191	12/2005	1,525	1,315	1,504
09/1999	1,093	850	1,029	12/2002	2,405	1,705	2,021	03/2006	1,600	1,410	1,489

Source: New York Board of Trade

COCOA

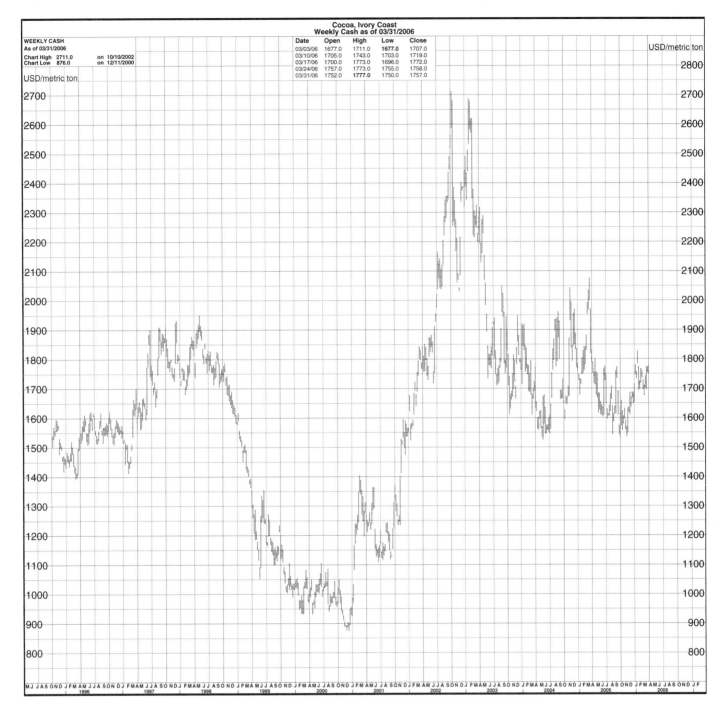

Quarterly High, Low and Close of Cocoa In Dollars per Metric Ton

Quarter	High	Low	Close	Quarter	High	Low	Close	Quarter	High	Low	Close
09/1996	1,618	1,512	1,577	12/1999	1,220	988	1,017	03/2003	2,686	2,200	2,247
12/1996	1,622	1,508	1,534	03/2000	1,081	933	980	06/2003	2,319	1,734	1,924
03/1997	1,662	1,412	1,633	06/2000	1,106	932	1,012	09/2003	2,049	1,710	1,899
06/1997	1,898	1,561	1,898	09/2000	1,087	940	975	12/2003	1,948	1,614	1,763
09/1997	1,910	1,638	1,864	12/2000	1,048	876	930	03/2004	1,920	1,611	1,713
12/1997	1,930	1,725	1,802	03/2001	1,405	925	1,311	06/2004	1,735	1,526	1,566
03/1998	1,876	1,682	1,865	06/2001	1,363	1,108	1,166	09/2004	1,960	1,547	1,655
06/1998	1,949	1,737	1,767	09/2001	1,312	1,116	1,312	12/2004	2,044	1,596	1,770
09/1998	1,828	1,705	1,727	12/2001	1,596	1,234	1,565	03/2005	2,074	1,679	1,832
12/1998	1,787	1,583	1,583	03/2002	1,843	1,524	1,777	06/2005	1,801	1,605	1,652
03/1999	1,616	1,377	1,387	06/2002	1,955	1,719	1,949	09/2005	1,774	1,535	1,614
06/1999	1,363	1,051	1,239	09/2002	2,521	1,977	2,521	12/2005	1,714	1,536	1,714
09/1999	1,272	1,098	1,212	12/2002	2,711	2,029	2,336	03/2006	1,828	1,677	1,757

Source: New York Board of Trade

COFFEE

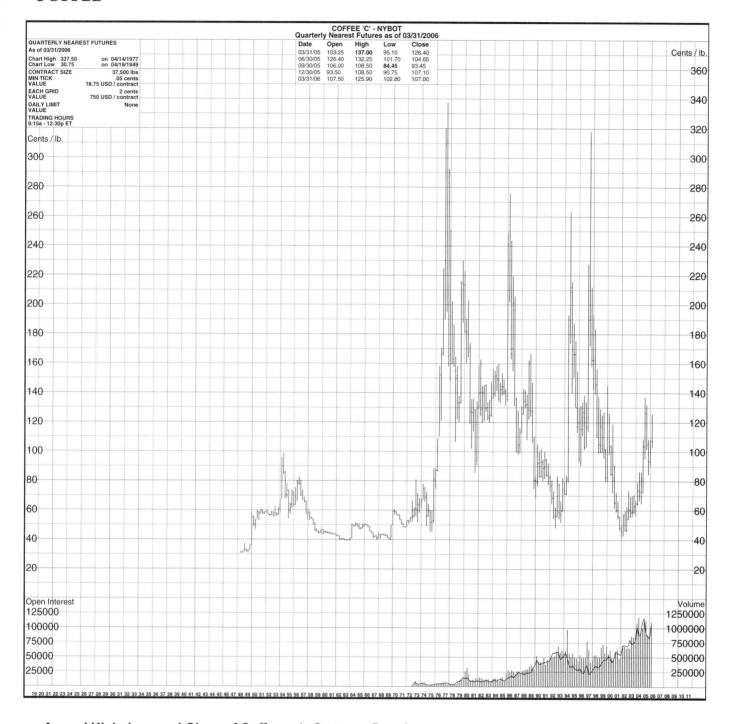

Annual High, Low and Close of Coffee   In Cents per Pound

Year	High	Low	Close	Year	High	Low	Close	Year	High	Low	Close
				1954	98.50	67.50	73.25	1961	45.00	42.75	42.75
1948	37.35	31.00	33.25	1955	74.00	54.00	63.50	1962	43.00	39.50	40.25
1949	58.75	30.75	54.75	1956	82.75	63.50	71.25	1963	41.00	39.00	41.00
1950	59.75	47.00	57.75	1957	73.75	53.00	58.00	1964	51.50	41.00	48.75
1951	60.50	57.00	59.25	1958	58.75	45.50	46.50	1965	51.00	47.25	50.25
1952	59.25	55.75	56.00	1959	48.00	44.00	44.00	1966	50.25	44.25	44.50
1953	66.87	55.50	66.87	1960	47.00	43.62	44.25	1967	45.00	40.00	43.25

Source: New York Board of Trade

COFFEE

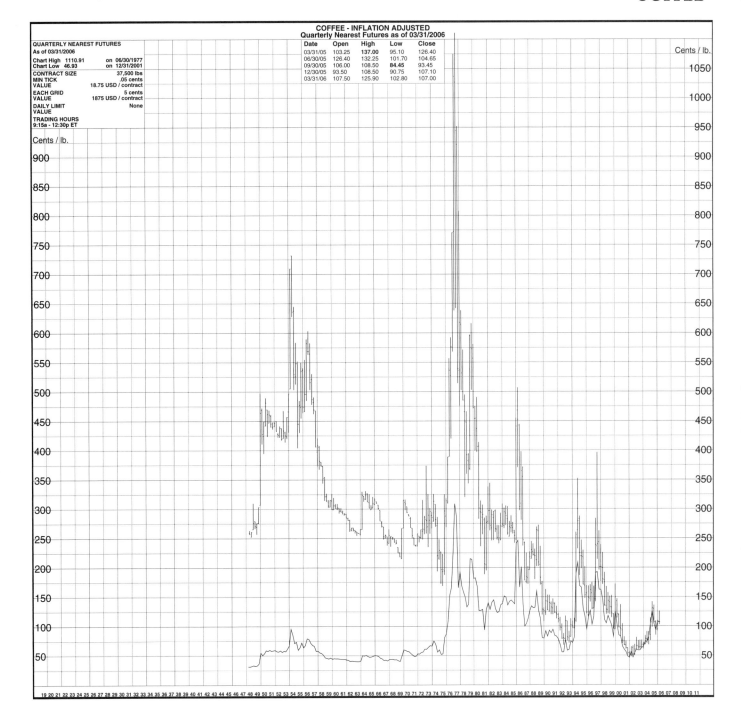

COFFEE

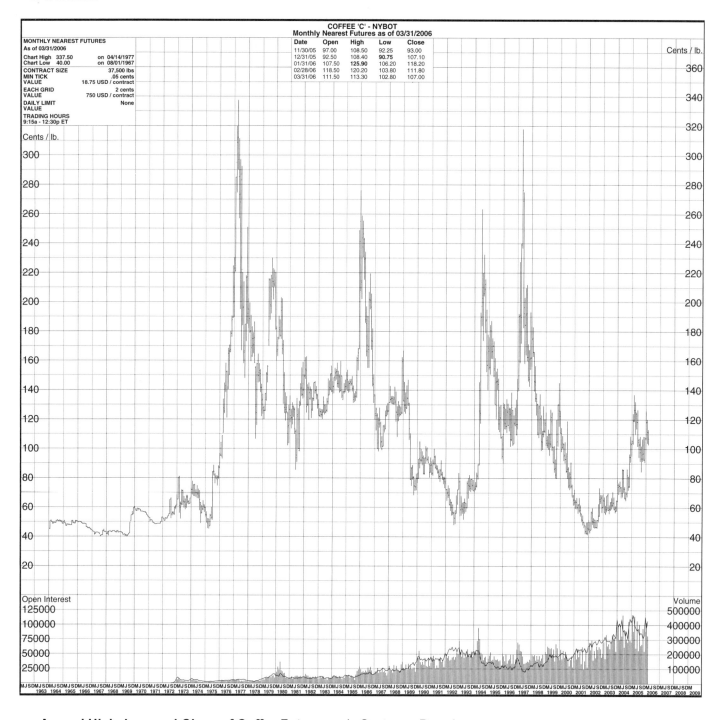

Annual High, Low and Close of Coffee Futures   In Cents per Pound

Year	High	Low	Close	Year	High	Low	Close	Year	High	Low	Close
1968	44.00	40.50	43.00	1981	159.00	85.50	139.71	1994	263.50	70.55	168.85
1969	59.50	40.00	59.50	1982	162.90	119.50	129.83	1995	187.25	93.15	94.90
1970	60.50	53.50	53.50	1983	156.50	120.10	138.79	1996	138.50	90.40	116.90
1971	53.50	48.25	53.00	1984	160.00	133.20	142.25	1997	318.00	113.60	162.45
1972	66.50	50.75	60.90	1985	249.00	131.25	241.29	1998	183.50	98.75	117.75
1973	81.00	52.00	66.00	1986	276.00	131.20	136.83	1999	145.00	80.00	125.90
1974	77.90	49.00	59.62	1987	136.90	98.10	125.96	2000	126.00	61.55	65.55
1975	88.75	45.25	87.22	1988	162.50	108.00	159.34	2001	72.50	41.50	46.20
1976	224.50	86.40	224.45	1989	166.90	68.30	79.57	2002	73.50	42.70	60.20
1977	337.50	148.00	192.03	1990	105.00	76.60	88.65	2003	70.75	55.30	64.95
1978	202.50	106.60	132.88	1991	100.00	73.25	77.70	2004	108.70	64.00	103.75
1979	230.05	120.00	181.56	1992	83.55	48.10	77.55	2005	137.00	84.45	107.10
1980	203.00	102.10	126.80	1993	82.20	51.70	71.55	2006	125.90	102.80	107.00

Source: New York Board of Trade

COFFEE

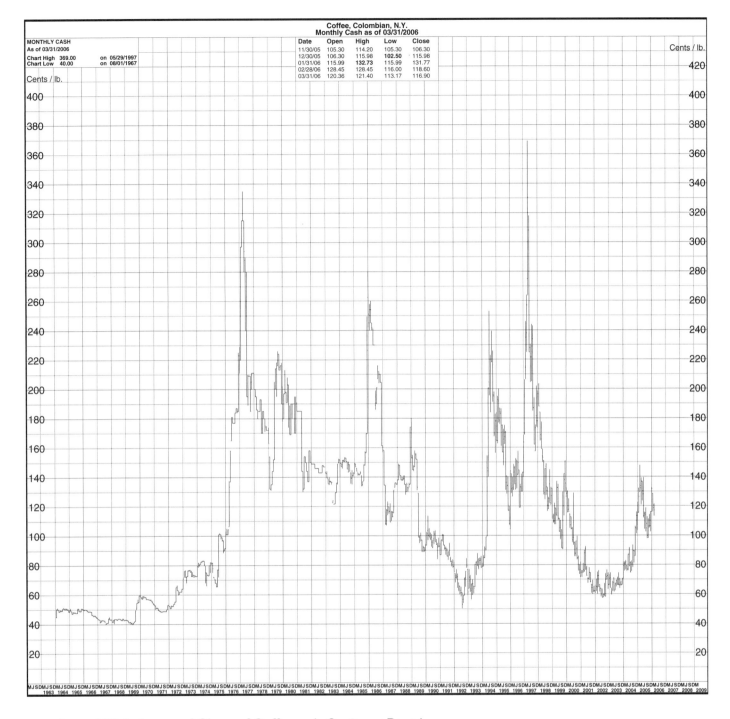

Annual High, Low and Close of Coffee   In Cents per Pound

Year	High	Low	Close	Year	High	Low	Close	Year	High	Low	Close
1968	44.00	40.50	43.00	1981	191.00	130.00	150.00	1994	253.00	78.50	178.00
1969	59.50	40.00	59.50	1982	150.00	143.00	147.00	1995	200.00	107.00	108.00
1970	60.50	53.50	53.50	1983	152.50	121.50	151.75	1996	157.50	104.50	143.00
1971	53.50	48.25	53.00	1984	153.50	135.05	143.00	1997	369.00	140.00	178.00
1972	66.50	50.75	64.00	1985	249.50	134.00	226.50	1998	203.50	116.50	127.00
1973	77.00	64.00	72.50	1986	280.00	161.25	161.25	1999	151.00	90.75	135.50
1974	83.50	66.00	82.00	1987	161.25	107.00	135.00	2000	132.50	73.50	76.50
1975	102.00	65.50	91.50	1988	174.00	128.00	174.00	2001	92.50	60.00	62.00
1976	225.00	91.50	223.00	1989	180.00	89.00	90.00	2002	76.50	57.50	66.25
1977	335.00	185.00	211.00	1990	113.50	84.00	93.00	2003	74.50	59.50	70.00
1978	211.00	170.00	172.00	1991	101.00	78.00	79.00	2004	116.00	70.00	113.25
1979	226.00	131.00	190.00	1992	84.50	50.50	79.50	2005	147.75	98.00	115.98
1980	213.00	169.00	190.00	1993	88.00	56.50	78.00	2006	132.73	113.17	116.90

Source: New York Board of Trade

COFFEE

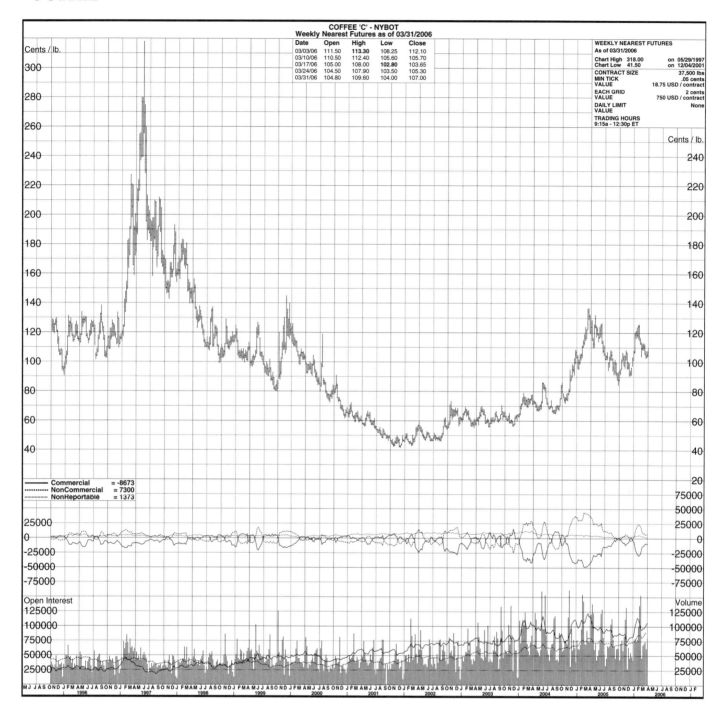

Quarterly High, Low and Close of Coffee Futures   In Cents per Pound

Quarter	High	Low	Close	Quarter	High	Low	Close	Quarter	High	Low	Close
09/1996	138.50	101.50	102.95	12/1999	145.00	80.00	125.90	03/2003	69.50	55.30	58.65
12/1996	133.70	103.50	116.90	03/2000	126.00	98.00	103.70	06/2003	70.00	55.80	58.90
03/1997	227.50	113.60	191.15	06/2000	104.70	84.00	84.85	09/2003	70.75	58.00	62.90
06/1997	318.00	172.00	192.40	09/2000	119.00	72.20	83.00	12/2003	66.90	56.40	64.95
09/1997	212.00	158.00	162.50	12/2000	91.00	61.55	65.55	03/2004	79.20	64.00	73.75
12/1997	193.25	142.50	162.45	03/2001	72.50	59.00	60.30	06/2004	86.50	66.80	73.10
03/1998	183.50	139.25	146.25	06/2001	66.80	54.10	56.10	09/2004	86.40	64.80	82.35
06/1998	156.50	109.50	111.25	09/2001	56.00	46.25	48.30	12/2004	108.70	71.90	103.75
09/1998	137.40	98.75	105.15	12/2001	50.00	41.50	46.20	03/2005	137.00	95.10	126.40
12/1998	129.25	99.50	117.75	03/2002	57.40	42.70	57.20	06/2005	132.25	101.70	104.65
03/1999	125.00	99.50	109.70	06/2002	59.70	46.10	46.50	09/2005	108.50	84.45	93.45
06/1999	127.00	95.50	101.40	09/2002	62.50	46.00	54.50	12/2005	108.50	90.75	107.10
09/1999	102.00	80.15	82.45	12/2002	73.50	54.25	60.20	03/2006	125.90	102.80	107.00

Source: New York Board of Trade

COFFEE

Quarterly High, Low and Close of Coffee   In Cents per Pound

Quarter	High	Low	Close	Quarter	High	Low	Close	Quarter	High	Low	Close
09/1996	157.50	119.00	119.00	12/1999	151.00	90.75	135.50	03/2003	74.50	59.50	61.25
12/1996	143.00	119.00	143.00	03/2000	132.50	115.50	116.00	06/2003	71.00	61.75	67.25
03/1997	246.00	140.00	235.00	06/2000	114.50	95.25	96.75	09/2003	74.50	65.00	66.00
06/1997	369.00	225.00	225.00	09/2000	129.00	85.75	96.00	12/2003	70.75	64.00	70.00
09/1997	244.00	185.00	187.00	12/2000	99.50	73.50	76.50	03/2004	83.00	70.00	81.75
12/1997	202.00	157.50	178.00	03/2001	82.00	71.50	76.50	06/2004	91.75	75.50	79.00
03/1998	203.50	164.50	168.50	06/2001	92.50	72.25	72.50	09/2004	93.50	74.50	89.50
06/1998	177.50	128.00	128.00	09/2001	78.00	67.50	68.50	12/2004	116.00	81.25	113.25
09/1998	149.00	116.50	120.50	12/2001	69.50	60.00	62.00	03/2005	147.75	103.25	132.25
12/1998	145.00	118.00	127.00	03/2002	75.00	60.00	72.25	06/2005	139.50	112.00	113.25
03/1999	132.00	107.50	118.50	06/2002	76.00	58.25	60.00	09/2005	118.75	98.00	99.76
06/1999	137.00	107.50	111.50	09/2002	67.25	57.50	58.50	12/2005	115.98	98.11	115.98
09/1999	111.50	91.25	91.75	12/2002	76.50	58.25	66.25	03/2006	132.73	113.17	116.90

Source: New York Board of Trade

ORANGE JUICE

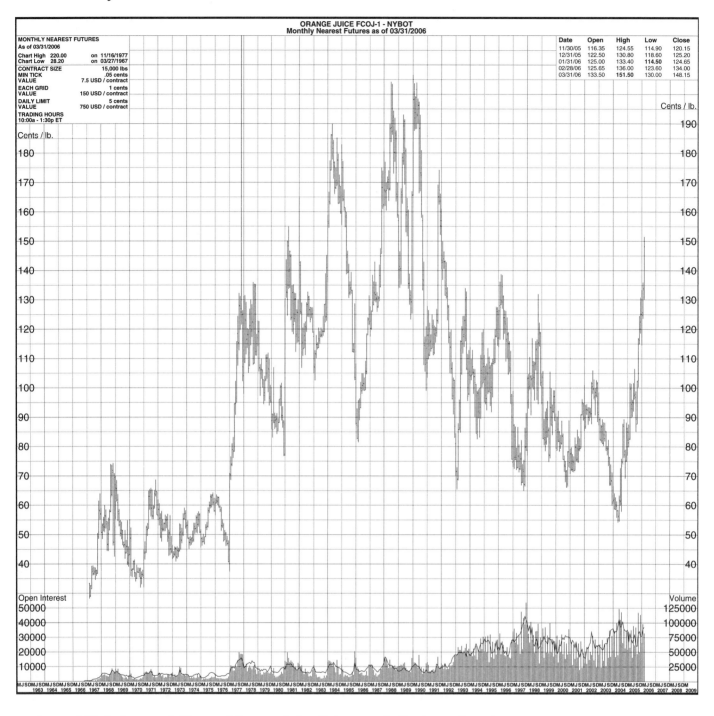

Annual High, Low and Close of Orange Juice Futures   In Cents per Pound

Year	High	Low	Close	Year	High	Low	Close	Year	High	Low	Close
1968	74.40	42.50	69.50	1981	155.10	76.90	117.20	1994	119.90	82.50	107.30
1969	69.90	39.10	43.00	1982	164.85	106.75	118.90	1995	127.60	91.75	117.00
1970	55.15	31.90	36.00	1983	145.25	102.50	140.90	1996	138.75	75.60	75.65
1971	68.75	32.00	56.70	1984	190.00	136.00	159.95	1997	99.00	65.00	80.00
1972	61.80	42.75	44.35	1985	183.00	102.60	103.50	1998	131.95	77.00	101.80
1973	59.10	40.85	52.60	1986	131.50	81.45	122.00	1999	105.75	74.80	88.95
1974	57.85	45.10	50.75	1987	175.00	117.50	161.95	2000	92.25	66.15	74.60
1975	64.35	45.60	58.00	1988	204.25	158.00	158.95	2001	96.20	70.80	89.10
1976	63.65	40.50	40.80	1989	193.10	123.30	165.65	2002	106.00	85.40	91.75
1977	220.00	37.40	107.10	1990	206.50	99.00	113.50	2003	98.50	60.05	60.75
1978	136.00	98.00	115.05	1991	174.25	103.50	155.15	2004	89.40	54.20	86.10
1979	122.95	93.95	95.75	1992	161.00	83.00	87.00	2005	130.80	77.00	125.20
1980	107.00	76.75	77.40	1993	134.00	65.45	104.40	2006	151.50	114.50	148.15

Source: *New York Board of Trade*

ORANGE JUICE

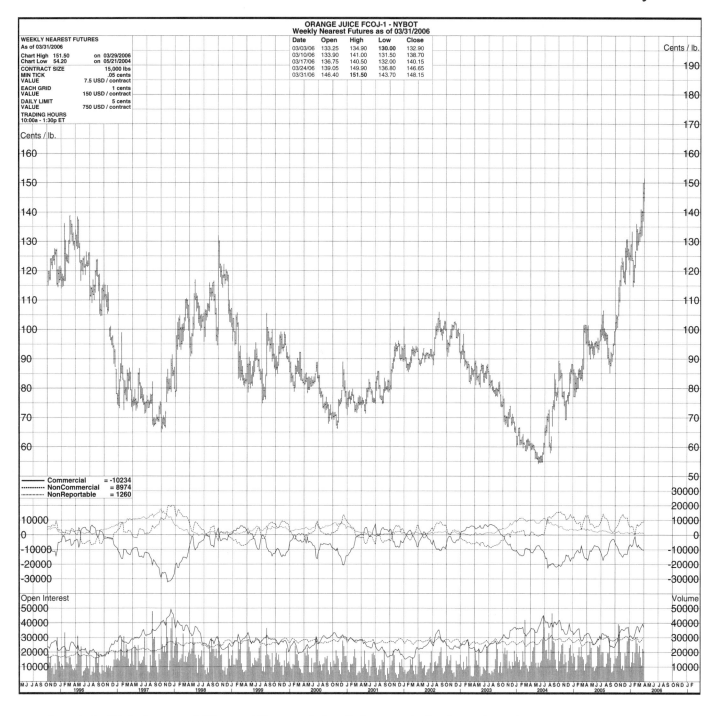

Quarterly High, Low and Close of Orange Juice Futures   In Cents per Pound

Quarter	High	Low	Close	Quarter	High	Low	Close	Quarter	High	Low	Close
09/1996	126.20	104.50	115.15	12/1999	99.25	84.00	88.95	03/2003	98.50	81.40	86.75
12/1996	115.95	75.60	75.65	03/2000	92.25	78.75	81.80	06/2003	89.40	80.25	85.30
03/1997	99.00	72.50	76.35	06/2000	88.90	78.25	83.75	09/2003	85.30	73.50	76.15
06/1997	86.75	71.30	72.55	09/2000	84.50	68.00	71.45	12/2003	76.50	60.05	60.75
09/1997	82.25	66.85	72.10	12/2000	89.00	66.15	74.60	03/2004	66.70	58.55	60.30
12/1997	91.50	65.00	80.00	03/2001	79.75	70.80	75.15	06/2004	63.40	54.20	61.75
03/1998	110.60	77.00	104.05	06/2001	83.10	71.35	75.50	09/2004	87.90	57.85	87.50
06/1998	117.00	90.75	103.65	09/2001	85.80	74.60	79.35	12/2004	89.40	69.20	86.10
09/1998	116.60	95.75	100.00	12/2001	96.20	79.50	89.10	03/2005	101.70	77.00	99.55
12/1998	131.95	94.50	101.80	03/2002	101.00	85.40	92.50	06/2005	101.70	89.85	96.35
03/1999	105.75	80.50	82.40	06/2002	93.50	87.50	91.20	09/2005	106.50	85.10	102.30
06/1999	95.60	78.50	85.50	09/2002	106.00	87.75	96.95	12/2005	130.80	100.20	125.20
09/1999	105.55	74.80	87.40	12/2002	102.70	88.50	91.75	03/2006	151.50	114.50	148.15

Source: New York Board of Trade

SUGAR

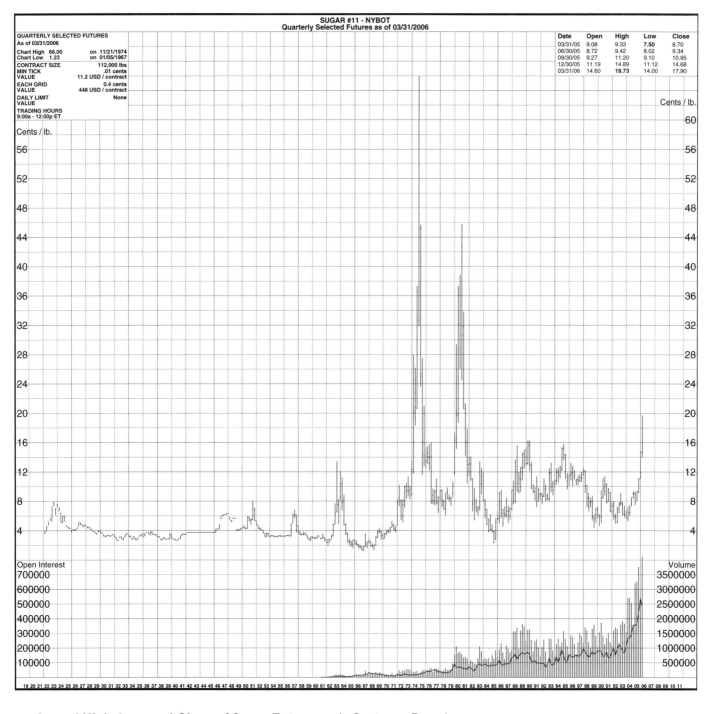

Annual High, Low and Close of Sugar Futures   In Cents per Pound

Year	High	Low	Close	Year	High	Low	Close	Year	High	Low	Close
1929	4.01	3.52	3.76	1942	3.74	3.72	3.74	1955	3.41	3.13	3.23
1930	3.70	3.14	3.29	1943	3.74	3.74	3.74	1956	5.00	3.22	4.85
1931	3.49	3.14	3.14	1944	3.75	3.74	3.75	1957	6.85	3.50	3.85
1932	3.16	2.59	2.83	1945	3.75	3.75	3.75	1958	3.85	3.35	3.67
1933	3.62	2.72	3.23	1946	5.94	3.76	5.94	1959	3.40	2.55	3.05
1934	3.32	2.67	2.67	1947	6.32	6.02	6.32	1960	3.40	2.85	3.25
1935	3.62	2.79	3.13	1948	5.82	5.14	5.67	1961	3.58	2.41	2.41
1936	3.82	3.27	3.82	1949	4.50	3.90	4.33	1962	4.95	1.95	4.80
1937	3.83	3.18	3.24	1950	5.95	4.15	5.45	1963	13.45	4.83	10.37
1938	3.21	2.69	2.88	1951	8.05	4.70	4.77	1964	11.24	2.42	2.50
1939	3.65	2.77	2.93	1952	4.75	3.62	3.62	1965	2.91	1.56	2.30
1940	2.91	2.64	2.91	1953	3.77	3.05	3.25	1966	2.76	1.32	1.32
1941	3.60	2.93	3.50	1954	3.43	3.05	3.17	1967	3.63	1.23	2.52

Source: New York Board of Trade

SUGAR

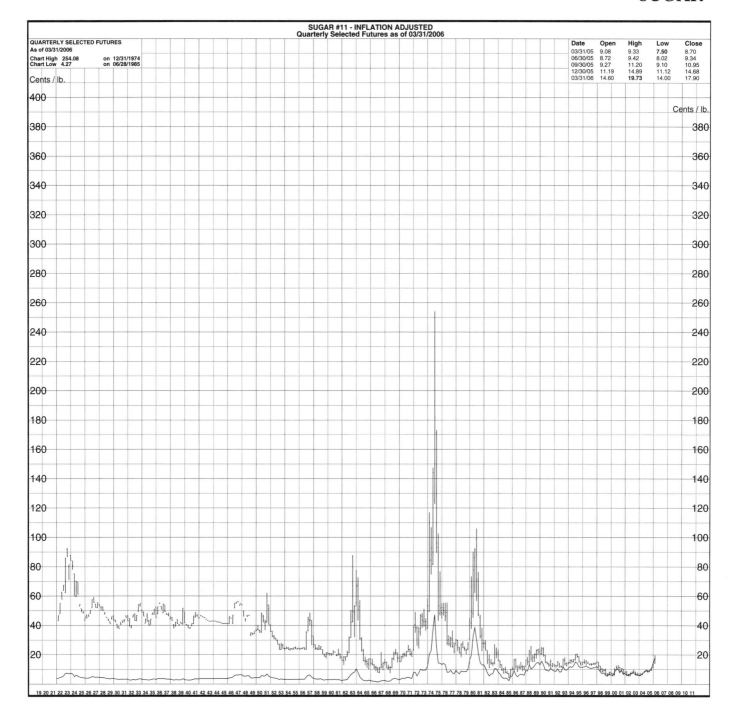

SUGAR

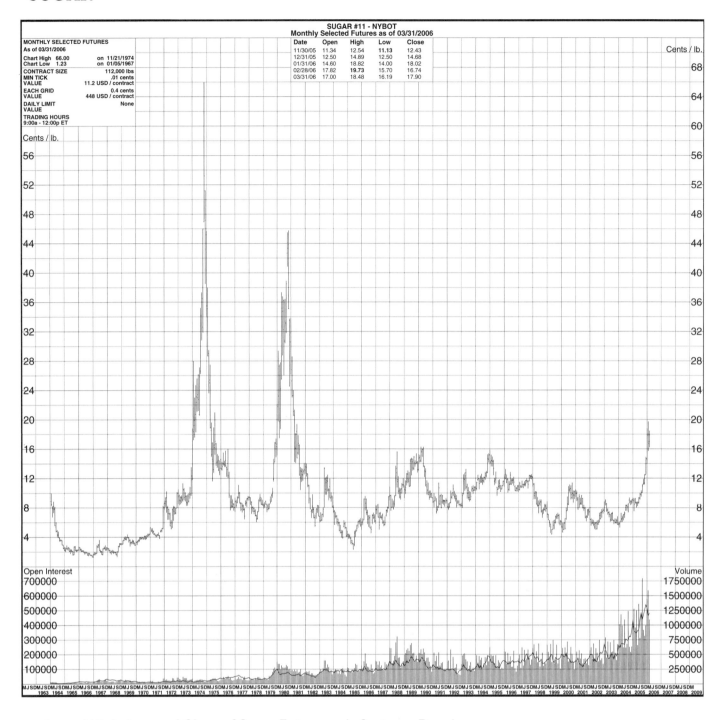

Annual High, Low and Close of Sugar Futures   In Cents per Pound

Year	High	Low	Close	Year	High	Low	Close	Year	High	Low	Close
1968	3.20	1.31	3.08	1981	33.85	10.41	13.18	1994	15.38	10.23	15.17
1969	4.36	2.74	2.88	1982	14.10	5.40	6.85	1995	15.83	9.62	11.60
1970	4.48	2.92	4.36	1983	13.47	6.05	8.18	1996	13.25	10.05	11.00
1971	8.25	3.79	7.99	1984	8.29	3.79	4.16	1997	12.55	10.10	12.22
1972	10.25	5.08	10.00	1985	6.56	2.30	5.62	1998	12.22	6.60	7.86
1973	13.53	8.25	12.33	1986	9.58	4.52	6.16	1999	8.82	4.36	6.12
1974	66.00	11.83	47.20	1987	9.55	5.00	9.49	2000	11.40	4.62	10.20
1975	45.70	11.60	13.37	1988	15.64	7.56	11.15	2001	10.49	6.11	7.39
1976	16.00	7.58	8.03	1989	15.38	9.26	13.16	2002	8.05	4.97	7.61
1977	11.10	6.40	9.40	1990	16.28	9.08	9.37	2003	9.13	5.66	5.67
1978	9.88	6.05	8.43	1991	11.40	7.18	9.00	2004	9.37	5.27	9.04
1979	17.40	7.37	16.31	1992	11.14	7.66	8.41	2005	14.89	7.50	14.68
1980	45.75	15.10	30.58	1993	13.26	7.96	10.77	2006	19.73	14.00	17.90

Source: New York Board of Trade

SUGAR

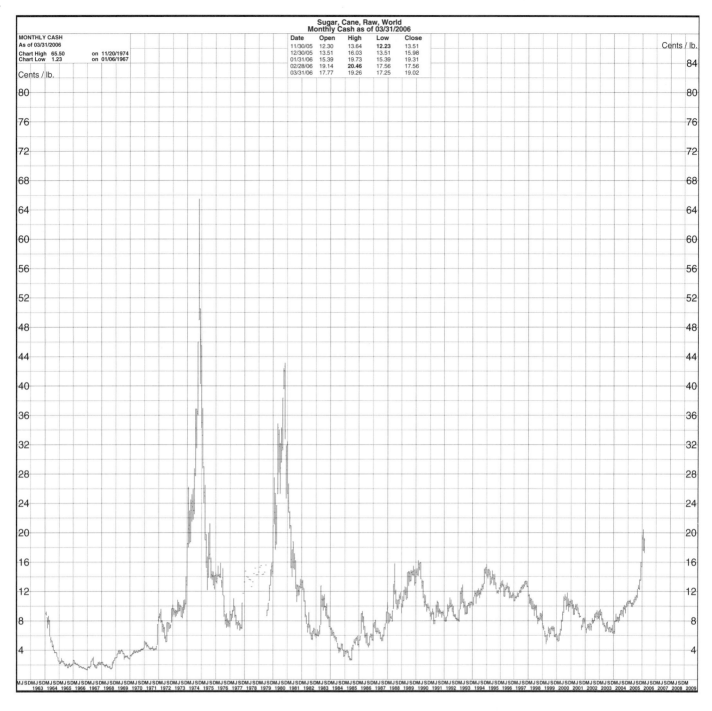

Annual High, Low and Close of Sugar   In Cents per Pound

Year	High	Low	Close	Year	High	Low	Close	Year	High	Low	Close
1968	2.95	1.37	2.95	1981	32.43	10.56	12.96	1994	15.29	10.04	15.02
1969	4.08	2.70	2.80	1982	13.60	5.37	6.20	1995	15.74	11.66	12.48
1970	4.25	2.80	4.25	1983	12.75	5.64	7.23	1996	13.53	11.04	11.82
1971	7.50	3.90	7.50	1984	7.25	3.08	3.16	1997	13.46	10.66	12.70
1972	9.65	5.10	9.65	1985	5.90	2.56	4.75	1998	12.70	7.56	8.54
1973	14.00	8.35	13.40	1986	9.31	4.34	5.43	1999	9.33	4.79	6.13
1974	65.50	12.70	46.30	1987	9.21	5.19	9.21	2000	11.84	5.17	10.64
1975	45.50	12.15	14.15	1988	15.83	7.61	10.93	2001	10.99	6.76	7.96
1976	15.90	7.05	7.45	1989	15.49	9.03	13.14	2002	9.43	6.30	8.42
1977	11.75	6.69	11.75	1990	16.25	9.24	9.42	2003	9.60	6.33	6.35
1978	15.17	12.63	14.25	1991	10.72	7.58	9.04	2004	10.49	6.22	10.45
1979	15.91	8.69	15.47	1992	11.16	7.85	8.23	2005	16.03	9.89	15.98
1980	43.13	14.38	28.55	1993	12.93	7.85	10.52	2006	20.46	15.39	19.02

Source: New York Board of Trade

SUGAR

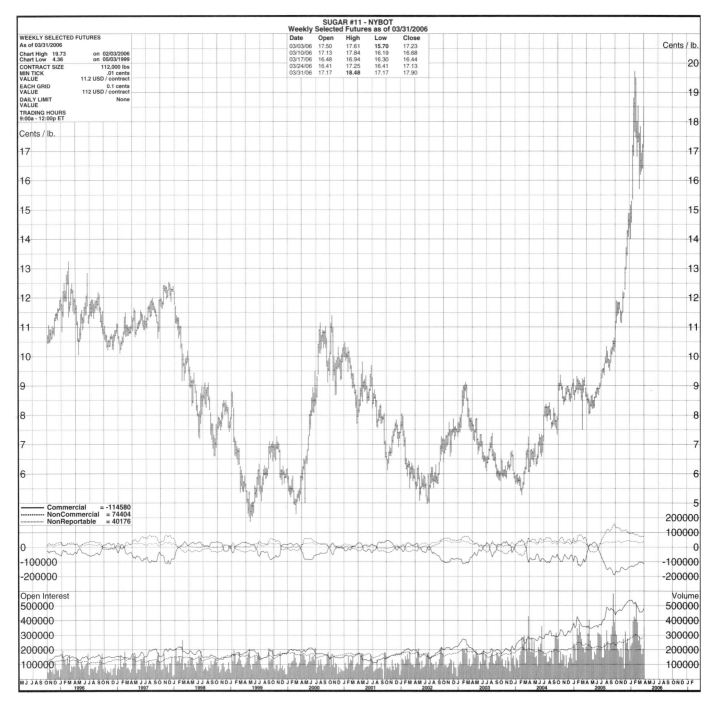

Quarterly High, Low and Close of Sugar Futures   In Cents per Pound

Quarter	High	Low	Close	Quarter	High	Low	Close	Quarter	High	Low	Close
09/1996	12.20	10.99	11.47	12/1999	7.27	5.62	6.12	03/2003	9.13	7.38	7.68
12/1996	11.05	10.21	11.00	03/2000	6.18	4.62	5.90	06/2003	7.90	6.07	6.33
03/1997	11.50	10.10	10.79	06/2000	9.50	5.00	8.50	09/2003	7.39	5.75	6.20
06/1997	11.66	10.65	11.19	09/2000	11.15	8.35	9.77	12/2003	6.79	5.66	5.67
09/1997	12.00	10.60	11.17	12/2000	11.40	8.67	10.20	03/2004	7.26	5.27	6.40
12/1997	12.55	11.59	12.22	03/2001	10.49	7.70	7.75	06/2004	7.43	6.05	7.24
03/1998	12.22	9.15	10.19	06/2001	9.82	7.93	9.59	09/2004	8.55	7.33	8.50
06/1998	10.19	7.20	8.46	09/2001	9.29	6.54	6.70	12/2004	9.37	8.35	9.04
09/1998	9.12	6.60	7.13	12/2001	7.85	6.11	7.39	03/2005	9.33	7.50	8.70
12/1998	8.50	7.15	7.86	03/2002	8.05	5.50	5.93	06/2005	9.42	8.02	9.34
03/1999	8.82	5.35	5.91	06/2002	6.30	4.97	5.91	09/2005	11.20	9.10	10.95
06/1999	6.17	4.36	5.60	09/2002	7.27	5.01	6.89	12/2005	14.89	11.12	14.68
09/1999	7.11	5.05	6.99	12/2002	7.89	6.38	7.61	03/2006	19.73	14.00	17.90

Source: New York Board of Trade

SUGAR

Quarterly High, Low and Close of Sugar   In Cents per Pound

Quarter	High	Low	Close	Quarter	High	Low	Close	Quarter	High	Low	Close
09/1996	13.17	11.04	11.22	12/1999	7.30	5.76	6.13	03/2003	9.60	8.10	8.31
12/1996	11.90	11.08	11.82	03/2000	6.23	5.17	6.23	06/2003	8.29	6.58	6.58
03/1997	11.77	10.66	11.12	06/2000	9.27	6.02	8.85	09/2003	7.89	6.47	7.08
06/1997	12.21	11.24	11.83	09/2000	11.60	9.08	10.01	12/2003	7.43	6.33	6.35
09/1997	12.97	11.79	12.54	12/2000	11.84	9.26	10.64	03/2004	8.96	6.22	8.07
12/1997	13.46	12.56	12.70	03/2001	10.99	8.85	8.85	06/2004	8.92	7.77	8.92
03/1998	12.70	10.16	11.07	06/2001	10.28	8.83	10.25	09/2004	9.83	8.51	9.83
06/1998	10.93	8.65	9.77	09/2001	9.78	8.46	8.64	12/2004	10.49	9.02	10.45
09/1998	10.15	7.56	8.36	12/2001	8.43	6.76	7.96	03/2005	10.86	9.98	10.55
12/1998	9.07	7.92	8.54	03/2002	8.46	6.30	7.47	06/2005	10.88	9.89	10.88
03/1999	9.33	5.82	6.24	06/2002	7.74	6.67	7.19	09/2005	12.26	10.55	12.26
06/1999	7.19	4.79	6.69	09/2002	8.95	7.60	8.61	12/2005	16.03	12.23	15.98
09/1999	7.29	5.74	6.97	12/2002	9.43	8.17	8.42	03/2006	20.46	15.39	19.02

Source: New York Board of Trade

COTTON

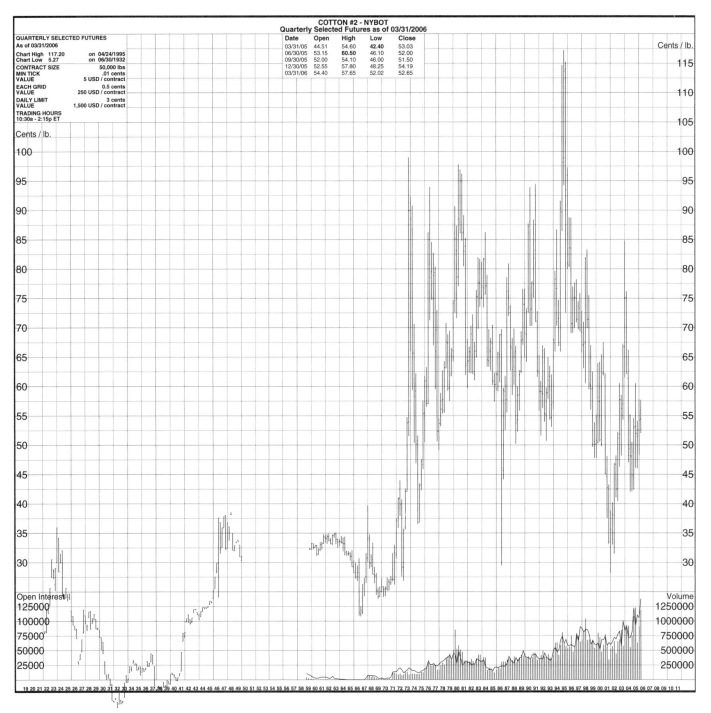

Annual High, Low and Close of Cotton Futures   In Cents per Pound

Year	High	Low	Close	Year	High	Low	Close	Year	High	Low	Close
1929	19.78	16.64	16.64	1942	20.23	18.57	19.67	1955	34.05	32.93	33.70
1930	16.56	9.55	9.55	1943	21.20	19.68	19.68	1956	35.52	31.94	32.02
1931	10.54	5.97	5.99	1944	21.64	20.17	21.55	1957	33.40	31.96	33.40
1932	7.55	5.13	5.85	1945	24.51	21.59	24.51	1958	33.35	32.95	32.95
1933	10.67	5.99	10.05	1946	36.88	24.71	32.38	1959	33.31	29.92	33.21
1934	13.36	11.09	12.94	1947	37.52	31.56	35.79	1960	33.20	31.12	32.12
1935	12.89	10.76	12.02	1948	37.55	31.18	32.17	1961	34.84	31.98	34.12
1936	13.30	11.66	13.17	1949	32.97	29.61	30.30	1962	34.93	32.95	34.64
1937	14.77	8.26	8.58	1950	42.59	31.03	42.59	1963	35.10	32.50	33.60
1938	9.34	8.41	8.74	1951	45.23	34.97	42.23	1964	34.50	31.15	31.43
1939	10.56	8.79	10.56	1952	41.88	33.09	33.09	1965	32.10	28.25	28.25
1940	10.80	9.38	9.86	1953	33.41	32.49	32.63	1966	30.75	20.80	21.80
1941	17.26	10.10	17.26	1954	34.94	33.21	34.94	1967	39.70	21.20	33.95

Source: New York Board of Trade

COTTON

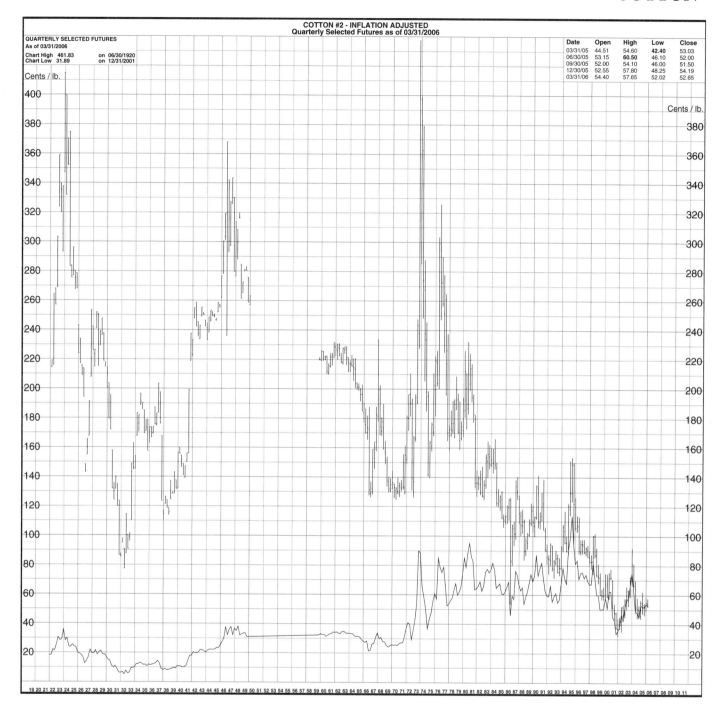

COTTON

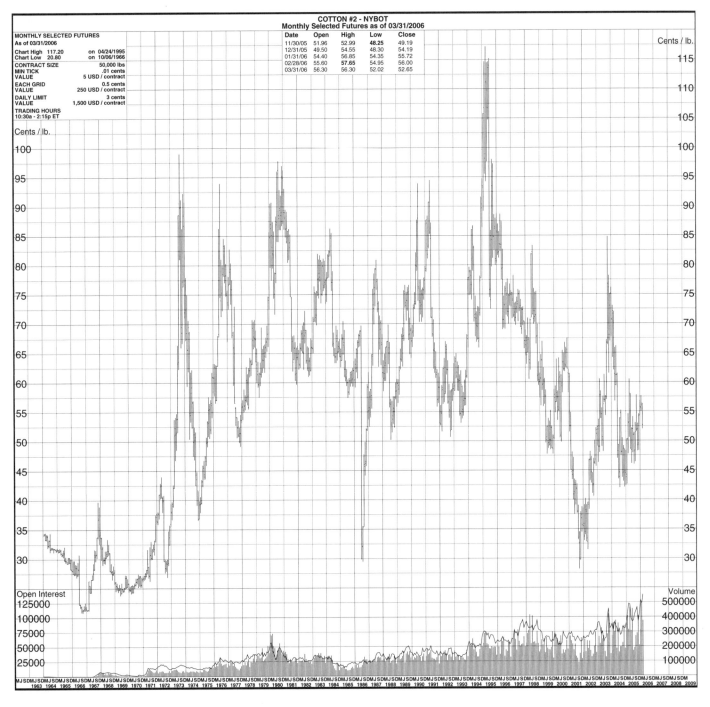

Annual High, Low and Close of Cotton Futures   In Cents per Pound

Year	High	Low	Close	Year	High	Low	Close	Year	High	Low	Close
1968	34.79	26.45	27.67	1981	96.20	59.67	64.27	1994	91.60	65.90	90.35
1969	28.19	23.75	25.75	1982	72.24	61.00	65.92	1995	117.20	72.50	81.05
1970	27.41	24.08	26.58	1983	81.95	64.90	77.11	1996	88.80	69.00	75.15
1971	37.46	26.15	37.20	1984	86.25	63.30	66.17	1997	78.25	65.75	67.07
1972	43.98	26.84	35.50	1985	70.45	57.40	62.06	1998	83.30	59.45	60.36
1973	99.00	35.60	88.50	1986	69.70	29.50	59.28	1999	67.00	47.75	50.74
1974	90.79	36.53	36.80	1987	80.90	52.50	66.76	2000	67.50	49.80	62.28
1975	61.75	36.85	60.87	1988	69.85	50.20	58.49	2001	62.20	28.20	35.59
1976	93.95	56.50	75.20	1989	76.60	55.85	69.07	2002	52.25	31.47	51.16
1977	82.75	49.10	53.69	1990	93.90	64.15	77.80	2003	84.80	46.30	75.07
1978	70.73	53.19	67.57	1991	94.45	55.85	59.17	2004	76.18	42.00	44.77
1979	74.70	57.50	74.06	1992	67.00	50.68	58.86	2005	60.50	42.40	54.19
1980	97.77	71.60	95.12	1993	68.18	53.10	67.88	2006	57.65	52.02	52.65

Source: New York Board of Trade

COTTON

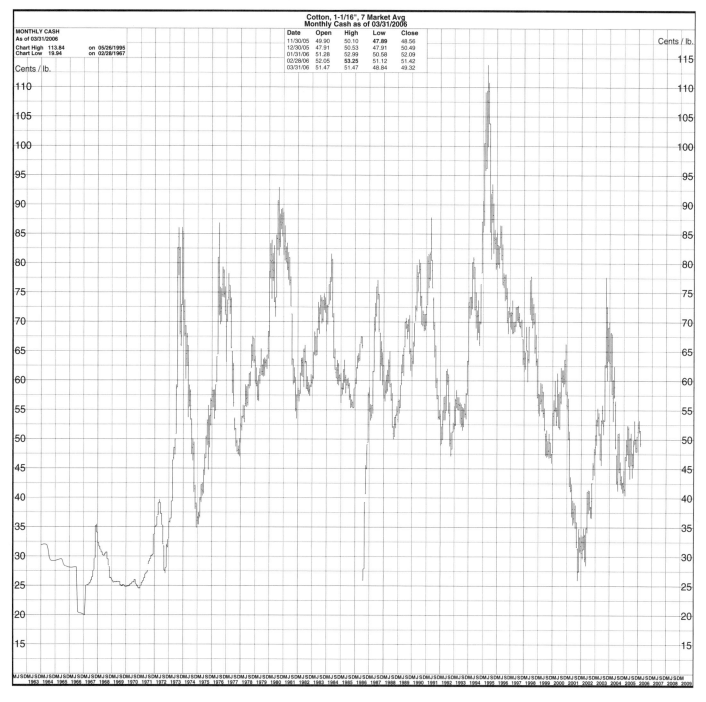

Annual High, Low and Close of Cotton   In Cents per Pound

Year	High	Low	Close	Year	High	Low	Close	Year	High	Low	Close
1968	34.01	26.22	26.25	1981	88.72	53.51	56.65	1994	87.07	62.74	87.07
1969	26.25	24.83	24.83	1982	66.04	56.40	59.68	1995	113.84	78.99	79.86
1970	25.99	24.46	24.53	1983	74.84	59.33	71.61	1996	86.48	68.00	71.43
1971	33.67	24.58	33.67	1984	81.61	59.17	60.31	1997	73.71	62.73	63.84
1972	39.69	27.08	32.81	1985	63.50	55.34	58.60	1998	77.79	57.06	57.19
1973	86.08	33.05	85.27	1986	67.48	25.94	57.60	1999	59.70	45.94	47.53
1974	84.98	34.93	34.93	1987	77.17	53.18	62.48	2000	66.27	47.84	57.70
1975	56.93	35.39	56.48	1988	64.96	50.05	54.71	2001	58.22	25.94	31.10
1976	86.84	53.43	71.87	1989	71.19	52.91	64.41	2002	48.48	28.44	47.83
1977	78.26	47.02	49.62	1990	80.67	60.69	71.29	2003	77.66	45.56	69.09
1978	67.57	49.27	63.47	1991	87.82	53.39	53.55	2004	69.99	40.87	42.67
1979	68.33	56.46	68.33	1992	62.02	47.11	52.11	2005	53.20	40.39	50.49
1980	92.96	67.54	88.37	1993	63.34	51.48	63.34	2006	53.25	48.84	49.32

Source: New York Board of Trade

COTTON

Quarterly High, Low and Close of Cotton Futures   In Cents per Pound

Quarter	High	Low	Close	Quarter	High	Low	Close	Quarter	High	Low	Close
09/1996	77.00	69.08	74.78	12/1999	55.20	47.75	50.74	03/2003	60.55	46.30	57.71
12/1996	77.65	69.90	75.15	03/2000	63.95	50.25	58.14	06/2003	58.50	48.15	56.20
03/1997	78.25	70.85	71.35	06/2000	64.15	50.50	50.88	09/2003	67.25	54.30	66.75
06/1997	74.50	69.70	73.70	09/2000	65.45	49.80	62.25	12/2003	84.80	61.50	75.07
09/1997	75.85	69.40	69.40	12/2000	67.50	61.80	62.28	03/2004	76.18	62.10	62.10
12/1997	72.85	65.75	67.07	03/2001	62.20	45.05	45.09	06/2004	66.19	47.00	48.25
03/1998	70.95	63.05	67.23	06/2001	48.10	37.50	42.75	09/2004	55.20	42.00	48.10
06/1998	81.95	60.50	81.80	09/2001	43.25	33.15	33.50	12/2004	50.50	42.10	44.77
09/1998	83.30	69.90	71.40	12/2001	38.75	28.20	35.59	03/2005	54.60	42.40	53.03
12/1998	75.50	59.45	60.36	03/2002	40.19	33.01	38.16	06/2005	60.50	46.10	52.00
03/1999	67.00	56.00	59.54	06/2002	46.80	31.47	46.80	09/2005	54.10	46.00	51.50
06/1999	62.50	49.65	50.10	09/2002	48.20	41.05	42.40	12/2005	57.80	48.25	54.19
09/1999	53.85	47.75	50.15	12/2002	52.25	40.50	51.16	03/2006	57.65	52.02	52.65

Source: New York Board of Trade

COTTON

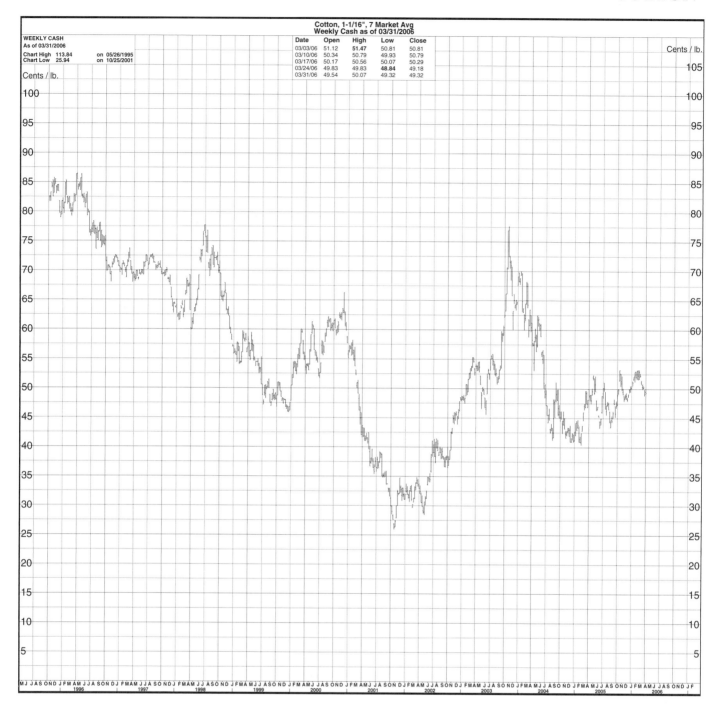

Quarterly High, Low and Close of Cotton In Cents per Pound

Quarter	High	Low	Close	Quarter	High	Low	Close	Quarter	High	Low	Close
09/1996	78.36	73.61	74.42	12/1999	50.99	45.94	47.53	03/2003	55.34	47.47	53.76
12/1996	75.82	68.00	71.43	03/2000	60.04	47.84	55.28	06/2003	54.56	45.56	53.18
03/1997	73.71	68.04	68.04	06/2000	61.30	52.04	52.04	09/2003	62.69	50.80	62.69
06/1997	72.58	68.13	72.48	09/2000	62.25	51.68	59.74	12/2003	77.66	60.06	69.09
09/1997	72.81	69.32	69.32	12/2000	66.27	57.70	57.70	03/2004	69.99	57.71	57.71
12/1997	70.41	62.73	63.84	03/2001	58.22	42.03	42.03	06/2004	62.43	48.43	48.64
03/1998	69.23	61.51	65.20	06/2001	43.63	35.39	37.57	09/2004	51.11	41.19	44.43
06/1998	77.14	59.82	77.14	09/2001	39.24	31.63	31.63	12/2004	46.19	40.87	42.67
09/1998	77.79	69.07	70.01	12/2001	34.73	25.94	31.10	03/2005	49.97	40.39	49.02
12/1998	71.59	57.06	57.19	03/2002	34.86	29.66	33.33	06/2005	52.30	43.28	50.23
03/1999	59.70	54.01	56.56	06/2002	41.04	28.44	41.04	09/2005	51.06	43.46	48.94
06/1999	59.49	51.45	51.78	09/2002	41.39	36.61	38.37	12/2005	53.20	47.89	50.49
09/1999	51.58	46.96	48.01	12/2002	48.48	36.56	47.83	03/2006	53.25	48.84	49.32

Source: New York Board of Trade

LUMBER

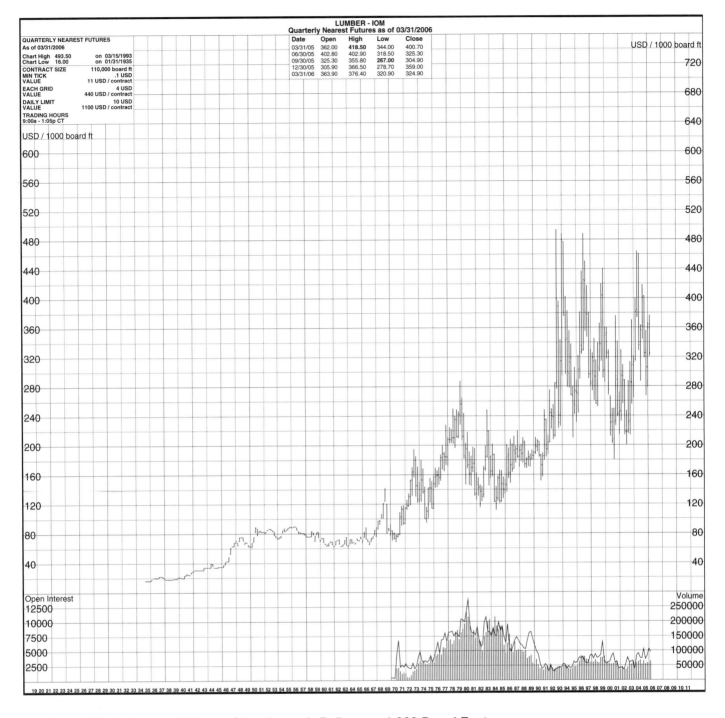

Annual High, Low and Close of Lumber   In Dollars per 1,000 Board Feet

Year	High	Low	Close	Year	High	Low	Close	Year	High	Low	Close
1935	16.00	16.00	16.00	1946	48.31	34.79	48.31	1957	81.99	75.61	75.61
1936	20.29	18.13	20.29	1947	70.59	52.74	70.59	1958	83.20	75.59	78.66
1937	22.05	18.50	18.50	1948	75.24	64.35	70.79	1959	82.00	69.00	71.00
1938	18.01	17.64	18.01	1949	68.31	62.72	63.21	1960	74.00	63.00	65.00
1939	21.07	18.42	21.07	1950	88.95	61.48	78.09	1961	69.00	63.00	63.00
1940	24.99	19.60	24.99	1951	83.94	81.37	81.37	1962	72.00	63.00	63.00
1941	29.20	24.01	29.20	1952	86.58	81.51	84.95	1963	75.00	62.00	64.00
1942	30.38	30.38	30.38	1953	84.67	73.12	73.41	1964	72.00	66.00	67.00
1943	33.81	30.38	33.81	1954	86.85	73.40	83.05	1965	76.00	68.00	71.00
1944	39.20	33.81	33.81	1955	89.32	83.97	88.10	1966	88.00	65.00	69.00
1945	34.79	33.81	34.79	1956	89.92	80.65	80.65	1967	88.00	69.00	88.00

Source: Chicago Mercantile Exchange

LUMBER

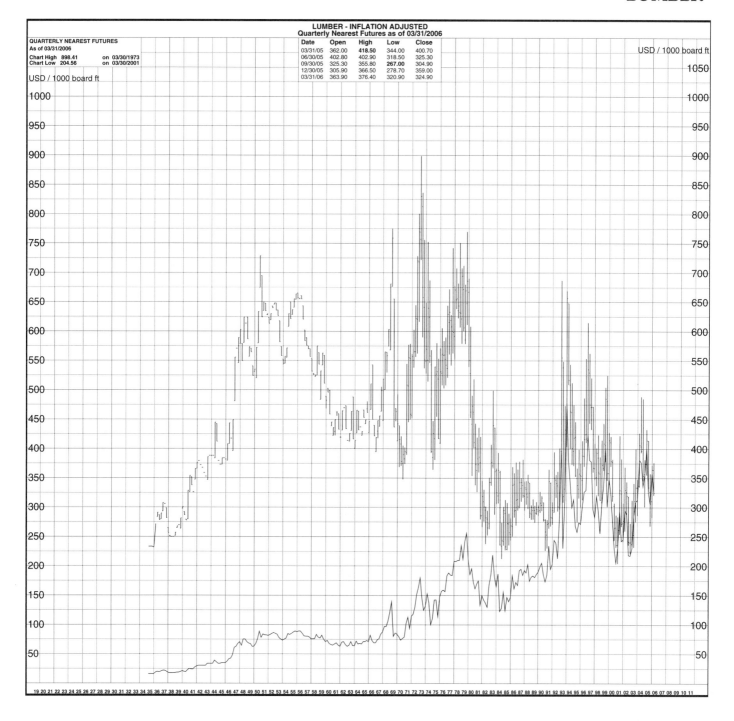

LUMBER

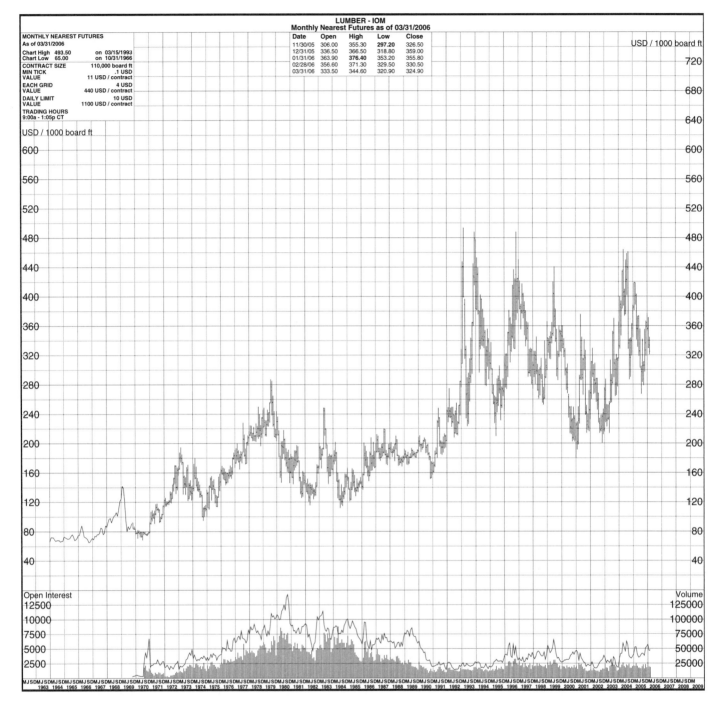

Annual High, Low and Close of Lumber Futures   In Dollars per 1,000 Board Feet

Year	High	Low	Close	Year	High	Low	Close	Year	High	Low	Close
1968	121.00	86.00	121.00	1981	197.60	125.50	149.90	1994	477.00	278.00	313.20
1969	93.00	78.00	83.50	1982	171.40	115.50	167.50	1995	337.90	209.60	271.50
1970	84.00	68.25	78.70	1983	248.50	145.00	165.00	1996	488.00	243.70	424.70
1971	118.20	78.00	114.60	1984	201.90	111.70	155.40	1997	450.50	280.60	282.90
1972	170.30	112.30	163.60	1985	166.50	121.10	147.20	1998	345.40	253.00	305.60
1973	194.70	121.50	131.80	1986	207.90	136.60	167.10	1999	440.80	285.60	349.00
1974	180.00	94.60	110.60	1987	219.70	168.00	192.90	2000	360.50	202.10	205.50
1975	158.70	100.50	147.52	1988	210.30	168.50	181.20	2001	376.00	180.40	245.10
1976	187.50	142.20	183.20	1989	193.50	170.30	189.90	2002	329.80	200.50	217.70
1977	228.00	164.60	208.40	1990	210.70	151.60	173.30	2003	370.40	213.50	312.60
1978	249.90	196.20	235.30	1991	248.30	157.00	203.50	2004	464.00	286.70	356.40
1979	287.30	207.10	211.50	1992	284.70	203.50	284.10	2005	418.50	267.00	359.00
1980	243.80	146.00	161.40	1993	493.50	223.00	479.00	2006	376.40	320.90	324.90

Source: Chicago Mercantile Exchange

LUMBER

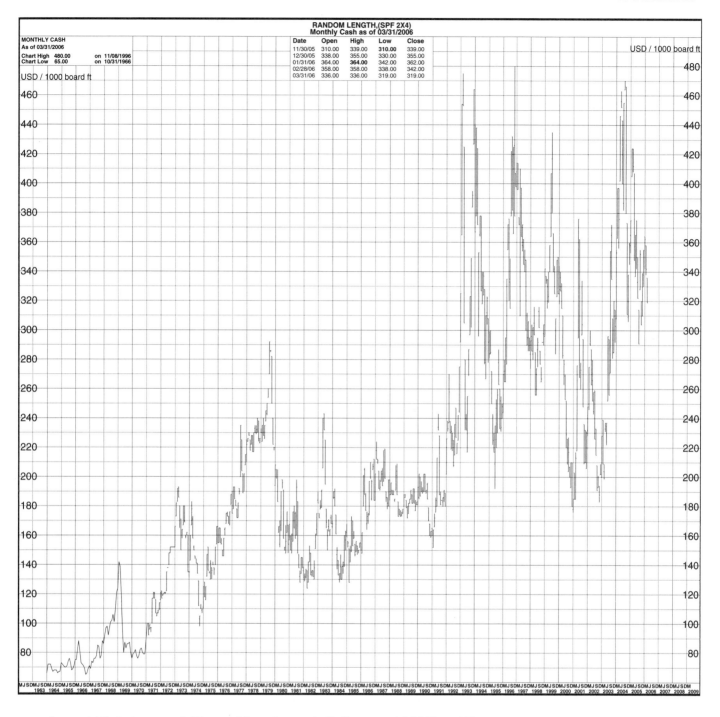

Annual High, Low and Close of Lumber   In Dollars per 1,000 Board Feet

Year	High	Low	Close	Year	High	Low	Close	Year	High	Low	Close
1968	121.00	86.00	121.00	1981	198.00	128.00	138.00	1994	440.00	267.00	292.00
1969	142.00	80.00	80.00	1982	175.00	124.00	175.00	1995	300.00	192.00	248.00
1970	83.00	76.00	79.00	1983	243.00	150.00	168.00	1996	480.00	244.00	398.00
1971	121.00	89.00	114.00	1984	192.00	128.00	163.00	1997	414.00	286.00	290.00
1972	152.00	116.00	152.00	1985	173.00	128.00	155.00	1998	316.00	256.00	304.00
1973	193.00	135.00	135.00	1986	212.00	148.00	184.00	1999	435.00	284.00	325.00
1974	183.00	98.00	110.00	1987	224.00	178.00	198.00	2000	344.00	180.00	180.00
1975	166.00	110.00	166.00	1988	209.00	173.00	178.00	2001	376.00	176.00	231.00
1976	188.00	146.00	188.00	1989	192.00	172.00	183.00	2002	300.00	183.00	202.00
1977	235.00	172.00	215.00	1990	202.00	159.00	163.00	2003	372.00	199.00	303.00
1978	240.00	210.00	226.00	1991	243.00	152.00	180.00	2004	470.00	306.00	358.00
1979	292.00	218.00	220.00	1992	275.00	202.00	275.00	2005	424.00	291.00	355.00
1980	208.00	148.00	154.00	1993	475.00	217.00	464.00	2006	364.00	319.00	319.00

Source: Chicago Mercantile Exchange

LUMBER

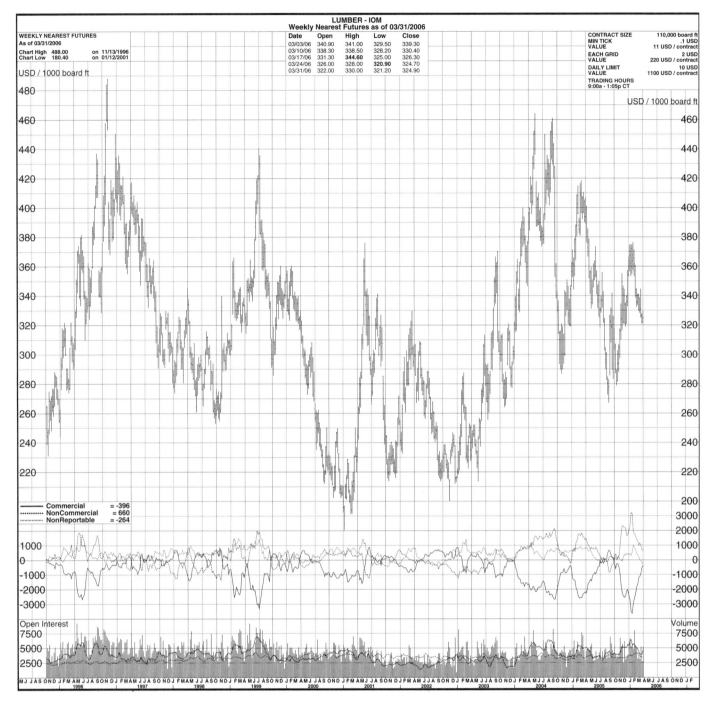

Quarterly High, Low and Close of Lumber Futures   In Dollars per 1,000 Board Feet

Quarter	High	Low	Close	Quarter	High	Low	Close	Quarter	High	Low	Close
09/1996	437.10	324.10	329.40	12/1999	360.50	285.60	349.00	03/2003	287.60	215.60	230.60
12/1996	488.00	328.40	424.70	03/2000	360.50	317.00	324.70	06/2003	313.50	213.50	285.50
03/1997	450.50	355.00	380.50	06/2000	329.50	268.00	275.50	09/2003	370.40	255.50	309.50
06/1997	417.50	347.10	378.00	09/2000	267.00	212.10	230.10	12/2003	321.00	264.10	312.60
09/1997	380.90	290.50	296.60	12/2000	249.70	202.10	205.50	03/2004	400.00	314.00	381.10
12/1997	330.00	280.60	282.90	03/2001	250.10	180.40	230.50	06/2004	464.00	373.50	376.50
03/1998	325.70	273.80	319.00	06/2001	376.00	226.50	293.30	09/2004	461.00	328.40	336.20
06/1998	345.40	260.80	293.40	09/2001	341.50	238.70	242.50	12/2004	363.30	286.70	356.40
09/1998	316.00	255.50	255.80	12/2001	272.00	213.80	245.10	03/2005	418.50	344.00	400.70
12/1998	340.00	253.00	305.60	03/2002	329.80	232.50	295.20	06/2005	402.90	318.50	325.30
03/1999	366.00	299.90	337.50	06/2002	309.30	256.30	287.50	09/2005	355.80	267.00	304.90
06/1999	419.70	314.30	403.60	09/2002	288.50	213.70	218.60	12/2005	366.50	278.70	359.00
09/1999	440.80	291.00	301.00	12/2002	247.00	200.50	217.70	03/2006	376.40	320.90	324.90

Source: Chicago Mercantile Exchange

LUMBER

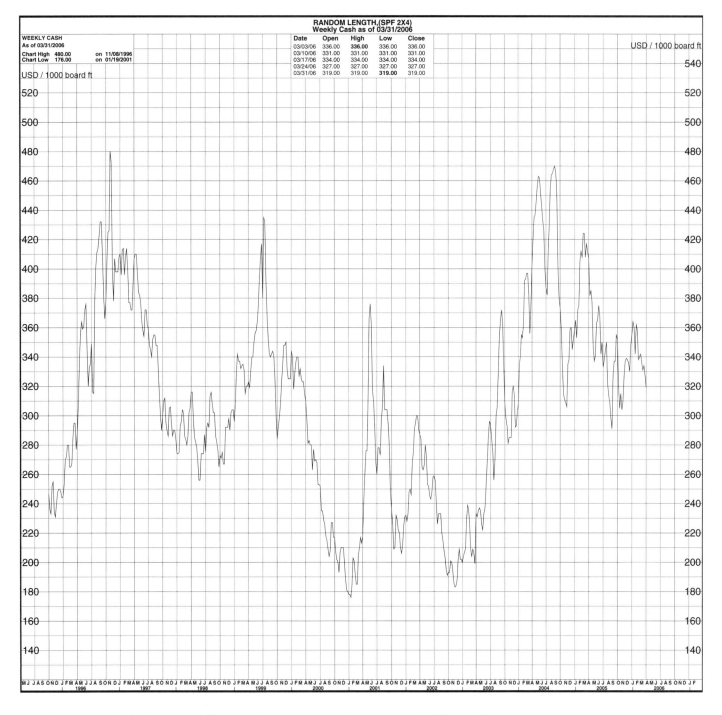

Quarterly High, Low and Close of Lumber   In Dollars per 1,000 Board Feet

Quarter	High	Low	Close	Quarter	High	Low	Close	Quarter	High	Low	Close
09/1996	432.00	315.00	382.00	12/1999	350.00	284.00	325.00	03/2003	239.00	199.00	199.00
12/1996	480.00	366.00	398.00	03/2000	344.00	315.00	315.00	06/2003	296.00	222.00	296.00
03/1997	414.00	372.00	372.00	06/2000	310.00	253.00	253.00	09/2003	372.00	256.00	335.00
06/1997	410.00	310.00	372.00	09/2000	252.00	204.00	217.00	12/2003	320.00	281.00	303.00
09/1997	362.00	300.00	300.00	12/2000	210.00	180.00	180.00	03/2004	397.00	308.00	376.00
12/1997	312.00	286.00	290.00	03/2001	217.00	176.00	213.00	06/2004	463.00	400.00	400.00
03/1998	304.00	274.00	302.00	06/2001	376.00	218.00	268.00	09/2004	470.00	380.00	380.00
06/1998	316.00	256.00	274.00	09/2001	334.00	248.00	248.00	12/2004	373.00	306.00	358.00
09/1998	316.00	275.00	277.00	12/2001	236.00	206.00	231.00	03/2005	424.00	353.00	412.00
12/1998	304.00	265.00	304.00	03/2002	300.00	228.00	290.00	06/2005	407.00	337.00	350.00
03/1999	342.00	296.00	320.00	06/2002	287.00	243.00	258.00	09/2005	355.00	291.00	352.00
06/1999	407.00	319.00	407.00	09/2002	259.00	191.00	191.00	12/2005	355.00	304.00	355.00
09/1999	435.00	325.00	325.00	12/2002	209.00	183.00	202.00	03/2006	364.00	319.00	319.00

Source: Chicago Mercantile Exchange

GRAINS & OILSEEDS

Long-term themes for grain and soybeans prices

The main long-term theme for corn, wheat and soybean prices is that prices on an inflation-adjusted basis have been trending lower since the 1960s. The nearby chart shows real grain and soybean prices back to 1960, with the historical price history adjusted with the CPI so that the price history is in terms of 2006 dollars.

The current soybean price near $5.75 per bushel is about one-third of the $15.40 price (in 2006 dollar terms) seen back in 1960. The current wheat price of $3.50 is about one-quarter of the $14.00 price (in 2006 terms) seen in 1960. The current price of corn near $2.40 is about one-third of the $7.86 price (in 2006 dollars) seen back in 1960.

The downward trend in the inflation-adjusted price of grain and soybean prices attests to the success of the world agriculture market in producing enough food to feed the world's growing population. The downward trend in real grain and soybean prices is a clear rejection of the Malthusian nightmare of global food shortages (Thomas Malthus in 1798 wrote: "the power of the population is indefinitely greater than the power in the earth to produce subsistence for man").

In fact, world agricultural producers are more than keeping up with demand. There is enough supply and competition among producers to force prices downward on an inflation-adjusted basis. Looking ahead, crop yields and output are likely to continue to grow with new advances in genetics and bio-engineering. Indeed, corn production in the central Midwest during the summer of 2005 surprised observers on the upside because drought-resistant corn was able to come through the summer drought much better than any corn in the past could have. In any case, high production and low real prices constitute welcome news for world consumers and for the governments that are ultimately responsible for feeding their people.

The downward trend in real grain and soybean prices, by contrast, offers pain for the world's farmers. Lower grain and soybean prices bring lower revenues to farmers. At the same time, the cost of production continually rises in the form of higher costs for labor, fuel, fertilizer, pesticides, irrigation and other inputs. This has put a tight squeeze on agricultural profits, particularly in the US and other industrialized countries where labor costs are high. Indeed, the squeeze on profitability has driven many small family farms out of business and turned US agriculture into an industry that is increasingly dominated by large corporations. Corporations can achieve lower costs and generate better profitability with economies of scale. Yet there is a sense of sadness as the US loses the family farms that through the 1800s and 1900s helped build the US agricultural industry into the global powerhouse that is it is today.

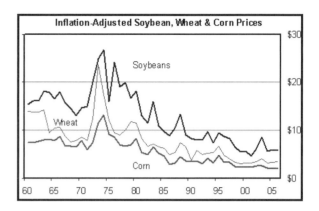

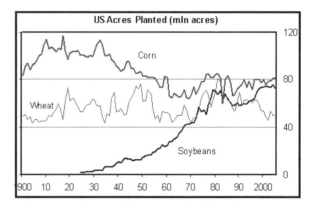

Long-term US acreage planting trends

The nearby chart of US planting trends, which incorporates data from the *CRB Commodity Yearbook 2006*, shows how corn a century ago in 1900 was the dominant crop in the US, with corn acreage about twice that of wheat acreage. Acres planted with wheat have fluctuated in a wide range but have moved basically sideways in the past 100 years and current wheat planting acreage in the US isn't much different than it was back in 1900.

The most striking aspect of the chart is the rise of soybeans as a US crop in the 1930s and 1940s, and particularly after World War II. In fact, US acres planted with soybeans is now only mildly below that of corn. Corn acres fell from 1930 through the 1970s to accommodate the higher acres planted with soybeans.

Soybeans after World War II became known as the "Miracle Bean." Soybean prices were higher than corn prices and soybeans were generally easier to grow. Demand for soybeans quickly surged due in part to the high protein content in soybeans. Soybean meal, with its high protein content, could be used as a super-charger for animal feed. Soybean oil found very strong demand since it is nearly tasteless and colorless and is ideal for use in processed foods.

GRAINS & OILSEEDS

Grain & Soybean Price History

Grain and soybean prices during the 1950s and 1960s were undoubtedly considered at the time to be volatile by farmers and market participants, as prices were buffeted by the usual fluctuations in supply due mainly to the weather. The US government tried to support and stabilize prices in order to support US farmers. However, by modern standards of volatility, grain and soybean prices during the 1950s and 1960s were remarkably stable. That stability ended in the early 1970s, however, when grain and soybean prices soared to levels that were unimaginable at the time.

In theory, the volatility of grain and soybean prices should be trending lower. The rise of South America as a major producer now provides a counter-cyclical harvest supply during the winter season in the Northern Hemisphere and also diversifies world production from a weather standpoint. Yet a quick look at the charts shows that grain and soybean prices remain about as volatile now as they were back in the 1980s and 1990s.

1972 Soviet Grain Purchases and Inflation

Starting in the summer of 1972, grain and soybean prices started to rally sharply. Soybean prices nearly quadrupled from $3.50 per bushel to a record high of $12.90 per bushel (nearest-futures) in early 1973. Corn prices more than tripled from $1.20 per bushel in mid-1972 to nearly $4 in 1973. Wheat prices more than tripled to as high as $6 per bushel from about $1.60 in mid-1972.

The main factor driving that rally was the fact that the Soviet Union secretly purchased 24 million metric tons of wheat, corn, soybeans and soybean meal during the summer of 1972. The Soviets were forced to make the purchases because of domestic shortages caused by poor crops in the Soviet Union starting in 1970. When the Soviet purchases came to light in late 1972 and early 1973, grain and soybean prices soared. Soybean inventories were so depleted that President Nixon had to impose an embargo on soy meal exports so that the US would have enough soy meal for its own needs.

Prices were also boosted in the first half of the 1970s by the general surge in inflation seen in response to the Federal Reserve's expansionary monetary policy and the surge in crude oil prices caused by the Arab Oil Embargo in October 1973 (US inflation reached 11% in 1975).

The surge in grain and soybean prices in 1972-73 caused the US government to drop its former policy of trying to restrict production in order to support prices. Instead, the US government adopted policies encouraging US farmers to plant as much acreage as they could to meet demand. In addition, Brazil during the early 1970s quickly ramped up its soybean production to take advantage of high prices. Brazilian soybean production soared by roughly six-fold from about 2 million metric tons in 1970-71 to 12.5 million metric

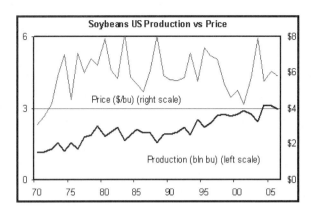

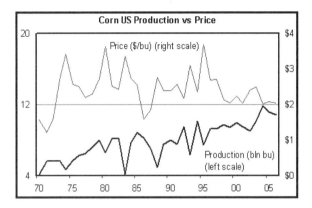

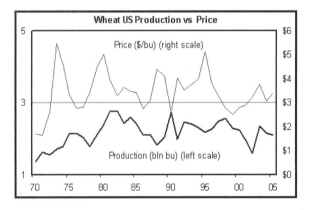

tons just 6 years later in 1976-77. This burst of world production created a production surplus of grain and soybeans, which led to extremely volatile prices through the 1970s.

1979 Soviet Grain Embargo

The Soviet Union in the latter half of 1979 entered the market again to make huge purchases of US grain and soybeans, thus pushing prices higher. However, in January 1980, President Carter announced a grain embargo against the Soviet Union in retaliation for its invasion of

GRAINS & OILSEEDS

Afghanistan. The US government was able to prevent a melt-down in prices in response to the embargo by placing the canceled Soviet grain purchases into government loan and reserve programs. The restrictions on keeping those inventories locked in loan and reserve programs were so tight that the inventories were not available on the open market when a drought occurred during the summer of 1980. The drought, combined with restricted inventories, resulted in a sharp rally in grain and soybean prices in the first three quarters of 1980. Prices then fell sharply in late 1980 and on into 1981-82 after the drought eased and large crops were harvested in 1981 and 1982. There was also the continued overhang from large government inventories. The plunge in grain and soybean prices in 1981-82 caused a farm recession tied to low prices and the buildup of debt that occurred in the 1970s as farmers expanded output.

1983 PIK program and drought

In order to allow huge US government inventories of grain and soybeans caused by the Soviet grain embargo to be worked down, the US government created the PIK program (payment-in-kind) where the government paid farmers in grain for not planting crops. However, this program succeeded in taking acreage out of production just as a severe drought hit during the summer of 1983(caused by El Nino conditions in the Pacific). The combination of the PIK program and the severe drought caused grain and soybean prices to soar in 1983.

Grain and soybean prices then fell sharply in 1984-86 as US production returned to normal and as the PIK grain that was paid to farmers came onto the market. This caused the return of the recessionary conditions for farmers that started in the early 1980s. There were widespread bankruptcies in the agriculture industry during that time. The first Farm Aid concert was organized in 1985 by Willie Nelson, Neil Young and John Mellencamp in an effort to help American farmers during those recessionary times (see www.FarmAid.org).

1988 Drought

Grain and soybean prices soared during spring-1988 as a severe winter drought extended into spring. However, rain in July eased conditions and improved yields, and prices quickly dropped back to more normal levels.

1993 Midwestern Flood

Grain and soybean prices were subdued in 1991-92 with generally favorable weather and big crops in 1992. However, the Midwest was swamped with rain in 1993 in a "500-year flood" that destroyed a significant part of Midwestern crops, thus leading to a moderate rally in grain and soybean prices in 1993.

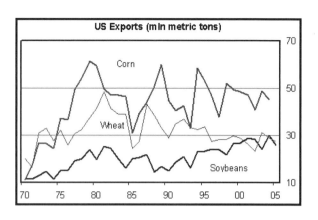

1996-97 demand-driven rally

Grain and soybean prices rallied in 1995-97 mainly because of strong demand by China, which in 1995 became a net importer, rather than an exporter, of corn. China also became a big buyer of vegetable oils and wheat.

1998-2000 bear market

US crops were relatively large during 1997-2002, which led to relatively high inventories and depressed prices in that time frame.

2003-04 spike on poor weather and low inventories

Inventory levels were already headed downward in 2000-02 when a spell of hot and dry weather hit in 2003. The US soybean crop in 2003 was the smallest in 7 years. Demand remained relatively strong, driving inventories to extremely low levels that produced the sharp rally in late 2003 and early-2004. Corn showed a smaller rally in 2003-04 since corn escaped from the hot and dry weather and the 2003-04 crop was large at 10.1 billion bushels.

2004-05 large crops produce subdued prices

The summer of 2004 saw ideal growing conditions with plenty of rain and cool temperatures. The result was record crops for soybeans and corn, and a large wheat crop as well. Crop sizes were large again in 2005 despite drought conditions in the Central Midwest. The result was a buildup in inventories into 2005 with a record carry-over in soybeans and a 12-year high carry-over in corn. The high production and carry-overs resulted in depressed soybean and corn prices in 2004 and 2005.

At the time, there were great concerns about soybean rust disease which first reached the US in late 2004 (see www.usda.gov/soybeanrust). Fortunately, soybean rust turned out to be a minor problem during the summer of 2005 and did not cause any significant yield losses. There were also concerns about the 2005 crop due to dry weather early in the summer, but there was enough rain in August to help the soybean and corn crops finish the season in relatively strong shape. In addition, the corn yield in drought-stricken Illinois was better than expected because of the new drought-resistant corn.

GRAINS & OILSEEDS

Soybeans-Current Situation & Outlook

Soybean prices in the first quarter of 2006 have traded on a weak note near 1-year lows. The market is trying to chew through the record US carry-over of 565 million bushels left over from the 2005 growing season. In addition, export demand has been poor with cumulative export inspections in the marketing year-to-date running 22% below the year-earlier level. Other bearish factors for soybeans include (1) a sharp 7% increase in soybean planting intentions by farmers for spring 2006 since soybean rust did not turn out to be a significant problem in 2005 and since soybeans are a less energy-intensive crop than corn, (2) expectations for a record South American crop during the March-April 2006 harvest which will push the world carry-over to a new record high, and (3) concerns about lower poultry feed demand due to bird flu (because of lower consumer poultry demand and the destruction of commercial poultry flocks). Despite all these bearish factors, soybean prices held their own during Q1-2006 because of buying by commodity index funds and because of mild El Nina ocean conditions in the Pacific which could lead to dry weather during the summer of 2006. In addition, soybean rust could turn out to be a larger problem in 2006 than in 2005.

The long-term 10-year outlook for soybeans is generally favorable, according to USDA projections in the "USDA Agricultural Baseline Projections to 2015" report, released in February 2006. The USDA forecasts increased soybean demand stemming mainly from higher feed demand to meet the world's expanding meat production. However, the USDA says feed demand for soybean meal will be tempered by competition from corn co-products from ethanol production. The USDA believes the planted area for soybeans will slowly decline from 2007 through 2015 as ethanol demand for corn causes farmers to shift acres from soybeans to corn. The USDA expects Brazil's market share of world soybean and soybean meal exports to grow to 45% by 2015 from about 32% in recent years, providing greater competition for US soybean exports. The USDA forecasts a slight rise in soybean prices to the low-$6 per bushel area in the 2007-08 timeframe as the market slowly works down the current high inventory levels. However, the USDA then expects soybean prices to move sideways in the following years as US exports drop off due to South American competition.

Corn-Current Situation and Outlook

Corn prices rallied sharply at the end of March 2006 on the surprise USDA Prospective Plantings report which indicated that US farmers plan to cut planted corn acres sharply by 5%. That added to other recent bullish factors such as (1) a significant improvement in export demand (exports are currently 7% ahead of last year), (2) dry weather in South America which reduced the size of the South American corn crop, and (3) concern about possible dry conditions in the spring and summer of 2006 due to mild El Nina conditions in the Pacific. However, corn prices still have overhead pressure from (1) the huge US carry-over from the 2005 harvest (an 18-year high of 2.351 bln bushels), and (2) concerns about lower poultry feed demand due to spreading bird flu.

The 10-year outlook for corn is favorable mainly because of the increased usage of corn for ethanol production, according to the USDA. The USDA in its "USDA Agricultural Baseline Projections to 2015" forecasts that corn used to produce ethanol in the US will more than double over the next 10 years. The Energy Policy Act of 2005 mandated renewable fuel use in gasoline to reach 7.5 billion gallons by 2012, which would be nearly double the 2005 level. However, corn demand will be undercut somewhat by the fact that a key co-product of ethanol, distillers dried grains (DDG), is used as livestock feed, thus reducing growth of non-ethanol corn demand for feed usage. The USDA believes that human consumption of corn and corn products will increase at only about one-half of the population growth rate because of dietary concerns about products such as high-fructose corn syrup, glucose and dextrose. The USDA expects the planted area for corn in the US to slowly increase over the next 10 years due to increased demand for corn for ethanol production. The USDA's baseline forecast is for slightly higher corn prices in the next 2 years and then for unchanged corn prices near $2.60 per bushel through 2015.

Wheat-Current Situation and Outlook

Wheat prices rallied sharply from December 2005 through early March 2006 because of a severe drought that hit the Southern Plains over the winter of 2005-06 that sharply reduced the winter wheat crop. The "poor" to "very poor" ratings for winter wheat were 87% in Texas and 70% in Oklahoma as of March 2006. However, wheat prices fell in the latter half of March after there was some moisture in the Central and South Plains. In addition, wheat prices were pressured by the facts that (1) wheat production has been on-trend for the last 3 marketing years and the US carry-over is steady near 500 million bushels, and (2) wheat exports have been below-trend in the current marketing year, thus undercutting wheat prices.

The long-term outlook for wheat is relatively stable, according to the "USDA Agricultural Baseline Projections to 2015." The USDA is forecasting that domestic wheat demand will slowly increase at a rate slower than population growth. The USDA expects a slow increase in the use of wheat as animal feed. The USDA expects US exports to increase a bit as income and population in developing countries grow, but that competition from other major wheat producers will keep the US market share constant near 23% through 2015. The USDA is projecting weak wheat prices near-term due to foreign competition, but then a slight increase in wheat prices starting in 2008 due to a small expansion in domestic demand and exports, along with a decline in inventories.

CORN

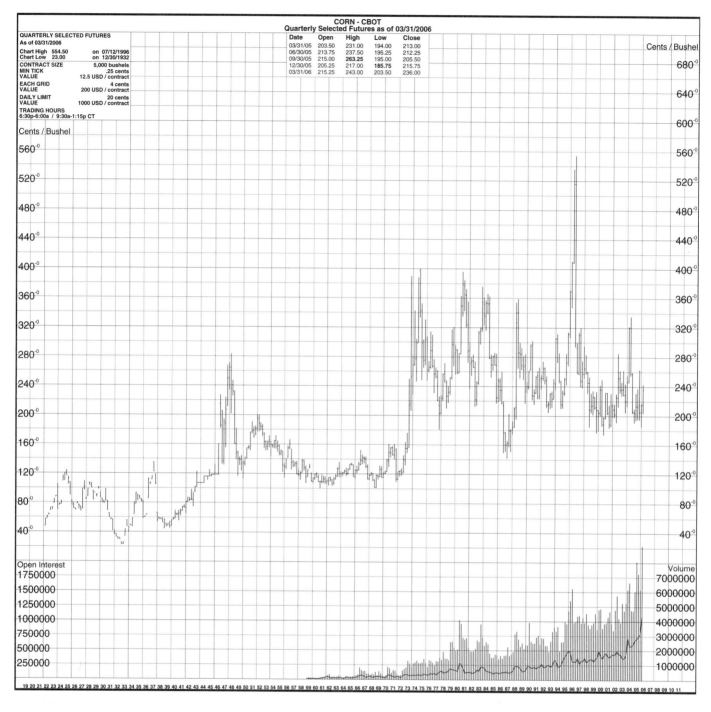

Annual High, Low and Close of Corn Futures In Cents per Bushel

Year	High	Low	Close	Year	High	Low	Close	Year	High	Low	Close
1929	101.25	87.38	87.50	1942	98.25	74.50	94.00	1955	159.13	114.50	128.75
1930	98.88	69.50	69.50	1943	123.00	95.25	107.00	1956	166.50	125.63	135.00
1931	65.38	37.13	37.13	1944	116.00	107.00	116.00	1957	138.38	116.13	118.13
1932	37.00	23.00	23.00	1945	132.25	115.50	118.50	1958	140.25	107.25	115.50
1933	55.88	23.13	46.50	1946	227.00	118.50	135.25	1959	133.25	107.38	113.88
1934	93.25	47.25	93.25	1947	271.00	131.75	264.00	1960	122.00	100.25	109.38
1935	90.75	59.00	59.00	1948	283.38	139.00	147.88	1961	119.13	105.75	110.75
1936	113.50	60.75	107.25	1949	150.50	113.00	134.25	1962	116.25	103.50	112.75
1937	135.00	53.38	56.13	1950	176.25	130.25	176.00	1963	136.00	112.25	120.13
1938	59.25	44.75	57.00	1951	200.13	168.63	195.75	1964	128.50	117.00	126.38
1939	56.25	45.00	56.25	1952	199.63	154.25	163.13	1965	135.25	113.75	124.88
1940	69.50	55.50	65.50	1953	171.88	143.00	159.00	1966	152.38	121.00	142.00
1941	82.00	62.00	81.00	1954	171.75	149.38	157.38	1967	144.00	111.63	118.38

Source: Chicago Board of Trade

CORN

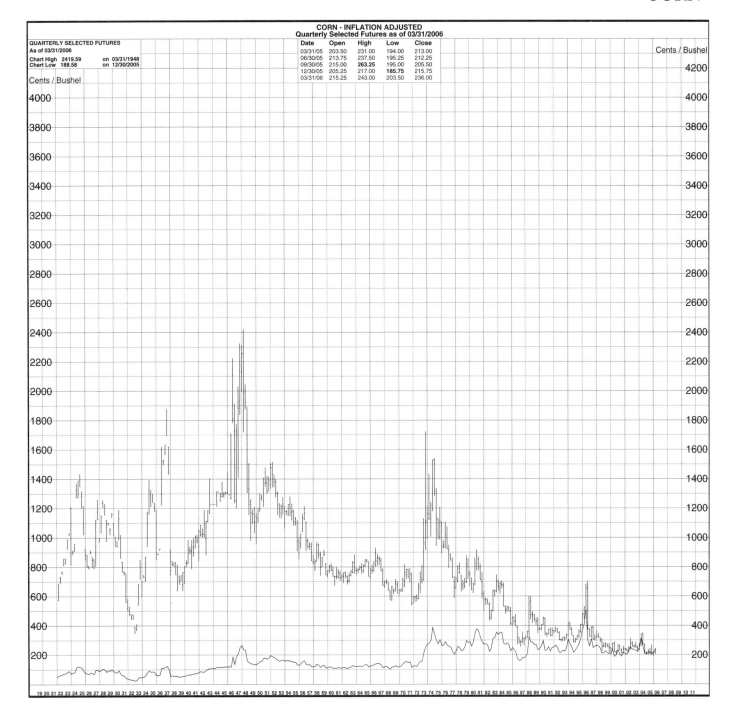

CORN

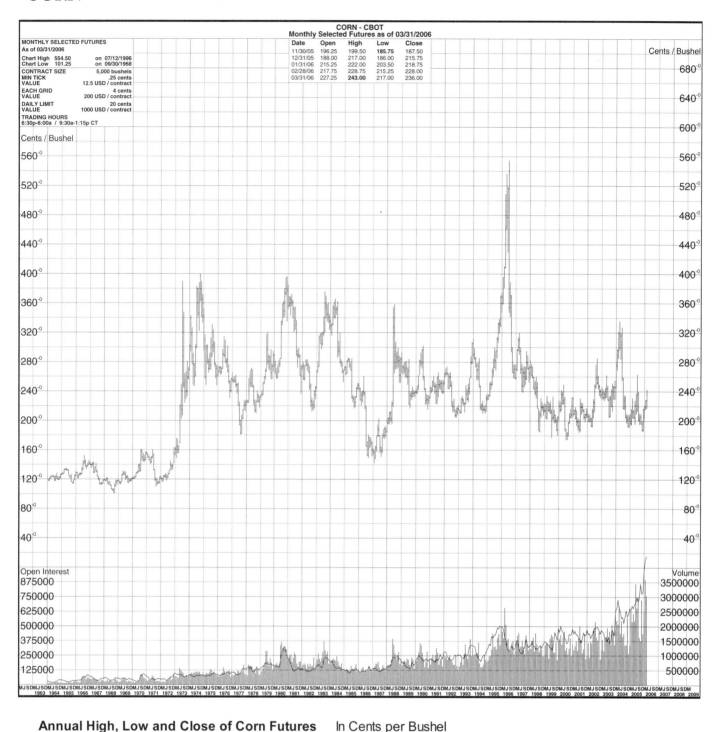

Annual High, Low and Close of Corn Futures   In Cents per Bushel

Year	High	Low	Close	Year	High	Low	Close	Year	High	Low	Close
1968	122.75	101.25	117.88	1981	384.75	236.00	270.50	1994	311.75	210.00	231.00
1969	131.50	112.50	121.13	1982	283.50	212.50	244.75	1995	370.50	227.75	369.25
1970	160.75	120.13	155.50	1983	376.00	242.25	337.25	1996	554.50	257.75	258.25
1971	160.75	109.50	123.38	1984	366.00	252.25	269.25	1997	320.00	238.25	265.00
1972	163.50	116.87	155.00	1985	286.00	217.00	248.25	1998	283.50	185.00	213.50
1973	390.00	148.50	268.75	1986	260.50	149.25	160.00	1999	234.25	177.00	204.50
1974	400.00	246.50	342.00	1987	202.75	142.00	184.75	2000	249.50	174.00	231.75
1975	352.50	247.75	261.50	1988	359.00	184.25	284.50	2001	232.00	184.00	209.00
1976	314.50	230.50	256.50	1989	292.75	217.00	239.75	2002	285.50	191.50	235.75
1977	265.50	180.75	223.75	1990	302.25	215.50	231.75	2003	262.00	204.50	246.00
1978	271.50	209.75	231.75	1991	266.00	223.00	251.50	2004	335.25	191.00	204.75
1979	320.75	228.00	289.50	1992	274.00	204.50	216.50	2005	263.25	185.75	215.75
1980	396.00	256.50	378.00	1993	306.75	210.00	306.00	2006	243.00	203.50	236.00

Source: Chicago Board of Trade

CORN

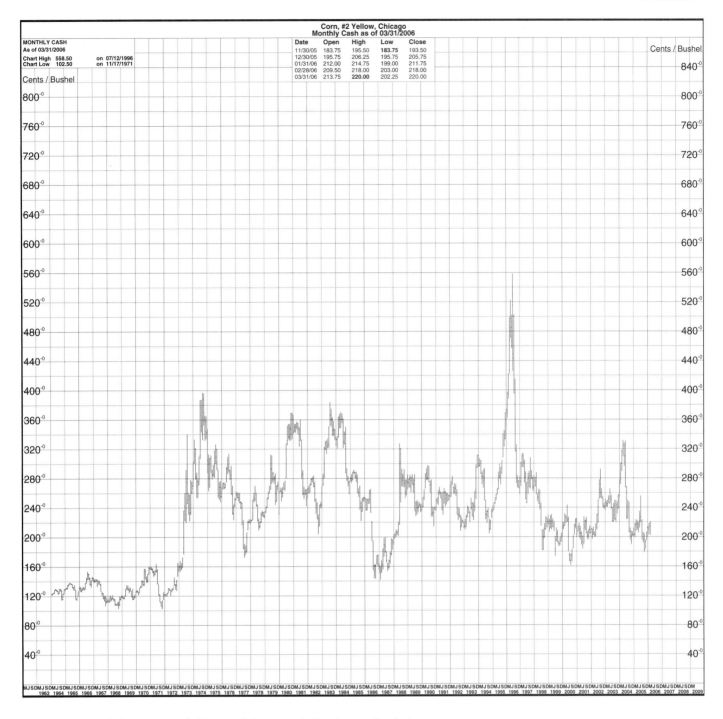

Annual High, Low and Close of Corn   In Cents per Bushel

Year	High	Low	Close	Year	High	Low	Close	Year	High	Low	Close
1968	121.50	103.00	119.00	1981	365.75	242.00	251.50	1994	311.75	204.75	236.00
1969	135.25	115.00	122.25	1982	284.00	204.00	242.75	1995	369.25	233.50	369.25
1970	159.88	121.50	157.50	1983	383.75	240.75	335.25	1996	558.50	266.50	268.25
1971	163.75	102.50	122.25	1984	370.25	259.25	275.25	1997	313.25	245.25	269.00
1972	165.50	120.00	156.25	1985	291.75	221.75	254.25	1998	287.75	182.25	213.25
1973	340.00	153.00	266.50	1986	265.00	143.00	160.00	1999	230.50	173.75	204.50
1974	396.50	253.50	341.75	1987	199.75	141.25	183.25	2000	243.75	161.75	222.25
1975	347.75	247.75	255.50	1988	327.50	189.50	277.50	2001	227.25	183.50	205.00
1976	313.75	223.25	251.75	1989	285.50	228.25	237.25	2002	292.50	196.75	240.75
1977	262.75	172.25	220.25	1990	297.25	214.50	237.75	2003	265.75	219.75	249.00
1978	270.25	209.50	228.75	1991	268.25	230.00	256.50	2004	331.50	189.50	202.75
1979	312.50	225.50	271.00	1992	282.75	208.00	219.00	2005	256.00	179.00	205.75
1980	369.00	230.25	362.00	1993	311.00	210.00	311.00	2006	220.00	199.00	220.00

Chicago.   *Source: Chicago Board of Trade*

CORN

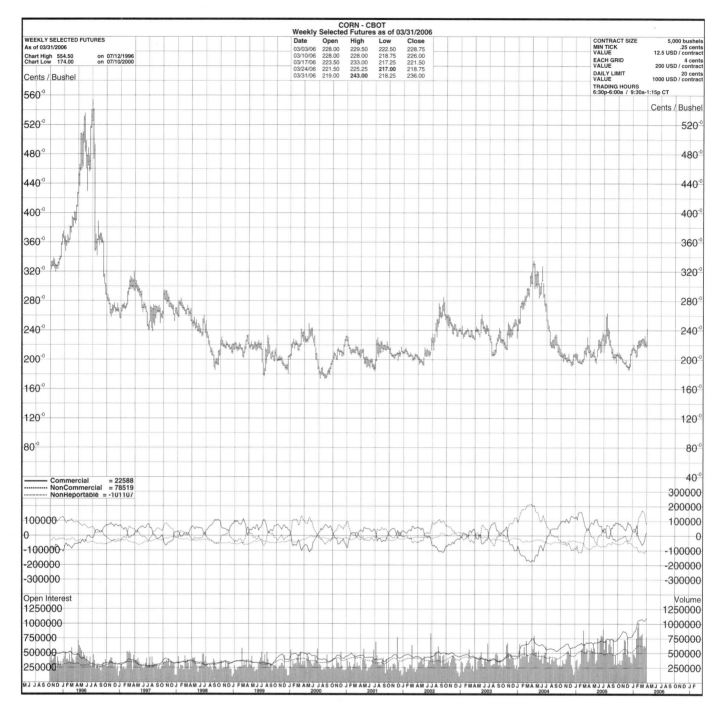

Quarterly High, Low and Close of Corn Futures   In Cents per Bushel

Quarter	High	Low	Close	Quarter	High	Low	Close	Quarter	High	Low	Close
09/1996	554.50	294.00	296.75	12/1999	208.50	180.00	204.50	03/2003	246.00	227.25	236.50
12/1996	300.50	257.75	258.25	03/2000	241.75	200.50	236.00	06/2003	262.00	228.00	228.50
03/1997	314.00	256.00	310.00	06/2000	249.50	186.50	187.50	09/2003	243.50	204.50	220.25
06/1997	320.00	240.00	248.00	09/2000	199.00	174.00	197.75	12/2003	255.00	213.25	246.00
09/1997	275.00	238.25	257.75	12/2000	232.00	196.75	231.75	03/2004	321.75	245.75	320.00
12/1997	295.00	252.00	265.00	03/2001	232.00	202.50	203.25	06/2004	335.25	254.50	257.50
03/1998	283.50	257.00	259.00	06/2001	214.75	184.00	188.75	09/2004	259.25	204.00	205.50
06/1998	260.50	230.75	245.25	09/2001	230.50	185.75	214.50	12/2004	209.50	191.00	204.75
09/1998	253.00	185.00	209.00	12/2001	217.50	198.25	209.00	03/2005	231.00	194.00	213.00
12/1998	231.00	204.50	213.50	03/2002	216.25	198.50	202.50	06/2005	237.50	195.25	212.25
03/1999	234.25	201.75	225.50	06/2002	230.00	191.50	225.50	09/2005	263.25	195.00	205.50
06/1999	226.50	209.50	211.25	09/2002	285.50	212.50	251.50	12/2005	217.00	185.75	215.75
09/1999	233.25	177.00	208.25	12/2002	261.75	231.25	235.75	03/2006	243.00	203.50	236.00

Source: Chicago Board of Trade

CORN

Quarterly High, Low and Close of Corn In Cents per Bushel

Quarter	High	Low	Close	Quarter	High	Low	Close	Quarter	High	Low	Close
09/1996	558.50	316.75	316.75	12/1999	204.75	186.75	204.50	03/2003	251.25	235.50	249.50
12/1996	325.75	266.50	268.25	03/2000	231.75	200.75	229.00	06/2003	265.75	238.50	238.50
03/1997	313.25	258.25	310.00	06/2000	243.75	180.75	180.75	09/2003	250.00	220.50	223.25
06/1997	313.00	251.25	252.00	09/2000	182.75	161.75	182.75	12/2003	257.75	219.75	249.00
09/1997	288.75	245.25	267.75	12/2000	224.75	184.75	222.25	03/2004	318.50	253.00	316.00
12/1997	308.25	263.00	269.00	03/2001	225.00	198.75	205.25	06/2004	331.50	267.50	267.50
03/1998	287.75	259.00	259.00	06/2001	214.25	183.50	188.25	09/2004	268.00	206.50	206.50
06/1998	265.00	236.75	248.25	09/2001	227.25	190.75	204.50	12/2004	212.25	189.50	202.75
09/1998	246.00	182.25	199.00	12/2001	215.25	196.00	205.00	03/2005	223.50	199.00	217.00
12/1998	227.00	198.75	213.25	03/2002	213.50	196.75	202.50	06/2005	234.75	205.50	216.25
03/1999	229.75	207.25	221.00	06/2002	231.00	200.25	230.00	09/2005	256.00	191.75	196.50
06/1999	230.50	208.00	208.25	09/2002	292.50	218.50	253.50	12/2005	206.25	179.00	205.75
09/1999	212.25	173.75	194.25	12/2002	266.00	237.75	240.75	03/2006	220.00	199.00	220.00

Chicago. *Source: Chicago Board of Trade*

OATS

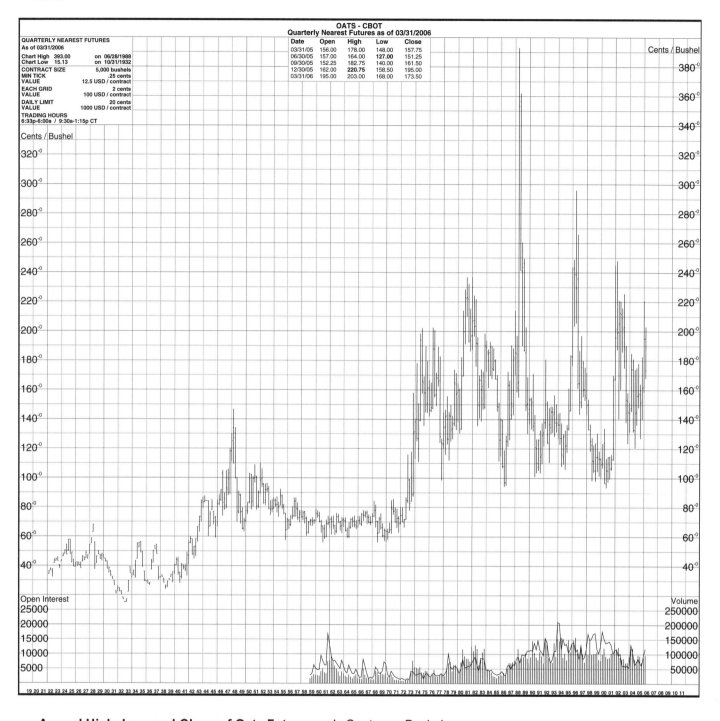

Annual High, Low and Close of Oats Futures   In Cents per Bushel

Year	High	Low	Close	Year	High	Low	Close	Year	High	Low	Close
1929	50.38	43.25	45.00	1942	59.75	44.75	58.50	1955	88.50	57.50	71.50
1930	44.75	32.50	33.63	1943	87.00	56.50	83.25	1956	86.50	65.00	84.00
1931	32.38	20.75	24.75	1944	87.75	60.00	75.00	1957	86.50	69.63	73.25
1932	24.63	15.13	15.38	1945	85.00	59.00	82.00	1958	77.50	60.50	69.38
1933	39.25	15.13	34.63	1946	105.00	74.00	79.00	1959	81.75	67.25	75.63
1934	55.75	31.75	55.75	1947	130.00	79.00	125.00	1960	77.75	56.00	64.88
1935	56.25	29.00	29.25	1948	146.75	70.00	88.13	1961	74.00	58.50	71.75
1936	50.38	26.63	50.38	1949	89.13	63.25	77.63	1962	76.00	61.13	73.63
1937	54.38	30.25	32.38	1950	103.25	75.13	99.50	1963	75.38	62.38	70.75
1938	33.50	24.00	29.25	1951	110.00	78.00	98.38	1964	73.00	59.00	71.63
1939	40.75	28.75	40.75	1952	106.25	81.25	92.50	1965	74.25	65.13	70.88
1940	45.75	28.00	41.25	1953	94.25	74.50	84.25	1966	78.00	67.13	76.13
1941	57.00	33.00	55.50	1954	92.50	73.25	88.00	1967	77.75	67.75	73.88

Source: Chicago Board of Trade

OATS

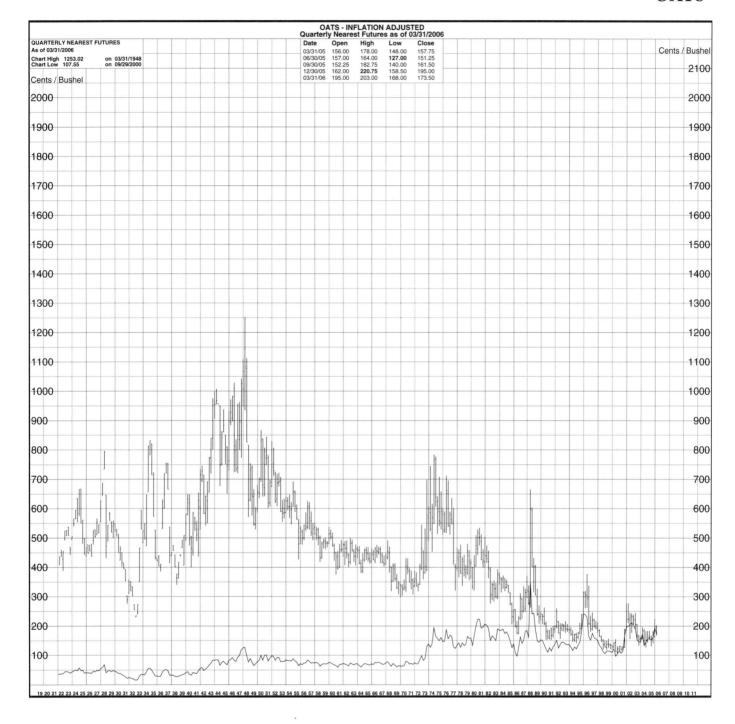

OATS

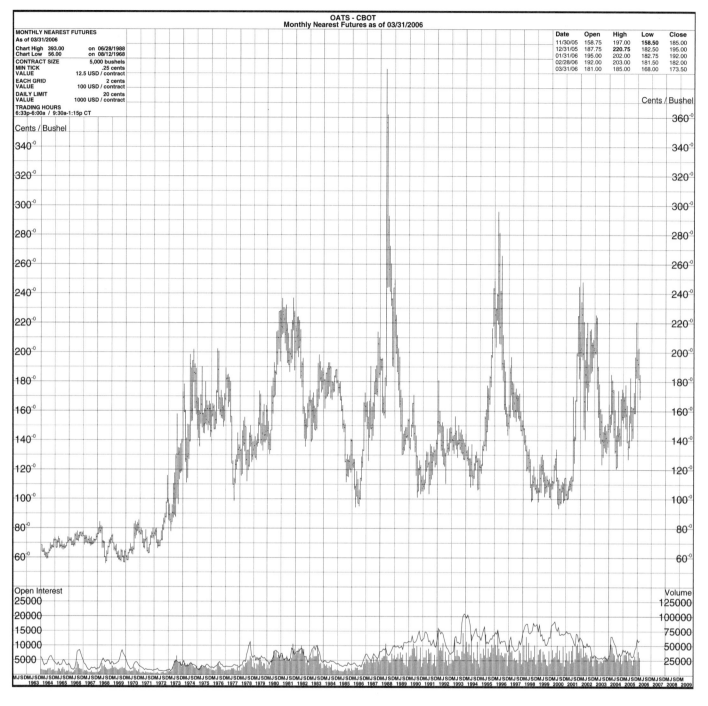

Annual High, Low and Close of Oats Futures   In Cents per Bushel

Year	High	Low	Close	Year	High	Low	Close	Year	High	Low	Close
1968	84.38	56.00	72.13	1981	237.00	186.50	207.00	1994	144.75	106.00	121.75
1969	75.88	56.50	63.63	1982	224.25	135.50	166.75	1995	243.75	117.50	242.25
1970	85.75	58.00	77.25	1983	198.50	138.75	186.00	1996	296.00	143.50	152.00
1971	80.00	62.75	74.50	1984	193.00	161.50	180.25	1997	197.00	143.25	149.75
1972	116.00	66.25	98.75	1985	181.00	111.50	139.50	1998	153.75	98.25	105.50
1973	158.00	77.75	138.50	1986	172.50	94.25	163.25	1999	130.50	98.00	109.25
1974	202.00	111.00	166.00	1987	214.00	126.00	185.50	2000	134.00	93.50	114.25
1975	190.00	135.50	146.25	1988	393.00	155.00	243.75	2001	245.00	99.50	195.75
1976	202.50	145.00	168.50	1989	249.50	130.25	153.50	2002	248.00	140.50	201.75
1977	189.50	98.50	134.50	1990	171.00	101.00	110.25	2003	225.50	123.50	146.25
1978	155.75	112.00	133.00	1991	140.50	103.50	138.00	2004	185.00	120.50	156.25
1979	173.75	126.50	159.75	1992	181.00	110.50	145.25	2005	220.75	127.00	195.00
1980	228.50	130.50	223.00	1993	156.50	126.75	136.75	2006	203.00	168.00	173.50

Source: Chicago Board of Trade

OATS

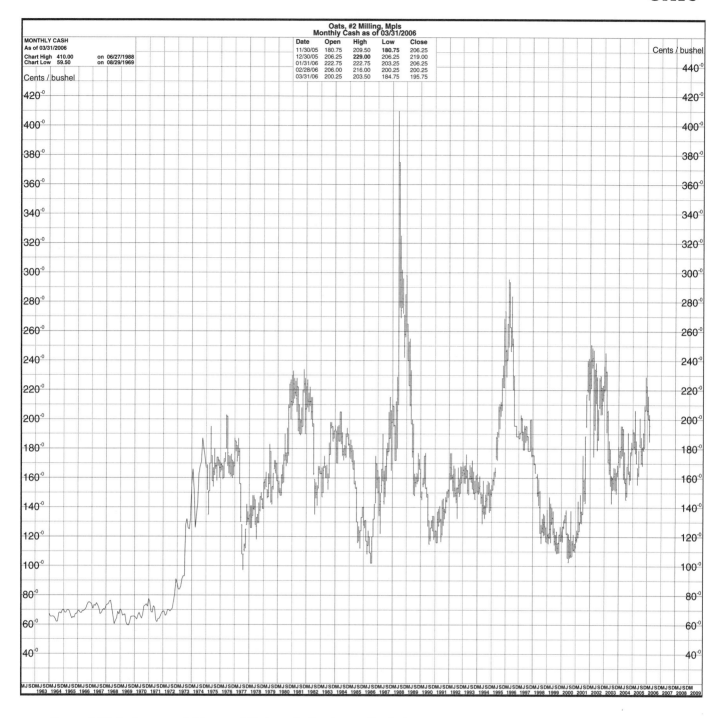

Annual High, Low and Close of Oats   In Cents per Bushel

Year	High	Low	Close	Year	High	Low	Close	Year	High	Low	Close
1968	76.25	60.38	67.00	1981	234.00	189.00	207.00	1994	163.00	128.75	149.00
1969	70.38	59.50	65.63	1982	227.00	135.00	163.00	1995	268.75	147.50	262.25
1970	73.88	63.50	72.25	1983	198.00	147.00	192.00	1996	295.50	188.25	188.25
1971	77.50	61.75	68.00	1984	205.00	170.00	183.00	1997	203.00	174.50	175.50
1972	91.00	66.00	91.00	1985	186.00	112.00	140.00	1998	181.25	115.50	116.75
1973	132.00	84.00	132.00	1986	175.00	102.00	159.00	1999	147.00	108.50	118.25
1974	187.00	126.00	174.00	1987	215.00	122.00	198.00	2000	138.25	102.75	115.25
1975	195.00	135.00	167.00	1988	410.00	172.00	285.00	2001	241.50	112.25	223.75
1976	203.00	159.00	168.00	1989	298.00	148.00	166.00	2002	251.00	174.50	216.75
1977	187.00	97.00	132.00	1990	177.00	115.00	120.00	2003	245.50	142.50	165.25
1978	150.00	118.00	139.00	1991	152.50	116.00	151.50	2004	195.50	145.25	179.75
1979	183.00	139.00	158.00	1992	177.00	132.25	163.75	2005	229.00	155.50	219.00
1980	227.00	146.00	212.00	1993	176.25	145.50	161.75	2006	222.75	184.75	195.75

Minneapolis.   Source: *Chicago Board of Trade*

OATS

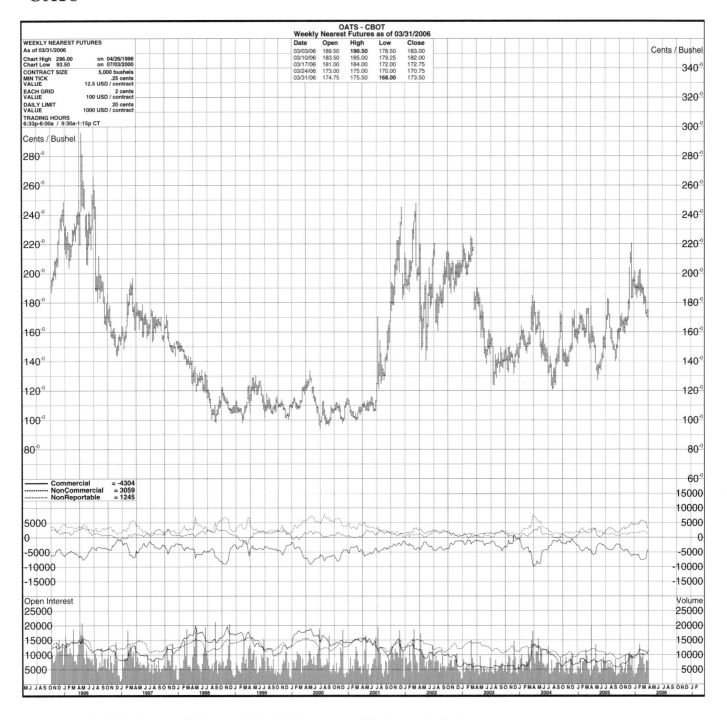

Quarterly High, Low and Close of Oats Futures   In Cents per Bushel

Quarter	High	Low	Close	Quarter	High	Low	Close	Quarter	High	Low	Close
09/1996	266.00	161.00	164.50	12/1999	114.00	100.50	109.25	03/2003	225.50	175.00	189.25
12/1996	187.00	143.50	152.00	03/2000	123.50	107.00	122.25	06/2003	190.50	138.00	153.25
03/1997	197.00	148.00	175.50	06/2000	134.00	96.75	96.75	09/2003	158.25	123.50	145.00
06/1997	180.25	155.50	160.25	09/2000	113.50	93.50	105.25	12/2003	151.75	131.25	146.25
09/1997	175.50	153.00	156.50	12/2000	114.50	97.50	114.25	03/2004	185.00	145.50	174.00
12/1997	172.00	143.25	149.75	03/2001	114.75	99.50	106.50	06/2004	181.25	131.50	132.75
03/1998	153.75	133.00	133.50	06/2001	116.00	105.50	113.00	09/2004	174.00	120.50	144.25
06/1998	136.75	118.25	125.25	09/2001	170.00	112.50	167.00	12/2004	175.00	136.25	156.25
09/1998	127.50	98.25	112.00	12/2001	245.00	166.75	195.75	03/2005	178.00	148.00	157.75
12/1998	122.50	104.00	105.50	03/2002	248.00	187.50	199.00	06/2005	164.00	127.00	151.25
03/1999	124.00	98.00	114.25	06/2002	221.00	140.50	205.50	09/2005	182.75	140.00	161.50
06/1999	130.50	104.50	114.50	09/2002	220.50	160.50	211.75	12/2005	220.75	158.50	195.00
09/1999	118.50	101.50	113.25	12/2002	216.00	186.00	201.75	03/2006	203.00	168.00	173.50

Source: Chicago Board of Trade

OATS

Quarterly High, Low and Close of Oats   In Cents per Bushel

Quarter	High	Low	Close	Quarter	High	Low	Close	Quarter	High	Low	Close
09/1996	283.75	195.50	195.50	12/1999	127.00	108.75	118.25	03/2003	245.50	191.00	205.25
12/1996	195.50	188.25	188.25	03/2000	131.25	116.50	131.25	06/2003	206.25	155.00	155.00
03/1997	203.00	187.00	201.00	06/2000	138.25	105.75	105.75	09/2003	167.25	142.50	161.50
06/1997	201.00	179.25	193.50	09/2000	137.75	102.75	106.25	12/2003	169.00	149.25	165.25
09/1997	195.25	178.50	178.50	12/2000	121.50	106.75	115.25	03/2004	195.50	167.50	181.50
12/1997	200.00	174.50	175.50	03/2001	144.25	112.25	122.00	06/2004	195.25	157.00	157.00
03/1998	181.25	163.50	163.50	06/2001	148.75	123.75	135.50	09/2004	191.00	145.25	163.25
06/1998	163.00	141.25	150.75	09/2001	188.50	135.50	188.50	12/2004	184.50	155.75	179.75
09/1998	151.50	115.50	126.00	12/2001	241.50	194.75	223.75	03/2005	206.25	177.00	177.00
12/1998	135.75	116.75	116.75	03/2002	251.00	217.75	237.00	06/2005	185.50	155.50	168.00
03/1999	147.00	115.25	125.25	06/2002	247.25	174.50	233.00	09/2005	201.00	168.25	180.50
06/1999	142.75	116.00	123.50	09/2002	229.00	178.75	226.75	12/2005	229.00	178.75	219.00
09/1999	126.00	108.50	115.25	12/2002	229.50	203.25	216.75	03/2006	222.75	184.75	195.75

Minneapolis.   Source: Chicago Board of Trade

RICE

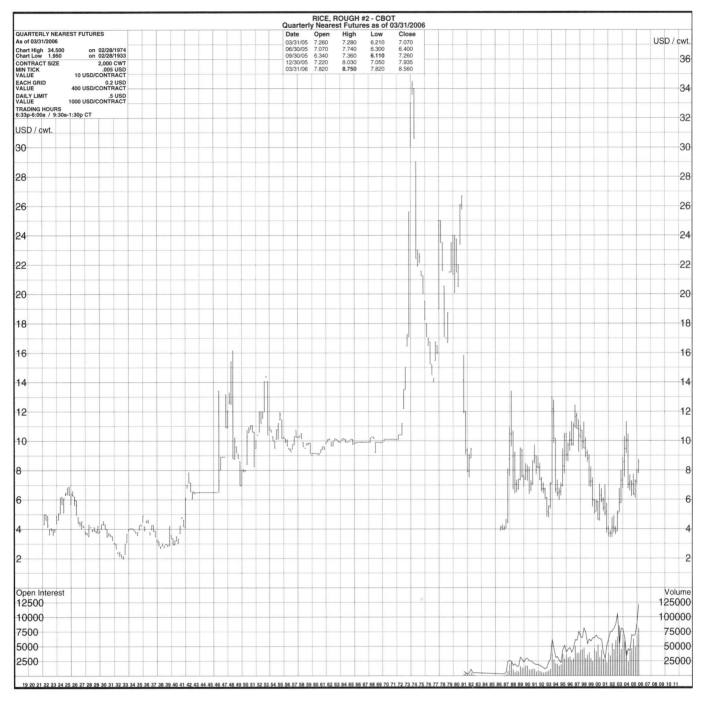

Annual High, Low and Close of Rice   In Dollars per Cwt.

Year	High	Low	Close	Year	High	Low	Close	Year	High	Low	Close
1929	4.25	3.72	3.84	1942	7.84	6.05	6.53	1955	11.95	10.10	10.20
1930	4.56	3.46	3.46	1943	6.55	6.40	6.50	1956	10.15	9.25	9.25
1931	3.75	3.00	3.06	1944	6.50	6.50	6.50	1957	10.70	9.45	10.25
1932	2.97	2.08	2.08	1945	6.50	6.50	6.50	1958	10.50	9.50	9.50
1933	3.99	1.95	3.99	1946	13.40	6.50	8.90	1959	9.85	9.05	9.15
1934	4.03	3.72	3.72	1947	13.15	8.90	12.05	1960	9.15	9.05	9.15
1935	4.90	3.56	4.90	1948	16.15	8.75	10.20	1961	9.90	9.20	9.90
1936	4.65	3.61	3.61	1949	9.60	6.95	8.00	1962	10.15	9.65	9.95
1937	4.26	3.12	3.12	1950	10.95	7.90	10.75	1963	10.15	9.90	9.90
1938	3.19	2.66	2.85	1951	11.05	8.25	10.00	1964	10.15	9.90	9.90
1939	4.19	2.82	3.38	1952	12.00	10.40	12.00	1965	10.10	9.75	9.85
1940	3.52	2.93	3.32	1953	14.40	10.40	10.90	1966	9.95	9.85	9.90
1941	6.12	3.71	6.12	1954	10.75	9.50	10.75	1967	9.90	9.90	9.90

Louisiana, Long grain.   *Source: U.S. Department of Agriculture*

RICE

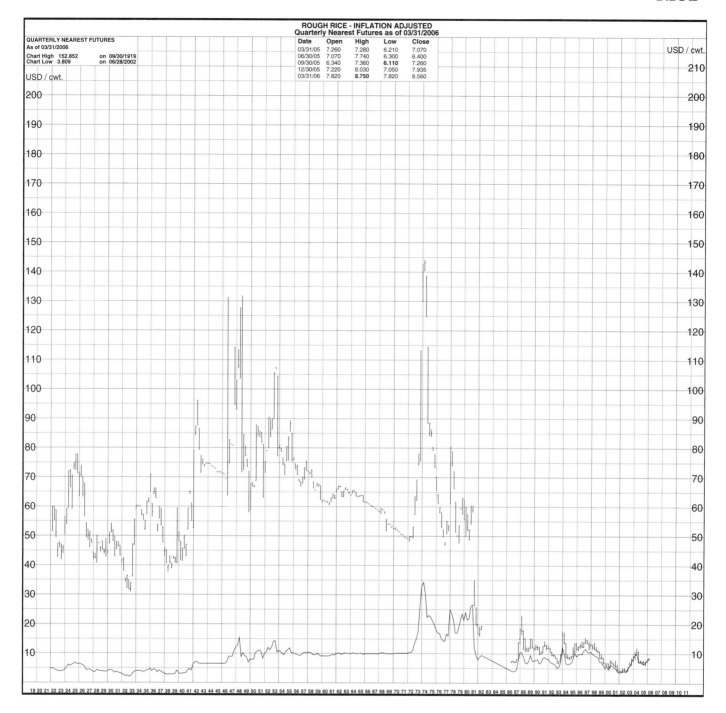

RICE

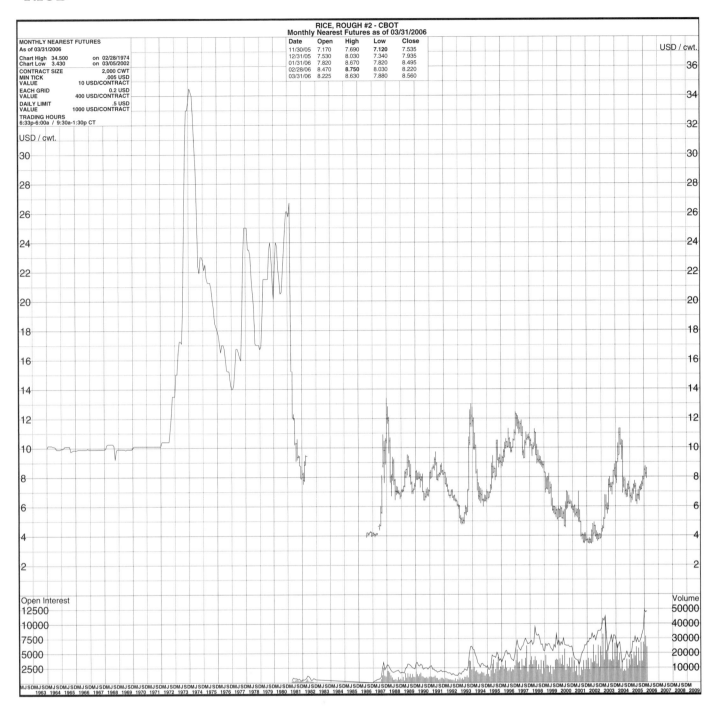

Annual High, Low and Close of Rice Futures — In Dollars per Cwt.

Year	High	Low	Close	Year	High	Low	Close	Year	High	Low	Close
1968	10.25	9.20	9.90	1981	28.00	20.85	20.85	1994	12.795	5.970	6.570
1969	9.90	9.85	9.90	1982	19.60	16.60	18.40	1995	10.520	6.260	9.030
1970	10.10	10.00	10.10	1983	19.00	17.50	19.00	1996	11.330	8.600	11.030
1971	10.10	10.10	10.10	1984	19.00	18.00	18.00	1997	12.450	9.250	10.720
1972	13.50	10.10	13.50	1985	18.00	17.25	17.25	1998	11.300	8.560	8.790
1973	33.00	13.50	33.00	1986	4.320	3.905	3.950	1999	9.070	5.060	5.140
1974	34.50	21.90	23.00	1987	10.920	3.900	10.460	2000	7.060	4.540	5.920
1975	22.75	18.25	18.25	1988	13.400	6.430	6.670	2001	7.030	3.460	3.690
1976	18.00	14.50	14.50	1989	9.520	6.670	7.430	2002	4.920	3.430	3.850
1977	25.00	14.00	25.00	1990	8.470	6.380	7.070	2003	8.880	3.840	8.540
1978	25.00	17.00	17.00	1991	9.730	7.020	8.190	2004	11.320	6.580	7.180
1979	24.00	16.70	21.35	1992	8.500	6.050	6.070	2005	8.030	6.110	7.935
1980	26.10	20.10	26.10	1993	13.000	4.760	12.200	2006	8.750	7.820	8.560

Source: *Chicago Board of Trade*

RICE

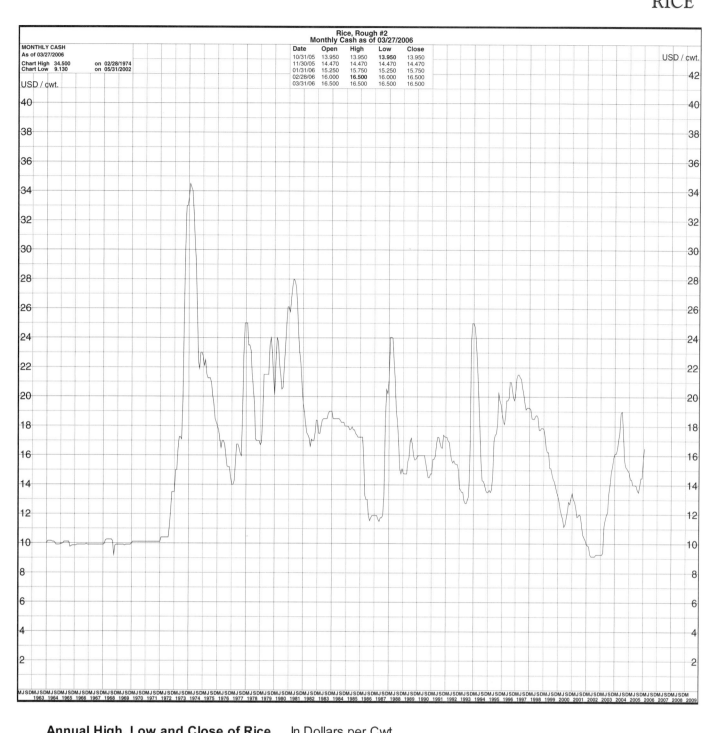

Annual High, Low and Close of Rice   In Dollars per Cwt.

Year	High	Low	Close	Year	High	Low	Close	Year	High	Low	Close
1968	10.25	9.20	9.90	1981	28.00	20.85	20.85	1994	25.00	13.50	13.50
1969	9.90	9.85	9.90	1982	19.60	16.60	18.40	1995	20.25	13.50	19.50
1970	10.10	10.00	10.10	1983	19.00	17.50	19.00	1996	21.00	18.13	19.75
1971	10.10	10.10	10.10	1984	19.00	18.00	18.00	1997	21.50	19.13	19.25
1972	13.50	10.10	13.50	1985	18.00	17.25	17.25	1998	19.25	17.75	17.88
1973	33.00	13.50	33.00	1986	17.25	11.55	11.90	1999	17.81	13.50	13.50
1974	34.50	21.90	23.00	1987	20.50	11.50	20.20	2000	13.25	11.13	13.13
1975	22.75	18.25	18.25	1988	24.05	14.75	15.10	2001	13.45	10.25	10.25
1976	18.00	14.50	14.50	1989	17.20	14.75	15.75	2002	9.97	9.13	9.25
1977	25.00	14.00	25.00	1990	16.00	14.50	14.75	2003	15.85	9.25	15.85
1978	25.00	17.00	17.00	1991	17.40	14.75	17.30	2004	19.00	15.00	15.00
1979	24.00	16.70	21.35	1992	17.25	15.05	15.05	2005	14.85	13.50	14.47
1980	26.10	20.10	26.10	1993	25.00	12.75	25.00	2006	16.50	15.25	16.50

Louisiana, Long grain.   *Source: U.S. Department of Agriculture*

RICE

Quarterly High, Low and Close of Rice Futures   In Dollars per Cwt.

Quarter	High	Low	Close	Quarter	High	Low	Close	Quarter	High	Low	Close
09/1996	11.330	9.650	9.780	12/1999	5.970	5.060	5.140	03/2003	5.220	3.840	5.120
12/1996	11.230	9.650	11.030	03/2000	5.990	5.180	5.835	06/2003	6.780	5.130	5.800
03/1997	12.450	10.860	11.650	06/2000	5.890	4.600	4.670	09/2003	8.000	5.750	7.310
06/1997	11.910	10.800	10.820	09/2000	7.060	4.540	6.310	12/2003	8.880	6.770	8.540
09/1997	11.450	9.250	10.365	12/2000	6.750	5.800	5.920	03/2004	10.300	7.540	9.450
12/1997	11.080	10.130	10.720	03/2001	6.120	5.220	5.400	06/2004	11.320	9.140	10.060
03/1998	10.730	9.410	9.940	06/2001	7.030	4.900	5.100	09/2004	10.470	6.760	7.040
06/1998	11.300	9.480	9.490	09/2001	5.750	3.720	4.050	12/2004	7.690	6.580	7.180
09/1998	10.220	8.880	9.170	12/2001	4.190	3.460	3.690	03/2005	7.280	6.210	7.070
12/1998	9.390	8.560	8.790	03/2002	3.920	3.430	3.720	06/2005	7.740	6.300	6.400
03/1999	9.070	6.910	7.235	06/2002	4.785	3.430	4.080	09/2005	7.360	6.110	7.260
06/1999	8.250	6.850	7.260	09/2002	4.920	3.730	4.035	12/2005	8.030	7.050	7.935
09/1999	7.500	5.500	5.970	12/2002	4.170	3.610	3.850	03/2006	8.750	7.820	8.560

Source: Chicago Board of Trade

RICE

Quarterly High, Low and Close of Rice   In Dollars per Cwt.

Quarter	High	Low	Close	Quarter	High	Low	Close	Quarter	High	Low	Close
09/1996	21.00	19.90	21.00	12/1999	14.22	13.50	13.50	03/2003	9.38	9.25	9.38
12/1996	20.50	19.75	19.75	03/2000	13.25	12.33	12.33	06/2003	11.95	11.19	11.95
03/1997	21.50	20.31	21.50	06/2000	11.94	11.13	11.13	09/2003	14.00	12.13	14.00
06/1997	21.50	21.20	21.20	09/2000	12.22	11.30	12.22	12/2003	15.85	14.88	15.85
09/1997	20.63	19.60	19.60	12/2000	13.13	12.69	13.13	03/2004	16.40	16.13	16.40
12/1997	19.25	19.13	19.25	03/2001	13.45	12.88	12.88	06/2004	18.90	17.03	18.90
03/1998	19.25	18.52	18.52	06/2001	12.45	11.81	11.88	09/2004	19.00	15.69	15.69
06/1998	18.70	18.50	18.70	09/2001	12.00	11.16	11.16	12/2004	15.25	15.00	15.00
09/1998	18.75	17.75	17.75	12/2001	10.59	10.25	10.25	03/2005	14.85	14.38	14.38
12/1998	17.88	17.75	17.88	03/2002	9.97	9.81	9.81	06/2005	14.00	14.00	14.00
03/1999	17.81	16.48	16.48	06/2002	9.25	9.13	9.13	09/2005	13.94	13.50	13.50
06/1999	16.22	15.15	15.15	09/2002	9.25	9.13	9.25	12/2005	14.75	13.95	14.75
09/1999	15.13	14.38	14.38	12/2002	9.25	9.25	9.25	03/2006	16.50	15.25	16.50

Louisiana, Long grain.   *Source: U.S. Department of Agriculture*

WHEAT, CHICAGO

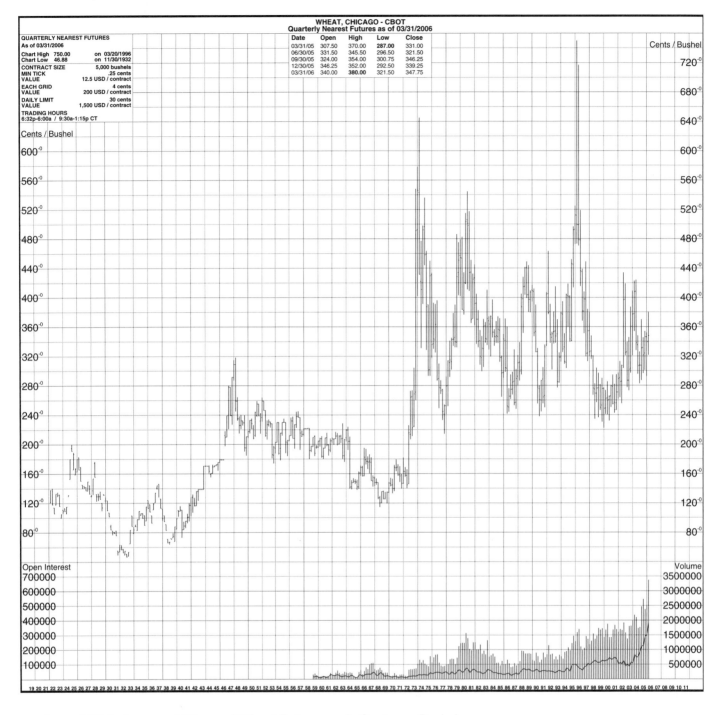

Annual High, Low and Close of Wheat Futures   In Cents per Bushel

Year	High	Low	Close	Year	High	Low	Close	Year	High	Low	Close
1929	136.13	109.50	128.75	1942	138.75	107.00	138.75	1955	235.00	184.00	211.75
1930	123.75	76.63	79.75	1943	170.50	138.75	170.50	1956	244.50	194.00	238.00
1931	82.75	49.38	58.00	1944	172.38	155.25	169.50	1957	245.00	192.50	221.50
1932	62.63	46.88	46.88	1945	180.00	164.25	179.00	1958	222.00	179.75	197.50
1933	102.88	48.25	83.88	1946	239.00	179.00	239.00	1959	212.00	184.00	204.25
1934	109.13	83.00	105.88	1947	315.00	221.00	309.00	1960	211.00	180.00	208.63
1935	124.00	90.00	113.00	1948	318.50	215.00	232.25	1961	215.75	184.63	207.25
1936	134.00	93.00	134.00	1949	239.50	184.75	217.75	1962	217.00	198.50	211.13
1937	146.00	96.00	99.00	1950	244.50	207.00	243.75	1963	228.63	176.00	219.50
1938	103.00	64.00	67.00	1951	263.50	214.75	259.00	1964	224.00	138.75	149.88
1939	99.00	68.00	99.00	1952	259.00	206.50	230.75	1965	170.75	138.00	168.63
1940	116.00	73.00	89.00	1953	230.75	174.00	202.75	1966	195.00	156.25	175.75
1941	127.50	86.25	127.50	1954	230.00	178.25	230.00	1967	186.25	142.38	147.88

Source: Chicago Board of Trade

WHEAT, CHICAGO

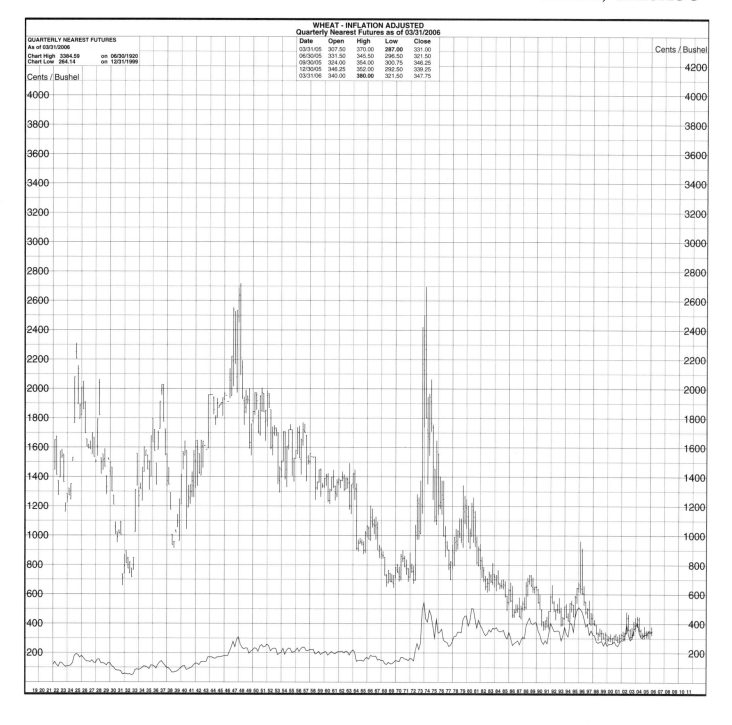

WHEAT, CHICAGO

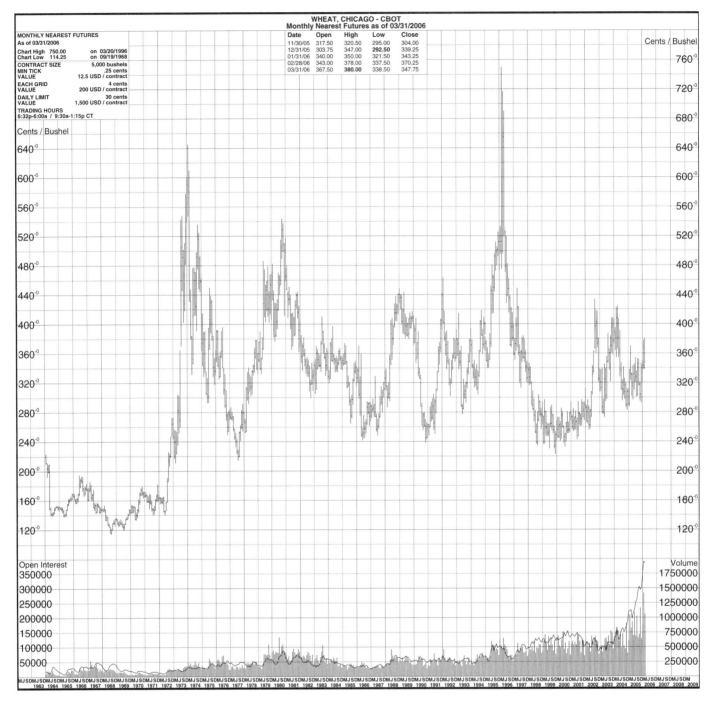

Annual High, Low and Close of Wheat Futures — In Cents per Bushel

Year	High	Low	Close	Year	High	Low	Close	Year	High	Low	Close
1968	153.25	114.25	135.50	1981	517.50	362.00	391.50	1994	418.75	303.50	401.50
1969	148.25	119.50	147.38	1982	405.00	299.25	330.75	1995	525.00	339.50	512.25
1970	179.38	133.25	168.50	1983	410.50	305.00	363.50	1996	750.00	368.00	381.25
1971	182.00	139.75	163.13	1984	397.00	319.50	347.75	1997	449.00	313.00	325.75
1972	272.75	140.00	264.00	1985	374.00	264.50	343.25	1998	348.00	234.50	276.25
1973	578.00	211.00	546.00	1986	371.00	241.50	274.50	1999	297.00	222.50	248.50
1974	645.00	331.00	458.00	1987	329.00	248.00	310.75	2000	285.50	232.00	279.50
1975	463.50	293.00	335.75	1988	441.50	286.50	440.00	2001	297.00	242.50	289.00
1976	396.00	249.00	277.50	1989	449.00	379.50	409.25	2002	434.00	255.50	325.00
1977	292.00	214.25	279.25	1990	412.00	238.00	260.50	2003	409.00	273.00	377.00
1978	378.75	251.75	343.25	1991	407.00	244.50	404.75	2004	424.00	282.50	307.50
1979	486.00	332.00	454.25	1992	463.25	301.50	353.75	2005	370.00	287.00	339.25
1980	544.50	376.50	501.00	1993	415.00	277.00	378.25	2006	380.00	321.50	347.75

Source: Chicago Board of Trade

WHEAT, CHICAGO

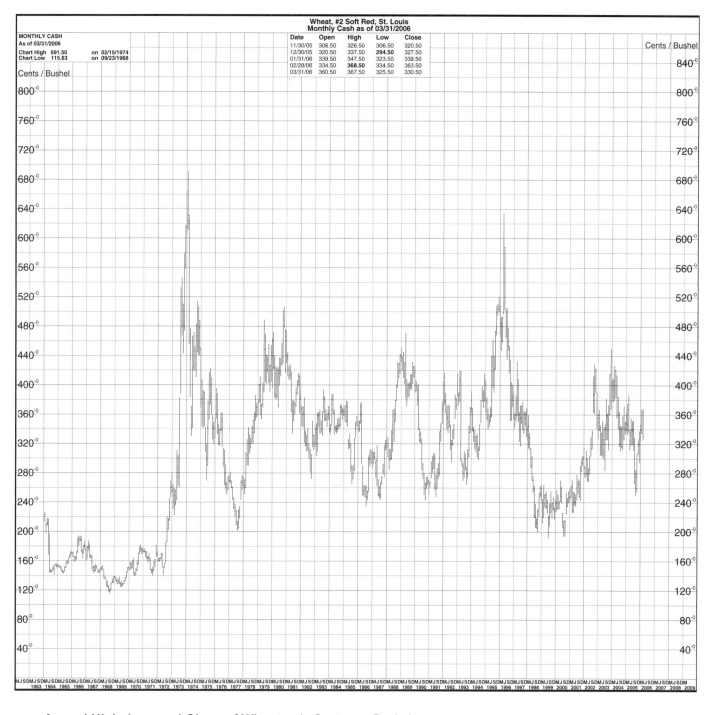

Annual High, Low and Close of Wheat   In Cents per Bushel

Year	High	Low	Close	Year	High	Low	Close	Year	High	Low	Close
1968	153.88	115.63	138.38	1981	473.50	333.50	381.50	1994	416.00	298.00	407.00
1969	151.00	124.63	150.50	1982	392.00	272.00	322.00	1995	520.00	340.00	513.00
1970	181.88	139.25	174.50	1983	394.50	304.00	370.50	1996	634.50	352.00	384.00
1971	181.75	140.00	170.00	1984	388.50	332.50	365.00	1997	432.50	317.00	330.00
1972	270.00	140.00	264.25	1985	379.50	265.00	356.50	1998	359.50	200.50	251.00
1973	618.50	222.00	605.00	1986	377.00	234.50	293.50	1999	265.50	192.00	228.50
1974	691.50	330.50	450.50	1987	325.00	243.50	312.00	2000	270.50	193.50	248.00
1975	449.75	269.50	324.75	1988	441.50	284.50	441.50	2001	304.50	226.50	300.50
1976	395.25	250.75	272.50	1989	471.50	371.00	412.50	2002	428.50	268.50	341.50
1977	281.25	201.00	273.00	1990	426.50	242.50	269.00	2003	450.00	283.50	377.50
1978	386.00	252.00	369.25	1991	378.50	248.00	371.50	2004	426.50	310.50	350.50
1979	488.75	353.50	444.25	1992	417.00	294.50	372.50	2005	386.50	249.50	327.50
1980	507.00	369.00	466.00	1993	419.50	264.00	369.00	2006	368.50	323.50	330.50

Chicago.   Source: *Chicago Board of Trade*

WHEAT, CHICAGO

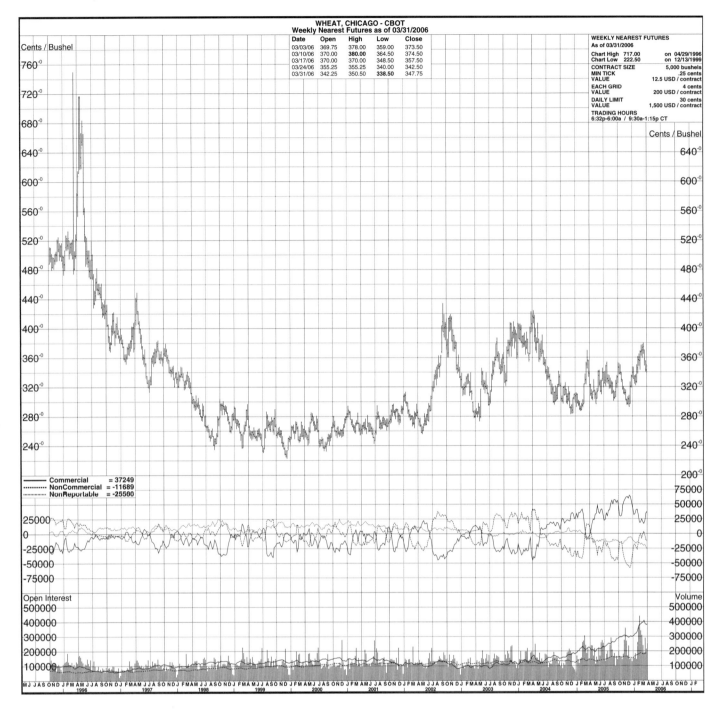

Quarterly High, Low and Close of Wheat Futures   In Cents per Bushel

Quarter	High	Low	Close	Quarter	High	Low	Close	Quarter	High	Low	Close
09/1996	519.00	415.50	436.00	12/1999	276.75	222.50	248.50	03/2003	339.50	277.50	286.75
12/1996	439.00	368.00	381.25	03/2000	273.50	241.00	262.25	06/2003	345.75	273.00	301.75
03/1997	408.00	351.00	397.50	06/2000	285.50	240.50	259.50	09/2003	387.00	297.00	360.25
06/1997	449.00	319.50	323.75	09/2000	266.00	232.00	265.00	12/2003	409.00	321.00	377.00
09/1997	384.00	313.00	354.25	12/2000	280.50	250.50	279.50	03/2004	422.75	354.00	408.00
12/1997	379.50	320.00	325.75	03/2001	294.50	254.00	255.00	06/2004	424.00	328.00	338.00
03/1998	348.00	316.00	320.25	06/2001	281.75	242.50	246.75	09/2004	348.00	295.50	306.75
06/1998	321.00	267.00	276.25	09/2001	295.00	246.25	270.75	12/2004	326.00	282.50	307.50
09/1998	282.50	234.50	269.25	12/2001	297.00	261.50	289.00	03/2005	370.00	287.00	331.00
12/1998	304.00	257.00	276.25	03/2002	313.25	263.75	285.00	06/2005	345.50	296.50	321.50
03/1999	297.00	236.50	280.25	06/2002	308.00	255.50	307.00	09/2005	354.00	300.75	346.25
06/1999	281.50	246.50	250.00	09/2002	434.00	304.00	396.50	12/2005	352.00	292.50	339.25
09/1999	290.00	230.50	275.75	12/2002	419.00	321.00	325.00	03/2006	380.00	321.50	347.75

Source: Chicago Board of Trade

WHEAT, CHICAGO

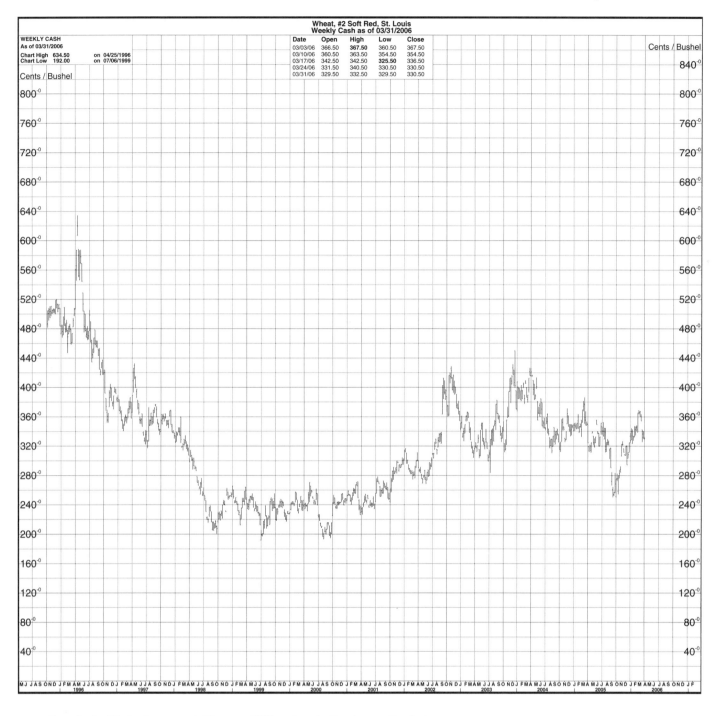

Quarterly High, Low and Close of Wheat   In Cents per Bushel

Quarter	High	Low	Close	Quarter	High	Low	Close	Quarter	High	Low	Close
09/1996	505.50	416.50	437.50	12/1999	247.50	217.50	228.50	03/2003	366.50	304.50	316.50
12/1996	434.50	352.00	384.00	03/2000	257.50	227.50	246.00	06/2003	351.50	299.50	304.50
03/1997	389.50	341.00	380.00	06/2000	270.50	231.50	239.50	09/2003	382.50	283.50	346.50
06/1997	432.50	324.00	324.00	09/2000	226.50	193.50	215.50	12/2003	450.00	312.00	377.50
09/1997	377.00	317.00	339.00	12/2000	255.50	225.00	248.00	03/2004	426.50	377.50	425.50
12/1997	369.00	330.00	330.00	03/2001	271.50	226.50	226.50	06/2004	421.50	341.50	341.50
03/1998	359.50	312.00	312.00	06/2001	254.45	226.50	241.00	09/2004	364.50	310.50	317.50
06/1998	314.50	253.50	258.50	09/2001	278.50	244.00	248.50	12/2004	371.50	312.50	350.50
09/1998	263.50	205.00	211.50	12/2001	304.50	242.50	300.50	03/2005	386.50	332.50	336.50
12/1998	263.00	200.50	251.00	03/2002	316.50	274.50	300.50	06/2005	355.50	311.50	337.50
03/1999	265.50	212.50	250.00	06/2002	304.50	268.50	301.50	09/2005	352.50	249.50	275.50
06/1999	255.50	224.50	228.50	09/2002	412.50	303.50	387.50	12/2005	337.50	254.50	327.50
09/1999	255.50	192.00	243.50	12/2002	428.50	341.50	341.50	03/2006	368.50	323.50	330.50

Chicago.   *Source: Chicago Board of Trade*

WHEAT, KANSAS CITY

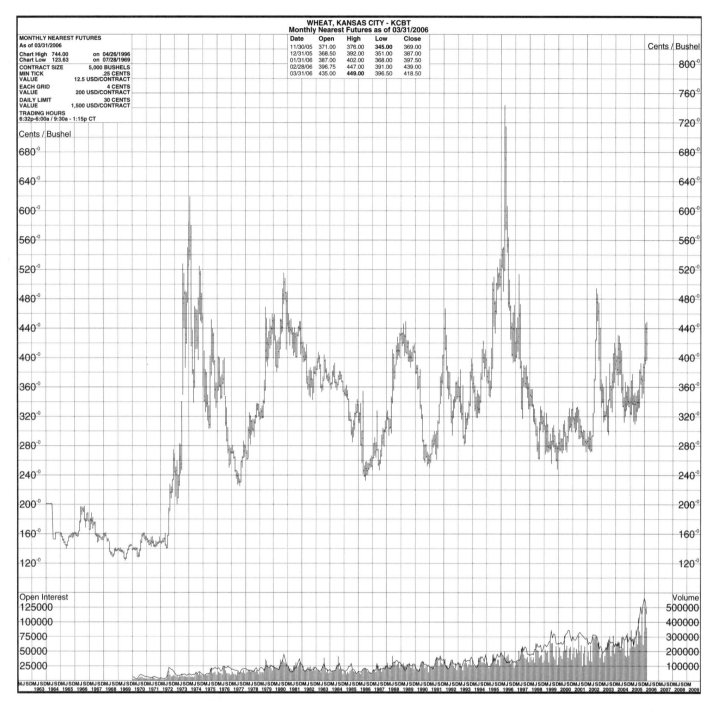

Annual High, Low and Close of Wheat Futures   In Cents per Bushel

Year	High	Low	Close	Year	High	Low	Close	Year	High	Low	Close
1968	162.25	128.63	138.50	1981	490.50	400.50	419.50	1994	423.25	318.00	399.00
1969	145.88	123.63	144.38	1982	428.75	342.50	378.25	1995	535.00	346.50	509.50
1970	162.00	127.63	154.63	1983	407.75	353.00	372.75	1996	744.00	393.00	395.25
1971	156.88	141.63	149.50	1984	393.00	354.00	354.00	1997	514.00	317.00	335.50
1972	275.00	139.63	262.25	1985	363.00	284.50	336.00	1998	358.00	262.00	314.00
1973	550.00	200.00	523.00	1986	354.75	232.50	252.00	1999	326.00	248.00	276.25
1974	619.00	338.50	452.50	1987	328.00	246.50	303.75	2000	331.50	270.00	330.00
1975	459.00	303.25	338.50	1988	433.50	293.50	431.00	2001	340.00	271.50	284.00
1976	402.00	250.00	272.00	1989	449.50	386.25	408.50	2002	495.00	271.25	359.75
1977	286.75	225.00	278.25	1990	409.50	252.25	261.00	2003	420.50	294.50	384.75
1978	338.00	260.50	321.00	1991	404.00	250.25	402.75	2004	431.00	312.00	338.00
1979	469.00	315.00	450.00	1992	467.00	294.00	347.25	2005	392.50	309.50	387.00
1980	515.50	380.00	477.25	1993	399.00	281.00	389.25	2006	449.00	368.00	418.50

Source: Kansas City Board of Trade

WHEAT, KANSAS CITY

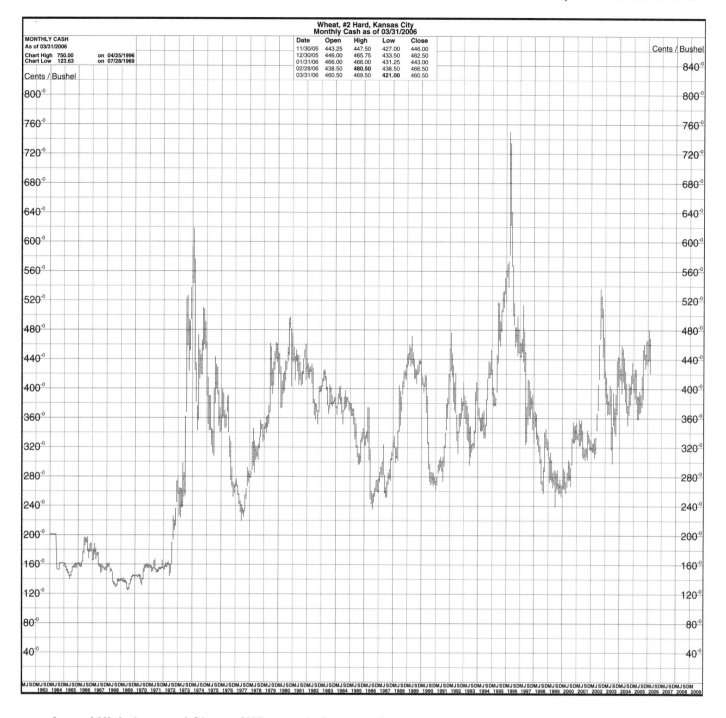

Annual High, Low and Close of Wheat   In Cents per Bushel

Year	High	Low	Close	Year	High	Low	Close	Year	High	Low	Close
1968	162.25	128.63	138.50	1981	475.00	404.25	427.00	1994	453.00	332.00	436.00
1969	145.88	123.63	144.38	1982	441.50	351.50	398.75	1995	551.00	376.50	549.00
1970	161.13	131.75	156.25	1983	426.00	365.25	384.25	1996	750.00	445.50	449.75
1971	167.50	148.63	155.38	1984	404.00	351.50	378.50	1997	514.00	324.00	345.00
1972	274.00	144.25	272.25	1985	380.50	296.00	343.75	1998	369.00	257.75	317.50
1973	537.50	223.63	537.50	1986	374.50	235.50	260.00	1999	329.25	238.75	265.75
1974	618.50	342.50	458.75	1987	324.00	251.50	304.25	2000	355.00	258.25	350.50
1975	463.25	308.25	340.50	1988	432.75	299.00	431.50	2001	358.50	302.00	318.50
1976	398.50	252.00	266.50	1989	471.50	406.50	435.50	2002	536.25	305.50	415.25
1977	292.50	219.75	283.75	1990	436.75	267.75	270.50	2003	444.00	298.00	417.25
1978	357.50	277.50	334.50	1991	420.00	261.00	419.00	2004	458.75	350.25	412.00
1979	463.00	328.50	452.50	1992	476.50	310.88	372.00	2005	465.75	358.00	462.50
1980	498.00	373.50	458.00	1993	409.00	296.00	407.00	2006	480.50	421.00	460.50

Kansas City.   *Source: Kansas City Board of Trade*

WHEAT, KANSAS CITY

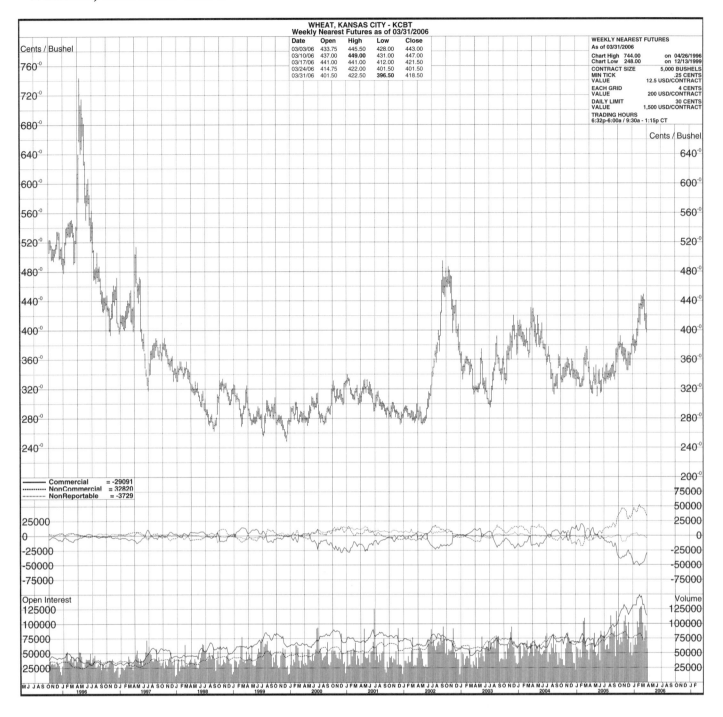

Quarterly High, Low and Close of Wheat Futures   In Cents per Bushel

Quarter	High	Low	Close	Quarter	High	Low	Close	Quarter	High	Low	Close
09/1996	564.00	424.50	442.00	12/1999	293.75	248.00	276.25	03/2003	370.75	312.25	320.75
12/1996	472.00	393.00	395.25	03/2000	302.50	270.25	286.50	06/2003	375.00	299.50	300.25
03/1997	455.00	395.50	422.50	06/2000	315.00	270.00	302.00	09/2003	392.50	294.50	356.75
06/1997	514.00	330.50	330.75	09/2000	320.00	271.00	320.00	12/2003	420.50	326.00	384.75
09/1997	389.50	317.00	365.00	12/2000	331.50	298.50	330.00	03/2004	431.00	362.00	412.50
12/1997	390.00	330.00	335.50	03/2001	340.00	298.00	301.50	06/2004	430.00	352.00	358.50
03/1998	358.00	330.00	335.50	06/2001	333.50	289.25	293.00	09/2004	378.00	312.00	336.75
06/1998	336.25	293.50	300.50	09/2001	317.50	281.00	292.50	12/2004	362.50	328.25	338.00
09/1998	313.00	262.00	303.25	12/2001	302.00	271.50	284.00	03/2005	378.00	322.00	338.00
12/1998	334.00	298.50	314.00	03/2002	300.00	273.50	290.00	06/2005	352.50	309.50	328.00
03/1999	326.00	268.50	308.25	06/2002	325.00	271.25	322.50	09/2005	384.00	326.50	380.25
06/1999	310.00	271.00	277.00	09/2002	495.00	325.00	475.25	12/2005	392.50	345.00	387.00
09/1999	308.75	255.50	294.25	12/2002	487.00	355.00	359.75	03/2006	449.00	368.00	418.50

Source: Kansas City Board of Trade

WHEAT, KANSAS CITY

Quarterly High, Low and Close of Wheat   In Cents per Bushel

Quarter	High	Low	Close	Quarter	High	Low	Close	Quarter	High	Low	Close
09/1996	568.50	456.75	479.50	12/1999	277.00	252.75	265.75	03/2003	425.00	364.75	382.25
12/1996	499.00	445.50	449.75	03/2000	291.75	263.00	275.00	06/2003	405.00	317.75	317.75
03/1997	468.75	443.50	457.00	06/2000	303.00	258.25	293.50	09/2003	395.00	298.00	361.25
06/1997	514.00	324.00	324.00	09/2000	331.50	267.50	331.50	12/2003	444.00	336.00	417.25
09/1997	412.00	326.75	363.50	12/2000	355.00	326.00	350.50	03/2004	458.75	393.50	449.50
12/1997	398.00	345.00	345.00	03/2001	358.50	322.00	322.00	06/2004	454.75	383.00	383.00
03/1998	369.00	326.00	342.00	06/2001	357.75	307.00	310.50	09/2004	408.00	350.25	383.25
06/1998	339.00	298.50	304.50	09/2001	320.25	302.00	314.00	12/2004	436.00	377.50	412.00
09/1998	304.50	257.75	287.75	12/2001	343.00	302.50	318.50	03/2005	426.50	380.50	380.50
12/1998	345.25	287.88	317.50	03/2002	330.00	313.50	323.50	06/2005	396.75	358.00	367.00
03/1999	329.25	272.50	301.75	06/2002	367.25	305.50	363.25	09/2005	452.75	368.50	452.75
06/1999	303.75	265.00	269.50	09/2002	536.25	371.25	516.75	12/2005	465.75	427.00	462.50
09/1999	289.50	238.75	275.75	12/2002	526.75	415.25	415.25	03/2006	480.50	421.00	460.50

Kansas City.   *Source: Kansas City Board of Trade*

WHEAT, MINNEAPOLIS

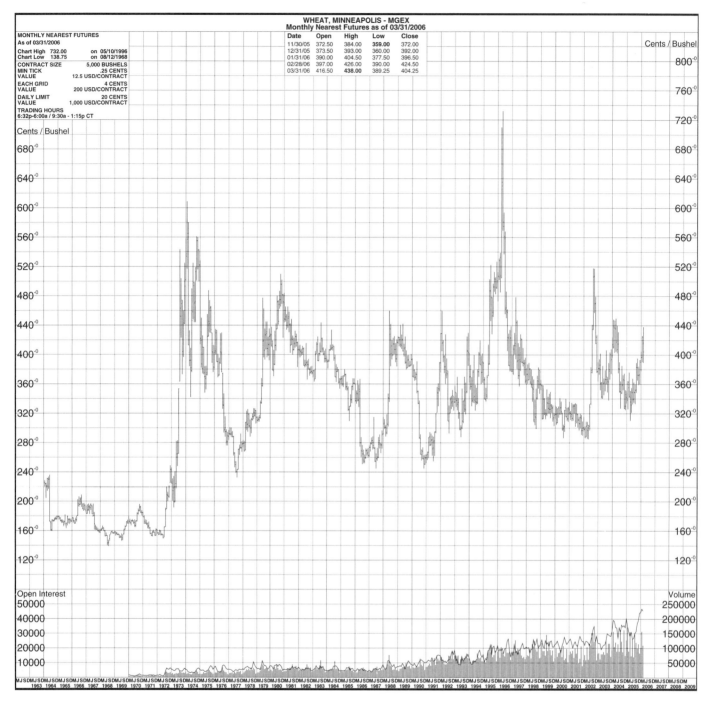

Annual High, Low and Close of Wheat Futures   In Cents per Bushel

Year	High	Low	Close	Year	High	Low	Close	Year	High	Low	Close
1968	166.63	138.75	156.63	1981	484.00	383.00	406.50	1994	419.50	324.00	390.00
1969	174.63	146.00	170.00	1982	415.75	366.00	375.00	1995	527.00	336.50	499.50
1970	196.00	164.75	184.63	1983	444.00	363.00	394.25	1996	732.00	377.50	377.75
1971	185.25	152.00	161.50	1984	434.00	353.50	367.00	1997	478.50	357.00	364.00
1972	249.00	149.75	243.50	1985	380.25	309.75	360.50	1998	389.00	299.00	359.25
1973	543.50	191.50	493.00	1986	367.00	251.00	262.75	1999	366.00	303.00	318.00
1974	609.00	342.00	522.00	1987	315.00	245.00	290.75	2000	341.00	286.50	327.25
1975	528.00	348.00	383.00	1988	460.00	288.50	417.00	2001	336.25	290.00	300.00
1976	435.00	276.00	289.25	1989	442.25	379.50	393.50	2002	518.00	285.00	377.25
1977	301.00	232.50	278.00	1990	395.00	245.00	259.50	2003	408.00	338.00	393.75
1978	327.00	267.75	314.50	1991	390.00	252.25	389.00	2004	449.50	325.00	346.00
1979	477.25	306.75	425.00	1992	460.00	292.75	335.75	2005	395.00	310.50	392.00
1980	510.00	370.50	472.00	1993	430.00	287.75	403.50	2006	438.00	377.50	404.25

Source: Minneapolis Grain Exchange

WHEAT, MINNEAPOLIS

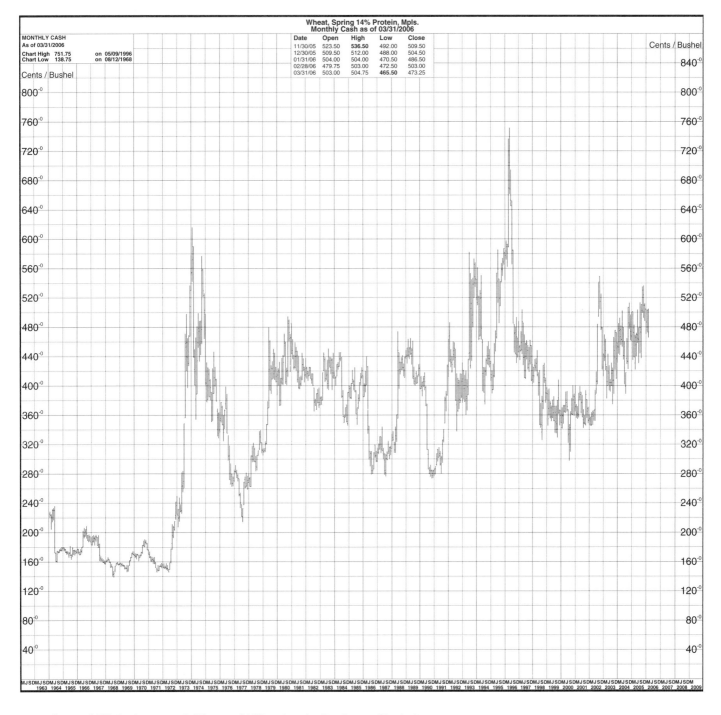

Annual High, Low and Close of Wheat   In Cents per Bushel

Year	High	Low	Close	Year	High	Low	Close	Year	High	Low	Close
1968	166.63	138.75	156.63	1981	484.50	395.75	414.38	1994	561.25	374.25	432.50
1969	174.63	146.00	170.00	1982	437.63	365.00	377.00	1995	587.00	389.25	587.00
1970	190.75	161.13	176.63	1983	450.75	373.50	417.13	1996	751.75	430.50	441.75
1971	177.00	146.00	158.25	1984	445.75	345.75	391.00	1997	503.75	406.50	406.50
1972	241.50	146.00	241.50	1985	425.00	346.75	420.50	1998	448.50	325.50	390.38
1973	537.00	207.25	508.00	1986	440.00	279.00	297.75	1999	408.00	329.00	365.50
1974	616.00	354.00	503.00	1987	344.00	276.25	310.75	2000	400.00	297.50	384.75
1975	497.50	328.50	339.00	1988	474.00	308.50	438.00	2001	400.00	342.00	352.50
1976	399.00	262.50	274.25	1989	464.75	400.00	423.50	2002	549.00	345.00	422.25
1977	291.88	214.00	271.00	1990	430.00	273.50	283.50	2003	475.50	374.50	436.25
1978	339.25	262.50	312.50	1991	428.00	276.50	428.00	2004	513.00	388.75	473.50
1979	479.50	305.13	412.88	1992	486.25	337.50	385.75	2005	536.50	421.75	504.50
1980	494.50	373.00	465.75	1993	582.25	360.25	546.00	2006	504.75	465.50	473.25

Minneapolis.   *Source: Minneapolis Grain Exchange*

WHEAT, MINNEAPOLIS

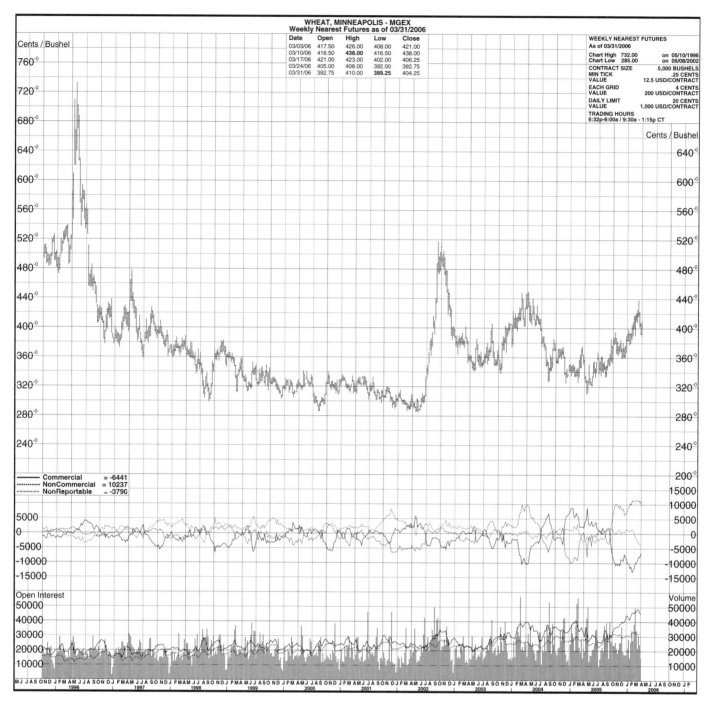

Quarterly High, Low and Close of Wheat Futures — In Cents per Bushel

Quarter	High	Low	Close	Quarter	High	Low	Close	Quarter	High	Low	Close
09/1996	568.00	405.25	423.75	12/1999	333.00	303.00	318.00	03/2003	402.00	352.00	361.25
12/1996	439.00	377.50	377.75	03/2000	331.00	304.50	327.00	06/2003	385.00	341.00	363.00
03/1997	430.00	372.75	412.50	06/2000	341.00	314.50	322.75	09/2003	406.50	349.00	364.00
06/1997	478.50	367.00	371.75	09/2000	325.00	286.50	324.50	12/2003	408.00	338.00	393.75
09/1997	428.00	357.00	389.25	12/2000	340.00	309.00	327.25	03/2004	448.00	396.00	436.75
12/1997	409.50	361.00	364.00	03/2001	336.25	310.00	313.50	06/2004	449.50	375.00	381.00
03/1998	389.00	359.00	380.50	06/2001	334.25	302.00	310.00	09/2004	390.00	327.00	358.25
06/1998	381.50	336.25	354.00	09/2001	333.00	297.00	306.75	12/2004	374.50	325.00	346.00
09/1998	366.50	299.00	341.25	12/2001	320.00	290.00	300.00	03/2005	376.00	326.00	343.75
12/1998	383.00	339.50	359.25	03/2002	315.50	287.00	303.00	06/2005	367.50	310.50	339.00
03/1999	366.00	312.00	339.75	06/2002	333.00	285.00	329.00	09/2005	389.00	333.25	383.00
06/1999	353.00	312.50	335.00	09/2002	518.00	332.00	506.25	12/2005	395.00	359.00	392.00
09/1999	349.50	314.00	331.50	12/2002	517.50	375.50	377.25	03/2006	438.00	377.50	404.25

Source: Minneapolis Grain Exchange

WHEAT, MINNEAPOLIS

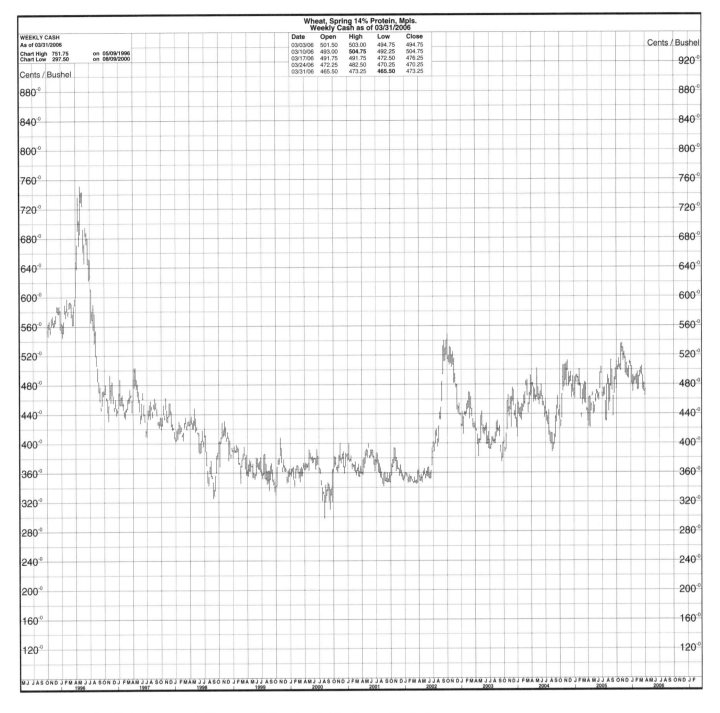

Quarterly High, Low and Close of Wheat   In Cents per Bushel

Quarter	High	Low	Close	Quarter	High	Low	Close	Quarter	High	Low	Close
09/1996	652.00	445.25	471.25	12/1999	408.00	329.00	365.50	03/2003	469.75	412.75	428.75
12/1996	493.50	430.50	441.75	03/2000	373.00	341.25	373.00	06/2003	443.50	382.25	404.25
03/1997	487.75	434.50	458.50	06/2000	392.50	363.50	371.50	09/2003	431.00	374.50	406.50
06/1997	503.75	410.50	410.50	09/2000	367.25	297.50	364.50	12/2003	475.50	388.50	436.25
09/1997	462.00	409.00	424.25	12/2000	400.00	359.00	384.75	03/2004	492.25	431.25	466.75
12/1997	462.00	406.50	406.50	03/2001	400.00	354.75	359.50	06/2004	502.25	435.38	441.00
03/1998	436.00	402.00	426.50	06/2001	399.25	356.50	377.50	09/2004	464.75	388.75	433.25
06/1998	448.50	386.25	403.75	09/2001	387.25	342.00	347.75	12/2004	513.00	422.50	473.50
09/1998	421.00	325.50	378.75	12/2001	393.75	345.50	352.50	03/2005	500.75	434.75	438.75
12/1998	431.00	368.00	390.38	03/2002	363.75	345.00	358.00	06/2005	503.50	421.75	464.50
03/1999	398.25	345.50	359.75	06/2002	394.00	346.25	388.25	09/2005	513.25	430.25	510.50
06/1999	380.75	351.50	371.25	09/2002	541.25	389.00	541.25	12/2005	536.50	488.00	504.50
09/1999	385.50	334.75	347.88	12/2002	549.00	422.25	422.25	03/2006	504.75	465.50	473.25

Minneapolis.   *Source: Minneapolis Grain Exchange*

CANOLA

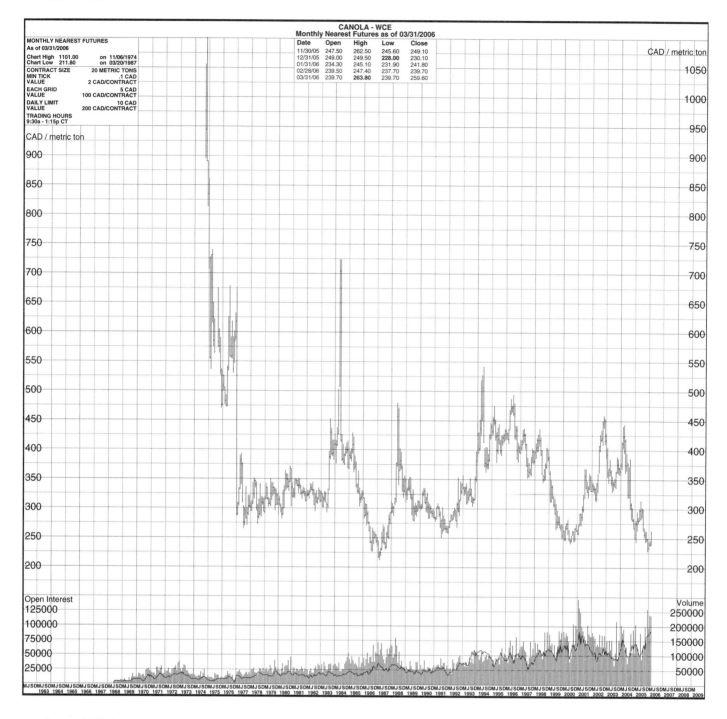

Annual High, Low and Close of Canola   In Canadian Dollars per Metric Ton

Year	High	Low	Close	Year	High	Low	Close	Year	High	Low	Close
1974	1,101.00	777.60	814.00	1985	429.20	303.10	326.30	1996	494.50	379.10	396.00
1975	861.00	470.00	476.40	1986	331.50	226.90	242.70	1997	437.50	352.00	380.90
1976	679.00	472.40	618.00	1987	293.20	211.80	292.60	1998	436.50	344.50	386.20
1977	677.00	265.00	302.00	1988	480.00	287.00	346.70	1999	390.70	250.00	254.00
1978	351.50	272.50	294.00	1989	354.00	278.50	301.60	2000	282.20	241.00	263.30
1979	351.00	290.50	306.00	1990	335.40	283.50	285.00	2001	369.00	256.60	331.00
1980	372.00	282.00	335.70	1991	309.00	250.00	260.00	2002	459.00	313.00	416.60
1981	351.20	311.00	313.00	1992	353.60	257.80	342.70	2003	428.90	328.50	364.50
1982	345.00	295.00	312.30	1993	398.00	304.00	395.90	2004	444.00	267.00	267.50
1983	453.00	292.80	416.10	1994	542.20	362.20	441.00	2005	314.00	228.00	230.10
1984	724.00	368.90	369.30	1995	475.50	378.50	432.50	2006	263.80	231.90	259.60

Source: Winnipeg Commodity Exchange

CANOLA

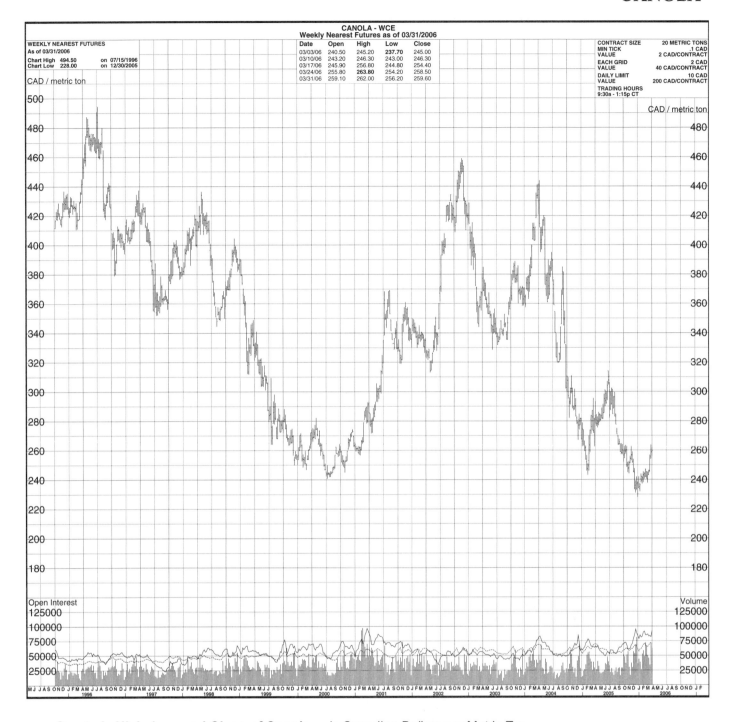

Quarterly High, Low and Close of Canola   In Canadian Dollars per Metric Ton

Quarter	High	Low	Close	Quarter	High	Low	Close	Quarter	High	Low	Close
09/1996	494.50	417.50	433.80	12/1999	288.40	250.00	254.00	03/2003	428.90	344.00	368.40
12/1996	441.00	379.10	396.00	03/2000	272.20	246.80	267.70	06/2003	385.00	328.50	340.00
03/1997	434.50	394.00	427.60	06/2000	282.20	246.50	246.90	09/2003	365.00	332.00	361.80
06/1997	437.50	373.00	373.00	09/2000	264.50	241.00	260.80	12/2003	388.90	358.30	364.50
09/1997	387.80	352.00	359.80	12/2000	274.50	245.00	263.30	03/2004	441.30	357.30	423.50
12/1997	403.50	356.10	380.90	03/2001	292.80	256.60	291.00	06/2004	444.00	360.80	380.20
03/1998	420.90	378.70	417.50	06/2001	325.00	271.50	316.80	09/2004	385.10	299.50	307.20
06/1998	436.50	391.30	399.20	09/2001	369.00	319.50	329.70	12/2004	311.00	267.00	267.50
09/1998	401.00	344.50	355.30	12/2001	361.00	319.00	331.00	03/2005	295.50	243.20	280.90
12/1998	404.50	350.00	386.20	03/2002	349.80	326.40	335.00	06/2005	314.00	275.50	283.90
03/1999	390.70	311.80	337.20	06/2002	360.20	313.00	360.00	09/2005	302.30	251.80	256.50
06/1999	341.00	291.50	292.50	09/2002	434.40	361.50	419.00	12/2005	263.40	228.00	230.10
09/1999	309.50	264.00	278.40	12/2002	459.00	408.50	416.60	03/2006	263.80	231.90	259.60

Source: Winnipeg Commodity Exchange

SOYBEANS

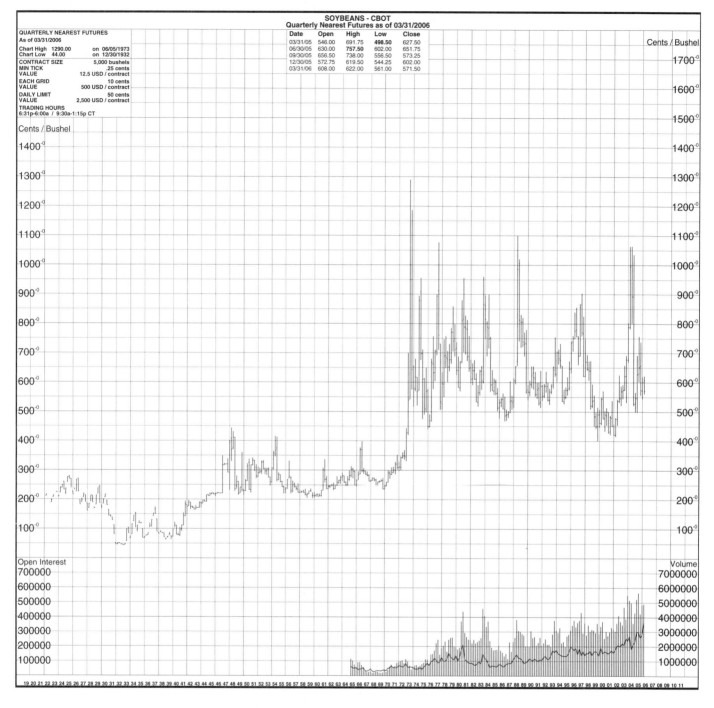

Annual High, Low and Close of Soybean Futures   In Cents per Bushel

Year	High	Low	Close	Year	High	Low	Close	Year	High	Low	Close
1929	246.00	170.00	172.00	1942	196.50	165.25	165.25	1955	284.00	220.00	239.50
1930	216.00	144.00	144.00	1943	192.00	165.25	186.00	1956	331.50	220.00	246.50
1931	146.00	47.00	47.00	1944	216.00	186.00	212.00	1957	257.50	222.50	223.50
1932	52.00	44.00	44.00	1945	222.00	210.00	219.00	1958	235.50	205.25	217.50
1933	104.00	45.00	73.00	1946	349.00	219.00	317.00	1959	237.00	204.13	212.38
1934	154.00	81.00	111.00	1947	401.25	231.50	394.00	1960	232.00	208.75	230.13
1935	127.00	68.00	72.00	1948	443.75	228.75	259.88	1961	337.00	231.50	243.63
1936	130.00	76.00	130.00	1949	360.00	214.25	229.63	1962	257.00	232.00	246.88
1937	174.00	83.00	83.00	1950	338.25	222.63	316.75	1963	291.50	246.38	281.25
1938	93.00	63.00	67.00	1951	342.13	271.63	291.00	1964	298.50	245.50	281.63
1939	97.00	64.00	97.00	1952	333.00	285.38	296.13	1965	313.50	244.50	264.75
1940	120.50	74.25	96.50	1953	309.75	247.75	306.50	1966	398.00	268.00	296.50
1941	194.00	91.25	174.50	1954	415.75	261.00	285.00	1967	298.00	261.25	266.12

Source: Chicago Board of Trade

SOYBEANS

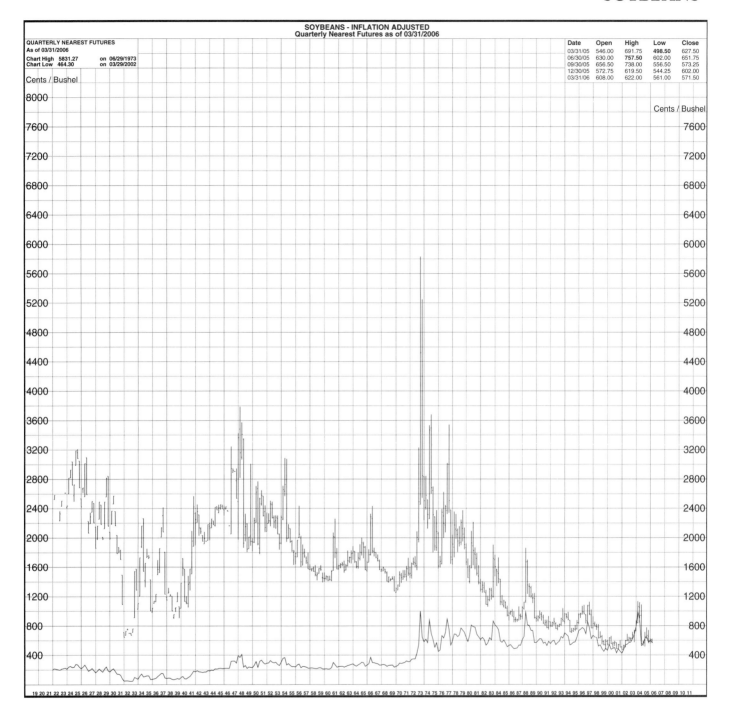

SOYBEANS

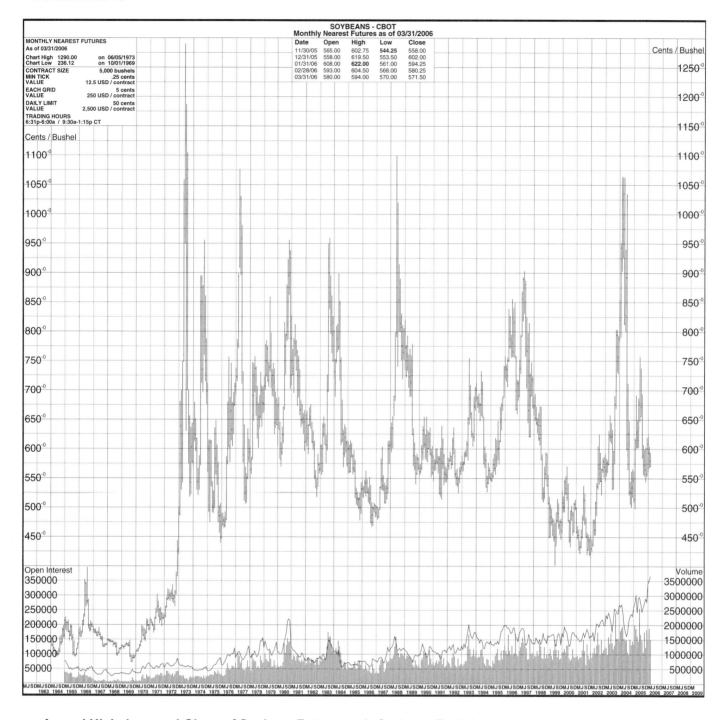

Annual High, Low and Close of Soybean Futures   In Cents per Bushel

Year	High	Low	Close	Year	High	Low	Close	Year	High	Low	Close
1968	275.75	247.25	260.50	1981	827.50	596.00	610.50	1994	732.50	526.75	550.75
1969	274.00	236.12	246.37	1982	675.50	518.00	564.50	1995	741.75	544.50	735.25
1970	310.25	246.00	292.75	1983	960.00	555.50	814.50	1996	856.00	659.75	690.50
1971	352.75	286.50	311.25	1984	899.00	568.50	572.25	1997	903.50	620.00	670.50
1972	444.00	301.25	426.25	1985	614.00	478.00	531.25	1998	694.00	509.25	537.75
1973	1,290.00	420.00	579.00	1986	563.00	467.50	490.75	1999	556.50	401.50	461.75
1974	956.00	521.00	697.00	1987	614.50	479.50	607.00	2000	570.50	433.50	499.50
1975	712.00	439.50	448.75	1988	1,099.50	594.50	804.75	2001	538.00	419.50	421.00
1976	757.00	446.00	706.50	1989	820.50	540.00	568.00	2002	625.00	415.50	569.50
1977	1,076.50	506.00	594.75	1990	655.00	552.00	559.75	2003	803.50	532.00	789.00
1978	758.00	550.25	676.50	1991	640.00	514.00	554.75	2004	1,064.00	501.00	547.75
1979	859.00	625.00	641.25	1992	637.00	524.50	568.75	2005	757.50	498.50	602.00
1980	956.00	569.50	788.75	1993	755.00	561.75	704.25	2006	622.00	561.00	571.50

Source: Chicago Board of Trade

SOYBEANS

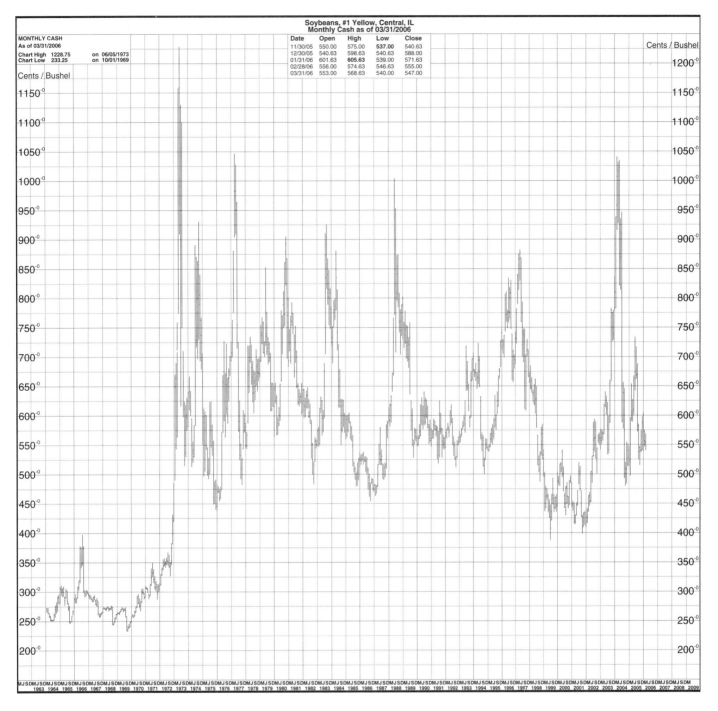

Annual High, Low and Close of Soybeans   In Cents per Bushel

Year	High	Low	Close	Year	High	Low	Close	Year	High	Low	Close
1968	276.63	243.88	262.00	1981	800.88	601.88	605.50	1994	723.50	500.00	545.50
1969	274.25	233.25	248.63	1982	648.50	483.50	551.00	1995	728.50	539.00	725.50
1970	306.00	248.25	290.00	1983	925.50	547.50	809.50	1996	835.00	657.50	688.00
1971	350.00	287.25	309.25	1984	881.00	550.00	571.50	1997	882.50	609.00	666.00
1972	431.88	301.63	421.25	1985	605.50	479.50	523.00	1998	685.00	488.00	526.00
1973	1,228.75	419.88	575.63	1986	537.50	454.00	475.50	1999	542.00	387.50	447.50
1974	931.00	513.00	694.63	1987	590.50	463.50	587.50	2000	541.50	429.50	487.50
1975	705.63	440.25	445.88	1988	1,004.00	581.50	789.00	2001	520.00	398.50	413.63
1976	727.63	436.88	701.63	1989	802.50	528.50	561.50	2002	594.00	410.00	560.63
1977	1,046.25	482.63	587.00	1990	641.00	548.00	557.00	2003	782.63	533.63	779.00
1978	734.63	543.63	672.63	1991	625.50	518.00	551.50	2004	1,040.63	480.00	540.63
1979	853.00	607.88	616.25	1992	619.50	511.50	555.50	2005	733.63	497.00	588.00
1980	905.00	563.00	770.88	1993	719.00	553.00	696.50	2006	605.63	539.00	547.00

Central Illinois.   *Source: Chicago Board of Trade*

SOYBEANS

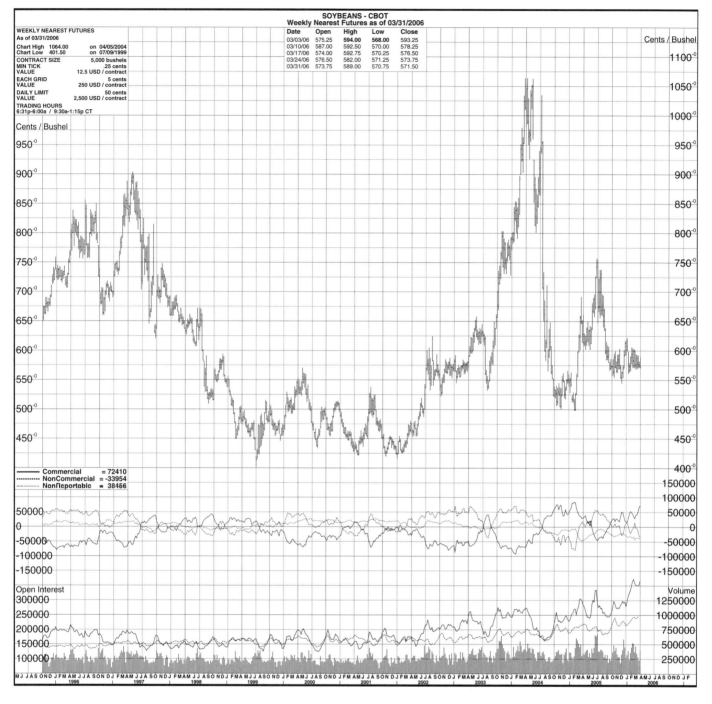

Quarterly High, Low and Close of Soybean Futures   In Cents per Bushel

Quarter	High	Low	Close	Quarter	High	Low	Close	Quarter	High	Low	Close
09/1996	856.00	755.50	758.00	12/1999	508.00	446.25	461.75	03/2003	592.50	544.75	574.50
12/1996	759.00	659.75	690.50	03/2000	548.50	455.75	545.50	06/2003	658.00	573.00	621.25
03/1997	868.00	690.00	855.75	06/2000	570.50	477.00	477.50	09/2003	691.00	532.00	677.25
06/1997	903.50	758.00	771.00	09/2000	504.00	433.50	490.50	12/2003	803.50	669.00	789.00
09/1997	825.00	620.00	621.50	12/2000	514.00	453.50	499.50	03/2004	1,063.75	782.50	995.00
12/1997	748.00	620.00	670.50	03/2001	500.00	428.00	428.50	06/2004	1,064.00	800.75	893.00
03/1998	694.00	641.00	645.00	06/2001	488.00	421.50	482.50	09/2004	1,035.00	521.50	527.00
06/1998	672.50	606.50	640.00	09/2001	538.00	450.50	451.25	12/2004	566.00	501.00	547.75
09/1998	673.00	509.25	520.75	12/2001	458.00	419.50	421.00	03/2005	691.75	498.50	627.50
12/1998	594.00	514.75	537.75	03/2002	480.50	415.50	476.25	06/2005	757.50	602.00	651.75
03/1999	556.50	449.00	483.75	06/2002	543.00	453.00	536.50	09/2005	738.00	556.50	573.25
06/1999	498.50	443.00	448.50	09/2002	625.00	532.00	545.75	12/2005	619.50	544.25	602.00
09/1999	515.50	401.50	491.25	12/2002	587.50	522.00	569.50	03/2006	622.00	561.00	571.50

Source: Chicago Board of Trade

SOYBEANS

Quarterly High, Low and Close of Soyeans   In Cents per Bushel

Quarter	High	Low	Close	Quarter	High	Low	Close	Quarter	High	Low	Close
09/1996	835.00	748.00	748.00	12/1999	466.00	435.00	447.50	03/2003	576.63	541.00	568.00
12/1996	738.50	657.50	688.00	03/2000	517.00	444.50	517.00	06/2003	640.63	568.00	612.00
03/1997	841.00	688.00	838.00	06/2000	541.50	471.00	471.00	09/2003	660.00	533.63	654.63
06/1997	882.50	759.50	759.50	09/2000	486.00	429.50	462.50	12/2003	782.63	658.00	779.00
09/1997	793.50	611.50	611.50	12/2000	497.50	441.50	487.50	03/2004	1,040.63	779.00	1,006.63
12/1997	730.00	609.00	666.00	03/2001	485.50	416.00	416.00	06/2004	1,034.63	814.00	881.00
03/1998	685.00	639.00	639.00	06/2001	472.00	414.50	472.00	09/2004	947.00	492.63	496.00
06/1998	662.50	603.00	627.50	09/2001	520.00	427.50	427.50	12/2004	554.63	480.00	540.63
09/1998	650.00	503.00	507.00	12/2001	435.63	398.50	413.63	03/2005	654.00	497.00	605.00
12/1998	585.50	488.00	526.00	03/2002	463.63	410.00	463.63	06/2005	733.63	589.63	642.63
03/1999	542.00	437.00	461.00	06/2002	530.63	445.63	530.63	09/2005	717.00	525.00	537.63
06/1999	476.00	426.00	426.50	09/2002	594.00	526.63	526.63	12/2005	598.63	515.00	588.00
09/1999	493.50	387.50	459.50	12/2002	569.63	501.00	560.63	03/2006	605.63	539.00	547.00

Central Illinois.   *Source: Chicago Board of Trade*

SOYBEAN MEAL

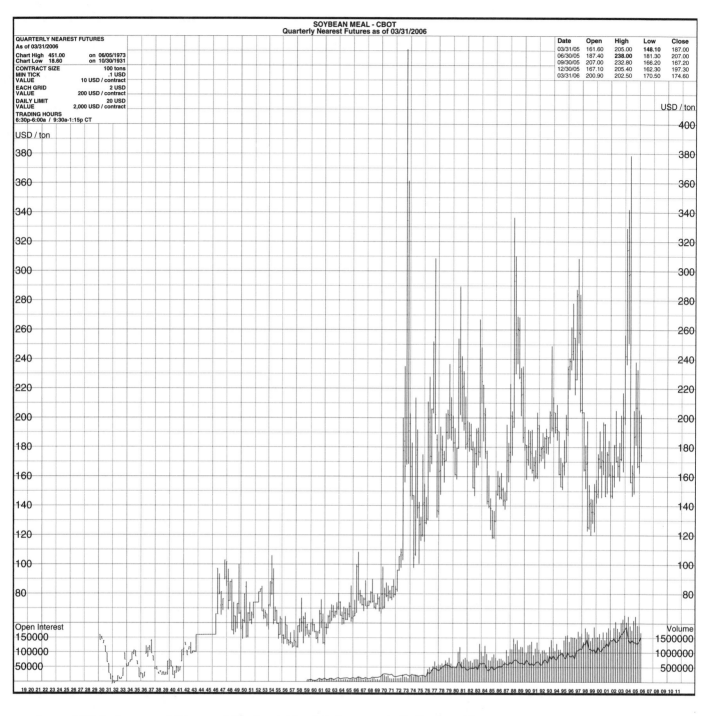

Annual High, Low and Close of Soybean Meal Futures   In Dollars per Ton

Year	High	Low	Close	Year	High	Low	Close	Year	High	Low	Close
1929	58.30	53.05	53.05	1942	46.60	37.90	39.00	1955	68.50	46.00	51.50
1930	51.80	40.00	40.00	1943	51.90	39.35	51.90	1956	64.50	44.50	46.50
1931	39.30	18.60	23.00	1944	52.00	51.90	52.00	1957	55.00	43.00	43.50
1932	23.70	18.75	21.70	1945	52.00	52.00	52.00	1958	77.00	43.00	63.00
1933	39.20	21.70	30.50	1946	97.00	52.00	80.70	1959	67.00	49.00	59.90
1934	41.20	30.60	41.20	1947	102.70	65.40	101.50	1960	62.75	46.15	53.75
1935	40.70	22.85	25.50	1948	96.50	52.00	64.50	1961	76.00	45.05	56.90
1936	44.30	22.30	43.00	1949	100.00	53.50	56.00	1962	72.50	52.30	67.80
1937	48.35	28.80	28.80	1950	88.00	49.00	66.50	1963	80.00	63.50	74.20
1938	30.00	24.40	26.20	1951	74.00	59.00	74.00	1964	74.60	58.85	62.40
1939	34.95	24.45	34.95	1952	85.00	68.00	68.00	1965	85.50	60.70	64.55
1940	33.90	22.25	29.60	1953	72.50	55.50	72.00	1966	108.50	64.75	78.65
1941	42.50	26.60	42.50	1954	106.00	59.00	68.00	1967	89.00	68.10	71.90

Source: Chicago Board of Trade

SOYBEAN MEAL

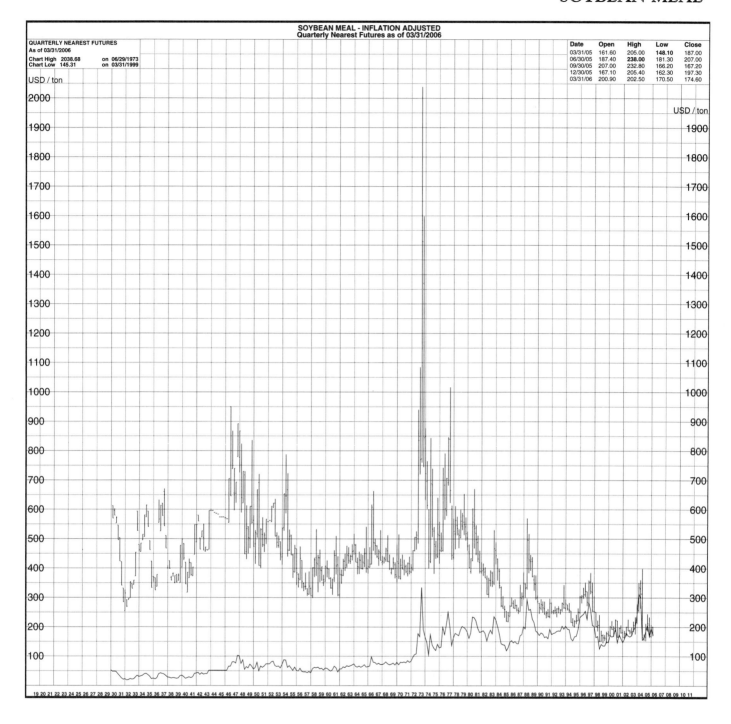

SOYBEAN MEAL

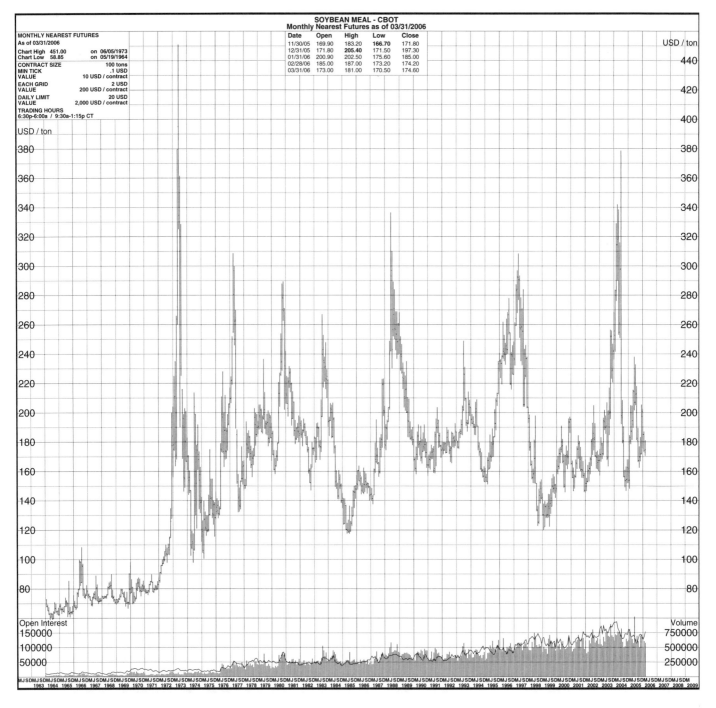

Annual High, Low and Close of Soybean Meal Futures   In Dollars per Ton

Year	High	Low	Close	Year	High	Low	Close	Year	High	Low	Close
1968	90.00	70.05	70.90	1981	242.00	178.50	184.20	1994	209.00	153.00	153.20
1969	90.50	66.50	79.70	1982	197.00	146.80	175.60	1995	235.00	151.10	233.20
1970	98.50	69.50	80.60	1983	267.00	166.00	224.70	1996	278.00	215.70	226.30
1971	89.70	75.70	83.00	1984	222.50	138.50	139.60	1997	308.50	203.00	203.80
1972	200.00	81.45	177.75	1985	150.50	117.50	148.20	1998	204.00	122.80	141.10
1973	451.00	146.50	167.00	1986	163.90	140.10	143.30	1999	158.00	120.00	146.70
1974	213.70	97.76	138.50	1987	223.20	137.50	201.50	2000	197.20	145.50	195.40
1975	175.00	100.50	128.40	1988	336.50	174.30	260.50	2001	196.00	145.80	147.10
1976	228.00	127.50	205.70	1989	268.40	177.80	181.60	2002	205.00	145.40	167.30
1977	308.70	132.00	163.40	1990	192.00	158.00	164.50	2003	256.50	157.10	241.90
1978	203.00	147.60	189.90	1991	203.70	157.00	174.70	2004	378.50	146.60	162.60
1979	236.50	177.00	182.80	1992	192.80	165.50	187.40	2005	238.00	148.10	197.30
1980	289.50	158.10	231.80	1993	249.00	175.20	203.80	2006	202.50	170.50	174.60

Source: Chicago Board of Trade

SOYBEAN MEAL

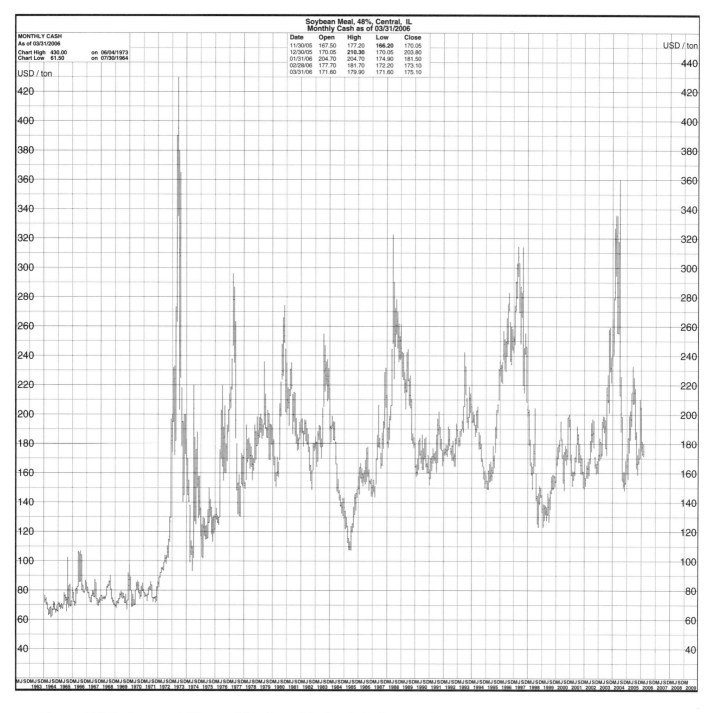

Annual High, Low and Close of Soybean Meal   In Dollars per Ton

Year	High	Low	Close	Year	High	Low	Close	Year	High	Low	Close
1968	90.00	70.00	70.50	1981	235.00	175.00	186.00	1994	205.50	150.00	153.00
1969	92.00	67.00	87.00	1982	197.00	148.50	179.75	1995	231.00	149.00	231.00
1970	98.00	68.50	79.50	1983	255.00	164.50	226.00	1996	283.00	221.00	244.00
1971	86.00	71.50	82.00	1984	217.50	131.00	131.00	1997	314.50	208.50	208.50
1972	197.00	80.50	185.00	1985	149.00	107.50	149.00	1998	206.25	123.00	143.50
1973	430.00	140.00	173.00	1986	178.00	144.00	147.00	1999	159.00	123.00	154.25
1974	220.00	93.00	135.00	1987	231.50	143.50	211.50	2000	200.00	148.00	199.00
1975	150.00	102.00	121.00	1988	322.50	177.00	250.50	2001	196.50	150.50	150.50
1976	220.00	121.00	203.00	1989	261.50	177.00	180.00	2002	197.00	149.50	166.50
1977	296.00	130.00	170.50	1990	186.25	157.50	160.50	2003	259.00	160.00	239.00
1978	198.50	149.50	187.00	1991	202.00	152.00	172.50	2004	360.00	148.00	165.60
1979	236.00	169.00	179.50	1992	194.00	164.50	192.00	2005	232.90	155.70	203.80
1980	274.50	150.50	223.00	1993	242.50	178.00	207.00	2006	204.70	171.60	175.10

Central Illinois.   *Source: Chicago Board of Trade*

SOYBEAN MEAL

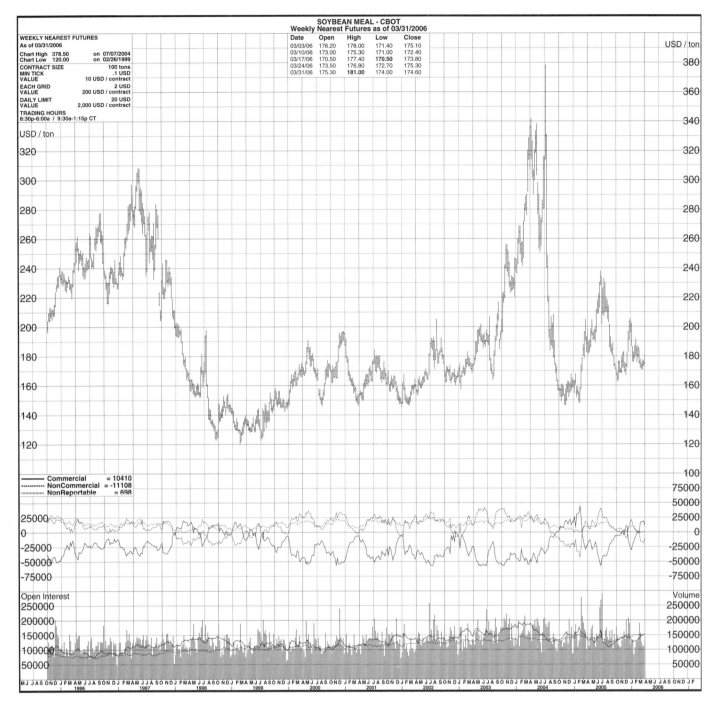

Quarterly High, Low and Close of Soybean Meal Futures   In Dollars per Ton

Quarter	High	Low	Close	Quarter	High	Low	Close	Quarter	High	Low	Close
09/1996	278.00	239.50	254.50	12/1999	158.00	141.80	146.70	03/2003	183.20	157.10	171.90
12/1996	254.50	215.70	226.30	03/2000	175.50	145.50	172.20	06/2003	201.80	170.80	190.80
03/1997	287.50	225.90	283.00	06/2000	191.00	165.50	166.90	09/2003	217.00	163.30	199.80
06/1997	308.50	251.00	258.00	09/2000	177.50	145.70	171.30	12/2003	256.50	195.60	241.90
09/1997	284.00	204.00	205.40	12/2000	197.20	161.50	195.40	03/2004	329.00	236.20	314.30
12/1997	246.20	203.00	203.80	03/2001	196.00	146.50	146.70	06/2004	342.00	250.70	297.50
03/1998	204.00	163.80	164.80	06/2001	177.00	148.20	175.20	09/2004	378.50	156.00	156.20
06/1998	181.50	151.80	168.70	09/2001	184.50	160.10	161.40	12/2004	168.00	146.60	162.60
09/1998	198.00	122.80	125.40	12/2001	170.00	145.80	147.10	03/2005	205.00	148.10	187.00
12/1998	154.50	124.10	141.10	03/2002	168.00	145.40	160.30	06/2005	238.00	181.30	207.00
03/1999	145.00	120.00	135.70	06/2002	181.80	153.00	180.40	09/2005	232.80	166.20	167.20
06/1999	144.50	128.10	135.90	09/2002	205.00	170.10	170.30	12/2005	205.40	162.30	197.30
09/1999	155.30	122.30	150.10	12/2002	174.00	160.20	167.30	03/2006	202.50	170.50	174.60

Source: Chicago Board of Trade

SOYBEAN MEAL

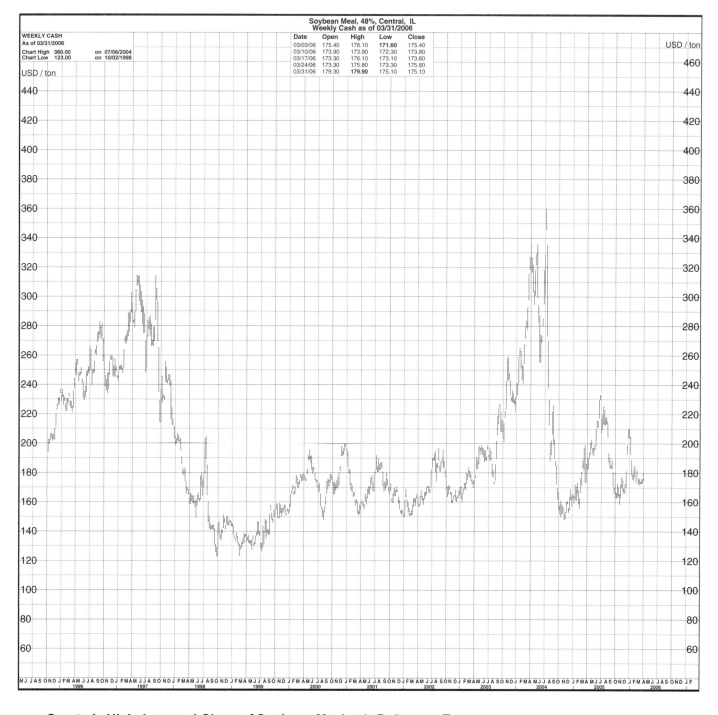

Quarterly High, Low and Close of Soybean Meal In Dollars per Ton

Quarter	High	Low	Close	Quarter	High	Low	Close	Quarter	High	Low	Close
09/1996	283.00	239.50	271.50	12/1999	159.00	149.00	154.25	03/2003	184.00	160.00	173.00
12/1996	263.00	234.00	244.00	03/2000	179.00	154.00	179.00	06/2003	199.00	172.00	192.00
03/1997	290.50	241.50	290.50	06/2000	195.50	170.50	170.50	09/2003	227.00	172.00	209.50
06/1997	314.50	269.50	269.50	09/2000	179.00	148.00	175.50	12/2003	259.00	201.00	239.00
09/1997	314.00	220.00	220.00	12/2000	200.00	165.50	199.00	03/2004	327.00	233.50	319.50
12/1997	255.50	208.50	208.50	03/2001	196.50	151.00	152.00	06/2004	336.00	255.00	309.50
03/1998	206.25	165.50	165.50	06/2001	179.00	155.00	179.00	09/2004	360.00	155.00	155.00
06/1998	180.00	149.00	175.00	09/2001	192.00	167.00	167.50	12/2004	168.90	148.00	165.60
09/1998	204.50	125.50	125.50	12/2001	172.50	150.50	150.50	03/2005	199.20	155.70	187.00
12/1998	151.50	123.00	143.50	03/2002	169.00	149.50	163.50	06/2005	232.90	182.70	207.50
03/1999	145.50	123.00	136.00	06/2002	182.00	156.50	182.00	09/2005	225.20	163.20	166.40
06/1999	146.50	127.50	140.00	09/2002	197.00	174.50	177.50	12/2005	210.30	158.80	203.80
09/1999	157.75	126.50	154.50	12/2002	171.50	159.50	166.50	03/2006	204.70	171.60	175.10

Central Illinois.   *Source: Chicago Board of Trade*

SOYBEAN OIL

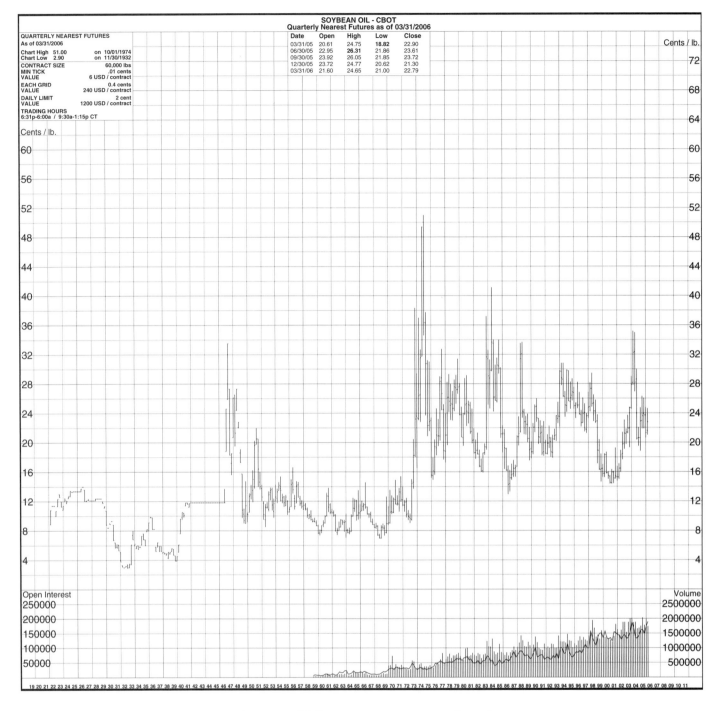

Annual High, Low and Close of Soybean Oil Futures   In Cents per Pound

Year	High	Low	Close	Year	High	Low	Close	Year	High	Low	Close
1929	12.38	8.80	8.80	1942	11.80	11.80	11.80	1955	12.88	10.13	10.90
1930	9.30	6.70	6.70	1943	11.80	11.80	11.80	1956	16.63	10.88	14.10
1931	6.40	3.80	3.80	1944	11.80	11.80	11.80	1957	14.63	10.88	11.40
1932	3.40	2.90	3.00	1945	11.80	11.80	11.80	1958	11.75	9.38	9.50
1933	8.00	3.00	6.20	1946	24.60	11.80	24.60	1959	9.75	7.51	7.66
1934	7.30	5.50	7.30	1947	33.50	15.60	26.10	1960	10.07	7.37	9.92
1935	9.10	6.00	9.10	1948	27.30	17.30	17.30	1961	13.85	9.93	10.43
1936	9.90	5.20	5.20	1949	15.75	9.00	10.20	1962	10.73	7.40	8.48
1937	6.40	5.00	5.10	1950	20.25	10.50	19.60	1963	10.30	7.05	8.06
1938	5.10	4.20	5.10	1951	22.00	12.00	12.60	1964	12.46	7.51	11.03
1939	5.60	3.90	4.50	1952	13.38	8.50	12.90	1965	13.50	9.36	10.61
1940	10.50	5.10	10.10	1953	14.25	9.75	12.60	1966	14.58	10.17	10.26
1941	11.80	11.20	11.80	1954	15.38	11.75	12.50	1967	10.55	8.37	8.44

Source: Chicago Board of Trade

SOYBEAN OIL

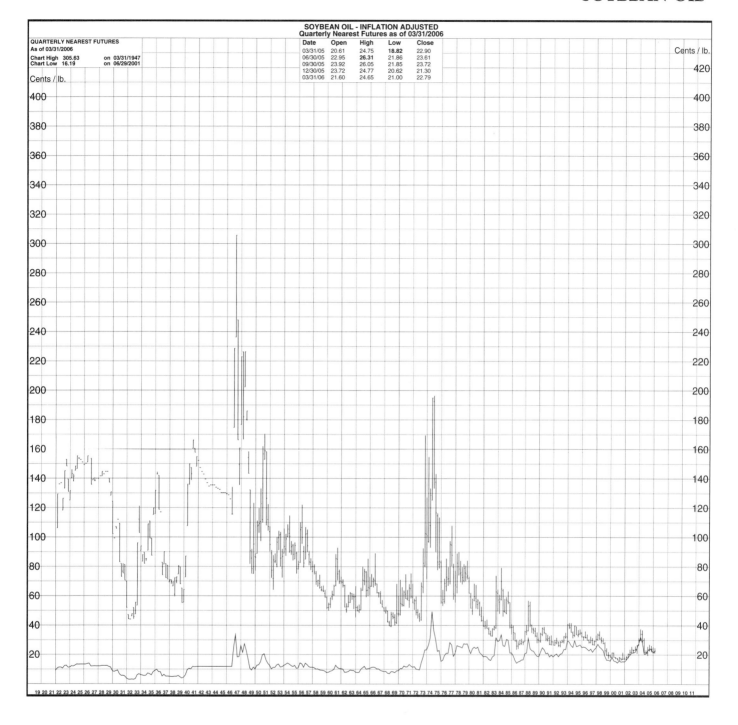

SOYBEAN OIL

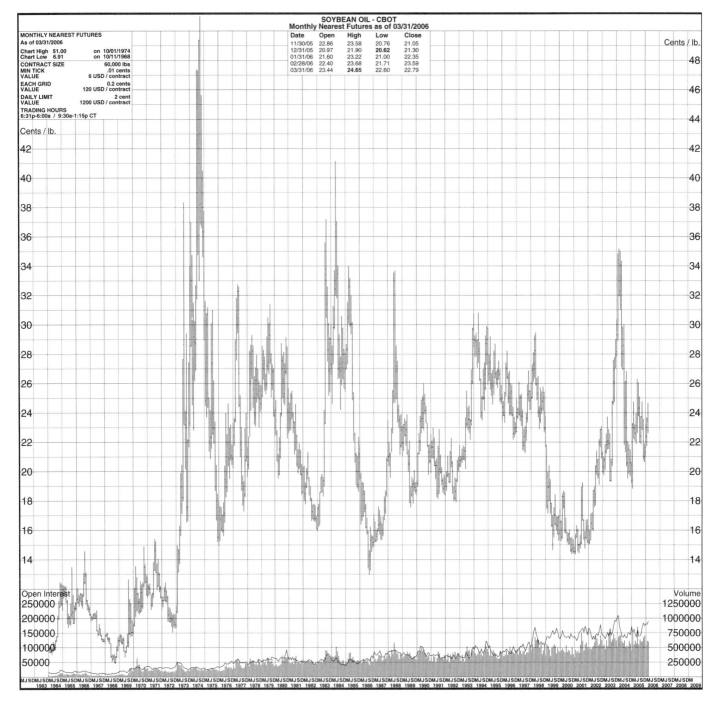

Annual High, Low and Close of Soybean Oil Futures — In Cents per Pound

Year	High	Low	Close	Year	High	Low	Close	Year	High	Low	Close
1968	9.04	6.91	8.45	1981	25.68	18.45	18.59	1994	30.82	23.48	29.83
1969	12.65	7.32	9.05	1982	21.32	16.08	16.08	1995	29.75	24.57	24.97
1970	14.90	8.95	11.62	1983	37.20	15.91	29.07	1996	28.23	22.16	22.71
1971	15.40	10.57	11.47	1984	41.15	24.21	25.72	1997	26.87	21.25	24.79
1972	12.43	9.03	9.60	1985	34.00	18.63	21.26	1998	29.46	22.65	22.83
1973	38.33	9.36	23.35	1986	21.82	12.95	15.18	1999	23.80	14.65	15.75
1974	51.00	22.80	36.35	1987	20.95	14.90	20.77	2000	18.70	14.36	14.53
1975	37.75	15.20	15.55	1988	33.70	19.57	22.82	2001	19.26	14.35	15.27
1976	24.65	14.92	20.90	1989	23.90	17.54	18.70	2002	23.08	14.99	21.24
1977	32.75	17.27	20.99	1990	26.00	18.37	20.74	2003	29.00	19.30	27.87
1978	29.30	19.63	24.60	1991	23.00	18.15	18.50	2004	35.18	19.50	20.61
1979	31.40	23.75	23.78	1992	22.29	17.89	20.47	2005	26.31	18.82	21.30
1980	29.15	19.53	24.25	1993	29.80	20.17	29.71	2006	24.65	21.00	22.79

Source: Chicago Board of Trade

SOYBEAN OIL

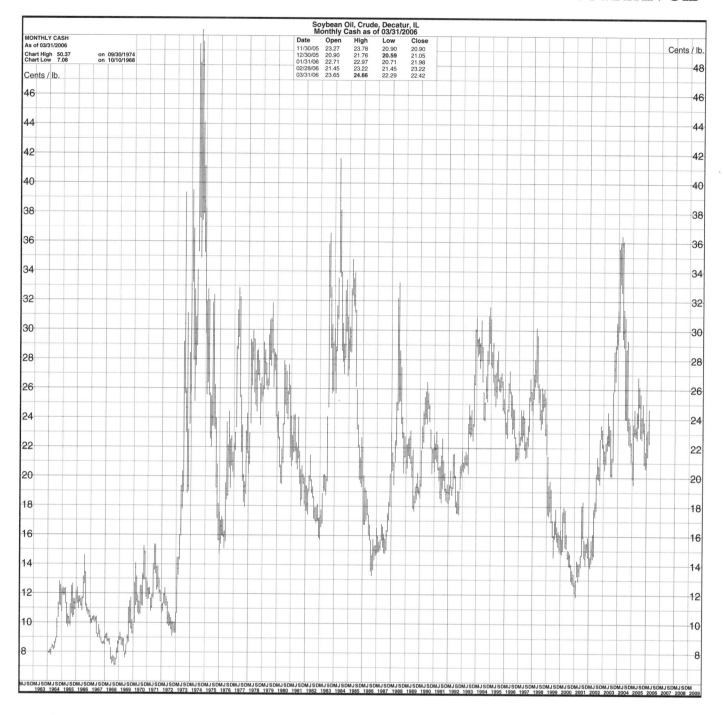

Annual High, Low and Close of Soybean Oil   In Cents per Pound

Year	High	Low	Close	Year	High	Low	Close	Year	High	Low	Close
1968	9.31	7.08	8.65	1981	24.26	18.00	18.27	1994	31.57	23.85	31.57
1969	11.73	7.61	9.36	1982	21.48	15.88	15.88	1995	30.75	24.38	24.56
1970	15.25	9.26	11.76	1983	36.60	15.73	29.01	1996	27.25	21.06	21.25
1971	15.38	10.79	11.47	1984	41.68	25.67	28.22	1997	26.72	21.32	25.04
1972	12.39	9.09	9.54	1985	34.83	19.34	21.79	1998	30.18	22.84	22.93
1973	39.35	9.35	25.68	1986	22.02	13.27	14.88	1999	23.67	14.53	15.15
1974	50.37	25.10	37.13	1987	20.20	14.76	20.17	2000	17.94	12.65	12.66
1975	38.25	15.65	15.65	1988	33.25	19.45	21.69	2001	18.35	11.83	14.62
1976	24.45	14.73	20.55	1989	23.18	17.65	18.93	2002	23.52	13.85	22.12
1977	32.87	17.90	21.59	1990	26.46	18.60	21.01	2003	30.52	20.05	29.25
1978	29.97	20.19	25.57	1991	23.13	18.25	18.30	2004	36.45	21.05	21.59
1979	31.85	24.10	24.10	1992	21.60	17.42	20.47	2005	26.83	19.49	21.05
1980	27.93	19.52	23.20	1993	30.07	20.20	30.07	2006	24.66	20.71	22.42

Decatur, Illinois.   *Source: Chicago Board of Trade*

SOYBEAN OIL

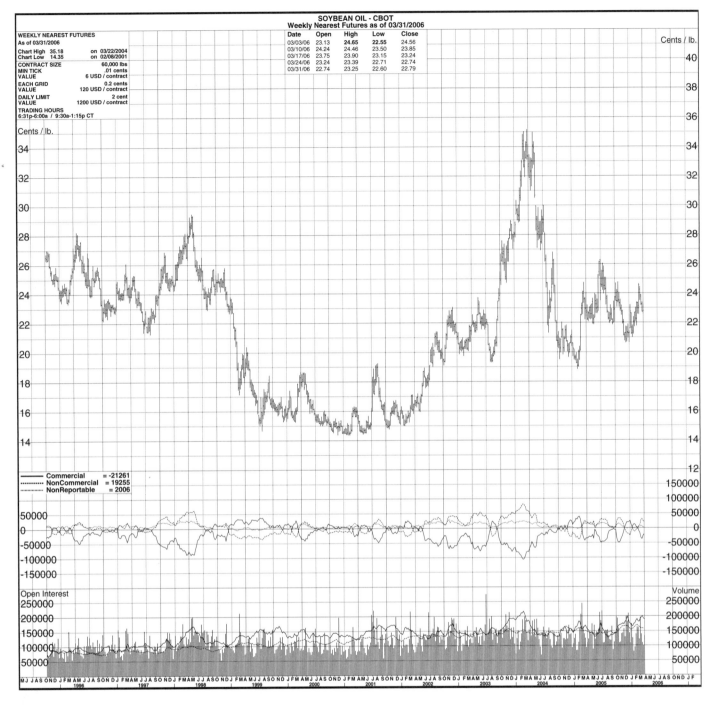

Quarterly High, Low and Close of Soybean Oil Futures   In Cents per Pound

Quarter	High	Low	Close	Quarter	High	Low	Close	Quarter	High	Low	Close
09/1996	26.85	23.78	23.86	12/1999	16.99	15.28	15.75	03/2003	21.86	19.75	21.37
12/1996	24.40	22.16	22.71	03/2000	18.48	15.25	18.31	06/2003	23.73	21.20	21.89
03/1997	26.10	22.68	23.92	06/2000	18.70	15.75	15.86	09/2003	24.82	19.30	24.71
06/1997	25.30	21.45	21.79	09/2000	16.05	15.01	15.49	12/2003	29.00	24.54	27.87
09/1997	24.00	21.25	23.60	12/2000	15.52	14.36	14.53	03/2004	35.18	27.80	32.23
12/1997	26.87	23.34	24.79	03/2001	16.33	14.35	15.95	06/2004	35.00	26.92	28.18
03/1998	28.15	24.20	27.33	06/2001	16.09	14.42	15.14	09/2004	30.00	20.34	20.52
06/1998	29.46	24.85	25.26	09/2001	19.26	15.05	15.40	12/2004	22.05	19.50	20.61
09/1998	26.50	22.89	24.28	12/2001	16.75	14.75	15.27	03/2005	24.75	18.82	22.90
12/1998	25.80	22.65	22.83	03/2002	17.13	14.99	16.46	06/2005	26.31	21.86	23.61
03/1999	23.80	17.13	18.91	06/2002	18.95	15.94	18.25	09/2005	26.05	21.85	23.72
06/1999	20.41	16.22	16.34	09/2002	21.40	17.67	19.74	12/2005	24.77	20.62	21.30
09/1999	18.45	14.65	16.39	12/2002	23.08	19.09	21.24	03/2006	24.65	21.00	22.79

Source: Chicago Board of Trade

SOYBEAN

Quarterly High, Low and Close of Soybean Oil   In Cents per Pound

Quarter	High	Low	Close	Quarter	High	Low	Close	Quarter	High	Low	Close
09/1996	25.63	22.68	22.68	12/1999	16.63	14.91	15.15	03/2003	22.37	20.51	22.00
12/1996	22.75	21.06	21.25	03/2000	17.63	14.75	17.63	06/2003	24.45	21.85	22.64
03/1997	24.62	21.37	22.56	06/2000	17.94	15.16	15.16	09/2003	25.84	20.05	25.84
06/1997	24.62	21.87	21.87	09/2000	15.04	13.89	14.11	12/2003	30.52	25.90	29.25
09/1997	23.55	21.32	23.35	12/2000	14.05	12.65	12.66	03/2004	35.98	29.09	35.03
12/1997	26.72	23.16	25.04	03/2001	14.33	11.83	14.20	06/2004	36.45	28.87	29.98
03/1998	28.02	24.26	27.33	06/2001	14.70	12.89	14.26	09/2004	30.90	23.27	23.27
06/1998	30.18	25.09	25.46	09/2001	18.35	14.52	14.52	12/2004	24.11	21.05	21.59
09/1998	26.12	23.26	24.85	12/2001	15.89	14.03	14.62	03/2005	24.62	19.49	23.28
12/1998	25.97	22.84	22.93	03/2002	15.71	13.85	14.84	06/2005	26.83	22.55	24.29
03/1999	23.67	17.33	18.68	06/2002	18.36	14.46	18.00	09/2005	26.19	22.59	24.10
06/1999	19.75	15.96	15.96	09/2002	21.39	17.71	20.22	12/2005	24.99	20.59	21.05
09/1999	17.84	14.53	16.15	12/2002	23.52	19.53	22.12	03/2006	24.66	20.71	22.42

Decatur, Illinois.   *Source: Chicago Board of Trade*

INDEXES - COMMODITIES

Commodity prices have been in a major bull market since late-2001. The 2001-06 rally is the second-largest in post-war history, second only to the 1971-74 rally.

The nearby chart shows the Reuters/Jefferies CRB index on both a nominal and inflation-adjusted basis (in 2006 dollars). The chart illustrates how commodity prices, despite the 92% bull market seen in the past several years, remain relatively cheap on an inflation-adjusted basis. In fact, the inflation-adjusted RJ/CRB index has not yet returned to where it was in 1985 and is currently one-half of the average value of about 700 seen during the 1960-70s. That tends to support Jim Roger's view expressed in his book, "Hot Commodities: How Anyone Can Invest Profitably in the World's Best Market," that the commodity bull market is still in its early innings.

From a macroeconomic standpoint, there are two main factors that drive commodity prices: inflation and the value of the dollar. Inflation and the dollar are similar in that inflation is a measure of the dollar in terms of the price of a basket of goods and services, whereas the dollar as a currency measures the value of the US currency in terms of the currencies of other nations (we use the Federal Reserve's dollar index here for the discussion). In either case, if the value of the dollar depreciates (i.e., higher inflation or a lower dollar in terms of foreign currencies), the price of commodities tends to rise simply because a dollar is worth less compared to the relatively stable value of a tangible commodity asset.

When inflation is rising or the dollar is falling, commodity prices tend to rise in unison. By the same token, commodity prices tend to fall in unison during a period of disinflation or a stronger dollar. Major commodity bull and bear markets therefore tend to emerge when inflation and/or the dollar are moving sharply. On the other hand, when inflation is low and the dollar is stable, there are no macroeconomic drivers for commodity prices and each commodity market then tends to move independently according to its own supply/demand fundamentals. With this background, we can better understand the drivers behind the major bull and bear markets in commodities seen in the past several decades.

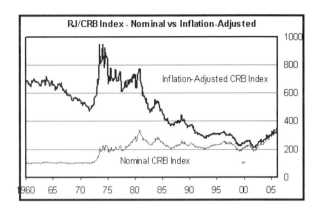

1970s Commodity Bull Market

The biggest commodity bull market in post-war history (so far) was the 146.7% rally in the RJ/CRB index seen in 1971-74. That rally was driven by a sharp increase in inflation and related weakness in the dollar. As the nearby table shows, US inflation during that bull market averaged +4.9% and the dollar averaged a yearly decline of -7.5%. Inflation at the time stemmed from the Federal Reserve's overly easy monetary policy. The weak dollar stemmed from inflation and the fact that the dollar was adjusting downward after the Bretton Woods agreement broke down and currencies started floating.

In addition to inflation and a weak dollar, there were supply/demand factors in particular markets that helped drive the 1971-74 commodity bull market. Grain and soybean prices soared during that time largely because of huge Soviet grain and soybean purchases in 1972 and 1973. The 1971-74 bull market was also driven in its latter stages by the October 1973 Arab Oil Embargo, which caused oil prices to triple, thus pushing the RJ/CRB index higher.

1977-80 Bull Market

After the RJ/CRB index peaked in 1974, commodity prices moved sideways during the mid-1970s as inflation and demand were undercut by the severe US recession seen in 1973-75. After the recession, however, commodity prices staged the third largest bull market in post-war history of +82.8% during 1977-80. Inflation was the key driver behind

Commodity Bull Markets Ranked by Percentage Gain (1960-2006)

	Low		High		Percent Rally	Rally Duration (months)	Avg CPI (yr-yr%)	Avg Dollar Index (yr/yr%)	Correlation CRB-CPI	Correlation CRB-DXY
1971-74	Oct 1971	96.40	Feb 1974	237.80	146.7%	28	4.9%	-7.5%	0.97	-0.79
2001-06	Oct 2001	182.83	Feb 2006	350.96	92.0%	53	2.5%	-5.2%	0.96	-0.71
1977-80	Aug 1977	184.70	Nov 1980	337.60	82.8%	39	10.2%	-5.2%	0.96	-0.93
1986-88	Jul 1986	196.16	Jun 1988	272.19	38.8%	23	3.2%	-13.3%	0.89	-0.68
1992-96	Aug 1992	198.17	Apr 1996	263.79	33.1%	44	2.8%	-0.6%	0.96	-0.32

Note: Data is current through March 31, 2006.   *Source: Commodity Research Bureau*

INDEXES - COMMODITIES

that rally. The US CPI during that commodity bull market averaged an extraordinarily high +10.2%. The dollar was also weak during that time with an average -5.2% yr/yr decline in the dollar index.

1980-2001 Bear Market

Fed Chairman Paul Volcker started to crack down on inflation in 1979, causing the double-dip recession in 1980 and 1981-82. Commodity prices were forced lower in the early-1980s by the double-dip recessions and the downward trend in inflation. Commodity prices were also pushed lower by the sharp rally in the dollar seen from 1980 until the 1985 Plaza Accord. Crude oil prices trended downward from 1981-85 and then plunged to $10 per barrel in March 1986, also undercutting the commodity indexes in the early to mid-1980s.

Although the RJ/CRB index was volatile in the 1980s and 1990s, the general trend was downward. On an inflation-adjusted basis (see chart on previous page), it is easy to see that in reality commodity prices were in a serious bear market from 1980 until 2001. The key causes for the bear market were (1) the success of global central banks in taming inflation, and (2) greatly expanded supply in nearly all commodity markets due to improved technology and new producers coming into the markets (e.g., Brazil in the agricultural markets).

2001-06 Bull Market

Commodity prices hit a post-war low in inflation-adjusted terms in October 2001. Commodity prices were depressed in 2001 due to the post-bubble plunge in the US stock market, the US recession in 2001, and a US inflation rate that fell sharply through 2001 (i.e., from 3.7% in Jan-2001 to +1.1% by mid-2002).

However, commodity prices bottomed out in October 2001 as the Federal Reserve was in the process of slashing interest rates to revive the economy and prevent a an extremely damaging deflationary episode such as the one Japan experienced from 1990-2005. The Fed during 2001 slashed the funds rate target by 4.75 percentage points from 6.50% to 1.75%, and then cut the funds rate by another 0.75 percentage points to 1.00% by mid-2003. The Fed left the funds rate target at an extraordinarily low 1.00% for a year until June 2004 to ensure that a US recovery would take hold.

The Fed's sharp easing of monetary policy was the key reason why the dollar started plunging in early 2002 and fell by a total of 33% through late 2004. The dollar also plunged during 2002-04 because of the soaring US current account deficit (which is the broadest measure of US trade). The US current account deficit as a percentage of GDP was also already at 4% of GDP in 2002, but then proceeded to balloon to 6.3% of GDP by the end of 2004 (widening further to 7.0% by the end of 2005).

The plunge in the dollar was the key reason behind the

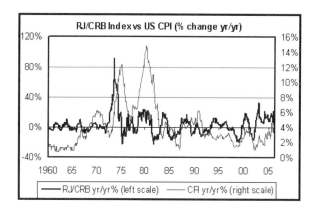

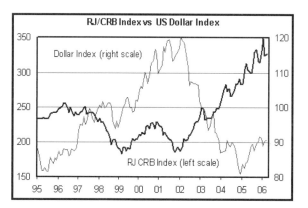

rally in the RJ/CRB index during the first 3 years of the bull market (i.e., 2002-04). The nearby chart illustrates the very strong negative correlation of -0.94 seen between the dollar index and the RJ/CRB index over the 2002-04 period. Simply put, as the dollar went straight down, commodity prices went straight up. Yet inflation remained low over this period because the market had confidence in the Fed's inflation-fighting intentions and because globalization increased the supply of goods available throughout the world. This new competition meant that US companies could not raise prices without losing market share. Inflation during the current commodity bull market has so far averaged only +2.5%.

The commodity rally continued in 2005 but for different reasons. In 2005, the dollar started to recover because of the Fed's tighter monetary policy. Yet the RJ/CRB index rallied even in the face of the stronger dollar because of strong demand in key commodity markets, driven in large part by China. China, with its truly massive scale of development, drove the prices of many commodity prices higher, particularly energy prices, metals prices, and construction materials prices.

Looking ahead, the outlook is generally favorable for commodity prices, assuming there are no economic stumbles in the US or China. Demand for most commodities remains strong and the dollar remains on thin ice because of the massive US current account deficit. Moreover, as seen earlier, commodity prices on average are still only half the real prices seen back in the 1960s.

REUTERS-CRB INDEX (CCI)

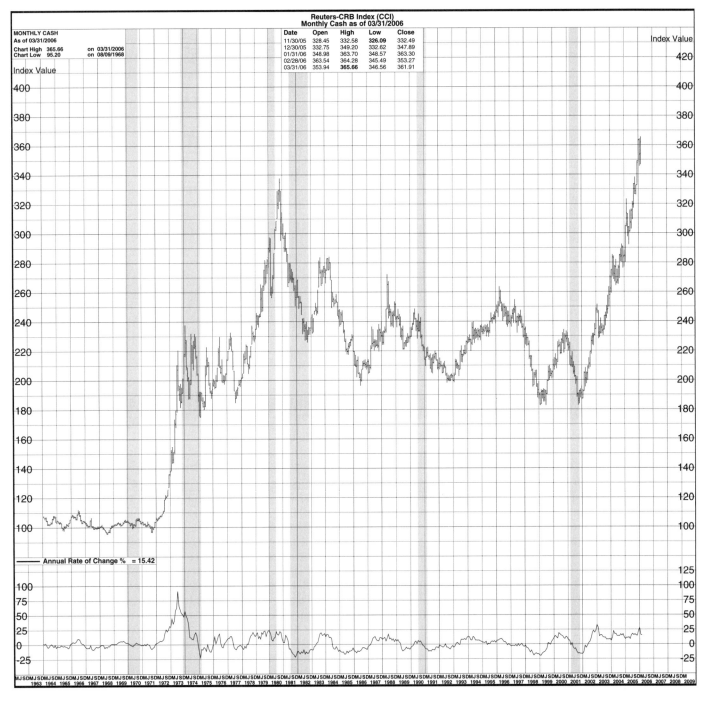

Annual High, Low and Close of Reuters-CRB Index (CCI)   Index Value

Year	High	Low	Close	Year	High	Low	Close	Year	High	Low	Close
1968	102.00	95.20	100.80	1981	314.50	250.50	254.90	1994	239.72	219.89	236.64
1969	105.40	100.90	103.90	1982	268.60	225.80	234.00	1995	246.47	229.31	243.18
1970	106.40	99.10	102.50	1983	283.80	232.10	277.60	1996	263.79	235.99	239.61
1971	104.10	96.40	103.40	1984	284.20	244.00	244.20	1997	254.79	228.84	229.14
1972	136.30	103.40	135.90	1985	248.10	217.30	229.37	1998	236.08	187.89	191.22
1973	220.70	135.10	200.60	1986	230.88	196.16	209.07	1999	209.91	182.67	205.14
1974	237.80	187.30	203.90	1987	238.21	204.24	232.53	2000	234.38	201.43	227.83
1975	222.90	175.10	191.00	1988	272.19	224.00	251.83	2001	232.58	182.83	190.61
1976	229.70	191.20	204.70	1989	252.37	220.82	229.93	2002	238.39	186.38	234.52
1977	232.70	184.70	200.30	1990	248.76	219.69	222.64	2003	263.60	228.10	255.29
1978	237.40	198.90	227.60	1991	222.96	204.43	208.08	2004	292.49	257.49	283.90
1979	282.80	228.40	281.50	1992	215.30	198.17	202.76	2005	349.20	277.07	347.89
1980	337.60	256.30	308.50	1993	226.76	198.38	226.31	2006	365.66	345.49	361.91

Source: Reuters

REUTERS-CRB INDEX (CCI)

Quarterly High, Low and Close of Reuters-CRB Index (CCI)   Index Value

Quarter	High	Low	Close	Quarter	High	Low	Close	Quarter	High	Low	Close
09/1996	252.04	240.09	245.63	12/1999	209.91	199.66	205.14	03/2003	251.59	228.10	232.15
12/1996	249.59	235.99	239.61	03/2000	217.88	201.43	214.37	06/2003	242.16	228.77	233.78
03/1997	248.01	236.14	245.17	06/2000	227.29	207.61	223.93	09/2003	246.07	230.36	243.66
06/1997	254.79	238.52	239.42	09/2000	232.20	217.42	226.57	12/2003	263.60	241.68	255.29
09/1997	245.30	232.01	243.06	12/2000	234.38	218.38	227.83	03/2004	285.28	257.49	283.77
12/1997	247.62	228.84	229.14	03/2001	232.58	210.24	210.26	06/2004	284.42	264.34	265.94
03/1998	236.08	221.56	228.88	06/2001	219.29	203.86	205.56	09/2004	285.37	265.20	284.98
06/1998	229.09	208.42	214.63	09/2001	209.27	188.24	190.49	12/2004	292.49	276.15	283.90
09/1998	216.75	195.18	203.30	12/2001	193.94	182.83	190.61	03/2005	323.33	277.07	313.57
12/1998	206.73	187.89	191.22	03/2002	205.45	186.38	204.92	06/2005	315.79	292.06	306.91
03/1999	198.96	182.76	191.83	06/2002	209.33	195.21	209.29	09/2005	333.58	302.71	333.33
06/1999	193.99	185.05	191.54	09/2002	229.62	207.24	226.53	12/2005	349.20	326.09	347.89
09/1999	209.41	182.67	205.19	12/2002	238.39	223.29	234.52	03/2006	365.66	345.49	361.91

Source: Reuters

REUTERS/JEFFERIES-CRB INDEX

Quarterly High, Low and Close of Reuters/Jefferies-CRB Index   Index Value

Quarter	High	Low	Close	Quarter	High	Low	Close	Quarter	High	Low	Close
09/1996	252.04	240.09	245.63	12/1999	209.91	199.66	205.14	03/2003	251.59	228.10	232.15
12/1996	249.59	235.99	239.61	03/2000	217.88	201.43	214.37	06/2003	242.16	228.77	233.78
03/1997	248.01	236.14	245.17	06/2000	227.29	207.61	223.93	09/2003	246.07	230.36	243.66
06/1997	254.79	238.52	239.42	09/2000	232.20	217.42	226.57	12/2003	263.60	241.68	255.29
09/1997	245.30	232.01	243.06	12/2000	234.38	218.38	227.83	03/2004	285.28	257.49	283.77
12/1997	247.62	228.84	229.14	03/2001	232.58	210.24	210.26	06/2004	284.42	264.34	265.94
03/1998	236.08	221.56	228.88	06/2001	219.29	203.86	205.56	09/2004	285.37	265.20	284.98
06/1998	229.09	208.42	214.63	09/2001	209.27	188.24	190.49	12/2004	292.49	276.15	283.90
09/1998	216.75	195.18	203.30	12/2001	193.94	182.83	190.61	03/2005	323.33	277.07	313.57
12/1998	206.73	187.89	191.22	03/2002	205.45	186.38	204.92	06/2005	313.91	292.06	300.00
03/1999	198.96	182.76	191.83	06/2002	209.33	195.21	209.29	09/2005	337.18	299.51	332.97
06/1999	193.99	185.05	191.54	09/2002	229.62	207.24	226.53	12/2005	336.42	310.81	331.83
09/1999	209.41	182.67	205.19	12/2002	238.39	223.29	234.52	03/2006	350.96	316.06	333.18

Source: Reuters

REUTERS/JEFFERIES-CRB TOTAL RETURN INDEX

Quarterly High, Low and Close of RJ/CRB Total Return Index — Index Value

Quarter	High	Low	Close	Quarter	High	Low	Close	Quarter	High	Low	Close
09/1996	213.34	203.67	209.55	12/1999	181.61	173.03	178.07	03/2003	214.03	197.50	200.92
12/1996	213.19	203.41	210.35	03/2000	189.08	174.04	186.68	06/2003	209.88	197.14	202.54
03/1997	222.54	211.11	221.21	06/2000	207.52	182.09	195.06	09/2003	212.32	200.34	210.87
06/1997	230.52	216.97	220.61	09/2000	202.74	189.98	200.19	12/2003	228.14	209.48	222.14
09/1997	228.34	213.89	227.92	12/2000	211.22	194.82	203.47	03/2004	250.33	224.03	249.10
12/1997	231.26	219.56	219.56	03/2001	207.07	187.62	189.30	06/2004	250.23	231.16	234.32
03/1998	225.25	212.57	218.08	06/2001	197.31	182.57	183.78	09/2004	249.35	229.06	249.04
06/1998	218.68	199.74	203.41	09/2001	187.56	169.25	170.11	12/2004	255.20	242.46	249.80
09/1998	203.00	183.20	188.69	12/2001	171.37	163.56	168.51	03/2005	284.41	243.43	276.15
12/1998	190.28	172.09	174.47	03/2002	179.41	164.07	178.98	06/2005	276.48	257.06	268.09
03/1999	179.31	163.26	170.85	06/2002	182.33	170.68	179.55	09/2005	297.97	263.63	295.06
06/1999	170.23	164.69	167.21	09/2002	195.57	179.38	192.98	12/2005	305.04	277.24	296.91
09/1999	188.85	159.09	177.22	12/2002	202.15	189.16	199.55	03/2006	315.23	285.17	301.44

Source: Reuters

CRB INDUSTRIALS SUB-INDEX

Annual High, Low and Close of CRB Industrials Sub-Index   Index Value

Year	High	Low	Close	Year	High	Low	Close	Year	High	Low	Close
1971	90.30	82.00	90.30	1983	281.90	242.70	249.00	1995	286.88	261.03	265.50
1972	122.90	89.70	122.80	1984	278.70	216.80	217.00	1996	280.33	247.96	271.12
1973	171.30	122.60	170.70	1985	224.70	202.10	211.70	1997	273.97	210.14	210.91
1974	214.80	132.10	132.10	1986	214.30	168.50	210.39	1998	223.07	182.56	185.30
1975	160.60	128.00	154.80	1987	272.33	210.71	252.47	1999	196.14	171.38	192.88
1976	192.20	152.50	173.60	1988	258.12	224.08	246.96	2000	227.84	189.34	210.99
1977	190.00	160.30	175.00	1989	261.00	240.59	249.64	2001	212.45	124.26	141.84
1978	228.30	176.10	222.10	1990	274.74	235.48	245.46	2002	183.06	142.65	176.61
1979	354.80	220.50	354.80	1991	242.99	214.28	217.18	2003	257.50	178.46	256.64
1980	429.00	289.40	324.60	1992	235.58	216.27	226.35	2004	292.64	213.10	232.09
1981	333.00	248.70	249.20	1993	251.97	223.94	251.73	2005	304.46	220.18	302.48
1982	254.60	195.50	249.90	1994	277.11	246.90	276.81	2006	336.66	299.60	330.91

Source: Reuters

CRB INDUSTRIALS SUB-INDEX

Quarterly High, Low and Close of CRB Industrials Sub-Index   Index Value

Quarter	High	Low	Close	Quarter	High	Low	Close	Quarter	High	Low	Close
09/1996	268.87	249.56	261.29	12/1999	194.59	182.52	192.88	03/2003	198.15	178.46	187.09
12/1996	271.94	261.62	271.12	03/2000	209.80	190.50	200.09	06/2003	196.23	178.98	195.93
03/1997	273.97	266.01	267.38	06/2000	212.95	189.34	199.39	09/2003	219.18	193.71	217.52
06/1997	271.65	260.97	267.62	09/2000	227.84	196.70	220.74	12/2003	257.50	217.16	256.64
09/1997	267.62	240.20	242.07	12/2000	225.65	210.82	210.99	03/2004	292.64	253.95	266.31
12/1997	243.16	210.14	210.91	03/2001	212.45	171.20	171.28	06/2004	267.65	219.24	228.16
03/1998	223.07	201.43	213.62	06/2001	181.27	155.17	161.63	09/2004	242.14	213.10	232.62
06/1998	222.31	200.56	218.11	09/2001	162.31	139.84	140.21	12/2004	241.64	214.81	232.09
09/1998	221.12	205.55	212.88	12/2001	157.33	124.26	141.84	03/2005	260.65	220.18	258.08
12/1998	213.90	182.56	185.30	03/2002	161.29	142.65	158.09	06/2005	269.67	239.04	264.67
03/1999	187.47	172.03	177.97	06/2002	181.24	144.45	180.95	09/2005	279.95	253.93	276.01
06/1999	194.26	171.38	187.67	09/2002	181.36	159.05	160.11	12/2005	304.46	275.91	302.48
09/1999	196.14	177.88	192.28	12/2002	183.06	154.54	176.61	03/2006	336.66	299.60	330.91

Source: Reuters

CRB GRAINS & OILSEEDS SUB-INDEX

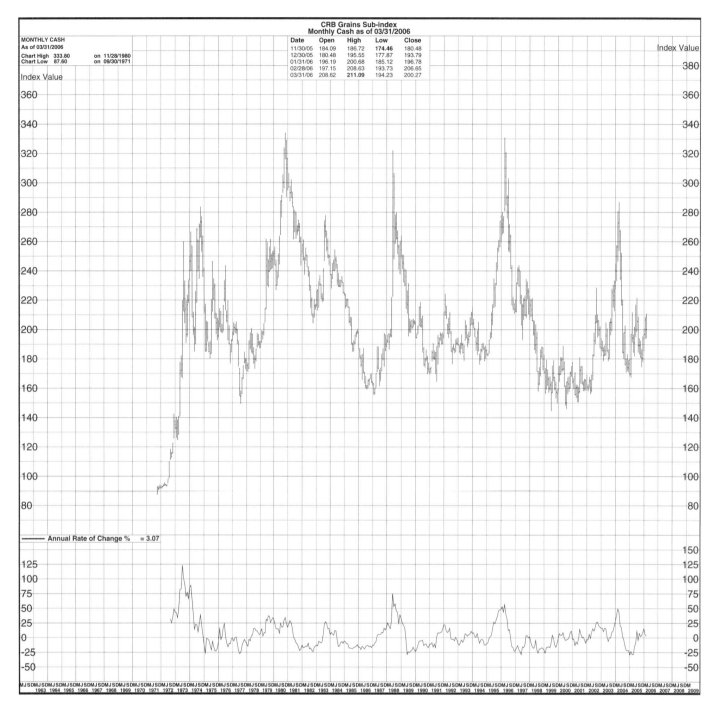

Annual High, Low and Close of CRB Grains Sub-Index   Index Value

Year	High	Low	Close	Year	High	Low	Close	Year	High	Low	Close
1971	94.20	87.60	92.50	1983	278.00	213.20	249.60	1995	274.01	182.24	274.01
1972	142.60	91.60	137.50	1984	254.50	224.50	224.90	1996	330.94	210.96	211.24
1973	259.80	124.70	228.90	1985	225.20	184.80	198.50	1997	244.02	193.03	210.67
1974	283.80	185.00	240.20	1986	198.50	159.10	164.63	1998	222.65	157.83	172.84
1975	246.70	180.60	195.60	1987	197.43	155.36	186.14	1999	182.96	144.63	156.64
1976	243.90	176.70	192.50	1988	322.00	186.45	258.47	2000	188.94	146.04	174.94
1977	205.50	149.50	179.00	1989	263.87	195.58	205.74	2001	181.12	150.62	159.04
1978	200.90	171.30	187.80	1990	218.72	169.68	171.18	2002	228.67	156.03	188.23
1979	262.00	187.40	251.90	1991	198.10	164.51	196.11	2003	233.61	178.33	225.75
1980	333.80	227.20	312.10	1992	224.36	176.25	190.43	2004	286.90	170.71	176.99
1981	317.10	243.60	251.30	1993	211.77	178.63	211.77	2005	221.67	167.32	193.79
1982	261.10	204.20	215.10	1994	215.14	176.01	185.50	2006	211.09	185.12	200.27

Source: Reuters

CRB GRAINS & OILSEEDS SUB-INDEX

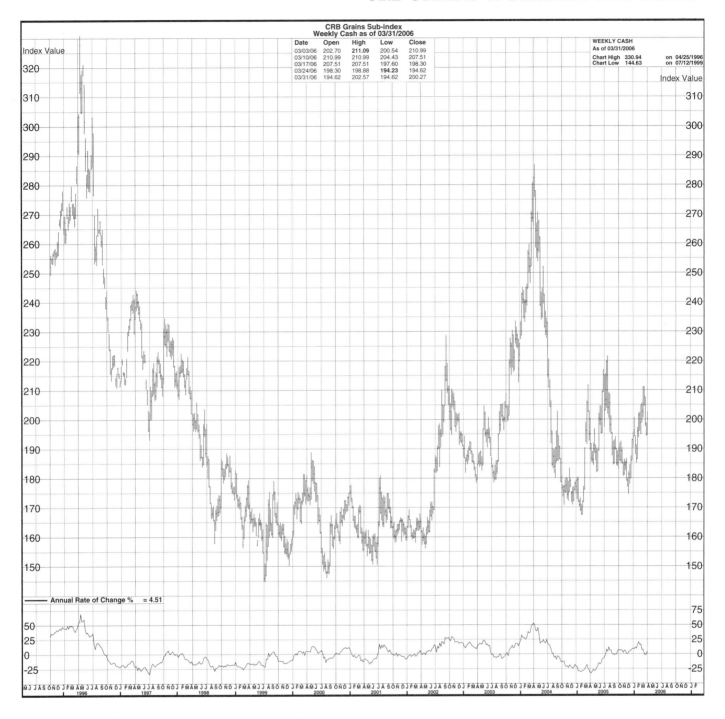

Quarterly High, Low and Close of CRB Grains Sub-Index Index Value

Quarter	High	Low	Close	Quarter	High	Low	Close	Quarter	High	Low	Close
09/1996	303.08	241.69	241.69	12/1999	167.61	150.21	156.64	03/2003	194.35	178.33	182.69
12/1996	243.99	210.96	211.24	03/2000	181.42	157.06	179.25	06/2003	204.78	182.10	185.66
03/1997	242.56	211.97	240.56	06/2000	188.94	161.19	161.43	09/2003	207.67	178.41	205.04
06/1997	244.02	203.05	203.05	09/2000	167.43	146.04	163.01	12/2003	233.61	199.09	225.75
09/1997	223.20	193.03	209.79	12/2000	174.96	157.60	174.94	03/2004	280.73	227.31	272.63
12/1997	234.56	208.02	210.67	03/2001	177.85	155.33	155.63	06/2004	286.90	216.33	218.92
03/1998	222.65	205.59	206.26	06/2001	162.56	150.62	157.73	09/2004	220.61	175.85	176.21
06/1998	206.26	183.79	194.41	09/2001	181.12	156.78	163.24	12/2004	183.42	170.71	176.99
09/1998	198.69	157.83	170.12	12/2001	166.66	158.06	159.04	03/2005	211.78	167.32	194.31
12/1998	188.53	168.12	172.84	03/2002	169.35	158.04	165.11	06/2005	216.95	181.94	198.97
03/1999	182.96	156.30	172.48	06/2002	183.37	156.03	182.72	09/2005	221.67	183.06	189.25
06/1999	172.48	157.08	162.09	09/2002	228.67	181.81	205.57	12/2005	195.55	174.46	193.79
09/1999	179.16	144.63	167.61	12/2002	210.47	187.47	188.23	03/2006	211.09	185.12	200.27

Source: Reuters

CRB LIVESTOCK & MEATS SUB-INDEX

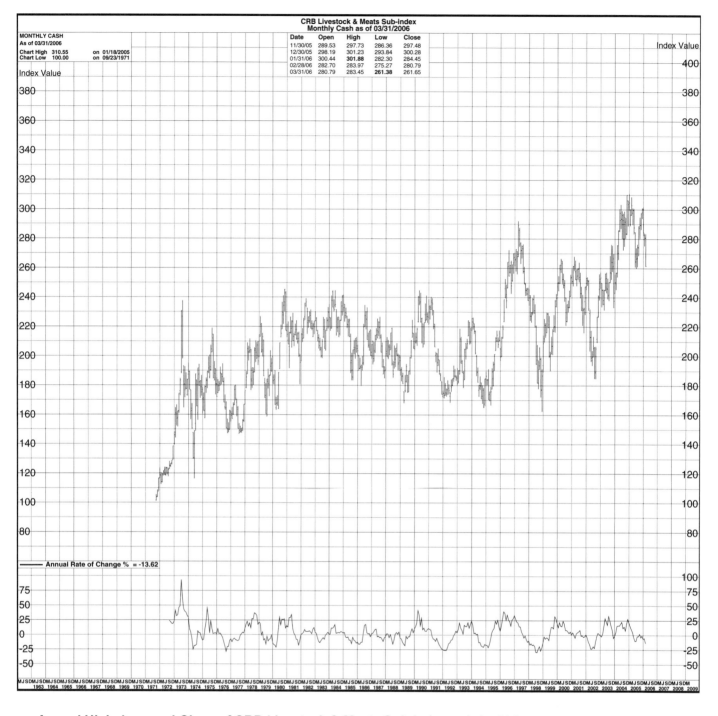

Annual High, Low and Close of CRB Livestock & Meats Sub-Index   Index Value

Year	High	Low	Close	Year	High	Low	Close	Year	High	Low	Close
1971	116.80	100.00	116.60	1983	233.20	198.40	229.70	1995	217.60	166.60	210.90
1972	138.50	112.50	138.50	1984	244.60	213.00	240.80	1996	272.44	196.70	270.14
1973	237.60	139.40	183.70	1985	241.40	183.40	206.90	1997	292.07	237.99	238.12
1974	195.00	116.40	175.20	1986	234.70	179.60	200.16	1998	246.01	162.42	186.70
1975	219.00	157.60	180.80	1987	226.70	184.87	189.85	1999	242.59	189.21	239.61
1976	194.70	147.30	162.50	1988	219.34	185.30	199.10	2000	266.65	220.93	253.56
1977	180.20	147.00	166.90	1989	224.70	167.91	206.45	2001	268.06	215.98	247.41
1978	211.80	167.00	196.40	1990	244.73	204.43	226.61	2002	256.16	184.73	250.97
1979	227.00	158.90	195.00	1991	240.38	174.01	174.01	2003	276.19	231.38	237.77
1980	245.30	163.20	217.40	1992	193.63	168.32	185.67	2004	310.11	242.99	303.64
1981	229.30	180.60	195.30	1993	224.28	178.38	219.25	2005	310.55	260.03	300.28
1982	239.20	196.40	219.90	1994	226.34	164.91	184.64	2006	301.88	261.38	261.65

Source: Reuters

CRB LIVESTOCK & MEATS SUB-INDEX

Quarterly High, Low and Close of CRB Livestock & Meats Sub-Index — Index Value

Quarter	High	Low	Close	Quarter	High	Low	Close	Quarter	High	Low	Close
09/1996	272.44	246.50	262.20	12/1999	242.59	216.37	239.61	03/2003	257.22	233.62	238.21
12/1996	270.14	242.60	270.14	03/2000	262.49	241.78	262.37	06/2003	257.32	231.38	246.04
03/1997	272.93	256.00	268.17	06/2000	266.65	246.44	248.49	09/2003	268.64	237.84	257.27
06/1997	292.07	263.06	272.16	09/2000	252.17	220.93	235.41	12/2003	276.19	233.12	237.77
09/1997	276.35	249.43	249.46	12/2000	255.82	229.94	253.56	03/2004	275.92	242.99	275.70
12/1997	250.15	237.99	238.12	03/2001	268.06	247.84	262.42	06/2004	303.47	265.88	293.58
03/1998	246.01	223.13	229.71	06/2001	265.47	247.97	259.64	09/2004	299.16	272.41	294.79
06/1998	241.81	219.83	220.07	09/2001	264.03	231.06	231.65	12/2004	310.11	280.26	303.64
09/1998	221.18	177.80	190.94	12/2001	247.48	215.98	247.41	03/2005	310.55	288.87	302.92
12/1998	206.34	162.42	186.70	03/2002	254.05	231.21	232.60	06/2005	301.13	260.92	264.65
03/1999	225.52	189.21	214.68	06/2002	232.08	193.67	199.71	09/2005	288.81	260.03	288.49
06/1999	229.90	199.22	200.18	09/2002	213.57	184.73	205.31	12/2005	301.23	280.27	300.28
09/1999	218.77	189.90	217.30	12/2002	256.16	209.38	250.97	03/2006	301.88	261.38	261.65

Source: Reuters

CRB ENERGY SUB-INDEX

Annual High, Low and Close of CRB Energy Sub-Index   Index Value

Year	High	Low	Close	Year	High	Low	Close	Year	High	Low	Close
				1991	251.19	175.46	182.16	1999	237.59	124.97	220.99
				1992	220.80	176.21	192.58	2000	399.38	210.45	355.78
1985	96.70	86.00	96.50	1993	205.70	151.12	151.83	2001	360.20	193.76	204.87
1986	172.18	93.70	172.18	1994	190.20	146.59	173.79	2002	335.31	186.36	320.67
1987	205.27	148.99	159.13	1995	186.34	162.55	180.01	2003	421.31	298.76	358.74
1988	176.77	124.17	156.52	1996	229.31	165.60	224.04	2004	621.83	338.00	457.27
1989	210.03	155.57	210.03	1997	234.45	178.55	180.36	2005	863.37	429.79	705.34
1990	333.86	176.38	245.95	1998	181.80	129.20	134.96	2006	735.62	600.97	662.56

Source: Reuters

CRB ENERGY SUB-INDEX

Quarterly High, Low and Close of CRB Energy Sub-Index   Index Value

Quarter	High	Low	Close	Quarter	High	Low	Close	Quarter	High	Low	Close
09/1996	219.66	185.87	218.29	12/1999	234.59	209.40	220.99	03/2003	421.31	303.30	320.87
12/1996	229.31	206.63	224.04	03/2000	273.82	210.45	251.03	06/2003	360.05	298.76	337.34
03/1997	227.54	190.31	196.01	06/2000	326.23	232.37	323.44	09/2003	354.37	303.08	324.77
06/1997	209.12	186.65	193.13	09/2000	388.56	285.37	348.94	12/2003	386.12	314.09	358.74
09/1997	227.17	188.11	221.83	12/2000	399.38	326.59	355.78	03/2004	390.65	338.00	379.91
12/1997	234.45	178.55	180.36	03/2001	360.20	289.17	305.88	06/2004	447.82	360.76	415.19
03/1998	181.80	151.79	175.97	06/2001	339.07	264.54	266.86	09/2004	537.91	412.67	534.50
06/1998	180.84	151.58	167.33	09/2001	286.15	211.27	233.41	12/2004	621.83	446.45	457.27
09/1998	176.91	144.05	175.97	12/2001	243.03	193.76	204.87	03/2005	600.24	429.79	597.25
12/1998	179.30	129.20	134.96	03/2002	263.73	186.36	260.35	06/2005	624.02	506.55	597.29
03/1999	167.45	124.97	166.90	06/2002	288.53	239.15	265.89	09/2005	863.37	599.93	847.12
06/1999	192.65	159.11	192.24	09/2002	314.43	249.49	311.86	12/2005	851.76	676.76	705.34
09/1999	237.59	189.56	231.43	12/2002	335.31	262.29	320.67	03/2006	735.62	600.97	662.56

Source: Reuters

CRB PRECIOUS METALS SUB-INDEX

Annual High, Low and Close of CRB Precious Metals Sub-Index — Index Value

Year	High	Low	Close	Year	High	Low	Close	Year	High	Low	Close
				1985	266.40	215.10	256.60	1996	295.79	252.09	252.57
1975	166.30	135.20	141.00	1986	342.40	255.10	296.63	1997	266.43	232.02	249.34
1976	182.80	133.50	149.50	1987	414.66	296.44	346.37	1998	278.48	222.21	234.27
1977	170.20	139.60	163.80	1988	378.36	309.34	318.67	1999	267.99	220.18	253.39
1978	241.60	165.10	230.40	1989	325.99	279.60	296.89	2000	280.60	238.96	265.73
1979	554.10	228.50	554.10	1990	311.28	246.50	257.76	2001	272.51	224.24	246.82
1980	760.90	360.50	409.20	1991	261.61	223.99	226.00	2002	289.36	233.27	289.09
1981	425.00	262.80	269.30	1992	238.94	216.49	219.06	2003	365.80	272.71	364.08
1982	294.20	181.60	288.60	1993	284.54	211.69	268.34	2004	431.01	334.51	396.59
1983	359.20	256.80	269.50	1994	287.73	259.12	269.62	2005	499.79	375.66	478.08
1984	354.50	242.50	243.30	1995	301.93	255.39	270.20	2006	567.76	479.68	558.69

Source: Reuters

CRB PRECIOUS METALS SUB-INDEX

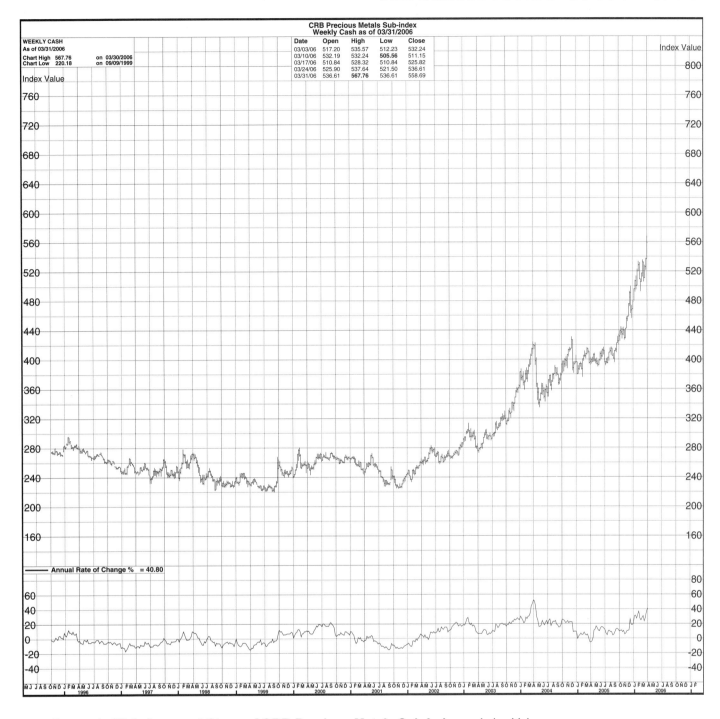

Quarterly High, Low and Close of CRB Precious Metals Sub-Index   Index Value

Quarter	High	Low	Close	Quarter	High	Low	Close	Quarter	High	Low	Close
09/1996	274.38	259.48	259.48	12/1999	264.42	239.99	253.39	03/2003	313.70	278.23	285.14
12/1996	265.52	252.09	252.57	03/2000	280.60	238.96	256.92	06/2003	305.10	272.71	293.27
03/1997	266.43	244.39	253.92	06/2000	273.12	243.09	271.44	09/2003	330.03	291.34	322.43
06/1997	259.92	243.98	250.40	09/2000	274.19	261.05	266.93	12/2003	365.80	310.58	364.08
09/1997	265.39	232.02	264.02	12/2000	270.70	257.94	265.73	03/2004	419.74	358.33	419.74
12/1997	265.19	238.62	249.34	03/2001	268.56	244.94	245.45	06/2004	424.05	334.51	350.90
03/1998	278.48	235.62	267.54	06/2001	272.51	241.78	251.04	09/2004	393.17	349.00	392.55
06/1998	273.86	230.17	243.49	09/2001	254.58	227.16	242.01	12/2004	431.01	380.99	396.59
09/1998	252.91	222.21	239.30	12/2001	246.96	224.24	246.82	03/2005	416.18	375.66	401.77
12/1998	242.22	226.01	234.27	03/2002	261.42	233.27	260.55	06/2005	416.77	389.86	404.47
03/1999	246.02	227.04	230.37	06/2002	283.09	256.01	269.78	09/2005	434.13	391.35	431.11
06/1999	238.98	221.49	227.89	09/2002	276.69	257.40	271.22	12/2005	499.79	424.70	478.08
09/1999	267.99	220.18	250.57	12/2002	289.36	264.58	289.09	03/2006	567.76	479.68	558.69

Source: Reuters

CRB SOFTS SUB-INDEX

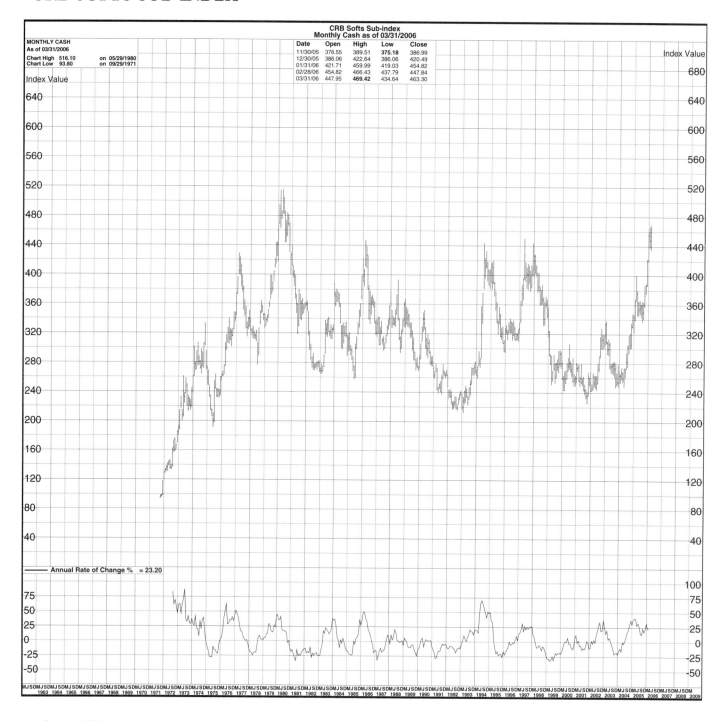

Annual High, Low and Close of CRB Softs Sub-Index   Index Value

Year	High	Low	Close	Year	High	Low	Close	Year	High	Low	Close
1971	118.00	93.80	116.50	1983	342.10	264.40	326.00	1995	418.91	295.38	297.01
1972	186.20	120.40	185.40	1984	388.20	288.90	291.70	1996	341.05	295.69	326.54
1973	261.10	180.10	238.40	1985	398.20	256.90	398.20	1997	449.99	320.88	408.73
1974	333.20	238.90	274.10	1986	446.40	317.81	321.24	1998	429.33	331.65	344.82
1975	274.60	191.10	259.40	1987	358.45	296.37	356.09	1999	357.33	250.81	280.94
1976	348.50	253.90	348.10	1988	393.52	293.37	359.82	2000	306.50	243.34	254.43
1977	428.90	314.70	334.80	1989	366.43	268.79	271.69	2001	282.20	225.16	252.80
1978	363.90	276.00	345.00	1990	352.28	273.29	276.03	2002	328.36	241.94	303.69
1979	444.90	325.70	425.30	1991	279.09	236.89	264.37	2003	338.30	247.22	250.46
1980	516.10	400.20	426.00	1992	262.90	215.15	237.65	2004	347.84	247.78	343.51
1981	439.80	318.50	357.00	1993	282.37	212.47	265.92	2005	422.64	322.21	420.49
1982	363.90	267.00	269.00	1994	443.57	259.55	402.42	2006	469.42	419.03	463.30

Source: Reuters

CRB SOFTS SUB-INDEX

Quarterly High, Low and Close of CRB Softs Sub-Index Index Value

Quarter	High	Low	Close	Quarter	High	Low	Close	Quarter	High	Low	Close
09/1996	338.66	311.18	312.64	12/1999	298.86	267.42	280.94	03/2003	338.30	292.39	299.56
12/1996	326.54	310.04	326.54	03/2000	282.08	243.34	259.39	06/2003	313.76	267.26	276.49
03/1997	387.54	320.88	374.74	06/2000	288.36	253.00	275.89	09/2003	283.26	260.67	272.18
06/1997	449.99	366.39	398.12	09/2000	306.50	262.22	268.86	12/2003	281.36	247.22	250.46
09/1997	415.95	380.43	393.94	12/2000	287.81	249.03	254.43	03/2004	274.56	252.81	267.49
12/1997	443.96	377.96	408.73	03/2001	282.20	253.46	256.15	06/2004	274.26	247.78	268.14
03/1998	429.33	397.90	403.67	06/2001	280.19	248.98	259.63	09/2004	318.60	272.34	318.29
06/1998	403.69	358.83	362.10	09/2001	262.10	232.02	236.13	12/2004	347.84	301.17	343.51
09/1998	387.40	331.65	336.95	12/2001	267.61	225.16	252.80	03/2005	400.82	322.21	376.04
12/1998	371.06	331.82	344.82	03/2002	269.36	241.94	262.05	06/2005	380.40	344.74	354.44
03/1999	357.33	277.96	289.85	06/2002	264.17	243.81	256.95	09/2005	364.91	336.91	359.61
06/1999	292.17	250.81	273.86	09/2002	316.65	252.44	305.15	12/2005	422.64	357.56	420.49
09/1999	286.22	252.88	274.93	12/2002	328.36	299.56	303.69	03/2006	469.42	419.03	463.30

Source: Reuters

CRB SPOT INDEX

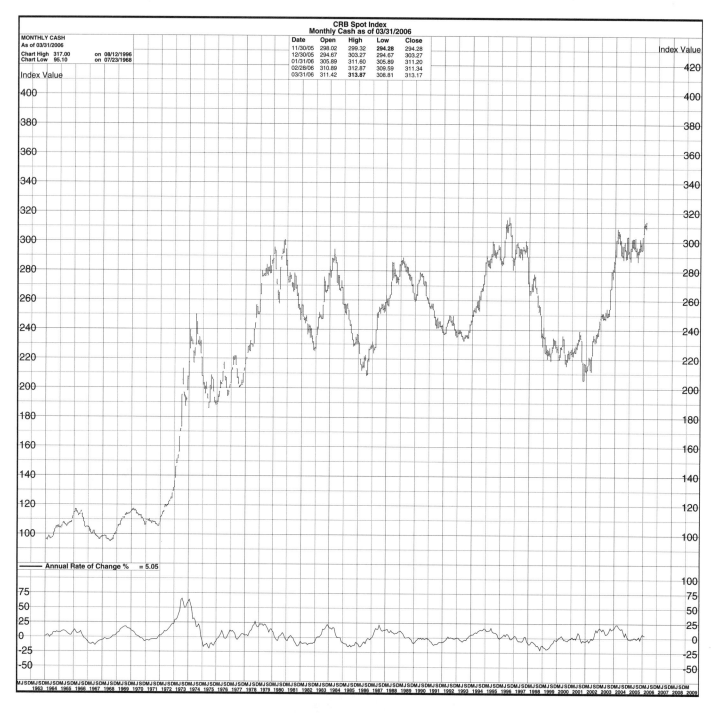

Annual High, Low and Close of CRB Spot Index   Index Value

Year	High	Low	Close	Year	High	Low	Close	Year	High	Low	Close
1968	101.50	95.10	100.80	1981	286.80	246.20	250.00	1994	286.32	245.33	285.98
1969	114.90	101.80	114.90	1982	256.80	225.20	227.40	1995	300.48	282.34	289.10
1970	117.40	106.20	106.20	1983	278.40	226.60	277.80	1996	317.00	280.81	288.22
1971	110.40	105.50	107.30	1984	294.80	257.20	257.20	1997	300.77	271.81	271.81
1972	131.60	108.20	131.60	1985	257.70	228.30	236.70	1998	278.23	228.66	235.22
1973	213.10	131.90	206.00	1986	236.00	208.40	228.33	1999	241.97	218.71	227.25
1974	249.90	207.30	207.90	1987	258.68	223.77	258.21	2000	236.22	215.29	223.99
1975	208.40	186.10	188.30	1988	286.12	255.73	284.35	2001	239.10	205.62	212.10
1976	217.30	188.70	201.90	1989	289.18	260.60	260.60	2002	246.42	211.20	244.31
1977	221.90	200.20	213.20	1990	279.24	257.93	258.13	2003	287.25	246.84	283.58
1978	256.50	216.20	250.30	1991	258.78	238.24	238.24	2004	309.10	285.36	292.97
1979	289.80	251.50	286.90	1992	250.00	234.98	235.27	2005	303.27	286.50	303.27
1980	300.90	257.40	283.50	1993	246.55	232.09	245.44	2006	313.87	305.89	313.17

Source: Commodity Research Bureau

CRB SPOT INDEX

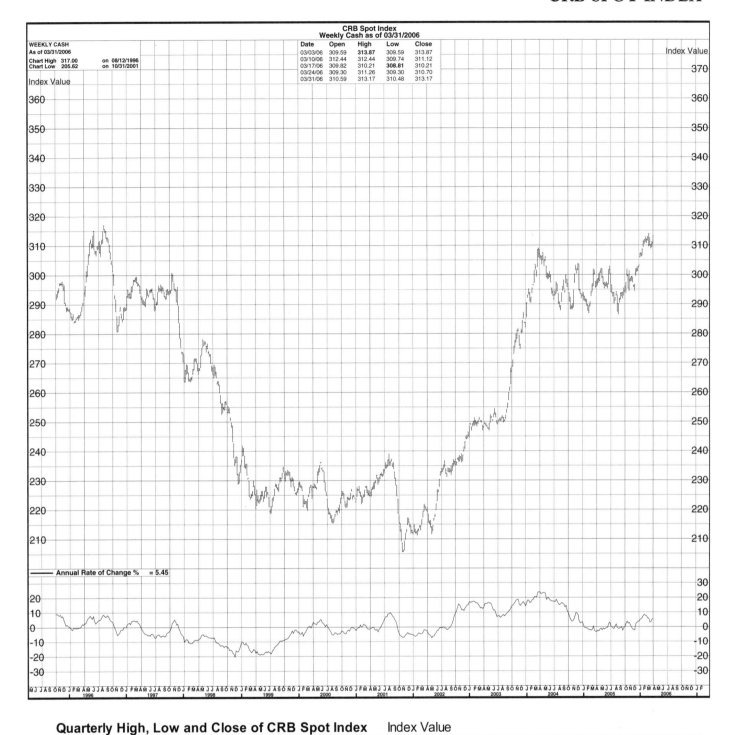

Quarterly High, Low and Close of CRB Spot Index   Index Value

Quarter	High	Low	Close	Quarter	High	Low	Close	Quarter	High	Low	Close
09/1996	317.00	304.17	304.17	12/1999	233.46	225.09	227.25	03/2003	251.55	246.84	248.06
12/1996	304.96	280.81	288.22	03/2000	229.71	219.78	228.01	06/2003	254.53	246.98	249.06
03/1997	299.57	288.26	296.34	06/2000	236.22	224.93	224.93	09/2003	268.24	249.11	268.11
06/1997	296.52	289.28	292.16	09/2000	223.95	215.29	223.95	12/2003	287.25	268.23	283.58
09/1997	296.77	287.90	293.80	12/2000	227.13	220.68	223.99	03/2004	309.10	285.36	305.43
12/1997	300.77	271.81	271.81	03/2001	228.10	222.01	224.72	06/2004	307.47	291.16	291.16
03/1998	273.05	263.59	269.06	06/2001	233.78	224.50	233.78	09/2004	299.97	287.80	294.98
06/1998	278.23	266.28	268.97	09/2001	239.10	218.65	218.65	12/2004	303.75	288.11	292.97
09/1998	269.36	252.46	256.78	12/2001	218.13	205.62	212.10	03/2005	301.81	286.82	298.11
12/1998	256.07	228.66	235.22	03/2002	221.82	211.20	219.64	06/2005	302.83	294.15	294.15
03/1999	241.97	223.48	225.71	06/2002	232.95	211.59	232.95	09/2005	296.40	286.50	294.61
06/1999	228.05	220.37	222.64	09/2002	237.21	231.05	237.21	12/2005	303.27	293.64	303.27
09/1999	234.73	218.71	233.60	12/2002	246.42	234.97	244.31	03/2006	313.87	305.89	313.17

Source: Commodity Research Bureau

CRB METALS SUB-INDEX

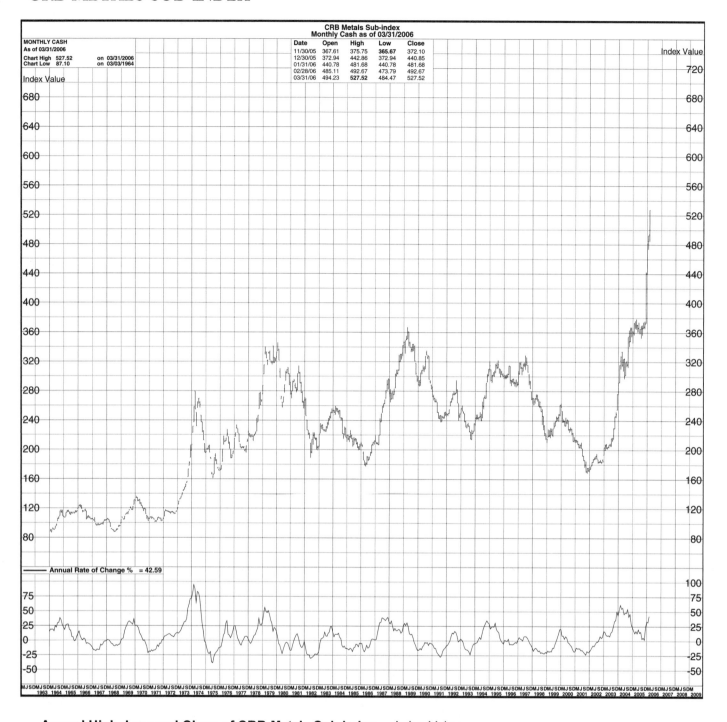

Annual High, Low and Close of CRB Metals Sub-Index   Index Value

Year	High	Low	Close	Year	High	Low	Close	Year	High	Low	Close
1968	105.60	87.80	96.00	1981	314.20	256.20	264.20	1994	310.10	233.68	310.10
1969	131.00	99.10	131.00	1982	270.80	188.80	202.30	1995	322.03	292.37	300.57
1970	136.40	102.60	102.60	1983	256.00	204.10	250.40	1996	314.72	285.88	289.90
1971	108.10	101.40	103.40	1984	259.00	214.70	216.90	1997	329.13	268.60	269.78
1972	117.90	105.70	116.00	1985	226.50	199.40	207.70	1998	276.33	214.38	218.51
1973	206.20	118.30	198.50	1986	211.98	177.30	211.98	1999	261.60	210.36	261.60
1974	279.00	196.10	196.10	1987	296.72	206.71	296.72	2000	264.00	211.82	214.03
1975	205.70	161.20	171.10	1988	342.43	264.83	342.43	2001	214.63	168.65	172.45
1976	227.70	172.00	197.80	1989	367.15	292.78	296.49	2002	195.23	171.46	184.50
1977	233.90	195.70	211.70	1990	335.30	282.81	283.16	2003	276.69	193.76	276.69
1978	278.00	211.50	267.30	1991	285.85	238.11	248.51	2004	367.73	275.47	357.69
1979	341.20	275.60	322.00	1992	295.04	240.36	248.79	2005	442.86	346.21	440.85
1980	346.00	257.60	288.30	1993	260.68	214.08	236.27	2006	527.52	440.78	527.52

Source: Commodity Research Bureau

CRB METALS SUB-INDEX

Quarterly High, Low and Close of CRB Metals Sub-Index   Index Value

Quarter	High	Low	Close	Quarter	High	Low	Close	Quarter	High	Low	Close
09/1996	297.04	287.61	291.95	12/1999	261.60	239.37	261.60	03/2003	208.56	193.76	202.43
12/1996	296.00	285.88	289.90	03/2000	264.00	238.39	239.01	06/2003	209.23	201.50	206.36
03/1997	319.94	288.97	311.71	06/2000	244.59	233.36	241.67	09/2003	230.27	205.55	229.08
06/1997	319.12	302.32	316.65	09/2000	240.65	224.05	227.89	12/2003	276.69	229.71	276.69
09/1997	329.13	305.87	306.28	12/2000	228.97	211.82	214.03	03/2004	328.64	275.47	327.01
12/1997	303.77	268.60	269.78	03/2001	214.63	207.97	207.97	06/2004	334.58	297.34	300.89
03/1998	271.95	261.28	270.12	06/2001	210.60	202.55	202.59	09/2004	354.08	301.72	354.08
06/1998	276.33	260.32	260.32	09/2001	202.11	176.59	180.41	12/2004	367.73	341.51	357.69
09/1998	267.02	234.74	246.35	12/2001	184.89	168.65	172.45	03/2005	376.26	346.21	369.95
12/1998	246.33	214.38	218.51	03/2002	184.12	171.46	183.85	06/2005	378.72	361.01	361.42
03/1999	228.23	210.36	219.77	06/2002	191.77	183.56	191.77	09/2005	370.53	352.78	366.01
06/1999	229.97	216.75	228.98	09/2002	195.23	182.37	184.25	12/2005	442.86	365.67	440.85
09/1999	246.30	229.89	244.16	12/2002	187.80	181.94	184.50	03/2006	527.52	440.78	527.52

Source: Commodity Research Bureau

CRB TEXTILES SUB-INDEX

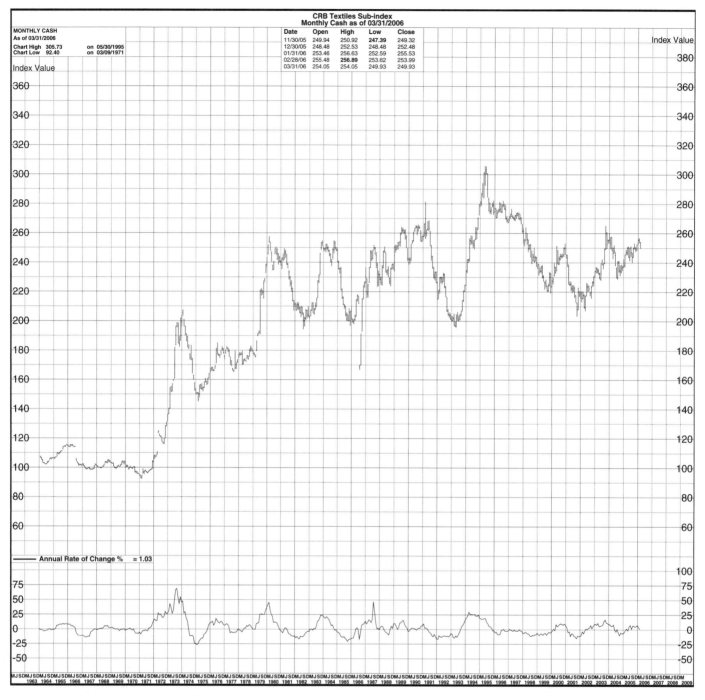

Annual High, Low and Close of CRB Textiles Sub-Index   Index Value

Year	High	Low	Close	Year	High	Low	Close	Year	High	Low	Close
1968	105.10	99.50	103.70	1981	249.50	207.00	211.00	1994	279.67	224.16	279.67
1969	104.60	99.00	104.00	1982	213.00	194.30	203.90	1995	305.73	272.62	274.31
1970	104.10	95.40	95.80	1983	254.90	201.30	251.20	1996	282.16	266.83	267.43
1971	104.80	92.40	103.90	1984	254.90	237.50	248.50	1997	276.78	260.32	261.54
1972	130.90	103.80	130.90	1985	249.80	196.70	206.70	1998	264.02	237.33	237.47
1973	201.90	131.70	201.90	1986	227.00	166.70	226.56	1999	239.23	219.16	223.75
1974	207.30	152.50	152.50	1987	251.88	215.72	231.79	2000	253.02	223.32	245.74
1975	164.30	145.00	164.30	1988	250.80	223.80	235.99	2001	245.85	203.36	217.41
1976	185.00	165.20	178.20	1989	264.16	234.03	243.02	2002	230.93	207.01	230.15
1977	182.90	165.00	173.50	1990	265.70	238.25	257.64	2003	265.16	227.81	255.19
1978	182.90	170.20	179.40	1991	281.41	226.23	226.23	2004	260.19	228.68	237.87
1979	238.90	175.00	238.00	1992	233.04	200.93	201.77	2005	253.23	237.00	252.48
1980	257.30	234.70	240.40	1993	224.69	195.96	224.69	2006	256.89	249.93	249.93

Source: Commodity Research Bureau

CRB TEXTILES SUB-INDEX

Quarterly High, Low and Close of CRB Textiles Sub-Index   Index Value

Quarter	High	Low	Close	Quarter	High	Low	Close	Quarter	High	Low	Close
09/1996	282.16	273.87	276.71	12/1999	233.80	219.16	223.75	03/2003	237.09	229.95	234.64
12/1996	279.39	266.83	267.43	03/2000	239.99	223.32	236.96	06/2003	239.47	227.81	239.47
03/1997	276.78	267.72	271.29	06/2000	251.45	232.66	239.05	09/2003	249.53	235.87	249.53
06/1997	272.59	268.27	272.27	09/2000	246.29	238.63	243.30	12/2003	265.16	249.13	255.19
09/1997	274.42	269.68	269.68	12/2000	253.02	243.46	245.74	03/2004	260.19	248.79	248.79
12/1997	273.26	260.32	261.54	03/2001	245.85	225.38	225.38	06/2004	251.97	238.12	238.38
03/1998	264.02	251.16	260.09	06/2001	227.49	219.40	222.71	09/2004	241.35	228.68	233.84
06/1998	260.04	247.25	251.71	09/2001	224.75	212.96	212.96	12/2004	238.66	231.05	237.87
09/1998	252.77	239.42	243.90	12/2001	222.79	203.36	217.41	03/2005	248.89	237.00	247.37
12/1998	250.35	237.33	237.47	03/2002	220.84	213.13	217.62	06/2005	251.27	241.21	250.35
03/1999	239.23	231.36	234.05	06/2002	226.08	207.01	226.08	09/2005	251.38	240.04	249.45
06/1999	238.44	227.25	227.76	09/2002	225.75	217.32	219.07	12/2005	253.23	247.39	252.48
09/1999	228.55	219.99	220.85	12/2002	230.93	215.61	230.15	03/2006	256.89	249.93	249.93

Source: Commodity Research Bureau

CRB RAW INDUSTRIALS SUB-INDEX

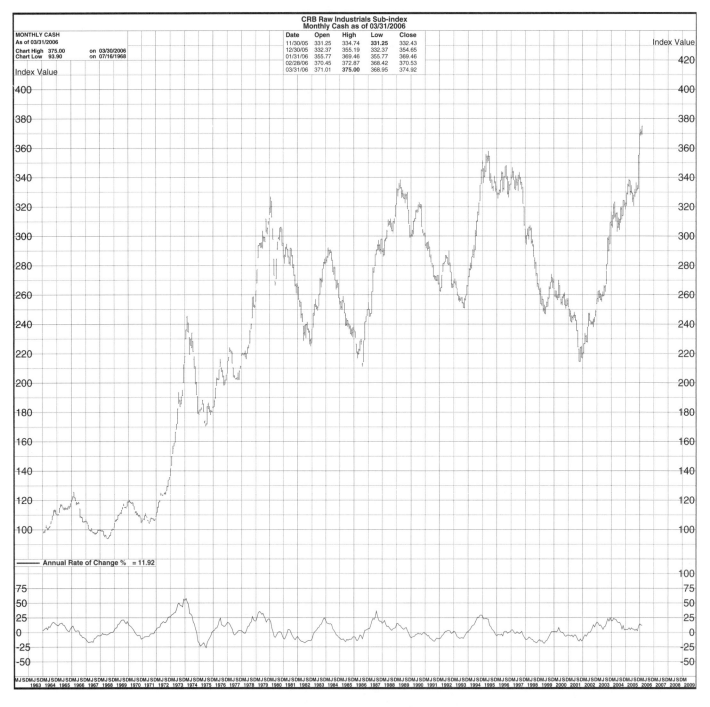

Annual High, Low and Close of CRB Raw Industrials Sub-Index   Index Value

Year	High	Low	Close	Year	High	Low	Close	Year	High	Low	Close
1968	100.70	93.90	100.20	1981	295.20	260.90	265.80	1994	345.12	265.81	345.12
1969	118.80	101.60	118.80	1982	267.50	224.90	226.90	1995	357.98	330.29	332.15
1970	120.20	104.70	104.70	1983	284.50	227.60	281.60	1996	348.08	325.50	334.92
1971	111.20	104.10	107.30	1984	292.00	258.00	258.00	1997	346.84	306.88	307.52
1972	135.60	109.00	135.60	1985	259.10	231.00	237.60	1998	307.26	263.49	265.32
1973	212.30	137.10	212.30	1986	249.98	211.00	249.76	1999	274.15	246.90	268.88
1974	245.60	179.20	179.20	1987	297.81	245.21	297.81	2000	270.87	250.46	255.81
1975	188.30	170.70	180.30	1988	321.14	286.05	321.14	2001	257.51	214.16	217.33
1976	216.30	183.10	205.40	1989	338.54	298.99	300.40	2002	249.48	216.70	248.56
1977	224.20	202.10	211.10	1990	322.85	299.31	301.21	2003	309.07	253.85	309.07
1978	258.60	216.30	251.90	1991	302.16	267.25	267.25	2004	324.30	302.90	321.50
1979	311.70	255.60	309.80	1992	290.01	261.96	265.22	2005	355.19	318.08	354.65
1980	326.90	266.40	293.50	1993	271.13	250.72	266.50	2006	375.00	355.77	374.92

Source: Commodity Research Bureau

CRB RAW INDUSTRIALS SUB-INDEX

Quarterly High, Low and Close of CRB Raw Industrials Sub-Index   Index Value

Quarter	High	Low	Close	Quarter	High	Low	Close	Quarter	High	Low	Close
09/1996	348.08	331.18	339.01	12/1999	274.15	264.02	268.88	03/2003	263.11	253.85	258.01
12/1996	340.89	326.26	334.92	03/2000	270.87	257.41	258.51	06/2003	262.12	255.20	259.47
03/1997	346.84	335.10	338.46	06/2000	270.02	256.54	257.98	09/2003	280.62	259.26	280.62
06/1997	341.33	331.56	336.32	09/2000	260.56	252.85	259.58	12/2003	309.07	280.95	309.07
09/1997	343.62	330.71	336.70	12/2000	261.55	250.46	255.81	03/2004	322.14	305.60	319.17
12/1997	336.74	306.88	307.52	03/2001	257.51	241.96	241.96	06/2004	323.51	302.90	306.03
03/1998	305.07	294.13	300.51	06/2001	248.25	240.99	246.21	09/2004	319.69	303.99	318.33
06/1998	307.26	294.73	296.20	09/2001	246.04	224.29	224.49	12/2004	324.30	311.29	321.50
09/1998	297.74	277.74	281.90	12/2001	225.07	214.16	217.33	03/2005	335.63	318.08	335.00
12/1998	282.44	263.49	265.32	03/2002	233.83	216.70	231.76	06/2005	338.83	327.95	329.32
03/1999	264.83	252.26	256.83	06/2002	247.34	227.43	247.34	09/2005	332.03	320.49	328.75
06/1999	256.84	246.90	251.66	09/2002	247.59	239.53	240.69	12/2005	355.19	329.50	354.65
09/1999	265.76	251.77	264.59	12/2002	249.48	237.87	248.56	03/2006	375.00	355.77	374.92

Source: Commodity Research Bureau

CRB FOODSTUFFS SUB-INDEX

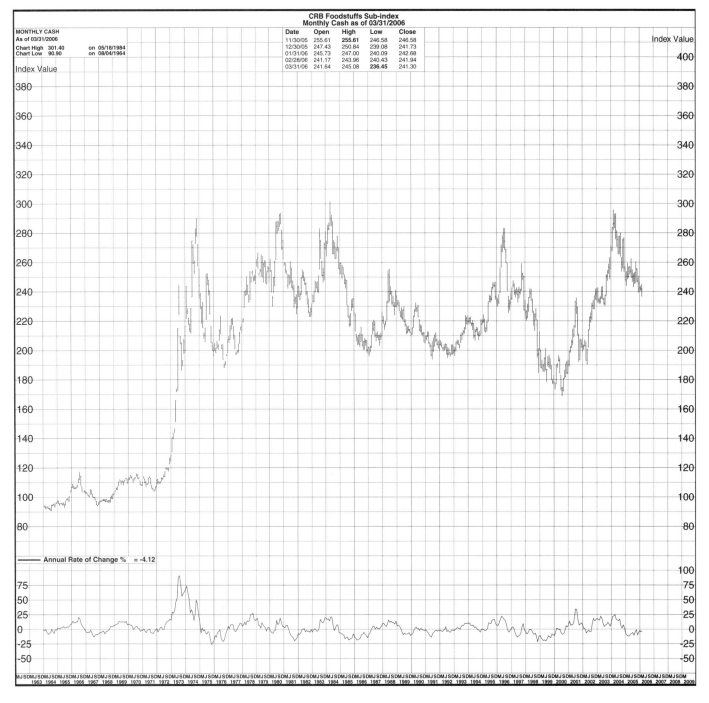

Annual High, Low and Close of CRB Foodstuffs Sub-Index   Index Value

Year	High	Low	Close	Year	High	Low	Close	Year	High	Low	Close
1968	102.60	95.90	101.70	1981	274.90	224.60	228.80	1994	223.58	206.53	217.82
1969	113.00	101.90	109.50	1982	255.30	222.80	228.00	1995	246.80	212.23	236.39
1970	115.90	108.20	108.20	1983	283.10	224.00	272.00	1996	283.18	225.39	231.83
1971	114.20	103.50	107.30	1984	301.40	255.90	255.90	1997	259.21	227.26	227.26
1972	127.10	107.00	126.00	1985	260.00	215.90	235.20	1998	242.06	184.37	197.52
1973	244.40	124.70	206.00	1986	235.00	198.48	200.41	1999	212.74	176.76	178.10
1974	290.00	198.30	257.50	1987	220.83	195.92	209.95	2000	196.59	168.61	184.74
1975	255.80	200.30	200.30	1988	255.28	209.71	238.33	2001	235.78	183.96	204.61
1976	223.60	188.10	196.70	1989	237.54	210.98	212.06	2002	241.87	190.17	238.10
1977	222.00	196.90	216.10	1990	232.42	205.33	206.39	2003	263.46	230.27	250.24
1978	254.50	212.50	247.90	1991	212.87	193.61	201.64	2004	295.90	253.41	255.97
1979	266.70	245.20	256.70	1992	207.45	194.55	197.72	2005	262.61	239.08	241.73
1980	293.50	230.30	269.50	1993	223.90	196.11	217.76	2006	247.00	236.45	241.30

Source: Commodity Research Bureau

CRB FOODSTUFFS SUB-INDEX

Quarterly High, Low and Close of CRB Foodstuffs Sub-Index   Index Value

Quarter	High	Low	Close	Quarter	High	Low	Close	Quarter	High	Low	Close
09/1996	283.18	259.86	259.86	12/1999	194.07	176.76	178.10	03/2003	242.51	231.51	234.18
12/1996	259.58	225.39	231.83	03/2000	190.05	173.16	190.05	06/2003	243.76	231.70	234.58
03/1997	247.61	230.84	244.39	06/2000	196.59	184.38	184.38	09/2003	251.66	230.27	250.82
06/1997	245.32	235.90	238.23	09/2000	182.89	168.61	180.79	12/2003	263.46	247.33	250.24
09/1997	243.40	232.34	241.11	12/2000	192.66	180.81	184.74	03/2004	295.90	255.58	286.39
12/1997	259.21	227.26	227.26	03/2001	202.82	183.96	201.79	06/2004	293.37	270.73	270.73
03/1998	233.90	220.31	229.17	06/2001	216.75	201.48	216.75	09/2004	279.80	264.04	264.04
06/1998	242.06	225.98	233.81	09/2001	235.78	210.32	210.32	12/2004	277.01	253.41	255.97
09/1998	235.21	213.55	224.22	12/2001	211.21	191.99	204.61	03/2005	259.37	243.81	251.68
12/1998	228.68	184.37	197.52	03/2002	208.28	199.18	203.09	06/2005	262.61	249.40	249.67
03/1999	212.74	187.15	187.15	06/2002	214.39	190.17	213.46	09/2005	255.10	242.91	251.27
06/1999	201.31	185.19	186.39	09/2002	232.08	213.80	232.08	12/2005	260.53	239.08	241.73
09/1999	196.90	178.25	194.98	12/2002	241.87	227.84	238.10	03/2006	247.00	236.45	241.30

Source: Commodity Research Bureau

CRB FATS & OILS SUB-INDEX

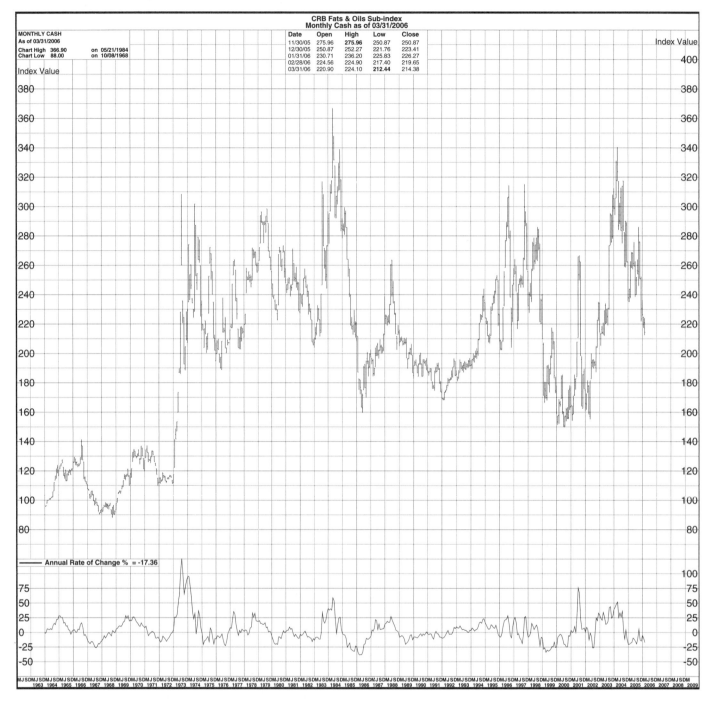

Annual High, Low and Close of CRB Fats & Oils Sub-Index   Index Value

Year	High	Low	Close	Year	High	Low	Close	Year	High	Low	Close
1968	98.50	88.00	92.40	1981	271.30	228.70	229.90	1994	244.05	189.45	236.17
1969	121.40	93.40	110.20	1982	257.70	205.70	205.70	1995	253.28	206.82	226.68
1970	136.70	111.20	121.30	1983	317.00	204.10	273.40	1996	314.46	202.26	246.42
1971	137.20	109.70	111.70	1984	366.90	273.20	287.10	1997	315.23	216.70	257.08
1972	118.90	111.40	111.40	1985	299.50	210.70	220.20	1998	285.99	220.04	236.01
1973	308.50	112.00	209.10	1986	220.80	159.60	199.79	1999	240.47	166.42	174.78
1974	301.70	207.40	225.30	1987	213.46	184.32	212.54	2000	185.48	149.78	163.62
1975	272.20	200.40	202.10	1988	263.51	202.43	214.70	2001	266.74	154.27	175.82
1976	237.80	188.90	207.40	1989	215.92	186.81	186.81	2002	235.00	155.22	234.00
1977	263.70	202.90	214.80	1990	200.23	182.74	188.67	2003	308.13	205.23	297.20
1978	271.70	211.00	255.20	1991	193.72	173.80	173.80	2004	340.45	258.58	262.55
1979	298.40	256.00	257.40	1992	196.60	168.16	184.97	2005	285.99	221.76	223.41
1980	273.20	222.50	255.90	1993	196.81	180.94	191.71	2006	236.20	212.44	214.38

Source: Commodity Research Bureau

CRB FATS & OILS SUB-INDEX

Quarterly High, Low and Close of CRB Fats & Oils Sub-Index   Index Value

Quarter	High	Low	Close	Quarter	High	Low	Close	Quarter	High	Low	Close
09/1996	314.46	276.42	278.46	12/1999	214.69	172.96	174.78	03/2003	234.37	205.23	214.32
12/1996	283.57	203.95	246.42	03/2000	178.25	151.39	166.32	06/2003	233.99	212.09	220.48
03/1997	264.19	242.47	242.47	06/2000	185.48	158.67	160.42	09/2003	273.36	219.11	273.36
06/1997	250.85	216.70	250.85	09/2000	162.75	149.78	161.64	12/2003	308.13	273.66	297.20
09/1997	264.96	244.84	264.90	12/2000	178.21	155.38	163.62	03/2004	331.13	294.23	317.85
12/1997	315.23	257.08	257.08	03/2001	177.66	154.27	169.03	06/2004	340.45	284.08	294.11
03/1998	255.80	227.56	238.89	06/2001	207.77	171.14	207.77	09/2004	317.40	274.90	283.74
06/1998	278.73	235.01	263.12	09/2001	266.74	198.52	198.52	12/2004	290.23	258.58	262.55
09/1998	285.99	261.02	283.96	12/2001	198.14	162.58	175.82	03/2005	262.77	235.02	259.41
12/1998	284.72	220.04	236.01	03/2002	181.66	161.01	177.49	06/2005	275.71	257.33	259.68
03/1999	240.47	166.42	175.85	06/2002	199.87	155.22	193.62	09/2005	263.95	238.50	254.11
06/1999	192.20	167.94	179.14	09/2002	195.81	189.70	192.23	12/2005	285.99	221.76	223.41
09/1999	217.55	173.42	215.25	12/2002	235.00	187.14	234.00	03/2006	236.20	212.44	214.38

Source: Commodity Research Bureau

CRB LIVESTOCK SUB-INDEX

Annual High, Low and Close of CRB Livestock Sub-Index   Index Value

Year	High	Low	Close	Year	High	Low	Close	Year	High	Low	Close
1968	97.80	87.80	96.50	1981	295.00	259.80	264.20	1994	321.75	276.72	319.33
1969	127.50	98.40	122.20	1982	313.60	250.90	254.40	1995	329.83	296.14	307.44
1970	136.20	106.80	106.80	1983	323.90	250.20	303.10	1996	399.67	292.73	363.01
1971	123.30	106.40	118.20	1984	366.40	302.90	308.20	1997	369.22	306.09	306.09
1972	163.40	120.10	163.10	1985	310.60	245.10	271.10	1998	320.31	201.75	232.28
1973	336.50	161.10	224.60	1986	276.80	217.30	268.07	1999	297.13	206.26	265.72
1974	263.50	190.10	192.80	1987	307.91	261.46	280.14	2000	272.11	234.91	265.51
1975	264.80	185.10	210.00	1988	319.70	257.00	285.74	2001	348.32	244.00	257.21
1976	232.40	198.70	223.90	1989	298.22	269.53	286.98	2002	320.63	243.62	317.79
1977	256.20	216.50	234.40	1990	310.15	275.28	292.73	2003	400.83	301.67	365.87
1978	308.20	239.10	305.10	1991	294.48	248.50	248.62	2004	407.25	343.74	365.02
1979	380.50	290.00	300.30	1992	296.91	247.91	286.64	2005	390.12	322.62	326.62
1980	302.50	223.10	281.00	1993	307.55	272.74	274.28	2006	337.79	311.11	313.84

Source: Commodity Research Bureau

CRB LIVESTOCK SUB-INDEX

Quarterly High, Low and Close of CRB Livestock Sub-Index   Index Value

Quarter	High	Low	Close	Quarter	High	Low	Close	Quarter	High	Low	Close
09/1996	399.67	341.71	373.38	12/1999	297.13	265.60	265.72	03/2003	323.77	301.67	306.09
12/1996	383.68	329.44	363.01	03/2000	270.08	236.60	254.21	06/2003	343.82	303.76	318.45
03/1997	369.22	335.80	341.37	06/2000	272.11	248.24	248.24	09/2003	377.45	317.28	375.53
06/1997	349.55	326.58	344.78	09/2000	256.89	234.91	256.89	12/2003	400.83	363.52	365.87
09/1997	348.26	334.35	341.85	12/2000	265.83	237.75	265.51	03/2004	382.21	343.74	364.12
12/1997	354.99	306.09	306.09	03/2001	272.45	245.34	260.60	06/2004	386.31	362.13	375.00
03/1998	317.13	259.80	274.46	06/2001	320.21	262.04	315.84	09/2004	407.25	384.23	384.23
06/1998	320.31	270.75	284.63	09/2001	348.32	279.03	279.03	12/2004	390.62	354.91	365.02
09/1998	291.36	254.26	258.13	12/2001	277.54	244.00	257.21	03/2005	369.79	333.63	363.04
12/1998	265.83	201.75	232.28	03/2002	280.13	243.62	272.14	06/2005	390.12	339.00	339.00
03/1999	264.91	206.26	227.24	06/2002	297.43	245.49	288.93	09/2005	358.65	322.62	347.21
06/1999	247.38	227.78	229.78	09/2002	292.45	260.01	283.63	12/2005	377.54	326.62	326.62
09/1999	293.83	226.97	293.83	12/2002	320.63	272.09	317.79	03/2006	337.79	311.11	313.84

Source: Commodity Research Bureau

GOLDMAN SACHS COMMODITY INDEX

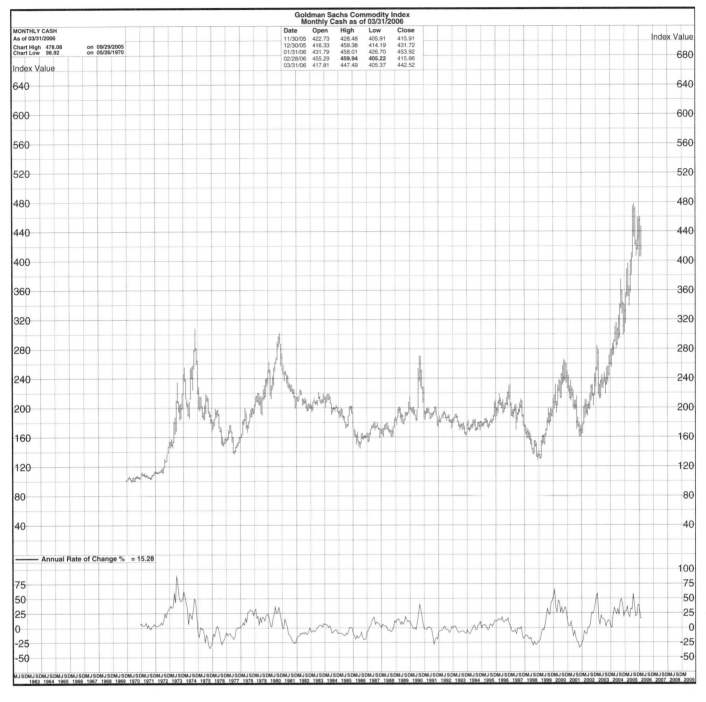

Annual High, Low and Close of Goldman Sachs Commodity Index   Index Value

Year	High	Low	Close	Year	High	Low	Close	Year	High	Low	Close
				1981	274.33	199.09	201.65	1994	185.01	163.41	180.84
1969	100.00	100.00	100.00	1982	225.07	194.93	201.46	1995	208.02	171.19	203.44
1970	107.73	98.92	104.91	1983	221.08	195.05	216.14	1996	229.87	182.66	215.26
1971	112.35	102.31	111.93	1984	219.40	190.55	195.53	1997	231.82	169.69	175.62
1972	147.16	110.50	147.14	1985	202.14	172.26	196.04	1998	177.62	127.94	133.02
1973	234.93	144.31	218.73	1986	193.08	144.33	159.27	1999	199.61	129.38	194.54
1974	308.10	185.44	264.03	1987	180.86	152.89	164.33	2000	265.93	187.73	246.92
1975	264.03	179.07	183.46	1988	184.41	159.39	184.41	2001	250.40	160.12	169.15
1976	199.06	147.92	158.10	1989	207.25	176.33	207.25	2002	246.53	161.72	235.15
1977	176.66	137.03	159.33	1990	270.41	181.56	219.97	2003	284.61	211.63	260.54
1978	199.85	153.97	193.07	1991	228.35	174.43	176.92	2004	374.89	254.74	310.47
1979	239.61	189.20	237.81	1992	196.04	171.70	181.01	2005	478.08	301.32	431.72
1980	302.21	212.05	268.69	1993	191.62	161.38	163.55	2006	459.94	405.22	442.52

Source: Goldman Sachs

GOLDMAN SACHS COMMODITY INDEX

Quarterly High, Low and Close of Goldman Sachs Commodity Index   Index Value

Quarter	High	Low	Close	Quarter	High	Low	Close	Quarter	High	Low	Close
09/1996	211.26	190.98	205.22	12/1999	199.61	174.91	194.54	03/2003	284.61	216.90	232.28
12/1996	229.87	201.28	215.26	03/2000	231.75	187.73	207.05	06/2003	244.68	211.63	233.20
03/1997	231.82	187.38	192.43	06/2000	238.44	192.36	235.71	09/2003	247.72	218.81	232.63
06/1997	204.72	169.69	185.17	09/2000	257.56	212.94	237.48	12/2003	271.86	230.33	260.54
09/1997	206.31	180.71	201.73	12/2000	265.93	233.33	246.92	03/2004	287.54	254.74	282.12
12/1997	212.13	175.11	175.62	03/2001	250.40	212.10	212.74	06/2004	315.77	271.52	286.35
03/1998	177.62	156.72	166.72	06/2001	237.45	199.19	202.66	09/2004	341.24	284.61	337.73
06/1998	170.52	149.25	155.20	09/2001	215.98	170.20	181.76	12/2004	374.89	298.57	310.47
09/1998	156.09	136.55	153.76	12/2001	186.92	160.12	169.15	03/2005	389.43	301.32	383.87
12/1998	154.93	127.94	133.02	03/2002	201.56	161.72	201.23	06/2005	400.58	337.98	380.05
03/1999	155.15	129.38	153.94	06/2002	211.08	186.38	202.78	09/2005	478.08	381.05	469.56
06/1999	163.62	148.11	163.36	09/2002	230.79	196.84	227.52	12/2005	472.38	405.91	431.72
09/1999	198.96	160.65	191.06	12/2002	246.53	202.51	235.15	03/2006	459.94	405.22	442.52

Source: Goldman Sachs

INDEXES - STOCKS

US Stock Market History

The nearby chart of the Dow Jones Industrial Average (DJIA) going back to 1900 clearly shows the major phases for the US stock market. US stocks moved sideways in a volatile range during the 1900-1920 period. US stocks rallied sharply during the Roaring Twenties, but then plunged in 1929-1932 during the Great Depression. US stocks recovered later in the 1930s but then moved sideways during World War II. After World War II, the US stock market entered a long-term uptrend, with interruptions in the 1970s and more recently in 2000-02.

The nearby chart of the S&P 500 of the post-World War II period shows how poorly investors did in US stocks during the 1970s and early 1980s on an inflation-adjusted basis when stagflation prevailed in the US. The chart also shows the long bull market that lasted from 1982 to 2000, and the 2000-02 downward correction that occurred after the technology bubble burst.

The lessons from these long-term charts are that stock investors tend to fare very well during periods of stable US economic growth and low inflation, and that they fare very poorly during periods of stagflation such as in the 1970s. The charts also show that the stock market occasionally goes through bubble periods, such as during the Roaring Twenties and in the late-1990s, which later prompt painful corrections. Over the long-term, however, US stocks have marched steadily higher. The Dow Jones Industrial Average has shown an average annual gain of +7.2% since 1900, which equates to a real average annual gain of +3.8% after subtracting the average annual CPI gain of +3.4% over that same period.

1929 Stock Market Crash

During the period from 1900 to 1920, the Dow Jones Industrial Average (DJIA) traded in a wide and volatile range. Several times during this period the DJIA fell by about 40% (e.g., in 1902-04, 1906-08, and 1910-15), but always rallied back within about 2 years.

After World War I ended in 1918, the US stock market traded in a volatile range for several years, but finally started to gather a head of steam after bottoming out in 1921. In fact, the DJIA from its low in 1921 (of 67.11) more than quintupled over the following 8 years to a record high of 381.17 in September 1929. The Roaring Twenties was a time of great optimism, with World War I in the past and with American industrial activity and productivity expanding greatly.

However, the 1929 Stock Market Crash brought the Roaring Twenties to an abrupt halt. The DJIA in just two days (October 28-29) plunged by an overall ?23.6%. In the following 2 months, the DJIA continued lower for an overall sell-off of ?47.9% from the peak. After a modest recovery in

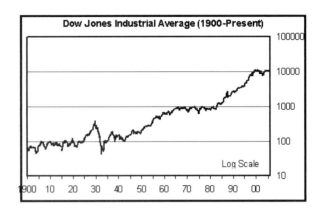

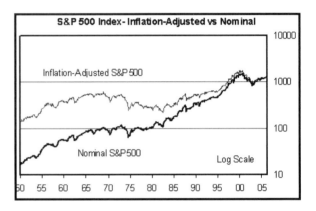

early 1930, the plunge resumed later in the year and the DJIA continued its plunge for another 2 years until finally bottoming in 1932 with a total loss of 90% from the 1929 peak. The 1929 Stock Market Crash helped set off the Great Depression, which of course resulted in mass poverty across America.

There have been a variety of reasons given for the 1929 Stock Market Crash, including (1) rampant speculation during the 1920s and the use of excessive margin (up to 90%) to buy stocks, (2) overvaluation of stocks, particularly highly-levered public utility stocks and investment trusts, and (3) the Smoot-Hawley trade tariff bill which was passed in the midst of the crash and which would go on to cause a plunge in world trade.

After the 1929-32 crash, the US stock market rallied through most of the rest of the 1930s as America slowly came out of the Depression and as the economy began to expand again. However, the DJIA would not exceed its 1929 peak until 2-1/2 decades later in November 1954.

Post-World War II Bull Market—1948 to 1973

The post-war period was a golden age for the US stock market. Stocks rallied sharply from 1949 to about 1966 as American business expanded its industrial base and profits. Moreover, macroeconomic conditions were very favorable with low inflation and low interest rates. The S&P 500 index rallied by a total of +675% from the end of World War II in August 1946 (15.51) to the stock market peak seen in January 1973 (102.24). That amounted to an average annual gain of +7.7%.

However, the stock market ran into trouble and turned sideways in the late-1960s on an inflation-adjusted basis as the US began to run a budget deficit in order to fund the Vietnam War and President Johnson's Great Society. The Federal Reserve monetized that deficit spending to keep interest rates low, thus allowing inflation to move higher. The US CPI, which averaged only 1.2% in the first-half of the 1960s, started rising in 1966 and by the end of 1969 it was over 6.0%.

1973-75 Bear Market

US macroeconomic conditions in the early 1970s deteriorated due to increased inflation, rising interest rates, and a decline in the dollar after the breakdown of the Bretton Woods agreement (which fixed the world's major currencies after World War II). The US economy and stock market were then hit with a major shock from the Arab Oil Embargo in October 1973, which was retaliation against the US for supporting Israel during the Yom Kippur War.

Crude oil prices (West Texas Intermediate oil) nearly tripled from $3.56 per barrel in July 1973 to $10.11 by early 1974. Crude oil prices then continued to rise steadily through the remainder of the 1970s, rising by another 50% to $15 per barrel by the end of 1978. The oil price shock caused inflation to soar from under 4.0% in 1972 to a peak of 12.3% two years later in 1974. The US experienced a long and grinding recession from November 1973 to March 1975.

The US stock market saw a serious bear market in 1973-74 due to the oil price shock and the US economic recession. The S&P 500 fell by a total of 48% during the 1973-74 bear market, from a high of 120.24 in January 1973 to the low of 62.28 in October 1974.

While the S&P 500 rose in the latter half of the 1970s on a nominal basis and recovered most of the losses seen in 1974-75, the earlier chart of the inflation-adjusted S&P 500 shows that the US stock market on an inflation-adjusted basis actually continued to grind lower through the latter half of the 1970s. Stock investors did poorly over that time frame due to high inflation and continued damage from high oil prices to the US economy and corporate profits.

The US stock market then received another oil shock in 1980. Oil prices in 1979-80 more than doubled from $15 a barrel at the beginning of 1979 to a peak of $39.59 in June 1980 (which equates to $94 a barrel in 2006 dollars). That spike was caused by a near shut-down of Iranian oil production due to the Iranian revolution against the Shah.

Also during that time, Paul Volcker took over as Fed Chairman in August 1979 and started cracking down on the money supply to tame inflation. The Fed drove the federal funds rate as high as 20% in March 1980 and then again to 20% in May 1981. The combination of the oil and interest rate shocks caused double dip recessions in 1980 (Jan-July) and again in 1981-82 (July-81 to Nov-82).

The S&P 500 dropped by a total of ?17% in Feb-March 1980, but then rallied through the remainder of 1980 as the US recession turned out to be short. However, the S&P 500 then again saw a bear market in 1981-82 totaling ?27% (from 140.52 in Nov 80 to 102.42 in Aug 1982) because of continued high oil prices and interest rates and the second phase of the double-dip recession.

1982 Bull Market Begins

Another golden age for the US stock market began in 1982 after the Federal Reserve got inflation under control and US interest rates started to fall. The devastating 1970s were finally over. The 10-year T-note yield, which peaked at about 16% in late 1981, moved lower through most of the 1980s and fell to 8% by 1990. The S&P 500 rallied sharply by a total of 229% from 1982 through 1987 (i.e., from a 102.42 low in August 1982 to a high of 336.77 in August 1987).

The infamous 1987 stock market crash then occurred on October 19, 1987, when the S&P 500 fell by ?20.5% in a single day. The Dow Jones Industrial on that same day plunged by ?22.6%, which remains the second largest single-day percentage loss to this day, behind only the ?24.4% loss on December 1914. The 1987 stock market crash of ?20.5% was just slightly less than the 1929 Stock Market Crash of ?23.6%, which was spread over two days (October 28-29, 1929).

The 1987 stock market crash was caused by a number of factors including (1) overvaluation in the stock market since the S&P 500 had rallied by 39% from the beginning of the year through the peak in August 1987, (2) the Fed's 150 basis point hike in the funds rate target to 7.50% in September 1987 from 6.00% in March 1987, and (3) suspicion that program trading and portfolio insurance worsened the slide due to sell stops and automated selling. The 1987 stock market crash was a global event as stock markets around the world plunged as well (UK ?26.4%, Germany ?9.3%, Japan ?14.9%, Canada ?22.5%, Australia ?41.8%, Hong Kong ?45.8%).

While the situation looked dire at the time, Fed Chairman Greenspan, who had only been on the job for two months, quickly stepped in to calm the markets. The Fed flooded the financial system with liquidity to prevent any banking system defaults. Moreover, US corporations also helped to stem the panic by announcing large stock buyback programs to show that they thought the sell-off was overdone and that their stocks were trading at unreasonably cheap levels.

INDEXES - STOCKS

The US stock market after the 1987 stock market crash stabilized at its lower level very quickly. Within just two months the correction was over and the stock market was headed higher again. There was surprisingly little damage to the US economy, despite the huge loss in shareholder and household wealth that had just occurred. In less than two years, the S&P 500 had regained all of the losses seen during the 1987 stock market crash. While a momentous event at the time, the 1987 stock market crash is now only a blip in the overall 1982-2000 bull market.

The S&P 500 in July-October 1990 saw a brief 3-month downdraft of ?20.3% due to America's first war against Iraq, which caused another oil price spike and a US recession from July 1990 to March 1991. However, the S&P 500 was able to regain those losses within just 4 months.

The US stock market in the first half of the 1990s benefited as the Federal Reserve continued to cut interest rates in response to an improved inflation situation. The S&P 500 rallied by a total of 64% from the low seen in October 1990 (294.51) to the high seen in January 1994 (482.85). Inflation fell from an average of 5% in 1989-90 to an average of 3% in 1992-96. That allowed the Fed to cut the federal funds rate target from 9.75% in early 1989 to 3.00% by the end of 1992 and the funds rate remained at 3.00% into early 1994. The 10-year T-note yield fell sharply over that period from 9% in 1990 to the 6-8% range during the 1994-97 period. US GDP averaged strong growth of +3.6% in 1992-94. S&P 500 annual profit growth during the 1992-94 period was very strong at an average +14.3%.

Bubble Market develops in the late-1990s

In the second-half of the 1990s, the US stock market entered an accelerated bull market that took the market to new record highs. The S&P 500 rallied by a total of +238% from the beginning of 1995 to the record high of 1552.87 posted in March 2000. The S&P 500 in the second half of the 1990s (1995-99) showed an average annual gain of an eye-popping +26.3% (+34.1% in 1995, +20.3% in 1996, +31.0% in 1997, +26.7% in 1998, +19.5% in 1999).

The late-1990s was a time of great optimism stemming from the technology and Internet boom, a structural increase in productivity, low interest rates, and low inflation-adjusted crude oil prices. The US economy performed very well in the latter half of the 1990s, averaging +4.0% annual GDP growth. Furthermore, earnings growth for the S&P 500 companies in 1995-2000 was very strong, with average annual earnings growth of +12.6%, far exceeding the long-term average of +7.5%, as seen on the nearby chart.

In addition, foreign investors piled into the US stock market in the latter half of the 1990s, helping to drive stock prices even higher. Specifically, foreign ownership of US equities more than tripled from about $500 billion in 1995

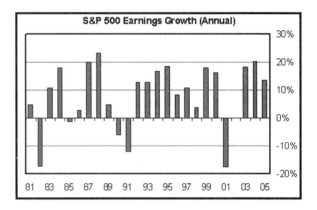

to $1.6 trillion in 1999. Foreign investors accounted for 10% of the ownership of all US equities in 1999, up 4 percentage points from 6% in 1995.

However, it was speculative fever that drove technology stocks higher during the 1995-2000 stock boom rather than rational analysis. The bubble in technology stocks is best demonstrated by the Nasdaq Composite index during the 1995-2000 period, which rose nearly 7-fold from 751.96 at the beginning of 1995 to the peak of 5,132.52 in March 2000.

As early as 1996, Fed Chairman Greenspan realized that an equity bubble might be developing. Mr. Greenspan, in a now-famous speech delivered on December 15, 1996, asked the question about how the Fed can know when "irrational exuberance" has "unduly escalated asset values." Mr. Greenspan's conclusion, as it developed in subsequent years, was that the Fed cannot know for certain when an asset bubble is emerging and that the Fed's best choice is therefore to focus on its overall goal of price stability and clean up after an asset bubble has burst, if needed. Mr. Greenspan believed that unnecessary damage can be done to the economy if the Fed tries to recognize and deflate asset bubbles before they become a problem.

By early 2000, stock market valuations had become extreme. The Nasdaq Composite was trading at a price/earnings ratio of about 150, meaning that investors were willing to pay $150 for each dollar of current earnings in technology stocks. The price/earnings ratio for the S&P 500 based on forward-looking earnings was trading at 26 in March 2000, which was far above the average P/E ratio of 18 seen in the pre-bubble 1985-95 period.

Equity bubble bursts, causing 2000-02 bear market

The US stock market reached its peak in March 2000 and subsequently started its descent into the 2000-02 bear market. A variety of factors finally caught up with the stock market. Technology spending started slowing in early 2000 since corporations had already made their technology investments ahead of Y2K on fears of massive disruptions when the year 2000 began (which fortunately never occurred). In addition, the Fed raised its funds rate target by 125 basis points from 4.75% in mid-1999 to 6.50% in mid-2000. The US economy also started to stumble in the latter half of 2000, with GDP falling ?0.5% in Q3-2000. After the equity bubble burst, household wealth plunged and consumer and business confidence was severely damaged. A full-blown, though short, recession then emerged from March to November 2001.

To make things worse, on September 11, 2001, al-Qaeda launched a terrorist attack on the World Trade Center and the Pentagon that shocked the nation. The attack occurred on a Tuesday morning, and the New York Stock Exchange remained closed for the remainder of the week (Sep 11-14) while New York City got back on its feet. The NYSE reopened the following Monday. The S&P 500 fell by ?13.5% in the subsequent 2 weeks, but then more than regained its losses within a month as confidence and resolve returned.

When 9/11 occurred, the Federal Reserve was already in the process of cutting interest rates because of the bursting of the equity bubble. However, 9/11 caused the Fed to continue to cut interest rates. In total, the Fed cut the federal funds rate by 4.75 percentage points from 6.5% in late 2000 to 1.75% by the end of 2001. The Fed then cut by another 0.75 percentage points to 1.00% by mid-2003.

The Fed was alarmed about the inability of the US economy to show sustained GDP growth of more than 2% annual growth in the 2001-02 time frame. The Fed was very worried that a deflationary period could emerge, such as the one seen in Japan from 1990-2005, in which the Fed would have trouble fighting a weak economy with monetary policy because the Fed would simply be "pushing on a string."

The US stock market finally bottomed out in October 2002. At the bottom of the bear market, the S&P 500 was down by a total of ?50.5%, and the Nasdaq Composite was down by a total of ?78.4%, from their record highs posted in March 2000.

2002-06 bull market begins

In October 2002, the US stock market finally started higher as the Fed's extraordinarily easy monetary policy started to stimulate asset prices, including home prices and the equity market. Moreover, US consumer spending held up well and pulled the rest of the US economy through the soft period seen in 2001-03. By the end of 2003, GDP growth had recovered and then averaged a strong +3.5% in 2004-05.

Since the US had escaped deflation and the US economy was on the mend, the Fed in June 2004 started raising its funds rate target in 25 basis point increments at each successive FOMC meeting. Through March 2006, the Fed had raised its funds rate target to 4.75%, up 3.75 percentage points from the 1.00% level that prevailed from mid-2003 to mid-2004. Yet the US economy was resilient enough to absorb the Fed's slow tightening process and the US economy performed well from 2003-05. The US economy was also able to absorb the shock of crude oil prices more than doubling in price from $30 per barrel in late 2003 to a record high of $70.85 in August 2005.

The 2002-06 stock market rally was driven largely by a surge in corporate earnings. US corporations were able to produce double-digit annual earnings growth averaging +17.3% per year in 2003-05. Strong earnings growth allowed valuation levels to remain at reasonable levels despite the rally in stock prices. In other words, the price/earnings ratio didn't rise sharply during the 2002-06 bull market because as stock prices rose (i.e., the numerator in the P/E ratio), earnings (the denominator) rose as well.

The price/earnings ratio for the S&P 500 in March 2006 was near 18, which is close to the long-term average seen back in 1985-95 before the 2000 bubble emerged. The modest valuation level means that the 2002-06 rally had sound underpinnings, unlike the bubble rally in the late-1990s.

The outlook for the US stock market going into Q2-2006 is generally favorable since (1) the Fed is nearly done tightening, (2) corporate profits are expected to continue to show double-digit gains through year-end, and (3) valuation levels are reasonable. However, there are still risks for the stock market, mainly involving the possibility of an upward spike in oil prices or the possibility that the Fed will go too far in its tightening process and cause an economic slump.

DOW JONES INDUSTRIALS

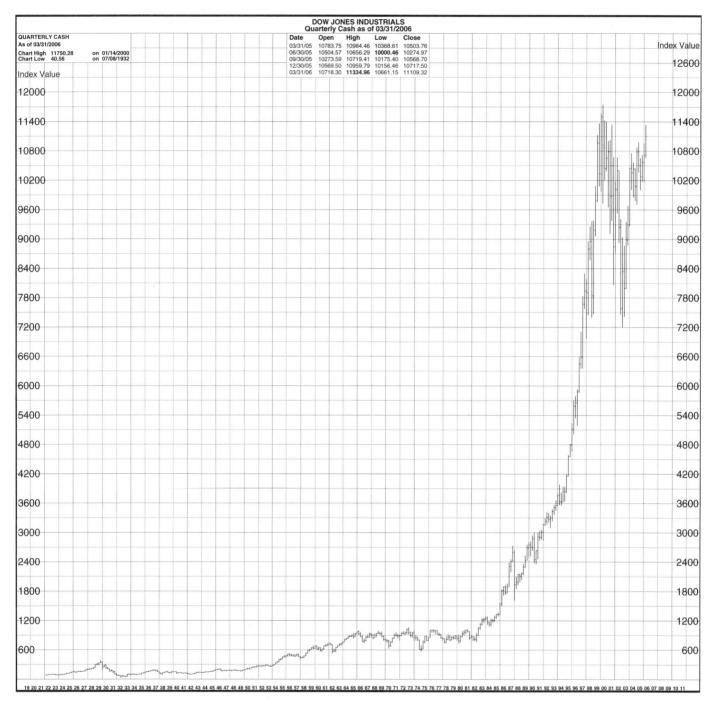

Annual High, Low and Close of Dow Jones Industrials Index   Index Value

Year	High	Low	Close	Year	High	Low	Close	Year	High	Low	Close
1929	386.10	195.35	248.48	1942	120.19	92.69	119.40	1955	490.75	385.65	488.40
1930	297.25	154.45	164.58	1943	146.41	118.84	135.89	1956	524.37	458.21	499.47
1931	196.96	71.79	77.90	1944	152.75	134.10	151.93	1957	523.11	416.15	435.69
1932	89.87	40.56	60.26	1945	196.59	150.53	192.91	1958	587.44	434.04	583.65
1933	110.53	49.68	98.67	1946	213.36	160.49	177.20	1959	683.90	571.73	679.36
1934	111.93	84.58	104.04	1947	187.66	161.38	181.16	1960	688.21	564.23	615.89
1935	149.42	95.95	144.13	1948	194.49	164.07	177.30	1961	741.30	606.09	731.14
1936	186.39	141.53	179.90	1949	200.91	160.62	200.52	1962	734.38	524.55	652.10
1937	195.59	112.54	120.85	1950	236.63	193.94	235.42	1963	773.07	643.57	762.95
1938	158.90	97.46	154.36	1951	277.51	234.93	269.23	1964	897.00	760.34	874.13
1939	157.77	120.04	149.99	1952	293.50	254.70	291.90	1965	976.61	832.74	969.26
1940	153.29	110.41	131.13	1953	295.03	254.36	280.90	1966	1,001.11	735.74	785.69
1941	134.27	105.52	110.96	1954	407.17	278.91	404.39	1967	951.57	776.16	905.11

Source: New York Stock Exchange

DOW JONES INDUSTRIALS

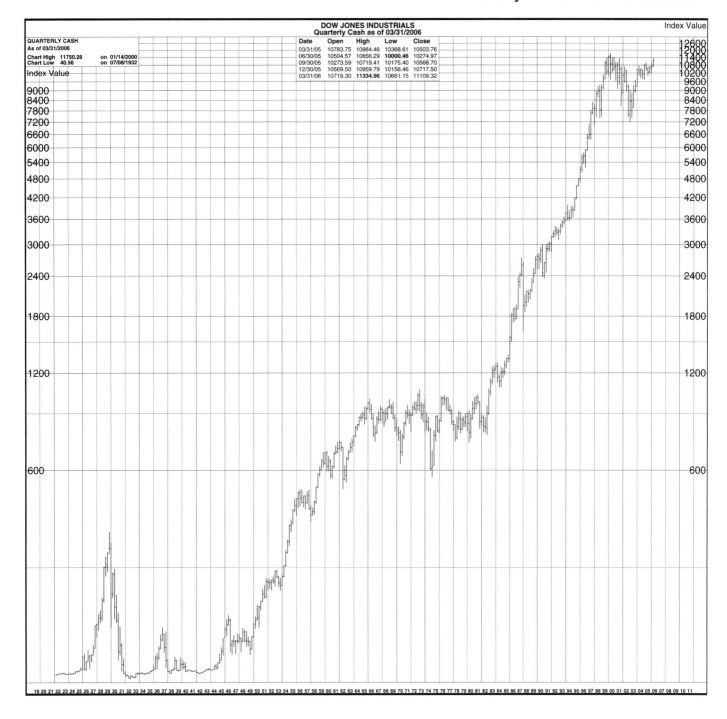

DOW JONES INDUSTRIALS

Annual High, Low and Close of Dow Jones Industrials Index   Index Value

Year	High	Low	Close	Year	High	Low	Close	Year	High	Low	Close
1968	994.65	817.61	943.75	1981	1,030.98	807.45	875.00	1994	3,985.69	3,552.48	3,834.44
1969	974.92	764.45	800.36	1982	1,074.32	769.98	1,046.54	1995	5,235.62	3,817.28	5,117.12
1970	848.23	627.46	838.92	1983	1,291.67	1,020.24	1,258.63	1996	6,589.53	5,014.52	6,448.27
1971	958.12	790.67	890.20	1984	1,291.87	1,082.05	1,211.57	1997	8,299.49	6,352.82	7,908.25
1972	1,042.44	882.75	1,020.02	1985	1,563.76	1,180.99	1,546.67	1998	9,380.20	7,400.30	9,181.43
1973	1,067.20	783.56	850.86	1986	1,961.47	1,497.71	1,895.11	1999	11,568.77	9,063.26	11,497.12
1974	904.02	570.01	616.24	1987	2,736.61	1,616.21	1,938.82	2000	11,750.28	9,654.64	10,786,85
1975	888.85	619.13	852.41	1988	2,188.04	1,850.96	2,168.57	2001	11,350.05	8,062.34	10,021.50
1976	1,026.26	848.63	1,004.65	1989	2,795.97	2,131.79	2,753.20	2002	10,673.10	7,197.49	8,341.63
1977	1,007.81	792.79	831.17	1990	3,010.64	2,354.21	2,633.66	2003	10,462.44	7,416.64	10,453.92
1978	917.27	736.75	805.01	1991	3,188.05	2,457.67	3,168.83	2004	10,868.07	9,708.40	10,783.01
1979	904.86	792.24	838.74	1992	3,422.01	3,095.80	3,301.11	2005	10,984.46	10,000.46	10,717.50
1980	1,009.39	729.95	963.98	1993	3,799.92	3,231.96	3,754.09	2006	11,334.96	10,661.15	11,109.32

Source: New York Stock Exchange

DOW JONES INDUSTRIALS

Quarterly High, Low and Close of Dow Jones Industrials Index — Index Value

Quarter	High	Low	Close	Quarter	High	Low	Close	Quarter	High	Low	Close
09/1996	5,929.88	5,182.32	5,882.17	12/1999	11,568.77	9,976.02	11,497.12	03/2003	8,869.29	7,416.64	7,992.13
12/1996	6,589.53	5,862.06	6,448.27	03/2000	11,750.28	9,731.81	10,921.92	06/2003	9,352.77	7,979.69	8,985.44
03/1997	7,112.10	6,352.82	6,583.48	06/2000	11,425.45	10,201.53	10,447.89	09/2003	9,686.08	8,871.20	9,275.06
06/1997	7,834.06	6,356.37	7,672.79	09/2000	11,401.19	10,393.09	10,650.92	12/2003	10,462.44	9,276.80	10,453.92
09/1997	8,299.49	7,580.85	7,945.26	12/2000	11,006.50	9,654.64	10,786.85	03/2004	10,753.63	10,007.49	10,357.70
12/1997	8,184.70	6,971.32	7,908.25	03/2001	11,035.14	9,106.54	9,878.78	06/2004	10,570.81	9,852.19	10,435.48
03/1998	8,959.24	7,443.41	8,799.81	06/2001	11,350.05	9,375.72	10,502.40	09/2004	10,448.09	9,783.91	10,080.27
06/1998	9,261.91	8,569.88	8,952.02	09/2001	10,679.12	8,062.34	8,847.56	12/2004	10,868.07	9,708.40	10,783.01
09/1998	9,367.84	7,400.30	7,842.62	12/2001	10,184.45	8,732.14	10,021.50	03/2005	10,984.46	10,368.61	10,503.76
12/1998	9,380.20	7,467.49	9,181.43	03/2002	10,673.10	9,529.46	10,403.94	06/2005	10,656.29	10,000.46	10,274.97
03/1999	10,085.31	9,063.26	9,786.16	06/2002	10,402.07	8,926.57	9,243.26	09/2005	10,719.41	10,175.40	10,568.70
06/1999	11,130.67	9,765.63	10,970.80	09/2002	9,410.38	7,460.78	7,579.58	12/2005	10,959.79	10,156.46	10,717.50
09/1999	11,365.93	10,081.13	10,336.95	12/2002	9,043.37	7,197.49	8,341.63	03/2006	11,334.96	10,661.15	11,109.32

Source: New York Stock Exchange

DOW JONES TRANSPORTS

Annual High, Low and Close of Dow Jones Transports Index   Index Value

Year	High	Low	Close	Year	High	Low	Close	Year	High	Low	Close
				1981	451.93	326.18	380.30	1994	1,874.87	1,353.96	1,455.03
				1982	468.90	288.97	448.38	1995	2,105.19	1,443.62	1,981.00
1970	184.04	115.76	171.52	1983	613.14	434.24	596.69	1996	2,336.43	1,858.88	2,255.67
1971	250.67	168.53	243.72	1984	615.19	439.61	557.68	1997	3,372.42	2,203.27	3,256.50
1972	278.27	210.19	227.17	1985	729.17	550.04	708.33	1998	3,701.42	2,282.18	3,149.31
1973	231.66	150.38	196.19	1986	876.32	677.20	807.17	1999	3,797.05	2,778.56	2,977.20
1974	204.89	124.30	143.44	1987	1,104.19	653.86	747.86	2000	3,017.18	2,260.78	2,946.60
1975	177.07	143.23	172.65	1988	966.63	732.43	960.92	2001	3,157.44	1,942.01	2,639.99
1976	238.06	172.07	237.03	1989	1,540.54	946.14	1,177.81	2002	3,050.98	2,008.31	2,309.96
1977	247.91	197.46	217.18	1990	1,216.06	812.68	910.23	2003	3,038.15	1,918.12	3,007.05
1978	264.95	198.19	206.56	1991	1,358.55	887.37	1,358.00	2004	3,823.96	2,743.46	3,798.05
1979	273.42	201.56	252.39	1992	1,472.53	1,202.67	1,449.23	2005	4,306.09	3,348.36	4,196.03
1980	430.18	229.79	398.10	1993	1,789.47	1,441.18	1,762.32	2006	4,615.83	4,059.87	4,568.00

Source: New York Stock Exchange

DOW JONES TRANSPORTS

Quarterly High, Low and Close of Dow Jones Transports Index Index Value

Quarter	High	Low	Close	Quarter	High	Low	Close	Quarter	High	Low	Close
09/1996	2,226.86	1,919.21	2,079.02	12/1999	3,102.89	2,778.56	2,977.20	03/2003	2,425.83	1,918.12	2,131.21
12/1996	2,336.43	2,031.08	2,255.67	03/2000	3,017.18	2,260.78	2,763.24	06/2003	2,557.47	2,116.65	2,412.86
03/1997	2,485.00	2,203.27	2,358.31	06/2000	2,979.25	2,605.43	2,645.37	09/2003	2,825.07	2,370.58	2,673.86
06/1997	2,786.68	2,321.94	2,713.61	09/2000	2,928.69	2,498.90	2,521.64	12/2003	3,038.15	2,672.64	3,007.05
09/1997	3,244.08	2,707.57	3,179.74	12/2000	2,964.07	2,348.70	2,946.60	03/2004	3,090.07	2,743.46	2,895.43
12/1997	3,372.42	2,929.94	3,256.50	03/2001	3,157.44	2,578.87	2,771.36	06/2004	3,205.56	2,785.50	3,204.31
03/1998	3,652.74	3,145.95	3,577.09	06/2001	3,010.24	2,606.26	2,833.56	09/2004	3,271.62	2,959.58	3,243.51
06/1998	3,701.42	3,249.68	3,475.29	09/2001	3,007.81	1,942.01	2,194.68	12/2004	3,823.96	3,245.20	3,798.05
09/1998	3,623.71	2,592.69	2,644.67	12/2001	2,662.08	2,119.77	2,639.99	03/2005	3,889.97	3,454.74	3,715.97
12/1998	3,166.17	2,282.18	3,149.31	03/2002	3,050.98	2,604.60	2,917.96	06/2005	3,758.59	3,348.36	3,487.76
03/1999	3,450.07	3,048.10	3,299.04	06/2002	2,919.96	2,578.71	2,730.32	09/2005	3,821.96	3,473.33	3,740.55
06/1999	3,797.05	3,290.73	3,404.36	09/2002	2,734.12	2,090.32	2,148.34	12/2005	4,306.09	3,550.55	4,196.03
09/1999	3,531.06	2,822.47	2,909.16	12/2002	2,416.91	2,008.31	2,309.96	03/2006	4,615.83	4,059.87	4,568.00

Source: New York Stock Exchange

DOW JONES UTILITIES

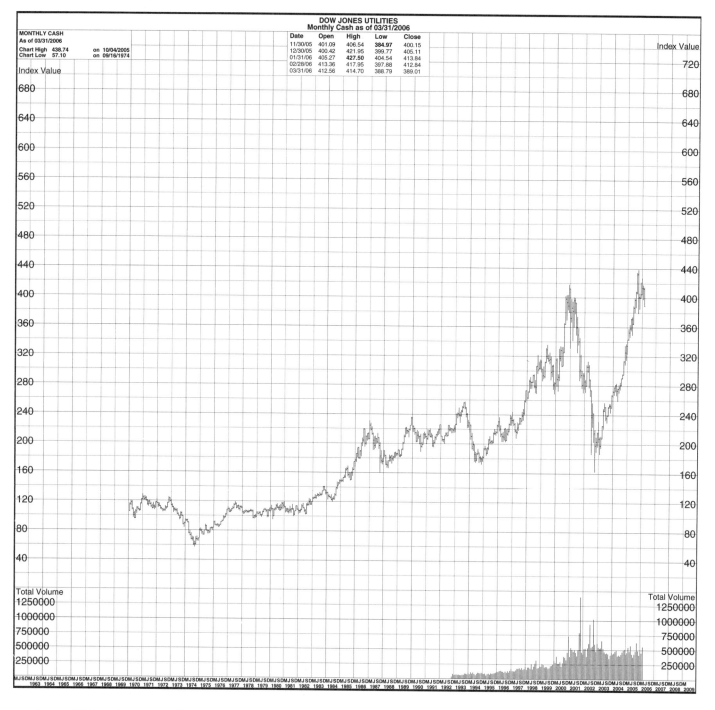

Annual High, Low and Close of Dow Jones Utilities Index   Index Value

Year	High	Low	Close	Year	High	Low	Close	Year	High	Low	Close
				1981	119.42	99.75	109.02	1994	229.77	172.03	181.52
				1982	124.17	102.21	119.46	1995	226.66	180.79	225.40
1970	122.48	95.09	121.84	1983	141.14	119.37	131.89	1996	239.59	202.84	232.53
1971	129.12	107.55	117.75	1984	150.13	119.56	149.36	1997	273.44	207.80	273.07
1972	125.32	104.58	119.50	1985	174.96	146.03	174.70	1998	322.21	260.51	312.30
1973	121.45	83.81	89.37	1986	219.75	168.09	205.84	1999	336.03	268.59	283.36
1974	95.83	57.10	68.76	1987	231.06	160.38	175.08	2000	418.25	272.37	412.16
1975	88.19	69.53	83.65	1988	190.02	166.25	186.28	2001	412.48	270.26	293.94
1976	108.64	83.53	108.38	1989	236.29	181.37	235.04	2002	313.25	162.52	215.18
1977	119.09	104.23	111.28	1990	236.23	188.76	209.70	2003	267.90	186.54	266.90
1978	111.84	96.04	98.24	1991	226.15	195.05	226.15	2004	337.79	259.08	334.95
1979	110.86	97.70	106.60	1992	226.02	200.23	221.02	2005	438.74	323.79	405.11
1980	118.69	95.23	114.42	1993	257.59	215.82	229.30	2006	427.50	388.79	389.01

Source: New York Stock Exchange

DOW JONES UTILITIES

Quarterly High, Low and Close of Dow Jones Utilities Index   Index Value

Quarter	High	Low	Close	Quarter	High	Low	Close	Quarter	High	Low	Close
09/1996	222.05	202.84	216.88	12/1999	308.89	268.59	283.36	03/2003	231.27	186.54	208.00
12/1996	239.59	216.25	232.53	03/2000	317.82	272.37	291.77	06/2003	256.99	207.85	250.99
03/1997	243.99	216.25	218.56	06/2000	334.14	286.64	306.91	09/2003	252.02	229.46	250.59
06/1997	229.74	207.80	226.79	09/2000	402.28	306.88	398.22	12/2003	267.90	243.26	266.90
09/1997	244.20	226.48	238.37	12/2000	418.25	369.31	412.16	03/2004	281.87	263.90	281.09
12/1997	273.44	232.48	273.07	03/2001	412.48	330.95	381.42	06/2004	283.52	259.08	277.89
03/1998	288.37	260.51	285.94	06/2001	400.69	348.92	359.34	09/2004	296.45	274.52	295.33
06/1998	295.01	275.50	293.87	09/2001	374.26	286.95	301.67	12/2004	337.79	295.30	334.95
09/1998	306.75	269.09	306.72	12/2001	322.75	270.26	293.94	03/2005	363.82	323.79	358.33
12/1998	322.21	296.21	312.30	03/2002	308.59	270.89	305.73	06/2005	389.28	349.25	386.59
03/1999	314.93	286.11	292.28	06/2002	313.25	265.45	273.88	09/2005	434.91	379.53	432.38
06/1999	336.03	290.54	316.82	09/2002	274.06	186.49	214.87	12/2005	438.74	378.95	405.11
09/1999	325.39	287.60	298.26	12/2002	220.08	162.52	215.18	03/2006	427.50	388.79	389.01

Source: New York Stock Exchange

CBOE VOLATILITY INDEX

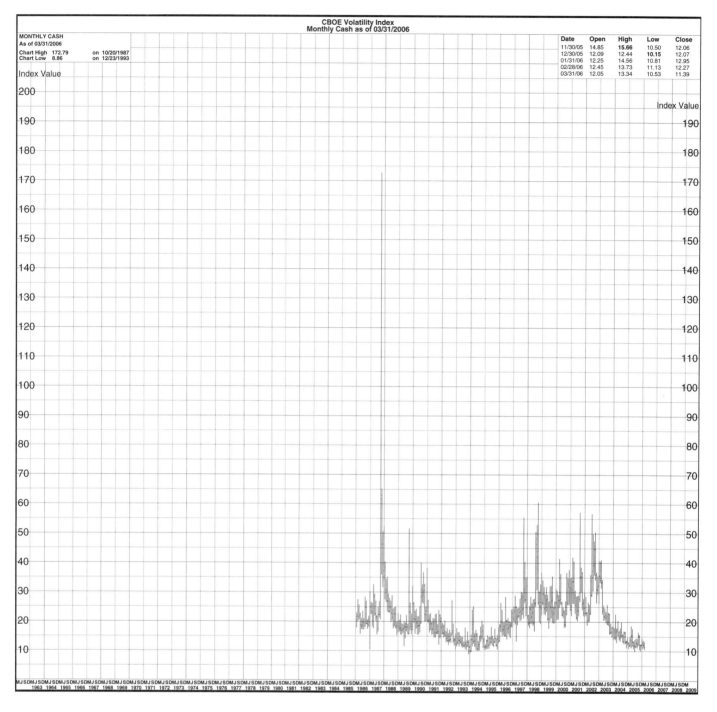

Annual High, Low and Close of CBOE Volatility Index — Index Value

Year	High	Low	Close	Year	High	Low	Close	Year	High	Low	Close
1986	28.41	15.75	18.71	1993	18.00	8.86	11.46	2000	41.53	18.06	30.23
1987	172.79	10.43	39.45	1994	25.31	9.25	13.44	2001	57.31	20.26	23.22
1988	52.60	15.22	18.53	1995	18.27	10.41	13.89	2002	56.74	18.87	32.03
1989	51.71	11.60	17.39	1996	28.45	12.66	21.67	2003	41.16	14.83	18.31
1990	40.01	15.51	23.55	1997	55.48	13.24	24.89	2004	22.67	11.14	13.29
1991	38.21	12.16	20.17	1998	60.63	16.73	25.41	2005	18.59	9.88	12.07
1992	27.28	11.89	13.55	1999	36.79	17.70	26.71	2006	14.56	10.53	11.39

Source: Chicago Board of Options Exchange

CBOE VOLATILITY INDEX

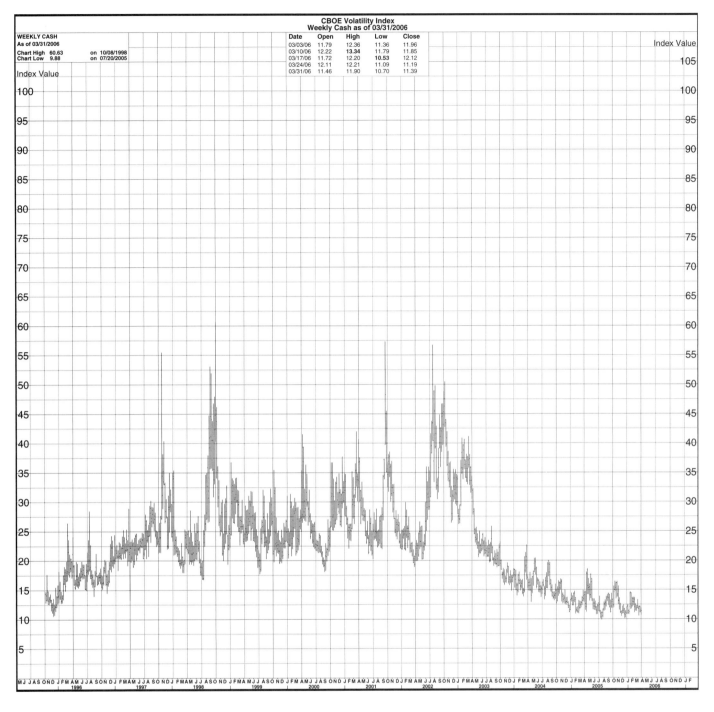

Quarterly High, Low and Close of CBOE Volatility Index   Index Value

Quarter	High	Low	Close	Quarter	High	Low	Close	Quarter	High	Low	Close
09/1996	28.45	13.94	17.87	12/1999	35.48	19.46	26.71	03/2003	41.16	26.19	33.37
12/1996	24.26	14.45	21.67	03/2000	31.37	20.41	27.21	06/2003	34.39	20.57	21.62
03/1997	28.89	18.34	24.99	06/2000	41.53	22.02	22.26	09/2003	25.88	18.79	22.72
06/1997	25.31	13.24	23.34	09/2000	27.04	18.06	23.85	12/2003	22.82	14.83	18.31
09/1997	30.25	20.32	24.30	12/2000	37.72	22.34	30.23	03/2004	22.67	13.83	16.74
12/1997	55.48	21.25	24.89	03/2001	41.99	22.05	33.82	06/2004	20.45	12.89	14.34
03/1998	35.41	17.92	24.25	06/2001	40.70	20.89	21.63	09/2004	19.97	13.16	13.34
06/1998	28.57	18.68	19.86	09/2001	57.31	20.26	35.19	12/2004	16.87	11.14	13.29
09/1998	53.08	16.73	41.94	12/2001	38.56	22.04	23.22	03/2005	14.89	10.90	14.02
12/1998	60.63	19.34	25.41	03/2002	29.92	18.87	19.32	06/2005	18.59	10.78	12.04
03/1999	36.79	22.26	24.45	06/2002	36.01	19.88	29.13	09/2005	14.41	9.88	11.92
06/1999	31.89	20.44	21.01	09/2002	56.74	28.63	44.57	12/2005	16.47	10.15	12.07
09/1999	32.33	17.70	26.89	12/2002	50.48	26.41	32.03	03/2006	14.56	10.53	11.39

Source: Chicago Board of Options Exchange

NASDAQ 100 INDEX

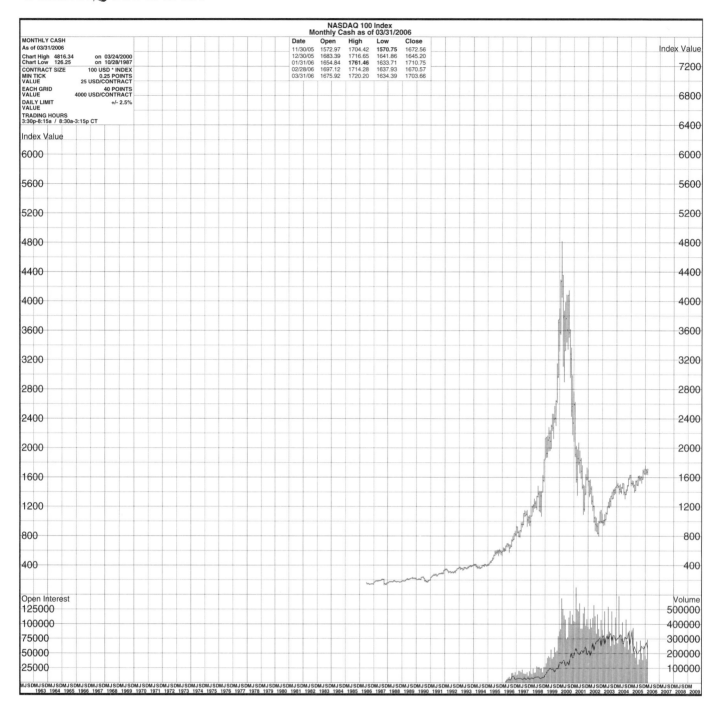

Annual High, Low and Close of NASDAQ 100 Index   Index Value

Year	High	Low	Close	Year	High	Low	Close	Year	High	Low	Close
1986	164.55	133.28	141.41	1993	401.81	326.56	398.28	2000	4,816.34	2,174.76	2,341.70
1987	214.03	126.25	156.25	1994	418.99	350.03	404.27	2001	2,771.63	1,088.96	1,577.05
1988	192.77	151.57	177.41	1995	623.53	394.59	576.23	2002	1,710.23	795.25	984.36
1989	238.85	172.95	223.84	1996	873.00	526.80	821.36	2003	1,474.24	938.52	1,467.92
1990	246.82	162.55	200.53	1997	1,153.89	779.17	990.80	2004	1,635.70	1,302.03	1,621.12
1991	332.67	190.90	330.70	1998	1,848.36	933.01	1,836.03	2005	1,716.65	1,394.49	1,645.20
1992	363.20	287.67	360.19	1999	3,750.41	1,838.65	3,707.83	2006	1,761.46	1,633.71	1,703.66

Source: NASDAQ

NASDAQ 100 INDEX

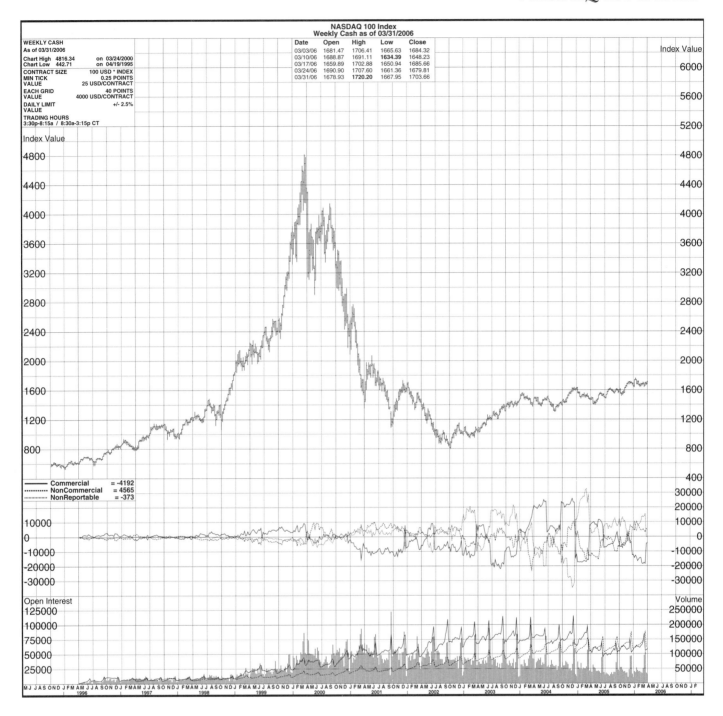

Quarterly High, Low and Close of NASDAQ 100 Index Index Value

Quarter	High	Low	Close	Quarter	High	Low	Close	Quarter	High	Low	Close
09/1996	757.83	572.92	737.57	12/1999	3,750.41	2,299.95	3,707.83	03/2003	1,104.32	938.52	1,018.66
12/1996	873.00	727.14	821.36	03/2000	4,816.34	3,314.75	4,397.84	06/2003	1,265.69	1,015.46	1,201.69
03/1997	938.11	784.54	797.06	06/2000	4,355.70	2,897.27	3,763.79	09/2003	1,406.61	1,180.11	1,303.70
06/1997	993.16	779.17	957.30	09/2000	4,147.19	3,341.83	3,570.42	12/2003	1,474.24	1,306.33	1,467.92
09/1997	1,151.82	947.78	1,097.17	12/2000	3,613.86	2,174.76	2,341.70	03/2004	1,559.47	1,368.08	1,438.41
12/1997	1,153.89	926.97	990.80	03/2001	2,771.63	1,530.14	1,573.25	06/2004	1,523.48	1,372.46	1,516.64
03/1998	1,230.92	933.01	1,220.66	06/2001	2,073.98	1,348.52	1,834.37	09/2004	1,514.82	1,302.03	1,412.74
06/1998	1,347.44	1,157.88	1,337.34	09/2001	1,864.20	1,088.96	1,168.37	12/2004	1,635.70	1,416.29	1,621.12
09/1998	1,485.97	1,118.12	1,345.48	12/2001	1,734.58	1,131.32	1,577.05	03/2005	1,635.45	1,458.26	1,482.53
12/1998	1,848.36	1,063.74	1,836.03	03/2002	1,710.23	1,329.93	1,452.81	06/2005	1,568.96	1,394.49	1,493.52
03/1999	2,168.69	1,838.65	2,106.72	06/2002	1,481.74	979.87	1,051.41	09/2005	1,628.57	1,484.46	1,601.66
06/1999	2,320.43	1,952.36	2,296.47	09/2002	1,066.28	825.80	832.52	12/2005	1,716.65	1,515.75	1,645.20
09/1999	2,573.50	2,120.26	2,407.90	12/2002	1,155.68	795.25	984.36	03/2006	1,761.46	1,633.71	1,703.66

Source: NASDAQ

NASDAQ COMPOSITE INDEX

Annual High, Low and Close of NASDAQ Composite Index   Index Value

Year	High	Low	Close	Year	High	Low	Close	Year	High	Low	Close
				1991	586.35	353.00	586.34	1999	4,090.61	2,193.13	4,069.31
1984	252.30	237.70	247.10	1992	676.95	545.95	676.95	2000	5,132.52	2,288.16	2,470.52
1985	325.60	245.80	324.90	1993	791.20	644.71	776.80	2001	2,892.36	1,387.06	1,950.40
1986	411.30	322.10	348.80	1994	804.43	690.95	751.96	2002	2,098.88	1,108.49	1,335.51
1987	456.30	288.50	330.50	1995	1,074.85	740.47	1,052.13	2003	2,015.23	1,253.22	2,003.37
1988	397.50	329.00	381.40	1996	1,328.45	977.79	1,291.03	2004	2,185.56	1,750.82	2,175.44
1989	487.50	376.90	454.80	1997	1,748.62	1,194.39	1,570.35	2005	2,278.16	1,889.91	2,205.32
1990	470.30	323.00	373.80	1998	2,200.63	1,357.09	2,192.69	2006	2,353.13	2,189.91	2,339.79

Source: NASDAQ

NASDAQ COMPOSITE INDEX

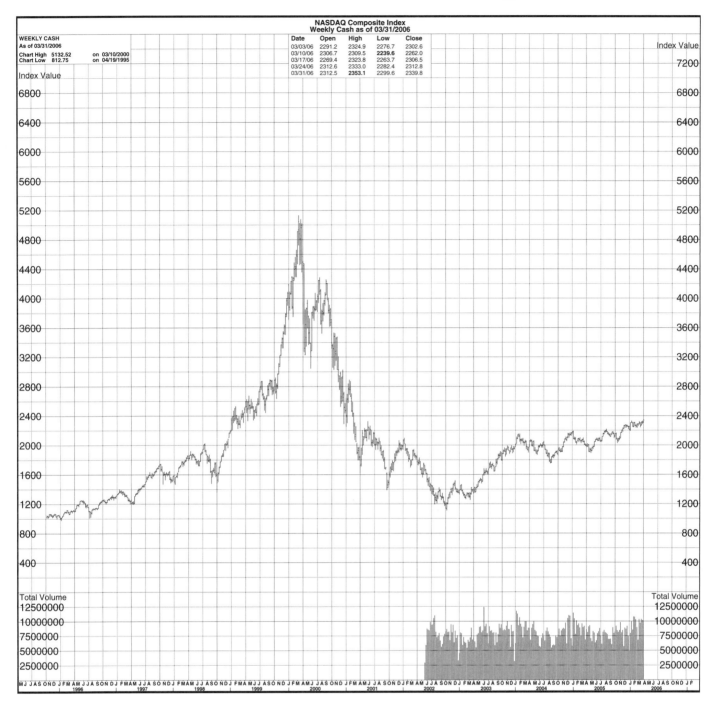

Quarterly High, Low and Close of NASDAQ Composite Index — Index Value

Quarter	High	Low	Close	Quarter	High	Low	Close	Quarter	High	Low	Close
09/1996	1,237.13	1,008.85	1,226.92	12/1999	4,090.61	2,632.01	4,069.31	03/2003	1,467.35	1,253.22	1,341.17
12/1996	1,328.45	1,202.55	1,291.03	03/2000	5,132.52	3,711.09	4,572.83	06/2003	1,686.10	1,338.23	1,622.80
03/1997	1,400.30	1,220.73	1,221.70	06/2000	4,504.36	3,042.66	3,966.11	09/2003	1,913.74	1,598.92	1,786.94
06/1997	1,467.19	1,194.39	1,442.07	09/2000	4,289.06	3,521.14	3,672.82	12/2003	2,015.23	1,796.09	2,003.37
09/1997	1,702.49	1,432.58	1,685.69	12/2000	3,714.48	2,288.16	2,470.52	03/2004	2,153.83	1,897.48	1,994.22
12/1997	1,748.62	1,468.84	1,570.35	03/2001	2,892.36	1,794.21	1,840.26	06/2004	2,079.12	1,865.40	2,047.79
03/1998	1,840.83	1,466.43	1,835.68	06/2001	2,328.05	1,619.58	2,160.54	09/2004	2,045.53	1,750.82	1,896.84
06/1998	1,921.10	1,715.19	1,894.74	09/2001	2,181.05	1,387.06	1,498.80	12/2004	2,185.56	1,899.33	2,175.44
09/1998	2,028.06	1,477.06	1,693.84	12/2001	2,065.69	1,458.41	1,950.40	03/2005	2,191.60	1,968.58	1,999.23
12/1998	2,200.63	1,357.09	2,192.69	03/2002	2,098.88	1,696.55	1,845.35	06/2005	2,106.57	1,889.91	2,056.96
03/1999	2,533.44	2,193.13	2,461.40	06/2002	1,865.37	1,375.53	1,463.20	09/2005	2,219.91	2,050.30	2,151.69
06/1999	2,696.87	2,329.87	2,686.12	09/2002	1,459.84	1,160.07	1,172.06	12/2005	2,278.16	2,025.95	2,205.32
09/1999	2,897.53	2,442.22	2,746.16	12/2002	1,521.44	1,108.49	1,335.51	03/2006	2,353.13	2,189.91	2,339.79

Source: NASDAQ

S&P 500 INDEX

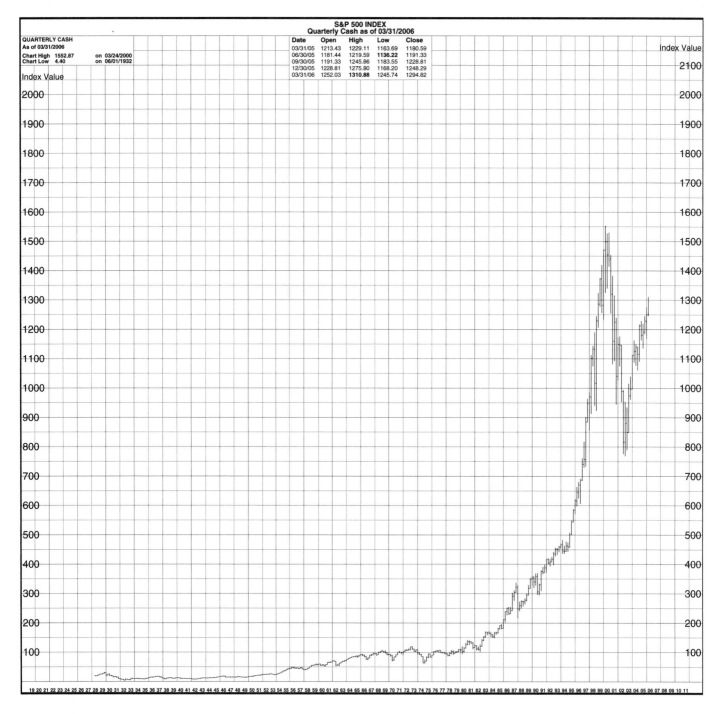

Annual High, Low and Close of S&P 500 Index   Index Value

Year	High	Low	Close	Year	High	Low	Close	Year	High	Low	Close
1929	31.83	17.66	21.45	1942	9.77	7.47	9.77	1955	46.41	34.58	45.48
1930	25.92	14.44	15.34	1943	12.64	9.88	11.67	1956	49.74	43.11	46.67
1931	18.17	7.72	8.12	1944	13.28	11.60	13.28	1957	49.13	38.98	39.99
1932	9.31	4.40	6.92	1945	17.67	13.21	17.36	1958	55.21	40.33	55.21
1933	12.20	5.56	9.97	1946	19.25	14.12	15.30	1959	60.71	53.58	59.89
1934	11.82	8.36	9.47	1947	16.14	13.74	15.30	1960	60.39	52.30	58.11
1935	13.46	8.06	13.43	1948	17.06	13.84	15.20	1961	72.64	57.57	71.55
1936	17.69	13.40	17.18	1949	16.79	13.55	16.79	1962	71.13	52.32	63.10
1937	18.67	10.17	10.55	1950	20.43	16.66	20.43	1963	75.02	62.69	75.02
1938	13.79	8.50	13.14	1951	23.83	20.69	23.73	1964	86.28	75.43	84.75
1939	13.23	10.31	12.46	1952	26.59	23.09	26.57	1965	92.63	81.60	92.43
1940	12.77	9.09	10.58	1953	26.66	22.71	24.81	1966	94.06	73.20	80.33
1941	10.86	8.38	8.69	1954	35.98	24.80	35.98	1967	97.59	80.38	96.47

Source: Chicago Mercantile Exchange

S&P 500 INDEX

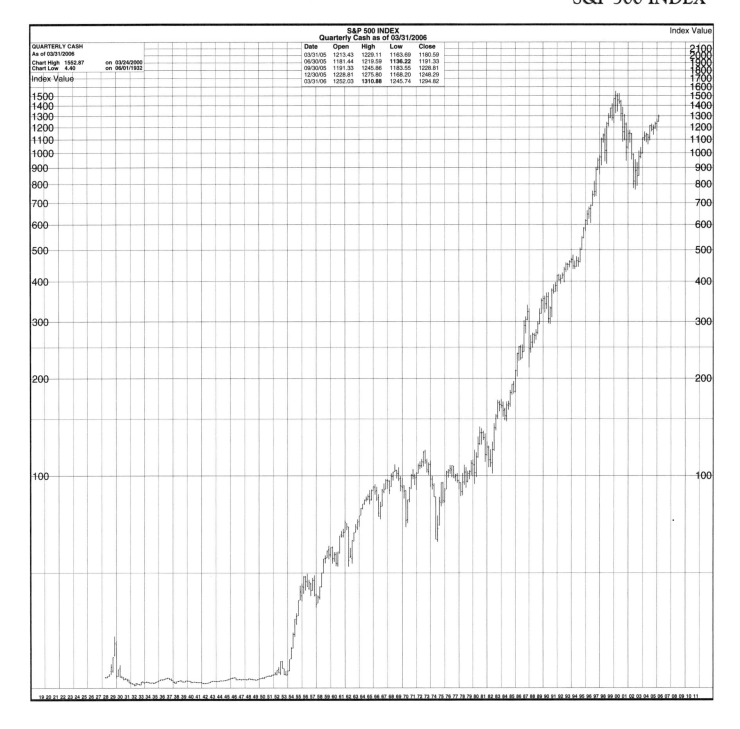

281

S&P 500 INDEX

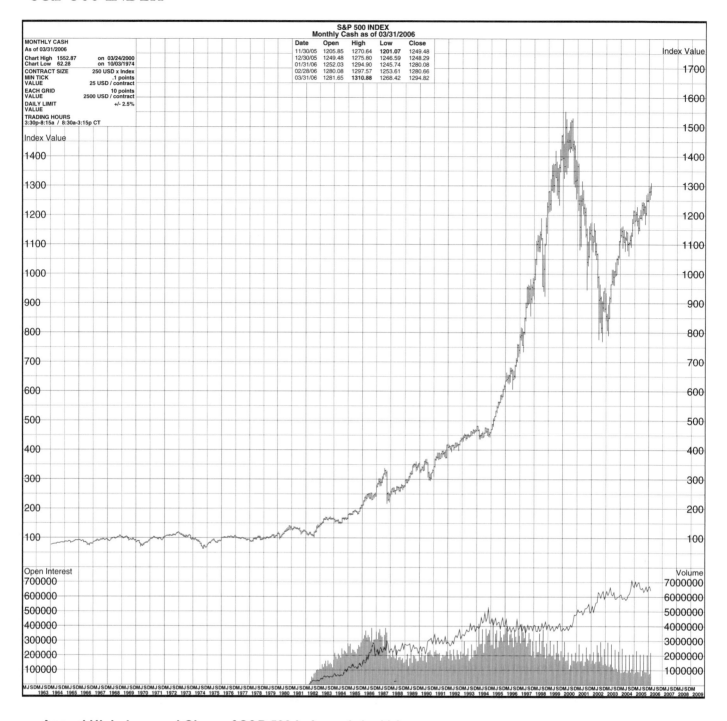

Annual High, Low and Close of S&P 500 Index   Index Value

Year	High	Low	Close	Year	High	Low	Close	Year	High	Low	Close
1968	108.37	87.72	103.86	1981	140.32	110.19	122.55	1994	482.85	435.86	459.27
1969	106.16	89.20	92.06	1982	145.33	101.44	140.64	1995	622.88	457.20	615.93
1970	93.46	69.29	92.00	1983	172.65	138.08	164.93	1996	762.12	597.29	740.74
1971	104.77	90.16	101.95	1984	170.41	147.26	167.24	1997	986.25	729.55	970.43
1972	119.12	101.67	118.05	1985	213.08	163.36	211.28	1998	1,244.93	912.83	1,229.23
1973	120.24	92.16	97.55	1986	254.86	202.60	242.16	1999	1,473.10	1,206.59	1,469.25
1974	99.80	62.28	68.56	1987	337.89	216.47	247.09	2000	1,552.87	1,254.07	1,320.28
1975	95.61	70.04	90.19	1988	283.77	240.17	277.72	2001	1,383.37	944.75	1,148.08
1976	107.83	90.90	107.46	1989	360.44	273.81	353.40	2002	1,176.97	768.63	879.82
1977	107.00	90.71	95.10	1990	369.78	294.51	330.23	2003	1,112.56	788.90	1,111.92
1978	108.05	86.45	96.11	1991	418.32	309.35	417.09	2004	1,217.33	1,060.72	1,211.92
1979	112.16	95.22	107.94	1992	442.65	392.41	435.71	2005	1,275.80	1,136.22	1,248.29
1980	141.96	94.24	135.76	1993	471.29	426.88	466.45	2006	1,310.88	1,245.74	1,294.82

Source: Chicago Mercantile Exchange

S&P 500 INDEX

Quarterly High, Low and Close of S&P 500 Index   Index Value

Quarter	High	Low	Close	Quarter	High	Low	Close	Quarter	High	Low	Close
09/1996	690.88	605.88	687.33	12/1999	1,473.10	1,233.66	1,469.25	03/2003	935.05	788.90	848.18
12/1996	762.12	684.44	740.74	03/2000	1,552.87	1,325.02	1,498.58	06/2003	1,015.33	847.85	974.50
03/1997	817.68	729.55	757.12	06/2000	1,527.19	1,339.40	1,454.60	09/2003	1,040.29	960.84	995.97
06/1997	902.09	733.54	885.14	09/2000	1,530.09	1,413.89	1,436.51	12/2003	1,112.56	997.12	1,111.92
09/1997	964.17	884.54	947.28	12/2000	1,454.82	1,254.07	1,320.28	03/2004	1,163.23	1,087.06	1,126.21
12/1997	986.25	855.27	970.43	03/2001	1,383.37	1,081.19	1,160.33	06/2004	1,150.57	1,076.32	1,140.84
03/1998	1,113.07	912.83	1,101.75	06/2001	1,315.93	1,091.99	1,225.71	09/2004	1,140.80	1,060.72	1,114.58
06/1998	1,145.15	1,074.39	1,133.84	09/2001	1,239.78	944.75	1,040.94	12/2004	1,217.33	1,090.19	1,211.92
09/1998	1,190.58	939.98	1,017.05	12/2001	1,173.62	1,026.76	1,148.08	03/2005	1,229.11	1,163.69	1,180.59
12/1998	1,244.93	923.32	1,229.23	03/2002	1,176.97	1,074.36	1,147.39	06/2005	1,219.59	1,136.22	1,191.33
03/1999	1,323.88	1,206.59	1,286.42	06/2002	1,147.84	952.92	989.82	09/2005	1,245.86	1,183.55	1,228.81
06/1999	1,375.98	1,277.31	1,372.66	09/2002	994.46	775.68	815.28	12/2005	1,275.80	1,168.20	1,248.29
09/1999	1,420.14	1,256.29	1,282.71	12/2002	954.28	768.63	879.82	03/2006	1,310.88	1,245.74	1,294.82

Source: Chicago Mercantile Exchange

S&P MIDCAP 400 INDEX

Annual High, Low and Close of S&P MidCap 400 Index   Index Value

Year	High	Low	Close	Year	High	Low	Close	Year	High	Low	Close
				1989	110.82	81.95	108.78	1998	392.31	268.66	392.31
1981	40.32	33.64	37.67	1990	112.88	85.39	100.00	1999	445.10	352.35	444.67
1982	43.56	31.46	43.56	1991	146.59	95.16	146.59	2000	549.63	415.98	516.76
1983	55.96	43.30	52.50	1992	160.58	135.12	160.56	2001	547.51	397.54	508.31
1984	53.56	44.37	50.63	1993	179.44	155.02	179.38	2002	554.01	370.83	429.79
1985	66.02	49.67	65.98	1994	184.95	161.55	169.44	2003	581.92	381.82	576.01
1986	80.76	64.52	74.34	1995	220.73	167.93	217.84	2004	666.99	548.29	663.31
1987	93.91	63.13	70.74	1996	259.29	206.34	255.58	2005	752.00	623.57	738.05
1988	83.11	70.75	82.78	1997	340.40	247.27	333.37	2006	795.50	732.57	792.11

Source: Chicago Mercantile Exchange

S&P MIDCAP 400 INDEX

Quarterly High, Low and Close of S&P MidCap 400 Index   Index Value

Quarter	High	Low	Close	Quarter	High	Low	Close	Quarter	High	Low	Close
09/1996	243.51	210.18	241.93	12/1999	445.10	366.05	444.67	03/2003	448.02	381.82	409.47
12/1996	259.29	240.49	255.58	03/2000	505.63	415.98	499.69	06/2003	495.12	407.81	480.21
03/1997	269.79	250.84	250.84	06/2000	506.90	425.65	481.77	09/2003	532.04	473.90	510.42
06/1997	291.51	247.27	286.65	09/2000	549.63	480.18	538.81	12/2003	581.92	510.42	576.01
09/1997	334.34	286.65	331.66	12/2000	540.65	471.17	516.76	03/2004	618.46	574.60	603.56
12/1997	340.40	299.28	333.37	03/2001	533.82	433.44	459.92	06/2004	616.94	557.37	607.69
03/1998	371.44	307.17	369.00	06/2001	547.51	432.38	518.56	09/2004	607.69	548.29	593.20
06/1998	381.31	344.92	360.08	09/2001	519.18	397.54	432.02	12/2004	666.99	580.67	663.31
09/1998	375.84	277.56	307.02	12/2001	514.51	420.03	508.31	03/2005	683.36	629.29	658.87
12/1998	392.31	268.66	392.31	03/2002	543.87	484.75	541.10	06/2005	695.91	623.57	684.94
03/1999	395.14	352.35	366.10	06/2002	554.01	469.31	489.52	09/2005	725.02	685.08	716.33
06/1999	419.24	361.18	416.68	09/2002	489.88	384.93	407.38	12/2005	752.00	665.23	738.05
09/1999	428.65	375.63	380.59	12/2002	457.22	370.83	429.79	03/2006	795.50	732.57	792.11

Source: Chicago Mercantile Exchange

S&P 100 INDEX

Annual High, Low and Close of S&P 100 Index   Index Value

Year	High	Low	Close	Year	High	Low	Close	Year	High	Low	Close
				1985	104.09	80.30	103.00	1996	369.87	285.16	359.99
1976	59.41	50.00	58.23	1986	121.49	97.91	115.54	1997	474.99	355.11	459.94
1977	57.92	48.76	51.03	1987	167.02	105.85	119.13	1998	615.90	431.76	604.03
1978	58.04	46.35	52.99	1988	134.12	115.06	131.93	1999	798.38	598.01	792.83
1979	58.19	52.39	55.53	1989	167.62	129.83	164.68	2000	846.19	656.67	686.45
1980	71.01	51.03	68.83	1990	175.95	139.67	155.24	2001	725.07	480.02	584.28
1981	70.58	56.13	59.77	1991	193.87	145.42	192.78	2002	600.80	384.96	444.75
1982	72.79	51.66	71.09	1992	202.18	181.69	198.32	2003	550.90	400.24	550.78
1983	87.33	69.78	83.06	1993	217.44	193.65	214.73	2004	578.13	518.67	575.29
1984	85.00	72.92	82.54	1994	223.60	201.17	214.32	2005	586.81	542.77	570.00
1980	141.96	94.24	135.76	1995	299.18	212.94	292.96	2006	596.28	568.37	587.75

Source: Chicago Mercantile Exchange

S&P 100 INDEX

Quarterly High, Low and Close of S&P 100 Index   Index Value

Quarter	High	Low	Close	Quarter	High	Low	Close	Quarter	High	Low	Close
09/1996	333.78	291.43	330.89	12/1999	798.38	644.35	792.83	03/2003	475.09	400.24	429.13
12/1996	369.87	329.21	359.99	03/2000	846.19	716.55	815.06	06/2003	512.67	429.54	490.39
03/1997	398.63	355.11	368.60	06/2000	830.09	721.58	790.25	09/2003	522.91	484.41	498.56
06/1997	440.37	356.04	430.59	09/2000	834.87	754.85	759.83	12/2003	550.90	499.25	550.78
09/1997	471.48	430.39	456.92	12/2000	773.97	656.67	686.45	03/2004	573.44	532.00	551.13
12/1997	474.99	407.51	459.94	03/2001	725.07	548.19	591.63	06/2004	562.86	526.53	553.87
03/1998	533.51	431.76	528.91	06/2001	680.02	554.43	632.00	09/2004	554.43	518.67	534.86
06/1998	560.41	521.14	554.56	09/2001	642.10	480.02	533.10	12/2004	578.13	521.90	575.29
09/1998	582.27	462.66	493.10	12/2001	599.97	526.93	584.28	03/2005	586.81	555.05	561.86
12/1998	615.90	454.92	604.03	03/2002	600.80	544.82	577.87	06/2005	574.37	542.88	558.07
03/1999	663.89	598.01	646.65	06/2002	577.19	471.24	490.12	09/2005	578.22	553.50	566.80
06/1999	704.50	644.67	704.42	09/2002	495.03	384.96	407.25	12/2005	584.33	542.77	570.00
09/1999	735.57	658.43	672.37	12/2002	487.94	387.80	444.75	03/2006	596.28	568.37	587.75

Source: Chicago Mercantile Exchange

RUSSELL 2000 INDEX

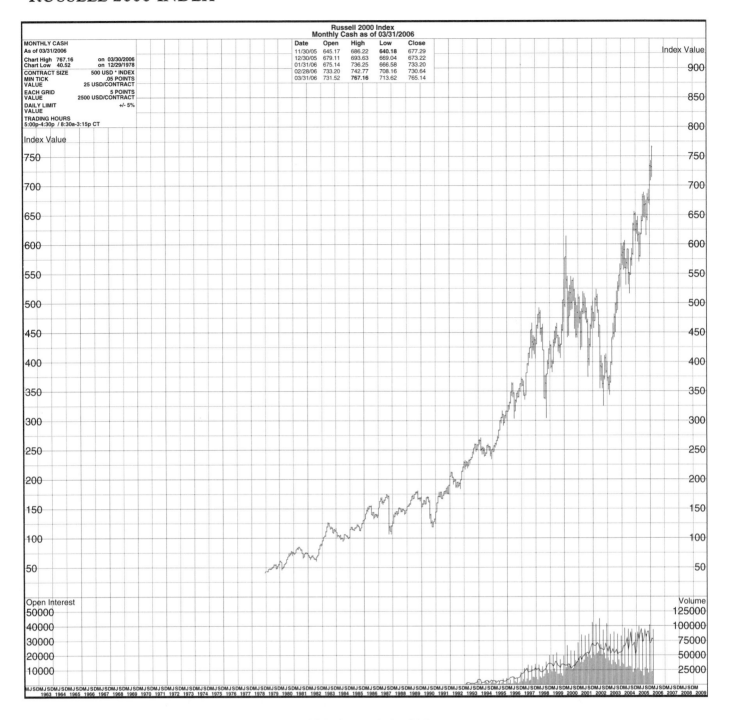

Annual High, Low and Close of Russell 2000 Index   Index Value

Year	High	Low	Close	Year	High	Low	Close	Year	High	Low	Close
				1987	174.44	106.07	120.42	1997	466.21	335.18	437.02
1978	40.52	40.52	40.52	1988	152.08	120.43	147.37	1998	492.28	303.87	421.97
1979	55.91	40.81	55.91	1989	180.95	146.33	168.30	1999	504.75	381.96	504.75
1980	77.70	45.36	74.80	1990	171.08	118.45	132.20	2000	614.16	440.76	483.53
1981	85.16	65.37	73.67	1991	189.93	124.52	189.91	2001	519.89	373.62	488.50
1982	91.01	60.33	88.90	1992	221.01	183.40	221.01	2002	523.79	324.90	383.09
1983	126.99	88.29	112.27	1993	260.41	216.43	258.59	2003	566.74	343.06	556.91
1984	116.69	93.95	101.49	1994	271.08	233.89	250.36	2004	656.11	515.90	651.57
1985	129.87	101.21	129.87	1995	316.98	246.38	315.97	2005	693.63	570.03	673.22
1986	155.30	128.23	135.00	1996	364.96	299.45	362.61	2006	767.16	666.58	765.14

Source: Chicago Mercantile Exchange

RUSSELL 2000 INDEX

Quarterly High, Low and Close of Russell 2000 Index   Index Value

Quarter	High	Low	Close	Quarter	High	Low	Close	Quarter	High	Low	Close
09/1996	347.83	303.04	346.39	12/1999	504.75	406.33	504.75	03/2003	399.55	343.06	364.54
12/1996	362.61	337.71	362.61	03/2000	614.16	467.56	539.08	06/2003	465.73	363.73	448.37
03/1997	373.17	342.49	342.56	06/2000	545.90	441.56	517.23	09/2003	520.61	441.22	487.68
06/1997	396.99	335.18	396.38	09/2000	545.71	487.39	521.37	12/2003	566.74	488.29	556.91
09/1997	453.82	392.99	453.82	12/2000	523.41	440.76	483.53	03/2004	603.16	556.13	590.31
12/1997	466.21	405.37	437.02	03/2001	515.22	419.70	450.53	06/2004	606.42	530.68	591.52
03/1998	480.68	404.86	480.68	06/2001	519.89	424.64	510.69	09/2004	591.38	515.90	572.94
06/1998	492.28	433.66	457.38	09/2001	508.59	373.62	404.86	12/2004	656.11	562.82	651.57
09/1998	464.33	335.87	363.59	12/2001	494.71	393.00	488.50	03/2005	654.30	603.75	615.07
12/1998	421.98	303.87	421.97	03/2002	509.19	457.05	506.46	06/2005	648.16	570.03	639.66
03/1999	435.30	381.96	397.63	06/2002	523.79	441.76	462.65	09/2005	688.51	638.93	667.80
06/1999	460.21	396.29	457.67	09/2002	461.79	354.11	362.27	12/2005	693.63	614.76	673.22
09/1999	465.80	414.20	427.30	12/2002	413.64	324.90	383.09	03/2006	767.16	666.58	765.14

Source: Chicago Mercantile Exchange

VALUE LINE INDEX

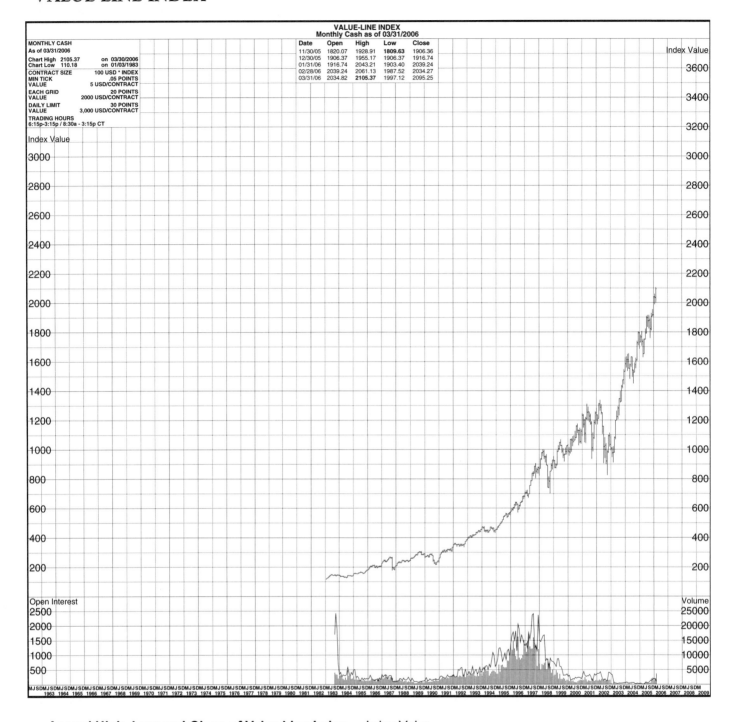

Annual High, Low and Close of Value-Line Index   Index Value

Year	High	Low	Close	Year	High	Low	Close	Year	High	Low	Close
1983	150.23	110.18	144.10	1991	335.32	229.57	335.30	1999	1,067.98	871.42	1,025.80
1984	148.69	124.60	140.18	1992	386.10	331.76	386.09	2000	1,176.20	956.69	1,124.76
1985	179.66	139.19	179.66	1993	456.15	382.19	455.88	2001	1,311.09	934.49	1,247.13
1986	213.82	176.68	203.14	1994	476.76	431.10	452.53	2002	1,337.54	824.77	1,033.75
1987	271.17	176.93	200.08	1995	571.20	450.32	569.91	2003	1,545.05	910.60	1,530.52
1988	248.56	201.85	245.51	1996	686.65	552.31	682.62	2004	1,803.83	1,448.33	1,794.19
1989	307.55	243.68	290.15	1997	906.20	670.94	876.84	2005	1,955.17	1,627.84	1,916.74
1990	294.88	215.35	241.52	1998	999.91	699.44	927.84	2006	2,105.37	1,903.40	2,095.25

Source: Kansas City Board of Trade

VALUE LINE INDEX

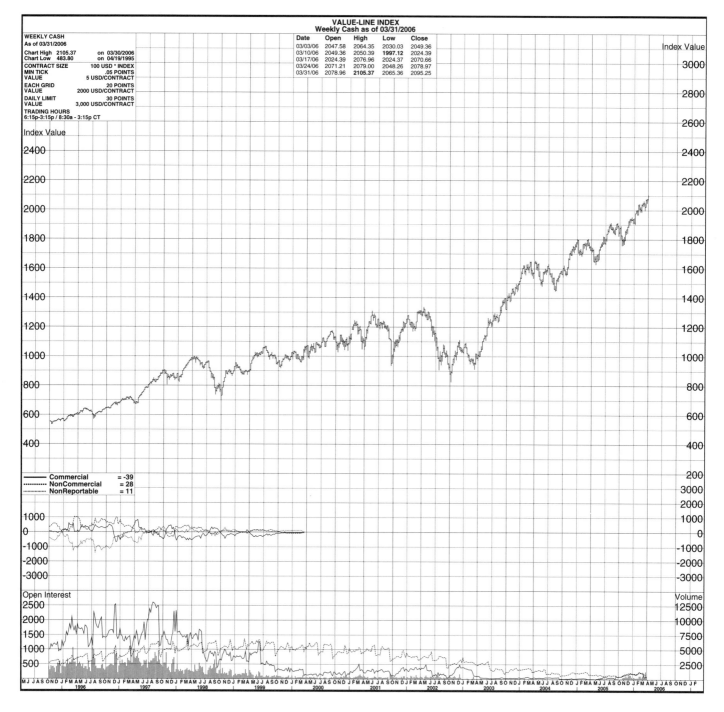

Quarterly High, Low and Close of Value-Line Index   Index Value

Quarter	High	Low	Close	Quarter	High	Low	Close	Quarter	High	Low	Close
09/1996	640.53	570.14	639.26	12/1999	1,025.80	917.15	1,025.80	03/2003	1,093.05	910.60	979.13
12/1996	686.65	637.53	682.62	03/2000	1,070.16	956.69	1,067.12	06/2003	1,263.64	976.80	1,222.44
03/1997	725.21	674.87	684.16	06/2000	1,093.79	982.56	1,062.57	09/2003	1,396.38	1,206.33	1,326.97
06/1997	791.22	670.94	786.51	09/2000	1,176.20	1,062.62	1,130.82	12/2003	1,545.05	1,326.97	1,530.52
09/1997	887.81	786.37	886.48	12/2000	1,147.64	1,027.11	1,124.76	03/2004	1,650.47	1,530.24	1,611.47
12/1997	906.20	804.71	876.84	03/2001	1,245.47	1,047.51	1,110.97	06/2004	1,655.20	1,479.53	1,631.15
03/1998	980.51	821.48	978.32	06/2001	1,311.09	1,041.98	1,254.79	09/2004	1,630.65	1,448.33	1,576.11
06/1998	999.91	910.85	948.57	09/2001	1,255.50	934.49	1,010.70	12/2004	1,803.83	1,551.30	1,794.19
09/1998	967.14	736.52	785.42	12/2001	1,258.03	985.79	1,247.13	03/2005	1,805.50	1,684.89	1,735.57
12/1998	927.87	699.44	927.84	03/2002	1,315.60	1,170.12	1,310.00	06/2005	1,822.31	1,627.84	1,791.95
03/1999	954.29	871.42	893.20	06/2002	1,337.54	1,104.72	1,158.78	09/2005	1,915.54	1,788.90	1,879.39
06/1999	1,049.80	892.25	1,047.35	09/2002	1,159.21	901.29	920.52	12/2005	1,955.17	1,757.86	1,916.74
09/1999	1,067.98	941.43	961.64	12/2002	1,114.29	824.77	1,033.75	03/2006	2,105.37	1,903.40	2,095.25

Source: Kansas City Board of Trade

DAX INDEX

Annual High, Low and Close of DAX Index — Index Value

Year	High	Low	Close	Year	High	Low	Close	Year	High	Low	Close
				1995	2,320.22	1,893.63	2,253.88	2001	6,795.14	3,539.18	5,160.10
1990	1,976.43	1,320.43	1,398.23	1996	2,914.61	2,271.40	2,888.69	2002	5,467.31	2,519.30	2,892.63
1991	1,728.30	1,311.82	1,577.90	1997	4,459.89	2,833.78	4,249.69	2003	3,996.28	2,188.75	3,965.16
1992	1,814.64	1,413.68	1,545.05	1998	6,217.83	3,833.71	5,002.39	2004	4,272.18	3,618.58	4,256.08
1993	2,284.56	1,514.31	2,266.68	1999	6,992.92	4,605.27	6,958.14	2005	5,469.96	4,157.51	5,408.26
1994	2,282.60	1,953.23	2,106.58	2000	8,136.16	6,110.26	6,433.61	2006	5,993.90	5,290.49	5,970.08

Source: Eurex

DAX INDEX

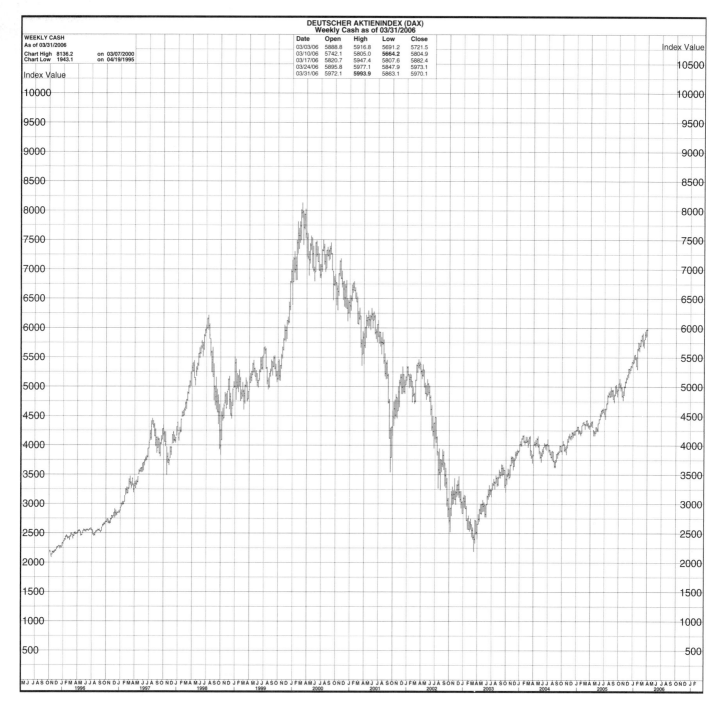

Quarterly High, Low and Close of DAX Index   Index Value

Quarter	High	Low	Close	Quarter	High	Low	Close	Quarter	High	Low	Close
09/1996	2,672.59	2,446.23	2,651.85	12/1999	6,992.92	5,078.59	6,958.14	03/2003	3,157.25	2,188.75	2,423.87
12/1996	2,914.61	2,645.90	2,888.69	03/2000	8,136.16	6,388.91	7,599.39	06/2003	3,324.44	2,395.72	3,220.58
03/1997	3,474.98	2,833.78	3,429.05	06/2000	7,641.53	6,794.08	6,898.21	09/2003	3,676.88	3,119.35	3,256.78
06/1997	3,827.52	3,192.33	3,785.77	09/2000	7,503.32	6,468.46	6,798.12	12/2003	3,996.28	3,217.40	3,965.16
09/1997	4,459.89	3,798.24	4,167.85	12/2000	7,185.66	6,110.26	6,433.61	03/2004	4,175.48	3,692.40	3,856.70
12/1997	4,347.30	3,487.24	4,249.69	03/2001	6,795.14	5,351.48	5,829.95	06/2004	4,156.89	3,710.02	4,052.73
03/1998	5,104.56	4,069.65	5,102.35	06/2001	6,337.47	5,383.99	6,058.38	09/2004	4,101.52	3,618.58	3,892.90
06/1998	5,900.59	5,012.57	5,897.44	09/2001	6,131.97	3,539.18	4,308.15	12/2004	4,272.18	3,838.98	4,256.08
09/1998	6,217.83	4,357.42	4,474.51	12/2001	5,341.86	4,157.60	5,160.10	03/2005	4,435.31	4,160.83	4,348.77
12/1998	5,176.27	3,833.71	5,002.39	03/2002	5,467.31	4,706.01	5,397.29	06/2005	4,637.34	4,157.51	4,586.28
03/1999	5,509.34	4,605.27	4,884.20	06/2002	5,379.64	3,946.70	4,382.56	09/2005	5,061.84	4,444.94	5,044.12
06/1999	5,500.93	4,779.04	5,378.52	09/2002	4,483.03	2,719.49	2,769.03	12/2005	5,469.96	4,762.75	5,408.26
09/1999	5,686.55	4,948.08	5,149.83	12/2002	3,476.83	2,519.30	2,892.63	03/2006	5,993.90	5,290.49	5,970.08

Source: Eurex

CAC 40 INDEX

Annual High, Low and Close of CAC-40 Index   Index Value

Year	High	Low	Close	Year	High	Low	Close	Year	High	Low	Close
1989	2,005.92	1,751.33	2,001.08	1995	2,025.15	1,711.80	1,871.97	2001	5,999.18	3,463.07	4,624.58
1990	2,141.13	1,472.59	1,517.93	1996	2,358.65	1,873.14	2,315.73	2002	4,720.04	2,612.03	3,063.91
1991	1,897.26	1,425.26	1,765.66	1997	3,114.00	2,251.53	2,998.91	2003	3,566.76	2,401.15	3,557.90
1992	2,080.80	1,577.74	1,857.78	1998	4,404.94	2,809.73	3,942.66	2004	3,856.01	3,452.41	3,821.16
1993	2,289.48	1,755.90	2,268.22	1999	5,979.54	3,845.77	5,958.32	2005	4,780.05	3,804.92	4,715.23
1994	2,360.98	1,796.82	1,881.15	2000	6,944.77	5,388.85	5,926.42	2006	5,247.31	4,719.33	5,220.85

Source: Euronext Paris

CAC 40 INDEX

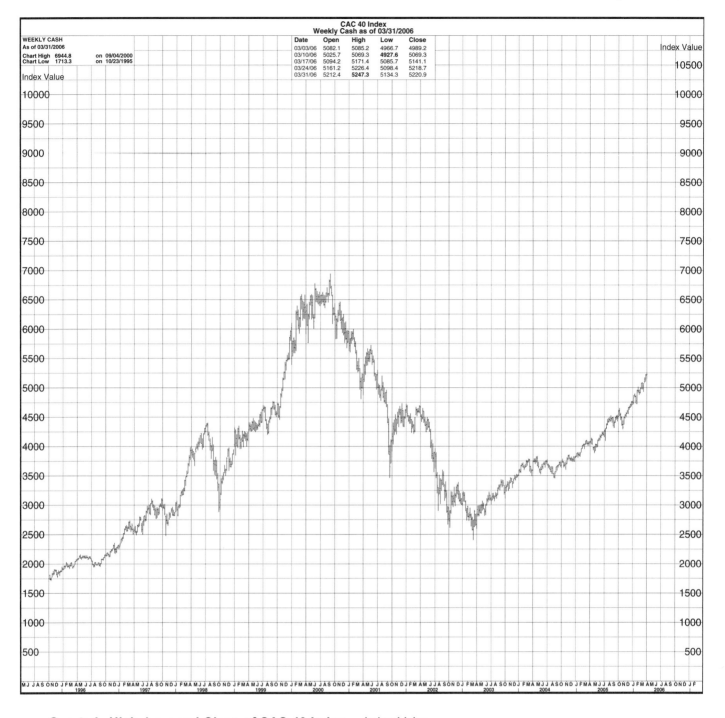

Quarterly High, Low and Close of CAC-40 Index   Index Value

Quarter	High	Low	Close	Quarter	High	Low	Close	Quarter	High	Low	Close
09/1996	2,133.08	1,939.64	2,132.81	12/1999	5,979.54	4,452.93	5,958.32	03/2003	3,232.34	2,401.15	2,618.46
12/1996	2,358.65	2,116.79	2,315.73	03/2000	6,590.35	5,388.85	6,286.05	06/2003	3,228.60	2,599.28	3,084.10
03/1997	2,736.71	2,251.53	2,656.68	06/2000	6,780.66	5,761.47	6,446.54	09/2003	3,435.79	3,008.72	3,134.99
06/1997	2,903.18	2,487.80	2,858.26	09/2000	6,944.77	6,085.40	6,266.63	12/2003	3,566.76	3,122.36	3,557.90
09/1997	3,107.31	2,765.55	3,008.26	12/2000	6,459.50	5,673.87	5,926.42	03/2004	3,789.33	3,489.53	3,625.23
12/1997	3,114.00	2,475.01	2,998.91	03/2001	5,999.18	4,804.40	5,180.45	06/2004	3,831.54	3,520.61	3,732.99
03/1998	3,886.06	2,809.73	3,875.81	06/2001	5,728.52	4,872.92	5,225.33	09/2004	3,773.64	3,452.41	3,640.61
06/1998	4,263.61	3,667.00	4,203.45	09/2001	5,299.90	3,463.07	4,079.02	12/2004	3,856.01	3,599.37	3,821.16
09/1998	4,404.94	3,187.06	3,197.95	12/2001	4,735.21	3,914.39	4,624.58	03/2005	4,108.00	3,804.92	4,067.78
12/1998	3,983.25	2,881.21	3,942.66	03/2002	4,720.04	4,210.30	4,688.02	06/2005	4,254.80	3,882.42	4,229.35
03/1999	4,354.29	3,845.77	4,197.88	06/2002	4,688.16	3,561.24	3,897.99	09/2005	4,620.85	4,089.27	4,600.02
06/1999	4,587.97	4,150.79	4,536.61	09/2002	3,973.93	2,666.04	2,777.45	12/2005	4,780.05	4,288.15	4,715.23
09/1999	4,773.82	4,197.38	4,591.42	12/2002	3,393.04	2,612.03	3,063.91	03/2006	5,247.31	4,719.33	5,220.85

Source: Euronext Paris

FTSE 100 INDEX

Annual High, Low and Close of FTSE 100 Index   Index Value

Year	High	Low	Close	Year	High	Low	Close	Year	High	Low	Close
1984	1,231.3	978.7	1,231.2	1992	2,848.9	2,260.9	2,846.5	1999	6,950.6	5,697.7	6,930.2
1985	1,460.7	1,199.6	1,412.6	1993	3,480.8	2,727.6	3,418.4	2000	6,900.2	5,915.2	6,222.5
1986	1,721.7	1,365.7	1,679.0	1994	3,539.2	2,844.7	3,065.5	2001	6,360.3	4,219.8	5,217.4
1987	2,449.1	1,515.0	1,712.7	1995	3,690.6	2,949.4	3,689.3	2002	5,362.3	3,609.9	3,940.4
1988	1,892.2	1,687.5	1,793.1	1996	4,123.2	3,612.6	4,118.5	2003	4,491.8	3,277.5	4,476.9
1989	2,435.7	1,782.4	2,422.7	1997	5,367.3	4,036.9	5,135.5	2004	4,826.2	4,283.0	4,814.3
1990	2,479.4	1,974.1	2,143.5	1998	6,183.7	4,599.2	5,882.6	2005	5,647.2	4,765.4	5,618.8
1991	2,683.7	2,052.3	2,493.1	1993	3,799.92	3,231.96	3,754.09	2006	6,047.0	5,618.8	5,964.6

Source: Euronext Liffe

FTSE 100 INDEX

Quarterly High, Low and Close of FTSE 100 Index   Index Value

Quarter	High	Low	Close	Quarter	High	Low	Close	Quarter	High	Low	Close
09/1996	3,994.1	3,612.6	3,953.7	12/1999	6,950.6	5,798.3	6,930.2	03/2003	4,025.5	3,277.5	3,613.3
12/1996	4,123.2	3,882.7	4,118.5	03/2000	6,900.2	5,972.7	6,540.2	06/2003	4,218.8	3,612.3	4,031.2
03/1997	4,466.3	4,036.9	4,312.9	06/2000	6,635.7	5,915.2	6,312.7	09/2003	4,329.6	3,951.5	4,091.3
06/1997	4,796.0	4,200.1	4,604.6	09/2000	6,838.6	6,075.1	6,294.2	12/2003	4,491.8	4,091.3	4,476.9
09/1997	5,269.2	4,597.1	5,244.2	12/2000	6,514.7	6,017.2	6,222.5	03/2004	4,566.2	4,291.3	4,385.7
12/1997	5,367.3	4,382.8	5,135.5	03/2001	6,360.3	5,279.6	5,633.7	06/2004	4,601.6	4,363.0	4,464.1
03/1998	6,105.8	4,988.3	5,932.2	06/2001	5,995.4	5,354.3	5,642.5	09/2004	4,630.7	4,283.0	4,570.8
06/1998	6,150.5	5,646.1	5,832.5	09/2001	5,726.1	4,219.8	4,903.4	12/2004	4,826.2	4,551.6	4,814.3
09/1998	6,183.7	4,899.6	5,064.4	12/2001	5,411.2	4,730.7	5,217.4	03/2005	5,077.8	4,765.4	4,894.4
12/1998	5,970.1	4,599.2	5,882.6	03/2002	5,362.3	5,015.5	5,271.8	06/2005	5,138.2	4,773.7	5,113.2
03/1999	6,365.4	5,697.7	6,295.3	06/2002	5,292.3	4,442.9	4,656.4	09/2005	5,508.4	5,022.1	5,477.7
06/1999	6,663.8	6,110.1	6,318.5	09/2002	4,708.7	3,609.9	3,721.8	12/2005	5,647.2	5,130.9	5,618.8
09/1999	6,649.5	5,868.4	6,029.8	12/2002	4,224.8	3,663.4	3,940.4	03/2006	6,047.0	5,618.8	5,964.6

Source: Euronext Liffe

HANG SENG INDEX

Annual High, Low and Close of Hang Seng Index — Index Value

Year	High	Low	Close	Year	High	Low	Close	Year	High	Low	Close
1986	2,543.00	1,645.00	2,524.00	1993	11,959.00	5,431.00	11,888.00	2000	18,397.57	13,596.63	15,095.53
1987	3,968.00	1,876.00	2,302.00	1994	12,599.00	7,670.00	8,191.00	2001	16,274.67	8,894.36	11,397.21
1988	2,774.00	2,199.00	2,687.00	1995	10,073.00	6,890.00	10,073.00	2002	12,021.72	8,772.48	9,321.29
1989	3,329.00	2,022.00	2,836.00	1996	13,744.00	10,070.00	13,451.00	2003	12,740.50	8,331.87	12,575.94
1990	3,559.00	2,697.00	3,024.00	1997	16,820.00	8,775.00	10,722.00	2004	14,339.06	10,917.65	14,230.14
1991	4,309.00	2,970.00	4,297.00	1998	11,926.00	6,544.00	10,048.58	2005	15,508.57	13,320.53	14,876.43
1992	6,470.00	4,284.00	5,512.00	1999	17,138.11	9,000.24	16,962.10	2006	15,999.31	14,843.97	15,805.04

Source: Hong Kong Futures Exchange

HANG SENG INDEX

Quarterly High, Low and Close of Hang Seng Index   Index Value

Quarter	High	Low	Close	Quarter	High	Low	Close	Quarter	High	Low	Close
09/1996	11,906.00	10,533.00	11,902.00	12/1999	17,138.11	12,066.65	16,962.10	03/2003	9,892.70	8,586.70	8,634.45
12/1996	13,744.00	11,857.00	13,451.00	03/2000	18,397.57	14,763.97	17,406.54	06/2003	10,067.86	8,331.87	9,577.12
03/1997	14,004.00	12,331.00	12,534.00	06/2000	17,458.06	13,596.63	16,155.78	09/2003	11,444.72	9,512.20	11,229.80
06/1997	15,322.00	11,951.00	15,196.00	09/2000	18,125.57	14,538.88	15,648.98	12/2003	12,740.50	11,372.50	12,575.94
09/1997	16,820.00	12,899.00	15,049.00	12/2000	16,245.61	13,894.19	15,095.53	03/2004	14,058.21	12,400.35	12,681.67
12/1997	15,242.00	8,775.00	10,722.00	03/2001	16,274.67	12,396.97	12,760.64	06/2004	13,126.15	10,917.65	12,285.75
03/1998	11,926.00	7,909.00	11,518.00	06/2001	13,989.16	12,061.55	13,042.53	09/2004	13,356.88	11,862.68	13,120.03
06/1998	11,506.00	7,351.00	8,543.00	09/2001	13,236.98	8,894.36	9,950.70	12/2004	14,339.06	12,743.42	14,230.14
09/1998	8,970.00	6,544.00	7,883.00	12/2001	11,957.83	9,758.98	11,397.21	03/2005	14,272.54	13,320.53	13,516.88
12/1998	10,979.31	7,540.00	10,048.58	03/2002	11,905.55	10,387.49	11,032.92	06/2005	14,365.05	13,337.44	14,201.06
03/1999	11,161.00	9,000.24	10,942.20	06/2002	12,021.72	10,291.16	10,598.55	09/2005	15,508.57	13,920.87	15,428.52
06/1999	14,124.42	10,850.11	13,532.14	09/2002	10,939.56	9,014.58	9,072.21	12/2005	15,493.00	14,189.47	14,876.43
09/1999	14,531.63	12,422.78	12,733.24	12/2002	10,246.86	8,772.48	9,321.29	03/2006	15,999.31	14,843.97	15,805.04

Source: Hong Kong Futures Exchange

NIKKEI 225 INDEX

Annual High, Low and Close of Nikkei 225 Index   Index Value

Year	High	Low	Close	Year	High	Low	Close	Year	High	Low	Close
1968	1,840.00	1,312.00	1,715.00	1981	7,867.00	7,150.00	7,682.00	1994	21,573.00	17,242.00	19,723.00
1969	2,360.00	1,759.00	2,360.00	1982	8,026.00	6,849.00	8,016.00	1995	20,023.00	14,295.00	19,868.00
1970	2,574.00	1,987.00	1,987.00	1983	9,893.00	7,803.00	9,893.00	1996	22,750.70	18,819.92	19,361.00
1971	2,714.00	2,099.00	2,714.00	1984	11,577.00	9,703.00	11,542.00	1997	20,910.79	14,488.21	15,258.74
1972	5,208.00	2,857.00	5,208.00	1985	13,128.00	11,558.00	13,083.00	1998	17,352.95	12,787.90	13,842.17
1973	5,226.00	4,307.00	4,307.00	1986	18,988.00	12,881.00	18,820.00	1999	19,036.08	13,122.61	18,934.34
1974	4,773.00	3,595.00	3,817.00	1987	26,646.00	18,525.00	21,564.00	2000	20,833.21	13,182.51	13,785.69
1975	4,533.00	3,886.00	4,359.00	1988	30,264.00	21,148.00	30,159.00	2001	14,556.11	9,382.95	10,542.62
1976	4,991.00	4,507.00	4,991.00	1989	38,957.00	30,082.00	38,915.00	2002	12,081.43	8,197.22	8,578.95
1977	5,264.00	4,866.00	4,866.00	1990	38,950.00	19,781.00	23,848.00	2003	11,238.63	7,603.76	10,676.64
1978	6,002.00	5,112.00	6,002.00	1991	27,270.00	21,123.00	22,983.00	2004	12,195.66	10,299.43	11,488.76
1979	6,591.00	6,073.00	6,569.00	1992	23,801.00	14,194.00	16,924.00	2005	16,445.56	10,770.58	16,111.43
1980	7,165.00	6,556.00	7,116.00	1993	21,281.00	15,671.00	17,417.00	2006	17,125.64	15,059.52	17,059.66

Source: Singapore Exchange

NIKKEI 225 INDEX

Quarterly High, Low and Close of Nikkei 225 Index   Index Value

Quarter	High	Low	Close	Quarter	High	Low	Close	Quarter	High	Low	Close
09/1996	22,600.10	19,920.00	21,556.40	12/1999	19,036.08	17,178.47	18,934.34	03/2003	8,829.06	7,824.82	7,972.71
12/1996	21,788.60	18,819.92	19,361.00	03/2000	20,809.79	18,068.10	20,337.32	06/2003	9,188.95	7,603.76	9,083.11
03/1997	19,500.90	17,019.56	18,003.40	06/2000	20,833.21	15,870.25	17,411.05	09/2003	11,160.19	9,078.74	10,219.05
06/1997	20,910.79	17,447.64	20,604.96	09/2000	17,661.11	15,394.71	15,747.26	12/2003	11,238.63	9,614.60	10,676.64
09/1997	20,698.67	17,563.66	17,887.71	12/2000	16,192.78	13,182.51	13,785.69	03/2004	11,869.00	10,299.43	11,715.39
12/1997	17,936.86	14,488.21	15,258.74	03/2001	14,186.62	11,433.88	12,999.70	06/2004	12,195.66	10,489.84	11,858.87
03/1998	17,352.95	14,546.25	16,527.17	06/2001	14,556.11	12,511.66	12,969.05	09/2004	11,988.12	10,545.89	10,823.57
06/1998	16,623.78	14,614.74	15,830.27	09/2001	12,929.66	9,382.95	9,774.68	12/2004	11,500.95	10,575.23	11,488.76
09/1998	16,756.89	13,406.39	13,406.39	12/2001	11,186.75	9,604.09	10,542.62	03/2005	11,975.46	11,212.63	11,668.95
12/1998	15,320.23	12,787.90	13,842.17	03/2002	12,034.04	9,420.85	11,024.94	06/2005	11,911.90	10,770.58	11,584.01
03/1999	16,437.23	13,122.61	15,836.59	06/2002	12,081.43	10,060.72	10,621.84	09/2005	13,678.44	11,540.93	13,574.30
06/1999	17,958.34	15,813.41	17,529.74	09/2002	11,050.69	8,969.26	9,383.29	12/2005	16,445.56	12,996.29	16,111.43
09/1999	18,623.15	16,652.04	17,605.46	12/2002	9,320.11	8,197.22	8,578.95	03/2006	17,125.64	15,059.52	17,059.66

Source: Singapore Exchange

SPI 200 INDEX

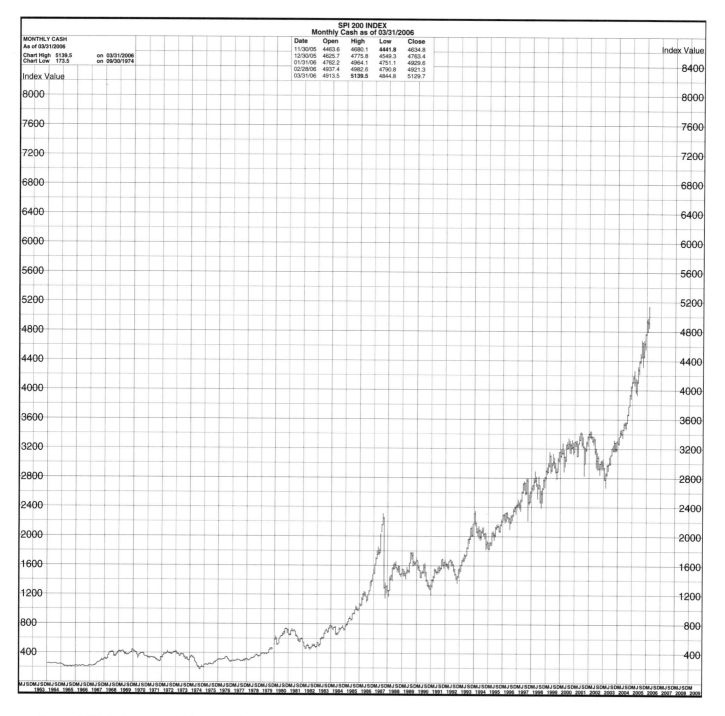

Annual High, Low and Close of SPI 200 Index   Index Value

Year	High	Low	Close	Year	High	Low	Close	Year	High	Low	Close
1968	419.7	300.1	405.5	1981	737.4	545.8	595.5	1994	2,350.1	1,814.5	1,912.7
1969	441.8	368.3	441.8	1982	595.5	443.1	485.4	1995	2,237.4	1,817.2	2,203.0
1970	448.2	320.2	348.7	1983	775.3	487.9	775.3	1996	2,426.5	2,092.4	2,424.6
1971	350.3	273.6	340.8	1984	787.9	646.3	726.1	1997	2,797.3	2,210.0	2,616.5
1972	431.9	331.1	408.6	1985	1,052.1	715.2	1,003.8	1998	2,893.7	2,386.7	2,813.4
1973	429.9	287.2	297.5	1986	1,473.2	1,010.8	1,473.2	1999	3,156.9	2,771.1	3,152.5
1974	362.1	173.5	201.6	1987	2,312.4	1,149.3	1,318.8	2000	3,343.7	2,883.0	3,154.7
1975	299.3	195.8	299.3	1988	1,657.6	1,169.6	1,487.2	2001	3,425.2	2,828.0	3,359.9
1976	353.0	273.5	291.4	1989	1,786.6	1,411.9	1,649.8	2002	3,443.9	2,842.6	2,975.5
1977	322.4	283.5	322.3	1990	1,713.7	1,266.5	1,280.7	2003	3,317.5	2,666.3	3,299.8
1978	382.9	298.0	366.1	1991	1,697.7	1,199.8	1,651.4	2004	4,055.0	3,252.9	4,050.6
1979	472.8	369.1	458.9	1992	1,688.9	1,355.6	1,549.9	2005	4,775.8	3,926.6	4,763.4
1980	746.2	509.1	713.5	1993	2,173.6	1,487.4	2,173.6	2006	5,139.5	4,751.1	5,129.7

Source: Sydney Futures Exchange

SPI 200 INDEX

Quarterly High, Low and Close of SPI 200 Index   Index Value

Quarter	High	Low	Close	Quarter	High	Low	Close	Quarter	High	Low	Close
09/1996	2,295.8	2,092.4	2,290.4	12/1999	3,156.1	2,779.3	3,152.5	03/2003	3,062.0	2,666.3	2,848.6
12/1996	2,426.5	2,271.6	2,424.6	03/2000	3,276.7	3,016.2	3,133.3	06/2003	3,089.0	2,829.8	2,998.9
03/1997	2,508.3	2,373.3	2,422.3	06/2000	3,260.0	2,883.0	3,257.6	09/2003	3,249.8	2,977.5	3,176.2
06/1997	2,728.5	2,341.1	2,725.9	09/2000	3,343.7	3,131.9	3,246.1	12/2003	3,317.5	3,158.8	3,299.8
09/1997	2,797.3	2,567.8	2,766.9	12/2000	3,321.8	3,120.5	3,154.7	03/2004	3,456.1	3,252.9	3,415.3
12/1997	2,793.1	2,210.0	2,616.5	03/2001	3,313.7	3,088.6	3,096.9	06/2004	3,556.4	3,341.0	3,532.9
03/1998	2,799.2	2,534.1	2,744.2	06/2001	3,425.2	3,100.5	3,425.2	09/2004	3,673.1	3,467.1	3,665.0
06/1998	2,893.7	2,511.2	2,668.4	09/2001	3,419.5	2,828.0	2,988.0	12/2004	4,055.0	3,654.6	4,050.6
09/1998	2,825.2	2,386.7	2,587.0	12/2001	3,376.0	2,994.8	3,359.9	03/2005	4,266.9	4,026.1	4,109.9
12/1998	2,813.4	2,457.1	2,813.4	03/2002	3,443.9	3,322.3	3,363.3	06/2005	4,321.7	3,926.6	4,277.5
03/1999	3,005.2	2,771.1	2,967.2	06/2002	3,372.1	3,124.5	3,163.2	09/2005	4,679.1	4,213.6	4,641.2
06/1999	3,156.9	2,865.1	2,968.9	09/2002	3,205.9	2,909.5	2,928.3	12/2005	4,775.8	4,311.1	4,763.4
09/1999	3,132.9	2,869.8	2,881.1	12/2002	3,047.6	2,842.6	2,975.5	03/2006	5,139.5	4,751.1	5,129.7

Source: Sydney Futures Exchange

LIVESTOCK & MEATS

Cattle

Cattle prices in February and March 2006 plunged on a combination of factors including (1) high slaughter numbers and cattle weights, (2) price competition tied to huge poultry inventories which resulted from bird flu overseas and reduced demand for US poultry exports, and (3) the fact that Japan's borders remained closed to US beef exports as of March 2006, thus eliminating a key source of demand.

US beef exports in early 2006 continued to be depressed because of Mad Cow disease. Japan on December 12, 2005 finally lifted the ban on US beef that had been in effect since December 2003 when a Washington state dairy cow was found to have Mad Cow disease. However, Japan quickly closed its borders to US beef again just a few weeks later in January 2006 when a shipment of beef to Japan accidentally violated Japan's rules by containing vertebrate material. That shipment raised questions about US inspection and quality control procedures and Japan therefore closed its borders to US beef again, thus undercutting cattle prices in early 2006.

The long-term outlook for the cattle market is for slow growth, according to the USDA in its "Agricultural Baseline Projections to 2015." The USDA is forecasting only slow growth in US domestic beef demand because higher demand from population growth will be offset by a slight decline in per capita beef consumption. However, the USDA expects overseas demand for beef to increase as incomes rise in rapidly developing countries such as China, thus allowing increased meat purchases. The USDA therefore expects US exports to rise in coming years. However, the USDA says it will take more than 10 years for US beef exports to reach the annual 2.5 billion pound level seen before US beef exports were shut-down by the Mad Cow scare in December 2003. The USDA is predicting slightly higher cattle prices near 80 cents per pound over the baseline period.

The sharp sell-off in cattle prices in early 2006 came after cattle prices posted a 2-year high in December 2005. Cattle prices were very strong during the 2002-05 period. Cattle prices in 2002-03 rallied sharply due to strong US domestic demand, strong export demand for high-quality grain-fed US beef, and the declining trend seen in the size of the US cattle herd since 1996 (and more generally since 1975). Prices surged on these factors in late 2003 to a record high. However, cattle prices then plunged in December 2003 and early 2004 after the dairy cow in Washington state was found to have Mad Cow disease. That led to more than 50 countries suspending US beef imports, including Japan which is the most important export destination for US beef. US beef exports plunged to near zero in a matter of days, causing cattle prices to plunge. However, cattle prices quickly recovered in 2004-05 due to continued strong US domestic demand and the relatively quick action by producers to reduce supplies.

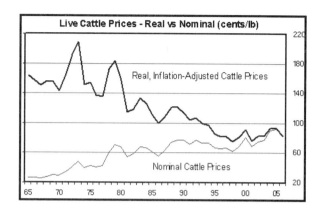

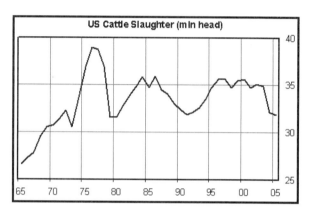

Cattle Market Events

1975—US cattle numbers peak—Cattle herd numbers in the US peak at 132 million head, having nearly doubled from 1940, but then enter a steady downtrend to current levels near 95 million.

1985—US per-capita beef consumption peaks—US per-capita beef consumption peaks in 1985 at 79.3 pounds per year but then falls sharply in the 1990s (due to health concerns about eating beef) and finally stabilizes near 66 pounds.

1989—World cattle numbers peak—World cattle numbers grow steadily in the 1980s but then peak in 1989 at 1.10 billion head, and then trend lower to 1.02 billion in 2005.

2001—Brazil cattle herd soars—Brazil cattle herd numbers, which were stable near 150 million head in the 1990s, surge starting in 2001 to 170 million by 2005, as Brazil puts more emphasis on meat production and the export of higher-value agriculture products.

May 2003—First case of Mad Cow disease (BSE) is found in Canada, prompting the US to suspend the import of Canadian cattle.

December 2003—First case of BSE is found in the US in a Canadian-born dairy cow in Washington state. More than 50 countries suspend US beef exports.

LIVESTOCK & MEATS

Hogs

Lean hog futures prices fell moderately in the first quarter of 2006 due to (1) heavy supply tied to record slaughter numbers and hog weights, and (2) the glut of poultry inventories which created heavy price competition for pork at the supermarket. Poultry inventories soared in Q1-2006 as bird flu spread overseas and caused a sharp drop in overseas consumer consumption and thus lower demand for US poultry exports. Extra US-produced poultry therefore ended up on US supermarket shelves, putting downward pressure on poultry prices and pork prices as well. Bird flu is expected by some experts to hit the US by late-2006, and that may cause a sharp drop in US domestic chicken consumption, thus creating even more severe price competition for pork.

However, counterbalancing the negative impact from the domestic poultry glut in Q1 was the fact that US pork exports were running very strong at +20% yr/yr. Pork export demand has been strong because some consumers overseas have switched to pork from poultry due to bird flu and have also switched to pork from beef because high-quality beef has been relatively scarce and expensive in key countries such as Japan because of the ban on US beef exports in place since December 2003.

The long-term outlook for the pork market is favorable, according to the USDA's "Agricultural Baseline Projections to 2015." Domestic demand for pork should grow at roughly the same rate as the US population since the USDA is projecting that US per-capita pork consumption will remain stable at 51-52 pounds per year over the next 10 years. The USDA is projecting steady growth in US pork exports, driven by increasing global demand for meat and the efficiency of US pork production facilities. However, the USDA expects strong pork competition from Canada and Mexico for exports to the Pacific Rim. Brazil is expected to become an even larger pork exporter, although it will continue to be prevented from exporting to the major export markets of Japan and South Korea because of ongoing problems with hoof and mouth disease.

Lean hog prices have been more volatile than usual in the past several years. There were major declines to 3-decade lows in 1998 and again in 2002. The plunge in hog prices in 1998 was caused by an overexpansion of pork production in 1996-97 when prices were high. That expansion caused a disaster in 1998 when prices plunged and many smaller hog farmers were forced out of business. In addition, Asian demand for pork was reduced in late-1997 and 1998 by the Asian financial crisis. Hog prices recovered in 2000-01 but then plunged again in 2002 as US hog farmers again overproduced and caused another pork glut. Over-supply was exacerbated by an increase in the flow of Canadian live hogs into the US by 1.9 million head annually from 1999 through 2001.

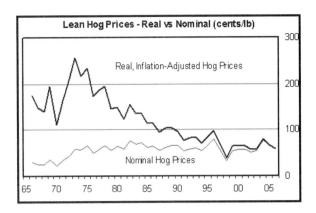

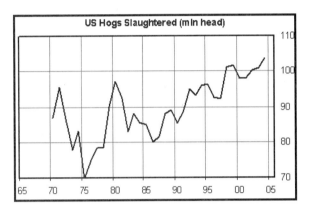

Hog Market Events

1970s—Hog prices rally—Hog prices rallied sharply in the early-1970s due to high inflation and a general rise in commodity prices. Hog prices in 1975 reached an inflation-adjusted record high close of 257 cents per pound (2006 dollars) due to tight supplies caused by a sharp drop in pork production in the first half of the 1970s. On an inflation-adjusted basis, hog prices are currently only about one-fourth of the record high of 257 cents per pound posted in 1975.

1980s—Lower pork production supports prices—In 1980, the number of US hogs slaughtered reached a then-record high of 97.2 million head, causing hog prices to plunge to 37 cents per pound. However, the number of hogs slaughtered then fell sharply by -4.8% in 1981 then and by -10.4% in 1982, leading to a sharp rally in pork prices to the all-time record high of 91.80 cents per pound in August 1982.

1990s—Pork exports surge in the 1990s—Between 1994 and 1998, the volume of US pork exports tripled due to efficient new plants, genetics, and the penetration of the Japanese market. In 1995, US pork exports exceeded imports for the first time in post-war history. US pork exports now account for more than 12% of production, versus 1% of production in the late 1980s.

1998—Hog prices drop to 30-year lows—Due to a severe production glut, hog prices in 1998 fell to levels not seen since the early-1970s and inflation-adjusted prices fall to levels not seen since the Depression.

CATTLE, FEEDER

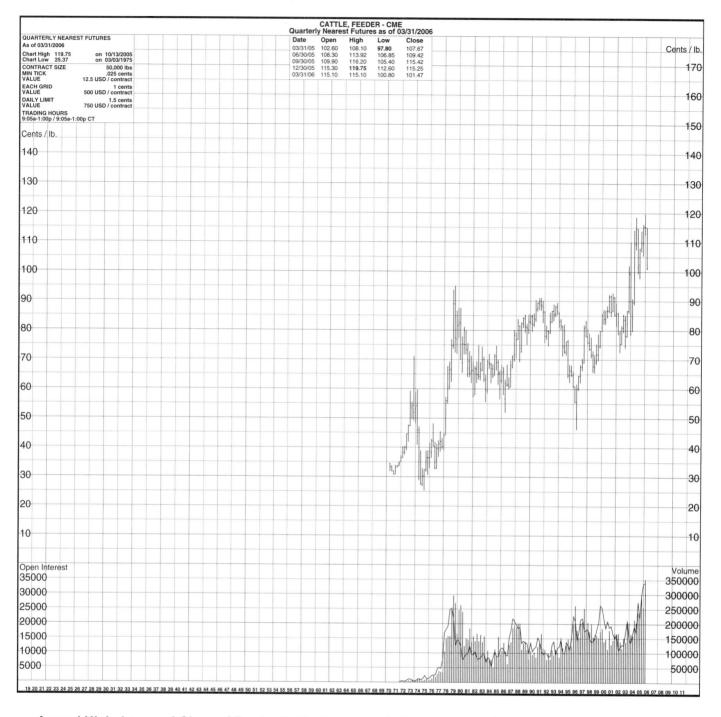

Annual High, Low and Close of Feeder Cattle Futures   In Cents per Pound

Year	High	Low	Close	Year	High	Low	Close	Year	High	Low	Close
				1981	75.70	57.25	57.35	1994	84.00	71.25	76.22
				1982	74.90	58.00	66.52	1995	76.90	60.45	61.02
1970	35.45	30.69	30.75	1983	74.45	55.50	69.22	1996	68.25	46.15	67.52
1971	37.40	30.85	36.30	1984	72.00	61.95	71.20	1997	83.40	66.25	75.87
1972	47.75	36.47	47.40	1985	74.75	56.50	65.45	1998	79.05	65.45	69.17
1973	71.20	47.25	54.00	1986	68.30	52.00	60.72	1999	85.85	68.45	85.35
1974	59.75	26.80	30.10	1987	80.20	60.72	76.87	2000	92.20	82.05	91.50
1975	41.65	25.37	38.65	1988	84.55	69.15	84.15	2001	92.75	81.40	86.02
1976	48.25	32.67	39.52	1989	85.60	75.15	84.85	2002	86.20	72.52	83.80
1977	45.50	36.80	44.10	1990	90.35	79.65	89.40	2003	110.17	73.95	78.92
1978	76.90	44.30	74.67	1991	91.10	75.70	78.05	2004	118.70	79.80	101.80
1979	95.15	71.95	82.70	1992	86.75	74.70	86.62	2005	119.75	97.80	115.25
1980	87.60	65.47	73.45	1993	89.50	81.00	83.05	2006	115.10	100.80	101.47

Source: Chicago Mercantile Exchange

CATTLE, FEEDER

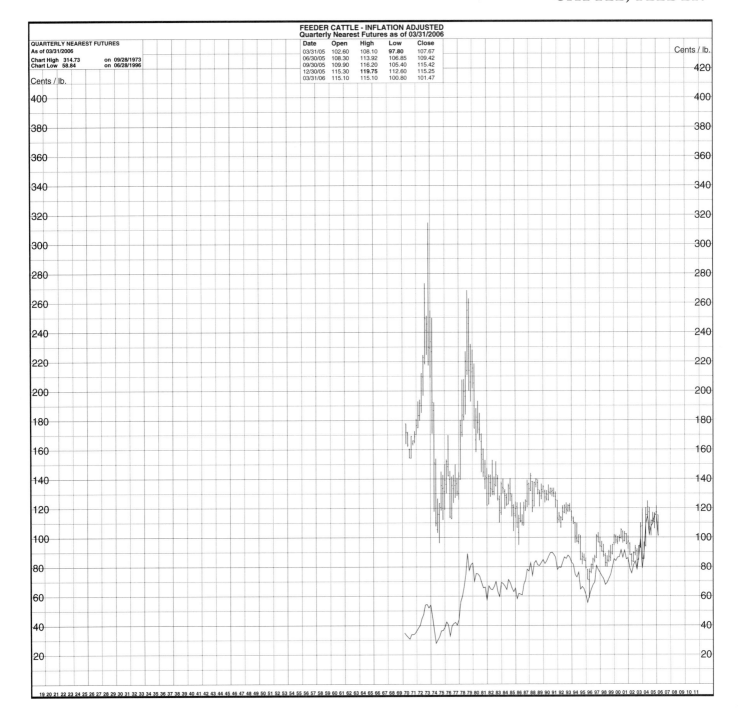

CATTLE, FEEDER

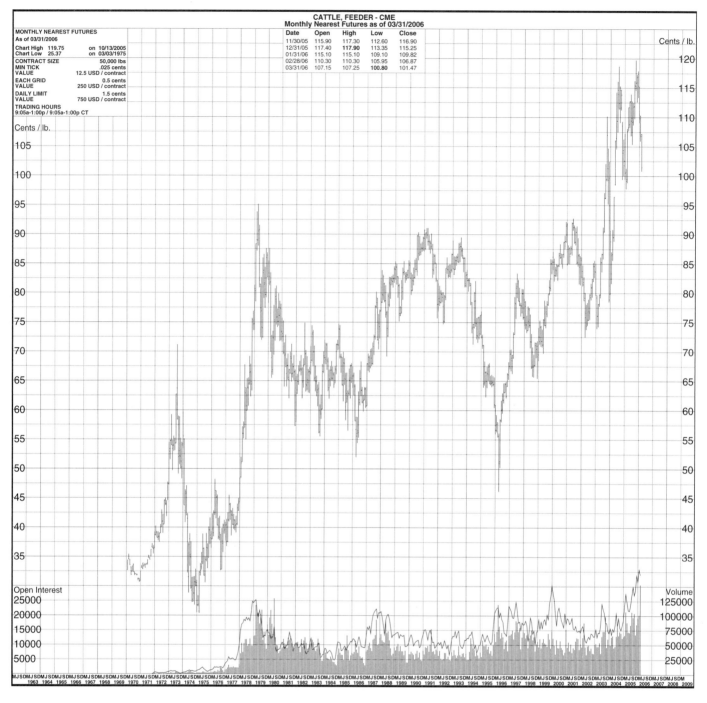

Annual High, Low and Close of Feeder Cattle Futures   In Cents per Pound

Year	High	Low	Close	Year	High	Low	Close	Year	High	Low	Close
				1981	75.70	57.25	57.35	1994	84.00	71.25	76.22
				1982	74.90	58.00	66.52	1995	76.90	60.45	61.02
1970	35.45	30.69	30.75	1983	74.45	55.50	69.22	1996	68.25	46.15	67.52
1971	37.40	30.85	36.30	1984	72.00	61.95	71.20	1997	83.40	66.25	75.87
1972	47.75	36.47	47.40	1985	74.75	56.50	65.45	1998	79.05	65.45	69.17
1973	71.20	47.25	54.00	1986	68.30	52.00	60.72	1999	85.85	68.45	85.35
1974	59.75	26.80	30.10	1987	80.20	60.72	76.87	2000	92.20	82.05	91.50
1975	41.65	25.37	38.65	1988	84.55	69.15	84.15	2001	92.75	81.40	86.02
1976	48.25	32.67	39.52	1989	85.60	75.15	84.85	2002	86.20	72.52	83.80
1977	45.50	36.80	44.10	1990	90.35	79.65	89.40	2003	110.17	73.95	78.92
1978	76.90	44.30	74.67	1991	91.10	75.70	78.05	2004	118.70	79.80	101.80
1979	95.15	71.95	82.70	1992	86.75	74.70	86.62	2005	119.75	97.80	115.25
1980	87.60	65.47	73.45	1993	89.50	81.00	83.05	2006	115.10	100.80	101.47

Source: Chicago Mercantile Exchange

CATTLE, FEEDER

Annual High, Low and Close of Feeder Cattle   In Cents per Pound

Year	High	Low	Close	Year	High	Low	Close	Year	High	Low	Close
				1981	75.13	59.00	59.50	1994	95.00	76.13	82.63
				1982	70.50	59.50	65.00	1995	85.75	62.63	64.13
1970	35.45	30.69	30.75	1983	74.50	59.75	65.00	1996	69.63	54.25	68.75
1971	37.40	30.85	37.38	1984	71.75	62.00	70.00	1997	93.75	68.75	85.37
1972	44.81	37.35	44.81	1985	74.50	60.38	65.00	1998	90.88	68.88	74.75
1973	65.40	45.31	47.50	1986	69.15	58.00	65.50	1999	97.00	75.63	95.75
1974	52.25	26.50	26.50	1987	88.75	65.50	82.00	2000	106.88	89.50	98.88
1975	41.20	24.75	39.50	1988	95.75	78.90	91.25	2001	109.88	83.63	95.31
1976	46.20	34.25	35.75	1989	96.40	84.50	90.25	2002	96.06	81.00	89.25
1977	43.50	35.45	42.75	1990	102.13	88.00	100.50	2003	112.25	75.00	75.70
1978	76.25	42.75	76.25	1991	105.25	86.00	86.00	2004	128.50	73.63	113.19
1979	97.75	75.50	85.75	1992	94.75	83.75	90.63	2005	131.80	108.00	122.63
1980	90.00	68.00	75.00	1993	102.50	89.00	91.25	2006	131.75	116.19	117.38

Source: Chicago Mercantile Exchange

CATTLE, FEEDER

Quarterly High, Low and Close of Feeder Cattle Futures   In Cents per Pound

Quarter	High	Low	Close	Quarter	High	Low	Close	Quarter	High	Low	Close
09/1996	64.70	59.50	64.45	12/1999	85.85	79.67	85.35	03/2003	85.10	73.95	78.15
12/1996	68.25	62.10	67.52	03/2000	87.10	82.05	84.02	06/2003	86.80	77.75	86.70
03/1997	70.45	66.25	69.37	06/2000	86.95	82.17	86.45	09/2003	102.10	85.85	99.37
06/1997	81.80	68.85	80.87	09/2000	88.40	84.25	86.65	12/2003	110.17	78.50	78.92
09/1997	83.40	77.85	77.95	12/2000	92.20	86.10	91.50	03/2004	90.84	79.80	89.50
12/1997	80.75	75.55	75.87	03/2001	92.05	84.80	86.30	06/2004	114.25	88.85	109.40
03/1998	79.05	73.25	73.62	06/2001	92.75	86.50	91.22	09/2004	118.70	107.50	114.62
06/1998	77.77	70.65	71.77	09/2001	91.60	85.02	85.20	12/2004	114.75	99.40	101.80
09/1998	73.10	65.67	67.72	12/2001	89.45	81.40	86.02	03/2005	108.10	97.80	107.67
12/1998	71.85	65.45	69.17	03/2002	86.20	78.75	78.75	06/2005	113.92	106.85	109.42
03/1999	75.37	68.45	71.85	06/2002	80.10	72.52	75.50	09/2005	116.20	105.40	115.42
06/1999	78.77	69.70	74.55	09/2002	81.70	75.40	80.95	12/2005	119.75	112.60	115.25
09/1999	79.90	74.10	79.90	12/2002	85.60	79.30	83.80	03/2006	115.10	100.80	101.47

Source: Chicago Mercantile Exchange

CATTLE, FEEDER

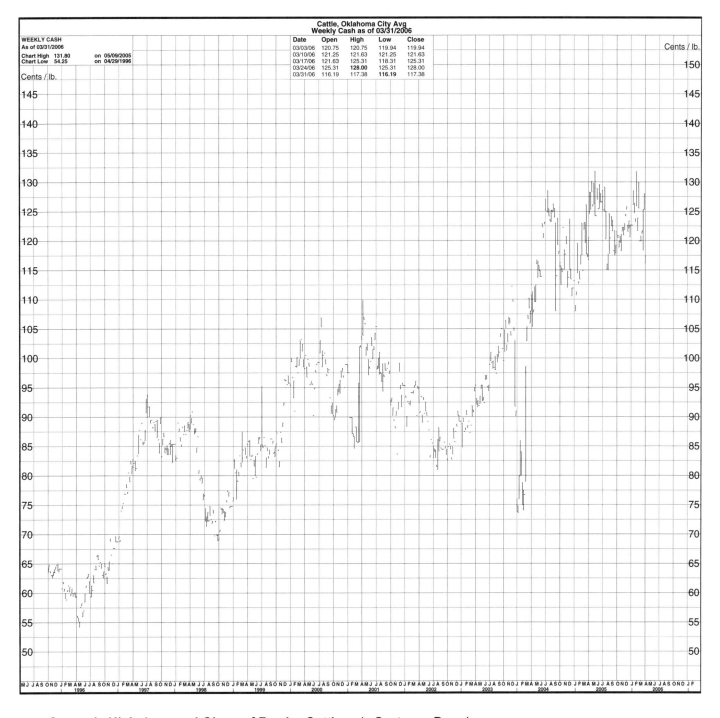

Quarterly High, Low and Close of Feeder Cattle   In Cents per Pound

Quarter	High	Low	Close	Quarter	High	Low	Close	Quarter	High	Low	Close
09/1996	66.50	59.38	62.63	12/1999	97.00	81.50	95.75	03/2003	95.38	84.81	95.38
12/1996	69.63	61.63	68.75	03/2000	103.25	91.00	99.75	06/2003	98.88	91.69	98.88
03/1997	82.50	68.75	80.38	06/2000	100.50	90.25	99.25	09/2003	105.06	97.38	99.56
06/1997	90.75	80.88	90.75	09/2000	106.88	90.50	90.50	12/2003	112.25	75.00	75.70
09/1997	93.75	83.86	89.88	12/2000	98.88	89.50	98.88	03/2004	110.75	73.63	108.00
12/1997	89.88	82.25	85.37	03/2001	102.13	84.63	101.88	06/2004	127.00	105.38	125.13
03/1998	89.12	82.50	87.50	06/2001	109.88	97.13	104.25	09/2004	128.50	108.06	116.31
06/1998	90.88	75.88	76.88	09/2001	105.38	94.38	97.81	12/2004	123.75	110.56	113.19
09/1998	76.88	69.75	69.88	12/2001	99.13	83.63	95.31	03/2005	126.13	108.00	118.75
12/1998	77.38	68.88	74.75	03/2002	96.06	88.38	94.81	06/2005	131.80	120.50	125.25
03/1999	87.50	75.63	83.25	06/2002	94.94	83.13	85.50	09/2005	129.13	115.13	120.88
06/1999	86.50	79.50	85.25	09/2002	88.13	81.00	82.81	12/2005	125.81	118.25	122.63
09/1999	95.25	81.38	84.75	12/2002	90.94	82.63	89.25	03/2006	131.75	116.19	117.38

Source: Chicago Mercantile Exchange

CATTLE, LIVE

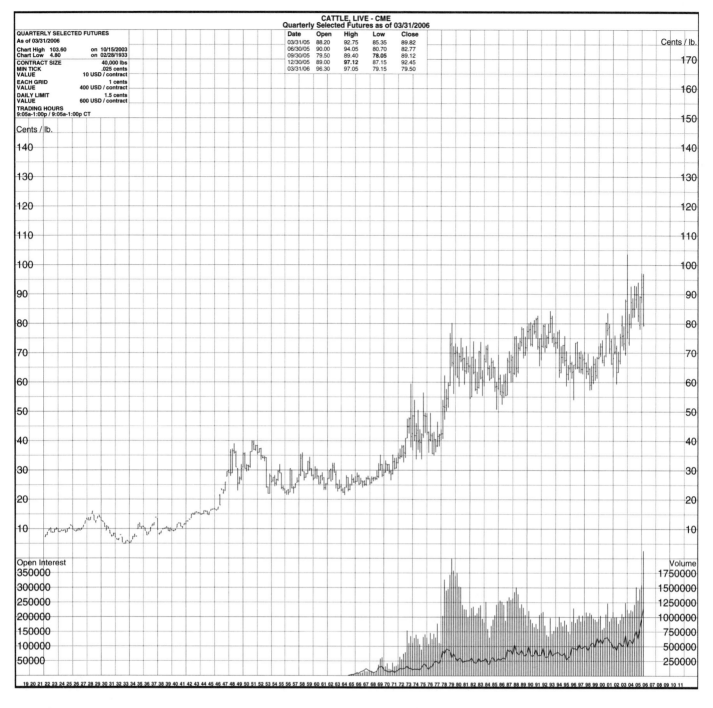

Annual High, Low and Close of Live Cattle Futures   In Cents per Pound

Year	High	Low	Close	Year	High	Low	Close	Year	High	Low	Close
1929	14.59	11.92	12.74	1942	15.30	12.39	14.85	1955	32.00	22.00	22.25
1930	12.62	9.42	10.17	1943	15.71	14.84	14.87	1956	30.50	21.50	24.00
1931	9.43	7.11	7.11	1944	16.07	14.81	14.87	1957	28.50	22.00	28.50
1932	7.91	5.44	5.44	1945	16.91	14.71	16.59	1958	36.00	26.50	28.75
1933	6.01	4.80	5.17	1946	23.64	16.14	23.19	1959	34.50	26.50	27.00
1934	8.06	5.35	7.41	1947	29.82	21.94	29.08	1960	31.25	25.25	28.00
1935	11.91	9.90	10.62	1948	39.00	28.00	31.00	1961	29.25	23.25	27.00
1936	10.38	7.80	10.38	1949	36.00	23.00	35.50	1962	32.50	26.25	29.25
1937	13.97	9.69	9.69	1950	36.25	29.50	36.25	1963	29.75	22.75	23.25
1938	10.16	7.91	10.16	1951	40.00	35.25	36.00	1964	28.25	21.50	23.45
1939	10.64	9.03	9.44	1952	37.50	33.00	34.25	1965	28.60	23.20	26.22
1940	12.06	9.08	11.85	1953	34.25	22.00	26.00	1966	29.20	24.10	25.95
1941	12.57	10.23	12.57	1954	30.00	24.50	29.50	1967	28.10	24.67	25.70

Source: Chicago Mercantile Exchange

CATTLE, LIVE

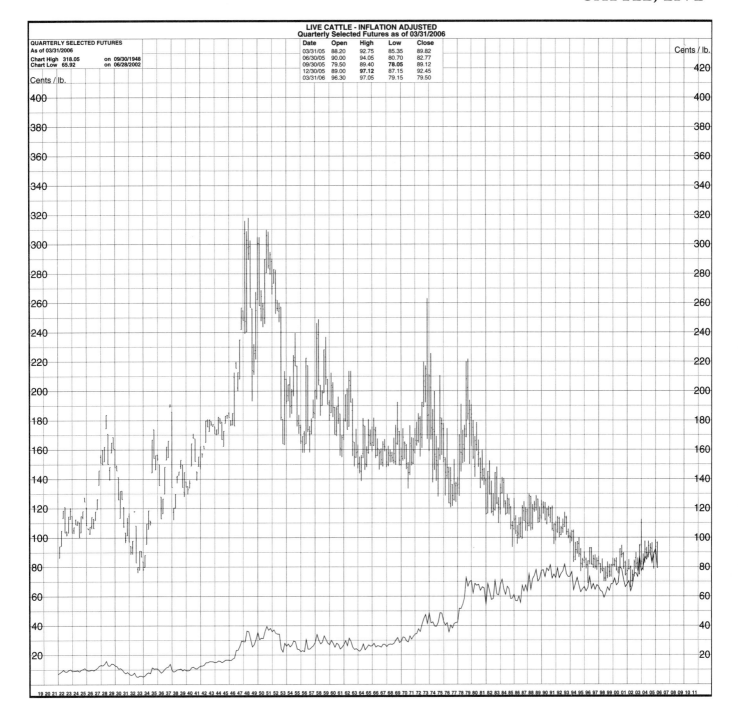

CATTLE, LIVE

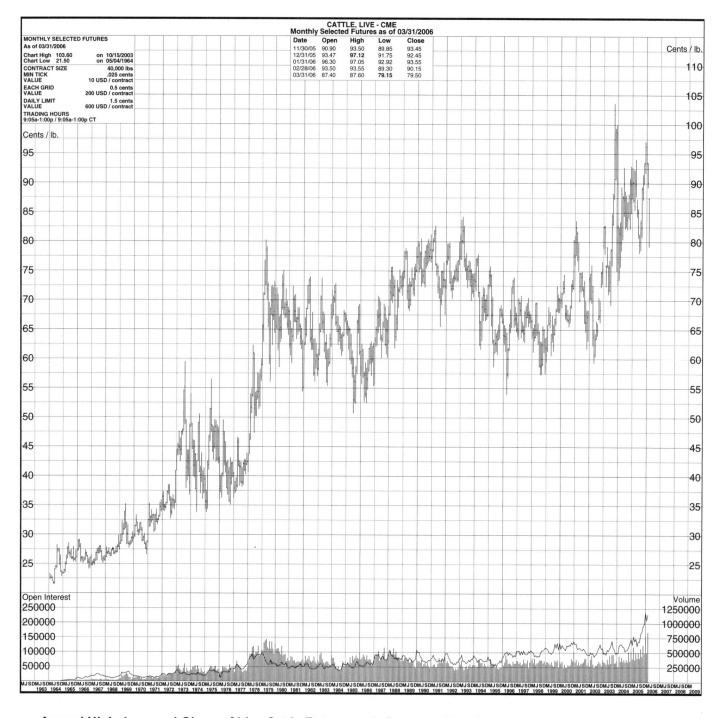

Annual High, Low and Close of Live Cattle Futures   In Cents per Pound

Year	High	Low	Close	Year	High	Low	Close	Year	High	Low	Close
1968	29.85	25.52	27.92	1981	72.40	54.37	54.65	1994	77.92	61.65	72.67
1969	35.25	27.40	29.30	1982	74.00	55.10	58.32	1995	75.82	58.65	66.42
1970	33.35	26.60	28.72	1983	73.82	55.35	67.85	1996	73.95	54.00	64.97
1971	35.90	28.55	34.20	1984	72.87	60.50	66.67	1997	70.80	62.80	66.45
1972	40.90	32.70	40.87	1985	69.35	50.72	61.15	1998	69.72	57.30	62.00
1973	59.50	36.75	48.60	1986	62.97	52.42	55.52	1999	72.45	59.45	68.47
1974	54.00	33.75	39.55	1987	70.72	55.70	63.12	2000	80.40	65.52	80.22
1975	56.50	33.75	42.92	1988	75.75	61.82	73.95	2001	83.60	61.75	68.17
1976	49.60	35.10	40.40	1989	79.15	68.15	77.37	2002	76.65	59.35	75.35
1977	46.60	36.15	42.37	1990	81.25	72.22	77.20	2003	103.60	69.17	77.20
1978	62.35	40.72	58.92	1991	82.70	65.50	72.40	2004	92.95	72.65	89.85
1979	80.25	56.05	70.67	1992	80.00	70.25	77.12	2005	97.12	78.05	92.45
1980	75.12	58.50	68.07	1993	84.30	70.00	73.45	2006	97.05	79.15	79.50

Source: Chicago Mercantile Exchange

CATTLE, LIVE

Annual High, Low and Close of Live Cattle   In Cents per Pound

Year	High	Low	Close	Year	High	Low	Close	Year	High	Low	Close
1968	29.75	26.50	29.15	1981	70.81	57.75	58.19	1994	77.25	60.25	71.00
1969	35.25	28.15	28.15	1982	74.75	55.50	59.75	1995	75.00	60.00	65.00
1970	32.75	27.00	28.00	1983	69.25	58.25	66.12	1996	73.00	54.50	66.00
1971	34.65	28.10	34.60	1984	70.00	60.40	65.88	1997	70.00	61.00	66.00
1972	39.00	32.40	37.50	1985	65.90	49.75	63.00	1998	67.00	56.00	60.25
1973	56.40	37.00	42.10	1986	63.75	53.10	59.12	1999	70.87	60.00	68.00
1974	49.50	35.00	36.90	1987	73.00	58.00	65.75	2000	78.00	64.00	78.00
1975	54.00	33.90	44.45	1988	77.75	65.25	74.75	2001	81.55	60.03	64.21
1976	46.50	34.40	39.10	1989	80.00	69.00	79.75	2002	74.46	60.00	74.00
1977	44.10	36.50	43.40	1990	82.25	74.00	81.00	2003	111.43	72.76	75.22
1978	61.50	43.30	55.55	1991	81.75	64.00	70.75	2004	91.38	73.86	87.35
1979	77.75	55.70	67.00	1992	79.75	71.00	78.25	2005	96.76	77.50	93.34
1980	73.95	60.00	63.62	1993	84.75	69.50	70.50	2006	96.56	84.03	84.03

Source: Chicago Mercantile Exchange

CATTLE, LIVE

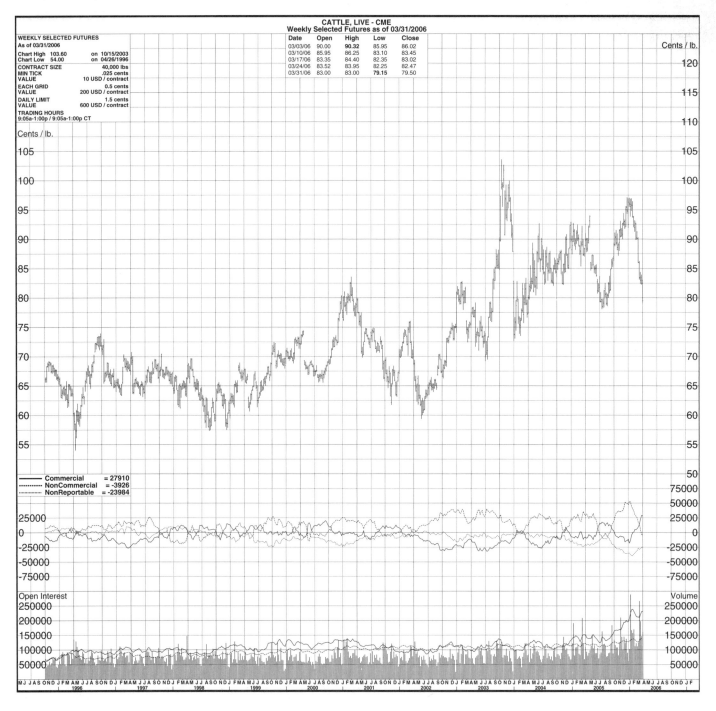

Quarterly High, Low and Close of Live Cattle Futures   In Cents per Pound

Quarter	High	Low	Close	Quarter	High	Low	Close	Quarter	High	Low	Close
09/1996	73.55	64.47	73.32	12/1999	72.45	67.92	68.47	03/2003	82.85	72.40	75.80
12/1996	73.95	64.60	64.97	03/2000	73.40	68.72	72.17	06/2003	79.20	71.00	73.22
03/1997	70.40	63.32	68.42	06/2000	74.45	66.57	67.47	09/2003	88.30	69.17	87.60
06/1997	70.80	63.10	64.45	09/2000	69.10	65.52	69.07	12/2003	103.60	74.97	77.20
09/1997	69.60	62.80	67.70	12/2000	80.40	68.65	80.22	03/2004	83.40	72.65	79.82
12/1997	70.50	65.25	66.45	03/2001	83.60	76.05	78.35	06/2004	92.70	78.50	87.25
03/1998	66.85	61.22	63.75	06/2001	79.95	69.82	71.52	09/2004	88.70	82.05	85.07
06/1998	69.72	62.52	62.97	09/2001	74.92	66.15	66.22	12/2004	92.95	82.20	89.85
09/1998	64.82	57.30	59.07	12/2001	69.90	61.75	68.17	03/2005	92.75	85.35	89.82
12/1998	65.65	57.45	62.00	03/2002	76.07	69.55	70.42	06/2005	94.05	80.70	82.77
03/1999	68.95	59.45	66.20	06/2002	72.60	59.35	63.40	09/2005	89.40	78.05	89.12
06/1999	68.09	60.62	63.75	09/2002	70.47	63.40	67.40	12/2005	97.12	87.15	92.45
09/1999	68.70	61.35	68.27	12/2002	76.65	66.25	75.35	03/2006	97.05	79.15	79.50

Source: Chicago Mercantile Exchange

CATTLE, LIVE

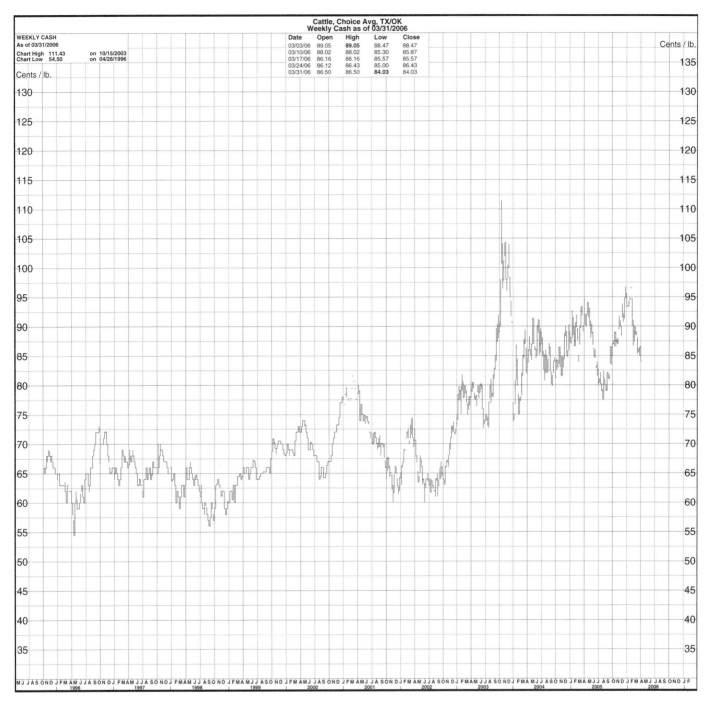

Quarterly High, Low and Close of Live Cattle   In Cents per Pound

Quarter	High	Low	Close	Quarter	High	Low	Close	Quarter	High	Low	Close
09/1996	72.00	60.00	72.00	12/1999	70.87	67.50	68.00	03/2003	81.78	72.85	77.88
12/1996	73.00	65.00	66.00	03/2000	73.00	68.00	72.00	06/2003	80.42	72.76	73.91
03/1997	69.00	63.00	67.00	06/2000	74.00	68.00	68.00	09/2003	92.00	72.78	89.75
06/1997	69.00	63.00	63.00	09/2000	68.00	64.00	67.00	12/2003	111.43	75.00	75.22
09/1997	67.00	61.00	66.00	12/2000	78.00	67.00	78.00	03/2004	89.38	73.86	84.60
12/1997	70.00	65.00	66.00	03/2001	81.55	76.75	77.58	06/2004	91.38	83.00	88.96
03/1998	66.00	59.00	61.00	06/2001	80.00	71.05	71.05	09/2004	88.00	79.92	82.34
06/1998	67.00	61.00	63.00	09/2001	72.04	65.93	65.93	12/2004	90.22	81.22	87.35
09/1998	63.00	56.00	57.00	12/2001	67.72	60.03	64.21	03/2005	94.75	84.00	94.69
12/1998	64.00	57.00	60.25	03/2002	74.46	63.00	69.48	06/2005	94.01	80.00	80.00
03/1999	65.00	60.00	64.00	06/2002	72.66	60.00	64.00	09/2005	87.02	77.50	87.01
06/1999	67.25	64.00	64.00	09/2002	66.90	61.00	64.99	12/2005	96.76	86.50	93.34
09/1999	66.50	64.00	66.50	12/2002	74.00	63.00	74.00	03/2006	96.56	84.03	84.03

Source: Chicago Mercantile Exchange

HOGS, LEAN

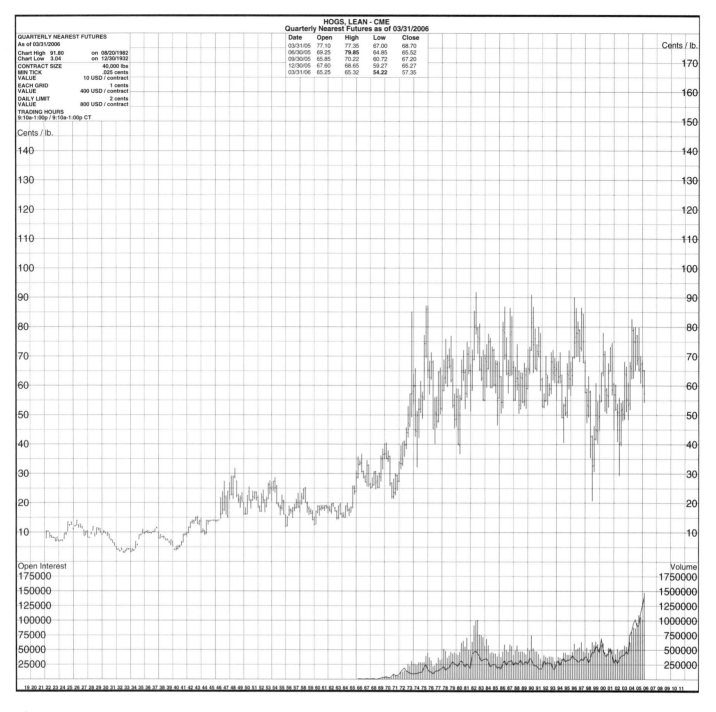

Annual High, Low and Close of Lean Hogs Futures   In Cents per Pound

Year	High	Low	Close	Year	High	Low	Close	Year	High	Low	Close
1929	11.44	9.06	9.34	1942	14.25	9.75	13.50	1955	22.75	11.75	12.00
1930	10.67	7.92	7.92	1943	15.50	9.50	10.25	1956	19.00	12.00	18.25
1931	7.65	4.20	4.20	1944	14.00	9.00	13.75	1957	23.35	16.75	20.00
1932	4.58	3.04	3.04	1945	14.25	13.25	14.00	1958	25.25	16.63	18.60
1933	4.51	3.12	3.25	1946	24.00	13.40	17.75	1959	18.75	12.50	12.50
1934	6.82	3.41	5.89	1947	27.50	14.75	22.75	1960	19.25	12.75	18.50
1935	10.95	7.70	9.57	1948	31.85	21.25	22.50	1961	19.25	16.50	18.25
1936	10.47	9.48	9.96	1949	23.65	15.75	16.25	1962	20.00	16.25	17.25
1937	11.77	7.90	7.90	1950	25.50	16.00	21.00	1963	20.00	14.35	15.50
1938	9.12	7.24	7.24	1951	24.10	18.25	18.85	1964	20.00	15.00	17.50
1939	7.77	5.38	5.38	1952	24.50	16.75	19.00	1965	31.00	16.75	28.70
1940	5.60	3.85	5.50	1953	27.70	18.50	25.35	1966	36.72	28.35	28.82
1941	10.00	5.55	9.70	1954	28.75	18.50	18.75	1967	34.56	24.84	25.31

Source: Chicago Mercantile Exchange

HOGS, LEAN

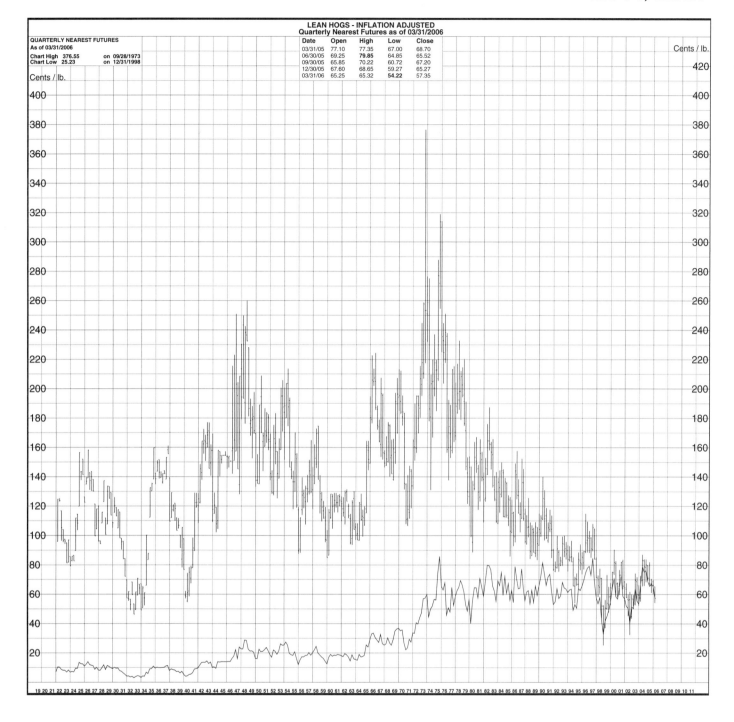

HOGS, LEAN

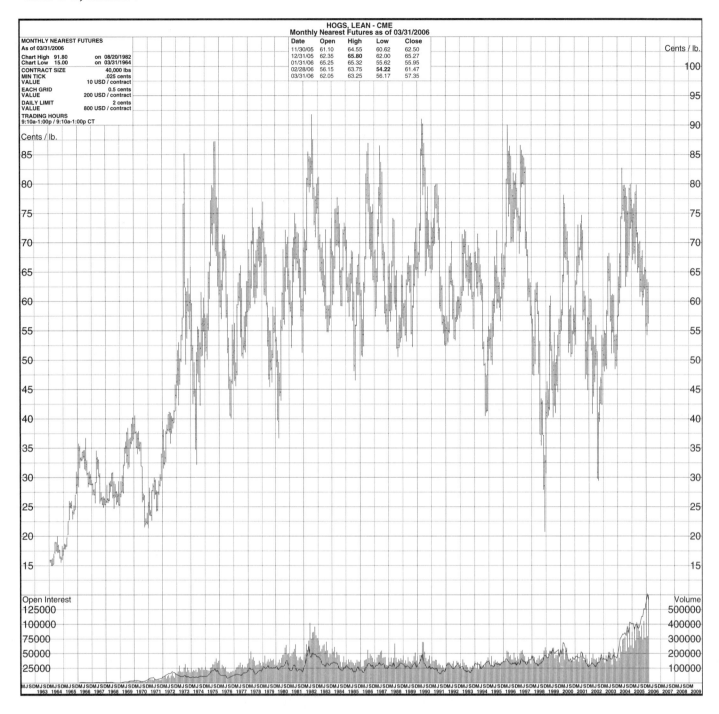

Annual High, Low and Close of Lean Hogs Futures — In Cents per Pound

Year	High	Low	Close	Year	High	Low	Close	Year	High	Low	Close
1968	30.87	24.64	25.25	1981	75.06	51.23	58.52	1994	71.48	40.46	53.12
1969	40.23	25.18	36.86	1982	91.80	58.25	76.61	1995	72.09	49.14	65.57
1970	40.57	21.47	22.10	1983	81.20	54.70	69.19	1996	90.07	60.08	79.22
1971	34.05	21.33	33.82	1984	77.72	59.13	71.98	1997	86.60	57.55	57.70
1972	45.83	31.52	44.01	1985	72.70	46.51	62.94	1998	63.27	20.70	32.65
1973	85.19	42.28	59.81	1986	86.94	50.56	63.79	1999	60.92	30.65	54.50
1974	65.84	32.13	56.57	1987	86.54	54.74	55.44	2000	78.10	50.50	56.82
1975	87.28	48.74	65.43	1988	74.18	50.49	62.80	2001	74.70	44.85	57.05
1976	71.37	40.10	50.79	1989	72.45	52.18	65.75	2002	60.42	29.40	51.60
1977	66.15	45.52	58.48	1990	91.06	63.92	65.97	2003	68.20	48.00	53.42
1978	75.96	58.12	66.29	1991	79.99	52.52	53.06	2004	82.70	51.75	76.40
1979	76.98	45.39	56.25	1992	70.20	52.41	58.89	2005	79.85	59.27	65.27
1980	72.16	36.65	64.46	1993	72.18	55.22	61.22	2006	65.32	54.22	57.35

Source: Chicago Mercantile Exchange

HOGS, LEAN

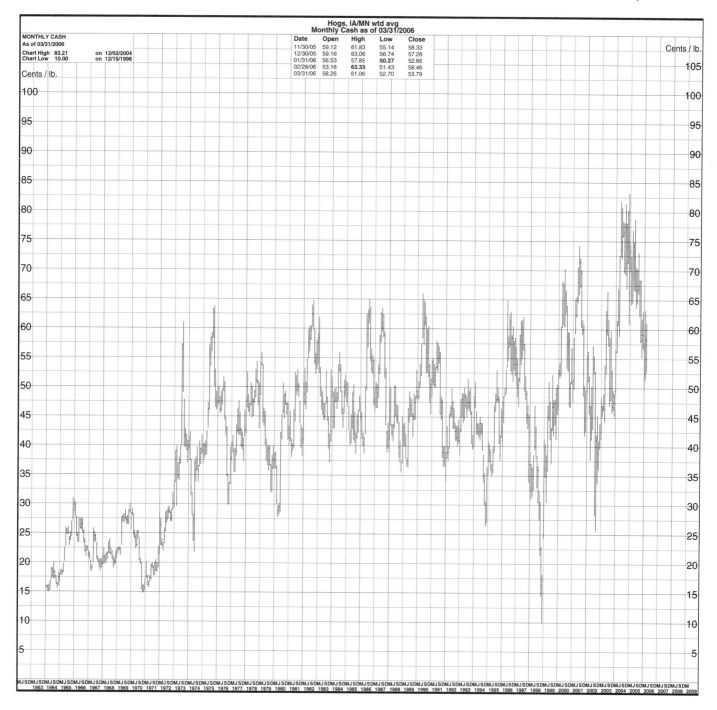

Annual High, Low and Close of Lean Hogs — In Cents per Pound

Year	High	Low	Close	Year	High	Low	Close	Year	High	Low	Close
1968	24.00	19.00	21.50	1981	53.00	38.00	40.40	1994	51.00	26.50	34.50
1969	30.00	20.75	29.00	1982	64.80	40.40	55.50	1995	53.00	35.00	43.00
1970	29.15	14.75	15.75	1983	62.00	37.10	49.25	1996	65.00	40.00	55.00
1971	22.80	15.15	22.25	1984	56.00	43.00	49.50	1997	62.00	34.00	34.00
1972	32.00	21.50	30.20	1985	51.00	38.65	48.00	1998	47.00	10.00	17.25
1973	61.00	29.50	40.75	1986	65.00	38.70	47.75	1999	52.22	24.48	45.53
1974	42.30	21.75	38.95	1987	63.50	39.00	41.25	2000	70.31	46.24	50.94
1975	63.90	36.80	46.50	1988	50.30	35.50	43.25	2001	74.24	41.83	49.57
1976	51.75	29.95	37.85	1989	53.00	36.50	49.35	2002	57.24	25.66	40.46
1977	47.70	35.55	42.80	1990	66.00	45.50	50.50	2003	66.46	41.39	48.53
1978	54.35	42.20	48.00	1991	58.00	36.50	36.70	2004	83.21	49.00	66.14
1979	55.90	32.00	37.50	1992	50.00	34.00	41.00	2005	78.82	55.14	57.26
1980	50.70	27.85	41.25	1993	51.50	38.50	39.75	2006	63.33	50.27	53.79

Source: Chicago Mercantile Exchange

HOGS, LEAN

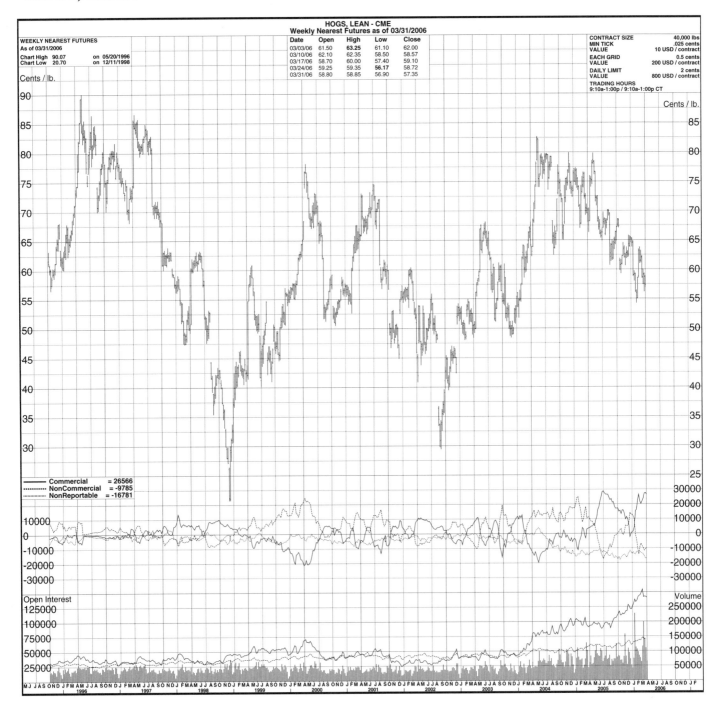

Quarterly High, Low and Close of Lean Hogs Futures   In Cents per Pound

Quarter	High	Low	Close	Quarter	High	Low	Close	Quarter	High	Low	Close
09/1996	86.47	69.93	77.92	12/1999	57.00	44.52	54.50	03/2003	54.95	48.00	50.32
12/1996	81.90	70.07	79.22	03/2000	64.50	54.45	64.35	06/2003	68.20	48.40	64.05
03/1997	79.25	68.05	72.97	06/2000	78.10	63.25	70.60	09/2003	66.52	51.10	55.52
06/1997	86.60	71.75	84.67	09/2000	71.90	51.22	58.35	12/2003	61.02	48.40	53.42
09/1997	84.40	67.70	67.80	12/2000	59.25	50.50	56.82	03/2004	68.15	51.75	66.65
12/1997	68.80	57.55	57.70	03/2001	67.67	52.60	64.47	06/2004	82.70	62.22	78.95
03/1998	59.15	47.30	53.52	06/2001	73.27	64.80	72.75	09/2004	79.80	62.50	75.00
06/1998	63.27	49.25	57.85	09/2001	74.70	56.75	58.60	12/2004	79.92	65.05	76.40
09/1998	58.35	35.40	42.62	12/2001	60.95	44.85	57.05	03/2005	77.35	67.00	68.70
12/1998	43.10	20.70	32.65	03/2002	60.42	51.55	51.87	06/2005	79.85	64.85	65.52
03/1999	46.35	30.65	41.85	06/2002	53.95	40.82	50.52	09/2005	70.22	60.72	67.20
06/1999	60.92	41.42	44.87	09/2002	55.92	29.40	40.20	12/2005	68.65	59.27	65.27
09/1999	54.75	40.20	48.97	12/2002	54.25	39.45	51.60	03/2006	65.32	54.22	57.35

Source: Chicago Mercantile Exchange

HOGS, LEAN

Quarterly High, Low and Close of Lean Hogs   In Cents per Pound

Quarter	High	Low	Close	Quarter	High	Low	Close	Quarter	High	Low	Close
09/1996	63.00	52.25	58.50	12/1999	50.64	41.22	45.53	03/2003	49.02	41.39	46.52
12/1996	60.50	51.00	55.00	03/2000	60.44	46.24	60.44	06/2003	66.46	44.25	59.13
03/1997	57.00	46.75	51.75	06/2000	70.31	60.34	65.94	09/2003	61.75	47.01	53.60
06/1997	61.50	51.00	61.50	09/2000	66.61	52.85	59.50	12/2003	52.98	45.16	48.53
09/1997	62.00	48.00	49.50	12/2000	59.42	46.66	50.94	03/2004	66.99	49.00	63.35
12/1997	49.50	34.00	34.00	03/2001	65.16	47.60	62.33	06/2004	81.82	58.83	76.00
03/1998	39.00	31.00	36.00	06/2001	74.24	62.18	71.46	09/2004	81.39	69.28	78.03
06/1998	47.00	32.50	38.00	09/2001	72.15	59.12	59.93	12/2004	83.21	60.93	66.14
09/1998	38.50	27.50	30.25	12/2001	60.85	41.83	49.57	03/2005	76.89	64.23	65.89
12/1998	30.50	10.00	17.25	03/2002	56.20	45.54	46.83	06/2005	78.82	63.69	63.72
03/1999	41.30	24.48	35.34	06/2002	57.24	37.69	53.20	09/2005	73.05	62.22	68.24
06/1999	51.10	35.87	41.25	09/2002	55.49	25.66	41.21	12/2005	68.28	55.14	57.26
09/1999	52.22	37.04	47.26	12/2002	45.29	33.72	40.46	03/2006	63.33	50.27	53.79

Source: Chicago Mercantile Exchange

PORK BELLIES

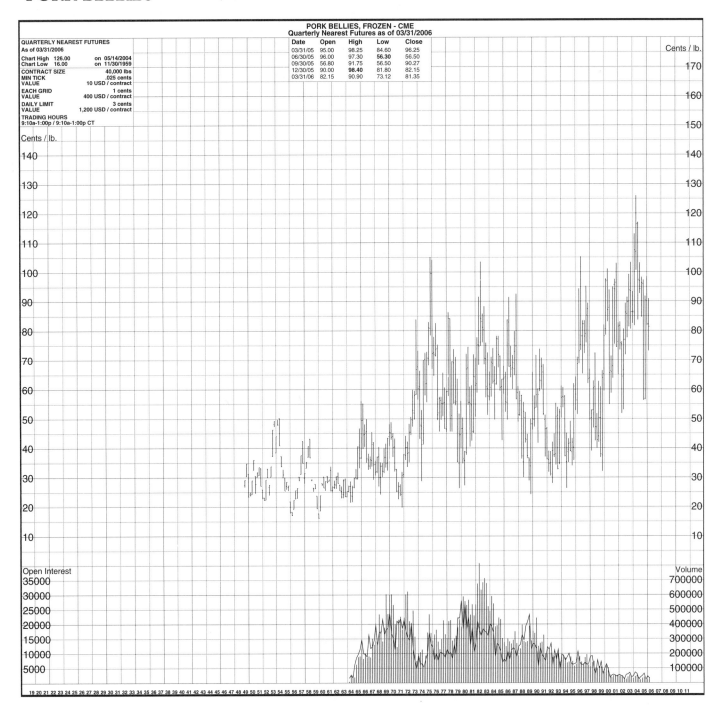

Annual High, Low and Close of Pork Belly Futures   In Cents per Pound

Year	High	Low	Close	Year	High	Low	Close	Year	High	Low	Close
				1954	50.25	30.00	31.00	1961	35.88	24.25	26.75
				1955	30.00	18.00	18.00	1962	31.75	25.50	25.50
1949	34.75	23.50	23.50	1956	26.38	17.00	26.38	1963	29.70	23.00	25.25
1950	36.00	23.88	27.75	1957	42.38	28.00	31.50	1964	30.00	21.42	29.75
1951	33.50	22.75	23.13	1958	43.13	28.88	29.25	1965	56.00	29.42	49.40
1952	33.00	22.25	27.50	1959	27.75	16.00	16.13	1966	55.25	32.65	34.25
1953	49.25	30.25	44.00	1960	30.25	18.63	28.75	1967	45.45	29.25	31.85

Source: Chicago Mercantile Exchange

PORK BELLIES

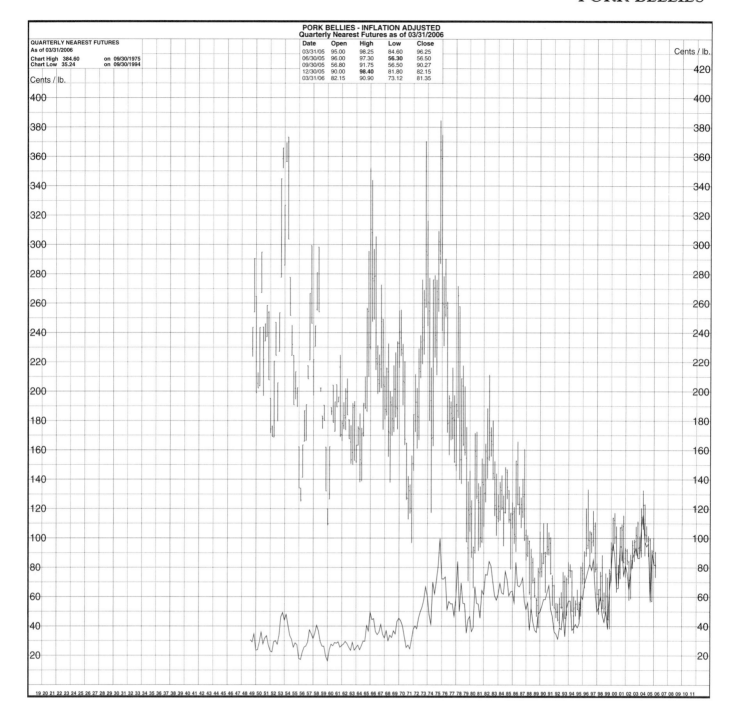

PORK BELLIES

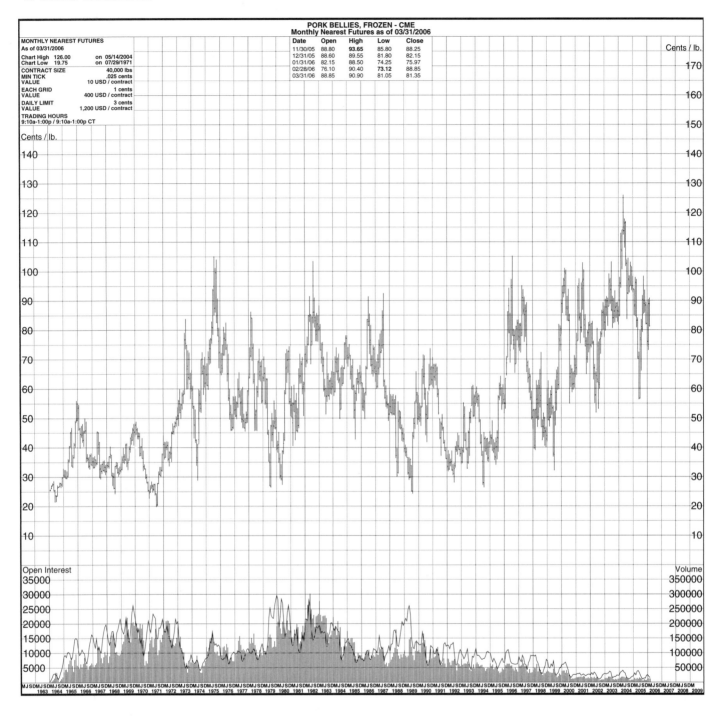

Annual High, Low and Close of Pork Belly Futures — In Cents per Pound

Year	High	Low	Close	Year	High	Low	Close	Year	High	Low	Close
1968	40.40	24.22	32.20	1981	71.95	40.45	61.37	1994	60.70	26.35	41.37
1969	48.10	31.55	45.40	1982	103.50	58.85	81.10	1995	64.30	34.00	58.27
1970	48.87	25.10	25.37	1983	88.30	51.25	61.72	1996	105.25	51.50	82.35
1971	37.95	19.75	37.90	1984	78.20	49.70	77.30	1997	95.20	49.50	50.02
1972	50.65	33.60	49.70	1985	78.20	42.65	63.82	1998	72.47	39.00	42.75
1973	83.80	47.35	60.30	1986	91.40	49.65	66.85	1999	81.95	32.10	78.15
1974	72.50	28.75	61.90	1987	92.50	49.00	51.32	2000	101.10	54.87	65.87
1975	105.10	55.65	72.25	1988	59.45	30.05	43.05	2001	103.00	63.77	81.42
1976	82.55	45.60	56.85	1989	65.90	24.27	49.90	2002	89.35	51.82	86.20
1977	65.65	45.40	59.40	1990	73.80	41.72	63.10	2003	103.30	77.60	86.47
1978	86.25	45.60	55.55	1991	70.75	36.07	36.22	2004	126.00	81.70	94.25
1979	71.05	26.35	46.65	1992	44.87	28.05	37.75	2005	98.40	56.30	82.15
1980	74.50	27.30	55.57	1993	61.15	32.70	57.15	2006	90.90	73.12	81.35

Source: Chicago Mercantile Exchange

PORK BELLIES

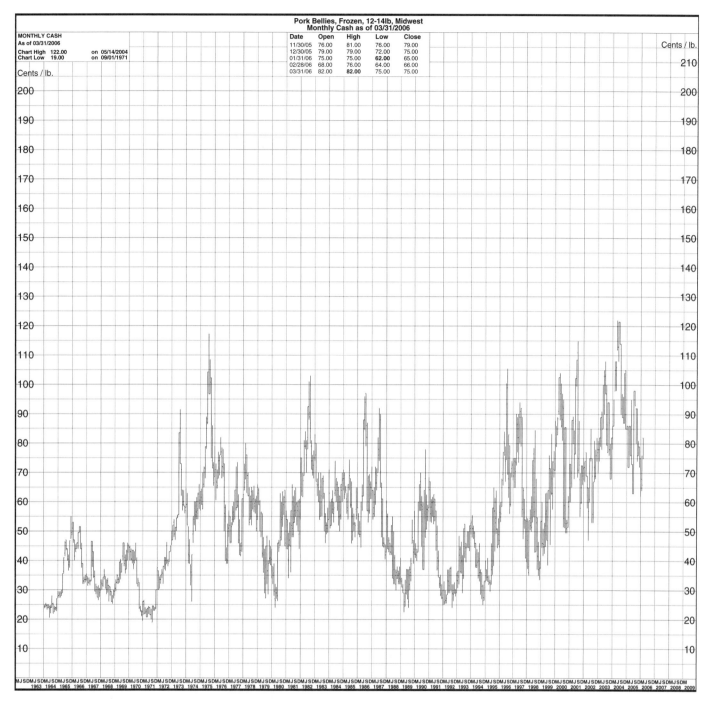

Annual High, Low and Close of Pork Bellies   In Cents per Pound

Year	High	Low	Close	Year	High	Low	Close	Year	High	Low	Close
1968	37.00	25.25	29.50	1981	66.00	34.00	60.00	1994	55.50	25.00	33.00
1969	46.00	28.00	45.00	1982	103.00	54.00	75.00	1995	65.00	29.50	49.00
1970	46.00	21.00	21.50	1983	83.00	46.00	54.00	1996	105.50	44.50	73.00
1971	30.00	19.00	30.00	1984	74.00	50.00	67.50	1997	94.00	41.00	41.00
1972	46.25	30.00	45.00	1985	74.50	46.00	55.50	1998	84.50	33.50	37.50
1973	91.50	45.50	57.00	1986	97.00	44.50	65.00	1999	83.25	37.50	71.00
1974	66.00	26.00	59.50	1987	92.00	40.50	42.00	2000	104.00	49.50	58.50
1975	117.25	57.00	66.50	1988	60.50	30.00	34.00	2001	115.00	55.13	69.00
1976	82.00	39.00	50.00	1989	54.00	22.50	43.00	2002	85.00	47.00	78.00
1977	73.50	41.50	61.00	1990	78.00	37.00	57.00	2003	108.00	68.00	82.00
1978	80.00	50.00	51.00	1991	68.50	27.00	27.50	2004	122.00	78.00	85.00
1979	66.00	27.25	38.50	1992	38.00	24.00	29.00	2005	98.00	63.00	75.00
1980	64.00	24.00	45.00	1993	52.50	29.00	52.00	2006	82.00	62.00	75.00

Source: Chicago Mercantile Exchange

PORK BELLIES

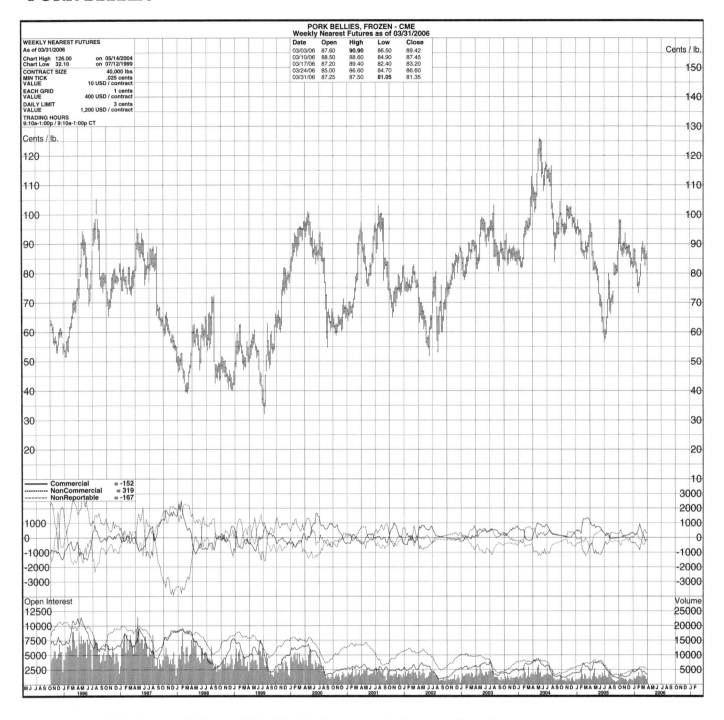

Quarterly High, Low and Close of Pork Belly Futures   In Cents per Pound

Quarter	High	Low	Close	Quarter	High	Low	Close	Quarter	High	Low	Close
09/1996	105.25	73.30	78.12	12/1999	81.95	59.50	78.15	03/2003	91.40	77.60	89.72
12/1996	83.42	65.30	82.35	03/2000	97.70	78.50	97.30	06/2003	99.20	81.30	93.85
03/1997	83.45	72.27	78.05	06/2000	101.10	83.05	87.07	09/2003	103.30	80.55	86.35
06/1997	95.20	75.90	85.22	09/2000	93.95	54.87	65.55	12/2003	93.40	82.52	86.47
09/1997	89.40	62.00	63.52	12/2000	71.40	58.70	65.87	03/2004	113.00	81.70	107.37
12/1997	66.90	49.50	50.02	03/2001	95.00	63.77	94.35	06/2004	126.00	100.60	116.27
03/1998	53.00	39.00	52.87	06/2001	97.55	75.40	94.15	09/2004	117.00	83.60	97.37
06/1998	62.90	46.90	60.42	09/2001	103.00	74.37	74.47	12/2004	103.15	92.65	94.25
09/1998	72.47	42.45	47.20	12/2001	82.60	64.92	81.42	03/2005	98.25	84.60	96.25
12/1998	51.77	40.00	42.75	03/2002	83.00	73.45	75.82	06/2005	97.30	56.30	56.50
03/1999	62.75	42.00	50.25	06/2002	76.27	51.82	64.35	09/2005	91.75	56.50	90.27
06/1999	60.90	36.80	37.95	09/2002	80.60	53.05	76.77	12/2005	98.40	81.80	82.15
09/1999	66.40	32.10	63.90	12/2002	89.35	71.80	86.20	03/2006	90.90	73.12	81.35

Source: Chicago Mercantile Exchange

PORK BELLIES

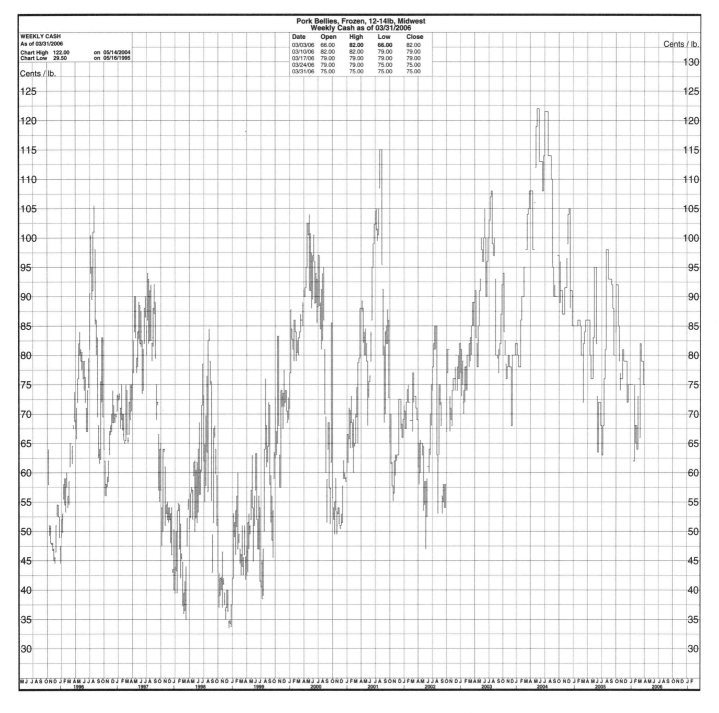

Quarterly High, Low and Close of Pork Bellies   In Cents per Pound

Quarter	High	Low	Close	Quarter	High	Low	Close	Quarter	High	Low	Close
09/1996	105.50	61.50	83.00	12/1999	83.25	57.50	71.00	03/2003	89.00	70.00	89.00
12/1996	79.25	56.00	73.00	03/2000	89.00	71.00	88.50	06/2003	105.00	78.00	100.00
03/1997	75.00	65.00	70.50	06/2000	104.00	85.50	86.00	09/2003	108.00	77.00	94.00
06/1997	90.00	72.50	90.00	09/2000	97.00	51.25	85.50	12/2003	94.00	68.00	82.00
09/1997	94.00	55.00	55.00	12/2000	85.50	49.50	58.50	03/2004	108.00	78.00	105.00
12/1997	65.00	41.00	41.00	03/2001	88.00	60.00	88.00	06/2004	122.00	98.00	121.50
03/1998	54.75	35.00	53.75	06/2001	102.25	68.00	102.25	09/2004	121.50	89.00	89.00
06/1998	74.25	50.00	74.25	09/2001	115.00	68.50	72.75	12/2004	105.00	85.00	85.00
09/1998	84.50	43.00	53.00	12/2001	72.50	55.13	69.00	03/2005	86.00	72.00	86.00
12/1998	54.75	33.50	37.50	03/2002	77.00	67.00	69.00	06/2005	95.00	63.00	63.00
03/1999	60.00	37.50	45.75	06/2002	75.00	47.00	75.00	09/2005	98.00	63.00	92.00
06/1999	63.25	42.50	52.00	09/2002	85.00	53.00	67.00	12/2005	92.00	72.00	75.00
09/1999	76.00	38.50	63.50	12/2002	82.00	67.00	78.00	03/2006	82.00	62.00	75.00

Source: Chicago Mercantile Exchange

HIDES

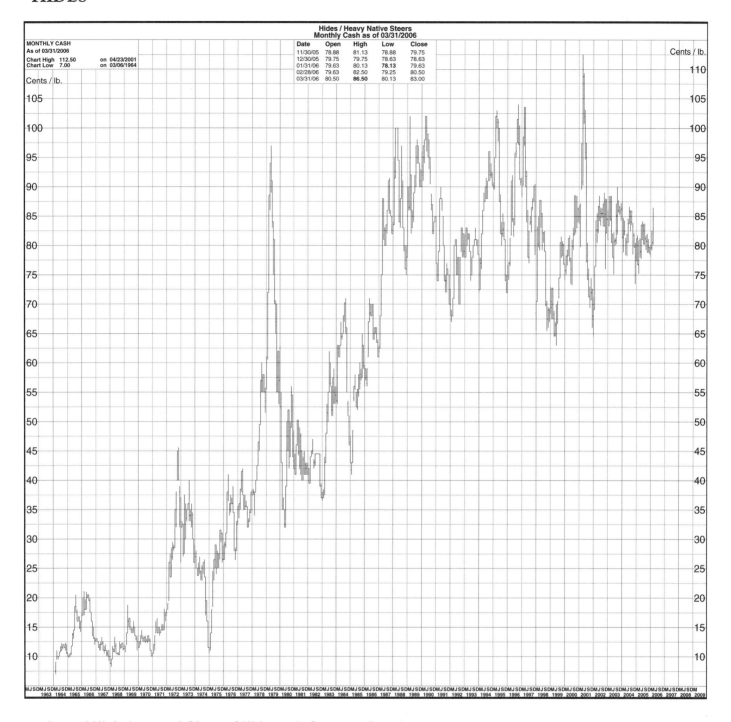

Annual High, Low and Close of Hides   In Cents per Pound

Year	High	Low	Close	Year	High	Low	Close	Year	High	Low	Close
1968	13.25	8.25	11.25	1981	50.25	40.00	41.00	1994	96.00	72.00	90.25
1969	18.75	10.75	12.50	1982	47.00	37.00	37.00	1995	103.00	72.00	72.00
1970	14.50	10.00	10.00	1983	62.00	36.50	54.50	1996	104.00	72.00	91.00
1971	18.00	10.00	17.00	1984	71.00	46.00	46.00	1997	103.50	77.00	78.50
1972	45.50	17.00	33.00	1985	65.00	41.00	59.50	1998	87.75	65.50	69.25
1973	40.00	26.00	26.00	1986	71.00	56.00	61.00	1999	81.50	63.00	77.00
1974	29.00	11.50	11.50	1987	91.50	61.00	82.00	2000	88.50	73.37	86.25
1975	31.50	10.50	26.50	1988	100.00	75.00	78.00	2001	112.50	66.00	68.00
1976	41.00	26.50	33.00	1989	102.00	78.00	90.00	2002	89.00	64.50	84.50
1977	42.00	32.00	38.00	1990	102.00	82.00	85.00	2003	90.00	75.13	86.25
1978	60.00	34.00	53.50	1991	90.00	70.00	70.00	2004	87.63	73.50	78.00
1979	97.00	53.00	57.00	1992	83.00	67.00	79.00	2005	84.13	75.25	78.63
1980	63.00	32.00	44.00	1993	83.00	74.00	78.50	2006	86.50	78.13	83.00

Source: U.S. Department of Agriculture

HIDES

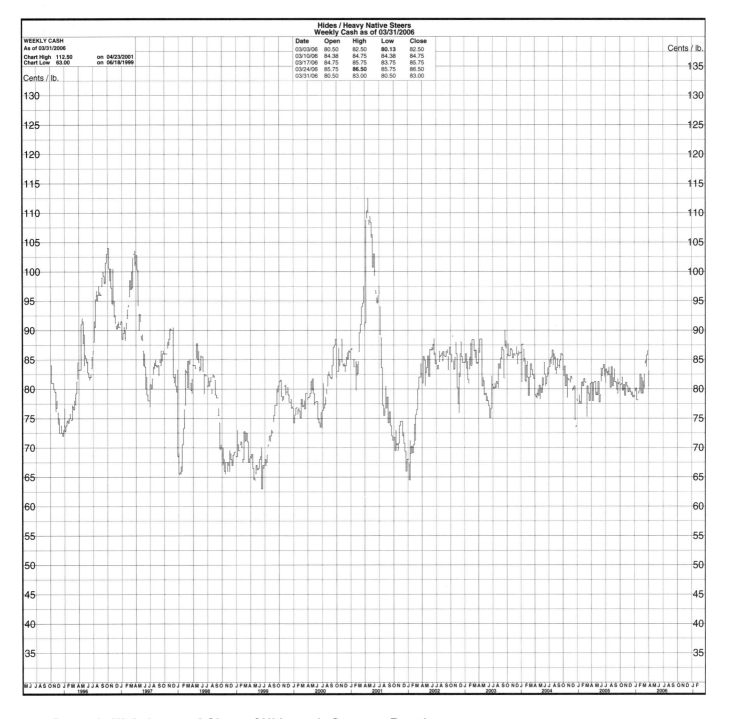

Quarterly High, Low and Close of Hides In Cents per Pound

Quarter	High	Low	Close	Quarter	High	Low	Close	Quarter	High	Low	Close
09/1996	101.50	83.50	101.50	12/1999	81.50	76.75	77.00	03/2003	88.38	81.00	84.50
12/1996	104.00	90.25	91.00	03/2000	79.25	74.25	79.25	06/2003	88.50	75.13	80.75
03/1997	103.50	88.25	103.50	06/2000	81.75	73.50	76.00	09/2003	90.00	80.00	85.25
06/1997	103.50	78.00	78.00	09/2000	88.50	73.37	88.50	12/2003	87.75	84.25	86.25
09/1997	86.50	77.00	86.50	12/2000	88.50	82.00	86.25	03/2004	87.63	78.88	82.38
12/1997	90.50	78.50	78.50	03/2001	97.50	79.75	97.50	06/2004	84.50	78.25	83.75
03/1998	85.00	65.50	79.75	06/2001	112.50	90.25	95.87	09/2004	86.63	82.50	85.75
06/1998	87.75	79.25	82.25	09/2001	97.50	71.25	71.25	12/2004	83.88	73.50	78.00
09/1998	82.50	69.75	69.75	12/2001	74.50	66.00	68.00	03/2005	81.75	75.25	80.88
12/1998	70.50	65.50	69.25	03/2002	84.25	64.50	84.25	06/2005	84.13	77.75	81.00
03/1999	73.00	67.50	68.25	06/2002	88.50	80.50	84.25	09/2005	83.75	79.25	80.75
06/1999	70.00	63.00	67.00	09/2002	87.13	83.25	87.13	12/2005	82.00	78.63	78.63
09/1999	80.50	66.75	80.50	12/2002	89.00	76.00	84.50	03/2006	86.50	78.13	83.00

Source: U.S. Department of Agriculture

TALLOW

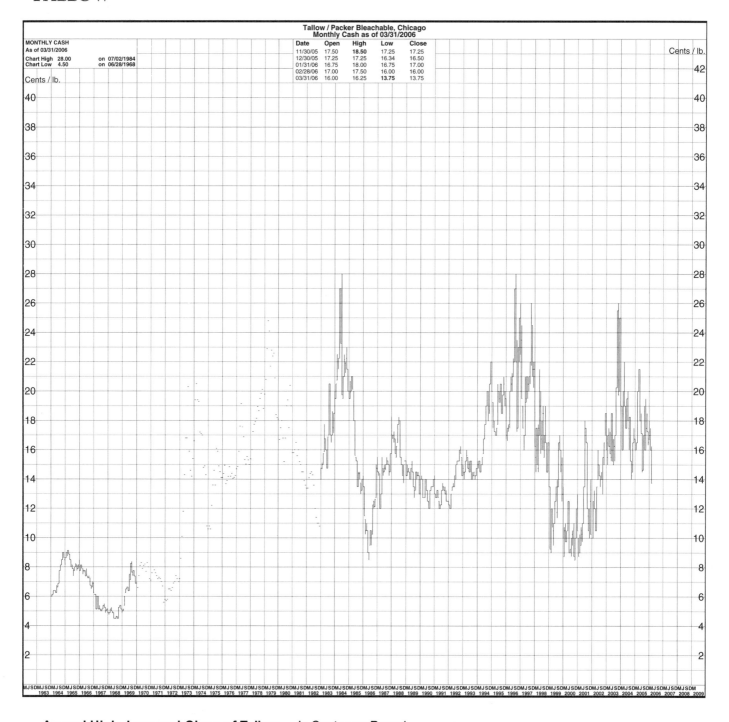

Annual High, Low and Close of Tallow   In Cents per Pound

Year	High	Low	Close	Year	High	Low	Close	Year	High	Low	Close
1968	5.38	4.50	5.13	1981	16.50	13.60	13.60	1994	22.00	14.50	22.00
1969	8.38	4.88	6.88	1982	14.50	10.80	10.80	1995	22.00	17.00	19.50
1970	8.30	6.60	7.20	1983	20.50	14.00	18.50	1996	28.00	16.63	25.00
1971	8.00	5.60	5.60	1984	28.00	18.50	20.00	1997	26.00	16.00	21.50
1972	7.40	5.70	7.00	1985	21.00	13.00	14.00	1998	22.00	14.50	16.50
1973	20.30	7.20	15.40	1986	15.00	8.50	14.75	1999	17.00	9.00	13.00
1974	20.50	10.80	10.80	1987	15.75	12.00	15.75	2000	13.50	8.50	12.00
1975	16.10	10.60	14.10	1988	18.25	13.75	15.25	2001	18.00	8.75	10.25
1976	14.95	13.69	14.25	1989	15.25	12.75	13.00	2002	18.50	10.00	18.50
1977	19.15	14.70	15.00	1990	14.25	12.00	14.00	2003	26.00	15.00	25.00
1978	20.12	15.38	18.83	1991	14.25	12.00	12.50	2004	25.00	14.00	16.75
1979	24.80	18.20	18.20	1992	16.25	12.00	14.25	2005	21.50	14.50	16.50
1980	20.40	15.20	19.00	1993	16.00	14.00	14.75	2006	18.00	13.75	13.75

Source: U.S. Department of Agriculture

TALLOW

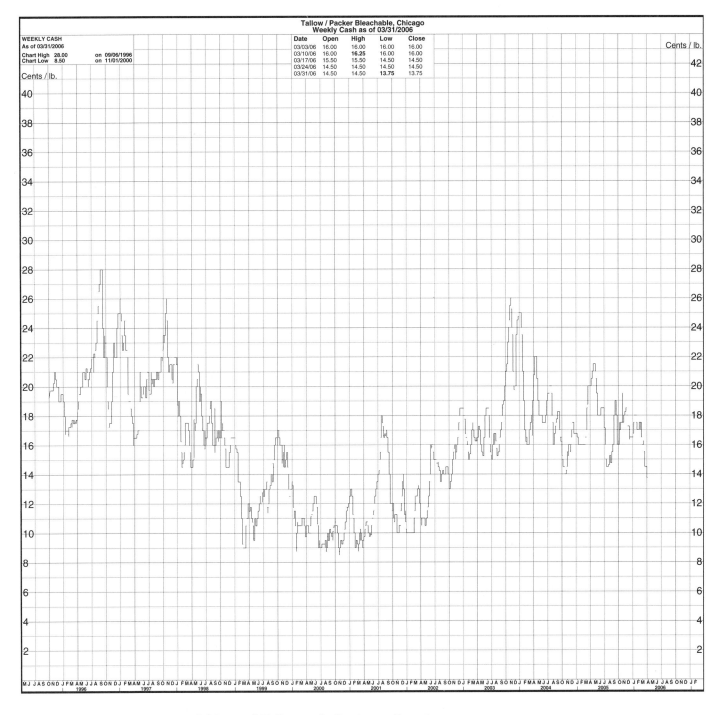

Quarterly High, Low and Close of Tallow   In Cents per Pound

Quarter	High	Low	Close	Quarter	High	Low	Close	Quarter	High	Low	Close
09/1996	28.00	21.00	22.00	12/1999	17.00	12.50	13.00	03/2003	18.50	15.00	16.25
12/1996	25.00	17.25	25.00	03/2000	13.50	8.75	9.75	06/2003	18.50	15.25	15.25
03/1997	26.00	17.50	17.50	06/2000	12.50	9.00	9.00	09/2003	20.25	15.00	20.25
06/1997	21.00	16.00	21.00	09/2000	10.50	8.75	10.50	12/2003	26.00	19.75	25.00
09/1997	22.00	19.50	22.00	12/2000	12.00	8.50	12.00	03/2004	25.00	16.00	19.00
12/1997	26.00	20.25	21.50	03/2001	13.00	8.75	9.00	06/2004	22.00	17.50	19.50
03/1998	22.00	14.50	15.00	06/2001	13.50	9.50	13.50	09/2004	20.00	15.25	15.25
06/1998	21.50	14.50	17.00	09/2001	18.00	12.00	12.00	12/2004	17.50	14.00	16.75
09/1998	19.00	15.50	17.00	12/2001	14.00	10.00	10.25	03/2005	20.00	16.00	20.00
12/1998	19.00	14.50	16.50	03/2002	13.25	10.00	12.00	06/2005	21.50	17.13	17.13
03/1999	16.50	9.00	12.00	06/2002	16.00	10.50	15.00	09/2005	19.00	14.50	16.00
06/1999	12.50	9.50	12.50	09/2002	15.00	13.50	14.00	12/2005	19.50	16.00	16.50
09/1999	16.50	11.37	16.50	12/2002	18.50	13.00	18.50	03/2006	18.00	13.75	13.75

Source: U.S. Department of Agriculture

METALS

Gold

Gold has earned its place in history as the world's most popular metal for using as a store of value. While modern currencies are no longer linked to gold, gold continues to be a precious metal that investors seek as a store of value and as a hedge against inflation. There is also strong demand for gold for jewelry and minor demand for industrial and dental purposes.

Current Gold Outlook

Gold prices doubled in value from 2001 through early 2006. Gold prices traded as low as $257 per ounce in early 2001, but then entered a steady rally up to $452 by late 2004. That rally was driven mainly by the 33% plunge in the US dollar index over that time frame. The plunge in the dollar increased the value of real assets such as gold in terms of the depreciated currency. The rally in gold was also driven by stagnant gold mine production in 2000-03 and a -6.2% yr/yr decline in production in 2004. Gold mine production showed a slight +0.8% recovery in 2005.

Gold in the first half of 2005 traded basically sideways in the range of $400-450. Gold was pressured in early 2005 by the recovery rally seen in the dollar in 2005. However, gold prices then soared in late 2005 and early 2006 to hit a 25-year high of $582.00 on March 31, 2006.

Gold prices were driven higher in late 2005 and early 2006 by strong fundamental demand and speculative buying. Gold demand in 2005 hit a record $53.7 billion, according to the World Gold Council. In 2005, investment demand rose +26%, jewelry demand rose +14%, and net inflows into ETF funds totaled 203 metric tons ($3 billion). The strong investment demand stemmed from both speculative fever and from inflation fears in light of sharply higher crude oil prices.

The recent 25-year high of $582.00 per ounce was still $268 below the record high of $850.00 seen on January 21, 1980 (London gold PM fix). Moreover the recent high of $582.00 is only about one-quarter of the record high of $2,169 per ounce when that record high of $850.00 is translated into inflation-adjusted 2006 dollars by using the Jan-2006 CPI as the base to deflate the gold series.

Gold prices during Bretton Woods (1945-71)

During the Bretton Woods period of 1945-1971, gold was fixed at about $35 per ounce. Bretton Woods was the global currency management system that fixed global currencies in terms of the dollar and also fixed gold in terms of the dollar at $35 per ounce. However, President Nixon on August 15, 1971 announced that the US Government would no longer convert dollars into gold. That was the end of the Bretton Woods system, and currency rates and gold prices have since floated freely.

Gold soars in the 1970s

After Bretton Woods broke down and gold started to trade freely, gold prices started to rally sharply. Gold prices were driven higher mainly by the sharp inflation pressures that emerged from (1) deficit spending for President Johnson's Great Society and the Vietnam war in the 1960s and early 1970s, (2) the oil spike in 1973 tied to the Arab oil embargo, and (3) monetary mismanagement by the Federal Reserve. The Fed at that time used interest rate targeting and refused to raise interest rates fast enough to curb inflation, trying to avoid a recession. But in the end, the Fed did more harm than good by waiting to curb inflation.

US inflation finally peaked at +14.8% yr/yr in March 1980, shortly after Paul Volcker took over from G. William Miller as Fed Chairman and started clamping down on the money supply. By no coincidence, gold peaked at roughly the same time in January 1980 at $850 (London PM gold fix) and then started a steep descent.

Gold moves lower during the 1980s and 1990s

Fed Chairman Volcker's stiff monetarist medicine took a toll on both the US economy and gold prices. The US economy experienced a double-dip recession in 1980 and 1981-82. Gold sold off sharply during that time as the double-dip recessions caused inflation to fall and caused reduced demand for gold. Gold was also undercut in the first half of the 1980s by the sharp rally in the dollar.

During the latter-half of the 1980s and the first half of the 1990s, gold was relatively stable and traded in the range of $300-500 per ounce. However, gold on an inflation-adjusted basis moved steadily lower from the early 1980s all the way until 2001. On an inflation-adjusted basis (in Jan 2006 dollars), gold fell from the peak of $2,169 in 1980, to $575 in 1990, and then to a 35-year low of $291 in 2001.

Gold was also pressured over this time frame by heavy selling by central banks. Confidence in the world's paper currencies has grown to the extent that gold has become somewhat an anachronism and has become an expensive proposition for the central banks to support. In fact, according to the World Gold Council, the world's central banks as a whole have slashed their ownership of gold by 18% from a peak of 38,300 metric tons in 1965 to the current level of 31,400 metric tons, which is the lowest level since about 1950. During the disinflationary 1980s and 1990s, the heavy selling by central banks forced gold prices lower. However, more recently, the strong demand seen in the marketplace has been able to absorb continued central bank selling.

The plunge in inflation-adjusted gold prices from 1980 through 2001 demoralized gold investors, and perhaps more importantly, mining companies. Gold mining almost doubled during the 1980s, but has been stagnant since 1990. Mining companies refused to invest the large amount of capital needed to open new mines because of low prices and rising mining expenses. Thus, by the time demand started to re-emerge in 2001, mining companies were caught flat-footed without the ability to boost supply to take advantage of higher prices. In fact, four years into the gold rally, there has still been no appreciable increase in gold mining output. Mining companies will slowly boost their production to extract the value from their gold reserves that remain in the ground, but that will take time. In the meantime, strong demand is snapping up scarce supply and driving gold prices sharply higher.

Silver

Silver, like gold, has also been a store of value and a medium of exchange for thousands of years. However, silver has more importance as a metal for use in photography and industrial applications. Data from the Silver Institute for 2004 shows that the bulk of silver supply goes to industrial applications (367 million ounces), photography (181 million ounces), and jewelry and silverware (248 million ounces). Only 41 million ounces goes for silver coins and medals, and another 41 million ounces for implied net investment. Silver therefore trades not only as a precious metal, but also as an industrial metal. The strength of the world economy and industrial demand is therefore an important demand driver for silver prices.

On the supply side, mining companies have steadily raised silver mining capacity, thus keeping the market supplied with silver. Since 1980, world silver mining production has risen by about 10,000 metric tons to the record high of 19,700 metric tons in 2004.

Silver in any case has been caught up in the metal buying frenzy. Industrial demand for silver has been strong, particularly from China. Moreover, investment and jewelry demand has also been strong. In addition, silver prices were driven higher in early 2006 by speculation that Barclay's would soon win approval for its silver Exchange Traded Fund (ETF), which would require Barclay's to purchase a large amount of physical silver.

New York cash silver prices soared in late 2005 and early 2006, reaching a 22-year high of $11.92 on March 31, 2006. That was the highest level seen since late 1983. However, that is far below the record high of $48.00 (NY daily close) that was posted back in January 1980. That high was equivalent to $122 per ounce in current 2006 dollars (using the Jan-2006 CPI as the base to deflate the silver series), which means the current price of silver in inflation-adjusted terms is less than one-tenth of the extreme level reached in 1980.

Silver was driven to that record high by the same inflation-driven fundamentals that caused the surge in gold prices. However, silver was also pushed sharply higher by Nelson Bunker Hunt's infamous attempt to corner the silver market. The Hunt family and a group of wealthy Arabs in 1973 started amassing more than 200 million ounces of silver, amounting to about one-half of the world's deliverable supply. However, the silver market then crashed when the New York Metals Exchange changed its trading rules and the Federal Reserve intervened. Nelson Bunker Hunt eventually filed for bankruptcy and was convicted of manipulating the markets.

Gold/silver ratio

When silver surged to a peak in January 1980, silver also reached a near-record value relative to gold. The gold/silver ratio fell to 17.1, which was lowest ratio seen since the post-war record low of 16.7 was posted in June 1968. However, when precious metals prices crashed from the January 1980 peak, silver sold off by much more than gold, and the gold/silver ratio rose sharply. The trend toward relative strength in gold stayed in place throughout the 1980s and early-1990s, when the gold/silver ratio moved sharply higher to a record peak of 98.8 in Feb 1991. Silver then regained ground against gold during the 1990s. The current gold/silver ratio of 48.8 shows that silver is currently close to its strongest level relative to gold in 20 years, illustrating silver's current popularity as both a precious metal and an industrial metal.

ALUMINUM

Annual High, Low and Close of Aluminum   In Cents per Pound

Year	High	Low	Close	Year	High	Low	Close	Year	High	Low	Close
1929	.2390	.2390	.2390	1942	.1500	.1500	.1500	1955	.2442	.2220	.2440
1930	.2430	.2330	.2330	1943	.1500	.1500	.1500	1956	.2710	.2440	.2710
1931	.2330	.2330	.2330	1944	.1500	.1500	.1500	1957	.2710	.2600	.2600
1932	.2330	.2330	.2330	1945	.1500	.1500	.1500	1958	.2600	.2400	.2470
1933	.2330	.2330	.2330	1946	.1500	.1500	.1500	1959	.2600	.2470	.2600
1934	.2330	.2050	.2050	1947	.1500	.1500	.1500	1960	.2600	.2600	.2600
1935	.2050	.2050	.2050	1948	.1500	.1500	.1500	1961	.2600	.2400	.2400
1936	.2050	.2050	.2050	1949	.1500	.1500	.1500	1962	.2400	.2250	.2250
1937	.2050	.2000	.2000	1950	.1500	.1500	.1500	1963	.2300	.2250	.2300
1938	.2000	.2000	.2000	1951	.1900	.1900	.1900	1964	.2450	.2300	.2450
1939	.2000	.2000	.2000	1952	.2000	.1900	.2000	1965	.2450	.2450	.2450
1940	.2000	.1700	.1700	1953	.2150	.2000	.2150	1966	.2450	.2450	.2450
1941	.1700	.1500	.1500	1954	.2220	.2150	.2220	1967	.2500	.2450	.2500

Source: New York Mercantile Exchange

ALUMINUM

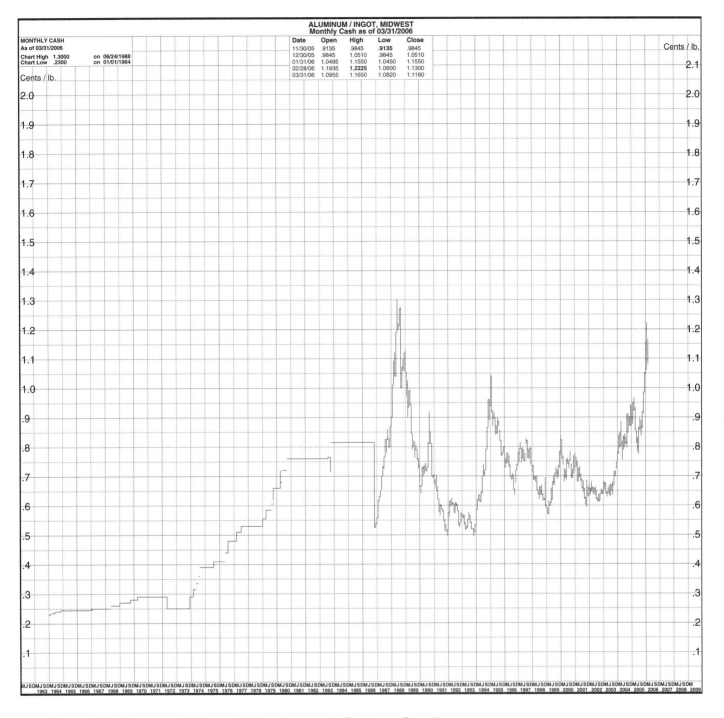

Annual High, Low and Close of Aluminum   In Cents per Pound

Year	High	Low	Close	Year	High	Low	Close	Year	High	Low	Close
1968	.2600	.2500	.2600	1981	.7600	.7600	.7600	1994	.9600	.5325	.9400
1969	.2800	.2600	.2800	1982	.7600	.7600	.7600	1995	1.0400	.7700	.7975
1970	.2900	.2800	.2900	1983	.8150	.7160	.8150	1996	.7975	.6350	.7400
1971	.2900	.2900	.2900	1984	.8150	.8150	.8150	1997	.8275	.7350	.7400
1972	.2900	.2500	.2500	1985	.8150	.8150	.8150	1998	.7350	.5950	.6000
1973	.2900	.2500	.2900	1986	.8150	.5250	.5400	1999	.7835	.5700	.7835
1974	.3900	.2900	.3900	1987	.8700	.5350	.8700	2000	.8385	.6800	.7465
1975	.4100	.3900	.4100	1988	1.3000	.8700	1.1200	2001	.7760	.5955	.6365
1976	.4800	.4100	.4800	1989	1.1300	.7250	.7350	2002	.6815	.6110	.6390
1977	.5300	.4800	.5300	1990	.9200	.6400	.7025	2003	.7470	.6290	.7460
1978	.5300	.5300	.5300	1991	.7075	.4963	.5175	2004	.9425	.7475	.9425
1979	.6600	.5300	.6600	1992	.6225	.5125	.5713	2005	1.0510	.7750	1.0510
1980	.7600	.6600	.7600	1993	.5763	.4950	.5325	2006	1.2225	1.0450	1.1180

Source: New York Mercantile Exchange

ALUMINUM

Quarterly High, Low and Close of Aluminum Futures   In Cents per Pound

Quarter	High	Low	Close	Quarter	High	Low	Close	Quarter	High	Low	Close
09/1996	.7100	.6550	.6550	12/1999	.7910	.6975	.7910	03/2003	.6840	.6385	.6410
12/1996	.7400	.6350	.7400	03/2000	.8375	.7350	.7350	06/2003	.6680	.6280	.6355
03/1997	.8150	.7350	.7925	06/2000	.7590	.6825	.7500	09/2003	.6815	.6310	.6705
06/1997	.7975	.7450	.7525	09/2000	.7835	.7285	.7580	12/2003	.7540	.6730	.7490
09/1997	.8275	.7500	.7900	12/2000	.7695	.6950	.7460	03/2004	.8465	.7510	.8270
12/1997	.7950	.7400	.7400	03/2001	.7760	.6860	.6860	06/2004	.8880	.7530	.8280
03/1998	.7350	.6875	.6950	06/2001	.7325	.6805	.6865	09/2004	.8950	.7960	.8950
06/1998	.7000	.6350	.6375	09/2001	.6890	.6220	.6310	12/2004	.9470	.8350	.9470
09/1998	.6700	.6200	.6350	12/2001	.6850	.5960	.6395	03/2005	.9700	.8725	.9420
12/1998	.6950	.5950	.6000	03/2002	.6965	.6330	.6620	06/2005	.9430	.7900	.7955
03/1999	.6150	.5700	.6150	06/2002	.6690	.6345	.6560	09/2005	.9010	.7750	.8730
06/1999	.6795	.6110	.6785	09/2002	.6515	.6110	.6160	12/2005	1.0595	.8700	1.0595
09/1999	.7345	.6670	.7315	12/2002	.6615	.6150	.6420	03/2006	1.2290	1.0500	1.1250

Source: New York Mercantile Exchange

ALUMINUM

Quarterly High, Low and Close of Aluminum   In Cents per Pound

Quarter	High	Low	Close	Quarter	High	Low	Close	Quarter	High	Low	Close
09/1996	.7100	.6550	.6550	12/1999	.7835	.6900	.7835	03/2003	.6825	.6380	.6405
12/1996	.7400	.6350	.7400	03/2000	.8385	.7395	.7395	06/2003	.6660	.6290	.6355
03/1997	.8150	.7350	.7925	06/2000	.7580	.6800	.7500	09/2003	.6810	.6310	.6675
06/1997	.7975	.7450	.7525	09/2000	.7835	.7260	.7540	12/2003	.7470	.6695	.7460
09/1997	.8275	.7500	.7900	12/2000	.7695	.6920	.7465	03/2004	.8465	.7475	.8000
12/1997	.7950	.7400	.7400	03/2001	.7760	.6820	.6820	06/2004	.8865	.7530	.8280
03/1998	.7350	.6875	.6950	06/2001	.7325	.6805	.6865	09/2004	.9095	.7960	.9095
06/1998	.7000	.6350	.6375	09/2001	.6890	.6220	.6250	12/2004	.9425	.8460	.9425
09/1998	.6700	.6200	.6350	12/2001	.6850	.5955	.6365	03/2005	.9655	.8685	.9440
12/1998	.6950	.5950	.6000	03/2002	.6815	.6320	.6600	06/2005	.9350	.7830	.7955
03/1999	.6150	.5700	.6150	06/2002	.6630	.6340	.6560	09/2005	.8980	.7750	.8660
06/1999	.6800	.5975	.6800	09/2002	.6515	.6110	.6130	12/2005	1.0510	.8630	1.0510
09/1999	.7300	.6700	.7200	12/2002	.6570	.6140	.6390	03/2006	1.2225	1.0450	1.1180

Source: New York Mercantile Exchange

ALUMINUM

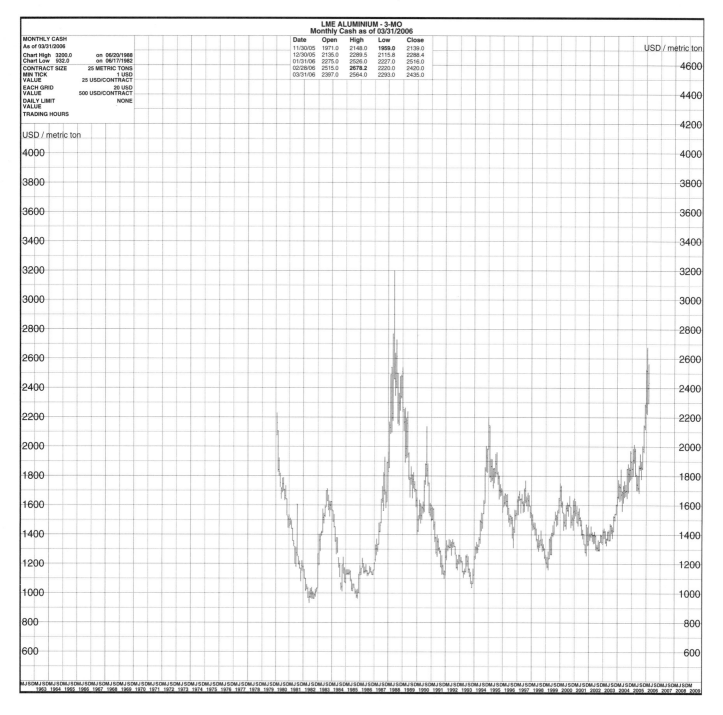

Annual High, Low and Close of Aluminum   In Dollars per Metric Ton

Year	High	Low	Close	Year	High	Low	Close	Year	High	Low	Close
1980	2,230.0	1,445.2	1,508.7	1989	2,540.0	1,587.0	1,630.0	1998	1,546.0	1,237.0	1,245.0
1981	1,605.4	1,079.2	1,181.6	1990	2,138.0	1,405.0	1,568.0	1999	1,651.0	1,158.0	1,650.0
1982	1,193.2	932.0	1,029.0	1991	1,605.0	1,097.0	1,150.0	2000	1,752.0	1,428.0	1,554.0
1983	1,711.8	1,035.2	1,621.9	1992	1,370.5	1,124.0	1,259.5	2001	1,649.0	1,255.0	1,355.0
1984	1,623.9	1,010.6	1,074.3	1993	1,267.0	1,037.0	1,124.0	2002	1,465.0	1,289.0	1,350.0
1985	1,162.6	961.9	1,129.7	1994	2,005.0	1,124.0	1,981.0	2003	1,607.0	1,324.0	1,600.0
1986	1,241.0	1,115.0	1,157.7	1995	2,194.0	1,640.0	1,706.0	2004	1,972.0	1,558.0	1,958.0
1987	1,930.0	1,157.1	1,892.0	1996	1,699.0	1,309.0	1,546.0	2005	2,289.5	1,681.0	2,288.4
1988	3,200.0	1,830.0	2,475.0	1997	1,770.0	1,514.0	1,552.0	2006	2,678.2	2,220.0	2,435.0

Source: London Metals Exchange

ALUMINUM

Quarterly High, Low and Close of Aluminum In Dollars per Metric Ton

Quarter	High	Low	Close	Quarter	High	Low	Close	Quarter	High	Low	Close
09/1996	1,540.0	1,377.0	1,377.5	12/1999	1,651.0	1,457.0	1,650.0	03/2003	1,444.0	1,335.0	1,346.0
12/1996	1,571.0	1,309.0	1,546.0	03/2000	1,752.0	1,548.0	1,549.5	06/2003	1,432.0	1,324.0	1,365.0
03/1997	1,698.0	1,533.0	1,642.0	06/2000	1,601.0	1,428.0	1,582.0	09/2003	1,475.0	1,359.0	1,420.5
06/1997	1,677.0	1,545.0	1,598.0	09/2000	1,664.0	1,525.0	1,595.5	12/2003	1,607.0	1,420.0	1,600.0
09/1997	1,770.0	1,555.0	1,644.0	12/2000	1,635.0	1,429.5	1,554.0	03/2004	1,775.0	1,594.0	1,724.0
12/1997	1,688.0	1,514.0	1,552.0	03/2001	1,649.0	1,481.0	1,487.0	06/2004	1,847.0	1,558.0	1,722.0
03/1998	1,546.0	1,430.0	1,447.0	06/2001	1,581.0	1,458.0	1,462.0	09/2004	1,850.0	1,645.0	1,845.5
06/1998	1,482.0	1,306.0	1,324.0	09/2001	1,500.0	1,334.0	1,339.0	12/2004	1,972.0	1,685.0	1,958.0
09/1998	1,430.0	1,285.0	1,331.0	12/2001	1,471.0	1,255.0	1,355.0	03/2005	2,015.0	1,782.0	1,970.0
12/1998	1,374.0	1,237.0	1,245.0	03/2002	1,465.0	1,328.0	1,403.0	06/2005	1,990.0	1,700.0	1,719.5
03/1999	1,287.0	1,158.0	1,235.0	06/2002	1,422.0	1,338.0	1,388.0	09/2005	1,951.0	1,681.0	1,851.0
06/1999	1,414.5	1,235.0	1,396.5	09/2002	1,398.0	1,289.0	1,295.0	12/2005	2,289.5	1,843.8	2,288.4
09/1999	1,558.0	1,385.0	1,513.0	12/2002	1,402.0	1,289.0	1,350.0	03/2006	2,678.2	2,220.0	2,435.0

Source: London Metals Exchange

COPPER

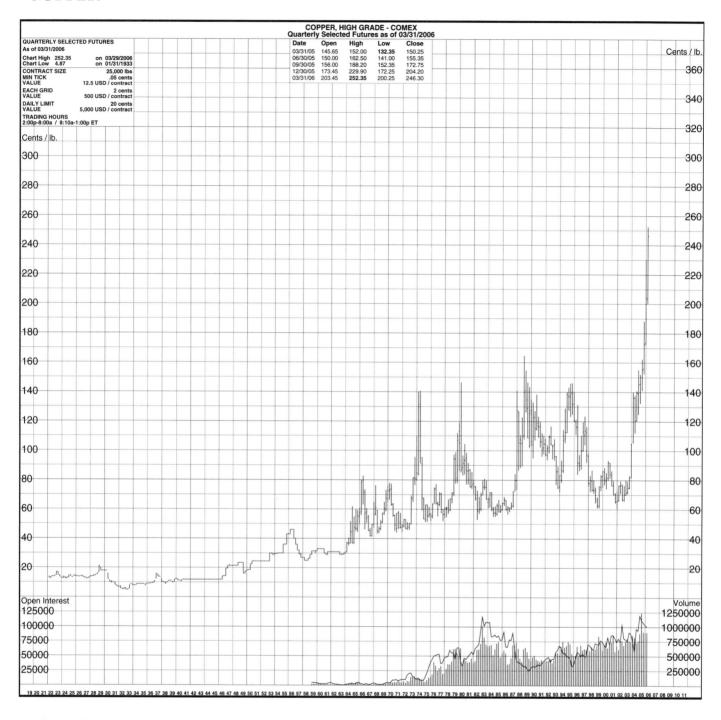

Annual High, Low and Close of Copper Futures   In Cents per Pound

Year	High	Low	Close	Year	High	Low	Close	Year	High	Low	Close
1929	21.26	16.72	17.87	1942	11.87	11.87	11.87	1955	43.00	30.00	43.00
1930	17.87	9.70	10.49	1943	11.87	11.87	11.87	1956	46.00	36.00	36.00
1931	10.02	6.67	6.72	1944	11.87	11.87	11.87	1957	36.00	27.00	27.00
1932	7.21	4.91	4.91	1945	11.87	11.87	11.87	1958	29.00	25.00	29.00
1933	8.87	4.87	8.00	1946	19.37	11.87	19.37	1959	35.35	27.44	31.68
1934	8.87	7.87	8.87	1947	22.19	19.45	21.37	1960	35.00	27.50	27.71
1935	9.12	7.87	9.12	1948	23.50	21.50	23.50	1961	32.60	26.67	30.21
1936	10.89	9.12	10.89	1949	23.50	16.00	18.50	1962	31.05	27.95	28.77
1937	15.87	10.11	10.11	1950	24.50	18.50	24.50	1963	30.59	28.67	30.50
1938	11.12	8.87	11.12	1951	24.50	24.50	24.50	1964	61.80	30.40	36.95
1939	12.37	9.87	12.37	1952	24.50	24.50	24.50	1965	60.85	36.25	57.25
1940	12.09	10.69	11.87	1953	30.00	24.50	29.50	1966	82.75	46.25	53.90
1941	11.87	11.87	11.87	1954	30.00	29.50	30.00	1967	64.90	41.40	56.50

Source: New York Mercantile Exchange

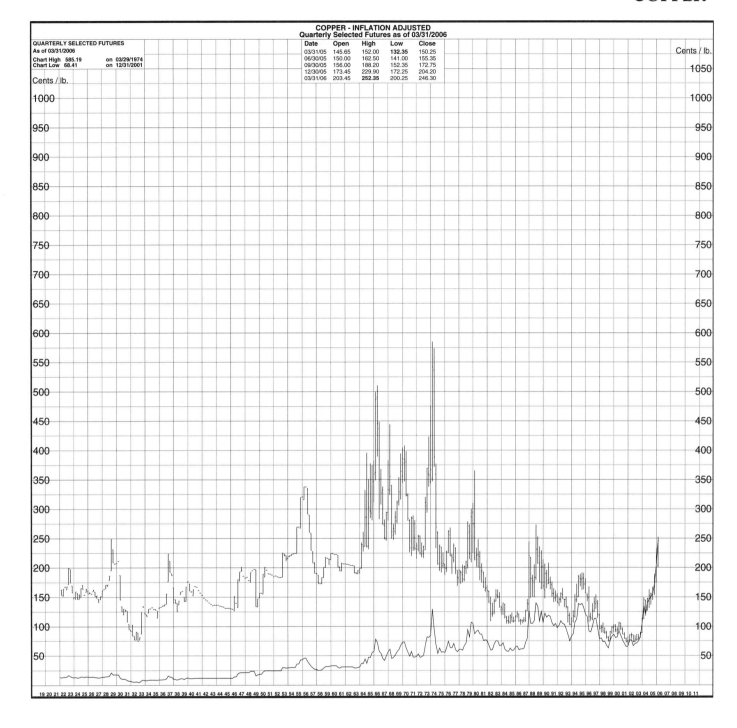

COPPER

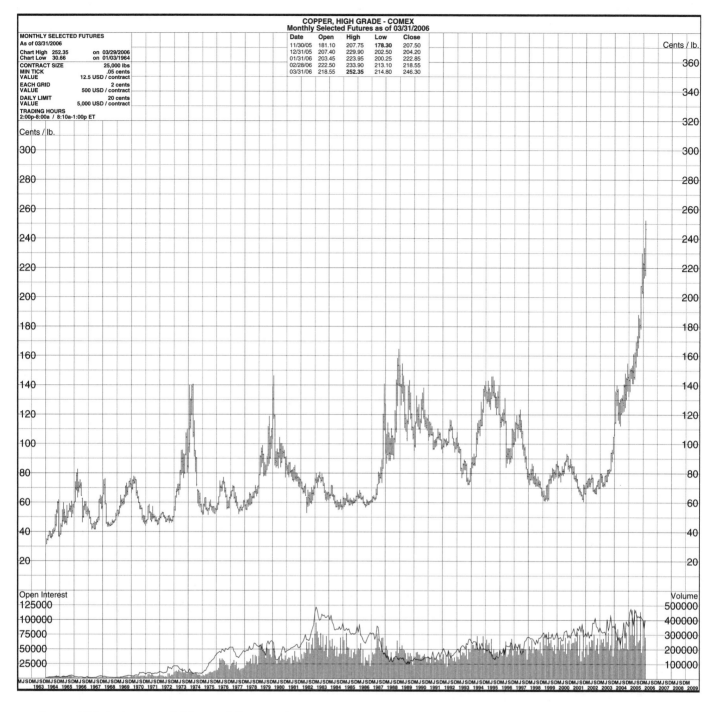

Annual High, Low and Close of Copper Futures   In Cents per Pound

Year	High	Low	Close	Year	High	Low	Close	Year	High	Low	Close
1968	76.30	43.30	50.80	1981	91.70	70.40	75.70	1994	140.00	78.50	138.60
1969	76.40	50.50	72.75	1982	76.10	52.80	69.65	1995	146.10	120.00	120.55
1970	78.00	45.05	48.90	1983	80.90	60.75	67.00	1996	131.40	83.90	100.25
1971	58.70	44.05	48.75	1984	71.80	54.90	57.20	1997	123.60	76.10	78.10
1972	53.40	45.85	50.25	1985	66.55	55.70	64.15	1998	86.70	64.40	67.20
1973	109.90	49.85	84.80	1986	68.55	56.60	61.15	1999	86.40	60.90	86.30
1974	140.70	53.20	53.60	1987	141.00	60.05	127.40	2000	93.40	74.10	84.30
1975	63.20	51.30	55.30	1988	164.75	86.50	139.75	2001	86.40	60.50	65.90
1976	77.30	53.80	63.20	1989	154.75	101.95	106.40	2002	79.45	65.65	70.25
1977	71.80	51.90	60.30	1990	138.40	95.00	116.85	2003	105.10	70.00	104.55
1978	71.75	54.70	71.05	1991	119.70	96.05	97.55	2004	155.00	105.40	145.25
1979	119.00	69.25	105.20	1992	116.70	93.70	103.60	2005	229.90	132.35	204.20
1980	146.50	77.05	86.55	1993	108.00	72.00	83.30	2006	252.35	200.25	246.30

Source: New York Mercantile Exchange

COPPER

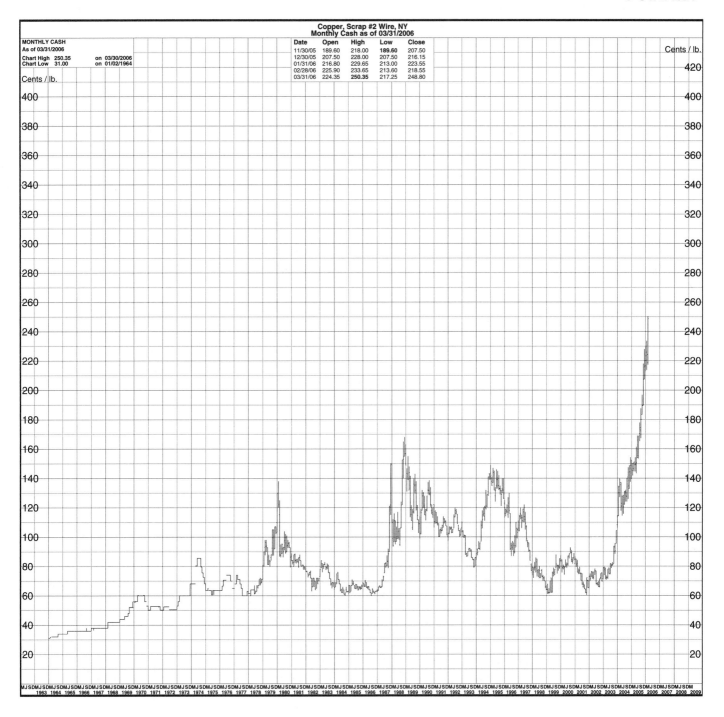

Annual High, Low and Close of Copper   In Cents per Pound

Year	High	Low	Close	Year	High	Low	Close	Year	High	Low	Close
1968	42.00	38.00	42.00	1981	89.00	78.00	78.00	1994	143.00	84.50	143.00
1969	56.00	42.00	52.00	1982	79.00	63.00	72.00	1995	149.00	121.00	126.00
1970	60.25	53.00	53.00	1983	84.00	65.00	68.00	1996	130.00	87.00	103.00
1971	53.00	50.00	50.25	1984	76.00	60.00	63.00	1997	122.00	77.00	77.00
1972	52.52	50.25	50.50	1985	71.00	61.00	66.50	1998	86.00	65.00	66.00
1973	68.10	50.50	68.10	1986	70.50	60.00	63.25	1999	88.00	61.00	85.25
1974	85.60	68.00	68.60	1987	150.00	62.50	150.00	2000	92.85	74.20	84.65
1975	68.60	60.60	63.60	1988	168.00	93.50	156.75	2001	86.70	60.40	65.30
1976	74.00	63.60	65.00	1989	163.00	102.75	109.00	2002	78.35	65.30	69.70
1977	74.00	60.00	63.00	1990	138.65	99.12	120.00	2003	104.30	70.90	104.30
1978	72.00	60.00	71.25	1991	122.00	100.25	101.25	2004	154.25	106.25	148.70
1979	107.00	71.25	103.00	1992	120.00	97.44	105.50	2005	228.00	139.50	216.15
1980	138.00	79.25	86.25	1993	110.50	79.00	86.00	2006	250.35	213.00	248.80

Source: New York Mercantile Exchange

COPPER

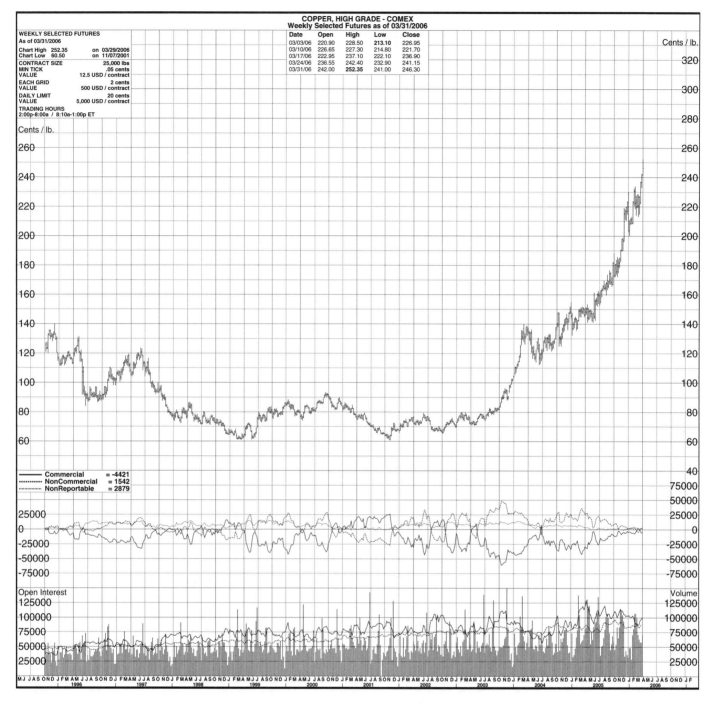

Quarterly High, Low and Close of Copper Futures   In Cents per Pound

Quarter	High	Low	Close	Quarter	High	Low	Close	Quarter	High	Low	Close
09/1996	97.20	86.40	90.10	12/1999	86.40	75.20	86.30	03/2003	79.85	70.00	71.45
12/1996	110.40	87.45	100.25	03/2000	88.50	76.90	80.50	06/2003	79.30	70.70	74.80
03/1997	119.60	99.50	113.00	06/2000	85.10	74.10	81.55	09/2003	83.20	74.25	81.85
06/1997	123.60	104.00	113.65	09/2000	93.40	80.05	92.05	12/2003	105.10	81.75	104.55
09/1997	116.50	92.00	97.00	12/2000	92.00	81.30	84.30	03/2004	139.85	105.40	136.00
12/1997	98.20	76.10	78.10	03/2001	86.40	76.30	76.40	06/2004	137.70	112.15	120.50
03/1998	83.15	72.20	79.85	06/2001	79.60	70.20	70.45	09/2004	140.80	120.50	139.60
06/1998	86.70	72.60	73.35	09/2001	71.50	64.40	65.20	12/2004	155.00	124.80	145.25
09/1998	80.30	71.05	73.75	12/2001	72.55	60.50	65.90	03/2005	152.00	132.35	150.25
12/1998	75.40	64.40	67.20	03/2002	76.60	65.65	76.35	06/2005	162.50	141.00	155.35
03/1999	68.50	60.90	62.75	06/2002	79.45	70.75	76.75	09/2005	188.20	152.35	172.75
06/1999	76.10	61.10	75.95	09/2002	77.20	65.95	66.60	12/2005	229.90	172.25	204.20
09/1999	83.85	72.85	82.65	12/2002	76.30	65.70	70.25	03/2006	252.35	200.25	246.30

Source: New York Mercantile Exchange

COPPER

Quarterly High, Low and Close of Copper   In Cents per Pound

Quarter	High	Low	Close	Quarter	High	Low	Close	Quarter	High	Low	Close
09/1996	97.00	87.00	94.00	12/1999	85.25	75.00	85.25	03/2003	79.50	71.25	71.25
12/1996	110.00	89.00	103.00	03/2000	87.50	75.75	80.00	06/2003	78.75	70.90	74.80
03/1997	120.00	104.00	115.00	06/2000	84.60	74.20	81.55	09/2003	82.75	74.60	81.30
06/1997	122.00	106.00	114.00	09/2000	92.85	80.35	91.55	12/2003	104.30	81.85	104.30
09/1997	117.00	93.00	96.00	12/2000	90.95	81.85	84.65	03/2004	139.45	106.25	135.55
12/1997	96.00	77.00	77.00	03/2001	86.70	75.85	75.85	06/2004	137.10	114.45	120.50
03/1998	83.00	72.00	79.00	06/2001	79.50	70.45	70.45	09/2004	140.00	122.00	140.00
06/1998	86.00	73.00	73.00	09/2001	75.00	64.60	64.60	12/2004	154.25	125.75	148.70
09/1998	80.00	72.00	73.00	12/2001	72.20	60.40	65.30	03/2005	152.35	139.50	151.05
12/1998	74.00	65.00	66.00	03/2002	76.60	65.30	76.05	06/2005	168.95	143.35	155.35
03/1999	68.00	61.00	62.00	06/2002	78.35	71.00	76.75	09/2005	187.65	153.65	180.15
06/1999	76.00	62.00	76.00	09/2002	76.80	66.00	66.00	12/2005	228.00	183.40	216.15
09/1999	88.00	73.00	82.00	12/2002	75.65	65.60	69.70	03/2006	250.35	213.00	248.80

Source: New York Mercantile Exchange

COPPER

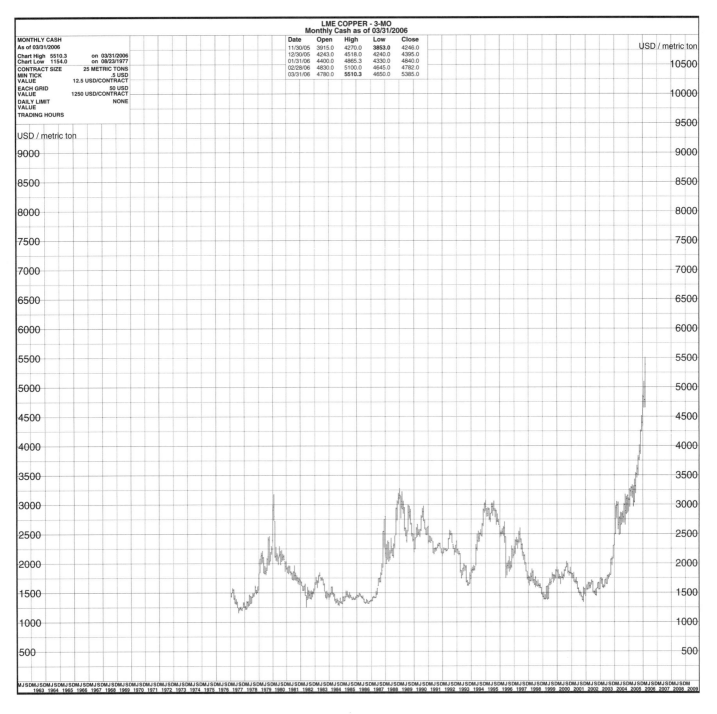

Annual High, Low and Close of Copper   In Dollars per Metric Ton

Year	High	Low	Close	Year	High	Low	Close	Year	High	Low	Close
1977	1,579.0	1,154.0	1,309.0	1987	2,750.0	1,356.0	2,750.0	1997	2,608.0	1,720.0	1,747.0
1978	1,620.0	1,210.0	1,604.0	1988	3,200.0	1,995.0	3,125.0	1998	1,905.0	1,466.0	1,485.0
1979	2,466.0	1,546.0	2,242.0	1989	3,280.0	2,353.0	2,400.0	1999	1,890.0	1,376.0	1,880.5
1980	3,181.0	1,856.0	1,949.0	1990	2,980.0	2,197.0	2,610.0	2000	2,036.0	1,639.0	1,833.0
1981	2,041.0	1,630.0	1,727.0	1991	2,640.0	2,160.0	2,193.0	2001	1,845.0	1,336.0	1,483.0
1982	1,713.0	1,250.0	1,538.0	1992	2,570.0	2,119.0	2,310.3	2002	1,719.0	1,440.0	1,560.0
1983	1,847.0	1,387.0	1,464.0	1993	2,392.0	1,613.0	1,785.0	2003	2,303.0	1,557.0	2,301.0
1984	1,603.0	1,274.0	1,318.0	1994	3,030.0	1,736.0	3,023.0	2004	3,179.5	2,307.0	3,150.0
1985	1,535.0	1,305.0	1,426.0	1995	3,072.0	2,650.0	2,657.0	2005	4,518.0	2,875.0	4,395.0
1986	1,500.0	1,313.0	1,369.0	1996	2,710.0	1,745.0	2,127.0	2006	5,510.3	4,330.0	5,385.0

Source: London Metals Exchange

COPPER

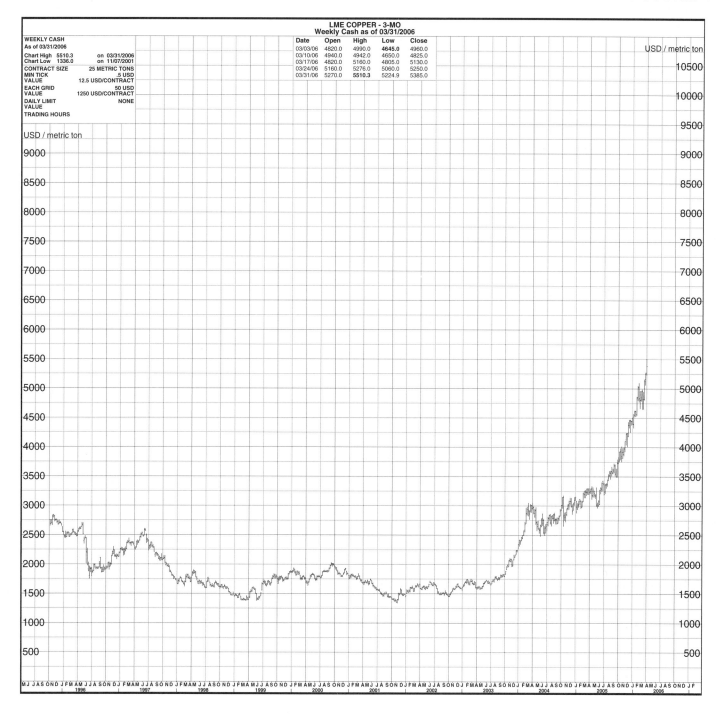

Quarterly High, Low and Close of Copper   In Dollars per Metric Ton

Quarter	High	Low	Close	Quarter	High	Low	Close	Quarter	High	Low	Close
09/1996	2,115.0	1,790.0	1,928.0	12/1999	1,890.0	1,666.0	1,880.5	03/2003	1,755.0	1,557.0	1,590.5
12/1996	2,300.0	1,886.0	2,127.0	03/2000	1,940.0	1,726.0	1,761.0	06/2003	1,738.0	1,571.0	1,655.0
03/1997	2,445.0	2,136.0	2,372.0	06/2000	1,851.0	1,639.0	1,790.0	09/2003	1,834.0	1,640.0	1,798.0
06/1997	2,608.0	2,245.0	2,422.0	09/2000	2,036.0	1,761.0	1,997.0	12/2003	2,303.0	1,798.0	2,301.0
09/1997	2,420.0	2,053.0	2,133.0	12/2000	1,987.0	1,783.0	1,833.0	03/2004	3,051.0	2,307.0	2,990.0
12/1997	2,150.0	1,720.0	1,747.0	03/2001	1,845.0	1,683.0	1,688.5	06/2004	3,044.0	2,475.0	2,649.0
03/1998	1,833.0	1,616.0	1,771.0	06/2001	1,753.0	1,556.0	1,568.0	09/2004	3,020.0	2,653.0	2,997.5
06/1998	1,905.0	1,625.0	1,636.0	09/2001	1,584.0	1,425.0	1,446.5	12/2004	3,179.5	2,650.0	3,150.0
09/1998	1,776.0	1,585.0	1,626.0	12/2001	1,595.0	1,336.0	1,483.0	03/2005	3,308.0	2,875.0	3,288.0
12/1998	1,654.0	1,466.0	1,485.0	03/2002	1,678.0	1,440.0	1,652.0	06/2005	3,435.0	2,960.0	3,319.0
03/1999	1,509.0	1,376.0	1,394.0	06/2002	1,719.0	1,563.0	1,687.0	09/2005	3,835.0	3,188.0	3,769.5
06/1999	1,650.0	1,377.0	1,569.0	09/2002	1,692.0	1,450.0	1,459.0	12/2005	4,518.0	3,750.0	4,395.0
09/1999	1,840.0	1,618.0	1,792.0	12/2002	1,677.0	1,441.0	1,560.0	03/2006	5,510.3	4,330.0	5,385.0

Source: London Metals Exchange

GOLD

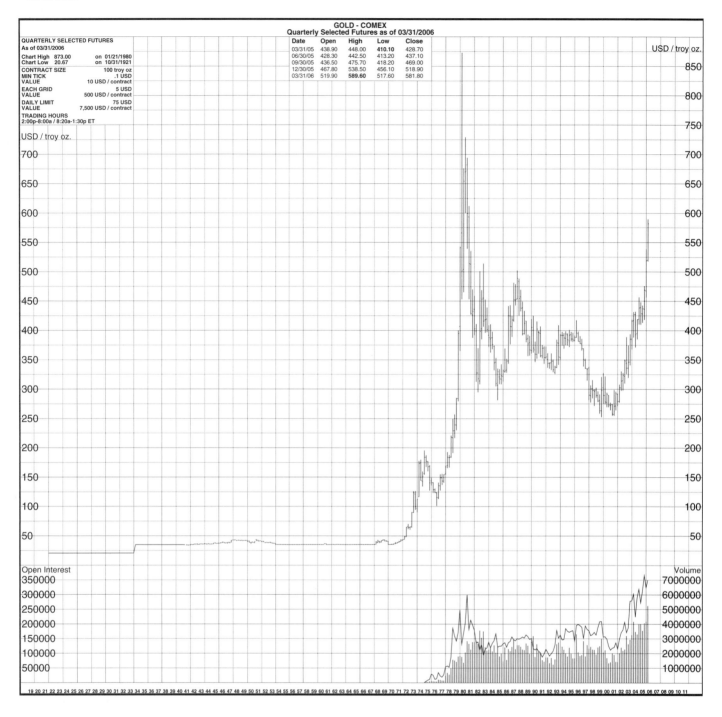

Annual High, Low and Close of Gold — In Dollars per Troy Ounce

Year	High	Low	Close	Year	High	Low	Close	Year	High	Low	Close
1929	20.67	20.67	20.67	1942	36.25	35.00	35.50	1955	35.25	35.15	35.15
1930	20.67	20.67	20.67	1943	36.50	35.50	36.50	1956	35.20	35.15	35.20
1931	20.67	20.67	20.67	1944	36.75	36.00	36.25	1957	35.25	35.15	35.25
1932	20.67	20.67	20.67	1945	38.25	36.25	37.25	1958	35.25	35.25	35.25
1933	20.67	20.67	20.67	1946	39.50	37.75	38.25	1959	35.25	35.25	35.25
1934	35.00	35.00	35.00	1947	43.25	37.50	43.00	1960	36.50	35.20	36.50
1935	35.00	35.00	35.00	1948	43.25	41.50	42.00	1961	36.50	35.15	35.50
1936	35.00	35.00	35.00	1949	42.50	40.50	40.50	1962	35.50	35.20	35.45
1937	35.00	35.00	35.00	1950	41.50	36.50	40.25	1963	35.42	35.25	35.25
1938	35.00	35.00	35.00	1951	44.00	40.00	40.00	1964	35.35	35.25	35.35
1939	35.00	35.00	35.00	1952	40.75	38.15	38.70	1965	35.50	35.28	35.50
1940	35.00	35.00	35.00	1953	39.25	35.25	35.50	1966	35.50	35.30	35.40
1941	35.50	34.25	35.50	1954	35.50	35.25	35.25	1967	35.50	35.27	35.50

Source: New York Mercantile Exchange

GOLD

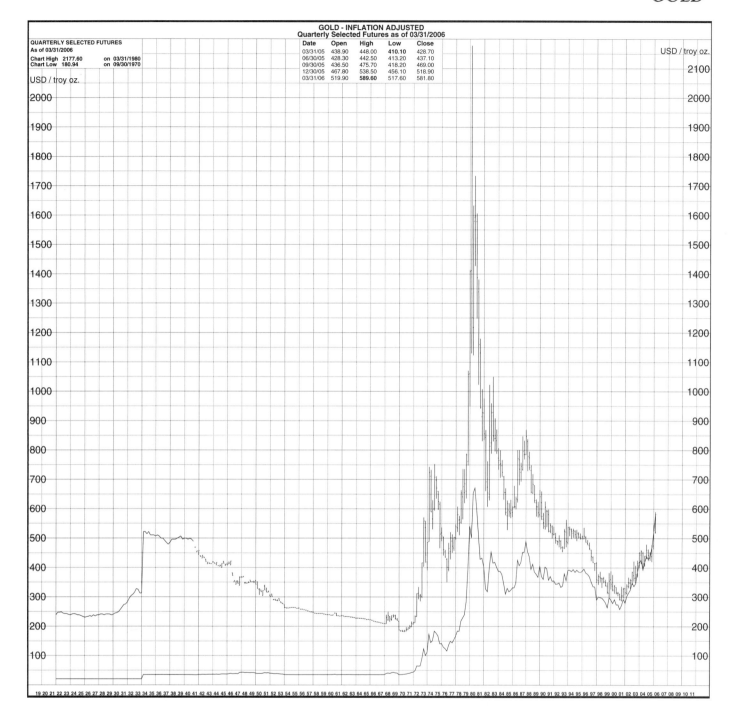

GOLD

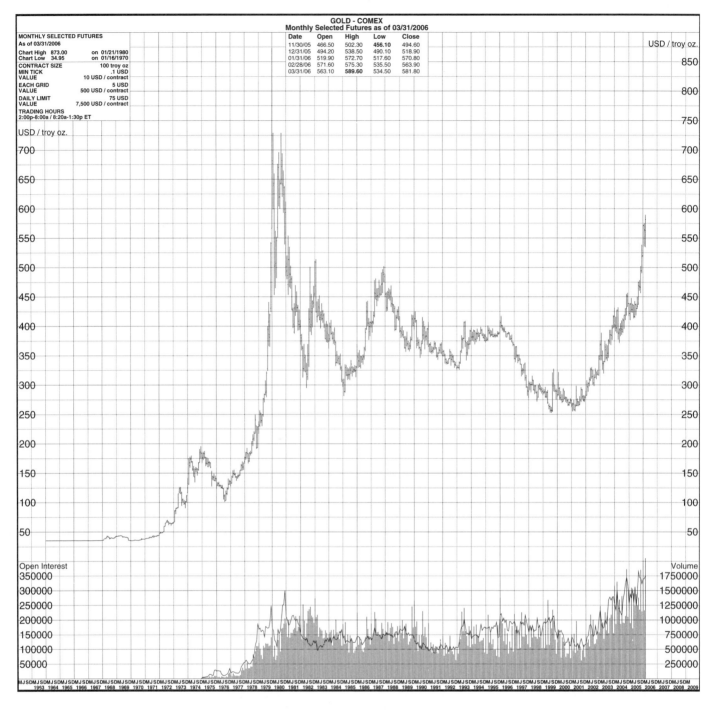

Annual High, Low and Close of Gold Futures   In Dollars per Troy Ounce

Year	High	Low	Close	Year	High	Low	Close	Year	High	Low	Close
1968	43.25	35.85	42.05	1981	612.00	387.50	402.80	1994	398.60	369.10	384.40
1969	44.05	35.20	35.45	1982	501.00	294.70	453.00	1995	401.00	372.00	388.10
1970	39.30	34.95	37.65	1983	514.00	372.00	388.00	1996	417.50	366.00	369.20
1971	44.25	37.70	43.85	1984	410.50	304.70	309.70	1997	369.40	281.50	289.90
1972	70.30	44.30	65.20	1985	342.20	281.20	331.10	1998	315.60	271.60	289.20
1973	126.45	64.20	112.30	1986	443.00	328.00	406.90	1999	327.50	252.50	289.60
1974	195.50	116.80	183.90	1987	502.30	389.00	488.90	2000	322.00	264.40	273.60
1975	187.50	127.40	141.00	1988	488.50	391.80	412.30	2001	298.60	255.00	279.00
1976	141.50	101.00	135.70	1989	419.70	356.50	405.20	2002	350.80	277.20	348.20
1977	169.90	127.50	167.50	1990	425.00	346.00	396.20	2003	418.40	319.30	416.10
1978	249.40	165.50	229.00	1991	406.90	343.00	355.20	2004	456.50	371.30	438.40
1979	543.00	216.60	541.00	1992	361.50	328.90	333.10	2005	538.50	410.10	518.90
1980	873.00	453.00	599.50	1993	409.00	325.80	391.90	2006	589.60	517.60	581.80

Source: New York Mercantile Exchange

GOLD

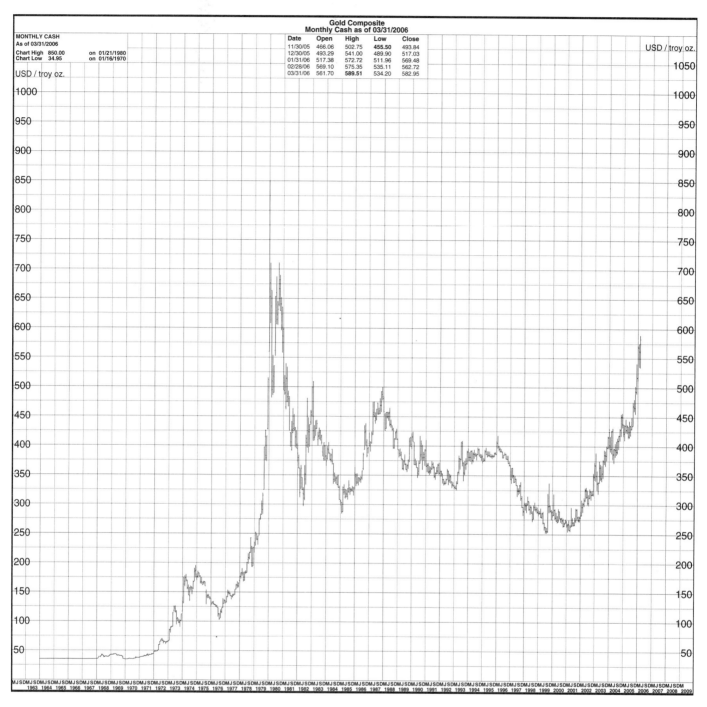

Annual High, Low and Close of Gold   In Dollars per Troy Ounce

Year	High	Low	Close	Year	High	Low	Close	Year	High	Low	Close
1968	43.25	35.85	42.05	1981	599.25	391.25	401.00	1994	398.00	369.50	382.70
1969	44.05	35.20	35.45	1982	481.00	296.75	456.90	1995	397.75	371.20	386.85
1970	39.30	34.95	37.65	1983	509.25	374.25	381.50	1996	417.90	366.30	367.45
1971	44.25	37.70	43.85	1984	405.85	307.50	308.30	1997	368.15	282.00	288.80
1972	70.30	44.30	65.20	1985	341.15	284.25	329.70	1998	314.70	271.50	288.00
1973	126.45	64.20	112.30	1986	438.35	326.55	397.00	1999	337.50	252.00	287.50
1974	195.50	116.80	186.75	1987	499.75	390.00	484.05	2000	319.00	262.62	271.90
1975	185.50	128.90	140.35	1988	483.90	395.30	410.90	2001	296.00	254.35	278.95
1976	139.20	102.20	134.75	1989	415.50	355.75	402.90	2002	354.25	277.05	348.05
1977	168.10	130.10	164.96	1990	423.75	345.85	394.00	2003	417.75	319.15	415.65
1978	242.75	165.95	226.00	1991	410.00	342.80	354.00	2004	456.87	371.70	438.44
1979	515.50	217.10	512.00	1992	361.00	328.80	333.10	2005	541.00	410.40	517.03
1980	850.00	481.50	586.00	1993	408.90	325.50	390.20	2006	589.51	511.96	582.95

Source: New York Mercantile Exchange

GOLD

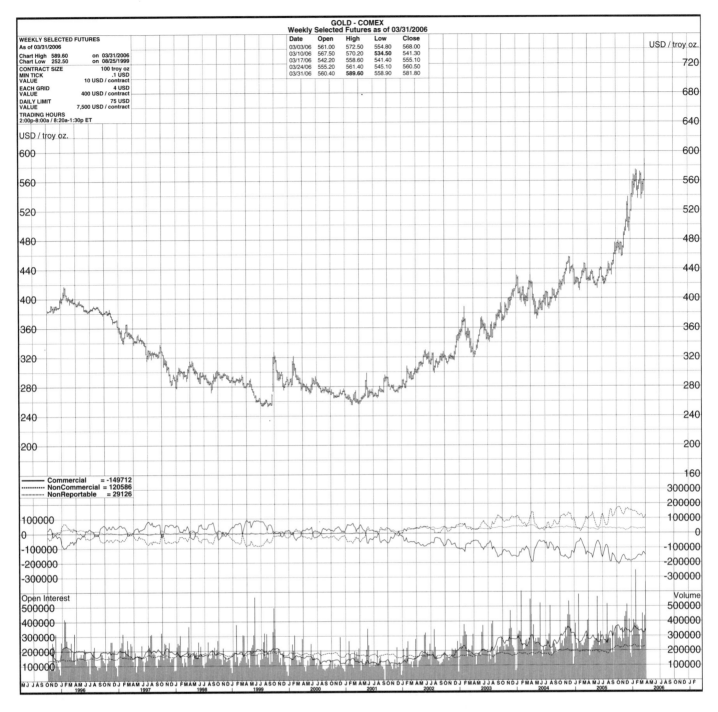

Quarterly High, Low and Close of Gold Futures — In Dollars per Troy Ounce

Quarter	High	Low	Close	Quarter	High	Low	Close	Quarter	High	Low	Close
09/1996	390.50	377.20	377.70	12/1999	327.50	275.00	289.60	03/2003	388.90	325.80	335.90
12/1996	385.80	366.00	369.20	03/2000	322.00	274.50	278.40	06/2003	374.90	319.30	346.30
03/1997	369.40	338.50	351.00	06/2000	294.30	269.50	291.50	09/2003	393.80	340.60	385.40
06/1997	352.20	334.60	335.30	09/2000	289.70	269.50	273.60	12/2003	418.40	368.00	416.10
09/1997	335.80	314.60	334.30	12/2000	277.20	264.40	273.60	03/2004	431.50	388.20	427.30
12/1997	338.00	281.50	289.90	03/2001	275.00	255.00	257.90	06/2004	432.00	371.30	393.00
03/1998	306.60	277.50	300.50	06/2001	298.60	255.00	271.30	09/2004	418.80	385.00	418.70
06/1998	315.60	284.60	298.10	09/2001	296.00	264.10	292.40	12/2004	456.50	410.30	438.40
09/1998	299.70	271.60	296.40	12/2001	292.90	271.20	279.00	03/2005	448.00	410.10	428.70
12/1998	302.70	285.50	289.20	03/2002	308.00	277.20	302.60	06/2005	442.50	413.20	437.10
03/1999	296.50	278.20	279.80	06/2002	330.30	297.50	313.90	09/2005	475.70	418.20	469.00
06/1999	291.20	258.60	263.60	09/2002	328.00	298.00	323.90	12/2005	538.50	456.10	518.90
09/1999	321.00	252.50	297.90	12/2002	350.80	309.80	348.20	03/2006	589.60	517.60	581.80

Source: New York Mercantile Exchange

GOLD

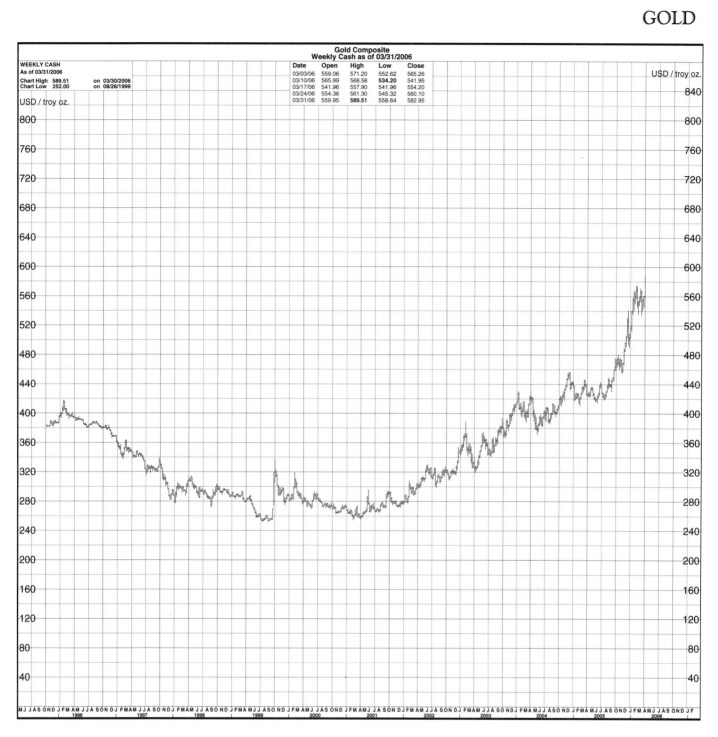

Quarterly High, Low and Close of Gold   In Dollars per Troy Ounce

Quarter	High	Low	Close	Quarter	High	Low	Close	Quarter	High	Low	Close
09/1996	389.80	378.50	378.50	12/1999	337.50	275.00	287.50	03/2003	389.05	325.70	337.35
12/1996	384.35	366.30	367.45	03/2000	319.00	275.50	278.40	06/2003	374.65	319.15	346.40
03/1997	368.15	336.85	350.80	06/2000	293.75	269.70	289.60	09/2003	393.75	340.55	385.35
06/1997	351.90	333.70	333.70	09/2000	289.50	268.85	273.65	12/2003	417.75	366.50	415.65
09/1997	334.50	314.20	334.00	12/2000	277.35	262.62	271.90	03/2004	430.40	387.95	426.40
12/1997	339.35	282.00	288.80	03/2001	274.40	254.35	257.45	06/2004	431.08	371.70	394.17
03/1998	305.80	277.10	300.70	06/2001	296.00	255.05	270.35	09/2004	419.09	385.55	418.51
06/1998	314.70	284.28	296.70	09/2001	294.50	264.75	292.45	12/2004	456.87	409.50	438.44
09/1998	299.60	271.50	296.70	12/2001	293.75	271.45	278.95	03/2005	447.05	410.40	428.55
12/1998	304.60	285.80	288.00	03/2002	308.55	277.05	302.45	06/2005	443.70	413.85	435.30
03/1999	294.60	278.80	279.80	06/2002	330.55	297.70	314.45	09/2005	475.50	418.25	469.35
06/1999	289.00	257.40	262.25	09/2002	327.95	298.95	323.55	12/2005	541.00	455.50	517.03
09/1999	320.00	252.00	297.70	12/2002	354.25	308.75	348.05	03/2006	589.51	511.96	582.95

Source: New York Mercantile Exchange

LEAD

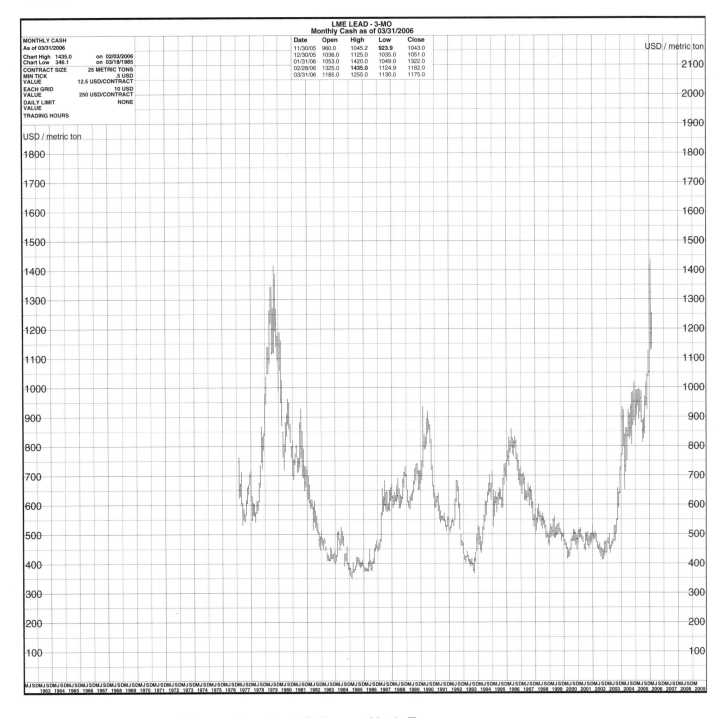

Annual High, Low and Close of Lead   In Dollars per Metric Ton

Year	High	Low	Close	Year	High	Low	Close	Year	High	Low	Close
1977	762.9	530.9	697.8	1987	684.1	438.8	656.9	1997	731.0	525.0	564.0
1978	867.4	540.7	843.4	1988	731.9	588.0	700.8	1998	603.0	466.0	474.0
1979	1,417.5	838.0	1,094.5	1989	743.0	584.5	707.0	1999	562.0	460.0	495.5
1980	1,190.6	719.2	768.3	1990	935.0	624.0	633.0	2000	517.0	415.0	484.0
1981	929.1	647.6	721.1	1991	643.0	509.0	560.0	2001	523.0	441.0	497.0
1982	719.1	445.1	487.4	1992	684.0	459.0	463.0	2002	530.0	409.0	436.0
1983	514.7	403.6	436.2	1993	499.0	365.0	488.0	2003	727.0	435.0	724.0
1984	522.8	378.6	378.6	1994	703.0	435.0	673.0	2004	1,019.0	651.0	1,004.0
1985	423.4	346.1	391.6	1995	742.0	523.0	714.0	2005	1,125.0	812.0	1,051.0
1986	480.6	371.1	462.4	1996	861.0	666.5	700.0	2006	1,435.0	1,049.0	1,175.0

Source: London Metals Exchange

LEAD

Quarterly High, Low and Close of Lead   In Dollars per Metric Ton

Quarter	High	Low	Close	Quarter	High	Low	Close	Quarter	High	Low	Close
09/1996	834.0	755.0	756.0	12/1999	517.0	475.0	495.5	03/2003	500.0	438.0	449.5
12/1996	775.0	666.5	700.0	03/2000	509.0	449.5	453.0	06/2003	483.0	435.0	479.0
03/1997	731.0	635.0	686.0	06/2000	454.0	415.0	450.0	09/2003	550.0	474.0	547.0
06/1997	696.0	610.0	627.0	09/2000	517.0	445.0	504.0	12/2003	727.0	547.0	724.0
09/1997	675.0	596.0	643.0	12/2000	513.0	446.0	484.0	03/2004	933.0	714.0	822.0
12/1997	650.0	525.0	564.0	03/2001	523.0	466.0	492.5	06/2004	862.0	651.0	837.0
03/1998	587.0	504.0	570.0	06/2001	498.0	447.0	455.0	09/2004	940.0	822.0	925.0
06/1998	603.0	527.0	547.0	09/2001	508.0	441.0	462.0	12/2004	1,019.0	805.0	1,004.0
09/1998	571.0	517.0	528.0	12/2001	503.0	451.0	497.0	03/2005	991.0	867.0	989.0
12/1998	528.0	466.0	474.0	03/2002	530.0	479.0	498.0	06/2005	996.0	880.0	880.0
03/1999	534.0	460.0	510.0	06/2002	500.0	445.0	461.0	09/2005	970.0	812.0	938.0
06/1999	562.0	486.0	498.5	09/2002	471.0	409.0	419.0	12/2005	1,125.0	923.9	1,051.0
09/1999	538.0	495.0	515.5	12/2002	477.0	413.0	436.0	03/2006	1,435.0	1,049.0	1,175.0

Source: London Metals Exchange

NICKEL

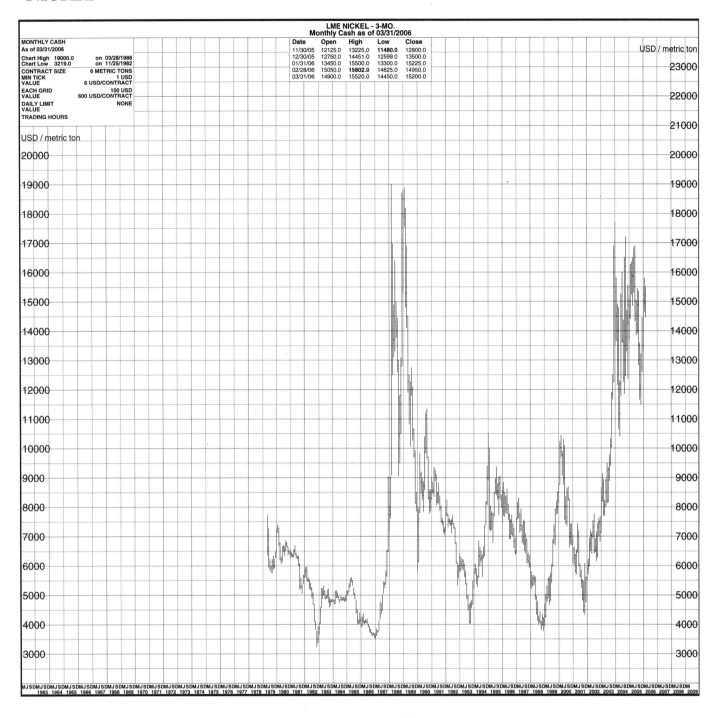

Annual High, Low and Close of Nickel In Dollars per Metric Ton

Year	High	Low	Close	Year	High	Low	Close	Year	High	Low	Close
				1987	9,039	3,484	8,995	1997	8,320	5,920	6,070
				1988	19,000	7,154	16,800	1998	6,080	3,775	4,170
1979	7,748	5,748	6,302	1989	18,900	7,850	8,000	1999	8,515	3,940	8,500
1980	7,404	6,057	6,477	1990	11,350	5,800	8,300	2000	10,450	6,610	6,830
1981	6,701	5,051	5,647	1991	9,350	7,050	7,215	2001	7,450	4,320	5,575
1982	5,962	3,219	3,906	1992	8,245	5,320	6,020	2002	7,760	5,470	7,130
1983	5,313	3,665	4,842	1993	6,440	4,030	5,305	2003	16,900	7,140	16,500
1984	5,168	4,701	4,825	1994	9,400	5,240	8,975	2004	17,700	10,400	14,875
1985	5,602	4,000	4,131	1995	10,500	6,770	8,010	2005	16,901	11,480	13,500
1986	4,356	3,541	3,568	1996	8,850	6,360	6,465	2006	15,802	13,300	15,200

Source: London Metals Exchange

NICKEL

Quarterly High, Low and Close of Nickel   In Dollars per Metric Ton

Quarter	High	Low	Close	Quarter	High	Low	Close	Quarter	High	Low	Close
09/1996	7,770	6,910	7,100	12/1999	8,515	6,690	8,500	03/2003	9,140	7,140	7,780
12/1996	7,450	6,360	6,465	03/2000	10,450	8,135	10,020	06/2003	9,500	7,700	8,210
03/1997	8,320	6,435	7,805	06/2000	10,300	7,550	8,010	09/2003	10,330	8,160	10,065
06/1997	7,940	6,765	6,860	09/2000	8,690	7,340	8,300	12/2003	16,900	10,025	16,500
09/1997	7,550	6,410	6,870	12/2000	8,260	6,610	6,830	03/2004	17,700	12,150	14,000
12/1997	6,930	5,920	6,070	03/2001	7,050	5,750	5,810	06/2004	15,250	10,400	15,175
03/1998	6,080	5,200	5,565	06/2001	7,450	5,710	6,020	09/2004	16,500	11,850	16,425
06/1998	5,670	4,340	4,390	09/2001	6,070	4,805	4,910	12/2004	17,200	12,350	14,875
09/1998	4,790	4,000	4,065	12/2001	6,090	4,320	5,575	03/2005	16,350	13,700	15,900
12/1998	4,360	3,775	4,170	03/2002	6,950	5,470	6,690	06/2005	16,901	14,325	14,590
03/1999	5,320	3,940	4,830	06/2002	7,540	6,410	7,160	09/2005	15,450	12,825	13,500
06/1999	5,755	4,660	5,490	09/2002	7,760	6,160	6,360	12/2005	14,451	11,480	13,500
09/1999	7,400	5,400	7,185	12/2002	7,680	6,260	7,130	03/2006	15,802	13,300	15,200

Source: London Metals Exchange

PALLADIUM

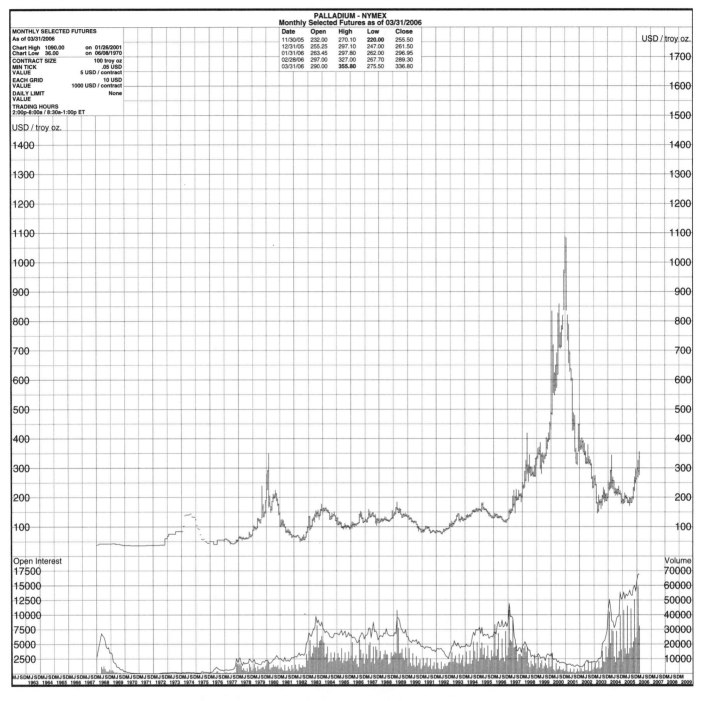

Annual High, Low and Close of Palladium Futures   In Dollars per Troy Ounce

Year	High	Low	Close	Year	High	Low	Close	Year	High	Low	Close
1968	42.00	37.00	42.00	1981	149.00	63.00	69.30	1994	164.00	122.50	160.25
1969	43.00	37.00	37.00	1982	102.00	48.00	97.50	1995	182.90	128.80	129.65
1970	37.00	36.00	36.00	1983	178.00	88.00	157.45	1996	147.00	114.50	124.05
1971	37.00	36.00	37.00	1984	166.75	120.00	121.50	1997	227.60	120.25	203.15
1972	60.00	37.00	60.00	1985	132.00	89.75	95.40	1998	419.00	200.00	332.15
1973	84.00	60.00	84.00	1986	153.00	94.00	118.30	1999	456.95	280.00	449.20
1974	143.80	84.00	132.50	1987	160.00	103.65	123.60	2000	975.00	430.20	954.45
1975	124.32	44.00	44.00	1988	155.95	113.00	129.00	2001	1,090.00	310.00	448.00
1976	55.00	40.00	55.00	1989	184.00	129.25	135.50	2002	447.00	229.70	238.00
1977	59.80	40.10	53.50	1990	139.90	80.55	81.25	2003	275.00	145.00	197.50
1978	83.35	52.40	72.50	1991	102.50	77.50	80.65	2004	344.70	177.75	185.25
1979	240.50	70.10	182.50	1992	112.00	74.50	104.45	2005	297.10	170.20	261.50
1980	350.00	139.00	142.25	1993	145.00	98.00	124.35	2006	355.80	262.00	336.80

Source: New York Mercantile Exchange

PALLADIUM

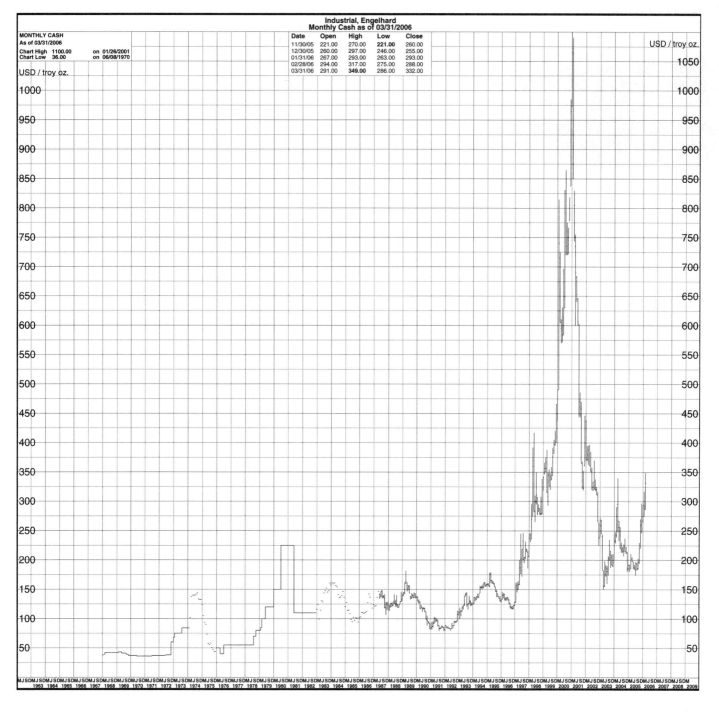

Annual High, Low and Close of Palladium — In Dollars per Troy Ounce

Year	High	Low	Close	Year	High	Low	Close	Year	High	Low	Close
1968	42.00	37.00	42.00	1981	225.00	110.00	110.00	1994	163.00	124.00	158.00
1969	43.00	37.00	37.00	1982	110.00	110.00	110.00	1995	179.00	130.00	130.00
1970	37.00	36.00	36.00	1983	160.69	99.55	160.69	1996	146.00	117.00	123.00
1971	37.00	36.00	37.00	1984	161.10	135.83	136.72	1997	246.00	122.00	207.00
1972	60.00	37.00	60.00	1985	127.88	94.50	94.50	1998	417.00	205.00	338.00
1973	84.00	60.00	84.00	1986	142.30	101.83	118.15	1999	466.00	293.00	466.00
1974	143.80	84.00	132.50	1987	148.50	106.50	125.50	2000	985.00	437.00	965.00
1975	124.32	44.00	44.00	1988	146.00	114.25	133.00	2001	1,100.00	319.00	446.00
1976	55.00	40.00	55.00	1989	181.50	131.00	135.50	2002	439.00	225.00	237.00
1977	55.00	55.00	55.00	1990	138.00	82.75	82.75	2003	273.00	150.00	196.00
1978	80.00	55.00	80.00	1991	102.50	79.00	81.00	2004	340.00	180.00	186.00
1979	120.00	80.00	120.00	1992	114.00	78.50	107.00	2005	297.00	174.00	255.00
1980	225.00	120.00	225.00	1993	145.00	100.00	124.00	2006	349.00	263.00	332.00

Source: New York Mercantile Exchange

PALLADIUM

Quarterly High, Low and Close of Palladium Futures   In Dollars per Troy Ounce

Quarter	High	Low	Close	Quarter	High	Low	Close	Quarter	High	Low	Close
09/1996	136.90	117.50	119.75	12/1999	456.95	363.00	449.20	03/2003	275.00	178.00	182.45
12/1996	124.70	114.50	124.05	03/2000	835.00	430.20	595.50	06/2003	208.00	145.00	181.35
03/1997	161.25	120.25	147.70	06/2000	692.15	547.50	647.95	09/2003	234.00	160.00	215.15
06/1997	225.00	147.25	174.90	09/2000	859.00	618.00	714.85	12/2003	225.00	182.50	197.50
09/1997	227.60	145.00	193.90	12/2000	975.00	712.25	954.45	03/2004	293.50	198.00	289.95
12/1997	224.45	183.00	203.15	03/2001	1,090.00	734.00	744.00	06/2004	344.70	213.00	214.95
03/1998	290.00	200.00	258.20	06/2001	789.90	595.00	599.95	09/2004	232.40	205.00	224.75
06/1998	419.00	253.10	285.45	09/2001	605.00	355.00	357.00	12/2004	239.20	177.75	185.25
09/1998	346.00	271.50	281.15	12/2001	449.50	310.00	448.00	03/2005	215.00	177.00	203.55
12/1998	334.00	270.00	332.15	03/2002	447.00	355.50	388.90	06/2005	207.00	180.50	181.95
03/1999	372.00	307.00	358.20	06/2002	394.00	314.00	318.80	09/2005	202.70	170.20	199.80
06/1999	387.00	280.00	320.30	09/2002	380.00	313.00	319.00	12/2005	297.10	192.10	261.50
09/1999	405.00	314.00	369.40	12/2002	329.00	229.70	238.00	03/2006	355.80	262.00	336.80

Source: New York Mercantile Exchange

PALLADIUM

Quarterly High, Low and Close of Palladium   In Dollars per Troy Ounce

Quarter	High	Low	Close	Quarter	High	Low	Close	Quarter	High	Low	Close
09/1996	137.00	118.00	121.00	12/1999	466.00	381.00	466.00	03/2003	273.00	183.00	183.00
12/1996	123.00	117.00	123.00	03/2000	815.00	437.00	605.00	06/2003	198.00	150.00	181.00
03/1997	163.00	122.00	158.00	06/2000	697.00	570.00	649.00	09/2003	235.00	160.00	211.00
06/1997	245.00	150.00	197.00	09/2000	865.00	630.00	722.00	12/2003	216.00	187.00	196.00
09/1997	246.00	172.00	205.00	12/2000	985.00	722.00	965.00	03/2004	290.00	200.00	290.00
12/1997	232.00	186.00	207.00	03/2001	1,100.00	744.00	744.00	06/2004	340.00	219.00	222.00
03/1998	296.00	205.00	270.00	06/2001	755.00	600.00	606.00	09/2004	230.00	207.00	221.00
06/1998	417.00	265.00	300.00	09/2001	602.00	365.00	365.00	12/2004	237.00	180.00	186.00
09/1998	350.00	277.00	288.00	12/2001	446.00	319.00	446.00	03/2005	211.00	180.00	202.00
12/1998	338.00	277.00	338.00	03/2002	439.00	363.00	388.00	06/2005	205.00	184.00	185.00
03/1999	375.00	318.00	367.00	06/2002	396.00	320.00	324.00	09/2005	203.00	174.00	196.00
06/1999	388.00	293.00	327.00	09/2002	370.00	318.00	321.00	12/2005	297.00	194.00	255.00
09/1999	392.00	320.00	377.00	12/2002	325.00	225.00	237.00	03/2006	349.00	263.00	332.00

Source: New York Mercantile Exchange

PLATINUM

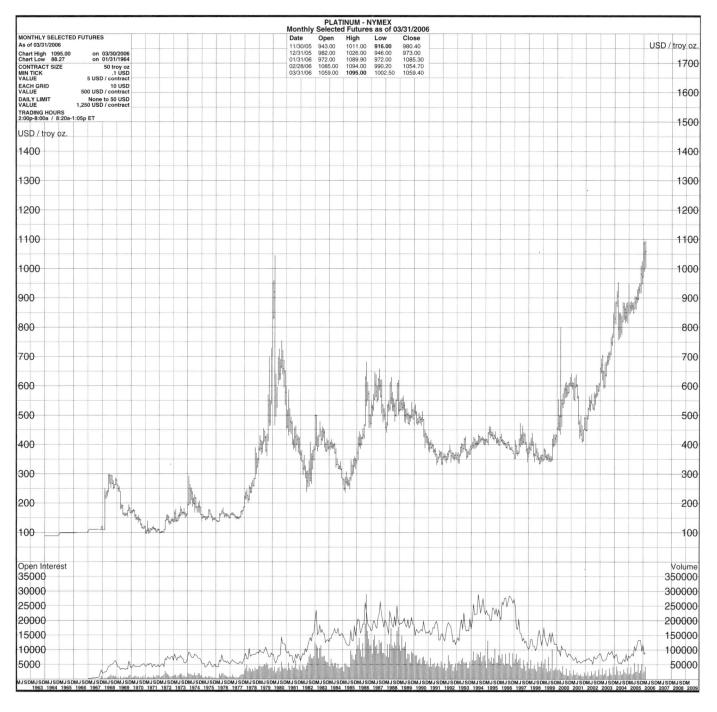

Annual High, Low and Close of Platinum Futures   In Dollars per Troy Ounce

Year	High	Low	Close	Year	High	Low	Close	Year	High	Low	Close
1968	300.50	214.00	280.00	1981	599.00	365.50	373.20	1994	435.40	379.00	414.70
1969	281.50	153.10	168.00	1982	409.00	238.00	383.10	1995	463.00	397.00	398.20
1970	180.10	112.50	120.50	1983	502.00	375.00	390.50	1996	436.90	369.00	369.30
1971	140.00	94.50	110.00	1984	417.50	285.50	287.70	1997	473.80	339.50	370.80
1972	161.60	96.00	141.70	1985	359.80	236.00	340.30	1998	440.00	332.00	364.50
1973	188.80	134.60	160.10	1986	682.00	334.00	470.70	1999	435.00	341.00	430.20
1974	293.50	159.50	159.50	1987	658.50	469.00	500.60	2000	800.00	408.00	609.60
1975	179.50	137.00	146.90	1988	630.00	439.50	516.60	2001	641.10	406.00	493.00
1976	184.50	135.00	149.50	1989	566.20	466.20	487.30	2002	610.50	445.20	604.40
1977	186.90	144.20	186.40	1990	536.90	387.50	408.70	2003	847.70	590.00	811.30
1978	390.00	183.00	349.00	1991	421.50	330.00	338.70	2004	954.00	756.00	863.70
1979	730.00	337.00	692.60	1992	400.00	330.00	354.10	2005	1,026.00	843.20	973.00
1980	1,045.00	465.00	578.00	1993	427.50	335.50	394.90	2006	1,095.00	972.00	1,059.40

Source: New York Mercantile Exchange

PLATINUM

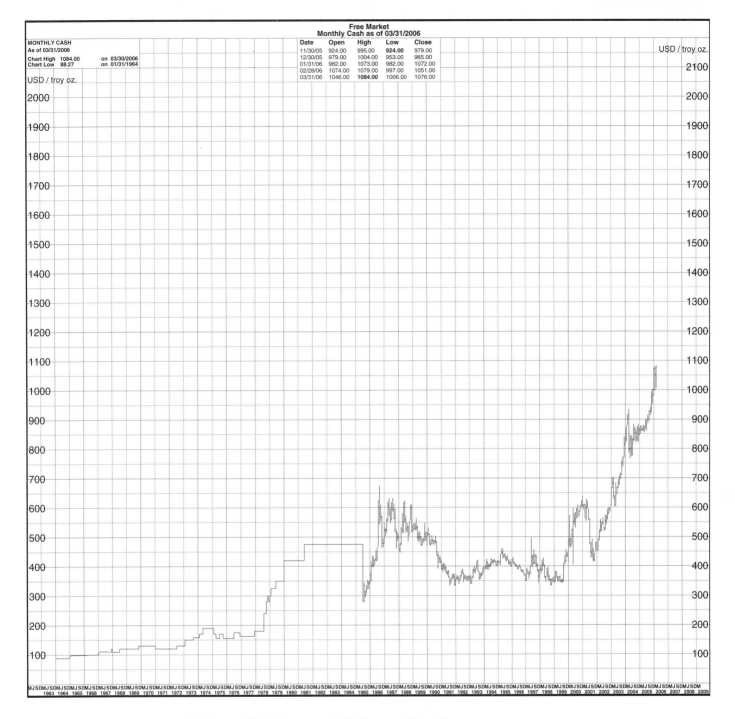

Annual High, Low and Close of Platinum   In Dollars per Troy Ounce

Year	High	Low	Close	Year	High	Low	Close	Year	High	Low	Close
1968	120.00	109.00	120.00	1981	475.00	420.00	475.00	1994	425.50	378.00	417.00
1969	130.00	120.00	130.00	1982	475.00	475.00	475.00	1995	461.50	398.25	398.25
1970	130.00	130.00	130.00	1983	475.00	475.00	475.00	1996	431.50	367.00	369.50
1971	130.00	120.00	120.00	1984	475.00	475.00	475.00	1997	497.00	342.50	363.00
1972	130.00	120.00	130.00	1985	475.00	276.75	340.30	1998	429.00	334.25	360.25
1973	158.00	130.00	158.00	1986	675.50	341.30	477.50	1999	457.00	342.00	443.00
1974	190.00	158.00	190.00	1987	632.00	461.00	500.00	2000	622.00	405.00	619.00
1975	190.00	155.00	155.00	1988	623.50	446.00	520.50	2001	637.00	415.00	480.00
1976	175.00	155.00	162.00	1989	563.75	470.00	488.50	2002	602.00	453.00	598.00
1977	180.00	162.00	180.00	1990	532.00	391.50	411.75	2003	840.00	603.00	813.00
1978	300.00	180.00	280.00	1991	423.00	333.00	338.25	2004	936.00	767.00	861.00
1979	350.00	280.00	350.00	1992	391.00	332.75	353.50	2005	1,004.00	844.00	965.00
1980	420.00	350.00	420.00	1993	422.00	338.25	394.00	2006	1,084.00	982.00	1,076.00

Source: New York Mercantile Exchange

PLATINUM

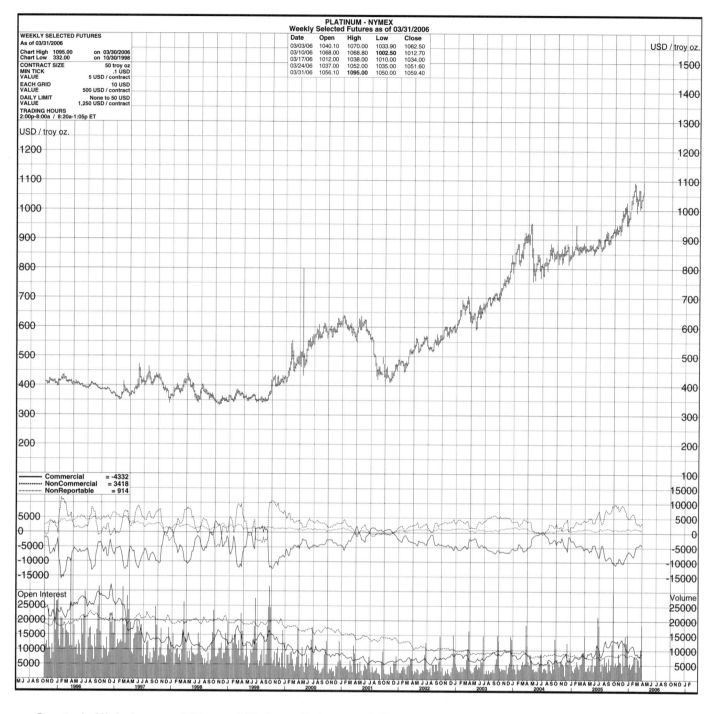

Quarterly High, Low and Close of Platinum Futures   In Dollars per Troy Ounce

Quarter	High	Low	Close	Quarter	High	Low	Close	Quarter	High	Low	Close
09/1996	412.00	383.50	384.60	12/1999	435.00	392.00	430.20	03/2003	707.00	599.50	648.40
12/1996	393.80	369.00	369.30	03/2000	555.00	408.00	496.40	06/2003	684.00	590.00	670.60
03/1997	415.00	351.00	368.80	06/2000	800.00	433.10	565.50	09/2003	718.80	669.00	706.90
06/1997	473.80	360.80	415.80	09/2000	614.00	539.00	578.80	12/2003	847.70	705.00	811.30
09/1997	466.00	398.00	432.50	12/2000	630.50	564.00	609.60	03/2004	924.00	810.00	908.70
12/1997	437.90	339.50	370.80	03/2001	641.10	554.50	555.00	06/2004	954.00	756.00	791.50
03/1998	423.50	355.50	408.50	06/2001	639.00	548.00	560.10	09/2004	885.80	775.00	861.00
06/1998	440.00	340.00	361.60	09/2001	567.20	420.10	433.30	12/2004	887.00	813.00	863.70
09/1998	405.00	346.00	353.40	12/2001	493.00	406.00	493.00	03/2005	950.00	843.20	870.60
12/1998	366.00	332.00	364.50	03/2002	527.00	445.20	521.70	06/2005	905.00	846.50	883.50
03/1999	388.00	342.20	359.10	06/2002	572.00	513.00	537.30	09/2005	938.50	860.30	930.30
06/1999	370.40	341.50	351.00	09/2002	578.00	516.00	564.50	12/2005	1,026.00	914.50	973.00
09/1999	420.00	341.00	388.90	12/2002	610.50	559.00	604.40	03/2006	1,095.00	972.00	1,059.40

Source: New York Mercantile Exchange

PLATINUM

Quarterly High, Low and Close of Platinum — In Dollars per Troy Ounce

Quarter	High	Low	Close	Quarter	High	Low	Close	Quarter	High	Low	Close
09/1996	404.50	383.00	383.00	12/1999	457.00	405.00	443.00	03/2003	704.00	603.00	642.00
12/1996	388.00	367.00	369.50	03/2000	573.00	414.00	482.00	06/2003	685.00	603.00	667.00
03/1997	392.00	349.50	373.50	06/2000	598.00	405.00	558.00	09/2003	718.00	665.00	710.00
06/1997	497.00	354.50	430.00	09/2000	610.00	532.00	569.00	12/2003	840.00	710.00	813.00
09/1997	457.00	396.00	434.25	12/2000	622.00	570.00	619.00	03/2004	917.00	815.50	917.00
12/1997	438.00	342.50	363.00	03/2001	637.00	563.00	563.00	06/2004	936.00	767.00	793.00
03/1998	422.00	358.00	407.00	06/2001	628.00	555.00	558.00	09/2004	885.00	776.00	854.00
06/1998	429.00	345.50	357.25	09/2001	560.00	429.00	429.00	12/2004	884.00	821.50	861.00
09/1998	397.50	349.00	350.00	12/2001	480.00	415.00	480.00	03/2005	877.00	844.00	864.00
12/1998	360.25	334.25	360.25	03/2002	524.00	453.00	516.00	06/2005	900.00	856.00	884.00
03/1999	383.00	342.00	361.00	06/2002	565.00	516.00	545.00	09/2005	930.00	860.00	929.00
06/1999	367.50	344.50	349.00	09/2002	574.00	520.00	563.00	12/2005	1,004.00	914.00	965.00
09/1999	409.00	343.50	393.00	12/2002	602.00	557.00	598.00	03/2006	1,084.00	982.00	1,076.00

Source: New York Mercantile Exchange

SILVER

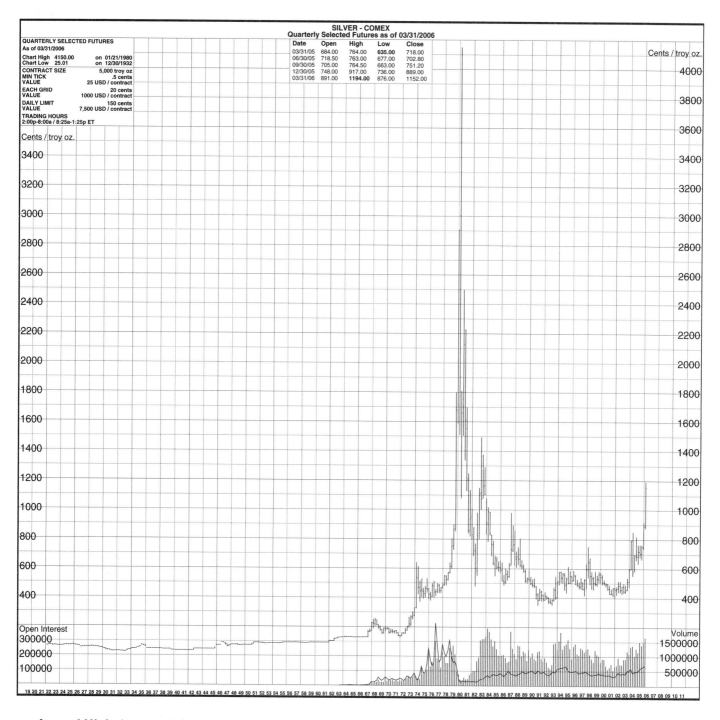

Annual High, Low and Close of Silver Futures   In Cents per Troy Ounce

Year	High	Low	Close	Year	High	Low	Close	Year	High	Low	Close
1929	57.00	48.47	48.47	1942	44.75	35.12	44.75	1955	92.00	85.25	90.50
1930	45.00	32.63	32.63	1943	44.75	44.75	44.75	1956	91.63	90.00	91.38
1931	32.22	26.77	30.12	1944	44.75	44.75	44.75	1957	91.38	89.63	89.63
1932	30.14	25.01	25.01	1945	70.75	44.75	70.75	1958	90.38	88.63	89.88
1933	43.55	25.40	43.55	1946	90.12	70.75	86.73	1959	91.63	89.88	91.38
1934	54.39	44.19	54.39	1947	86.25	59.75	74.63	1960	91.50	91.38	91.38
1935	74.36	54.42	58.42	1948	77.50	70.00	70.00	1961	104.75	91.38	104.75
1936	47.25	44.75	45.35	1949	73.25	70.00	73.25	1962	122.00	101.00	120.50
1937	45.46	43.81	43.81	1950	80.00	71.75	80.00	1963	129.50	121.00	129.50
1938	44.75	42.75	42.75	1951	90.16	80.00	88.00	1964	131.70	128.50	131.70
1939	42.75	34.75	34.96	1952	88.00	82.75	83.25	1965	131.80	128.00	129.70
1940	34.95	34.75	34.75	1953	85.25	83.25	85.25	1966	131.20	128.70	130.90
1941	35.12	34.75	35.12	1954	85.25	85.25	85.25	1967	230.25	128.80	226.00

Source: New York Mercantile Exchange

SILVER

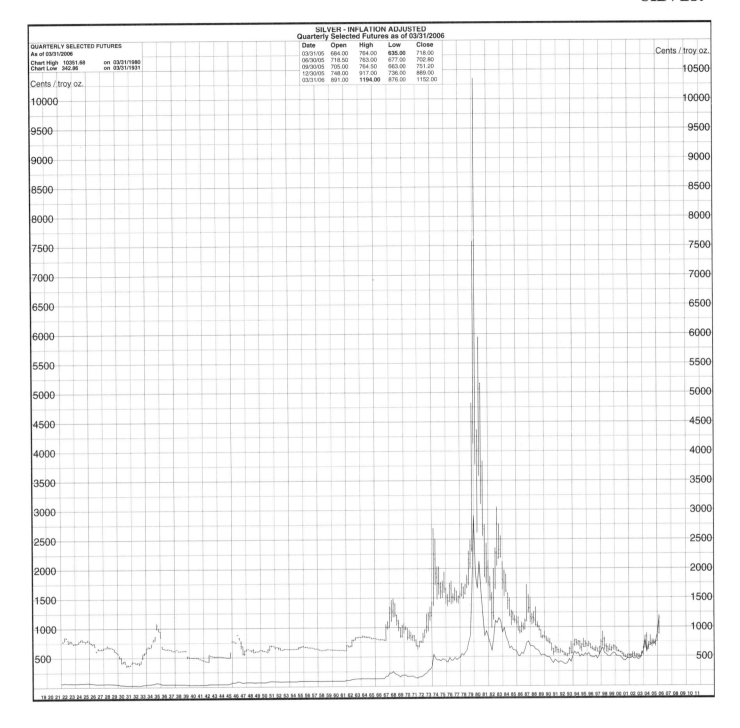

SILVER

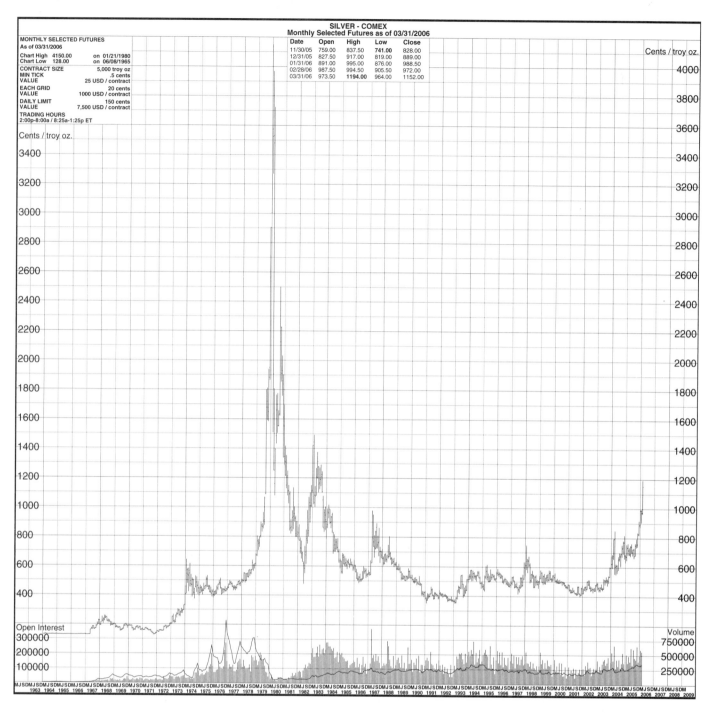

Annual High, Low and Close of Silver Futures   In Cents per Troy Ounce

Year	High	Low	Close	Year	High	Low	Close	Year	High	Low	Close
1968	259.00	184.00	198.20	1981	1,697.00	797.00	829.00	1994	582.00	453.00	491.70
1969	206.90	151.00	184.10	1982	1,150.00	478.00	1,110.00	1995	616.00	434.00	520.70
1970	195.00	152.10	166.00	1983	1,493.00	832.00	915.50	1996	589.00	464.00	479.00
1971	177.20	128.20	138.40	1984	1,017.00	624.50	638.00	1997	635.00	415.50	598.80
1972	205.50	138.70	204.70	1985	689.00	548.00	590.50	1998	750.00	456.00	502.00
1973	331.30	195.40	329.70	1986	642.00	485.00	546.00	1999	581.00	482.00	545.30
1974	643.00	326.10	447.00	1987	979.50	536.50	677.00	2000	560.00	455.00	463.50
1975	532.00	388.00	423.60	1988	806.00	598.00	613.00	2001	488.00	401.50	458.80
1976	515.00	380.00	439.00	1989	631.00	502.00	527.30	2002	515.00	421.00	481.20
1977	500.00	430.50	484.90	1990	544.50	393.00	424.70	2003	605.00	434.60	596.50
1978	640.00	482.20	613.70	1991	464.00	350.50	391.20	2004	850.00	549.50	683.70
1979	2,905.00	598.00	2,905.00	1992	441.00	362.00	369.00	2005	917.00	635.00	889.00
1980	4,150.00	1,080.00	1,612.00	1993	547.00	351.00	511.70	2006	1,194.00	876.00	1,152.00

Source: New York Mercantile Exchange

SILVER

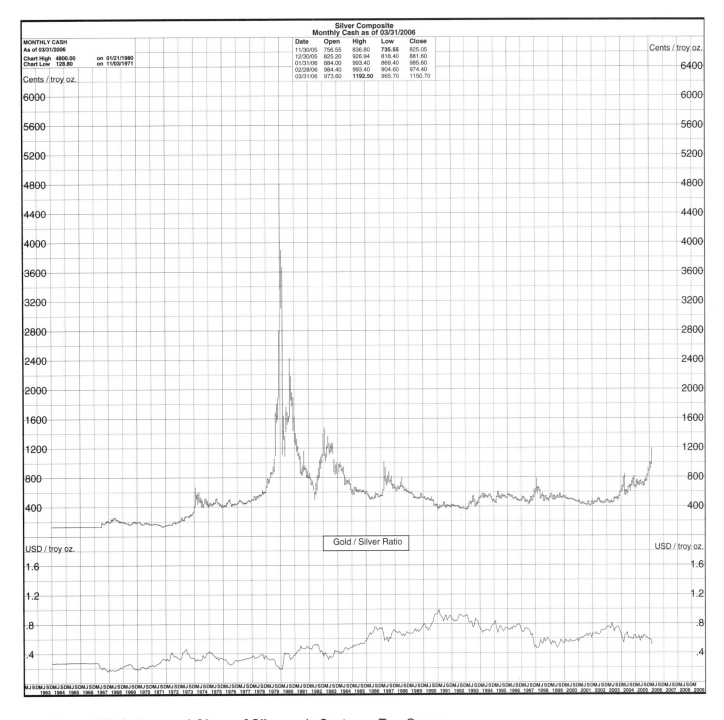

Annual High, Low and Close of Silver   In Cents per Troy Ounce

Year	High	Low	Close	Year	High	Low	Close	Year	High	Low	Close
1968	256.50	181.00	190.00	1981	1,645.00	795.00	825.00	1994	585.00	454.00	488.00
1969	202.50	154.00	180.00	1982	1,121.00	488.50	1,090.00	1995	613.00	436.00	518.00
1970	193.00	157.00	163.50	1983	1,474.50	834.00	895.00	1996	587.00	468.00	477.00
1971	175.20	128.80	138.00	1984	1,003.50	626.00	636.00	1997	638.00	418.00	593.00
1972	204.80	138.70	204.20	1985	673.50	557.00	583.00	1998	787.00	462.00	502.00
1973	328.40	196.20	328.40	1986	619.50	487.00	536.50	1999	582.00	482.00	540.00
1974	670.00	327.00	437.00	1987	1,020.00	536.00	669.50	2000	551.00	455.00	457.00
1975	522.50	391.00	416.50	1988	799.00	601.00	602.00	2001	484.00	404.00	462.00
1976	510.00	381.50	437.50	1989	617.00	501.50	518.00	2002	515.00	423.00	478.00
1977	496.00	430.00	478.00	1990	539.00	392.00	422.00	2003	601.00	434.00	594.00
1978	629.60	482.90	607.40	1991	463.00	352.00	390.00	2004	845.00	545.50	682.28
1979	2,800.00	596.10	2,800.00	1992	439.00	363.00	368.00	2005	926.94	632.60	881.60
1980	4,800.00	1,080.00	1,565.00	1993	551.00	353.00	510.00	2006	1,192.50	869.40	1,150.70

Source: New York Mercantile Exchange

SILVER

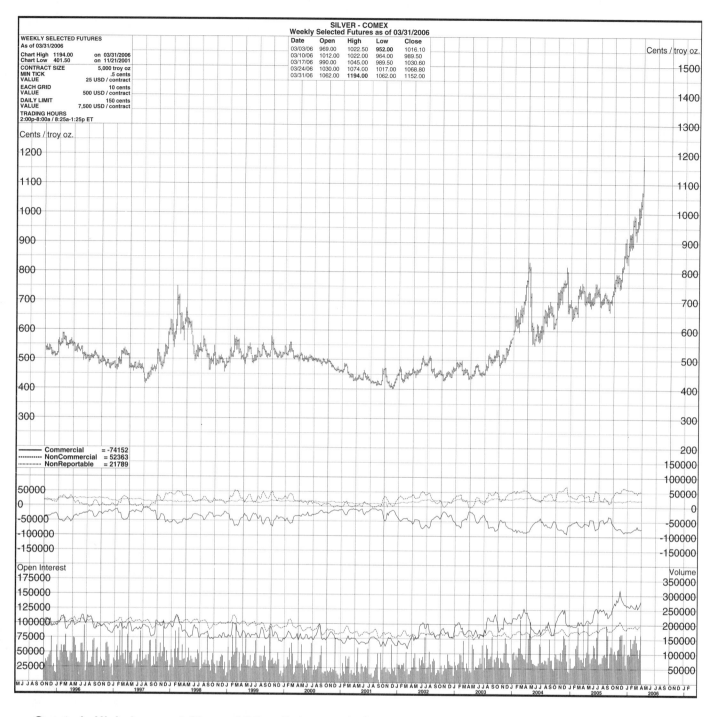

Quarterly High, Low and Close of Silver Futures   In Cents per Troy Ounce

Quarter	High	Low	Close	Quarter	High	Low	Close	Quarter	High	Low	Close
09/1996	528.00	480.50	487.70	12/1999	576.50	502.50	545.30	03/2003	498.00	434.60	446.50
12/1996	509.50	464.00	479.00	03/2000	560.00	492.00	504.50	06/2003	488.00	435.00	455.70
03/1997	539.00	461.00	507.50	06/2000	524.00	490.00	503.30	09/2003	536.50	454.50	514.20
06/1997	508.50	457.00	460.00	09/2000	504.50	477.50	494.80	12/2003	605.00	474.50	596.50
09/1997	533.00	415.50	523.20	12/2000	498.50	455.00	463.50	03/2004	795.00	595.00	794.50
12/1997	635.00	463.00	598.80	03/2001	488.00	427.00	429.50	06/2004	850.00	549.50	577.60
03/1998	750.00	538.50	646.70	06/2001	463.50	427.00	429.20	09/2004	701.00	583.00	693.80
06/1998	674.50	492.00	550.70	09/2001	471.80	411.00	467.50	12/2004	819.00	660.00	683.70
09/1998	579.00	461.50	536.00	12/2001	473.00	401.50	458.80	03/2005	764.00	635.00	718.00
12/1998	547.50	456.00	502.00	03/2002	477.50	421.00	465.00	06/2005	763.00	677.00	702.80
03/1999	581.00	486.00	497.00	06/2002	515.00	439.00	483.30	09/2005	764.50	663.00	751.20
06/1999	556.00	482.00	529.10	09/2002	514.00	438.00	454.80	12/2005	917.00	736.00	889.00
09/1999	580.50	503.00	561.50	12/2002	482.00	428.00	481.20	03/2006	1,194.00	876.00	1,152.00

Source: New York Mercantile Exchange

SILVER

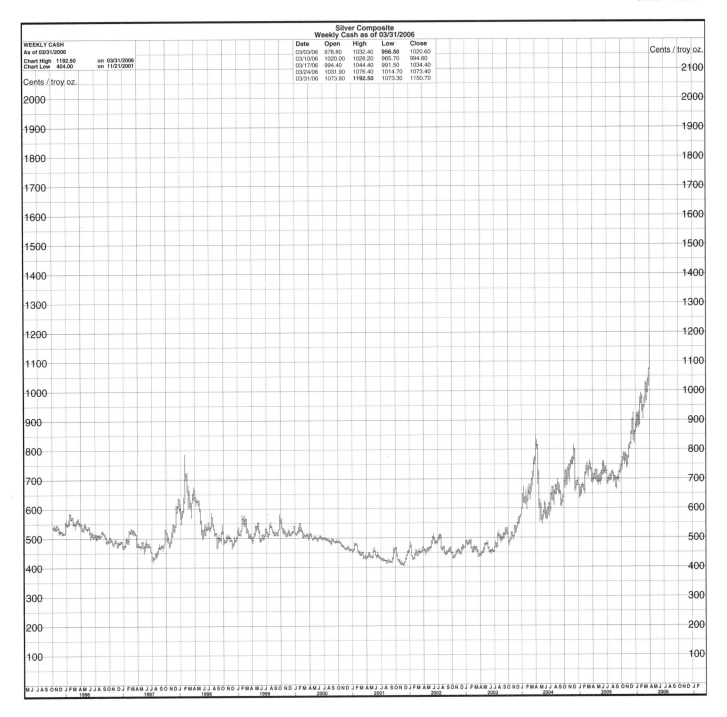

Quarterly High, Low and Close of Silver   In Cents per Troy Ounce

Quarter	High	Low	Close	Quarter	High	Low	Close	Quarter	High	Low	Close
09/1996	528.00	480.00	488.00	12/1999	573.00	504.00	540.00	03/2003	496.00	434.00	446.00
12/1996	506.00	468.00	477.00	03/2000	551.00	492.00	500.00	06/2003	489.00	435.00	456.00
03/1997	534.00	463.00	506.00	06/2000	519.00	489.00	501.00	09/2003	535.00	454.00	512.00
06/1997	514.00	447.00	463.00	09/2000	503.00	475.00	484.00	12/2003	601.00	473.00	594.00
09/1997	532.00	418.00	521.00	12/2000	493.00	455.00	457.00	03/2004	792.80	593.00	791.50
12/1997	638.00	467.00	593.00	03/2001	484.00	428.00	428.00	06/2004	845.00	545.50	576.80
03/1998	787.00	546.00	650.00	06/2001	468.00	428.00	429.00	09/2004	699.80	581.80	689.00
06/1998	675.00	495.00	552.00	09/2001	467.00	413.00	463.00	12/2004	817.00	655.50	682.28
09/1998	588.00	465.00	535.00	12/2001	469.00	404.00	462.00	03/2005	764.08	632.60	715.53
12/1998	546.00	462.00	502.00	03/2002	488.00	423.00	466.00	06/2005	761.00	676.60	704.40
03/1999	579.00	496.00	496.00	06/2002	514.00	440.00	484.00	09/2005	759.60	664.40	745.40
06/1999	555.00	482.00	525.00	09/2002	515.00	438.00	454.00	12/2005	926.94	731.50	881.60
09/1999	582.00	502.00	556.00	12/2002	481.00	428.00	478.00	03/2006	1,192.50	869.40	1,150.70

Source: New York Mercantile Exchange

TIN

Annual High, Low and Close of Tin   In Dollars per Metric Ton

Year	High	Low	Close	Year	High	Low	Close	Year	High	Low	Close
1989	10,440.0	6,570.0	7,100.0	1995	7,310.0	5,170.0	6,325.0	2001	5,320.0	3,630.0	3,940.0
1990	7,150.0	5,650.0	5,705.0	1996	6,650.0	5,680.0	5,840.0	2002	4,550.0	3,630.0	4,280.0
1991	5,990.0	5,500.0	5,605.0	1997	6,130.0	5,235.0	5,420.0	2003	6,570.0	4,260.0	6,525.0
1992	7,250.0	5,447.0	5,850.0	1998	6,210.0	5,100.0	5,170.0	2004	9,650.0	6,150.0	7,765.0
1993	6,130.0	4,360.0	4,900.0	1999	6,150.0	4,960.0	6,100.0	2005	8,650.0	5,850.0	6,500.0
1994	6,400.0	4,730.0	6,210.0	2000	6,175.0	5,160.0	5,180.0	2006	8,325.0	6,450.0	8,150.0

Source: London Metals Exchange

TIN

Quarterly High, Low and Close of Tin   In Dollars per Metric Ton

Quarter	High	Low	Close	Quarter	High	Low	Close	Quarter	High	Low	Close
09/1996	6,460.0	6,000.0	6,020.0	12/1999	6,150.0	5,355.0	6,100.0	03/2003	4,820.0	4,260.0	4,540.0
12/1996	6,170.0	5,680.0	5,840.0	03/2000	6,175.0	5,320.0	5,345.0	06/2003	4,850.0	4,480.0	4,650.0
03/1997	6,130.0	5,750.0	5,885.0	06/2000	5,550.0	5,270.0	5,510.0	09/2003	5,070.0	4,585.0	5,035.0
06/1997	5,910.0	5,520.0	5,570.0	09/2000	5,605.0	5,275.0	5,390.0	12/2003	6,570.0	5,030.0	6,525.0
09/1997	5,730.0	5,290.0	5,660.0	12/2000	5,410.0	5,160.0	5,180.0	03/2004	8,480.0	6,150.0	8,475.0
12/1997	5,890.0	5,235.0	5,420.0	03/2001	5,320.0	4,950.0	4,975.0	06/2004	9,650.0	8,150.0	8,760.0
03/1998	5,640.0	5,100.0	5,635.0	06/2001	5,115.0	4,610.0	4,660.0	09/2004	9,235.0	8,410.0	9,140.0
06/1998	6,210.0	5,470.0	5,555.0	09/2001	4,625.0	3,630.0	3,740.0	12/2004	9,250.0	7,600.0	7,765.0
09/1998	5,700.0	5,300.0	5,335.0	12/2001	4,295.0	3,650.0	3,940.0	03/2005	8,650.0	7,200.0	8,125.0
12/1998	5,580.0	5,125.0	5,170.0	03/2002	4,070.0	3,630.0	4,040.0	06/2005	8,300.0	7,150.0	7,300.0
03/1999	5,410.0	4,960.0	5,260.0	06/2002	4,480.0	3,700.0	4,460.0	09/2005	7,500.0	6,300.0	6,555.0
06/1999	5,740.0	5,100.0	5,270.0	09/2002	4,550.0	3,720.0	4,120.0	12/2005	7,050.0	5,850.0	6,500.0
09/1999	5,580.0	5,190.0	5,390.0	12/2002	4,415.0	4,010.0	4,280.0	03/2006	8,325.0	6,450.0	8,150.0

Source: London Metals Exchange

ZINC

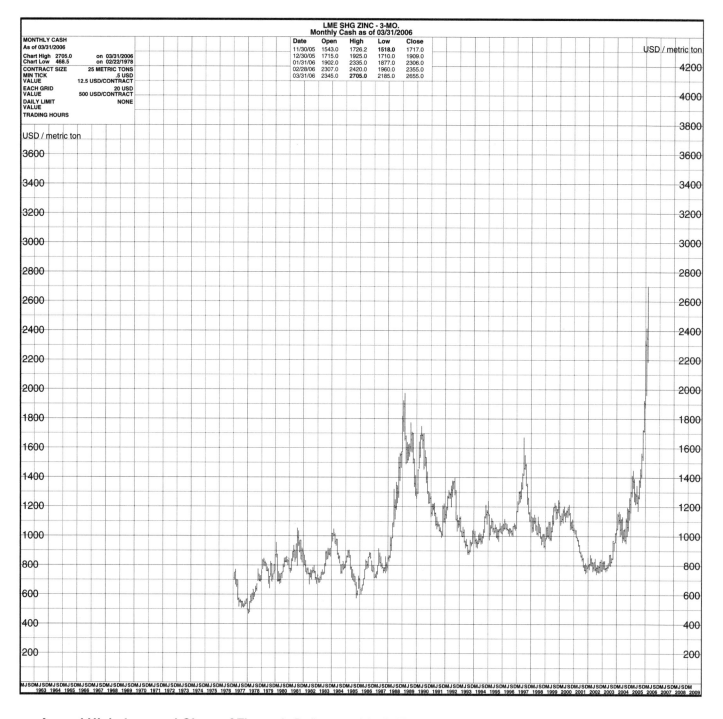

Annual High, Low and Close of Zinc   In Dollars per Metric Ton

Year	High	Low	Close	Year	High	Low	Close	Year	High	Low	Close
1977	771.6	507.2	559.6	1987	916.2	711.3	787.8	1997	1,674.0	1,054.5	1,107.0
1978	775.2	468.5	726.3	1988	1,575.0	771.0	1,555.0	1998	1,185.0	923.0	934.0
1979	848.3	641.0	759.1	1989	1,975.0	1,275.0	1,292.0	1999	1,245.0	914.0	1,245.0
1980	956.4	670.5	828.6	1990	1,750.0	1,220.0	1,257.0	2000	1,235.0	1,042.0	1,042.0
1981	1,054.5	746.1	903.3	1991	1,273.0	989.0	1,115.0	2001	1,081.0	745.0	787.0
1982	895.0	667.9	690.0	1992	1,397.0	1,032.0	1,081.0	2002	874.5	738.0	767.0
1983	918.5	680.3	914.6	1993	1,134.0	873.5	1,030.0	2003	1,023.0	757.0	1,017.0
1984	1,049.3	740.2	782.7	1994	1,214.0	918.0	1,162.0	2004	1,262.0	950.0	1,246.0
1985	905.2	574.8	708.7	1995	1,239.0	963.0	1,024.0	2005	1,925.0	1,160.0	1,909.0
1986	890.4	601.4	794.3	1996	1,118.0	1,000.5	1,060.0	2006	2,705.0	1,877.0	2,655.0

Source: London Metals Exchange

ZINC

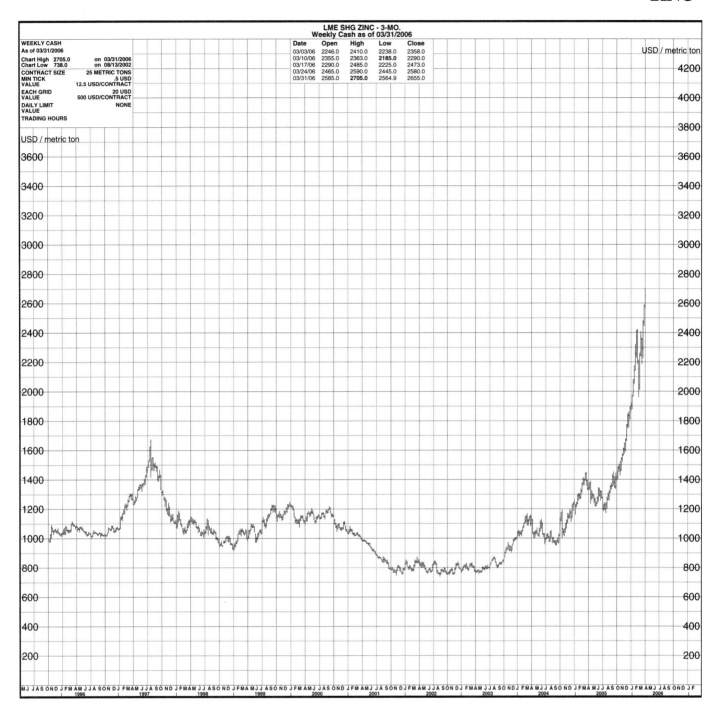

Quarterly High, Low and Close of Zinc In Dollars per Metric Ton

Quarter	High	Low	Close	Quarter	High	Low	Close	Quarter	High	Low	Close
09/1996	1,056.0	1,002.0	1,016.0	12/1999	1,245.0	1,114.0	1,245.0	03/2003	834.0	763.0	777.0
12/1996	1,089.0	1,000.5	1,060.0	03/2000	1,235.0	1,073.0	1,116.0	06/2003	819.0	757.0	800.0
03/1997	1,307.0	1,054.5	1,295.0	06/2000	1,204.0	1,090.0	1,161.0	09/2003	877.0	795.0	844.0
06/1997	1,430.0	1,230.5	1,418.0	09/2000	1,216.0	1,128.0	1,152.0	12/2003	1,023.0	843.0	1,017.0
09/1997	1,674.0	1,345.0	1,350.0	12/2000	1,160.0	1,042.0	1,042.0	03/2004	1,169.0	1,010.0	1,110.0
12/1997	1,360.0	1,098.0	1,107.0	03/2001	1,081.0	992.0	993.5	06/2004	1,153.5	958.0	992.0
03/1998	1,185.0	1,025.0	1,100.0	06/2001	994.0	889.0	890.0	09/2004	1,124.0	950.0	1,108.0
06/1998	1,148.0	1,011.0	1,021.0	09/2001	895.0	788.0	799.5	12/2004	1,262.0	1,000.0	1,246.0
09/1998	1,135.0	987.0	988.0	12/2001	818.0	745.0	787.0	03/2005	1,450.0	1,160.0	1,375.0
12/1998	1,018.0	923.0	934.0	03/2002	874.5	771.0	842.0	06/2005	1,392.0	1,215.0	1,230.0
03/1999	1,068.0	914.0	1,005.0	06/2002	854.0	758.0	822.0	09/2005	1,460.2	1,170.0	1,420.0
06/1999	1,100.0	970.0	1,031.5	09/2002	849.0	738.0	759.0	12/2005	1,925.0	1,399.0	1,909.0
09/1999	1,229.0	1,030.0	1,200.0	12/2002	844.0	748.0	767.0	03/2006	2,705.0	1,877.0	2,655.0

Source: London Metals Exchange

CRB ENCYCLOPEDIA CD

Table of Contents

Chapter 1: Installation
    QuickSearch 378

Chapter 2: Searching and Browsing
    Selecting Text to Search 378
    Types of Searches 378
    Search Operators 379
    Conducting a Search 379
    Search Results 380
    Reader Preferences 380
    Table of Contents Browsing 380

Chapter 3: Viewing Images
    Finding Images 381
    Finding Embedded Images 381
    Zooming Hyper-linked Images 381

Chapter 4: Printing
    Print Hints 382
    Printing Text or Images 382
    Print Setup 383
    Page Layout 383

Chapter 5: User Annotations
    Using Bookmarks 383
    Using Notes 383

CRB Encyclopedia CD Copyright © Commodity Research Bureau All rights reserved.

QuickSearch is a trademark of dataDisc, Inc.
Segments of this manual reprinted with permission by dataDisc, Inc.

Factual information contained in the CRB Encyclopedia CD has been obtained from sources believed to be reliable but are not necessarily inclusive and are not guaranteed in any way and should not be construed as a representation by us.

Chapter 1: Installation

Installing QuickSearch

To run QuickSearch, you will need:
- A computer with a 120 Mhz or faster processor, running any current Windows or Macintosh operating system
- At least 32 MB of total RAM installed on your computer; for best performance, we recommend at least 64 MB
- A CD-ROM drive

To Install:
1) Place the disc in the CD-ROM drive. If installation does not start automatically proceed to step 2.
2) Click Start; Select Run
3) Type D:\Autoplay, where D is the letter representing your CD-ROM drive. Press the enter key and follow the instructions.

Chapter 2: Searching and Browsing

Selecting Text to Search

Searches can be conducted across all the text in a *QuickSearch* document (full-text), restricted to a specific field (fielded search), or restricted to a selected table of contents section.

Everywhere in text - searches the full text of the *QuickSearch* document (except for user-defined notes and bookmarks). Choose **Everywhere in text** in the Search dialog box to specify a full-text search.

Fielded Search - searches a specific field and ignores all text outside of that field. To specify a fielded search:

1) Click **Selected field** under **Select where to search.**
2) Select a field from the list of available fields.

Current Table of Contents section - restricts a research only to a Table of Contents (TOC) section.

1) Click the TOC section in the TOC window.
2) Click the Search button on the toolbar OR select Search/Search from the main menu.
3) Click *Current Table of Contents section* under *Select where to search.*

Note: Search results will represent the selected TOC Section and its sublevels.

Types of Searches

Search for Phrase
Type an exact phrase you wish to find, e.g. "Business is the key." Use quotation marks around the search text to distinguish a *phrase search* from a *word search* or choose *Search for phrase* in the **Search/More>>** dialog box. The QuickSearch default setting is a phrase search.

Search for Words
Two types of word searches may be conducted - single words or words in proximity as determined by **Search Operators**. To conduct a word search, choose *Search for word(s)* in the **Search/More>>** dialog box.

1) **Single Word** - Enter any single word, e.g. BUSINESS, to find all occurrences in the document.
2) **Words in Proximity** - Enter any series of words that you wish to find near each other (e.g. BUSINESS INCREASE). Before conducting a *proximity search*, define a search range/proximity in the **Search/ More>>** dialog box. The default setting is 4 words. A typical sentence has 10 words, a typical paragraph has 25 words, and a typical page has 500 words.

Refine Last Search

The **Refine last search** feature can be used to modify your most recent search. (See the Advanced Searching section of this chapter.)

Search Operators

Boolean, wildcard and phrase search operators are available by selecting **MORE>>** in the **Search** dialog box. Double-click on any operator to add it to the Search command line *or* type the operator in the **Type the text to find** box.

To see example of each operator:
- Click the **Search** button and then the **More>>** button.
OR
- Select **Search/Search** from the main menu and **More>>**.
- Click once on the operator you wish to view.

The following operators are available for a word search:

AND (&) - BUSINESS AND INCREASE - Returns all occurrences of BUSINESS and INCREASE in the specified search range that are near each other. "Near" is defined using the Word Proximity setting in the **Search/ More>>** dialog box.

OR (|) - BUSINESS OR INCREASE - Returns all occurrences of the words in the specified search range without regard to proximity.

NOT (~) - BUSINESS NOT INCREASE - Returns all occurrences of the word BUSINESS that are not near the word INCREASE in the specified search range. "Near" is defined using the Word Proximity setting in the **Search/ More>>** dialog box.

Wildcard (*) - Use the asterisk (*) at the end of any part of a word to represent any character or combination of characters. For example, BUSI* may return hits such as *business, businesses, busing,* and *Businowski*. The wildcard operator cannot be used in a phrase search.

Conducting a Search

Basic Searching

1) Click the Search button on the Reader toolbar OR select Search/Search from the main menu.
2) In the **Search** dialog box, select where to search choosing one of the following:
- Everywhere in text
- Selected field*
- Current Table of Contents

*Note: Click a field or a TOC entry before choosing Selected field or Current Table of Contents section.

3) Type the search text (word, words within proximity or phrase) in the *Type the text to find* box or double click on any entry in the **Word Wheel** to select it as search text.
4) Click **Search** in the dialog box. "Hits" will be highlighted in the text and displayed in context in a separate **Hit List** window. The number of hits also will be displayed on the status bar at the bottom of the screen.

Advanced Searching

Search for Words

1) Begin a search by completing steps 1-3 of a Basic Search.
2) Select **More>>** to expand the Search dialog box and change to a *Search for Word(s)* and/or select other **Search Operators** which alter the nature of the search to be conducted. A *Search for Phrase* is conducted unless you select another type of search.
3) Specify the **Word Proximity** in the **Search/ More>>** dialog box, if you are conducting an AND or NOT search. The default proximity is 4 words.
4) Click **Search** in the dialog box. "Hits" will be highlighted in the text and displayed in context in a separate **Hit List** window. The number of hits also will be displayed on the status bar at the bottom of the screen.

Refine Last Search

To refine the last research:
1) Begin a search by completing steps 1-3 of a Basic Search. Click the **More>>** button on the **Search** dialog box to access all search parameters.
2) Click the **Refine last search** box in the lower left corner of the **Search** dialog box.
3) Select the **Boolean** operator to be applied to the refined search (just to the right of the *Refine last search* check box).
4) Preview the format for the refined search in the *Refined Search box* at the bottom of the **Search** dialog box.
5) Type the **[New text to Find]** word(s) in the *Type the text to find* box at the top of the **Search** dialog box.
6) Click **Search**.

Example:

Your first search in the Constitution was for the word "House." If you want to narrow the search results to include only hits of "House" which are not near "senate," you can return to the **Search** dialog box, select **Refine last search**, select the *NOT* operator, specify the word proximity, type "Senate" in the *Type the text to* find box at the top of the **Search** dialog box and click the **Search** button. The **Hit List** will display only hits of "House" which were not located near "Senate" ("near" depends on the proximity that you specified). The final search command would look as follows:

(House) ~ (Senate)

This search could be further refined by selecting **Refine last search** and repeating the steps above.

Example:

If you want to find only occurrences of "House *NOT* Senate" which are near "Representative," return to the Search dialog box, select **Refine last search**, select the *AND* operator, specify the word proximity, type "Representatives" in the *Type the text to find* box at the top of the **Search** dialog box and click on the **Search** button. The **Hit List** would display only hits of "House" which were near "Representatives" but not located near "Senate" ("near" depends on the proximity that you specified). The final search command would look as follows:

[(House) ~ (Senate)] & (Representatives)

Search Results

Browsing Search Results

Hit List

After conducting a search, each occurrence of the e search text in the document will be displayed in context in a separate **Hit List** window. Double click on any entry in the **Hit List** to move to the corresponding section of text.

Highlighted Hits in the Text

After conducting a search, each occurrence of the search text is highlighted in the text of the document.

1) Click the **First/Previous/Next/Last (Hit)** buttons to move between highlighted hits in the text.
2) The number of the current hit being viewed and the total number of hits are displayed in the Status bar at the bottom of the screen.

Removing the Hit List

1) Click the **Clear** button on the toolbar **OR** select **Search/Clear Search** from the main menu to remove the current **Hit List** window and the highlighting from the hits in the text.
2) Turn off the **Hit List** for future searches by selecting **Edit/Preferences** to open the **Document Preferences** dialog box. Click the **Reader** tab to open **Reader Preferences.** Deselect *Show Hit List?*.

Reader Preferences

Select **Edit/Preferences** from the main menu to open the **Document Preference** dialog box. The box includes three tabs: **Reader, Author,** and **Stopper Word List.**

Reader Preferences include:

CD-ROM Drive Letter

Every CD-ROM player is assigned a drive letter. (It is usually the last drive letter after your other drives.)

Default Word Search Proximity

Set the default proximity (the number of words between selected words) to be applied in multiple word (non-phrase) searches.

Show Hit List?

Click **Show Hit List?** to open a **Hit List** automatically after conducting a Search. The Hit List shows "hits" - items found - when you do a search. Browse hits by clicking the **Next/Previous Hit** buttons on the toolbar or selecting **Search/Search** from the main menu. All hits will be highlighted in the text even if a **Hit List** is not activated.

TOC Window Color

Click the **TOC Window Color** button to open a dialog box containing table of Contest background color options. Select from a present color chart, or create a custom color and select it. Click **OK**.

SAVE YOUR DOCUMENT after you select preferences!

Table of Contents Browsing

Hyperlinks

The Table of Contents (TOC) provides a convenient method for accessing any section of the ***QuickSearch*** document. Each TOC entry is hyper-linked to the corresponding section of text; just click on an entry and ***QuickSearch*** automatically will move the corresponding section to the text window.

Multiple Levels

QuickSearch TOC's may include up to 32 levels. If there are sublevels in a TOC section, a "+" will appear in front of the TOC entry. To open the next level, click on the "+".

Automatic Tracing

As you move through a ***QuickSearch*** document (scroll, Next Hit, Previous Hit, etc.) the Table of Contents will "track" your location in the document automatically. A box outline indicates the current TOC section.

Chapter 3: Viewing Images

A ***QuickSearch*** document may contain ***hyperlinked*** or ***embedded*** images. Different methods are used for finding and viewing each type of image

Finding Images

Finding Hyperlinked Images
You can find hyperlinked images in a ***QuickSearch*** document by using any of the following options:
- **List** of images
- **Next/Previous Image** buttons or menu selections
- **Search** feature
- **Special formatting**/camera icon

Image List - Open a comprehensive list of hyperlinked images in the document.
1) Click the **Image List** button on the Toolbar *OR* select **Search/Image List** from the main menu.
2) Double click on an image title in the **Image List** to open the image.

Browsing Images - You can browse through images using the **Next/Previous Image** buttons or menu selections.
1) Select Nest/Previous Image buttons OR Search/First (Nest, Previous, Last) Image from the main menu.
2) The **Next and Previous Image** buttons or menu selections move the reader sequentially through images in the document.
3) The **First** and **Last Image** menu selections move only to the first or last image in the document.

Searching for Words in Hyperlinked Image Titles - As each hyper-linked image file is added to a ***QuickSearch*** document, it is given an ***Image Title.*** The Image Title appears with an optional camera icon at the point you have chosen in the text window. The Image Title is indexed with other text and may be found using a word or phrase search (see Chapter 1 - *Searching & Browsing*).

Look for Special Formatting/Camera Icon – Hyperlinked images can be found by looking for words that have special formatting (the default is double-underlined text). Double click on the specially formatted text to open the image. A camera icon may precede the specially formatted image title. The image can also be opened by clicking on the camera icon.

Finding Embedded Images

Embedded images appear in the text at the point you have chosen. They may be found by:
- Scrolling through text
- Conducting a search for words/phrases that appear near the image.

Scrolling for an Embedded Image
Use the vertical scroll bar to scan text and locate embedded images.

Searching for an Embedded Image*
Search for text that has been placed near an image and marked as hidden.

*Note: **Titles of embedded images will NOT appear on an Image List.** The Image List feature is only for hyperlinked images.

Zooming Hyper-linked Images

Marquee Image Zooming*

Marquee Image Zooming allows you to select a portion of a **hyper-linked image** and enlarge it to the size of the image window. ***QuickSearch*** allows you to zoom to a single pixel.

*Note: Marquee Image Zooming **is available ONLY for hyper-linked images.**

1) Click a **hyperlinked image title** or camera icon to open the image window.
2) Click on and hold the **left mouse** button and drag a box around the image area you want to enlarge.
3) When the area is defined, release the mouse button. The area selected will fill the **Image Window**.
4) Steps 2 and 3 may be repeated to continuing zooming.
5) To return the image to its original size, click once on the image with the **left mouse** button.

Image Panning

Image Panning allows you to use the horizontal/vertical scroll bars* to move around a **hyperlinked** image that has been enlarged by Marquee zooming.
Click an arrow on the scroll bar *OR* click and drag the horizontal or vertical scroll bar button to move the image across the screen.
*Note: **Scroll bars do not appear on-screen until an image has been zoomed.**

Scale to Gray

Some 1 bit (black & white) hyperlinked images can be sharpened by using the **Scale to Gray** feature. **Scale to Gray** will fill in missing pixels to improve the quality of an image. This feature is particularly useful for viewing scanned document images.

To use Scale to Gray:
1) Open a hyperlinked image
2) Select **View/Scale to Gray** from the main menu
3) **Scale to Gray** will remain active until it is deselected.

381

Chapter 4: Printing

The **Print** feature will print **text** and **images** in the following forms:
- Highlighted lines or blocks of text
- Selected Tables of Contents section(s)
- Search results ("hit" lists)
- Embedded images
- Hyper-linked images
- Zoomed portions of Hyper-linked images

Print Hints

Highlighted text, images and TOC sections will print in order as they are found in the document.

The printed size of Zoomed and Hyper-linked images may vary between portrait and landscape page orientation settings (found via **File/Print Setup**).

You can print *multiple* TOC sections by:
- Using the **Shift** key to select a series of *adjacent* TOCs.
- Using the **CTRL** key to individually select *specific* TOCs.
- Using the **Shift** and **CTRL** keys alternately to select specific TOC groupings.

Printing specifications can be set from the Windows Print Manager utility.
Make **Print Setup** modifications *before* you **Print.**

Printing Text or Images

To Print portions of a document:
1) Highlight lines and/or block(s) of text.
2) Click the **Print** button on the toolbar.
OR
Select the **File/Print** from the main menu.
OR
Press **CTRL+P**.

To Print a Single TOC section:
1) Click the TOC heading in the **Table of Contents** window.
2) Click the **Print** button on the toolbar.
OR
Select the **File/Print TOC selection(s)** from the main menu.
OR
Click the **right mouse** button and select **Print TOC selection(s).**
OR
Press **CTRL+P**.
*Note: All the sublevels in the TOC section will be printed.

To Print Multiple TOC sections:
1) Click the first TOC section you want to print from the **Table of Contents** window.
2) Press and hold the **CTRL** key while you click the order TOC sections you want to print. They do not have to be adjacent.
3) When you have finished selecting TOCs, click the **Print** button on the toolbar.
OR
Select **File/Print TOC selection(s)** from the main menu.
OR
Click the **right mouse** button and select **Print TOC selection(s).**
OR
Press **CTRL+P**.

To Print adjacent TOC sections:
1) Click the *first* TOC section you want to print from the **Table of Contents** window.
2) Press and hold the **Shift** key, and click the last TOC section in the series (all TOC sections between the first and last will be selected automatically).
3) Click the **Print** button on the toolbar.
OR
Select **File/Print TOC selection** from the main menu.
OR
Click the **right mouse** button and select **Print TOC selection(s).**
OR
Press **CTRL+P**.

*Note: **Multiple TOC Selection functions (highlighting using the** Shift **and/or** CTRL **keys) can be used in combination to select specific TOC groupings.**

To Print Embedded Images:
1) Highlight (double click) the embedded image(s) you want ant to print.
2) Click the **Print** button on the Toolbar.
OR
Select **File/Print** from the main menu.
OR
Press **CTRL+P**.

To Print a Hyperlinked Image:
You can print a **Hyperlinked Image** or a zoomed portion of a Hyperlinked Image.
1) Open the image by double clicking the **Image title** and/or the **camera icon.**
OR
Click the **Image List** button on the toolbar and double click the **Image title** from the list.
2) Click the **Print** button on the Toolbar.
OR
Select **File/Print** from the main menu.
OR
Press **CTRL+P**.

Print Setup

The Print Setup option allows you to select printer type, page orientation, paper size, paper source, and printer properties (paper, graphics, fonts, device options). Make these selections **before** you print.

To change the Print Setup:
1) Select **File/Print Setup** from the main menu.
2) In the **Print Setup** dialog box, click the down arrow in the **Name** pull down menu, select a printer type and enter it in the **Name** window (or click **Network** to access Network printer options).
3) To select new printer properties select **Properties** and make modifications.
4) Select **Landscape** or **Portrait**.
5) Select **OK** to exit.

Page Layout
You can adjust the top, bottom, left, and right margins of a printed page as follows:
1) Select **File/Page Layout** from the main menu.
2) In the **Page Parameters** dialog box, set margins (in inches) and click **OK**.

Chapter 5: User Annotations

The reader may customize a *QuickSearch* document by adding "margin" Bookmarks and Notes.

Annotate functions enable the reader to make customized **Bookmarks** in the text and make private, unsearchable comments about a document with **Notes**. The **Bookmark** feature enables the reader to "save his place," while the **Notes** feature allows the reader to "write in the margins" of the text.

Using Bookmarks

To add a Bookmark to a document:
1) Highlight a portion of text or place the cursor where you would like to add the Bookmark.
2) Click on the **Bookmark** icon on the Reader toolbar *OR* select **Annotate/Bookmark** from the main menu or select **Insert Bookmark** from the **right mouse** button menu. If text has been highlighted, it is shown in the **Edit Bookmark/Name** text box. If not, enter a name for the bookmark in the text box.
3) Click **Add** to place the selected text in the **Current Bookmarks** list.
4) Click **Go to** to scroll text to the point where the bookmark appears.
5) Click **Close** to close the Bookmark dialog box.

To go to a Bookmark:
1) Click on the **Bookmark** button on the toolbar *OR* select **Insert Bookmark** from the **right mouse** button menu to open the list of Current Bookmarks.
2) Highlight the bookmark you want to move to in the text.
3) Click **Go to.** The selected text will move to the top of the text window.

To edit a Bookmark:
1) Click on the **Bookmark** icon on the toolbar *OR* select **Annotate/Bookmark** from the main menu *OR* select **Insert Bookmark** from the **right mouse** button menu to open the dialog box containing current bookmarks.
2) In the **Current Bookmarks** list, click on the bookmark you wish to edit. It will appear in the **Edit Bookmark/Name** window.
3) Make changes and click **Add**.

To remove a Bookmark:
1) Click the **Bookmark** icon on the Reader toolbar or select **Insert Bookmark** from the **right mouse** button menu to open the dialog box containing current bookmarks.
2) In the **Current Bookmarks** list, click on the bookmark you wish to remove. It will appear in the **Edit Bookmark/Name** text box.
3) Click **Remove.**

Using Notes

To add a Note to a document:
1) Place the cursor in the text window where you want the note to appear.
2) Click on the **Notepad** button *OR* select **Annotate/Notes/Insert** from the main menu *OR* select **Insert Note** from the **right mouse** button menu to open the **Notepad** dialog box.
3) Type in the note and click **Save**; a Notepad icon appears in the left margin next to the specified line of text.

To View a Note:
1) Double click the **Notepad** icon in the left margin.
2) The **Notepad** dialog box displays the note.

To Edit a Note:
1) Double click the icon of the note you want to edit.
2) Make changes to text.
3) Click **Save.**

To Remove a Note:
1) Place the cursor on the **Notepad** icon and select **Annotate/Note/Delete** from the main menu *OR* select **Delete Note** from the **right mouse** button menu.
2) A dialog box will ask you to confirm the note deletion.
3) Click **Yes.** The icon will disappear after scrolling in the document.

CRB Wall Charts and Desk Sets

Designed to help you easily spot market reversals and critical turning points, CRB Historical Wall Charts and Desk Sets will show you in one quick look how seasonal patterns and long-term trends create profitable trading opportunities. Our charts let you plot trendlines according to actual market performance, rather than charting on market averages. Each chart offers plenty of room for updating and adding trendlines.

Historical Wall Charts

Printed each fall, Wall Charts are available for the top 35 markets. More than just a poster measuring 22½"h x 34"w, these ten-year charts use the nearest futures contract and show open/high/low/settle prices with total volume and total open interest and Commitment of Traders data for each week through the last week of September.

Agricultural Markets: Corn, Oats, Soybeans, Soybean Meal, Soybean Oil, Wheat, Kansas City Wheat, Cotton #2, Cocoa, Coffee, Sugar #11, Feeder Cattle, Live Cattle, Lean Hogs and Pork Bellies.

Financial Markets: U.S. Dollar Index, British Pound, Canadian Dollar, Euro FX, Japanese Yen, Swiss Franc, Eurodollars, 5-Year T-Notes, 10-Year T-Notes 30-Year T-Bonds, Copper, Gold Silver, Crude Oil, Heating Oil #2, Unleaded Gasoline Natural Gas, S&P 500 Index, NASDAQ 100 Index and Dow Jones Industrials

Historical Desk Sets

Printed each spring and fall, the Desk Set includes 48 markets*. By allowing you to take the longest possible view of these markets, our Desk Set helps you identify potential trends and plan your strategy accordingly. Measuring 12½"h x 17"w, this spiral-bound set includes 10 years of weekly trading ranges with total volume and open interest and Commitment of Traders data and 30 years of monthly price activity with total volume and open interest on adjacent pages.

*Additional Markets: Lumber, Orange Juice, Australian Dollar, Mexican Peso, 2-Year T-Notes, Palladium, Platinum, SPI 200 Index, DAX Index, Hang Seng Index, Nikkei 225 Index, FTSE 100 Index and Reuters-CRB Futures Index.

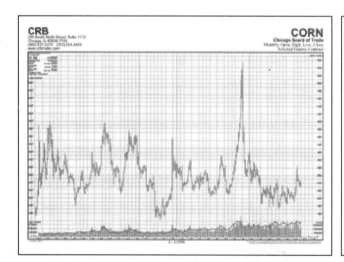
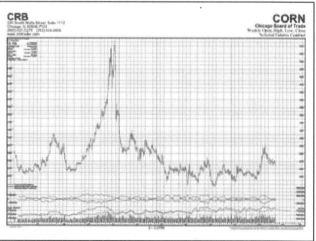

For more information, visit www.crbtrader.com, or call 800-621-5271

Commodity Research Bureau • 330 South Wells Street, Suite 612 • Chicago IL, 60606 USA
Phone: 312.554.8456 or 800.621.5271 • Fax: 312.939.4135 • info@crbtrader.com • www.crbtrader.com